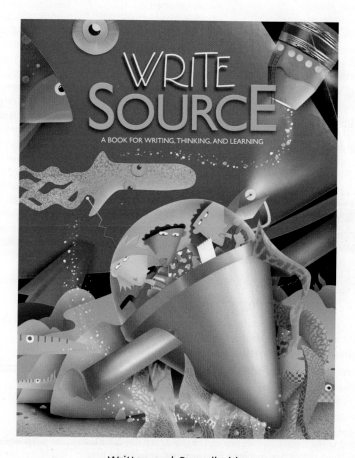

WRITE SOURCE

A BOOK FOR WRITING, THINKING, AND LEARNING

Written and Compiled by

Dave Kemper, Patrick Sebranek, and Verne Mey

Illustrated by

Chris Krenzk

WRITE SOURCE®

GREAT SOURCE EDUCATION GROUP
a division of Houghton Mifflin Company
Wilmington, Massachusetts

Reviewers

- -

Technology Connection for *Write Source*

Visit our Web site for additional student models, writing prompts,
updates for citing sources, multimedia reports, information about
submitting your writing, and more.

The Write Source Web site. . . . **www.thewritesource.com**

- -

Printed in the United States of America

International Standard Book Number: 978-0-669-50705-8 (hardcover)

5 6 7 8 9 10 -RRD- 11 10 09 08

International Standard Book Number: 978-0-669-50702-7 (softcover)

5 6 7 8 9 10 -RRD- 11 10 09 08

Using the Write Source Book

Your *Write Source* book is loaded with information to help you learn about writing. One section that will be especially helpful is the "Proofreader's Guide" at the back of the book. This section covers all of the rules for language and grammar.

The book also includes four units covering the types of writing that you may have to complete on district or state writing tests. At the end of each unit, there are samples and tips for writing in science, social studies, and math.

The *Write Source* will help you with other learning skills, too—study-reading, test taking, note taking, and speaking. This makes the *Write Source* a valuable writing and learning guide in all of your classes.

Your *Write Source* guide . . .

With practice, you will be able to find information in this book quickly using the guides explained below.

The **TABLE OF CONTENTS** (starting on the next page) lists the six major sections in the book and the chapters found in each section.

The **INDEX** (starting on page 751) lists the topics covered in the book in alphabetical order. Use the index when you are interested in a specific topic.

The **COLOR CODING** used for "The Basic Elements of Writing (blue)," "A Writer's Resource," (green) and the "Proofreader's Guide" (yellow) make these important sections easy to find.

The **SPECIAL PAGE REFERENCES** in the book tell you where to turn for additional information about a specific topic.

If, at first, you're not sure how to find something in the *Write Source*, ask your teacher for help. With a little practice, you will find everything quickly and easily.

contents

The Writing Process

The Forms of Writing

DESCRIPTIVE WRITING

EXPOSITORY WRITING

PERSUASIVE WRITING

RESPONSE TO LITERATURE

CREATIVE WRITING

RESEARCH WRITING

Speaking and Writing to Learn

SPEAKING TO LEARN

WRITING TO LEARN

The Basic Elements of Writing

WORKING WITH WORDS

CONSTRUCTING STRONG PARAGRAPHS

A Writer's Resource

Strengthening Word Choice and Vocabulary

Improving Sentence Fluency

Enhancing Your Presentation

Proofreader's Guide

Why Write?

When Walter was a toddler, he lost his mother. His father was too poor to raise him, so he ended up as a foster child. He also suffered from a speech impairment. Walter didn't have much going for him, did he?

Of course, he hated to speak in front of the class in school. Then in fifth grade, Walter was asked to read something he had written for a speech assignment. His own writing contained words that he was able to pronounce. Afterward, he felt much better about himself and continued to write stories and poems. So began the incredible writing life of Walter Dean Myers, the award-winning author of *Hoops* and *Fast Sam, Cool Clyde, and Stuff.*

We now know how important writing has been to Walter Dean Myers. Read on to find out how writing can be important to you.

Mini Index

- **Reasons to Write**
- **Starting Points for Writing**

Reasons to Write

Why should you write? Actually, there are many good reasons to write, and four of the most important are listed below. If you write for one or more of these reasons, you can expect good things to happen.

1. To Review Your Experiences

You can write about your experiences by keeping a personal journal. Just set aside 10 or 15 minutes every day and write about the people, places, and events in your life. (See pages **431–434** for more information.)

 Writing in a personal journal helps you make sense of everything that is happening in your world. It also helps you gain confidence in your ability to write.

2. To Learn

Writing about new or complex ideas presented in your classes will help you to understand the ideas better. It's best to do this kind of writing in a special notebook or learning log. Think of the writing that you do in a learning log as an ongoing conversation about the subjects you are studying. (See pages **435–438** for more information.)

3. To Show Your Understanding

You are assigned paragraphs, essays, and reports to see how well you are learning. You are also asked to answer prompts on assessment tests. These types of assignments require that you (1) understand your subjects, and (2) use your best writing skills.

4. To Share Ideas

Writing narratives, stories, and poems allows you to use your imagination and creativity. These forms of writing are meant to be shared.

 Write to learn. Write nonstop for 5 to 8 minutes about one of your classes. Discuss any new concepts you may be covering in that class. Decide how this new information relates to what you already know. Try to sort out any ideas that confuse you.

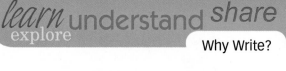

Starting Points for Writing

Every day you do things that you feel good about. You hear things that make you angry. You become curious about how something works. These common, everyday thoughts and happenings make excellent starting points for writing. The list of prompts below will also help you get started on your own writing.

Writing Prompts

Best and Worst, First and Last

My worst day
My craziest experience
The hardest thing I've ever done
My best moment
My greatest creation

Inside Education

My best class ever
Dear Blackboard,
A good assembly
I memorized every word.
A classmate I admire

It could only happen to me!

It sounds crazy, but . . .
Putting my foot in my mouth
Guess what I just heard?
Creepy, crawly things
Whatever happened to my . . .
I got so mad when . . .

Where? What? Why?

Where do I draw the line?
What should everyone know?
What should I do next?
Why are people always in such a rush?

As My World Turns

My secret snacks
A day in the life of my pet
When I played the rebel
When I'm in charge
Last time I went shopping, I . . .

Find a topic. On a piece of paper titled "Writing Prompts," list the five headings shown above—"Best and Worst, First and Last," "Inside Education," and so on. Leave space between each heading, and write one or two new prompts under each. Add others to the list throughout the school year. Use these prompts as starting points for your personal writing.

4

Using the Writing Process

Understanding the Writing Process

Take your time. These three words may be the best advice you will ever receive when it comes to writing. No one can write well by trying to do everything at once. As author Lloyd Alexander says, "Unless you're a genius, I don't see how you could get everything right the first time."

To do your best work, you need to take your writing through a series of steps—the writing process. The steps are *prewriting, writing the first draft, revising, editing,* and *publishing.* As you complete each step, your writing will get closer and closer to a finished product that will please both you and your readers.

This chapter will help you learn more about the writing process and build some valuable writing habits.

Mini Index

Building Good Writing Habits

Someone once said that writing is too much fun to be left to professional writers. This is very true, especially when you make writing an important part of your life. If you're ready to get into writing, follow the tips below.

Write as well as you can during each writing experience.

You will feel good about your writing if it is the result of your best efforts.

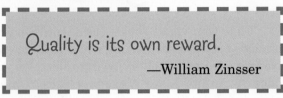

Quality is its own reward.
—William Zinsser

Try different forms of writing.

Stories, letters, e-mail messages, essays, poems—they all have something to teach you about writing.

I wrote my first poems and short stories perched on a fire escape high above the backyards.
—Sharon Bell Mathis

Become a student of writing.

Learn as much as you can about writing, including the traits of effective writing. (See pages 33–44.)

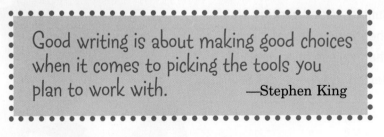

Good writing is about making good choices when it comes to picking the tools you plan to work with.
—Stephen King

Write about a quotation. Write nonstop for 5 to 8 minutes about one of the quotations above. Consider what it means to you.

The Writing Process

The best writers use the writing process to help them complete their work. The steps in the process are described below.

The Steps in the Writing Process

Prewriting

At the start of an assignment, a writer explores possible topics before selecting one to write about. Then the writer collects details about the topic and plans how to use them.

Writing

During this step, the writer completes the first draft using the prewriting plan as a guide. This draft is a writer's *first* chance to get everything down on paper.

Revising

After reviewing the first draft, the writer changes any ideas that are not clear or complete. A wise writer will ask at least one other person to review the draft, as well.

Editing

A writer then checks his or her revised writing for correctness before preparing a neat final copy. The writer proofreads the final copy for errors before sharing or publishing it.

Publishing

This is the final step in the writing process. Publishing is to a writer what an exhibit is to an artist—an opportunity to share his or her work with others.

Analyze your process. On your own paper, explain the parts of the writing process that you find are (1) the easiest, and (2) the hardest to complete. Share your analysis with your classmates.

The Process in Action

This page and the next show you the writing process in action. Use this information as a general guide for each of your writing assignments. The graphic below reminds you that, during an assignment, you can move back and forth between the steps in the writing process.

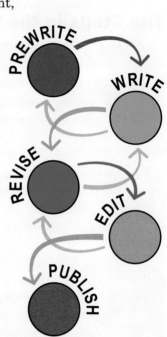

Prewriting Selecting a Topic

- Search for possible writing topics that meet the requirements of the assignment.
- Select a specific topic that really interests you.

Gathering Details

- Learn as much as you can about the topic before you start writing.
- Consider what to emphasize in the writing—either an interesting part of the topic or your personal feelings about it. This will be the focus, or thesis, of your writing.
- Decide which details you want to include in your writing. Also decide on the best way to organize the details.

Writing Developing the First Draft

- When you write your first draft, concentrate on getting your ideas on paper. Don't try to produce a perfect piece of writing.
- Use the details you collected and your prewriting plan as general guides, but feel free to add new ideas as you go along.
- Make sure your writing has a beginning, a middle, and an ending.

 Write on every other line and on only one side of the paper when using pen and paper. Double-space on a computer. This will give you room for revising, the next step in the process.

Revising **Improving Your Writing**

- Review your first draft after setting it aside for a while.
- Use these questions as a general revising guide:
  - **Do I sound interested in my topic?**
  - **Do I say enough about my topic?**
  - **Are the ideas clear and in the right order?**
  - **Does the beginning draw the reader into the writing?**
  - **Does the closing remind the reader about the importance of the topic?**
  - **Are the nouns specific and the verbs strong?**
  - **Are the modifiers (adjectives and adverbs) clear and well chosen?**
  - **Are the sentences varied? Do they read smoothly?**
- Try to have at least one other person review your work.
- Make as many changes as necessary to improve your first draft.

Editing **Checking for Conventions**

- Edit for correctness by checking for punctuation, capitalization, spelling, and grammar errors. Also ask someone else to check your writing for errors.
- Then prepare a neat final copy of your writing. Proofread this copy for errors before sharing it.

Publishing **Sharing Your Writing**

- Share your finished work with your classmates, teacher, friends, and family members.
- Consider including the writing in your portfolio.
- Think about submitting your writing to your school newspaper or some other publication. (See pages **57–64** for ideas.)

Consider the process. Each step in the writing process is important. However, some experts say that prewriting and revising are especially important steps. In a brief paragraph, explain the importance of either prewriting or revising.

Getting the Big Picture

Many questions will come to mind each time you write: What *ideas* do I want to include? What is the best way to *organize* these ideas? How can I add *voice* to my writing? Are my *words* well-chosen and specific?

Luckily, you won't have to answer these questions all at once. Instead, you can deal with them as they become important at different times in the writing process. *Remember:* The writing process helps you slow down and think about what you are writing. You can give each of the traits, the six qualities of writing listed below, the proper attention.

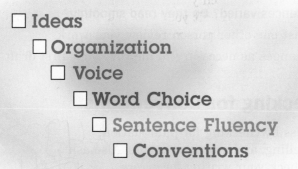

- ☐ Ideas
  - ☐ Organization
    - ☐ Voice
      - ☐ Word Choice
        - ☐ Sentence Fluency
          - ☐ Conventions

Use the writing process. Imagine that you are working on a writing assignment. On your own paper, match each activity on the left to its proper place in the writing process on the right.

___ **1.** Review the first draft for voice. ("Voice" relates to the writer's personality.)

___ **2.** Gather the important ideas about a topic.

___ **3.** Share the final copy with classmates.

___ **4.** Double-check the spelling of all names.

___ **5.** Write a beginning that gets the reader's attention.

A. Prewriting
B. Writing
C. Revising
D. Editing
E. Publishing

Extra Credit: Suppose you had to explain the writing process to a group of younger students who were just beginning to write paragraphs and brief stories. On your own paper, write down what you would say to them.

One Writer's Process

Many people dream about becoming "black belts" in judo, but not everyone succeeds at it. Why? Because mastering a martial art is a lot tougher than just putting on a belt. It takes discipline, courage, and a great deal of determination.

Writing well takes these same three traits. If you have the *discipline* to search for interesting topics and gather plenty of details, your writing will be full of great ideas. If you then have the *courage* to pour words onto a blank page—or computer screen—you'll watch your ideas come to life. Finally, if you have the *determination* to revise and edit your writing, it will be unbeatable.

This chapter shows you how seventh-grader Kaylie Brandt used the writing process to share information about the sport of judo. As you will see, Kaylie is well on her way to becoming a skilled writer.

Mini Index

- **Previewing the Goals**
- **Prewriting**
- **Writing**
- **Revising**
- **Editing**
- **Publishing**
- **Assessing the Final Copy**
- **Reflecting on Your Writing**

Previewing the Goals

Before Kaylie began writing, she looked at the goals for her expository assignment, which are shown below. These goals helped her get started. She also previewed the rubric for expository writing. (See pages **194–195**.)

GOALS OF EXPOSITORY WRITING

Ideas

Select a topic that truly interests you, write a clear focus statement, and present the important details about the topic.

Organization

Include a beginning that attracts the reader, a middle that supports the focus, and a closing that connects everything. Use transitions to link ideas.

Voice

Write the essay in a way that sounds informative and confident. Let the reader know that you are sincerely interested in the topic.

Word Choice

Use specific nouns, vivid verbs, and well-chosen modifiers. Explain or define any unfamiliar terms.

Sentence Fluency

Use a variety of sentence styles that flow smoothly and clearly from one idea to the next.

Conventions

Make sure that you follow the rules for punctuation, capitalization, spelling, and grammar.

 To understand the important goals for Kaylie's assignment, answer the following questions:

1. What type of topic should Kaylie select? Why?
2. What should she do in the middle part of her essay?
3. How should she sound in her essay?
4. What types of words should she use?

Prewriting Selecting a Topic

Kaylie was given the following assignment: *Write an expository essay that informs readers about an activity that promotes physical fitness.* To select a topic, she listed physical activities that she has tried and ones that interest her.

swimming	*volleyball*	*biking*
soccer	*judo* ✳	*aerobics*

Kaylie chose judo because she loves it and wants other students to learn about it.

 List your own possible activities on a piece of paper and put a star next to the one that would make the best topic. Write a brief paragraph (several sentences) explaining why you would write about this topic.

Gathering and Organizing Details

After thinking about what she already knew, Kaylie did some additional research. She then listed the main points about judo that she wanted to cover: *background information, equipment, techniques,* and *benefits.* Kaylie then used a collection sheet to gather details for each main point.

Collection Sheet

background	equipment	techniques	benefits
—started around 1882	—white uniform called a "gi"	—throws: have to take partner down	—builds muscle strength
—based on jujitso	—color of belt tells skill level	—grapple: how to control partner	—improves mental discipline
—means "the gentle way"	—mats	—break-falls: how to fall	—helps opponents respect each other
—not like karate			

Kaylie also stated the focus of her essay. This *focus statement* expresses her main feelings about the topic. She then planned her middle paragraphs by turning each main point into a topic sentence.

Focus Statement:
Students involved in judo keep their bodies in top shape.
First Topic Sentence (background):
Most people have heard of judo, but they don't know much about it.

Writing Developing Your First Draft

Kaylie sat down to write her essay. She used the ideas she had gathered on her collection sheet as a basic guide. Her head was full of thoughts, and she wanted to get them all down on paper. **(There are errors in Kaylie's first draft.)**

The Gentle Way

The first paragraph introduces the topic and gives the focus statement.

There are different ways to be active. People like to skate board or bike. Others like to play sports. Others enjoy working out or something else. A few people stay fit by doing judo. Judo is a fun sport and a health program. Students involved in judo keep their bodies in top shape.

Most people have herd of judo, but they don't know much about it. Neither punching nor kicking is used in judo. A man named professor Jigoro Kano created the sport. Professor Kano based judo on jujitsu. Judo focused on how to stay in shape, self discipline, and character development.

Each body paragraph covers one part of the topic.

Judo equipment is very simple. Each student has a uniform that is tied with a belt that shows the student's rank. Junior students begin with a white belt and then move up. These belts help partners know each other's level so they can train and compete safely. Training is done on mats.

The three basic judo techniques include throws,

grapples, and break-falls. Throws are ways to take an opponent down. They are made with specific movements. Grapples allow a student to control an opponent. A main objective in a judo match is to hold an opponent on his back. Break-fall techniques help students avoid injury. These techniques are practiced over and over again during training sessions.

Details explain the topic.

Judo has benefits for your body. It helps people lose weight if they are heavy and gain solid muscle if they are really skinny. It develops flexibility. Students are constantly bending and twisting. Judo makes people stronger because most of the training involves pushing against somebody. It improves a student's reflexes because they learn how to react quick to their opponent's moves.

The ending summarizes the essay and gives the reader a final thought.

Judo students have self confidence and discipline. Judo keeps them mentally fit. The goal is to master the basic techniques, not to smash somebody. Students can feel safe because judo has different belt levels. The instructors know what they're doing and have respect and confidence, too. Students learn that judo is an honorable and gentle way of life.

Try It On page 13, Kaylie used a collection sheet to gather details for her essay. Does her first draft include all of the details from this sheet? Does she add any new details? Explain.

Revising Focusing on the Big Picture

After Kaylie finished her first draft, she looked again at the goals on page 12 and used them as a revising guide. Her thoughts, which are shown below, tell you what changes she planned to make.

Ideas

Select a topic that truly interests you, write a clear focus statement, and present the important details about the topic.

> "I need to add more details to support my main points."

Organization

Include a beginning that attracts the reader, a middle part that supports the focus, and a closing that connects everything. Use transitions to link ideas.

> "I should check my transitions to make sure that they help the reader follow my ideas."

Voice

Write the essay in a way that sounds informative and confident. Let the reader know that you are sincerely interested in the topic.

> "I must remember to sound confident and knowledgeable about my topic."

 Team up with a partner to review Kaylie's first draft. Write down at least two things that you like about the draft and one or two things that could be improved.

Reviewing Kaylie's First Revision

After Kaylie reviewed her first draft, she made the following revisions, or changes.

Transitions improve the flow of ideas.

There are different ways to be active. ^Some^ People like to skate board or bike. ^while^ Øthers like to play sports. ^Still^ Øthers enjoy working out or something else. ~~A few people~~ ^Then there are those who^ stay fit by doing judo. Judo is a fun sport and a health program. Students involved in judo keep their bodies in top shape.

New details support the paragraph's main point.

Most people have herd of judo, but they don't know much about it. Neither punching nor kicking is used in judo. ^Judo became a sport in the early 1880s^ A man named professor Jigoro Kano created the sport. Professor Kano based judo on jujitsu. ~~Judo~~ ^He called his new sport the gentle way. It^ focused on how to stay in shape, self discipline, and character development.

Details also make the voice sound more knowledgeable.

Judo equipment is very simple. Each student ^wares a gi. This uniform^ ~~has a uniform that~~ is tied with a belt that shows the student's rank. Junior students begin with a white belt and then move up. ^to yellow, orange, and green belts^ These belts help partners know each other's level so they can train and compete safely. Training is done on mats. ^often in a dojo^

The three basic judo techniques include throws, grapples, and break-falls. Throws are ways to . . .

Try It Review Kaylie's changes. Identify two changes that seem the most effective. Explain your choices.

Revising Using a Peer Response Sheet

One of Kaylie's classmates read her essay. He used a rubric like the one on pages 194–195 and spotted more places that could use improvements. Kaylie's classmate wrote his comments on a "Peer Response Sheet."

Peer Response Sheet

Writer: **Kaylie Brandt**   Responder: **Chris Williams**

Title: **"The Gentle Way"**

What I liked about your writing:

* You selected an interesting topic.

* You shared a lot of good information.

* Your ideas were easy to follow.

Changes I would suggest:

* Make sure that the beginning attracts the reader.

* The second paragraph is kind of jumbled.

* How do you become a black belt?

 Review the classmate's suggestions for improvements listed above. Which one do you think is the most important? Explain. Also add one suggestion of your own. Focus on the ideas, organization, and voice in the writing.

Revising with a Peer Response

Using the comments made by her classmate, Kaylie revised her story again. These changes made her essay even more effective.

> The beginning should attract the reader.

Teenagers have ~~There are~~ different ways to ~~be active.~~ *stay in shape* Some ~~people~~ *teens* like to skate board or bike, while others like to play ~~sports.~~ *basketball or soccer* Still others enjoy working out or something else. Then there are those who stay fit by doing judo. Judo is a fun sport, ~~and~~ *and a way of life all rolled into one* a health program. Students involved in judo keep their bodies in top shape.

Most people have herd of judo, but they don't know much about it. Neither punching nor kicking is used in judo. Judo became a sport in the early 1880s A man named professor Jigoro Kano created the sport. Professor Kano based judo on jujitsu. He called his new sport the gentle way. It focused on how to stay in shape, self discipline, and character development.

> Move the second sentence to the end of the paragraph.

Judo equipment is very simple. Each student wares a gi. This uniform is tied with a belt that shows the student's rank. Junior students begin with a white belt and then move up to yellow, orange, and green belts. *A student moves up to blue, brown, and black belts.* These belts help partners know each other's . . .

> How do you become a black belt?

Try IT Have you ever used peer responding during a writing assignment? Discuss the experience with your classmates. Consider why peer responding is (or can be) helpful.

Revising **Focusing on Words and Sentences**

Once Kaylie had finished revising her ideas, organization, and voice, she began checking the style of her writing. She thought about what she had written and considered what she should change to make everything sound more effective.

Word Choice

Use specific nouns, vivid verbs, and well-chosen modifiers. Explain or define any unfamiliar terms.

> *"Some words are too general. I should define tough words."*

Sentence Fluency

Use a variety of sentence styles that flow smoothly and clearly from one idea to the next.

> *"I could use sentence combining to improve the smoothness of certain parts."*

 Team up with a partner to review Kaylie's revised writing on page 19 for style. Identify two nouns, two verbs, or two adjectives that could be more specific, vivid, or colorful. Then find one or two sentences that could be improved.

Checking Kaylie's Improvements in Style

Kaylie's next step was to concentrate on the style or sound of her ideas. She paid special attention to the effectiveness of the words and the sentences.

> The word choice is improved.

Teenagers have different ways to stay in shape. Some teens like to skate board or bike, while others like to play basketball or soccer. Still others enjoy working out or ~~something else~~ *jogging*. Then there are those who stay fit by ~~doing~~ *practicing* judo. Judo is a fun sport, a ~~health~~ *fitnes* program, and a way of life all rolled into one. Students involved in judo keep their bodies in top shape.

> Combining clauses using transitions improves the flow of ideas.

Most people have herd of judo, but they don't know much about it. Judo became a sport in the early 1880s. *At that time* A man named professor Jigoro Kano created the sport. Professor Kano based judo on *an ancient combative activity called* jujitsu. He called his new sport the gentle way. *because* It focused on ~~how to stay in shape~~ *fitness*, self discipline, and character development. Neither punching nor kicking is used in judo.

> Difficult words are defined.

Judo equipment is very simple. Each student *a white, long-sleeved uniform called* wares a gi. This uniform is tied with a belt that shows the student's rank. Junior students begin with a white belt and then move up to yellow, orange, and green . . .

 Compare your comments about the style of Kaylie's writing (page 20) with the changes she has made. How are those changes alike or different from your recommendations?

Editing Checking for Conventions

Once Kaylie was pleased with the way her essay read, she checked her work for conventions. (Conventions deal with the rules for correct spelling, grammar, punctuation, and capitalization.)

Conventions

Make sure that you follow the rules for punctuation, capitalization, spelling, and grammar.

> *"I'll check word by word and look at all my punctuation."*

For help with writing rules, Kaylie turned to the "Proofreader's Guide" in the back of her *Write Source* book. She also used the editing checklist shown below.

Editing Checklist

PUNCTUATION

_____ **1.** Do I use end punctuation after all my sentences?

_____ **2.** Do I use commas correctly?

_____ **3.** Do I use apostrophes to show possession (*a boy's bike*)?

CAPITALIZATION

_____ **4.** Do I start all my sentences with capital letters?

_____ **5.** Do I capitalize all proper nouns?

SPELLING

_____ **6.** Have I spelled all my words correctly?

_____ **7.** Have I double-checked words my spell checker might miss?

GRAMMAR

_____ **8.** Do I use correct forms of verbs (*had gone*, not *had went*)?

_____ **9.** Do my subjects and verbs agree in number? (*Each* of them *has* a chance to win.)

_____ **10.** Do I use the right word (*to, too, two*)?

Try IT Team up with a partner. Using the checklist above, find two or three errors in Kaylie's revised draft on page 21.

Checking Kaylie's Editing for Conventions

Before writing a final copy, Kaylie checked her essay for conventions—spelling, punctuation, capitalization, and grammar. (See inside the back cover of this book for a list of the common editing and proofreading marks.)

Corrections are made to spelling.

Grammar errors are corrected.

Punctuation errors are fixed.

Teenagers have different ways to stay in shape. Some teens like to skate board or bike, while others like to play basketball or soccer. Still others enjoy working out or jogging. Then there are those who stay fit by practicing judo. Judo is a fun sport, a ~~fitnes~~ *fitness* program, and a way of life all rolled into one. Students involved in judo keep their bodies in top shape.

Most people have *heard* ~~herd~~ of judo, but they don't know much about it. Judo became a sport in the early 1880s. At that time, a man named professor Jigoro Kano created the sport. Professor Kano based judo on an ~~ancient~~ *ancient* combative activity called jujitsu. He called his new sport the "gentle way" because it focused on fitness, self-discipline, and character development. Neither punching nor kicking is used in judo.

Judo equipment is very simple. Each student *wears* ~~wares~~ a white, long-sleeved uniform called a "gi." This uniform is tied with a belt that shows the student's rank. Junior students begin with a white belt and . . .

Try IT Review Kaylie's editing for conventions in the paragraphs above. Did you find some of the same errors when you edited her earlier draft on page 21?

Publishing Sharing Your Writing

Kaylie used the tips below to help her write the final copy of her story. (See pages **25–26**.)

Focus on Presentation

Tips for Handwritten Copies

- Use blue or black ink and write neatly.
- Write your name following your teacher's instructions.
- Skip a line and center your title; skip another line and start your writing.
- Indent every paragraph and leave a one-inch margin on all four sides.
- Write your last name and page number on every page after page 1.

Kaylie Brandt

Brandt 2

The Gentle Way

Teenagers have different ways to stay in shape. Some teens like to skateboard or bike, while others like to play basketball or soccer. Still others enjoy working out or jogging. Then there are those who stay fit by practicing judo. Judo is a fun sport, a fitness program, and a way of life all rolled into one. Students involved in judo keep their bodies in top shape.

Most people have heard of judo, but they don't know much about it. Judo became a sport in the early 1880s. At that time, a man named Professor Jigoro Kano created the sport. Professor Kano based judo on an ancient combative activity called jujitsu. He called his new sport the "gentle way" because it focused on fitness, self-discipline, and character development. Neither punching nor kicking is used in judo.

Judo equipment is very simple. Each student wears a white, long-sleeved uniform called a "gi." This uniform is tied with a belt that shows the student's rank. Junior students begin with a white belt and then move up to yellow, orange, and green belts. After that, a student moves up to blue, brown, and black belts. These belts help partners know each other's level so they can train and compete safely. Training is done on mats, often in a special school called a "dojo."

The three basic judo techniques include throws, grapples, and break-falls. Throws are ways to take an opponent down. They are made with specific hand, foot,

Brandt 2

Kaylie Brandt

The Gentle Way

Teenagers have different ways to stay in shape. Some teens like to skateboard or bike, while others like to play basketball or soccer. Still others enjoy working out or jogging. Then there are those who stay fit by practicing judo. Judo is a fun sport, a fitness program, and a way of life all rolled into one. Students involved in judo keep their bodies in top shape.

Most people have heard of judo, but they don't know much about it. Judo became a sport in the early 1880s. At that time, a man named Professor Jigoro Kano created the sport. Professor Kano based judo on an ancient combative activity called jujitsu. He called his new sport the "gentle way" because it focused on fitness, self-discipline, and character development. Neither punching nor kicking is used in judo.

Judo equipment is very simple. Each student wears a white, long-sleeved uniform called a "gi." This uniform is tied with a belt that shows the student's rank. Junior students begin with a white belt and then move up to yellow, orange, and green belts. After that, a student moves up to blue, brown, and black belts. These belts help partners know each other's level so they can train and compete safely. Training is done on mats, often in a special school called a "dojo."

Tips for Computer Copies

- Use an easy-to-read font and a 10- or 12-point type size.
- Double-space and leave a one-inch margin around each page.

PROCESS

Kaylie's Final Copy

Kaylie was proud of her final essay. It introduced the reader to her favorite physical activity.

Kaylie Brandt

The Gentle Way

Teenagers have different ways to stay in shape. Some teens like to skateboard or bike, while others like to play basketball or soccer. Still others enjoy working out or jogging. Then there are those who stay fit by practicing judo. Judo is a fun sport, a fitness program, and a way of life all rolled into one. Students involved in judo keep their bodies in top shape.

Most people have heard of judo, but they don't know much about it. Judo became a sport in the early 1880s. At that time, a man named Professor Jigoro Kano created the sport. Professor Kano based judo on an ancient combative activity called jujitsu. He called his new sport the "gentle way" because it focused on fitness, self-discipline, and character development. Neither punching nor kicking is used in judo.

Judo equipment is very simple. Each student wears a white, long-sleeved uniform called a "gi." This uniform is tied with a belt that shows the student's rank. Junior students begin with a white belt and then move up to yellow, orange, and green belts. After that, a student moves up to blue, brown, and black belts. These belts help partners know each other's level so they can train and compete safely. Training is done on mats, often in a special school called a "dojo."

The three basic judo techniques include throws, grapples, and break-falls. Throws are ways to take an opponent down. They are made with specific hand, foot, and hip movements. Grapples allow a student to control an opponent. A main objective in a judo match is to hold an opponent on his back, much like in wrestling. Break-fall techniques help students avoid injury when they are being thrown to the mat. These techniques are practiced over and over again during training sessions.

Judo offers a wide range of physical benefits. Generally, it helps students lose weight if they are heavy and gain solid muscle if they are really skinny. Judo also makes students stronger because most of the training involves reacting to physical resistance. Specifically, judo helps develop flexibility. During training, students are constantly bending and twisting. In addition, it improves students' reflexes because they learn how to act as quickly as possible to their opponents' moves.

As judo students train, they become more self-confident and disciplined. In this way, judo promotes physical and mental fitness. The overall goal is to master the basic techniques, not to show up opponents in competitions. Students of all ability levels can feel safe because judo is so structured. The instructors are highly trained and approach judo with respect and confidence. As students advance with their training, they often come to see judo as an honorable and gentle way of life.

Assessing the Final Copy

Kaylie's teacher used a rubric like the one that appears on pages 194–195 to assess Kaylie's final copy. A 6 is the very best score that a writer can receive for each trait. The teacher also included comments under each trait.

4 Ideas

Your essay introduces an activity you love. I still want to know more about the physical part of judo.

5 Organization

Your writing has a clear beginning, middle, and ending.

4 Voice

I wanted to hear more about your experiences as a student of judo.

4 Word Choice

You explain new terms, but your nouns and verbs could be more specific.

4 Sentence Fluency

Your sentences are easy to follow. You could have varied some of your sentence beginnings.

6 Conventions

Your essay is free of careless errors.

Review the assessment. Do you agree with the comments and scores made by Kaylie's teacher? Why or why not? Explain your feelings in a brief paragraph.

Reflecting on Your Writing

After the whole process was finished, Kaylie filled out a reflection sheet. This helped her think about the assignment and plan for future essays.

Kaylie Brandt

My Expository Essay

1. **The best part of my essay is . . .**
   that I have introduced my classmates to a new physical activity. They now know some basic information about judo.

2. **The part that still needs work is . . .**
   my voice. I should've sounded more interested in my topic. Still, I came a long way!

3. **The main thing I learned about writing an expository essay is . . .**
   it must contain information that truly interests readers.

4. **In one of my next essays, I would like to . . .**
   write more about actual judo competitions.

5. **Here is one question I still have about writing an expository essay:**
   How important is it to add my personal thoughts and feelings?

Peer Responding

In 1609, Galileo started experimenting with lenses and tubes. He was trying to create an instrument that would magnify things that were very small or very far away. He and others eventually devised microscopes and telescopes. With these two tools, people suddenly could see their world in a whole new way.

Sometimes a classmate can act as a microscope or telescope for your writing. Through another person's eyes, you can see things in your writing that you never knew were there. A peer response can point out not only what could be improved but also what is already working well!

Mini Index

- **Peer-Responding Guidelines**
- **Sample Peer Response Sheet**

Peer Response Sheet
Responder: Angie

Writer: Keisha
Title: "My Own Room"
What I liked about your writing:
• The opening background details about sharing a room with your sister are great.
• Your writing voice shows that you love your new room.
• The comparison you make in the first paragraph helps me picture your closet.

Changes I would suggest:
• In the second paragraph, check your description of what is on your walls. Are the details organized by location?
• You could add to the ending. Maybe you could share a final feeling about your room.

Peer-Responding Guidelines

At first, you may work with only one person: a teacher or a classmate. This person does not expect your writing to be perfect. He or she knows that you are still working on your paper.

Later, you may have a chance to work with a small group. After a while, you will find that responding to someone's writing is much easier than you thought it would be.

The Author's Role

Select a piece of writing to share and make a copy of it for each group member.

GUIDELINES	SAMPLE RESPONSES
● **Introduce your piece of writing.** But don't say too much about it.	This paper is about Wilma Mankiller. I got interested in her from a TV show.
● **Read your writing out loud.** Or ask group members to read it silently.	Ms. Mankiller was the first woman chief of the Cherokee Nation. . . .
● **Invite your group members to comment.** Listen carefully.	Okay, everyone, now it's your turn to talk. I'm listening.
● **Take notes** so you will remember what was said.	Did I make it clear that she had a muscle disease?
● **Answer all questions** the best you can. Be open and polite.	Yes, she did have a kidney transplant.
● **Ask for help from your group** with any writing problems you are having.	What do you think of my title? Does the ending seem right?

The Responder's Role

Responders should show an interest in the author's writing and treat it with respect.

GUIDELINES	SAMPLE RESPONSES
● **Listen carefully.** Take notes so that you can make helpful comments.	Notes: Why did Ms. Mankiller want to be chief?
● **Look for what is good** about the writing. Give some positive comments. Be sincere.	Your explanation of her childhood is very clear.
● **Tell what you think could be improved.** Be polite when you make suggestions.	You could use more details about her actual time as chief.
● **Ask questions** if you need more information.	What does she do now?
● **Make other suggestions.** Help the writer improve his or her work.	Could you include a picture of Ms. Mankiller?

Helpful Comments

In all your comments, be as specific as you can be. This will help the writer make the best changes.

Instead of . . .	Try something like . . .
Your writing is boring.	**Most of your sentences begin with "There" or "It."**
I can't understand one part.	**The part about her schooling isn't very clear.**
What about the final quotation?	**Perhaps you should check the wording of the final quotation.**

 In a class discussion, share your experiences with peer responding. When have you done it? Was it helpful? What would you do differently next time?

Sample Peer Response Sheet

Your teacher may want you and a classmate to react to each other's first draft by completing a response sheet like the one below. (Sample comments are included.)

Peer Response Sheet

Writer: _Keisha_   Responder: _Angie_

Title: _"My Own Room"_

What I liked about your writing:

 * In the opening, background details about sharing a

   room with your sister are great.

 * Your writing voice shows that you love your new room.

 * The comparison you make in the first paragraph helps

   me picture your closet.

Changes I would suggest:

 * In the second paragraph, check your description of

   what is on your walls. Are the details organized by

   location?

 * You could add to the ending. Maybe you could share a

   final feeling about your room.

Practice. Exchange a recent first draft with a classmate.

1 Read the draft once to get an overall feel for it.

2 Then read the paper again, paying careful attention to its strengths and weaknesses.

3 Fill out a response sheet like the one above.

Understanding the Traits of Writing

When a dedicated hairstylist gives a haircut, she has two people to please—the customer, so the person comes back for more haircuts, and herself, because this is her chosen profession.

This holds true for professional writers, too. First, they want to please the readers so that they become loyal fans; and second, they want to please themselves because their writing reflects directly on their own thoughts and feelings.

Good writers know that they must pay careful attention to the *ideas, organization, voice, word choice, sentence fluency,* and *conventions* in everything they write. You should do the same in each of your writing assignments. This chapter discusses the six traits found in all good writing. Once you understand them, you will know how to make your own essays and stories the best they can be.

Mini Index

- **Introducing the Traits**
- **Understanding Ideas**
- **Understanding Organization**
- **Understanding Voice**
- **Understanding Word Choice**
- **Understanding Sentence Fluency**
- **Understanding Conventions**

Introducing the Traits

Writing is made up of six main traits, or qualities. Each of these traits is important for every essay, story, or report that you develop. This page explains how the traits work in the best writing.

Ideas

Effective writing has a clear message, purpose, or focus.
The writing contains plenty of specific ideas and details.

Organization

Strong writing has a clear beginning, middle, and ending.
The overall writing is well organized and easy to follow.

Voice

The best writing reveals the writer's voice—or special way of saying things. The voice also fits the audience and purpose.

Word Choice

Good writing contains strong words, including specific nouns and verbs.
Strong words help deliver a clear message.

Sentence Fluency

Effective writing flows smoothly from one sentence to the next.
Sentences vary in length and begin in a variety of ways.

Conventions

Good writing is carefully edited to make sure it is easy to understand.
The writing follows the rules for punctuation, grammar, and spelling.

One additional trait to consider is the presentation of your writing. Good writing looks neat and follows guidelines for margins, spacing, indenting, and so on. The way the writing looks on the page attracts the reader and makes him or her *want* to read on.

conventions ideas sentence fluency
VOICE organization *word choice* **35**
Traits of Writing

Understanding Ideas

Ideas are the beginning and the end of good writing. That is why the best writers are constantly thinking of good ideas for their stories and essays. Author Jane Yolen knows the importance of good ideas: "I keep an idea file. I always scribble down ideas when I get them."

What types of ideas will you find in good writing?

The best writing (1) starts with a **well-chosen topic**—one that interests you (the writer) and works well for the assignment, (2) continues with **main points** that support the topic, and (3) ends with **important details** that explain the main points.

What makes a writing topic good?

Good writing topics are neither too general nor too specific. They cover just the right amount of information for the assignment.

Sample Assignment: Share an unforgettable experience—a specific event that has meant a lot to you.

Possible Topics

- *Too Broad*   Being a baseball fan
- *Too Narrow*   Buying a pack of baseball cards
- *Just Right*   Visiting the Mets' training camp

How should I write about a topic?

Effective writing has focus. In other words, the story or essay pays special attention to a certain part of a topic or to a specific feeling you have about the topic. Notice how the following statement puts a topic into clear focus.

Focus statement:
During my visit to the Mets' training camp (topic), **I was able to get autographs from my two favorite players** (a certain part).

Try IT Identify a specific topic and write an effective focus statement based on the following assignment: *Recall an unforgettable experience—a specific event that has meant a lot to you.*

How many main points do I need to support my topic and focus?

In most cases, you should have at least two or three main points to help support your writing idea. However, don't try to cover too much territory. If you do, your writing may become hard to follow. Each main point should be covered in a separate paragraph.

> **Focus statement:** *During my visit to the Mets' training camp, I was able to get autographs from my two favorite players.*

Main supporting points:

- Waiting in the parking lot for players to arrive
- Getting an autograph from one of my favorite players
- Getting an autograph from another favorite player

Where do I find the best details?

Make sure to use a variety of details to develop or explain each main point. Many of these details will come from your personal thoughts; others will come from talking to other people or reading about the topic in books and articles. Here are the three main types of personal details.

Personal Details

Sensory details come from the writer's senses.

> **I saw my favorite player get out of his van.**

Reflective details come from the writer's thoughts and feelings.

> **I was so excited that I thought I would drop my cards.**

Memory details come from the writer's experience and knowledge.

> **He made the all-star team last year.**

 Review one of your personal narratives or essays. On a piece of paper, list at least one sensory, one reflective, and one memory detail that you used.

How can I gather more details?

Sometimes you may need a jumpstart to find additional details for your writing. Here are some different ways to find the information you may need.

Ask questions: You can list questions that come to mind and then find answers to them. You can ask the 5 W's—*who? what? when? where?* and *why?*—about your topic. Add *how?* for even better coverage. (See "Analyze" below for more structured questions.)

Analyze: Think about your topic very carefully by answering two or more of the following questions.

- What parts does my topic have? *(Break it down.)*
- What do I see, hear, or feel when I think about it? *(Describe it.)*
- What is it similar to? What is it different from? *(Compare it.)*
- What are its strengths and weaknesses? *(Evaluate it.)*
- What can I do with it? How can I use it? *(Apply it.)*

Freewriting: Write freely about your topic from a number of different angles. Doing this can often help you uncover new ideas to use in your writing.

tip Try to write nonstop for at least 5 to 8 minutes to keep your mind open to all kinds of ideas. (See page **439** for more information.)

Try IT Select one of the topics below. Then, on your own paper, answer three of the questions from "Analyze" above. What new thing did you learn about the topic?

Possible topics: earning extra money, getting in shape, a locker room, a junk drawer, a personal injury

How can I hold my reader's interest?

The best writing has something to say. It contains a lot of specific details that grab the reader's attention.

PASSAGE WITH FEW DETAILS

The leadership council raised a lot of money and then gave some of that money to a local mission.

SAME PASSAGE WITH SPECIFIC DETAILS

The McKinley Leadership Council raised $3,000 for local charities and then gave $400 to the Lake Street Mission to help feed homeless people.

Understanding Organization

Strong writing is well organized from start to finish. Writer Stephen Tchudi (pronounced "Judy") calls organizing a paper the "framing" process: "Just as a carpenter puts up a frame of a house before tacking on the outside walls, a writer needs to build a frame for a paper."

How should I organize my writing assignments?

Each of your essays should have a meaningful beginning, middle, and ending. The graphic that follows shows the basic shape of effective writing.

BEGINNING

Start with interesting information and state the focus (underlined).

> Last year, my grandpa gave me the best present ever. He took me to three baseball training camps. . . . <u>During my visit to the Mets' camp, I was able to get autographs from my two favorite players.</u>

MIDDLE

Present the main supporting points and details.

> We arrived at the Mets' camp early and waited in the parking lot. . . .
>
> All of a sudden, a black custom van parked in the area reserved for the players. . . .
>
> Later a red sports car pulled into the lot. . . .

ENDING

Review the essay and offer a final thought.

> Was I ever lucky! I got autographs from my two favorite Mets. . . .
>
> I guess you could say on that day the ball really bounced my way.

How can transitions help me organize my writing?

Linking words and phrases (transitions) can help you organize the details in your narratives, descriptions, and essays. (Also see pages **572–573**.)

Personal narratives: You can use the following transitions, which show time, to arrange details in your narratives. These types of transitions also work well for "how-to" or process essays.

after	before	during	first	second	today	next	then

Next I got Sammy Sosa's autograph. He is my favorite player. I was speechless. Then I watched for other players to arrive just for the fun of it. . . .

Descriptions: You can use the following transitions, which show location, to arrange details in your descriptions.

above	across	below	in the front	on the right	near	in the back

In the front of the snack shop, you will find a small counter on the right surrounded by rows and rows of candy bars. Across from the counter, bags of chips, pretzels, and popcorn are neatly stacked. In the back of the shop, a cooler contains sports drinks, bottled water, and sodas. . . .

Comparison-contrast essays: You can use the following transitions to organize comparisons.

(when comparing)	like	also	both	in the same way		similarly
(when contrasting)	but	still	yet	on the other hand		unlike

Both red blood cells and white blood cells play important roles. Red blood cells transport oxygen throughout your body, and white blood cells protect your body against infection. Unlike red blood cells, most white blood cells live only a few days.

Persuasive essays: You can use the following transitions to organize the details in your persuasive essays.

first of all	in addition	equally as important	most importantly

First of all, carrying out the death penalty is a very slow process. . . . In addition, capital punishment is very expensive. . . . Most importantly, many believe that capital punishment is morally wrong. . . .

Try It Review a narrative, a description, or an essay that you have written. Underline any transitions that you find. Do they organize your writing, making it easier to follow? Could you add any more transitions?

Understanding Voice

Writer Donald Murray says that voice is the "person in the writing." When the writer's voice or personality is strong, the reader stays interested. Something about the writer's way of using words attracts the reader.

How can I write with voice?

If the real you shines through in your writing, it will have voice. To have voice, you must be honest and sincere in what you write.

> **This passage lacks voice because you can't hear the writer.**
>
> **Coach Brown requires us to complete pull-ups in a very specific way. He doesn't allow any unnecessary movements. He positions himself close to the bar with a yardstick in hand. As soon as there is any movement . . .**

> **This passage has voice because you can hear the writer.**
>
> For Coach Brown, there is only one way to complete a pull-up—his way. For one thing, he doesn't allow any kicking, wriggling, or squirming. He stands right next to the bar and taps us on the stomach if . . .

How important is audience when it comes to voice?

Your audience is very important because it impacts the tone of your voice. For example, in a letter to the school board, you would try to sound formal and respectful. In a personal narrative shared with classmates, you would try to sound more casual and relaxed.

Audience	Adults (school administrators, businesspeople, city officials)
Voice	Serious, formal, respectful, and thoughtful
	Art classes greatly benefit all students. . . .
Audience	Peers (classmates, friends, and students in other schools)
Voice	Engaging, usually informal, casual, and relaxed
	Art classes give kids a chance to be creative. . . .

Try IT Write a brief note to a teacher explaining something that you really like about the class. Then write another note, this time to a friend in the class, about the same topic. The tone of each note should be different.

PROCESS

Understanding Word Choice

Author Gloria D. Miklowitz says, "Write visually, write clearly, and make every word count." If you follow her advice, you will create a lot of specific images (word pictures), making your writing very enjoyable to read. *Remember:* Your writing is only as good as the words that you use.

What should I know about descriptive words?

The best writing contains specific adjectives and adverbs. For example, you may tell readers that Beau is a farm dog, but telling them that he is a *bossy* farm dog says so much more. On the other hand, remember to use descriptive words selectively. Writing sounds unnatural if it contains too many of them.

> **A sentence containing too many adjectives**
> **Josie served delicious, spicy, homemade beef tamales.**
>
> **A sentence containing the right number of adjectives**
> Josie served delicious beef tamales.

tip Avoid overusing the following adjectives: *cool, big, pretty, small, fun, bad, nice,* and *good.* They are used so much that they carry little meaning.

Use adverbs when they are needed to describe the action in a sentence. For example, the adverb *barely* makes the action clearer in the following sentence: "We barely squeezed through the subway door before it shut."

How do words affect the feeling of my writing?

The words that you use directly affect the **connotation,** or feeling, of your writing. Let's say that you are describing a scary dream. You wouldn't use the word "dream" or "fantasy" because neither one has the right feeling. The word "nightmare," however, does have the right feeling. Check a thesaurus if you have trouble finding a word with both the right meaning and the right feeling.

 Look through a classroom thesaurus. On your own paper, write one entry that interests you. Under that word, list three or four synonyms. Share your findings with a classmate. Try to explain the connotation, or feeling, of each synonym.

Understanding Sentence Fluency

Writing that succeeds shares the main message in an effective way. That is why good writers pay careful attention to each sentence they write. As author Cynthia Ozick states, "I never go to the next sentence until the previous one is perfect."

What does it mean to write fluent sentences?

Sentences are fluent when they all work together to make your writing enjoyable to read. When checking for sentence fluency, you should be able to say these things about your writing :

- Every sentence in my paper is important.
- Someone else could read my paper aloud and like the sound of it.
- Short, choppy sentences have been combined. (See pages **512–514**.)
- My sentence beginnings and lengths are varied. (See pages **511** and **522**.)
- Transition words and phrases—*first, for example*—connect the ideas.

How can I improve my sentence style?

The information above identifies two key things that you can do to improve your sentence style: (1) Combine short, choppy sentences, and (2) vary your sentence beginnings and lengths. You can also improve your sentence style by expanding your simple sentences in a number of ways. (See pages **512–517**.)

■ **You can expand simple sentences before the subject and verb.**

Simple sentence: **Todd completed his assignment.**

Expanded sentence: Before first hour, **Todd completed his assignment.**

■ **You can expand simple sentences after the subject and verb.**

Simple sentence: **Tisha spoke.**

Expanded sentence: **Tisha spoke** confidently during the meeting.

■ **You can expand a simple sentence from within.**

Simple sentence: **Coach Brown explained the play.**

Expanded sentence: **Coach Brown** carefully **explained the** new running **play** at the start of practice.

 On your own paper, expand each of the sentences below in at least two different ways.

Erin talked to her friend.   Richard studied.

PROCESS

What sentence structures should I avoid?

Avoid writing too many sentences that begin with "There is" and "There are" or that contain "be" verbs *(is, are, was, were)*. You should also avoid rambling sentences that contain too many *and*'s.

Sentences beginning with "There is" and "There are"

There is **a funny-looking cat sitting on our front porch.**
There are **three annoying crows cawing in our backyard.**

Sentences are improved by deleting "There is" and "There are."

A funny-looking cat is sitting on our front porch.
Three annoying crows are cawing in our backyard.

Sentences containing "be" verbs *(is, are, was, were)*

Rosa is **a persuasive speaker in debates.**
Ellis and Roy are **creative painters.**

Sentences are improved by making another word in each sentence into a verb.

Rosa speaks **persuasively in debates.**
Ellis and Roy paint **creatively.**

Rambling sentences containing too many *and's*

After the *Titanic* sank, the International Ice Patrol was formed and its job was to report icebergs and the United States gave this vital job to the U.S. Coast Guard.

A rambling sentence is improved by deleting an *and* and making two sentences.

After the *Titanic* sank, the International Ice Patrol was formed, and its job was to report icebergs. The United States gave this vital job to the U.S. Coast Guard.

 On your own paper, write three sentences that begin with "There is" or "There are." Exchange papers with a classmate and rewrite each other's sentences, deleting "There is" and "There are."

Understanding Conventions

Good writing follows the conventions, or basic rules, of the language. These rules cover punctuation, capitalization, grammar, and spelling. When you follow these rules, the reader will find your writing much easier to understand and enjoy.

How can I make sure my writing follows the rules?

A checklist like the one below can guide you as you look over your writing for errors. When you are not sure about a certain rule, refer to the "Proofreader's Guide" (pages **578–749**).

Conventions

PUNCTUATION

_____ **1.** Do I use end punctuation after all my sentences?

_____ **2.** Do I use commas correctly in compound sentences?

_____ **3.** Do I use commas correctly in a series?

_____ **4.** Do I use apostrophes correctly to show possession (*that girl's purse* and *those girls' purses*)?

CAPITALIZATION

_____ **5.** Do I start every sentence with a capital letter?

_____ **6.** Do I capitalize the proper names of people and places?

SPELLING

_____ **7.** Have I checked my spelling using a spell checker?

_____ **8.** Have I also checked the spelling by myself?

GRAMMAR

_____ **9.** Do I use correct forms of verbs (*had gone*, not *had went*)?

_____ **10.** Do my subjects and verbs agree in number (*The boy eats* and *the boys eat*)?

_____ **11.** Do I use the right word (*to, too,* or *two*)?

tip Have at least one other person check your writing for conventions. Professional writers have trained editors to help them with this step in the process. You should ask your classmates, teachers, and family members for help.

Using a Rubric

Some things you read are red-hot, and other things leave you cold. The problem is that you can't use a thermometer to measure how "hot" a piece of writing is. Instead, you measure writing by using a rubric.

This chapter explains how to use a rubric. Rubrics are charts that help you evaluate writing. This book contains rubrics for four important kinds of writing: narrative, expository, persuasive, and responses to literature. Each rubric rates writing for the six traits: *ideas, organization, voice, word choice, sentence fluency,* and *conventions.*

Mini Index

- **Understanding Rubrics**
- **Reading a Rubric**
- **Getting Started with a Rubric**
- **Revising and Editing with a Rubric**
- **Assessing with a Rubric**
- **Assessing in Action**
- **Assessing a Narrative**

Understanding Rubrics

Once you understand how to use these rubrics, you will find it easy to assess your writing. And more importantly, you will understand what you need to do to improve as a writer.

| **6** | **5** | **4** | **3** | **2** | **1** |
| Amazing | Strong | Good | Okay | Poor | Incomplete |

Your essays, reports, and stories can be rated for each of the main traits of writing—*ideas, organization, voice, word choice, sentence fluency,* and *conventions.* For example, in one of your essays, the ideas may be "strong" and the organization may be "good." That would give you a 5 for ideas and a 4 for organization.

Rating Guide

This guide will help you understand the rating scale.

A **6** means that the writing is truly amazing.
It goes way beyond the requirements for a certain trait.

A **5** means that the writing is very strong.
It clearly meets the main requirements for a trait.

A **4** means that the writing is good.
It meets most of the requirements for a trait.

A **3** means that the writing is okay.
It needs work to meet the main requirements for a trait.

A **2** means that the writing is poor.
It needs a lot of work to meet the requirements for a trait.

A **1** means that the writing is incomplete.
It is not yet ready to assess for a trait.

PROCESS

Reading a Rubric

For the rubrics in this book, each trait has its own color bar (green for *ideas*, pink for *organization*, and so on). There is a description for each rating to help you evaluate for a particular trait.

Rubric for Narrative Writing

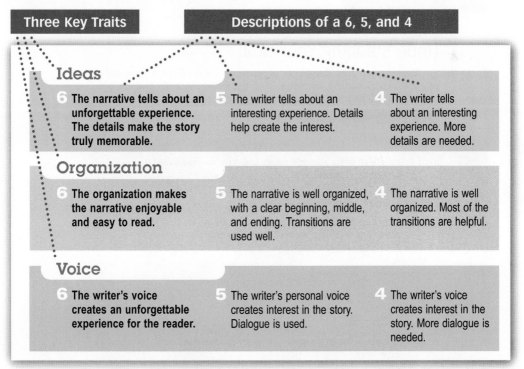

Three Key Traits	Descriptions of a 6, 5, and 4		
Ideas	**6** The narrative tells about an unforgettable experience. The details make the story truly memorable.	**5** The writer tells about an interesting experience. Details help create the interest.	**4** The writer tells about an interesting experience. More details are needed.
Organization	**6** The organization makes the narrative enjoyable and easy to read.	**5** The narrative is well organized, with a clear beginning, middle, and ending. Transitions are used well.	**4** The narrative is well organized. Most of the transitions are helpful.
Voice	**6** The writer's voice creates an unforgettable experience for the reader.	**5** The writer's personal voice creates interest in the story. Dialogue is used.	**4** The writer's voice creates interest in the story. More dialogue is needed.

Guiding Your Writing

Learning how to use a rubric helps you . . .

- **think like a writer**—understanding your goal,
- **make meaningful changes in your writing**—using the traits of writing, and
- **assess your final copies**—rating their strengths and weaknesses.

Reflect on your work with rubrics. On your own paper, explain your experience with rubrics. When have you used them? How well did they work for you? What have they taught you about writing? If you've never used a rubric, explain how you have generally evaluated your writing. Share your thoughts with your class.

Getting Started with a Rubric

At the beginning of each main writing unit, you will see a page like the one below. This page, which is arranged according to the traits of writing, explains the main requirements for developing the writing in the unit.

Understanding Your Goal

Your goal in this chapter is to write an essay about a memorable personal experience. As you write, keep the following traits and goals in mind. They will help you plan and create your personal narrative.

TRAITS OF NARRATIVE WRITING

Ideas

Include all of the important details and make the reader want to know what happened next.

Organization

Make sure that the beginning, middle, and ending are clear to the reader and the events are in chronological order.

Voice

Create a personal voice and use dialogue to show each individual's personality.

Word Choice

Use words that let the reader know how you feel about the experience.

Sentence Fluency

Use a variety of sentence lengths to create an effective style.

Conventions

Be sure your punctuation, capitalization, spelling, and grammar are correct.

 Get the big picture. Look at the rubric on pages 130–131. You can use this rubric to assess your progress. Your goal is to write an essay about a memorable personal experience.

A Closer Look at Understanding Your Goal

To use the "Understanding Your Goal" rubric at the beginning of each writing unit, follow these steps.

 Review the entire chart to get the big picture about the form of writing.

 Focus your attention on *ideas, organization,* and *voice* at the beginning of a writing project because these traits are so important. (See the chart below.)

 Read the requirements under each of these three traits. When you consider *ideas*, for example, try to do these things:
- Include all of the important details.
- Make the reader want to know what happened next.

 Make sure to talk to your teacher if you have any questions about the requirements for the assignment.

A Special Note About the Traits

At each step in the writing process, certain traits are more important than others. Keep this point in mind as you use a rubric.

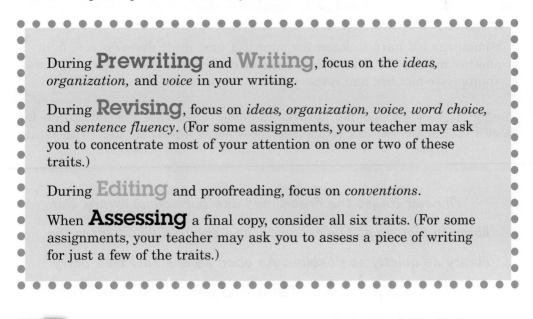

During **Prewriting** and **Writing**, focus on the *ideas, organization,* and *voice* in your writing.

During **Revising**, focus on *ideas, organization, voice, word choice,* and *sentence fluency.* (For some assignments, your teacher may ask you to concentrate most of your attention on one or two of these traits.)

During **Editing** and proofreading, focus on *conventions.*

When **Assessing** a final copy, consider all six traits. (For some assignments, your teacher may ask you to assess a piece of writing for just a few of the traits.)

Write a paragraph. Review the traits rubric on page 48. Then write a short paragraph sharing a learning experience, keeping these traits in mind.

Revising and Editing with a Rubric

6 My narrative tells about one experience. My ideas and details are presented in a memorable way.

5 My narrative tells about one experience and "shows" my ideas.

4 My narrative tells about one experience. I need to "show" more of my ideas instead of "tell" about them.

In each main writing unit, you will find a strip at the top of the pages dealing with revising and editing. Each strip covers one of the traits of writing and will help you improve your first drafts. The strip at the top of these two pages focuses on *ideas* for narrative writing.

How can I use each strip to evaluate my first draft?

To use the strip, start by reading the number 5 description. Number 5 in the strip above says that your first draft should tell about one experience and "show" your ideas. Decide if your writing should get a 5 for ideas. If not, check the description for 6 or 4 and so on. Remember that a 5 means that the writing is *strong* for that trait.

Sometimes it's hard to know for sure if a first draft deserves a 6, 5, or another number for a trait. Just come as close as you can to choosing the appropriate number, and revise your writing as needed.

 Review the sample paragraph below. Then rate the paragraph for ideas and explain your rating. (See pages **46–47** for help with rating a paper.)

> I'll never forget the first time I saw our school library. Our librarian met us at the entrance, and she told us to enter the library as quietly as possible. As soon as she said this, Jerry Howell collided with Yvonne Davis, who yelled, "You klutz!" The librarian said, "Shhhh!"

3 I need to focus on one experience. I need more sensory details.

2 I need to focus on one experience. Also, I need to use sensory details.

1 I need to choose a different experience to write about.

How can the strip help me revise my first draft?

After you find the proper rating on the strip for your paper, you will know what changes you should make. Here's what the writer of the paragraph on page 50 thought about her first draft.

- **Important details:** *I need to give the librarian's name.*
- **Keep the reader's interest:** *I could add an idea to make the reader want to read on.*

Making Changes

After deciding how to improve the ideas in her paragraph, the writer made the following changes.

An important detail is added.

A new idea creates interest.

> I'll never forget the first time I saw our school
> Ms. Witte,
> library. Our librarian ∧met us at the entrance, and
>
> she told us to enter the library as quietly as
>
> possible. As soon as she said this, Jerry Howell
>
> collided with Yvonne Davis, who yelled, "You klutz!"
> Ms. Witte   and we immediately stood at attention.
> ~~The librarian~~ said, "Shhhh!"

Revise your paragraph. Review and revise the paragraph you wrote on page 49. Use the strip on these two pages as a guide.

Assessing with a Rubric

Follow the three steps below when you use a rubric—like the one on page 53—to assess a piece of writing.

1 **Create an assessment sheet.** On your own paper, list the key traits from the rubric (*ideas, organization,* and so on). Draw a line before each trait for your score and skip two or three lines between each trait for comments.

2 **Read the final copy.** Get an overall feeling for the writing to help you evaluate it.

3 **Assess the writing using the rubric.** To get started, read the descriptions for *ideas,* starting with the 5 rating. Decide which rating best

```
ASSESSMENT SHEET          Title: _____

____  IDEAS


____  ORGANIZATION


____  VOICE


____  WORD CHOICE


____  SENTENCE FLUENCY


____  CONVENTIONS


                          Evaluator: _____
```

fits the writing and put that number on your assessment sheet. Make comments as needed. Then go on to the other traits.

Assess your experience paragraph. Create an assessment sheet like the one above. Then evaluate your paragraph using the narrative rubric on pages 130–131. For each trait, try to write down something you did well and then something you'd like to improve. (See the sample on page 55.)

PROCESS

130

Rubric for Narrative Writing

Use the following rubric for help as you assess and improve your narrative writing using the six traits.

Ideas

6 **The narrative tells about an unforgettable experience. The details make the story truly memorable.**

5 The writer tells about an interesting experience. Details help create the interest.

4 The writer tells about an interesting experience. More details are needed.

Organization

6 **The organization makes the narrative enjoyable and easy to read.**

5 The narrative is well organized, with a clear beginning, middle, and ending. Transitions are used well.

4 The narrative is well organized. Most of the transitions are helpful.

Voice

6 **The writer's voice creates an unforgettable experience for the reader.**

5 The writer's personal voice creates interest in the story. Dialogue is used.

4 The writer's voice creates interest in the story. More dialogue is needed.

Word Choice

6 **The writer's exceptional word choice captures the experience.**

5 Specific nouns, strong verbs, and well-chosen modifiers create vivid pictures and express clear feelings.

4 Specific nouns and strong verbs are used. Modifiers are needed to create a clearer picture.

Sentence Fluency

6 **The sentences are skillfully written and original. They keep the reader's interest.**

5 The sentences show variety and are easy to read and understand.

4 The sentences are varied, but some should flow more smoothly.

Conventions

6 **Grammar and punctuation are correct, and the writing is free of spelling errors.**

5 The narrative has a few minor errors in punctuation, spelling, or grammar.

4 The narrative has several errors in punctuation, spelling, or grammar.

Each complete rubric helps you assess a final copy for the traits of writing.

mber
rate **131**

an Experience

The writer needs to tell about an experience and use details.

The narrative needs to be organized.

The writer has not gotten involved in the story. Dialogue is needed.

NARRATIVE

3 Strong nouns, verbs, and modifiers are needed to create a clear picture.

2 General and overused words do not create a clear picture.

1 The writer has not yet considered word choice.

3 A better variety of sentences is needed. Sentences do not read smoothly.

2 Many short or incomplete sentences make the writing choppy.

1 Few sentences are written well. Help is needed.

3 Some errors confuse the reader.

2 Many errors make the narrative confusing and hard to read.

1 Help is needed to make corrections.

The rubrics are based on a six-point rating scale. A 6 is the highest rating, and a 1 is the lowest rating.

Assessing in Action

On this page and on page 55, you can see how one student used a rubric to assess her writing.

Narrative Writing

In the following narrative, the writer shares a memorable baby-sitting experience. As you read the narrative, pay special attention to its strong points and weak points. (The writing does contain errors.)

Moms Can Be Right

"Baby-sitting is alot harder then it looks," my mom said. "Are you sure you want your first job to be for three kids?"

"Mom," I said, "I'll be fine. I've gone baby-sitting with Ellie a bunch of times. She and I have taken care of there kids before."

"Well, I really think you should have some jobs with one child."

"I'll be fine," I said. "You'll see."

I don't know if I could of been more wrong! I showed up on Friday night just as planned. The boys were already changed into there pjs and I just had to watch them. Mrs. Taylor ran thru the list of things they could and couldn't do and then headed for an office party.

The first twenty minutes was fine but then the show they were watching ended. So they got out some toys and started playing. Alex was good and wanted to sit on my lap, so I let him.

Then Robbie was in tears. Robbie screamed and yelled but Max just smiled and run into another room. I couldn't get up fast enough because Alex didn't want me to. He kept crawling up on me.

I had only just gotten them to bed when the Taylor's walked back in. I hadn't even got a chance to clean up. Their place was a total mess. They didn't say anything, but I could tell they weren't too happy. They paid me and I felt bad for not listening to my mom.

Sample Assessment

To complete the response to "Moms Can Be Right," the student writer used the rubric for narrative writing on pages 130–131. Beneath each trait, she identified one strength (*1.*) and one weakness (*2.*) in her writing.

RESPONSE SHEET   Title: Moms Can Be Right

__4__   IDEAS
  1. The details in the first part are effective.
  2. More specific details would help the rest of the essay.

__3__   ORGANIZATION
  1. The narrative starts right in the middle of the action.
  2. Transitions besides "then" should be used.

__3__   VOICE
  1. The writer's voice can sometimes be heard.
  2. Dialogue is needed in the second part of the narrative.

__3__   WORD CHOICE
  1. The words are easy to follow.
  2. Some words could be more specific ("good," "bad").

__4__   SENTENCE FLUENCY
  1. The sentences in the first part read smoothly.
  2. Sentence combining could help the last paragraph.

__4__   CONVENTIONS
  1. The dialogue is punctuated correctly.
  2. There are spelling and grammar errors.

                    Evaluator: Maria Peña

Review the assessment. On your own paper, explain why you agree with the response above (or why you don't). Consider each trait carefully.

Assessing a Narrative

As you read through the essay below, pay attention to the strengths and weaknesses in the writing. Then follow the directions at the bottom of the page. (This writing does contain errors.)

Cookies, Anyone?

Chocolate chip muffins, carmel rolls, peanut butter cookies, fudge brownies. Do these things make your mouth water? Baking these snacks and deserts is my specialty.

It started one year when my mom and I walked through Ryan's Discount Store. It was the start of summer vacation and I was looking for something to keep me busy. I saw a beautiful chrome Home-Bake oven.

I said, "Mom, look at this oven. It would be so much fun!"

She replied, "Well, your birthday is coming up. We'll see what we can do."

Luckily, I did get the oven and started baking right away. After a few weeks of making prepackaged cookies and cakes in my Home-Bake, my Mom bought me a new cookbook. Now I could make more complicated breakfasts, dinners, and snacks.

I remember the first time I made dinner for my family. Using my new cookbook, I made Tacos. I read the recipe over at least five times before begining. My family was so impressed.

Although I like making dinners for my family my favorite thing to do is baking. I started with easy recipes that didn't have alot of ingredients. I practiced making things like cookies and brownies. Now I like to make things that take longer like candy and layer cakes.

The thing I like best about baking is sharing it. Sometimes I bake cookies for older people in church. I love to see their smiles when I share my baking with them, I've learned that the best thing about having a talent is sharing it with others.

Use a narrative rubric. Assess the narrative essay you have just read using the rubric on pages 130–131 as a guide. Before you get started, create an assessment sheet like the one on page 55 in this chapter. *Remember:* Leave room after each trait for comments.

Publishing Your Writing

Publishing refers to the different ways that you can present your finished writing. Sharing a story in class is one form of publishing. Posting a poem on your own Web site is another form. In one way, publishing is the most important step in the writing process because it helps you take pride in your work. It is also one of the best ways to connect in a meaningful way with others.

Your writing is ready for publication when it reflects your true thoughts and feelings from start to finish. Your writing must also be as close to error-free as you can make it.

This chapter will help you get your writing ready to publish and give you a variety of publishing ideas. (Also see "Creating a Portfolio" on pages 65–69.)

Mini Index

- **Sharing Your Writing**
- **Preparing to Publish**
- **Designing Your Writing**
- **Making Your Own Web Site**
- **Publishing Online**

Jason Costello

Serving Your Library

Libraries are community treasures that contain information on just about any subject imaginable. They provide a quiet space to read and reflect, and they help people become lifelong learners. Because libraries offer so much, everyone in the community should support them. One way to offer support is to volunteer your services to your local library.

Working with Books

A community library contains CD's tapes, computers, and other sources of information. Still, when people think of a library, they usually think of all of the books it contains. Here are two easy ways volunteers can work to keep the book collection in top shape.

1. **Shelving books.** Reshelving books keeps the library in order. Volunteers can learn about the Dewey decimal system and find good books to read.

2. **Repairing books.** Popular books get a lot of use, and often the covers and pages get torn. When volunteers repair books, they enable more people to use and enjoy them.

Sharing Your Writing

Some publishing ideas are easy to carry out, like sharing your writing with your classmates. Other publishing ideas take more time and effort, like entering a writing contest. Try a number of these publishing ideas during the school year. All of them will help you grow as a writer.

Performing

- Sharing with Classmates
- Reading to Various Audiences
- Preparing a Multimedia Presentation
- Videotaping for Special Audiences
- Performing Onstage

In School

- School Newspapers
- School Literary Magazines
- Classroom Collections
- Writing Portfolios

Self-Publishing

- Family Newsletters
- Greeting Cards
- Bound Writings
- Online Publications

Posting

- Classroom Bulletin Boards
- School or Public Libraries
- Hallway Display Cases
- Business Windows
- Clinic Waiting Rooms
- Literary/Art Fairs

Sending It Out

- Local Newspapers
- Area Historical Society
- Young Writers' Conferences
- Magazines and Contests
- Various Web Sites

Plan your publishing. Identify one piece of writing that you would like to perform. Explain why and how you would perform this writing. Then identify another piece that you would like to send out. Explain why you would send this writing out and where you would send it.

PROCESS

Preparing to Publish

Your writing is ready to publish when it is clear, complete, and correct. Getting your writing to this point requires careful revising and editing. Follow the tips below to help you prepare your writing for publication.

Publishing Tips

- **Ask for advice during the writing process.**
  Be sure your writing answers any questions your readers may have about your topic.

- **Check the ideas, organization, voice, word choice, and sentence fluency in your writing.**
  Every part of your writing should be clear and complete.

- **Work with your writing.**
  Continue working until you feel good about your writing from beginning to end.

- **Check your writing for conventions.**
  In addition, ask at least one classmate to check your work for this trait. Another person can catch errors that you miss.

- **Prepare a neat finished piece.**
  Use a pen (blue or black ink) and one side of the paper if you are writing by hand. If you are writing with a computer, use a font that is easy to read. Double-space your writing.

- **Know your options.**
  Explore different ways to publish your writing. (See page 58.) As you become more confident in your writing ability, you will become more interested in publishing your writing.

- **Follow all publication guidelines.**
  Just as your teacher wants assignments presented in a certain way, so do the newspapers, magazines, or Web sites that review the writing you submit.

Save all drafts for each writing project. This will help you keep track of the changes you have made. If you are preparing a portfolio, you may be required to include early drafts as well as finished pieces.

Designing Your Writing

Whenever you write, always focus on the content or information first. Then think about how you want your paper to look. For handwritten papers, write neatly in blue or black ink on clean paper. When using a computer, follow the guidelines below.

Typography

- Use an easy-to-read font. Generally, a serif font is best for the body, and a sans serif style is used for contrast in headings.

     The letters of serif fonts have "tails"—as in this sentence.
     The letters of sans serif styles are plain—as in this sentence.

- Use a title and headings. Headings break writing into smaller parts, making the writing easier to follow.

Spacing and Margins

- Use one-inch margins on all sides of your paper.
- Indent the first line of every paragraph.
- Use one space after every period and comma.
- Avoid awkward breaks between pages. Don't leave a heading or the first line of a paragraph at the bottom of a page or a column. Never split a hyphenated word between pages or columns.

Graphic Devices

- If possible, use bulleted lists in your writing. Often, a series of items works best as a bulleted list (like the ones on this page).
- Include graphics where appropriate. A table, a chart, or an illustration can help make a point clearer. But keep each graphic small enough so that it doesn't dominate the page. A larger graphic can be displayed by itself on a separate page.

Share effective design. Find an article in a magazine or newspaper that contains many design features. Share the article with the class and identify the features. Do all of the features work effectively?

Computer Design in Action

The following two pages show a well-designed student essay. The side notes explain all of the design features.

Jason Costello

The title is 18-point type.

Serving Your Library

Libraries are community treasures that contain information on just about any subject imaginable. They provide a quiet space to read and reflect, and they help people become lifelong learners. Because libraries offer so much, everyone in the community should support them. One way to offer support is to volunteer your services to your local library.

The main text is 12-point type and double-spaced throughout.

Working with Books

A community library contains CD's, tapes, computers, and other sources of information. Still, when people think of a library, they usually think of all of the books it contains. Here are two easy ways volunteers can work to keep the book collection in top shape.

Headings are 14-point type.

A graphic is inserted for visual interest.

Numbered lists identify options.

1. **Shelving books.** Reshelving books keeps the library in order. Volunteers can learn about the Dewey decimal system and find good books to read.

2. **Repairing books.** Popular books get a lot of use, and often the covers and pages get torn. When volunteers repair books, they enable more people to use and enjoy them.

The writer's name and page number appear on every page starting with page 2.

A bulleted list helps organize the essay.

Margins are at least one inch all around.

Working with People

Another way to help out at the library is to work with others. Volunteers can use their people skills in one of the following ways:

- **Reading out loud.** Most libraries have children's story hours and need extra people to read to children. This is a good choice for people who like entertaining others.

- **Being read to.** Sometimes children have trouble reading, and it may be helpful for them to read out loud to another person. Volunteers can be good listeners and help struggling readers improve.

- **Matching people with materials.** Another volunteer job is helping people locate books or other library resources.

Finding Your Place

Stop in and have a talk with your local librarian after deciding which services you can offer. See how you can volunteer to make your library the best it can be for everyone in your community.

Design a page. Create an effective design for an essay or a report you've already written. Share your design with a classmate to get some feedback: Does your design make the writing clear and easy to follow? Does your design distract the reader in any way?

Making Your Own Web Site

You can make your own Web site if your family has an Internet account. Ask your provider how to get started. If you are using a school account, ask your teacher for help. Then start designing your site. Use the questions and answers below as a starting point.

How do I plan my site?

Think about the purpose of your Web site and how many pages you need. Will one page be enough space, or will you require several pages? Check out other sites for ideas. Then make sketches to plan your pages.

How do I make the pages?

Start each page as a text file by using your computer. Many new word processing programs let you save a file as a Web page. If yours doesn't, you will have to add HTML (Hypertext Markup Language) codes to format the text and make links to graphics and other pages. You can find instructions for HTML on the Net or at the library.

How do I know whether my pages work?

You should always test your pages. Using your browser, open your first page. Then follow the links to make sure they work correctly and that all the pages look right.

How do I get my pages on the Net?

You must upload your finished pages to the Internet. (Ask your Internet provider how to do this.) After the upload, visit your site to make sure it still works. Also, check it from other computers if possible.

How do I let people know about my site?

Once your site is up, e-mail your friends and tell them to visit it!

Visit a number of different sites for ideas. On your own paper, answer these questions about each one: What is especially good about this site? What could be better? Also talk about these sites with your classmates and friends. When designing your own pages, refer to your research for ideas.

Publishing Online

The Internet offers many publishing opportunities, including online magazines and writing contests. The information below will help you submit your writing on the Net. (At home, always get a parent's approval first. In school, follow all guidelines for computer use.)

How should I get started?

Check with your teacher to see if your school has its own Web site where you can post your work. Also ask your teacher about other Web sites. There are a number of online magazines that accept student writing. Visit some of these magazines to learn about the types of writing they usually publish.

How do I search for possible sites?

Use a search engine to find places to publish. Some search engines offer their own student links.

How do I submit my work?

Before you do anything, make sure that you understand the publishing guidelines for each site. Be sure to share this information with your teacher and your parents. Then follow these steps:

- **Send your writing in the correct form.**
  Some sites have online forms. Others will ask you to send your writing by mail or e-mail. Always explain why you are sending your writing.

- **Give the publisher information for contacting you.**
  However, don't give your home address or any other personal information unless your parents approve.

- **Be patient.**
  A site should contact you within a week to confirm that your work has arrived. However, it may be several weeks before you hear whether your writing will be used or not.

Does Write Source have a Web site?

Yes. You can visit our Web site at www.thewritesource.com. The "Publish It" link also lists other Web sites that accept student submissions.

Visit the Write Source Web site. Use the "Publish It" link. Find out what forms of writing the Write Source is accepting. (Check for your grade level.) Also visit at least two of the other publishing sites listed by the Write Source.

Creating a Portfolio

Would it be fair if people judged your overall writing ability by looking at the very first thing that you wrote in the fall? Not at all. It would be like meeting someone for the first time as you shuffled down to breakfast, still half asleep. Obviously, you would not make your best impression at such a moment.

Your writing skills can be judged best by looking at a collection of your writing developed throughout a grading period. This type of collection is often called a *writing portfolio,* and it gives a clear, complete picture of you as a writer.

This chapter will help you develop a writing portfolio. It includes information about the types and parts of portfolios, plus planning ideas.

Mini Index

- **Types of Portfolios**
- **Parts of a Portfolio**
- **Planning Ideas**
- **Sample Portfolio Reflections**

Types of Portfolios

There are four basic types of portfolios you should know about: a showcase portfolio, a growth portfolio, a personal portfolio, and an electronic portfolio.

Showcase Portfolio

A showcase portfolio presents the best writing you have done in school. A showcase is the most common type of portfolio and is usually put together for evaluation at the end of a grading period.

Growth Portfolio

A growth portfolio shows your progress as a writer. It contains writing assignments that show how your writing skills are developing:

- writing beginnings and endings,
- writing with voice,
- using specific details, and
- using transitions.

Personal Portfolio

A personal portfolio contains writing you want to keep and share with others. Many professional people—including writers, artists, and musicians—keep personal portfolios. You can arrange this type of portfolio according to different types of writing, different themes, and so on.

Electronic Portfolio

An electronic portfolio is any type of portfolio (showcase, growth, or personal) available on a CD or a Web site. Besides your writing, you can include graphics, video, and sound with this type of portfolio. This makes your writing available to friends and family members no matter where they are!

Rate your growth. On your own paper, list two or three skills that show how your overall writing ability is developing. Also list one or two skills that you need to work on. Make sure to review several pieces of writing before you make your choices.

PROCESS

Parts of a Portfolio

A showcase portfolio is one of the most common types of portfolios used in schools. It may contain the parts listed below, but always check with your teacher to be sure.

- A **table of contents** lists the writing samples you have included in your portfolio.
- A **brief essay** or **letter** introduces your portfolio—telling how you put it together, how you feel about it, and what it means to you.
- A **collection of writing samples** presents your best work. Your teacher may require that you include all of your planning, drafting, and revising for one or more of your writings.
- A **cover sheet for each sample** explains why you selected it.
- **Evaluations, reflections,** or **checklists** identify the basic skills you have mastered, as well as those skills that you still need to work on.

Gathering Tips

- **Keep track of all your work.** Include prewriting notes, first drafts, and revisions for each writing assignment. Then, when you put together a portfolio, you will have everything that you need.

- **Store all of your writing in a pocket folder or computer file.** This will help you keep track of your writing as you build your portfolio.

- **Set a schedule for working on your portfolio.** You can't put together a good portfolio by waiting until the last minute.

- **Take pride in your work.** Make sure that your portfolio shows you at your best.

Write a cover sheet. Think of the best piece of writing you've done this year. Why is it your best piece? What parts are especially good? How did other people react to the writing? Then write a sample cover sheet for this writing, explaining why you would include it in your portfolio.

Planning Ideas

The following tips will help you choose your best pieces of writing to include in your portfolio.

1 Be patient.

Don't make quick decisions about which pieces of writing to include in your portfolio. Just keep gathering everything—including all of your drafts—until you are ready to review all of your writing assignments.

2 Make good decisions.

When it's time to choose writing for your portfolio, review each piece. Remember the feelings that you had during each assignment. Which piece makes you feel the best? Which one did your readers like the best? Which one taught you the most?

3 Reflect on your choices.

Read the sample reflections on page 69. Then answer these questions about your writing:

- Why did I choose this piece?
- Why did I write this piece? (What was my purpose?)
- How did I write it? (What was my process?)
- What does it show about my writing ability?
- How did my peers react to this writing?
- What would I do differently next time?
- What have I learned since writing it?

4 Set future writing goals.

After putting your portfolio together, set some goals for the future. Here are some goals that other students have set:

I will write about topics that really interest me.
I will spend more time on my beginnings and endings.
I will make sure that my sentences read smoothly.
I will support my main points with convincing details.

Plan a portfolio cover. On a piece of plain paper, design a cover for a portfolio folder. Include your name and an interesting title. Add sketches or photos related to your writing, your classes, your favorite pastime, and so on.

Sample Portfolio Reflections

When you take time to reflect on your writing assignments, think about the process that you used to develop each one. Also think about what you might do differently next time. The following samples will help you with your own reflections.

Student Reflections

> If I had to write another comparison essay, I would think more carefully about my topics. To make effective comparisons, there must be a number of meaningful similarities and differences to write about. I would also do a lot more research before I started my writing. When my classmates rated my essay, I could tell that they had a lot of questions about the information I included. Next time, I will seek their advice much earlier in the writing process.
>
> —Anna Hernandez

> My persuasive essay on proposing a solution turned out really well. This happened because I felt so strongly about my topic. I really do think that students would become better writers if we had a writing lab open before and after school. I learned from this essay that the words and ideas come easy if I have strong feelings about a topic. I also learned that these strong feelings helped make my writing voice sound really convincing.
>
> —Roy Baker

Professional Reflections

> I wrote *Mad Merlin* by combining legends of Camelot with histories and myths. As I look back at the novel, though, I see it is mostly about my own life. Good fiction is that way—creative in the details, but otherwise full of truth.
>
> —J. Robert King

> With each book I write, I become more and more convinced that the books have a life of their own, quite apart from me.
>
> —Madeleine L'Engle

SPECIFY *picture*

express describe portray

Descriptive Writing

Descriptive Writing

Descriptive Paragraph

All kids have a favorite place where they like to spend time, either alone or with their friends. It could be a room at home, a particular spot in the park, or maybe a neighborhood restaurant with the "World's Juiciest Burgers."

In this chapter, you will write a paragraph to describe a favorite place. You will need to use plenty of sensory details to re-create this place. Your goal is to help readers see the sights, smell the aromas, feel the atmosphere, and hear the sounds as if they were right there with you.

Writing Guidelines

Subject:	**A favorite place**
Form:	**Descriptive paragraph**
Purpose:	**To describe one of your favorite places**
Audience:	**Classmates**

Descriptive Paragraph

In a descriptive paragraph, you use details to paint a vivid picture of one person, place, thing, or event. You start with a **topic sentence** that tells what the paragraph is about. Then, in the **body** of the paragraph, you add the specific details. The **closing sentence** brings the description to an end.

**Topic
sentence**

Body

**Closing
sentence**

Bob's Deli

When I walk through the door at Bob's Deli, familiar sights and smells greet me. As usual, Bob is wiping the counter, even though it's spotless. "Hey, you," he says. He greets all his regular customers this way. Above him on the wall, giant pictures of sandwiches and salads make me even hungrier than I already am. At least six kinds of pie fill a round display case that stands next to the counter. It looks as though someone has already had a piece of the lemon meringue. A sign on the cash register announces today's special—a bowl of vegetable beef soup and half a sandwich. I sit down at the cold, shiny chrome counter and watch Bob pour a thick smoothie into a tall glass. As he plops a fresh strawberry on top, my stomach growls, and I am ready to place my order.

Respond to the reading. On your own paper, answer the following questions.

☐ **Ideas** (1) What details did the writer use to "paint" a picture? Name three of them.

☐ **Organization** (2) Which order of location pattern did the writer use (left to right, right to left, top to bottom, far to near)?

☐ **Voice & Word Choice** (3) What phrases show that the writer really likes Bob's Deli? List two of them.

Prewriting **Selecting a Topic**

To get started, think about places you could write about. Clustering is one way to begin. The writer of the paragraph on page 72 used a cluster like the one below to remember some favorite places.

Select a topic. Create your own cluster to identify possible places to write about in your paragraph. Then "star" one place you'd like to describe.

Gathering Details

Collect plenty of sensory details about your topic, even though you might not use all of them in your paragraph. Choose details that will help you create a clear, vivid description.

Collect your details. Use the following questions to help you remember important details.

- What are the main sights and sounds?
- Are there any parts in this place that stand out?
- What colors are important?
- What smells and tastes do you connect with this place?
- What feelings do you have about it?
- What happens in this place?

Writing Creating Your First Draft

The goal of a first draft is to get all of your ideas and details down on paper. Remember that everything does not have to be perfect in a first draft. You can make as many changes as you want later on.

- Start your paragraph with a topic sentence that identifies a favorite place and interests your reader.
- Think about how you want to organize your sentences. Order of location (top to bottom, left to right, near to far) works well for many descriptions. See page **551** for information about other patterns.
- Choose transitions from the list below to help you show location. See pages **572–573** for more transitions.
  above, below, beside   to the left, to the right   on top of, next to
- End with a sentence that brings your description to a close. See the closing sentence in the model on page 72.

 Write your first draft. Use the guidelines above when you write. Be sure to add specific details that appeal to your reader's senses.

Revising Improving Your Writing

When you revise, focus first on the ideas and organization in your writing. You may move, delete, or change parts of your writing as necessary.

 Revise your paragraph. Use the following questions as a guide.

1 Does my topic sentence identify the place I'm describing?

2 Have I included enough sensory details?

3 Have I put the details in the best order?

4 Do I use specific nouns, verbs, and adjectives?

5 Do I use complete sentences that read smoothly?

Editing Checking for Conventions

Carefully edit your revised paragraph for punctuation, capitalization, spelling, and grammar.

 Edit and proofread your work. Use the conventions checklist on page 128 as you edit. Then write a neat final copy.

Descriptive Writing
Describing a Place

"Ah, my room. . . . Let me show you around. Do you see how I display all my stylish clothes across the floor? Do you hear the gentle snoring of my dog Urfie as he warms the foot of my bed? Do you detect that strange odor coming from the closet? Ah hah! That must be my gym shoes."

When you describe a familiar place, you take your reader on a tour using your best words. Your goal is to let the reader see the things around you, hear what is happening, and maybe even smell the gym shoes!

Writing Guidelines

Subject:	A place you know well
Form:	Descriptive essay
Purpose:	To describe a familiar place
Audience:	Classmates

Descriptive Essay

In the sample essay that follows, the writer describes his locker. As you read the description, look at the notes in the left margin. They explain the important parts of the essay.

My Home Away from Home

BEGINNING

The beginning shows why this place is special.

Blue metal lockers line the hallways in our school. Each locker is identical except for the brass number attached to the door. Locker number 379 is mine. This locker is my home away from home for the year.

When I click open my locker, the smell of peanut butter escapes from a brown paper lunch bag on the top shelf. Under the bag, the sleeve of my old olive green sweatshirt dangles off the shelf. On top of everything is my favorite blue cap. Some magazines that I've shoved up there, way in the back, almost hide my dead CD player.

MIDDLE

The middle paragraphs describe the locker from top to bottom.

All winter long, my ski jacket was stuffed in the middle part of my locker. Now the only things hanging on the hooks are my red warm-up jacket and my bag full of dirty gym clothes. Phew. That smell mixed with the peanut butter is almost enough to make me gag.

The bottom of my locker is like a mini dump site. It is filled with my muddy shoes, broken pencils, and a pile of sticky candy wrappers. Buried underneath all of that are dozens of old assignments and, probably, some things I've been looking for all year. I'll know for sure when I dig everything out in June.

DESCRIPTIVE

MIDDLE
Special attention is given to the locker door.

ENDING
• • • • • • • • • • • •
The ending gives more insight into the writer's personality.

Some of my most important stuff is attached to the inside of my locker door. Near the top, I've taped two pictures of my favorite rock group. Around the edges, I've jammed in a bunch of notes from my friends. Below the notes, a collection of fridge magnets from my favorite pizza places hold up a huge photo of me with the 10-pound bass I landed last summer.

On the last day of school, I'll take down the pictures and throw out the candy wrappers and trash. I'll stuff all the important things into my backpack and grab those smelly gym clothes. When I close my locker for the last time and head for home, it will feel as if I've just completed another chapter in my life.

Respond to the reading. Answer the following questions about the essay.

☐ **Ideas** (1) What comparison does the writer make to introduce the topic? (2) Which details rely on a sense other than sight? Name two.

☐ **Organization** (3) How is the essay organized?

☐ **Voice & Word Choice** (4) Which details reveal the most about the writer's personality?

Prewriting Selecting a Topic

The topic for your essay should be a place that is very familiar to you. Make sure that you choose a place that isn't too big or too small. Think of places that you can describe in a few paragraphs with many interesting details. A topic chart like the one below can help you organize your thoughts.

Topic Chart

Places	Specific Topics
Home	– my bedroom – our backyard – the kitchen
School	– (my locker) – the music room – the office
Other	– Gus's Pizza – my grandma's kitchen – the city beach

Create a topic chart. Make a chart like the one above, using *Home, School,* and *Other*. Think of two or three specific topics for each category. Circle the one specific topic that you would like to write about.

Gathering Details

One way to gather details is to make a list of sensory details. Sensory details help the reader see, feel, smell, taste, and hear what is being described.

Collect details. Gather sensory details for your description by answering the following questions.

1 What do you see when you look around your place? (Think about colors, shapes, and sizes.)

2 What sounds do you hear?

3 What smells do you notice?

4 What textures can you touch?

5 What tastes or feelings come to mind?

Organizing Your Details

You can use order of location (spatial order) to arrange the details in a description. For example, you may decide to organize the details from top to bottom or from left to right or farthest to nearest. The writer of the essay on pages 76–77 organized the details from top to bottom on a list.

Organizing List

1. Open the locker door.
2. Describe what's on the top shelf.
3. Tell what's hanging in the middle part.
4. Draw a mental picture of what's on the bottom.
5. Describe the inside of the locker door.
6. Share the details of the last day of school.

Prewrite

Organize your details. Decide which order works best for your description (top to bottom, left to right, far to near). Then write an organizing list like the one above for your essay.

Using Similes and Metaphors

Similes and metaphors can make descriptive writing clearer and more creative. They can help readers see the description in their minds. The writer of the essay on pages 76–77 uses a metaphor in the opening paragraph and a simile in the third middle paragraph.

- A **simile** compares two different things using *like* or *as*.

  The bottom of my locker is like a mini dump site.

- A **metaphor** compares two different things without using *like* or *as*.

  This locker is my home away from home for the year.

Try IT Write a simile and a metaphor to compare your place with other things. If you like how your comparisons turn out, include them in your essay.

Writing Starting Your Descriptive Essay

The beginning paragraph should get your reader's attention and identify your topic—a familiar place. Here are two ways to get started.

Beginning Paragraph

- **Put yourself in the description.** You can do this by serving as the narrator. This means that you will use "I" and describe the place through your eyes.

> The writer tells how she feels.
>
> *When I stand on our back step and look out, I see more than just a backyard. I see my family's "summer home," a small, relaxing plot of land protected by a redwood fence.*

- **Begin with background information.** This information will help your reader better understand or appreciate your topic.

> The writer shows why this place is special.
>
> *When my mom's job forced us to move into the city, she decided to create a quiet place for us to relax. That's just what she did in our backyard. With a lot of work, we now have a peaceful "getaway" to enjoy.*

Using Words with Feeling

Don't settle for just any word to capture the description of the place you are describing. Use words that have the right meaning and the right feeling, or connotation. (*Connotation* means "the feeling that a word suggests.")

The writer of each of the beginning paragraphs above uses words like "summer home," "relaxing," "quiet," and "peaceful" because they all have the right feeling—the backyard is a place to unwind and enjoy yourself.

Write your beginning paragraph. Write a beginning that catches your reader's interest and focuses on your topic. Make sure to use words with the right feeling. If you don't like how your first opening turns out, try again.

Developing the Middle Part

In the middle paragraphs of the essay, describe your familiar place. Use your organizing list from page 79 as a guide for your writing.

Middle Paragraphs

In the middle paragraphs, the writer first describes the three sides of the backyard before focusing on the lawn in the center.

> Along the fence at the left side of the yard are my mom's famous red rosebushes. They explode with color all summer long. A flat stone walkway running in front of the bushes makes it easy to admire and smell the flowers. These stones are smooth and warm against my bare feet.
>
> Against the back fence is a small white shed. The shed holds my mom's garden tools and an old push mower. It also holds our bicycles and a lot of sports equipment, including my favorite basketballs. On rainy days, I like to stand in the shed and hear the raindrops hitting the metal roof.
>
> My mother's vegetable garden runs next to the fence on the right side of the yard. Mom always plants beans in that space. As the bean plants grow, she carefully ties them to stakes to keep them from falling over. In the front of this garden is a row of golden yellow marigolds. Their distinct smell is supposed to keep the rabbits away from the beans.
>
> The heart of our yard is the lawn itself. A crab apple tree towers over the back of the yard and provides plenty of shade. In front of the tree is a wooden lawn swing that gets plenty of use, especially in the evening. To the right of the swing is a yellow plastic sand box where my little brother and sister play for hours at a time.

Each middle paragraph focuses on a different part of the yard.

The underlined phrases show the organization of the essay.

Write your middle paragraphs. Use sensory details in your paragraphs to help the reader imagine how your place looks, feels, sounds, and smells.

Writing Ending Your Essay

The ending paragraph should clearly signal that your description is complete. In the last sentence or two, leave your reader with a final idea or image—something that will keep him or her thinking about your topic.

Ending Paragraph

The writer makes a final comment about the topic.	*Beyond my yard lies a busy city. On hot summer nights, when we relax in the yard, I can hear the rush of freeway traffic and the call of far-off train whistles. I'm sure that someday I'll join the traffic or follow the train whistles, but for now, I'm happy right here.*

 Write your ending paragraph. Use interesting details that will keep this place in your reader's memory for some time.

Revising and Editing

You can improve your first draft by adding, deleting, or changing some details. Keep these questions in mind when you revise.

 Revise your first draft. Revise your first draft using the questions below as a guide.

- ☐ **Ideas** Have I included enough sensory details about the place?

- ☐ **Organization** Do I use order of location to organize the details?

- ☐ **Voice** Do I sound like I really care about the subject and the reader?

- ☐ **Word Choice** Do I use descriptive words from start to finish?

- ☐ **Sentence Fluency** Do my sentences flow smoothly? Do I vary sentence lengths and beginnings?

 Edit your description. Once you have completed your revising, use the checklist on page 128 to correct any errors in your essay. Then write a neat final copy to share.

AWK!!

Descriptive Writing
Across the Curriculum

Wouldn't it be great if you could teach a parrot to recite the Gettysburg Address? Wouldn't it be even greater if you could teach your parrot not to recite the speech all day and all night? Finally, wouldn't it be the greatest if you could write an ad that describes your parrot so well that a kind and caring bird lover comes to buy him? Descriptive writing can be useful.

Sometimes, descriptive writing can also be useful in completing class assignments. For example, in social studies, you could describe a famous person or place. In math, you could describe a geometric object, or in science, you could describe the result of a lab experiment.

Mini Index

- **Social Studies:**
  Describing a Famous Place
- **Math:** Writing a Geometric Riddle
- **Science:** Writing a Lab Report
- **Practical Writing:** Writing a Classified Ad

FOR SALE

Social Studies:
Describing a Famous Place

Use descriptive writing when you need to explain the features of a famous place. Think about a modern or an ancient structure that you have read about or visited. The writer below chose to write about the ancient Roman Colosseum.

The Roman Colosseum

The **beginning** shares important background information.	A modern football stadium is about the same size as the Roman Colosseum was. Between 50,000 and 75,000 spectators attended events there for hundreds of years after it was completed in 80 C.E.
	Without using modern machinery, the Romans built the huge Colosseum on the site of a marsh. They drained water and then cut an oval donut shape into the clay base. On top of the base, they poured layers of cement, more than 36 feet thick. Next, they built supporting brick walls, about 9 feet wide, around both the inner and outer walls of the foundation.
The **middle** describes the place from the bottom to the top.	Just below ground level, the Romans built a maze of tunnels, rooms, and passages on top of the concrete base. This area held equipment, scenery, and even wild animals. Huge hoists lifted both gladiators and animals to the ground level.
	At ground level, sand covered the wooden floor of the arena. Nets attached to tall poles protected the audience from the wild beasts.
	Above the arena, spectators sat and viewed the events of the day. Just like today, there were sections of preferred seating. The outer walls of the Colosseum stood four stories high and enclosed the seating area. Each of the first three stories had 80 identical arches, and each arch held a statue. Forty rectangular windows circled the fourth story.
The **ending** gives the reader something to think about.	When people visit the Colosseum today, they will see the ruins, but they can still imagine sitting among the ancient Romans in this famous place.

DESCRIPTIVE

Writing Tips

Before you write . . .

- **Choose a famous place that interests you.**
  Select a place related to a subject you are studying in social studies class.
- **Do your research.**
  Learn about your place. Look at pictures of it and read about its history and culture.
- **Take notes.**
  Collect important details that will help create a clear description in the reader's mind.

During your writing . . .

- **Write a clear beginning, middle, and ending.**
  Begin with a little-known fact or a comparison. In the middle, describe the place using precise words. End with a final thought that inspires your reader to find out even more about your famous place.
- **Organize your thoughts.**
  Describe your place in order of location, from top to bottom, from left to right, or from near to far.
- **Use an engaging voice.**
  Your writing should give the impression that you know a lot about the place and are interested in it.

After you've written a first draft . . .

- **Check for completeness.**
  Make sure that you have included enough information so that the reader can imagine your place in his or her mind.
- **Check for correctness.**
  Proofread your essay to make sure there are no mistakes in punctuation, capitalization, spelling, or grammar.

 Choose a famous place that interests you and learn more about it. Then write a clear, complete description to share with your classmates.

Math: Writing a Geometric Riddle

Descriptive writing can be used to write about objects. Below, a student writes a riddle for math class using geometrical terms.

The writer uses personification to describe the object.

The writer rhymes the second and fourth lines.

An Ancient Wonder

I stand upon a giant square

And have four triangle faces.

My polyhedron family

Lives near a large oasis.

What am I?

Answer: An Egyptian pyramid

More About Riddles

Riddles are rewarding mental exercises. They encourage you to use your imagination and build new language skills. Riddles are also creative forms of descriptive writing. The simplest form of riddle, the "What Am I?" riddle, has been around for a long time. Court jesters used this type of riddle to entertain kings and queens for centuries.

DESCRIPTIVE

Writing Tips

Before you write . . .

- **Think about different geometric shapes and figures.** There are many to choose from such as the triangle, rectangle, square, parallelogram, pentagon, cube, sphere, and arc.
- **Look at the world around you.** Choose an object to describe that contains specific geometric shapes and figures. The object is the answer to your riddle.
- **Study your object.** Find out as much as you can about the object. Reading about it and answering the 5 W's are two ways to gather information for your description.
- **Jot down details.** Write down specific words and phrases to describe your object. Be sure to include some geometric terms.

During your writing . . .

- **Be creative.** Think of different ways to write your riddle. Here are a few suggestions.

  Use metaphors. Compare the appearance of the object to something else.

  Use personification. Describe the object as if it were a living thing.

  Create a surprise ending. Let the ending take a funny or unexpected twist.

  Make it rhyme. Try to make your riddle rhyme. It's a great exercise for your mind.

After you've written a first draft . . .

- **Check for completeness.** Have you used the best words to describe your object? Have you included enough information for readers to answer the riddle?
- **Check for correctness.** Are the words spelled correctly? Do you use the correct words (*angle, angel; right, write*)?

Try IT Write a geometrical "What Am I?" riddle of your own following the tips above. Share your riddle with your classmates.

Science: Writing a Lab Report

In science class, you may be asked to write a lab report. The student report below describes which variables (variety of conditions) make mold grow fastest on bread.

In the **beginning** the purpose is stated, variables are listed, and a hypothesis is given.

The **middle** clearly describes the experiment and what the writer observed.

The **ending** reports the writer's conclusion.

A Moldy Problem

PURPOSE: Find out what conditions will make mold grow fastest on bread.

VARIABLES: Temperature and moisture

HYPOTHESIS: Mold will grow fastest on bread that is kept warm and moist.

EXPERIMENT: I put three slices of freshly baked white bread into sandwich bags. I labeled them A, B, and C. I added a small amount (2 T.) of water to the bread in Bag A, and I put the bag inside a warm, dark cabinet. Bags B and C got no water. I put Bag B in the refrigerator and Bag C inside a cool, dark cabinet. I made sure that all of the bags were tightly sealed. I checked each bag daily for one week, and I recorded any changes I observed.

OBSERVATIONS: Nothing happened until the fifth day. The bread in the refrigerator appeared fresh. The bread in the cool, dark cabinet had no mold. The moist bread in the warm cabinet was starting to grow spots of greenish-gray mold on the crust.

CONCLUSION: My hypothesis that mold will grow fastest on bread that is kept warm and moist was correct. I expected, though, that the mold would appear sooner than it did.

DESCRIPTIVE

Writing Tips

Before you write . . .

- **Choose a topic that interests you.**
  Select a science topic related to a subject you are studying in school.
- **Research your topic and plan your experiment.**
  Read about your topic and jot down important details. Then decide what your experiment will be.

During your writing . . .

- **State the purpose, the variables, and your hypothesis.**
  Write a statement that describes what you want to do. Tell which variables you will test. Then write a hypothesis telling what you think you will find out from your experiment.
- **Organize your details.**
  Use time order to describe the procedure you followed (what happened first, second, next, and so on).
- **Use strong, colorful words.**
  A good description contains strong verbs, and specific nouns, adjectives, and adverbs.
- **Clearly state your observations and conclusion.**
  Your observations should describe what happened during your experiment. Your conclusion should tell whether or not your hypothesis was correct.

After you've written a first draft . . .

- **Check for completeness.**
  Make sure that you have clearly stated the purpose, variables, hypothesis, and conclusion. Check your experiment and observation. Make sure you haven't left out any important details.
- **Check for correctness.**
  Proofread your report for punctuation, capitalization, spelling, and grammar.

 Select and perform a science experiment. Then describe it in a lab report using the tips above as a guide.

Practical Writing:
Creating a Classified Ad

In everyday life, you will find descriptive writing used in many ways. Classified newspaper ads usually contain lots of descriptive writing. Students created the ads below.

Real Ads

FOUND: Small black and white cat. Red collar with silver bell and pearls. Found near 5th and Walnut. Call Julie, 555-4321, after 3:00 p.m.

FOR SALE: Radio-controlled boat. Bright yellow racer. Dual, rechargeable, nickel-cadmium battery. Like new. $10. Call Colin at 555-1234.

Just-for-Fun Ads

LOST: Blue denim backpack. Tuna sandwich, dirty gym clothes, and math book inside. Need by 3rd period tomorrow. Reward. Call Jake, 555-4231.

FOR SALE: Parrot named Lincoln. Recites Gettysburg Address. $20, cage included. Call 555-1342 and ask to talk to Lincoln.

Specific details, such as color, size, location, and price, are listed.

Contact information, names, and phone numbers are included.

Writing Tips

Before you write . . .

- **Do some research.**
  Look at classified ads in your local newspaper. Find some ads with clear descriptions to use as models.
- **Select a topic for your ad.**
  Choose an animal or an item that can be lost, found, or for sale.
- **Gather specific details.**
  List important features to describe your item.
- **Jot down contact information.**
  Think about how and when you would like the reader to contact you.

During your writing . . .

- **Organize your thoughts.**
  Name the animal or item that is lost, found, or for sale. Clearly describe it. End by telling the reader how to contact you.
- **Use colorful words.**
  A good description contains strong verbs, and specific nouns, adjectives, and adverbs.
- **Be brief.**
  Most newspapers charge by the word for classified ads. The more words you use, the more your ad will cost. So make every word count.

After you've written a first draft . . .

- **Check for completeness.**
  Do you name the item? Have you included enough details to make your description clear? Is your contact information complete? Is your ad interesting to read?
- **Check for correctness.**
  Proofread your ad to make sure there are no mistakes in spelling, capitalization, punctuation, or grammar.

Try IT Create a classified ad. It can be real or imagined (see the examples on the facing page). Use the tips above as a guide.

Narrative Writing

Narrative Writing
Narrative Paragraph

Think of a time when something really exciting happened to you. Maybe you won a basketball game, or caught a big fish, or got an "A on a tough test. Now imagine telling a friend all about it. That's what a "narrative" is—a story about something that has happened. We all tell such stories at one time or another.

In this chapter, you will write a paragraph that tells about a great moment in your life. Once you are finished, you and your classmates can share these personal stories with each other.

Writing Guidelines

Subject: A great moment
Form: Narrative paragraph
Purpose: To entertain
Audience: Classmates

Narrative Paragraph

By remembering the great experiences in your life and telling stories about them, you can relive those times over and over. In the following narrative paragraph, Devon opens with a **topic sentence** that identifies the experience. Next, the **body** of his paragraph recalls the events. Finally, the **closing sentence** tells how the experience ended.

Topic sentence

Body

Closing sentence

Getting Game

The teachers were winning the annual student-faculty basketball game 42 to 40. One minute remained, and Coach Williams had the ball. He tried to dodge around me at midcourt, but I reached in and swatted the ball away from him. The crowd roared as the ball bounced toward our basket, but Mrs. Jenkins was too quick. She snatched the ball up. Ten seconds remained on the clock. Mrs. Jenkins tried to pass, but one of my teammates knocked the ball right into my hands. Two seconds remained, and Coach Williams was guarding me. In desperation, I hurled a half-court shot over his head. The ball sailed up—beautiful—and the crowd held its breath. BUZZ! With a silent swish, the shot dropped through the hoop. Our score flipped to 43. The stands erupted, and Coach Williams gave me a high five, saying, "I guess I've found next year's shooting guard."

Respond to the reading. Answer the following questions on your own paper.

☐ **Ideas** (1) What details create excitement in the paragraph? Name two.

☐ **Organization** (2) How does Devon begin his narrative?

☐ **Voice & Word Choice** (3) What verbs re-create the action? List three or four.

Prewriting **Selecting a Topic**

How do you choose a great moment to write about? Devon used a listing strategy to help him think about exciting moments he had experienced. Part of his list follows.

> *Rode the "Plunge"*
>
> *Got a first at the solo and ensemble contest*
>
> *Fed a sea lion*
>
> *Scored the winning shot in basketball*
>
> *Did my first gainer dive*

List your ideas. On your own paper, write a list of exciting experiences or great moments you have had. Choose one experience to write about.

Gathering Details

Once you know your topic, you can gather details for your paragraph. To collect details for his narrative paragraph, Devon decided to make a time line. This graphic organizer helped him remember details and get them in the right order. Not every detail ended up in the final draft, but the time line did give Devon a good plan for starting to write.

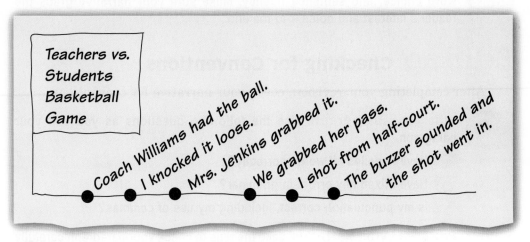

Teachers vs. Students Basketball Game

Coach Williams had the ball.

I knocked it loose.

Mrs. Jenkins grabbed it.

We grabbed her pass.

I shot from half-court.

The buzzer sounded and the shot went in.

List your details. Make a time line of details for the event you will write about. Make sure to list them in the correct order.

Writing Creating Your First Draft

A narrative paragraph has a topic sentence, a body, and a closing sentence. Each part serves a different purpose.

- The topic sentence introduces the narrative.
- The body uses details to describe what happened.
- The closing sentence wraps up the narrative.

 Write your first draft. Review your time line and then write your narrative paragraph. Include details to make your readers feel that they are experiencing the event for themselves.

Revising Improving Your Paragraph

In a piece of writing as short as a narrative paragraph, it's important for every sentence to work well. Keep these tips in mind as you revise.

- **Revise with a reader's eye.** Pretend you are reading the paragraph for the first time. What parts work well? What parts still need work?
- **Keep the action moving.** Use strong action verbs and specific nouns to hold the reader's interest. Cut any unnecessary details.
- **Build to a climax.** Have the events in your paragraph lead up to a moment of crisis. Then resolve the crisis at the end.

 Revise your paragraph. Revise with a focus on ideas, organization, voice, word choice, and sentence fluency. Make sure your narrative grabs the reader's interest and holds it to the end.

Editing Checking for Conventions

After completing your revision, check your narrative for conventions.

 Edit your paragraph. Use the following questions as you edit your paragraph.

1 Have I spelled all words correctly?

2 Have I fixed any errors in grammar?

3 Is my punctuation correct, including my use of commas?

Proofread your narrative. Take the time to check your paragraph carefully for any errors. Then make a clean final copy to share with your classmates.

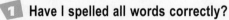

Narrative Writing

Sharing a Learning Experience

"The writer steps up to the plate. She looks cool and focused. She takes a couple of practice swings with her pencil, and then settles in. Here comes the first idea. The writer takes a swing at it by starting her first sentence . . . , but then decides to cross it out. She gets ready for the next idea. She swings. Crack! The idea is a real hit, and the writer is off and running with her story."

Writing a personal narrative can be just as exciting as playing baseball. All kinds of ideas will enter your mind; it's your job to connect with the best ones. Personal narratives allow readers to experience the thrill of your life stories and learn from them just as you did. They will cheer whenever you make a hit.

Writing Guidelines

Subject:	An important learning experience
Form:	Personal narrative
Purpose:	To share a true experience that has taught you something
Audience:	Classmates

Understanding Your Goal

Your goal in this chapter is to write an essay about a personal experience that taught you something. As you write, keep in mind the following traits of narrative writing. These traits will help you to plan and create your personal narrative.

TRAITS OF NARRATIVE WRITING

Ideas

Use specific details that make the reader want to know what happens next.

Organization

Write a beginning, a middle, and an ending that are clear to the reader, and put the events in chronological (time) order.

Voice

Create a personal voice, and use dialogue to show each individual's personality.

Word Choice

Use words that express how you feel about the experience, and experiment with participles for added description.

Sentence Fluency

Use a variety of sentence lengths to create an effective style.

Conventions

Be sure that your punctuation, capitalization, spelling, and grammar are correct.

Get the big picture. Look at the rubric on pages 130–131. You can use this rubric to assess your progress. Your goal is to develop a well-written essay about a personal experience.

Personal Narrative

In this personal narrative, the student writer remembers an experience from his first day in middle school. The key parts of the narrative are described in the left margin.

BEGINNING

The beginning starts in the middle of an action and then gives the reader background information.

Home Team or Visitor?

"Time to leave!" my mother yelled up the stairs.

My heart kicked against my ribs. This was it—my first day at school in Chicago! Before this, we had lived in a town that had a total population of 2,114. I could walk from the cornfields at one end of town to the bean fields at the other end in 20 minutes. Mom had changed jobs, though, and now we were Chicagoans. I had no idea what to expect from this big-city school.

I took one last look in the mirror. My brand-new Chicago Cubs jersey looked great with my faded jeans and new tennis shoes. I slapped my old Cubs cap on my head, snatched my backpack from the kitchen table, and ran for the waiting school bus.

MIDDLE

The middle includes the writer's feelings.

When the bus came, it was nearly full. I walked down the aisle slowly, looking for an empty seat. I felt as if everybody was staring at me, even though most of them were busy talking to each other. However, as I glanced toward the back, I noticed a couple of guys laughing. They were pointing at me.

"Hey, it looks like we have a super fan riding on our bus today!" one of them shouted over the noise.

At that moment, everyone got quiet and all eyes were glued on me. I could feel my face getting hot. The last thing I wanted to be was the center of attention.

MIDDLE

The middle includes dialogue that connects the action and gives information.

Suddenly, this big kid stood up and said, "Slide in here." I was glad to get out of the aisle, away from all those eyes. I slid in next to the window and breathed a sigh of relief. The big kid sat down beside me, and the bus started moving.

"I'm Al," he said, shaking my hand. "Don't let those two bother you. You'll soon find out that they're some of the biggest baseball fans in our school."

"I'm Lewis," I said.

Al grinned and said, "You know, you do kind of look like a tourist."

We both laughed, and suddenly I felt a lot better. Right then I decided that the next day I'd wear the same kind of clothes I had worn at my old school. I wouldn't worry about fitting into the city scene.

ENDING

The ending tells what the writer learned from his experience.

I thought I needed to impress everyone, but I learned that it's always best to just be myself. I also realized that every day is full of surprises. How could I know that in the middle of an embarrassing moment, I'd meet someone like Al, who would become a great friend?

Respond to the reading. What makes "Home Team or Visitor?" a well-written narrative? To find out, answer the following questions.

☐ **Ideas** **(1)** What specific experience does the writer choose to share with the reader?

☐ **Organization** **(2)** How does the writer organize the narrative? **(3)** What is the purpose of the ending part?

☐ **Voice & Word Choice** **(4)** What words and phrases show how the writer feels about this experience?

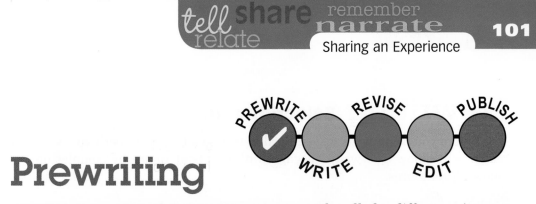

Prewriting

Choosing a topic that interests you can make all the difference in your personal narrative. Along with choosing an interesting topic, you will also gather and organize details in this prewriting section.

Keys to Effective Prewriting

NARRATIVE

1. Select an experience that you remember well.

2. Think about the lesson you learned from the experience.

3. Write freely about your experience and then check to see how many of the 5 W and H questions you can answer.

4. Use a list or graphic organizer to put the events in time order.

5. Gather details about sights, sounds, smells, and other sensory details related to your experience.

6. Consider how you can use dialogue in your narrative.

Prewriting Selecting a Topic

Before you begin writing, you need to choose a topic that both you and your reader will enjoy. One writer began thinking about topics by completing the following sentences.

Sentence Starters

1. I was being helpful when . . .
   — I helped my uncle install a CD player in his car.
   — I kept the little kids away from the fire equipment. ✳

2. I was inspired when . . .
   — I saw how well everyone liked my science-fair project.
   — the guest teacher from Kenya spoke to our class.

3. I was exhausted when . . .
   — I came home from my cousin's sleepover.
   — I hiked up the giant sand dunes. ✳

4. I was excited when . . .
   — my uncle from Puerto Rico visited us.
   — I placed third in the gymnastic competition. ✳

Prewrite

Complete some sentence starters. On your own paper, finish the sentence starters above with your own ideas. Put stars next to three ideas that you think would make interesting topics for a personal narrative.

Focus on the Traits

Ideas If you can't think of anything to write about, look through old photos and souvenirs and read through your personal journal. That's how many professional writers get ideas.

Focusing on Your Topic

You've identified some possible experiences to write about. Now you need to think about what you have learned from each of them. Below, the writer used a chart to list three interesting experiences and the lessons learned.

My Experiences   *Lessons I Learned*

Climbing the sand dunes ——→ *I shouldn't hike alone.*
Watching the warehouse burn ——→ *I want to be a firefighter.*
Placing in a competition ——→ *The more I practice,*
                                        the better I perform.

Prewrite

Focus on a topic. Using your three starred ideas from the activity on page 102, make a chart like the one above. List what you learned from each of your experiences. Then circle the experience you could write about in your narrative.

Remembering the Details

Isabella used two gathering techniques. First, she wrote freely, and then she answered the 5 W and H questions.

> *My brother was shouting. I heard sirens. Fire trucks flew past. I ran down to the corner. Smoke was coming out of the warehouse's windows. One firefighter asked me to help her. I did. I kept watching her. I'd like to be a firefighter.*

Who was in the experience?—my brother, the firefighter, me
What happened?—a warehouse caught on fire
When did it happen?—last summer
Where did it happen?—in my neighborhood
Why did I get interested?—a firefighter asked for help
How did I change?—now want to be a firefighter

Prewrite

Remember your details. Write nonstop about your topic for 5 minutes to see what you remember. Also answer the 5 W and H questions about your topic. If you can't come up with enough details, try another topic.

Prewriting Putting Events in Order

Once you've gathered your details, it's time to put the main events in order. Most narratives are organized in chronological (time) order. That means the events, or scenes, appear in the order in which they happened. Isabella used a quick list to get her events in order.

Quick List

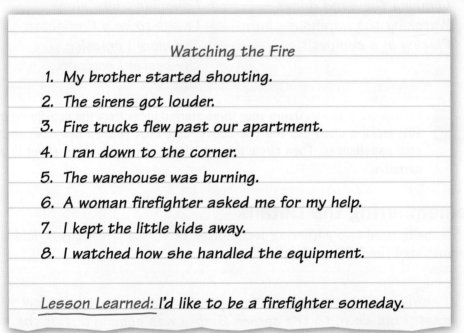

> *Watching the Fire*
>
> 1. My brother started shouting.
> 2. The sirens got louder.
> 3. Fire trucks flew past our apartment.
> 4. I ran down to the corner.
> 5. The warehouse was burning.
> 6. A woman firefighter asked me for my help.
> 7. I kept the little kids away.
> 8. I watched how she handled the equipment.
>
> <u>Lesson Learned</u>: I'd like to be a firefighter someday.

Make your quick list like the one above. Look back at your details to get started. List the main scenes of your experience. Then add the lesson you learned. You may find that you need to add more information.

Focus on the Traits

Organization As you begin your first draft, keep in mind that the beginning, the middle, and the ending are equally important. Carefully develop each part so that when the parts are put together, they form an inspiring narrative.

Gathering Sensory Details

Sensory details help the reader see, hear, smell, taste, and feel what is being described. The chart below shows some of the sensory details Isabella remembered.

Sensory Detail Chart

I saw...	I heard . . .	I smelled . . .	I felt . . .
racing fire trucks	screaming sirens	smoke	the spray of water
shooting flames	firefighters shouting orders	burning tires	waves of heat
dark smoke	shattering windows	chemical fumes	
heavy hoses	noisy kids	exhaust fumes	
leaning ladders			

NARRATIVE

Prewrite **Create a sensory detail chart.** Make a chart of sensory details for your experience. Then write down words or phrases that describe the events in your quick list on page 104.

Focus on the Traits

Voice It's important to use your writer's voice to show feelings. For example, the phrases *bolted out the front door* and *heart pumping fast* show excitement and fear.

Prewriting Adding Dialogue

There are many different reasons to use dialogue, or conversation, in your narrative. You can use it to show a speaker's personality, to keep the action moving, or to add information. The chart below shows different ways the writer can express the same idea. The dialogue examples are taken from the model on pages 99-100.

Use dialogue to . . .	WITHOUT DIALOGUE	WITH DIALOGUE
Show a speaker's personality	One of the kids started shouting that I looked like a super fan.	"Hey, it looks like we have a super fan riding on our bus today!" one of them shouted over the noise.
Keep the action moving	Suddenly this big kid stood up and told me to slide in next to him. I was glad to get away from all of those eyes.	Suddenly, this big kid stood up and said, "Slide in here." I was glad to get out of the aisle, away from all those eyes.
Add information	The big kid told me his name and not to be bothered by the other kids. I told him my name, too.	"I'm Al," he said, shaking my hand. "Don't let those two bother you. . . ." "I'm Lewis," I said.

Prewrite

Plan some dialogue for your narrative.
Plan to use dialogue in at least three places in your essay—one time for each of the ways listed above. (See pages 126 and 556 for more about punctuating dialogue.)

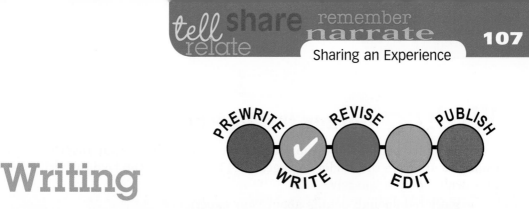

Writing

After you have finished gathering and organizing your ideas, you are ready to begin writing the first draft of your narrative. Write as if you were telling a friend about your experience.

Keys to Effective Writing

1. Use the ideas you gathered to help create your narrative.

2. Focus on getting all your ideas on paper.

3. Write on every other line to make room for changes later.

4. Include action words to show the reader what is happening.

5. Use sensory details to let the reader experience the event.

6. Use dialogue to show a speaker's personality, to keep the action moving, or to add information.

NARRATIVE

Writing Getting the Big Picture

The chart below shows how a personal narrative is put together. (The examples are from the model on pages 109–112.) Before you begin to write your first draft, be sure you have . . .

- gathered enough details about your experience.
- organized the events in chronological order.

BEGINNING

The **beginning** introduces the topic and grabs the reader's attention.

Opening Sentences
"Something's burning. I hear sirens. Something's burning!" Marcus shouted.

MIDDLE

The **middle** gives details that appeal to the senses and tells what happened first, second, and so on. It also uses dialogue show personalities and to keep the action going.

I rushed to the corner . . .

The firefighter shouted thanks . . .

Suddenly, giant flames shot . . .

I kept watching the firefighters . . .

ENDING

The **ending** reflects on the experience and tells what the writer learned.

Closing Sentences
I now had a dream. I wanted to be a firefighter. I knew that, someday, I wanted to be the person opening a hydrant to help put out a fire.

Starting Your Personal Narrative

Now that you have a plan, you can begin writing about your experience. Your first paragraph should get your reader's attention and introduce your topic. Write freely, using words that sound as if you were talking to a friend. You can begin your narrative in several different ways.

■ **Start with interesting details.**

> It's common to hear sirens wailing through the city. In fact, I usually don't pay attention to them. Then one day the sirens came screaming right past my apartment and stopped at the corner.

■ **Use sensory details to grab the reader's attention.**

> When was the last time you were at the scene of a fire? Every time I think about the warehouse fire, I remember the thick smoke reaching into the air and the stench of burning tires.

■ **Begin with a person speaking.**

> "Something's burning. I hear sirens. Something's burning!" Marcus shouted.

Beginning Paragraph

NARRATIVE

The writer grabs the reader's attention with dialogue. The writer introduces her experience.	*"Something's burning. I hear sirens. Something's burning!" Marcus shouted. I usually don't pay too much attention to my little brother. However, as the wailing sirens got louder, I thought maybe this time he was right. Just then, two fire trucks flew past our apartment building. I bolted out the front door and immediately felt my heart pumping fast. The trucks had stopped at the end of our block.*

Write your beginning. On your own paper, write the beginning for your narrative. Try using one of the three suggestions above.

Writing **Developing the Middle Part**

You have your reader's attention. Now you need to keep it by adding just the right details. Remember that even though you may be interested in every little thing that happened, your reader may not be. Stay focused and include only those details that make your experience come alive. Here are a few things to remember as you write your middle paragraphs.

- **Put your events in the order in which they happened.**
- **Appeal to your reader's senses.**
- **Create a clear picture with action words.**
- **Use dialogue to show a speaker's personality, to keep the action moving, or to add information.**

Middle Paragraphs

Dialogue moves the action along.

Sensory details let the reader "see" and "hear" the experience.

I rushed to the corner and saw the firefighters charging toward the abandoned warehouse across the street. A firefighter in a bulky coat, a yellow helmet, and big boots was attaching a huge snakelike hose to the hydrant. "Do me a favor," she said. "Stand back and keep those kids away from my rig." I could see a group of neighborhood kids, including my brother, running up to the fire truck.

"Marcus, Paulo, Maria!" I shouted. "You and your friends come here and stay away from that truck!"

The firefighter shouted thanks as she ran toward the burning, smoking warehouse. Then more sirens screamed to the scene. Suddenly,

NARRATIVE

Sensory details capture the excitement.

Dialogue adds information.

Dialogue shows personality.

giant flames shot into the sky, and a dark tower of smoke swirled into the air like a tornado. Above the shouts of firefighters, an explosion rocked the ground, and windows shattered. I watched my firefighter friend handle the hose as the powerful spray of water poured down on the blaze. "Some of those firemen aren't men," Marcus said, tugging on my shirt.

"You're right, Marcus, but they are all working together to put out the fire." I kept watching the firefighters wrestling with the huge hoses, smashing holes in the smoking roof, and climbing the leaning ladders.

"Bet you couldn't do that," Marcus said.

"Bet I could!" I answered.

Write your middle paragraphs. As you begin to write your middle paragraphs, be sure you look at all of the details you collected on pages 103–105. Also keep the following tips in mind.

Drafting Tips

- **Remember that your purpose** is to tell your classmates about an experience that taught you something.

- **Write freely.** Don't worry about getting everything just right. Just relax and let your ideas flow.

- **Add any new ideas** you remember as you write your first draft.

Writing Ending Your Personal Narrative

There are two important things to remember as you get ready to write your ending: (1) reflect on the experience, and (2) share what you learned from it. *Note:* The writer of this model used dialogue to add a final detail.

Beginning

Middle

Ending

Ending Paragraph

The writer tells the reader what she learned from her experience.

> By early evening the firefighters had gone, but the people were still standing around on the sidewalk talking about the fire. I heard a man say, "Some squirrels chewed on electrical wires." Maybe tomorrow things would get back to normal, but I would never be the same. I now had a dream. I wanted to be a firefighter. I knew that, someday, I wanted to be the person opening a hydrant to help put out a fire.

Write

Write your ending. In a final paragraph, tell the reader what you learned from your experience. Remember to keep it simple but interesting.

Form a complete first draft. Put together a complete copy of your first draft. Then you will be ready to revise your writing.

Drafting Tip

- **If you are having trouble writing your ending, wait awhile.** Then read through the narrative aloud. Think about all the ways this experience is important and how it has changed you.

Revising

As you revise, you get the chance to take your essay to the next level. You've already written about the major ideas. Now it's time to add, delete, or move certain parts in order to make your narrative even better.

Keys to Effective Revising

1. Put your narrative aside for a while. Then, when you're ready to revise, you'll have a fresh outlook about it.

2. Read your narrative out loud. Be sure your writing voice sounds like you.

3. Check your beginning, middle, and ending. Make sure each part works well.

4. Mark any parts that seem confusing.

5. Make sure your words capture your experience.

6. Use the editing and proofreading marks inside the back cover of this book.

NARRATIVE

Revising for Ideas

6 My narrative tells about one experience. My ideas and details are presented in a memorable way.

5 My narrative tells about one experience and "shows" my ideas.

4 My narrative tells about one experience. I need to "show" more of my ideas instead of "tell" about them.

When you revise for *ideas*, be sure you have focused on one experience. Check to see that you use a variety of sensory details to "show" your ideas. The rubric above will guide you as you improve your ideas.

Have I used a variety of sensory details?

You have used a variety of sensory details if you have appealed to most of the reader's senses.

 In the paragraph below, some of the sensory details have been underlined. Identify each numbered detail, using "S" for See, "H" for Hear, "F" for Feel, or "SM" for Smell.

> *F*
> With a groan, I pulled on my <u>heavy backpack</u> and headed off
> *S*
> barefoot up the <u>giant sand hills</u> at Sleeping Bear Dunes. At first, I
>
> thought this hike would be easy. Then, about halfway up, I began
>
> <u>huffing and puffing</u> like an <u>old steam engine</u>. My feet sank deep
>   **(1)**   **(2)**
> into the <u>cold</u> <u>white sand</u>. Although my leg muscles were <u>burning</u>,
>   **(3)**   **(4)**   **(5)**
> I kept trudging up and up. Once at the top, I saw the <u>icy-blue lake</u>
>   **(6)**
> and enjoyed the <u>cool breeze</u> blowing a <u>fresh scent</u> my way.
>   **(7)**   **(8)**

 Check your sensory details. Read through your first draft. Underline and label each sensory detail, using the following labels: "S"—See, "H"—Hear, "SM"—Smell, "T"—Taste, and "F"—Feel. Have you included a variety of sensory details? Have you used sensory details in your beginning, middle, and ending?

3 I need to focus on one experience. I need more sensory details.

2 I need to focus on one experience. Also I need to use sensory details.

1 I need to choose a different experience to write about.

NARRATIVE

Do I "show" instead of "tell"?

If you have created a detailed picture of your experience by using vivid descriptions in your writing, then you have *shown* your ideas.

Telling: **I saw damage from the tornado.**

Showing: **The tornado ruined our street. The winds roared out of the southwest about 3:00 p.m. and hit us hard. Along our street, all the houses are now missing either a roof or a front porch. A huge oak tree smashed down on four parked cars. Broken glass, tree limbs, and dangling electrical wires made moving on our street impossible. No one was seriously injured, although two people were taken to the clinic for cuts.**

Try It Use one of the following sentences for a topic sentence. Write a paragraph full of details that *show* rather than *tell*.

1. Yesterday's class was a blast.

2. My mother works very hard.

Revise   **Review your details.** Make sure your details "show" your ideas. Use action verbs and concrete nouns.

Ideas
Sensory details are checked for vivid pictures that "show" the experience.

> SM—Smell   H—Hear
> "Something's burning. I hear sirens. Something's
>   H—Hear
> burning!" Marcus shouted. I usually don't pay too
> much attention to my little brother. However, as the
>   H—Hear
> wailing sirens got louder, I thought maybe this time
>   S—See
> he was right. Just then, two fire trucks flew past
> our apartment building. I bolted out the . . .

Revising for Organization

6 My organization makes my narrative enjoyable and easy to read.

5 My events are in time order, and I use transitions well. I have a clear beginning, middle, and ending.

4 My events are in time order. Most of my transitions are helpful. I have a beginning, a middle, and an ending.

Your narrative needs to have a strong beginning, middle, and ending. As you revise for *organization*, use the rubric strip above to guide you.

Did I choose the best way to begin my narrative?

You can check how well your beginning works by answering the following questions. (See page 109 for ideas.)

1. What method do I use to grab the reader's attention?

2. As I read over my narrative again, can I see that a different beginning would work better? (If you answered "yes" to the second question, try another beginning.)

 Reread your opening. Make any necessary changes to improve your beginning.

How do I know if the middle is well organized?

Your middle is well organized if you put your events in the order in which they happened. It's also important that your middle be organized in such a way that your reader can move through it easily. Transition words can help tie ideas, sentences, and paragraphs together. The transitions below tie things together by time and work well in narratives.

before	while	immediately	soon	then
during	suddenly	next	later	after
finally	when	afterward	until	as soon as

 Review for time order. Check the middle paragraphs of your narrative to make sure your events are in chronological order. Rearrange the events if necessary. Also check to see how well you have used transitions to help the reader move easily through your narrative. (See pages 572–573 for more transitions.)

3 Some of my events are out of order. I need more transitions. My beginning or ending is weak.

2 I need to use time order and transitions in order to create a clear beginning, middle, and ending.

1 My narrative is confusing. I need to learn about time order.

Does my ending work well?

You will know whether your ending is successful after you answer the following questions.

1. Does my narrative end soon after the most important or intense moment?

2. Does my whole narrative lead up to the lesson I learned?

3. Will the reader be left with unanswered questions? (If you answered "yes," make changes to bring the reader to a satisfying ending.)

Revise   **Check your ending.** Use the questions listed above to see if you have written a winning ending.

Organization
Transitions are added to move the events along.

The firefighter shouted thanks as she ran toward the burning, smoking warehouse. *Then* More sirens screamed to the scene. *Suddenly,* Giant flames shot into the sky, and a dark tower of smoke swirled into the air like a tornado. Above the shouts of firefighters, an explosion rocked the ground, and windows shattered. I watched my firefighter . . .

Revising **for** Voice

6 My writer's voice creates an unforgettable experience for the reader. I use dialogue well.

5 My voice is sincere and expresses feelings. My dialogue shows each speaker's personality.

4 My voice is sincere and expresses feelings, but I need to check my dialogue.

When you revise for *voice*, check to make sure your writer's voice is sincere and shows feelings. Also make sure that the dialogue you use helps to reveal each speaker's personality. The rubric above will guide you as you improve the voice in your writing.

Is my personal voice heard in my narrative?

Your voice will come through if you express yourself sincerely and with real feelings. This is usually not difficult to do when you are sharing a personal experience. On the other hand, writers sometimes turn uninteresting, or dull, as soon as they put pen to paper (or fingers to the keyboard).

WRITING THAT LACKS VOICE: Uninteresting/Dull

When we walked home, I saw the moon. The night was foggy. I heard one dog bark and then others.

WRITING THAT CONTAINS VOICE: Sincere and Full of Real Feelings

While we were walking home, I looked up and saw the moon through the fog. Off in the distance, I heard a dog bark and then a chorus of barks. I felt a shiver crawl up my spine. It was probably just the cold.

 Write the first part of your narrative in the form of an e-mail message or a note to your closest friend. "Talk" to this person as if he or she were sitting right next to you. Afterward, underline any thoughts and feelings that sound like the real you.

 Check for voice. Rewrite any parts of your narrative that don't sound like the real you. Consider adding some of the thoughts and feelings you underlined in the previous activity.

3 My voice is sometimes dull. I need to improve the dialogue I've used.

2 My voice sounds uninteresting and dull. I need to add dialogue.

1 I need to understand how to write my story.

Does my dialogue show each speaker's personality?

Your dialogue shows each speaker's personality if it sounds natural and expresses true thoughts and feelings. Dialogue that works well helps the reader get to know each speaker. (See page **556**.)

> **SAMPLE DIALOGUE: Shows Each Speaker's Personality**
>
> "Well, don't just stand there. Grab a shovel. We've got a garden to plant," Mrs. Walters, our next-door neighbor, bellowed at me.
> "Me? Garden? I don't think so," I replied.
> "Here. Put on these gloves. We don't want to hurt those tender hands of yours," she said.
> "Come on, Mrs. Walters. I don't do gardens," I pleaded.
> "Nonsense. Your mother said that you needed a project, so let's get to work," she barked.

Revise **Check the dialogue in your narrative.** Do I include enough dialogue? Does it sound realistic and show each speaker's personality? If you can't answer "yes" to these questions, then revise the dialogue in your narrative.

Voice
Dialogue helps reveal the personality of the writer and of Marcus.

I kept watching the firefighters wrestling with the huge hoses, smashing holes in the smoking roof, and climbing the leaning ladders.

"Bet you couldn't do that," Marcus said.

"Bet I could!" I answered.

Revising **for** Word Choice

6 My exceptional word choice captures the experience.

5 I use specific words that add feeling. I use participles to improve my writing.

4 Most of my words add the feeling I want to create. I experiment with participles.

When you revise for *word choice*, check that you've used words that express specific feelings. Also check to see whether you have used participles correctly.

Have I used words that express the right feeling?

You know you have chosen words with the right feeling if the words express your *attitude* about your topic. The examples below demonstrate how certain words show different feelings.

 Read the examples and decide which one expresses *determination*, which one *nervousness*, and which one *enthusiasm*. What specific words help to express each feeling? Write your answers on your own paper.

Example 1

The applause signals that I'm next. My stomach begins doing flips. Heart throbbing and knees trembling, I make my way up what seems like a dozen steps. Reaching the mat, I take a deep breath, plaster on the expected smile, and take the first shaky step into my routine.

Example 2

In a few minutes, I'll show the world my routine. With every move locked in my brain, I glance in the mirror. My hair, makeup, and costume are ready and so am I! Bolts of energy travel from my toes to my fingertips as the announcer calls my name.

Example 3

After the competition, I march over to my coach and ask, "What do I have to do to place in the top three?" He instantly sits me down and finds his calendar. From now on, I'll be camping out at the gym.

 Revise for word choice. Think about the feeling you want to express. List words that fit that feeling. Have you used them in your narrative? Make changes to express the correct feeling in your writing.

3 I need to add more words that express specific feelings. I also need to use participles.

2 I keep using the same words again and again. I need to use words that express specific feelings.

1 I need help choosing words that express the feelings in my narrative.

How can participles improve my writing?

Participles are powerful adjectives that help writers strengthen their writing. They are formed by adding *ing* and *ed* to verbs. Compare the following sentences. (See page **485** and **730.3**.)

> **WITHOUT A PARTICIPLE**
>
> **Leaves decay and fill the forest with a rich smell.** (verb)
>
> **WITH A PARTICIPLE**
>
> **The rich smell of decaying leaves fills the forest.** (*ing* participle)

Try IT Change the verbs in parentheses into participles by adding *ing* or *ed*. For each item, write the participle along with the noun it modifies. Then write a sentence using the new word group.

1. (close) door
2. (crackle) campfire
3. (laugh) children
4. (whine) puppies
5. (surprise) faces
6. (annoy) sounds

Expand your choice of words. Look through your narrative. Are there any nouns that could be modified with a participle?

Word Choice
Participles replace wordy phrases and modify nouns.

I kept watching the firefighters wrestling with
the huge hoses, smashing holes in the ^smoking roof that
had smoke coming out of it, and climbing the
^leaning ladders that were leaning against the warehouse.

NARRATIVE

Revising for Sentence Fluency

6 My sentences are skillfully written and keep the reader's interest throughout.

5 My sentences flow smoothly. I use both long and short sentences.

4 Most sentences flow smoothly. I use long sentences well. Some of my short sentences need work.

When you revise for *sentence fluency*, check to see if you have used a variety of sentence lengths. Use the rubric above as you revise your sentences.

How can I write longer sentences?

Writers often use prepositional phrases and word groups that start with participles to expand their sentences. (See **730.3** and **742.1**.)

USE PREPOSITIONAL PHRASES

Before winter comes to Wyoming, **I hike** in the Snowy Mountain Range **where elk graze and eagles soar.**

USE WORD GROUPS THAT START WITH PARTICIPLES

Munching my trail mix, I watch soaring eagles **in a patch of sky** sandwiched between the canyon's walls.

 Read the following short sentences. Add prepositional phrases and participle word groups from the lists below to create sentences that flow smoothly.

1. Fire trucks arrived.

2. Sirens wailed.

3. Flames leaped.

4. Hoses sprayed.

Prepositional Phrases	Participial Word Groups
in the neighborhood	**roaring and racing**
around the warehouse	**hissing terribly**
through the windows	**rising suddenly**
with a terrific noise	**flaring and flashing**

 Check your sentences. Add important details to your narrative by using prepositional phrases and word groups that begin with participles. Include a variety of sentence lengths.

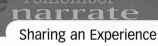

3 Most of my sentences flow smoothly. I need to use a few long sentences.

2 My sentences are all the same length. I need to expand or shorten some.

1 Most of my sentences need to be rewritten.

How can I use short sentences effectively?

You can sometimes use short sentences to draw attention to important points in your writing. Notice how the writer of the paragraph below uses two short sentences.

> My great-grandmother's school had a fascinating name connected to a mystery. Long before the school was built, maybe even before Grandma was born, Native Americans had discovered a strange pit on the land. <u>The pit was full of broken bones.</u> Maybe an ancient hunter had dug the pit to trap animals, which would fall into it and break their bones when they hit bottom. Maybe the pit had been a dump where a long-ago tribe threw its garbage. The mystery of the pit was never solved, but it did provide a name for Grandma's school. <u>The name was Broken Bone.</u>

Review your narrative. Find a place where you can use a short sentence to stress an important idea. Reread that part of the essay to see if your special sentence is effective.

NARRATIVE

Sentence Fluency
A prepositional phrase adds a detail, and a short sentence stresses an important idea.

By early evening
⋀The firefighters had gone, but the people were still standing around on the sidewalk talking about the fire. I heard a man say, "Some squirrels chewed on electrical wires." Maybe tomorrow things would get back to normal, but I would never be the same.⋀ *I now had a dream.* I wanted to be a firefighter. I . . .

Revising **Using a Checklist**

Check your revising. On a piece of paper, write the numbers 1 to 12. If you can answer "yes" to a question, put a check mark after that number. If not, continue to work with that part of your essay.

Ideas

_____ **1.** Do I focus on one experience?

_____ **2.** Do I include a variety of sensory details?

_____ **3.** Do I "show" my readers my ideas?

Organization

_____ **4.** Are my beginning, middle, and ending effective?

_____ **5.** Are the events arranged in chronological order?

_____ **6.** Do the transitions work well?

Voice

_____ **7.** Have I created a personal voice?

_____ **8.** Does the dialogue show each speaker's personality?

Word Choice

_____ **9.** Have I chosen words that express the right feeling?

_____ **10.** Have I used any participles?

Sentence Fluency

_____ **11.** Have I used a variety of sentence lengths?

_____ **12.** Have I used a short sentence or two to stress a point?

Make a clean copy. When you've finished revising your essay, make a clean copy before you begin to edit.

PREWRITE · REVISE · PUBLISH · WRITE · EDIT

Editing

After you've finished revising your narrative, it's time to edit it for your use of conventions: punctuation, capitalization, spelling, and grammar.

Keys to Effective Editing

1. Use a dictionary, a thesaurus, and the "Proofreader's Guide" in the back of this book.

2. Check for any words or phrases that may be confusing to the reader.

3. Check your writing for correct punctuation, capitalization, spelling, and grammar.

4. If you use a computer, edit on a printed computer copy and then enter your changes on the computer.

5. Use the editing and proofreading marks inside the back cover of this book.

NARRATIVE

Editing for Conventions

6 My grammar and punctuation are correct, and the copy is free of spelling errors.

5 I have a few minor errors in punctuation, spelling, or grammar.

4 I have some errors in punctuation, spelling, or grammar.

When you edit for *conventions*, you fix any errors in spelling, grammar, capitalization, and punctuation. The rubric above will help you edit for conventions.

Did I punctuate my dialogue correctly?

You will know your dialogue is punctuated correctly if you remember to follow the rules. (See page **556**, and pay special attention to the examples below.)

When a speaker is identified in the middle of a quotation . . .

"Did I tell you," asked Luis, **"that I rented the DVD you like?"**

- Quotation marks set off the first part of the quotation. The words identifying the speaker follow a comma and quotation marks.
- The words that interrupt the quotation (sometimes called a *dialogue tag*) are followed by a comma.
- Quotation marks set off the last part of the quotation.

When both parts of the quotation are complete sentences . . .

"Tell me what you think," said Eric. **"That movie is full of action."**

- Quotation marks are placed before and after each quotation.
- A period follows the words that identify the speaker.

 Rewrite the following sentences using the correct punctuation.

1. Dad called my sister said to let you know that he'll pick you up after practice.
2. Owen is coming with us said Antonio Do you want to come along?
3. Mom will be home any minute Marcus said We better clean up the kitchen.

 Edit your dialogue. Review the dialogue in your narrative and fix any punctuation errors that you find.

3 Some of my errors confuse the reader. I need to fix punctuation in my dialogue.

2 I need to correct many errors that make my narrative and dialogue hard to read.

1 I need help making corrections, especially with my dialogue.

Have I punctuated equal adjectives correctly?

Commas are used to separate equal adjectives. How can you tell if the adjectives are equal? Try two tests: (1) put the word *and* between the adjectives, or (2) reverse the adjectives' order. Then read the sentence. If the meaning of the sentence remains clear, the adjectives are equal. (See **586.2**.)

EQUAL ADJECTIVES SEPARATED WITH A COMMA

The loud, squealing **tires warned the pedestrians of a speeding car.** (*loud* and *squealing*) or (*squealing, loud*)

UNEQUAL ADJECTIVES WITHOUT A COMMA

Many curious **spectators gathered to watch the firefighters.** (*Many* and *curious* do not modify spectators equally. They cannot be interchanged.)

Edit

Check your adjectives. Find a place where you have equal adjectives and make sure they are punctuated correctly.

NARRATIVE

Conventions
Quotation marks are added to the dialogue.

A comma separates equal adjectives.

"Marcus, Paulo, Maria!" I shouted. "You and your friends come here and stay away from that truck!"

The firefighter shouted thanks as she ran toward the burning, smoking warehouse. Then more sirens screamed to the scene. Suddenly, giant . . .

Editing Using a Checklist

Check your editing. On a piece of paper, write the numbers 1 to 12. If you can answer "yes" to a question, put a check mark after that number. If not, continue to edit for that convention.

Conventions

PUNCTUATION

_____ **1.** Do I use end punctuation after all my sentences?

_____ **2.** Do I use commas after introductory word groups and transitions?

_____ **3.** Do I use commas between equal adjectives?

_____ **4.** Do I punctuate dialogue correctly?

_____ **5.** Do I use apostrophes to show possession (a *boy's bike*)?

CAPITALIZATION

_____ **6.** Do I start all my sentences with capital letters?

_____ **7.** Do I capitalize all proper nouns?

SPELLING

_____ **8.** Have I spelled all my words correctly?

_____ **9.** Have I double-checked the words my spell checker may have missed?

GRAMMAR

_____ **10.** Do I use correct forms of verbs (*had gone*, not *had went*)?

_____ **11.** Do my subjects and verbs agree in number?
(She and I *were* going, not She and I *was* going.)

_____ **12.** Do I use the right words (*to, too, two*)?

Adding a Title

- Use strong, colorful words: **The Perfect Mask**
- Give the words rhythm: **Sirens, Firefighters, and a Dream**
- Be imaginative: **Home Team or Visitor?**

Publishing **Sharing Your Narrative**

After you have worked so hard to improve your narrative, make a neat, final copy to share. You may also decide to present your story in the form of an illustrated book, a script, or a reading. (See the suggestions below.)

Make a final copy. Follow your teacher's instructions or use the guidelines below to format your story. (If you are using a computer, see page 60.) Create a clean copy of your narrative and carefully proofread it.

Focus on **Presentation**

- Use blue or black ink and write neatly.
- Write your name in the upper left corner of page 1.
- Skip a line and center your title; skip another line and start your writing.
- Double-space your essay.
- Indent every paragraph and leave a one-inch margin on all four sides.
- Write your last name and the page number in the upper right corner of every page after the first one.

NARRATIVE

Read to an Adult

Share your narrative with an adult. Have the adult tell you what he or she liked best.

Write a Script

Turn your narrative into a play. Write a script for the events in your narrative. Assign parts. Practice and perform your play for another class.

Create an Illustrated Book

Make a neat copy of your essay, including illustrations of the main events. Add a cover and share your book with younger students.

Rubric for Narrative Writing

Use the following rubric for help as you assess and improve your narrative writing using the six traits.

Ideas

6 **The narrative tells about an unforgettable experience. The details make the story truly memorable.**

5 The writer tells about an interesting experience. Details help create the interest.

4 The writer tells about an interesting experience. More details are needed.

Organization

6 **The organization makes the narrative enjoyable and easy to read.**

5 The narrative is well organized, with a clear beginning, middle, and ending. Transitions are used well.

4 The narrative is well organized. Most of the transitions are helpful.

Voice

6 **The writer's voice creates an unforgettable experience for the reader.**

5 The writer's personal voice creates interest in the story. Dialogue is used.

4 The writer's voice creates interest in the story. More dialogue is needed.

Word Choice

6 **The writer's exceptional word choice captures the experience.**

5 Specific nouns, strong verbs, and well-chosen modifiers create vivid pictures and express clear feelings.

4 Specific nouns and strong verbs are used. Modifiers are needed to create a clearer picture.

Sentence Fluency

6 **The sentences are skillfully written and original. They keep the reader's interest.**

5 The sentences show variety and are easy to read and understand.

4 The sentences are varied, but some should flow more smoothly.

Conventions

6 **Grammar and punctuation are correct, and the writing is free of spelling errors.**

5 The narrative has a few minor errors in punctuation, spelling, or grammar.

4 The narrative has several errors in punctuation, spelling, or grammar.

3 The writer needs to focus on one experience. Some details do not relate to the story.

2 The writer needs to focus on one experience. Details are needed.

1 The writer needs to tell about an experience and use details.

3 The order of events needs to be corrected. More transitions need to be used. One part of the narrative is weak.

2 The beginning, middle, and ending all run together. The order is unclear.

1 The narrative needs to be organized.

3 A voice can usually be heard. More dialogue is needed.

2 The voice is weak. Dialogue is needed.

1 The writer has not gotten involved in the story. Dialogue is needed.

3 Strong nouns, verbs, and modifiers are needed to create a clear picture.

2 General and overused words do not create a clear picture.

1 The writer has not yet considered word choice.

3 A better variety of sentences is needed. Sentences do not read smoothly.

2 Many short or incomplete sentences make the writing choppy.

1 Few sentences are written well. Help is needed.

3 Some errors confuse the reader.

2 Many errors make the narrative confusing and hard to read.

1 Help is needed to make corrections.

Evaluating a Narrative

As you read the narrative below, focus on the writer's strengths and weaknesses. (The essay contains some errors.) Then read the student self-evaluation on page 133.

The Perfect Mask

The slippery wet paper mashay felt good in my hands. I put the first strips over the form of a mask that I made in art class. It was the start of the project that I planned to enter in the school art fair. The art fair was a big deal at our school, so I wanted to make sure my project would win.

I didn't listen much to my art teacher, Mr. Cardinelli. He talked about color, style, texture, and stuff like that. I was good at art. I was probably one of the best students in my class. So, I just did my own thing.

I wanted my mask to look like a beautiful medeavil woman. I gave her beautiful eyes and a beautiful nose and mouth. Mr. Cardinelli said that I didn't have to do her so perfect. I also gave her thick, black curls and a beautiful, white headdress. Mr. Cardinelli said I should use more colors, but I wanted to use only black and white.

The day of the art fair came and all the masks were hung on a wall in the gym. I noticed that mine looked different from all the others. Above the masks there was a huge sign that said, USING COLOR IN ABSTRACT ART. I realized then that I had missed the whole point of the assignment.

My mask didn't win a prize. On that day, I learned that listening to the teacher's instructions might be a good idea.

Student Self-Assessment

The assessment below shows how the writer of "The Perfect Mask" rated her essay. She used the rubric and number scales on pages 130–131 to rate each trait. Then she made two comments for each trait. The first one showed something she liked in her essay. The second comment pointed out something that she felt could be done better.

4 Ideas

1. *I wrote about one main experience.*
2. *I could have added more sensory details.*

3 Organization

1. *I did a good job organizing things by time.*
2. *My ending is weak.*

4 Voice

1. *I like the way my voice sounds.*
2. *I could have used some dialogue between Mr. C and me.*

2 Word Choice

1. *I like the description in my first sentence.*
2. *I used the word "beautiful" too many times.*

4 Sentence Fluency

1. *I used a variety of sentences.*
2. *A couple of my sentences are confusing.*

5 Conventions

1. *I punctuated my sentences correctly.*
2. *I wasn't sure how to spell two words.*

Use the rubric. Assess your narrative using the rubric shown on pages 130–131.

1 On your own paper, list the six traits. Leave space after each trait to write one strength and one weakness.

2 Then choose a number (from 1 to 6) that shows how well each trait was used.

NARRATIVE

Reflecting on Your Writing

You've worked hard to write a narrative that your classmates will enjoy. Now take some time to think about your writing. Finish each sentence starter below on your own paper. Thinking about your writing will help you see how you are growing as a writer.

My Narrative

1. The best part of my narrative is . . .

2. The part that still needs work is . . .

3. The main thing I learned about writing a personal narrative is . . .

4. In my next narrative, I would like to . . .

5. Here is one question I still have about writing a narrative:

Narrative Writing

Phase Autobiography

The *Saturn V* rocket that carried the first astronauts to the moon used three stages. The first stage was basically an engine with a big fuel tank of hydrogen and oxygen. Its job was to push the rocket past the atmosphere. The second stage propelled the rocket into space, toward the moon. The third stage of the rocket included the space capsule and the landing module. Each stage had its own purpose.

Our lives also have stages, or phases. Each phase serves a different purpose. In a phase autobiography, you tell about a stage or phase in your own life and what effect it has had on you. Your goal is to entertain your readers while showing them a little bit about who you are.

Writing Guidelines

Subject:	**A time of personal change**
Form:	**Phase autobiography**
Purpose:	**To tell about a phase in your life**
Audience:	**Classmates**

Phase Autobiography

We all go through phases or stages. Sometimes those stages are school related, like graduating from elementary school and beginning middle school. Other stages are more personal, like moving to a new town, learning to play chess, or making a new friend. A phase autobiography tells how events over a period of time affect a person. In the following sample, Andy tells about a summer he spent drawing.

Rocket to Mars

BEGINNING

The beginning introduces the stage.

At the beginning of last summer, my dad gave me a sketchbook. At first I wondered what I would do with it. I wasn't planning to be an artist or anything, and I figured I'd catch up on a few TV shows. Then Dad lost his job. He was home all day every day, and the TV was his. We were living in a cramped apartment in Brooklyn, and Dad and I were always stumbling over each other. Since I couldn't watch my shows, I started drawing. With just a pencil and my sketchbook, I could be in another world. And that world was full of rockets.

The first drawing in my sketchbook showed a needle-tipped rocket just as it was bounding from the launchpad. I sketched in ice cracking from the hull and falling toward the firestorm below. It was a rocket caught in the moment of breaking free. The next pages had more rockets blasting off, ripping through clouds, and reaching for the stars.

MIDDLE

The middle provides details about the stage.

"We're just about out of money, Son," Dad told me one day. "We can't afford to stay here. We're going to have to move."

MIDDLE
A series of events occur during this stage.

Suddenly, I couldn't draw rockets. Each time I tried, the hull would shift this way or that. Nothing was sleek anymore, but clunky and bent. My rockets evolved into space stations—pages and pages of space stations. They just floated there above the earth. I'd put little windows in them, and inside you could see me sitting at a table, drawing pictures, or Dad tending pots with space plants in them.

"Son, I got a new job!" Dad told me near the end of summer. "We don't have to move after all!"

Dad started his new job, and I had the TV back. The funny thing was, I didn't care about watching TV so much anymore. I was too busy drawing. My space stations got land put under them, and they became Mars bases. And I drew my dad and me standing outside, waving, next to a field of space plants.

ENDING
· · · · · · · · · · · · · · ·
The ending shows how the person changed.

Now I'm taking art classes in school, learning to draw people. One of these days, maybe I'll be an artist for NASA.

NARRATIVE

Respond to the reading. Answer the following questions on your own paper.

☐ **Ideas** (1) What details does Andy provide about his art and his home during this phase?

☐ **Organization** (2) What problem is identified in the beginning? (3) How is this problem resolved in the end?

☐ **Voice & Word Choice** (4) What words and phrases give you clues about Andy's personality? Name two.

Prewriting **Selecting a Topic**

You've been through many stages in your life, but which one should you write about? A life map can help you decide on a topic.

A life map begins at your birth and continues to the present. The pictures represent important events in your life, and the numbers or dates indicate your age or the year for each event. Andy made the following life map.

Age 10 had my appendix out

Age 9 met my best friend Jeremy

Age 8 spent the summer with Uncle Grady

Age 7 learned to swim

Age 0 my birth

Age 13 TODAY

Age 5 a newspaper took my picture at the state fair

Age 11 won a talent contest with my puppet show

Age 12 Dad got a new job. We got a bigger apartment

Age 12 moved to a tiny apartment in Brooklyn

Prewrite

Make a life map. Draw your own life map. Then review it, looking for a stage to write about. The stage must include a number of events over a period of time. For example, Andy could have written about learning to swim or spending the summer with his uncle. Select a stage to write about.

Gathering Details

To write your phase autobiography, you'll need to list events in time order. A time line can help you gather and organize these details. Remember that you can't include everything that happened, so you must focus on the most important events.

Write the first event at the top of the time line and list other events in order below it. Andy made the following time line to gather details for his phase autobiography.

Time Line

1	Dad gave me a sketchbook.
2	Dad lost his job.
3	I started drawing rockets.
4	Dad said we'd have to move.
5	My rockets became space stations.
6	Dad got a better job.
7	My space stations became Mars bases.
8	I started taking drawing classes.

NARRATIVE

Prewrite **Make a time line.** Put together a time line showing the story details of the stage you've chosen. Start with the first detail at the top and then list the rest in the order they happened.

Another good way to gather details for a narrative is to make a 5 W's chart. Label the columns *Who? What? When? Where?* and *Why?* Then fill in the table with answers to those questions. (See page **549**.)

Writing Creating Your First Draft

With your time line in mind, begin writing your phase autobiography. Use the tips below to guide your writing.

BEGINNING Draw the reader in and introduce the stage you are describing. Consider using one of the following strategies for your opening.

- **Start with the first event.** Tell what began this stage in your life. Andy, for example, started by saying that his dad gave him a sketchbook.
- **Start in the middle of the action.** Begin with action or dialogue to draw the reader in quickly. Imagine, for instance, the effect of Andy starting with the quotation, "What am I going to do with a sketchbook?"
- **Start with an interesting fact.** Find a fact that the reader might want to know: Did you know that NASA uses artists to paint scenes from other worlds?

MIDDLE Let your story unfold and bring it to a high point.

- **Be selective.** Include events that keep the story moving along. Leave out unneeded details.
- **Use sensory details.** Use sights, sounds, and other sensory details so that the reader feels involved in the story.
- **Use action and dialogue.** Show, don't tell. Let your reader see things happening and hear what is said. Don't just tell about what happened.
- **Build to a high point.** Increase the action to a point of excitement or tension. Make your reader want to keep reading to find out what happens next.

ENDING Describe how the stage ends. Consider using one of the following approaches for your ending.

- **Reveal why the stage was important.** Make sure your reader understands the significance of this stage.
- **Tell how the experience changed you.** Tell what you learned from the stage or how you are different because of it.

Write the first draft. Review your time line and then write your phase autobiography. Include details that make the story clear and interesting.

Revising Improving Your Writing

Revise your first draft with the following traits in mind.

☐ **Ideas** Have you focused on the key or most important details?

☐ **Organization** Are your ideas in the best order?

☐ **Voice** Does your personality show in the way you tell the story? Does the dialogue in your story sound natural?

☐ **Word Choice** Have you used strong nouns and verbs?

☐ **Sentence Fluency** Does your story carry the reader along smoothly from sentence to sentence? Are your sentences varied?

NARRATIVE

Voice
More natural wording is used.

Ideas
An unnecessary detail is cut.

Sentence Fluency
Sentences are changed for variety.

Word Choice
A more colorful adjective is used.

Organization
A sentence is moved for better order.

At the beginning of last summer,
~~When the hot season arrived,~~ my dad gave me

a sketchbook. At first I wondered what I would

do with it. ~~Who gives a kid a sketchbook?~~ I wasn't

planning to be an artist or anything. *and I figured* I'd catch

up on a few TV shows. Then Dad lost his job.

He was home all day every day, and the TV

was his. We were living in a ~~small~~ *cramped* apartment in

Brooklyn, and Dad and I were always stumbling

over each other. With just a pencil and my

sketchbook, I could be in another world. And that

world was full of rockets. Since I couldn't watch

my shows, I started drawing.

Revise to improve your first draft. Revise your phase autobiography. Make sure your writing grabs the reader's interest and holds it to the end.

Editing Checking Your Work

While a phase autobiography is not as formal as a report, it should still be free of errors in punctuation, capitalization, spelling, and grammar.

Conventions

Once your autobiography sounds the way you want it to, check your punctuation, capitalization, spelling, and grammar. Use the following checklist.

PUNCTUATION

_____ **1.** Do I use end punctuation after all my sentences?

_____ **2.** Do I use commas correctly?

_____ **3.** Do I use apostrophes to show possession (*a boy's bike*)?

CAPITALIZATION

_____ **4.** Do I start all my sentences with capital letters?

_____ **5.** Do I capitalize all proper nouns?

SPELLING

_____ **6.** Have I spelled all my words correctly?

GRAMMAR

_____ **7.** Do I use correct forms of verbs (*had gone,* not *had went*)?

_____ **8.** Do my subjects and verbs agree in number?
(She and I *were* going, not She and I *was* going.)

_____ **9.** Do I use the right words (*to, too, two*)?

Edit your autobiography. Make sure your words are lively and that your sentences flow smoothly. Also carefully proofread your final copy.

Publishing Sharing Your Writing

A phase autobiography shouldn't be allowed to gather dust. It should be shared! This type of writing is perfect for sending to family and friends by mail or e-mail. It also makes an interesting addition to a family Web site. Magazines that accept student writing are also good places for a phase autobiography. Finally, this sort of writing should definitely be kept in a journal or portfolio to be read again in later years.

Share your phase autobiography. Find one way to share your phase autobiography with relatives or friends. (See page 129.)

Narrative Writing

Across the Curriculum

What is a kite? Paper, wood, string . . . but when you put those pieces together in the right way, the kite suddenly soars to the skies.

What is a narrative? People, events, places . . . but when you carefully build a narrative, it can soar to the sky. Sometimes a narrative soars so far and so fast, it carries you away with it.

For example, in social studies, a firsthand observation report can carry you away to another culture. In math, learning-log entries can help you explore new concepts. In science, a story script can explain a topic you are studying. And in any class, incident reports give you the opportunity to record events you have personally observed. The following chapter will lead you through these kinds of narrative writing and also prepare you for a narrative writing test.

Mini Index

Social Studies:
Writing About a Cultural Experience

You don't have to travel to another country to have a cultural experience. Restaurants, festivals, and exhibits can give you interesting information about other cultures. The following narrative, written for a social studies class, tells about an ethnic meal.

The **beginning** introduces the experience.

The **middle** provides details.

The **ending** reflects on the experience.

An Indian Meal

My grandma came from India, so to celebrate her 60th birthday, my family went to an Indian restaurant. Grandma wanted me to try the foods she had eaten as a young woman. It turned out to be a very interesting experience.

As we walked into the restaurant, we were greeted by a hostess in a silk sari decorated with gold. She seated us. Then Grandma ordered samosas for each of us. The samosas were crispy, fried pastry pockets stuffed with mashed potatoes, peas, and other spicy vegetables or ground lamb. My samosa was very hot, but very good!

Then the waitress brought out several more dishes. A big silver bowl held mounds of steaming white rice. Two small baskets had large slices of nan bread. In the middle of the table, a round pot held spicy chicken curry. Grandma showed me how to tear off some bread and use it to scoop up my curry. The curry was unbelieveably hot! Soon I was using the nan bread between dishes just to cool off my mouth!

Grandma ordered dessert, which included kheer—a rice pudding with almonds, pistachios, cardamom, and saffron. It was better than ice cream. Sitting there, eating my kheer, I could just imagine when Grandma was my age, eating the same food in India.

Writing Tips

Before you write . . .

- **Select a topic.**
  Write about the specific experience your teacher assigns or choose an experience that relates to what you are studying in social studies.
- **Take notes about what you experience.**
  Record specific details. Use all your senses: sight, hearing, smell, taste, and touch.

During your writing . . .

- **Set the scene.**
  Describe where and when you had the experience.
- **Include specific details.**
  Use concrete nouns and vivid verbs.
- **Explain new terms.**
  Give the reader any background information that is needed to understand the experience.

After you've written a first draft . . .

- **Revise your first draft.**
  Make sure that your narrative is complete, easy to follow, and interesting.
- **Check for accuracy.**
  Double-check your facts and details.
- **Edit for correctness.**
  Check for spelling, punctuation, and grammar errors.

NARRATIVE

Try IT Think about cultural events that happen where you live: parades, festivals, holiday services, concerts, and so forth. Choose one event you would feel comfortable attending, and write an eyewitness account of your experience.

Math: Writing a Learning-Log Entry

When you write in a learning log, you make a personal connection to the things you are learning in class. In his math class, Ethan wrote a learning-log entry based on his experience of building kites. (Also see page **437**.)

The **beginning** tells what is being studied.

The **middle** contains explanations and examples.

The **ending** relates the information to the student's experience.

Friday, September 24:

Today in math class we learned about angles. Angles are created when two lines extend from a point. Three types of angles are vertical, complementary, and supplementary.

— Vertical angles are opposite each other. They share one point called a vertex.

— Complementary angles add up to 90°.

— Supplementary angles add up to 180°.

Angles can be found in places besides math books. For example, last summer when my brother and I made kites, the kites had all sorts of angles created by the wood frame. Now, by learning to recognize and measure different angles, the next kites I build will be even better!

supplementary angles add up to 180°

vertical angles

complementary angles add up to 90°

Writing Tips

Before you write . . .

- **Format your learning log.**
  Set up your learning log so that you like the way it looks. Also, make sure to follow your teacher's guidelines.
- **Pay attention in class.**
  Take notes to make sure you understand the material your teacher presents.

During your writing . . .

- **Record the date.**
  Write the date of each learning-log entry.
- **Write down what you are learning.**
  Record the most important facts.
- **Reflect on the information.**
  Relate what you are learning to your own experiences.
- **Include sketches.**
  Make sketches in your learning log if your teacher shows you a picture of something interesting. Also copy and label any important diagrams that help explain a concept.

After you've written a first draft . . .

- **Reread your work.**
  Read your learning-log entries to review the material and decide if you need to add any details.
- **Use your learning log.**
  Return to your learning log whenever you are asked to write a paper for that class. It will be full of excellent topics for writing assignments.

NARRATIVE

Try**IT** Write a learning-log entry about something you recently learned in math class. Record the facts and include sketches or equations to explain concepts. (See page **437** for another math learning log.)

Science: Writing a TV Script

When you write a factual TV script, you are telling a story to make an idea clearer. This type of narrative writing is helpful for learning a scientific concept. In the sample below, a student used a classroom experience to help explain the different types of clouds.

The **beginning** sets the scene.

Characters:	Student, Tai; Teacher, Mr. Hynek
Setting:	School courtyard

Tai: Why are these clouds all feathery, Mr. Hynek? Shouldn't clouds be fluffy?

Mr. Hynek: Clouds have many different shapes. Remember the clouds yesterday?

Tai: They looked like a gray blanket. What were they?

Mr. Hynek: They were stratus clouds, Tai. Since stratus clouds are low to the ground, they make everything look gray. Fog is a type of stratus cloud at ground level. Stratus clouds bring rain or drizzle.

The **middle** uses dialogue to explain the scientific ideas.

Tai: They did yesterday! Which clouds are fluffy?

Mr. Hynek: Those are cumulus clouds. When they are small and fluffy, cumulus clouds usually mean fair weather. If they grow really tall, they can become thunderheads and bring rain or storms.

Tai: Today I see feathery clouds reaching across the sky. The sun is shining, and the sky is bright blue. It looks like good weather for today.

Mr. Hynek: Right, Tai. Cirrus clouds tend to be high in the sky. Sometimes the ends of cirrus clouds curl in thin streamers. Cirrus clouds usually mean fair weather.

The **ending** closes the scene.

Tai: Now when I look at the clouds, I see a lot more than just fluff!

Writing Tips

Before you write . . .

- **Select an interesting science topic.**
  Review the chapters you have recently studied in your science book. Select a topic that interests you and isn't too complicated.
- **Get your science facts correct.**
  Check into the facts behind your topic.
- **Imagine ways to dramatize the topic.**
  Think in terms of storytelling—characters, settings, actions, and dialogue.

During your writing . . .

- **Let the story tell itself.**
  Experiment with your script and have fun as you write.
- **Be clear and direct.**
  Explain the idea or concept as simply and clearly as possible.
- **Keep it conversational.**
  Write natural-sounding dialogue.

After you've written a first draft . . .

- **Revise your first draft.**
  Make sure that your script is conversational, easy to follow, and interesting.
- **Check for accuracy.**
  Double-check your facts and details.
- **Edit for correctness.**
  Check for punctuation, capitalization, spelling, and grammar errors.

Try IT Search for a science topic that you would like to write a TV script about. Invent characters, situations, and dialogue that could help you explain the topic. Then write your script.

Practical Writing:
Creating an Incident Report

When you see an accident, you may be asked to write up an incident report telling just what you observed. It's important that you include everything you saw in a clear way. The following incident report was written by the student set director of a middle school play.

INCIDENT REPORT

The **beginning** names the student and gives the date.

Ronnette Williams
May 13, 2005

An accident happened today at 4:15 p.m. on the auditorium stage. I was there as student set director, and so were Ms. Davis and the following students: Randy Dover, Danielle Walters, Maylie Royce, and Sumey Lee.

The **middle** answers each of the 5 W's: *who, what, where, when,* and *why*.

Here's what happened. We were moving the flats for *Phantom of the Country Opera* when one tipped over and fell on Randy Dover. Ms. Davis saw the flat fall, shouted a warning, and tried to catch it herself. The flat hit Randy's shoulder and knocked him down. Ms. Davis pulled the flat off Randy, and he scrambled out.

The **ending** tells the outcome of the incident.

Randy said he wasn't hurt, but Ms. Davis found a small scrape on his shoulder. She sent him to Nurse Hollenkomf. Randy was checked by the nurse, who treated his scrape and released him. Ms. Davis asked me to write up a report of what I saw. She also asked Randy to write a report.

Writing Tips

Before you write . . .

- **Follow a proper format.** Ask your teacher or school administrator if there is an incident report form you should fill out. Otherwise, base your report on the sample on page 150.
- **Review the facts.** Jot down notes to yourself that answer the 5 W's: *who, what, when, where,* and *why.*

During your writing . . .

- **Be objective.** Report what happened in a straightforward way. Avoid blaming anyone or adding your own opinion. Simply tell what happened.
- **Be honest.** Record what you witnessed. Don't tell half-truths or change events slightly to produce a certain outcome.
- **Be complete.** Provide all the information that teachers, advisors, or administrators would need.

After you've written a first draft . . .

- **Review your statements.**
  Make sure that your sentences are clear and complete. Check to see that you have answered all the 5 W's.
- **Check for accuracy.**
  Double-check dates, times, facts, and details.
- **Edit for correctness.**
  Check punctuation, capitalization, spelling, and grammar.

NARRATIVE

Try IT Using the report on page 150 as a guide, write an incident report as if you had witnessed the following accident.

Who:	Todd MacFarland
What:	Hit his thumb with a hammer
When:	At 4:30 p.m. on May 14, 2005
Where:	In the wings of the auditorium stage
Why:	Working on the set for *Phantom of the Country Opera*
Follow-up:	Nurse Hollenkomf checked to make sure the thumb wasn't broken, and she washed and bandaged it, and sent Todd home for the night.

Writing for Assessment

Many state and school writing tests ask you to respond to a narrative prompt. A narrative prompt asks you to recall a personal experience or respond to a "what if" question. Study the following sample prompt and student response.

Narrative Prompt

Suppose that you lived in a world where there were no televisions, computers, or video games. Tell a story about what you and your friends did one Saturday.

The **beginning** states the focus of the narrative (**underlined**).

Last Saturday was the first nice spring day this year. My friends and I spent the whole day together. We hadn't made any special plans, but we still had a fun-filled day.

I woke up just before 8:00 that morning because there was a scraping noise outside my bedroom window. Looking out, I saw my friend Cal digging a hole near our back fence. My other friend Rob was standing there watching, and his little sister Marcie, who follows Rob everywhere, was holding a can.

"What do you think you're doing?" I yelled from my window.

Each **middle** paragraph tells a main part of the story.

"Digging worms," said Cal. "Find your fishing stuff and get down here!"

By 8:30 we were on our way to the lake. The sun was already warming us up, and soon it was too hot for jackets, so we tied them around our waists. When we got to the lake, we settled down on a pier, tossed our lines in the water, and watched the sun's reflection dance on the waves. Soon the fish started nibbling the worms off our hooks.

Specific details are used throughout the narrative.

That annoyed Rob because he is afraid of worms, and every time Marcie had to bait his hook for him, Cal and I laughed. By lunchtime we had a stringer full of bluegills and rock bass.

When we got home, Mom made lunch for us, and for the first time this year, it was warm enough to eat outside at the picnic table. After lunch, we played cards for a while. We had to play war because Marcie doesn't know any other games, but it was fun to play it again because you can yell and act up like a little kid.

Pretty soon five or six other kids showed up looking for something to do. We decided to play baseball in the lot near the cemetery. A great thing happened during that game. I became the first one in the neighborhood to hit a home run over the cemetery fence. I came close a couple of times last year, so this was a turning point in my career. We'll play ball after supper every night this summer.

The ending paragraph reflects on the experience.

All in all, it was a great day. It's amazing that all a guy like me needs to have fun is a can of worms, a deck of cards, a baseball, and a few friends.

Respond to the reading. Answer the following questions about the sample response.

☐ **Ideas** **(1) What is the focus of the writer's response? (2) What are some of the key details in the writing?**

☐ **Organization** **(3) How is the response organized?**

☐ **Voice & Word Choice** **(4) Do the writer's feelings come through in his word choice? Give examples.**

Writing Tips

Use the following tips as a guide when responding to a narrative writing prompt.

Before you write . . .

- **Understand the prompt.**
  Remember that a narrative prompt asks you to tell a story.
- **Plan your time wisely.**
  Spend several minutes planning before you start writing. Use a time line to help you put your ideas in order.

Time line

Subject:
① —
② —
③ —
④ —
⑤ —

During your writing . . .

- **Decide on a focus for your narrative.**
  Use key words from the prompt as you write your focus statement.
- **Be selective.**
  Tell only the main events in your narrative.
- **End in a meaningful way.**
  Reflect on the importance of the narrative.

After you've written a first draft . . .

- **Check for completeness and correctness.**
  Present events in order. Delete any unneeded details and neatly correct any errors.

Narrative Prompts

- Make up a story in which you accidentally broke something that belonged to someone else. What did you do as a result?
- Think of something important that happened in your life. It doesn't have to be earthshaking, but it should be something that has meaning for you. Tell the story of what happened and why it has made a difference to you.

Plan and write a response. Respond to one of the prompts listed above. Complete your writing within the time limit your teacher sets. Afterward, list one part of your response that you like and one part that could be better.

Narrative Writing in Review

Purpose: In narrative writing, you *tell a story* about something that has happened.

Topics: Narrate . . . an experience that taught you something,
a time of personal change, or
a memorable event.

Prewriting

Select a topic from your own life. Look through old photos or your journal for ideas. Also, use sentence starters to get you thinking about possible topics. (See page **102**.)

Remember the details by writing freely and answering the 5 W's. (See page **103**.)

Organize details about the people involved and the order of events. List sensory details to use in the narrative. Add dialogue to show the speaker's personality or to keep the action moving. (See pages **104–106**.)

Writing

In the beginning, grab the reader's attention by using interesting details or dialogue. (See page **109**.)

In the middle, tell the events of the story in time order. Use sensory details, dialogue, and action words to create a clear picture for the reader. (See pages **110–111**.)

In the ending, tell why the experience was important and how it taught you something. (See page **112**.)

Revising

Review the ideas, organization, and voice first. Then check **word choice** and **sentence fluency**. Use "showing" instead of "telling" in your narrative. (See pages **114–124**.)

Editing

Check your writing for conventions. Review punctuation of dialogue, and ask a friend to check the writing, too. (See pages **126–128**.)

Make a final copy and proofread it for errors before sharing it with other people. (See page **129**.)

Assessing

Use the narrative rubric to assess your finished writing. (See pages **130–131**.)

Expository Writing

Expository Writing

Expository Paragraph

What's the difference between a school bus driver and a cold? One knows the stops, and the other stops the nose!

All kidding aside, when you explain the similarities and differences between two things, you are comparing and contrasting them. Doing this helps you to understand each thing better. In an expository paragraph (a paragraph that *explains*), you can compare and contrast all sorts of things: soul music and R & B, science fiction and fantasy, or even tacos and pizza.

In this chapter you will write a comparison-contrast paragraph about two similar things. Maybe next time someone says, "What's the difference between . . . ?," you'll already know the answer!

Writing Guidelines

Subject: Two things to compare and contrast

Form: Expository paragraph

Purpose: To share knowledge

Audience: Classmates

Expository Paragraph

The simplest form of expository writing is the expository paragraph. It usually starts with a **topic sentence**, which lets the reader know what the paragraph will be about. The **body** sentences give details that support the topic sentence, and the **closing sentence** ends the explanation. The paragraph below compares and contrasts a student's two favorite foods.

Topic sentence
· · · · · · · · · · · · · ·

Body

Closing sentence
· · · · · · · · · · · · · ·

What'll It Be: Tacos or Pizza?

Tacos and pizza might seem totally different, but they actually have a lot in common. Even though tacos come from Mexico, and pizza comes from Italy, each food is an American favorite. Both are foods with a solid base you can pick up and eat. Tacos have a tortilla shell made from ground corn or flour. Pizzas are cooked on a crust that is basically a flat loaf of bread. Both foods are loaded with toppings. One way they are different is that taco fixings get cooked separately and then put together, but pizza ingredients get baked right along with the crust. Ingredients for both tacos and pizza include meats, cheeses, sauces, and vegetables. These foods have one more thing in common: They go fast, so make plenty!

Respond to the reading. On your own paper, answer each of the following questions.

☐ **Ideas** (1) What is the topic of the paragraph?

☐ **Organization** (2) Does the essay focus on one food at a time (subject by subject) or compare tacos and pizza together (point by point)?

☐ **Voice & Word Choice** (3) Is the voice of this paragraph formal or informal? Which words make it that way?

Prewriting Selecting a Topic

Selecting a topic for a comparison-contrast paragraph is easy. Start by listing things that interest you. Then, for each item on your list, write down at least one other thing you could compare it to. The two things should have some similarities and some differences.

The writer of the paragraph on page 158 created the following list of topics. Afterward he crossed out ideas that were too similar or too different.

<u>Topics to Compare</u>

~~Cars~~   ~~Boats~~

Skateboards   Scooters

~~Mountains~~   ~~Clouds~~

Baseball   Softball

Tacos   Pizza

Make a list and select a topic. Using the list above as a guide, jot down a few topics or items that interest you. For each, write at least one thing that might make an interesting comparison and contrast. Choose two items with enough similarities and differences to write a comparison-contrast paragraph.

Writing a Topic Sentence

Once you have two things to compare, it's time to write a topic sentence that introduces your comparison-contrast paragraph. Your topic sentence should (1) name the two things and (2) sum up your comparison and contrast.

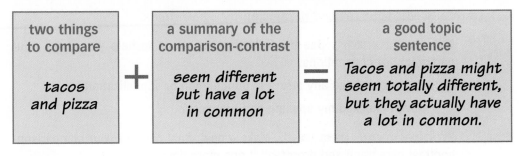

two things to compare	a summary of the comparison-contrast	a good topic sentence
tacos and pizza	seem different but have a lot in common	Tacos and pizza might seem totally different, but they actually have a lot in common.

Write your topic sentence. Use the basic formula above to write a topic sentence for your paragraph. You may need to try a few different versions to make sure this sentence says what you want it to say. (See page 553.)

EXPOSITORY

Writing Creating Your First Draft

Now it's time to think about your two topics and write the first draft of your paragraph. The following suggestions can help you.

- Start with your topic sentence.
- Include your details point by point.
- Create a closing sentence that shows your interest in the topic.

Write your first draft. Get all of your important ideas down on paper. Put the details in an order that makes the most sense.

Revising Improving Your Paragraph

When you have finished your first draft, read it over. Then check the *ideas, organization, voice, word choice,* and *sentence fluency* in your paragraph.

Review and improve your paragraph. Think about the questions below as you work on your writing.

1 Is my topic sentence clear and interesting?

2 Have I organized my details point by point?

3 Does my closing sentence show my interest in the topic?

4 Do I use specific nouns and strong action verbs?

5 Have I written complete sentences that flow smoothly and begin in a variety of ways?

Editing Checking for Conventions

Carefully edit your revised paragraph for *conventions*.

Edit your writing. Use the following questions to help you check your paragraph for conventions.

1 Have I corrected any errors in punctuation or capitalization?

2 Have I checked my spelling and grammar?

Proofread your paragraph. Make a neat, final copy of your comparison-contrast paragraph and proofread it one more time.

Expository Writing

Comparing
Two Subjects

"What is that, a bee or a yellow jacket?"
"What's the difference? Both can sting me!"
"The big difference is how many times they can sting you!"
Sometimes it's very important to understand the
similarities and differences between two things like stinging
insects. A comparison-contrast essay can help you form
this understanding. In this chapter, you will write a
comparison-contrast essay that explains the similarities
and differences between two animals.

Writing Guidelines

Subject: **Two animals**

Form: **Comparison-contrast essay**

Purpose: **To explain similarities and differences**

Audience: **Classmates**

Understanding Your Goal

Your goal in this chapter is to write a well-organized expository essay that compares and contrasts two animals. The traits listed in the chart below will help you plan and write your essay.

TRAITS OF COMPARISON-CONTRAST WRITING

Ideas

Select two interesting subjects, write a clear focus statement, and use details to compare and contrast the subjects.

Organization

Introduce your comparison in the beginning and provide the point-by-point comparison in the middle part.

Voice

Write with an original voice that shows your enthusiasm.

Word Choice

Choose precise words and define unfamiliar terms.

Sentence Fluency

Write sentences that connect your subjects with clear comparisons and contrasts.

Conventions

Check your essay for correct punctuation, capitalization, spelling, and grammar.

Get the big picture. Look at the rubric on pages 194–195. You can use that rubric to assess your progress as you write. Your goal is to develop an expository essay that compares and contrasts two animals.

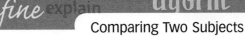

Comparison-Contrast Essay

In the following essay, a student writer tells about two insects that look similar but are very different.

BEGINNING

The beginning introduces the two insects and gives a focus statement (**underlined**).

MIDDLE

The first middle paragraph compares and contrasts the physical characteristics of the animals.

The second middle paragraph deals with the insects' diets.

What's the Buzz?

Last summer, my grandma's backyard overflowed with flowers and with stinging insects. At first, whenever I heard a buzz, I grabbed the flyswatter. Then Grandma showed me that not all buzzes are created equal. For example, honeybees and yellow jackets (wasps) may look similar, but they're really very different creatures.

At first glance, anybody could mistake a honeybee for a yellow jacket. Both are about an inch long, with black and yellow stripes on their abdomens. Also, both have a pair of wings that buzz as they fly. A closer look shows differences, though. First, honeybees are fuzzy, but yellow jackets have a smooth, hard skin. Second, honeybees have little pollen baskets on their legs, while yellow jackets have none. Third, each insect has a stinger, but a honeybee uses its stinger only as a last defense. It actually dies after it stings once. A yellow jacket can sting over and over and not die.

Honeybees and yellow jackets have completely different diets. Honeybees eat honey, of course. They make it out of flower nectar, which is a sweet liquid that flowers create. As honeybees go from flower to flower, they pollinate the plants. That's why people want as many honeybees around as possible. Yellow jackets, on the other hand, don't pollinate flowers. If a yellow jacket has to choose between a flower and a can of soda, it'll take the soda every time. Yellow jackets also like to eat garbage and even other insects. So, if a honeybee comes to your window box, it is there to visit the flowers. If a yellow jacket comes, it is probably planning to eat the dead flies in the windowsill.

Both insects build nests, but the two kinds of nests are really different. A honeybee's nest is a honeycomb made out of wax. Many of the little cells inside a honeycomb are full of honey, but others hold pupae, which are baby bees. Yellow jackets make their nests out of a paper-like substance that holds no honey. Another difference between the homes of bees and yellow jackets is their size. Beehives can be very large, with tens of thousands of bees. One queen rules a complicated society, with different jobs for male drones and female workers and guards. Yellow jackets' nests are usually smaller, with only a dozen or so insects and no complex organization.

Though honeybees and yellow jackets might seem the same, they really are quite different. Honeybees are gentle helpers, but yellow jackets are mean scavengers. Grandma summed it up pretty well: "In my garden, bees are guests, but yellow jackets are pests."

MIDDLE
The third paragraph explains their habitats.

ENDING
. . . .
The ending sums up the comparison and gives the reader something to think about.

Respond to the reading. Answer the following questions about the sample essay.

☐ **Ideas** (1) How does the writer capture your interest? (2) What two details in the essay are most interesting to you?

☐ **Organization** (3) How does the writer organize the middle paragraphs?

☐ **Voice & Word Choice** (4) What words or phrases make the writer sound knowledgeable? (5) What words does she define in the essay?

Prewriting

You may not have any idea what to write about yet. Don't worry. That's what prewriting is all about. It can help you select a topic, gather details, and organize them in the best way.

Keys to Effective Prewriting

1. Select two subjects that could be made into an interesting comparison-contrast essay.

2. Gather details about each subject, making sure you have enough information for an essay.

3. Write a focus statement that names your subjects and sums up the similarities and differences.

4. Write topic sentences that tell what each body paragraph will be about.

5. Organize your details with a list or an outline.

EXPOSITORY

PROD. NO.
SCENE
TAKE
ROLL
SOUND

Prewriting Selecting a Topic

Your first job is to find two animals that you would like to compare and contrast. You can begin by checking the list below to find out which animal groups interest you most.

birds	spiders	amphibians	sea creatures	mammals
fish	insects	reptiles	single-celled animals	primates

Using this list, Luc chose his favorite categories and listed them in a chart. Under each category, he wrote pairs of animals he would enjoy comparing and contrasting.

Topics Chart

Birds	Reptiles	Sea Creatures
eagle and buzzard	king cobra and rattler	white shark and dolphin
hummingbird and finch	anaconda and python	octopus and squid
pigeon and falcon		orca and blue whale

Prewrite

Create your own chart. Use the example above as a model to create your own animal chart.

1 Choose three categories of animals you are interested in and list them across the top.

2 Under each category, write pairs of animals you would like to compare and contrast.

3 Circle the pair of animals that you want to write about.

Focus on the Traits

Ideas For this assignment, select two animals with a fairly equal number of similarities and differences. A whale and a brine shrimp, for example, are too different to make a balanced point-by-point comparison-contrast. Then again, a gray squirrel and a red squirrel may be too similar.

Gathering Details

Well-written comparison-contrast essays are full of details. Luc used a gathering grid to collect details about his topic—sharks and dolphins. When he needed more information, he checked encyclopedias and Web sites.

Gathering Grid

Physical Characteristics

Questions	WHITE SHARKS	DOLPHINS
What size is it?	— many grow up to 16 feet long	— around 8 feet long
What shape is it?	— long body, pectoral fins, dorsal fin, vertical tail	— long body, pectoral fins, dorsal fins, horizontal tail
What covers it?	— rough skin made up of millions of sharp scales	— rubbery skin over a layer of blubber
What color is it?	— light gray back and white belly	— dark gray back and white belly
What special features does it have?	— gills for breathing water, as other fish do	— blowhole for breathing air, as other mammals do

EXPOSITORY

Luc continued his gathering grid, asking the following questions about the diet and habitat of each animal.

Diet: *What does it eat? How does it gather food? How does it eat its food?*

Habitat: *Where does it live? Does it live alone or with others?*

Create a gathering grid. Use the example above as a model to make your own grid.

 In the first column, write the questions listed above about physical characteristics, diet, and habitat. Add other questions about behavior, history, or the animals' future if you wish.

 In the second and third columns, write your answers.

3 Check your science book or the Internet if you don't know an answer.

Prewriting Organizing Point by Point

Your comparison-contrast essay will be organized **point by point**. That means that you will discuss one point about both subjects before you move on to the next point.

Paragraphs in a Point-by-Point Essay

In point-by-point organization, each paragraph is about one main idea.

- The **first body paragraph** should discuss *physical characteristics* of both animals (the first block in your gathering grid).
- The **second body paragraph** should discuss *diet*.
- The **third body paragraph** should discuss *habitat*.
- **Other body paragraphs** may deal with *behaviors, history,* or the animals' *future outlook*.

Details in a Point-by-Point Essay

Within each body paragraph, details are also arranged point by point. If the size of one animal is given, the size of the other is given next. That way, each detail can be separately compared or contrasted.

 In each example below, decide if the details are organized point by point. If not, rewrite the sentences, using point-by-point organization. Use details from Luc's grid on page 167 to fill in information.

1. Dolphins grow to about 8 feet in length. Sharks, on the other hand, eat anything they find.
2. Both dolphins and sharks have dorsal fins and pectoral fins, but dolphins have a blowhole for breathing, while sharks use gills.
3. Sharks have rough skin, but dolphins are very smart.

Focus on the Traits

Organization The gathering grid you created (page 167) can give you a general order for your details. The questions about physical characteristics already appear in a logical organization—size, shape, color, and so forth. As you add more questions and answers to the grid, make sure to organize those details in a logical order, too.

Writing Topic Sentences

Now that you have gathered details and learned about point-by-point organization, you are ready to write topic sentences for your body paragraphs. Each topic sentence should sum up the paragraph's main idea (physical characteristics, diet, and so on) for both animals. (See pages 552–553 for more information about topic sentences.)

For his essay on white sharks and dolphins, Luc referred to his gathering grid (page 167) and wrote a topic sentence for each main idea.

- ■ ***Topic sentence 1:*** *(physical characteristics)* Both white sharks and dolphins have bodies that are perfect for life at sea.
- ■ ***Topic sentence 2:*** *(diet)* Both of these great ocean hunters enjoy the same favorite foods.
- ■ ***Topic sentence 3:*** *(habitat)* Even though both white sharks and dolphins live in warm ocean waters, they lead very different lives.

Write your topic sentences. Refer to the models above as you create your topic sentences.

 Review the first part of your gathering grid, the part that deals with physical characteristics. Sum up the animals' similarities and differences in your first topic sentence.

 Review the next part about diet. Sum up the animals' similarities and differences in diet in your second topic sentence.

3 Repeat the process for each part of your gathering grid.

Writing a Focus Statement

With your topic sentences written, you are ready to write a focus (thesis) statement. Your focus statement should name the two animals and sum up their similarities and differences for the whole essay.

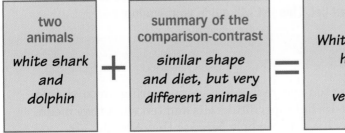

two animals		summary of the comparison-contrast		a focus statement
white shark and dolphin	**+**	similar shape and diet, but very different animals	**=**	*White sharks and dolphins have similar shapes and diets but are very different animals.*

Write your focus statement. Use the formula above to write a focus statement for your comparison-contrast essay.

Prewriting Organizing Your Ideas

Before you write your essay, you should create an organized list to plan your essay. The directions below can guide you.

Directions

Organized List

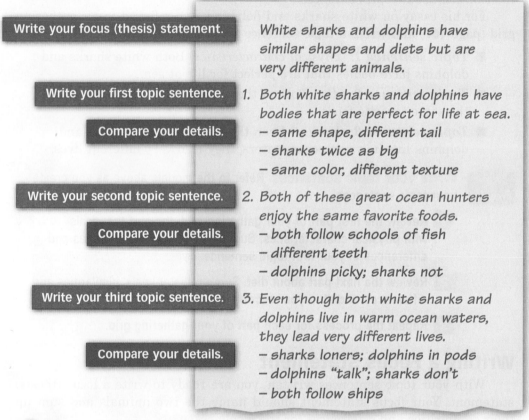

Write your focus (thesis) statement.

White sharks and dolphins have similar shapes and diets but are very different animals.

Write your first topic sentence.

1. Both white sharks and dolphins have bodies that are perfect for life at sea.

Compare your details.

 – same shape, different tail
 – sharks twice as big
 – same color, different texture

Write your second topic sentence.

2. Both of these great ocean hunters enjoy the same favorite foods.

Compare your details.

 – both follow schools of fish
 – different teeth
 – dolphins picky; sharks not

Write your third topic sentence.

3. Even though both white sharks and dolphins live in warm ocean waters, they lead very different lives.

Compare your details.

 – sharks loners; dolphins in pods
 – dolphins "talk"; sharks don't
 – both follow ships

Create your organized list. Use the directions above to help you create your own organized list. This list will guide your writing.

Focus on the Traits

Voice In a comparison-contrast essay, your writing voice should sound knowledgeable. Include specific details and tell what they mean. For example, dolphins have a blowhole *because* they breathe air.

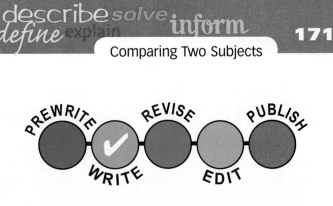

PREWRITE REVISE PUBLISH
WRITE EDIT

Writing

Once you've finished your prewriting, it's time to write your first draft. You're ready to write a first draft when you know enough about your topic and have written a clear focus statement.

Keys to Effective Writing

1. Use your organized list or an outline as a writing guide.

2. Get all your ideas on paper in your first draft.

3. Include your focus statement in your first paragraph.

4. Begin each middle paragraph with a clear topic sentence.

5. Compare your two subjects point by point within each paragraph.

6. Sum up your comparison and contrast thoughtfully in your final paragraph.

EXPOSITORY

Writing Getting the Big Picture

After finishing your prewriting, you are ready to write a first draft of your comparison-contrast essay. The graphic below shows how the parts of your essay will fit together. (The examples are from the student essay on pages 173–176.)

BEGINNING

The **beginning** introduces the two animals and gives a focus statement.

Focus Statement

White sharks and dolphins have similar shapes and diets but are very different animals.

MIDDLE

Each **middle paragraph** covers one main point of comparison.

Topic Sentences

Both white sharks and dolphins have bodies that are perfect for life at sea.

Both of these great ocean hunters enjoy the same favorite foods.

Even though both white sharks and dolphins live in warm ocean waters, they lead very different lives.

ENDING

The **ending** thoughtfully sums up the comparison and contrast.

Closing Sentences

That's one final difference between sharks and dolphins. Dolphins are very smart, curious, and friendly, so our swimmer can breathe easily— just like his friend, the dolphin.

Starting Your Essay

The first paragraph of your essay should grab your reader's attention and introduce your topic. Here are some strategies you can use to begin your first paragraph.

- ■ **Share an experience.**

  When I looked into the eyes of the dolphin at Sea World, I felt as though I had met a friend.

- ■ **Give interesting information.**

  Swimmers may fear sharks, but sharks fear dolphins!

- ■ **Create a dramatic scene.**

  A man paddles in the ocean, unaware that a large gray hunter is eyeing him.

Beginning Paragraph

Luc begins his essay with a dramatic scene. Then he introduces the two animals he will compare by asking a question. Finally, he adds his focus statement.

The writer gets the reader's attention.

The focus statement is given (underlined).

> A man paddles in the ocean, unaware that a large gray hunter is eyeing him. The creature suddenly swims toward him, and its dorsal fin breaks the surface. Is it a white shark or a dolphin? These creatures might look alike, but the difference between them could mean life or death. White sharks and dolphins have similar shapes and diets but are very different animals.

EXPOSITORY

Write a beginning paragraph. Write the opening of your comparison-contrast essay. Use one of the three strategies above to get your reader's attention. Then add your focus statement.

Writing **Developing the Middle Paragraphs**

Remember to use your organized list and follow these tips.

- The **first middle paragraph** compares and contrasts the animals' *physical characteristics*.
- The **second middle paragraph** compares *diets*.
- The **third middle paragraph** compares *habitats*.
- **Other middle paragraphs** are optional and may cover such things as *behavior, history,* or *future outlook*.

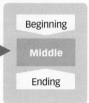

Using Comparison-Contrast Words

Certain words can help you make a comparison, while others create a contrast. (See pages **572–573** for additional transitions.)

COMPARISON		
like	same	also
as	identical	both
alike	similar	each

CONTRAST		
while	still	different
although	yet	however
whereas	but	even though

Middle Paragraphs

The topic sentence tells about physical characteristics (underlined).

The writer uses comparison-contrast words (in blue).

The closing sentence contains a final detail.

<u>Both white sharks and dolphins have bodies that are perfect for life at sea.</u> They have similar shapes, with long bodies, dorsal fins on their backs, pectoral fins on their bellies, and tails. The shark's tail is vertical, but the dolphin's tail is horizontal. On the whole, white sharks are bigger than dolphins. Most dolphins are no more than 8 feet long, but white sharks often grow to be 16 feet! Though sharks and dolphins have similar coloring, with gray backs and white bellies, their skin feels completely different. Sharkskin is like sandpaper because it is made up of millions of sharp scales. Dolphins have smooth, rubbery skin with blubber underneath. One other difference is

that a shark has gills since it breathes water as other fish do. A dolphin, however, is a mammal, so it has a blowhole for breathing air.

Topic sentence

Both of these great ocean hunters enjoy the same favorite food. They follow schools of fish and swim in to snatch them up. White sharks have rows of flat, triangular teeth, like knives. These teeth are made for cutting their food so they can swallow it in chunks. That's how sharks eat giant ocean tuna. Dolphin teeth are smaller and shaped like cones. They're perfect for biting into a fish or squid and holding on. Then dolphins swallow the food whole. Dolphins are picky eaters, unlike sharks, which also eat marine mammals like seals and otters. In fact, white sharks will eat just about anything, including license plates, tin cans, and even other sharks!

The writer covers details in point-by-point fashion.

Closing sentence

Topic sentence

Even though both white sharks and dolphins live in warm ocean waters, they lead very different lives. White sharks tend to cruise the oceans alone, but dolphins swim in pods, or schools, of between 10 and 500 creatures. Amazingly, dolphins have been seen in groups of more than 2,000! In their pods, dolphins make clicks and squeals for communication and echolocation, which is using sound to locate objects. Sharks don't make any sound except the crunch of bones! Both sharks and dolphins like to follow ships. Sharks follow them because someone might dump garbage out, but dolphins think it's fun to swim alongside them, leaping and playing.

The writer's voice shows genuine interest in the topic.

Closing sentence

EXPOSITORY

Write your middle paragraphs. Create the body of your comparison-contrast essay using your organized list as a guide.

Writing Ending Your Essay

The ending of your essay should sum up the comparison and contrast and leave your reader with something to think about. Here are some effective strategies for ending your essay.

Beginning

Middle

Ending

- **Emphasize a key idea.**

  White sharks and dolphins are both great hunters of the deep, but only sharks are known for attacking humans.

- **Add a new insight.**

  Perhaps the biggest difference between sharks and dolphins is that dolphins are smart, friendly mammals, but sharks are small-brained and cold-blooded fish.

- **Refer back to your beginning.**

  The gray dorsal fin comes out of the water—but is this a shark or a dolphin?

Ending Paragraph

> The comparison-contrast is summed up in a thoughtful way.

So whatever happened to our swimmer? The gray dorsal fin comes out of the water—but is this a shark or a dolphin? Look! There's a blowhole! The creature leaps over the swimmer and squeaks a greeting before diving again. That's one final difference between sharks and dolphins. Dolphins are very curious and very friendly, so our swimmer can breathe easily—just like his friend, the dolphin.

Write your ending. Write the final paragraph of your essay. Try one of the three strategies listed above to give the reader something to think about.

Form a complete first draft. Write a complete copy of your essay. Skip every other line if you write by hand or double-space if you use a computer. This will give you room for revising.

Revising

Now that you have all your ideas on paper, it's time to begin revising. You might add or remove details, shift sentences around, and refine your writing to make it clear and smooth.

Keys to Effective Revising

1. Read through your entire draft to get a feeling of how well your essay works.

2. Make sure your focus statement clearly names the two things you compare and contrast.

3. Revise your paragraphs to make sure each one begins with a topic sentence and covers one main point.

4. Make sure you sound interested and knowledgeable.

5. Check your words and sentences to be sure you make clear comparisons and contrasts.

6. Use the editing and proofreading marks inside the back cover of this book.

Revising **for** Ideas

6 I make my topic fascinating, and my essay contains many interesting details.

5 My topic is interesting, and I balance comparison and contrast details.

4 My topic is clear and balanced, but I could use a few more interesting details.

To revise your comparison-contrast essay for *ideas,* check to see if you have included interesting details. Also make sure you have a balance of similarities and differences. The rubric strip above and the following questions and answers can help you.

How do I know if my details are interesting?

If your essay contains only details that everybody knows, the reader will be bored. Look for information that amazes, entertains, or informs.

Amazing
Cows have four stomachs, one of which can hold up to 40 gallons.

Entertaining
Pigs and people have about the same percentage of body fat.

Informative
A peregrine falcon can dive at 200 miles per hour.

 Read the following details. For each, indicate whether you think the detail is interesting and why.

1. A typical box turtle lives longer than a human being.
2. Dolphin brains are seven times larger than human brains.
3. Parrots have feathers of different colors.
4. As arthropods, crabs are giant spiders of the sea.
5. Dogs come in all shapes and sizes.

 Review your details. Do you have several details that are amazing, entertaining, or informative? If not, check encyclopedias or the Internet to find a few more interesting details that relate to your main points.

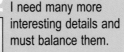

3 My topic isn't clear, and some details are boring. I need to balance my comparisons and contrasts.

2 I need many more interesting details and must balance them.

1 I need a new topic and help figuring out how to gather interesting details.

Do I have a balance of similarities and differences?

The quickest way to tell if you have balanced similarities and differences is to look for comparison and contrast words in your essay (see page **174**). Do you use about the same number of comparison words (*similar, like, also*) and contrast words (*instead, even so, but*)?

Read the following paragraph. On your own paper, list comparison words used in the paragraph. Then read the paragraph again and list contrast words. Is the paragraph balanced?

> Jellyfish and octopi have similar body structures, but they also have many differences. Both have a large head or dome with tentacles around a central mouth. Even so, a jellyfish does not have a true brain, whereas an octopus has a large brain. Octopi have big, sensitive eyes, but jellyfish have no eyes. Instead, their head is light-sensitive, and that helps to guide them through the water. Each creature uses tentacles to bring food to its mouth. Also, octopi and jellyfish are similar because they lack bones.

Check for comparisons and contrasts. Review your first middle paragraph for comparison words. Then check for contrast words. Do you have about the same number of each? If not, revise your essay to balance the number of similarities and differences.

EXPOSITORY

Ideas
An interesting detail helps balance comparisons and contrasts.

They have similar shapes, with long bodies, dorsal fins on their backs, pectoral fins on their bellies, and tails. ∧*On the whole, white sharks are bigger than dolphins. . . .*

The shark's tail is vertical, but the dolphin's tail is horizontal.

Revising **for** Organization

6 I use clear point-by-point organization that helps my reader understand and appreciate my essay.

5 I use clear point-by-point organization in my details, and my paragraphs have unity.

4 Each paragraph is about one main point, though a few of my details aren't in the best order.

When you revise your essay for *organization,* make sure that you have covered your details point by point. Also make sure your paragraphs have unity. The rubric strip above can guide your revision.

Did I organize my details point by point?

One way to check your essay for point-by-point organization is to make a "hopscotch chart" for each middle paragraph. A chart like this can help you see if you covered each detail for both subjects. If you write about the body shape of the shark, you should also write about the body shape of the dolphin. (The hopscotch chart to the right was created by Luc to check the details in his first middle paragraph on page 174.)

 Create your own hopscotch chart. In the body of your paper, choose one of your middle paragraph and graph the details in it using a hopscotch chart.

1 Write the first type of detail (for example, "Body shape") in a single box.

2 Draw double boxes below.

3 If you covered that detail for an animal, write its name in one of the double boxes.

4 Don't "hop" to the next single box until you have covered the detail for both animals.

5 Repeat the process for each detail in the paragraph.

Revise your details. If you forgot to cover one type of detail for a specific animal, revise your essay to include the detail.

Body shape
Shark | Dolphin

Body size
Shark | Dolphin

Body color
Shark | Dolphin

Body texture
Shark | Dolphin

3 Some details are in the wrong paragraphs or in the wrong order.

2 The reader may be confused about my main points and the order of the details.

1 I need help understanding point-by-point organization and unity.

How can I check my paragraphs for unity?

You'll know that your paragraphs have unity if each one deals with one main point, a point that is stated in the topic sentence. Every sentence in the paragraph should support the topic sentence. (Also see page **538**.)

 Read the following paragraph. Pay special attention to the main point stated in the topic sentence. Then indicate which details should be removed because they do not support the topic sentence.

> Both lions and tigers are carnivores that hunt for their meat, though they go about it in different ways. Among lions, the lionesses are the best hunters. They stalk and bring down prey and then drag it back to the pride. Male lions are the ones with manes. Tigers, on the other hand, are solitary, so both males and females must know how to hunt. Tigers live in India, but lions live in Africa. Although lions and tigers have been known to attack humans, both great cats prefer hunting and eating wild game.

 Check the unity of your paragraphs. Read through each paragraph, checking to see whether all the details support the main point in the topic sentence. Remove any details that do not.

EXPOSITORY

Organization
A new detail corrects the point-by-point organization, and an unrelated detail is deleted.

> Dolphins are picky eaters, unlike which
> Then dolphins swallow the food whole. Sharks also
> eat marine mammals like seals and otters. ~~White~~
> ~~sharks have many teeth.~~ In fact, white sharks will
> eat just about anything, including license plates, . . .

Revising for Voice

6 My voice is original, and I sound eager to share my knowledge with the reader.

5 My voice is original, and I show interest in informing the reader.

4 My voice is original, but in places I could sound more interested.

When you check your essay for *voice,* you want to make sure your writing sounds original and enthusiastic. The rubric strip above can guide your revision.

Is my voice original, or is it too predictable?

Your voice sounds predictable if you repeat the same sentence pattern over and over. Read the following paragraph. Notice how predictable the writing becomes.

> Both butterflies and moths come from larvae. Both insects go through metamorphosis. Butterflies create a chrysalis. Moths create a cocoon. Both insects turn into pupae. Butterflies come out with colorful wings. Moths come out with pale wings. Both insects let their wings dry. Butterflies fly off during the day. Moths fly off during the night. Butterflies drink nectar from flowers. Moths eat leaves from trees.

The reason this voice sounds so predictable is that the writer uses just one pattern for his comparisons: "Both A and B do the same thing." He also uses just one pattern for his contrasts: "A does one thing. B does a different thing." Here are some other patterns that the writer should try.

COMPARISON	CONTRAST
A and B are similar in that . . .	Even though A does one thing, B . . .
A does one thing, and B also . . .	A and B are completely different because . . .
B is like A because both . . .	Unlike A, B . . .
Just as A does one thing, B also . . .	On the one hand, A . . . On the other hand, B . . .

 Rewrite the predictable paragraph above. Use some of the comparison and contrast patterns shown above to make the voice sound original.

 Revise for voice. Review your essay and look for places where your voice sounds too predictable. Try some of the patterns from above to make your voice sound more original.

EXPOSITORY

3 Sometimes my voice sounds predictable. I need to show more interest.

2 I sound predictable. I need to show interest.

1 I need help understanding what voice is.

Does my voice sound enthusiastic?

Your voice is enthusiastic if it sounds like you want to share information with the reader. When your teacher is enthusiastic about a subject, he or she will use verbal cues to show that enthusiasm: "Here's the really amazing part," "Look how easy this is," "Can you believe that?" In your writing, you can also use cues like these to show your enthusiasm.

 Read the following enthusiastic paragraph. Find verbal cues that show the writer is eager to share information with the reader.

> Of course, black bears have black fur, and polar bears have white fur, but let's look a little deeper. Under a black bear's fur is light gray skin, but under a polar bear's fur is black skin. Why would that be? It's an incredible adaptation. A polar bear's fur is translucent, like fiber optics. The hairs actually carry sunlight down to the black skin, which absorbs it, warming up the bear. So when it comes to black bears and polar bears, their color isn't as black-and-white as it might seem.

 Add cues to show enthusiasm. Review your essay. Are there places where you list facts without showing any real interest in them? If so, add a verbal cue (words or phrases) to show enthusiasm. Don't overdo it, however.

Voice
Changes make the voice less predictable and more enthusiastic.

White sharks tend to cruise the oceans alone,

but dolphins swim in pods, or schools, of between

Amazingly,
10 and 500 creatures. Dolphins have been seen in
of more than 2,000!^
groups. In their pods, dolphins make clicks and . . .

Revising **for** Word Choice

6 Precise and accurate words and definitions make my essay informative and enjoyable to read.

5 Precise words and definitions help make my essay clear.

4 Most of my words are specific enough, though maybe I need to define some.

To revise your essay for *word choice,* make sure you have used precise and accurate terms to describe your animals. Also, if you use a term that might be unfamiliar to your reader, always provide a definition. The rubric strip above can help you revise for word choice.

Do I use terms that are precise and accurate?

There are precise terms to describe every animal. For example, ducks have *bills* instead of *beaks,* and chickens have *beaks* instead of *bills.* You might write about a *flock* of geese or sheep, but you wouldn't write about a *herd* of geese. In your essay, make sure you use terms that fit the animals you are describing.

Try IT Read the following sentences. From the terms in parentheses, choose the one that is precise and accurate.

1. The young of both a lion and a bear is called a *(foal, cub).*
2. A lion lives in a *(clan, pride).*
3. Bears tend to be solitary, and they live in *(dens, burrows).*
4. The male lion has a *(beard, mane).*
5. Lions and bears both have thick *(coats, coverings)* of *(hair, fur).*
6. Each of these large beasts has long *(nails, claws).*
7. Since lions eat only meat, they are strict *(carnivores, scavengers).*
8. Because bears eat berries, roots, insects, and meat, they are considered to be *(vegetarians, omnivores).*
9. Due to overhunting, both animals have become *(extinct, endangered).*
10. Now many lions and bears are protected and live on wildlife *(farms, preserves).*

Revise for precise words. Read over your essay, looking for words that aren't precise or accurate for the animal you are describing. Underline them and then replace them with more precise words. You may need to check your science book, an encyclopedia, or a Web site to find the right words to use.

3 In places, I might have used words that are unclear or too general.

2 Many of my words are too general, and some are incorrect.

1 I need help finding precise words and definitions for my essay.

When should I explain words?

Sometimes when you use a precise word for an animal, your reader might not be familiar with the meaning of the word. For words like this, you need to add a definition or an explanation. Your explanation should make the word clear without disrupting the flow of the essay. See the sample definition below.

> A male orangutan makes a long call, which is the sound that marks his territory.

 For each sentence that follows, choose an ending that explains the word without interrupting the flow.

1. An orangutan gets around by brachiating,
   a. a word that means moving around.
   b. using its arms to swing from branch to branch.

2. A chimpanzee gets around by knuckle-walking,
   a. using its fists and feet to amble across the ground.
   b. which means that it gets its hands dirty.

3. Both animals are frugivores,
   a. or "fruit eaters."
   b. which comes from the Latin word for "fruit" (*fructus*) and the Latin word for "eating" (*vore*), much like *carnivore* comes from "meat" (*carne*) and "eat" (*vore*).

 Add definitions. Check your essay for difficult words. Add explanations that make the meaning clear without interrupting the flow of the essay.

Revise

EXPOSITORY

Word Choice
An explanation is added.

In their pods, dolphins make clicks and squeals for
    which is using sound to locate objects.
communication and echolocation.
                    ∧

Revising **for** Sentence Fluency

6 My sentences are polished, and my ideas are clearly connected.

5 My sentences flow well, and I use coordinating and subordinating conjunctions.

4 Most sentences flow well, and I use a few conjunctions, but I might need more.

When you revise your essay for *sentence fluency*, you need to consider using conjunctions. Conjunctions are the workhorses of comparison-contrast writing because they help you connect similarities and differences. The rubric strip above and the questions below can guide your revision.

How can coordinating conjunctions help me compare and contrast?

Coordinating conjunctions can help you compare and contrast equal ideas smoothly and clearly.

| **COMPARISON** and, so | **CONTRAST** but, yet, or |

Fish and sea mammals **need oxygen to breathe.**
(This sentence uses *and* to compare two nouns.)
Fish get oxygen from water, but sea mammals breathe air.
(This sentence uses *but* to contrast two clauses.)
Sea mammals are at home in the water or on land.
(This sentence uses *or* to contrast two phrases.)

 Read each sentence below and find any coordinating conjunctions. List what kind of equal ideas are being joined—words, phrases, or clauses. Finally, tell whether the two ideas are being compared or contrasted.

1. Seals and sea otters are marine mammals.
2. Both animals are playful and sleek.
3. Seals hunt fish, but otters dive for oysters on the seafloor.
4. Both animals enjoy sunbathing, but seals do so in huge groups.

 Review your use of coordinating conjunctions. Read your essay. Find one place where you use a coordinating conjunction to compare equal ideas. Find another where you use a coordinating conjunction to contrast equal ideas. Look for other places where coordinating conjunctions could help you compare and contrast.

3 My sentences are a little choppy in spots, and I need to use subordinating conjunctions.

2 My sentences do not read smoothly. I need to use conjunctions.

1 I need help understanding sentence fluency and conjunctions.

How can subordinating conjunctions help me compare and contrast?

Subordinating conjunctions connect unequal ideas. These conjunctions are especially useful for creating strong contrasts. (Also see pages **744** and **746**.)

STRONG CONTRASTS

although, even though, where, though, even so, however, because

 In the paragraph below, find subordinating conjunctions that create strong contrasts. For each, indicate what is being contrasted.

> Although seals are clever hunters, otters have developed an ingenious technique for opening oysters. Otters float on their backs and balance stones on their bellies. Even though this may look silly, the technique allows otters to crack oysters open by hitting them on the stones. Though seals are known for performing tricks, this oyster trick is one they'll never master because they have no hands.

EXPOSITORY

 Check your use of subordinating conjunctions. Read your essay and look for a sentence where you used a subordinating conjunction to create a strong contrast. If you don't find one, create a strong contrast by combining two short sentences using a subordinating conjunction.

Sentence Fluency
Adding conjunctions improves sentence fluency.

> Most dolphins are no more than 8 feet long. ^but^
> ^Though^
> ⁁White sharks often grow to be 16 feet! Sharks and
> dolphins have similar coloring, with gray backs and
> white bellies. Their skin feels completely . . .

Revising **Using a Checklist**

Check your revising. On a piece of paper, write the numbers 1 to 12. If you can answer "yes" to a question, put a check mark after that number. If not, continue to work with that part of your essay.

Ideas

_____ **1.** Do I have a clear and focused topic?

_____ **2.** Have I included plenty of interesting details for both subjects?

_____ **3.** Do I have enough comparisons and contrasts?

Organization

_____ **4.** Have I written an effective beginning?

_____ **5.** Have I used point-by-point organization?

_____ **6.** Do my body paragraphs have unity?

Voice

_____ **7.** Does my voice sound original?

_____ **8.** Does my voice sound enthusiastic?

Word Choice

_____ **9.** Do I use precise and accurate words?

_____ **10.** Do I define difficult words?

Sentence Fluency

_____ **11.** Do I use coordinating conjunctions to compare and contrast?

_____ **12.** Do I use subordinating conjunctions to create strong contrasts?

Make a clean copy. When you've finished revising, make a clean copy of your essay before you edit. This makes checking for conventions easier.

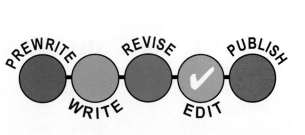

Editing

After you are done revising, your essay is ready for editing. As you edit, focus on conventions: punctuation, capitalization, spelling, and grammar.

Keys to Effective Editing

1. Use a dictionary, a thesaurus, and the "Proofreader's Guide" in the back of this book.

2. Check for any words or phrases that may be confusing to the reader.

3. Check your writing for correct punctuation, capitalization, spelling, and grammar.

4. If you are using a computer, edit on a printed computer copy. Then enter your changes on the computer.

5. Use the editing and proofreading marks located inside the back cover of this book.

Editing for Conventions

6 Grammar and punctuation are correct, and I have no spelling errors.

5 I must fix a few minor errors in punctuation, spelling, or grammar.

4 I need to correct some errors in punctuation, spelling, or grammar.

When you edit your essay for *conventions*, you check your capitalization, grammar, spelling, and punctuation. On these two pages, you'll also learn to look for errors common to comparison-contrast writing. The rubric strip above can guide your editing.

How can I check subject-verb agreement?

Your subjects and verbs must agree in number. This can be tricky in comparison-contrast writing, because you often will use compound subjects. The following rules will help you check for subject-verb agreement with compound subjects. (Also see pages **508–509**.)

COMPOUND SUBJECTS JOINED BY "AND"

If the compound subject is joined by the word *and,* the verb should be plural.

> **An ant and an aphid form a partnership.**
> *singular   singular plural*

COMPOUND SUBJECTS JOINED BY "OR" (OR "NOR")

If the compound subject contains two singular subjects joined by the word *or* (or *nor*), the verb should be singular.

> **An ant or an aphid relies on its partner.**
> *singular singular singular*

If the compound subject has a singular subject and a plural subject joined by *or* (or *nor*), the verb should agree with the subject closest to the verb.

> **Neither aphids nor the ant minds this partnership.**
> *plural   singular singular*

Check your compound subjects. Read your essay, watching for places where you use compound subjects. Check to make sure the verb agrees in number with the compound subject. Then check for subject-verb agreement in all your sentences.

3 Some of my errors may confuse the reader. I need to fix them.

2 I need to correct many errors that make my essay confusing and hard to read.

1 I need help making corrections, especially with my commas.

Have I used commas to set off explanations?

When you created definitions or explanations for the difficult words on page 185, you may not have realized that these definitions must often be set off with commas. (See **588.4**.) Notice the use of commas with the following explanatory phrase and clause.

Phrase: **Orcas, or killer whales, are related to dolphins.**

Clause: **Orcas, which are commonly called killer whales, are related to dolphins.**

Try IT Rewrite the following sentences on your own paper. Use commas to set off each explanatory phrase or clause that defines a word.

1. *Cetacea* the scientific name for whales and dolphins are marine mammals.
2. They get this name from *cetus* the Latin word for whale.
3. Some cetaceans feed on plankton tiny floating animals and plants.
4. Such creatures have baleen or whalebone filters instead of teeth.
5. The baleen filters thousands of krill or tiny creatures living in the water.

Edit

Check your comma use. Find places where you have defined difficult terms. Use commas to set off these explanatory phrases or clauses.

EXPOSITORY

Conventions
The punctuation of an explanatory clause is corrected.

In their pods, dolphins make clicks and squeals for communication and echolocation $\wedge$*which is using*

sound to locate objects. Sharks don't make . . .

Editing **Using a Checklist**

Edit

Check your editing. On a piece of paper, write the numbers 1 to 13. If you can answer "yes" to a question, put a check mark after that number. If not, continue to edit for that convention.

Conventions

PUNCTUATION

_____ **1.** Do I use end punctuation after all my sentences?

_____ **2.** Do I use commas to set off definitions?

_____ **3.** Do I use commas between items in a series?

_____ **4.** Do I use commas in all my compound sentences?

_____ **5.** Do I use quotation marks around any direct quotations?

CAPITALIZATION

_____ **6.** Do I start all my sentences with capital letters?

_____ **7.** Do I capitalize all proper nouns and proper adjectives?

SPELLING

_____ **8.** Have I spelled all my words correctly?

_____ **9.** Have I double-checked the words my spell checker may have missed?

GRAMMAR

_____ **10.** Do I form comparative and superlative forms correctly?

_____ **11.** Do I use correct forms of verbs *(had gone,* not *had went)*?

_____ **12.** Do my subjects and verbs agree in number? (The girl or the boy *is* going, not The girl or the boy *are* going.)

_____ **13.** Do I use the right words *(to, too, two)*?

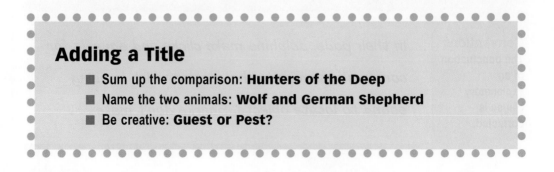

Adding a Title

■ Sum up the comparison: **Hunters of the Deep**

■ Name the two animals: **Wolf and German Shepherd**

■ Be creative: **Guest or Pest?**

Publishing **Sharing Your Essay**

After writing, revising, and editing your comparison-contrast essay, make a neat final copy to share. You may also want to include an illustrated copy in your portfolio, publish your paper online, or even turn it into a mini-documentary.

Make a final copy. Follow your teacher's instructions or use the guidelines below to format your essay. (If you are using a computer, see page 60.) Create a clean final copy of your essay and carefully proofread it.

Focus on Presentation

- Use blue or black ink and write neatly.
- Write your name in the upper left corner of page 1.
- Skip a line and center your title; skip another line and start your writing.
- Indent every paragraph and leave a one-inch margin on all four sides.
- Write your last name and the page number in the upper right corner of every page after the first one.

Create a Mini-Documentary

Turn your essay into a script for a wildlife documentary. Ask friends to help you act it out and film it. Include animals—if possible—to enliven the presentation.

Illustrate Your Essay

Prepare an illustrated copy of your comparison-contrast essay for your classroom portfolio or e-portfolio. If possible, include diagrams of each animal.

Submit Your Paper Online

Look for Web sites that accept student submissions (such as www.thewritesource.com) and submit your paper for publication.

EXPOSITORY

Rubric for Expository Writing

Use this rubric for guiding and assessing your expository writing.
Refer to it to help you improve your writing by using the six traits.

Ideas

6 The topic, focus, and details make the essay truly memorable.

5 The essay is informative with a clear focus and specific details.

4 The essay is informative with a clear focus. More specific details are needed.

Organization

6 The organization makes the essay informative and easy to read.

5 The beginning interests the reader. The middle supports the focus. The ending works well. Transitions are used.

4 The essay is divided into a beginning, a middle, and an ending. Some transitions are used.

Voice

6 The writer's voice sounds confident, knowledgeable, and enthusiastic.

5 The writer's voice sounds knowledgeable and confident.

4 The writer's voice sounds well-informed most of the time.

Word Choice

6 The word choice makes the essay very clear, informative, and fun to read.

5 Specific nouns and action verbs make the essay clear and informative. Unfamiliar terms are defined.

4 Some nouns and verbs could be more specific. Unfamiliar terms are defined.

Sentence Fluency

6 The sentences flow smoothly, and people will enjoy reading them.

5 The sentences read smoothly. A variety of sentences is used.

4 Most of the sentences read smoothly, but more variety is needed.

Conventions

6 Punctuation and grammar are correct. Spelling is correct.

5 The essay has a few minor errors in punctuation, spelling, or grammar.

4 The essay has several errors in punctuation, spelling, or grammar.

3 The focus of the essay needs to be clearer, and more specific details are needed.

2 The topic needs to be narrowed or expanded. Many more specific details are needed.

1 A new topic needs to be selected.

3 The beginning or ending is weak. The middle needs a paragraph for each main point. More transitions are needed.

2 The beginning, middle, and ending all run together. Paragraphs and transitions are needed.

1 The essay should be reorganized.

3 The writer sometimes sounds unsure.

2 The writer sounds unsure.

1 The writer needs to learn about voice.

3 Too many general words are used. Specific nouns and verbs are needed. Some words need to be defined.

2 General or missing words make this essay hard to understand.

1 The writer needs help finding specific words.

3 Many short, choppy sentences need to be combined to make a better variety of sentences.

2 Many sentences are choppy or incomplete and need to be rewritten.

1 Most sentences need to be rewritten.

3 Some errors confuse the reader.

2 Many errors make the essay confusing and hard to read.

1 Help is needed to make corrections.

EXPOSITORY

Evaluating an Expository Essay

Read the comparison-contrast essay below and focus on the writer's strengths and weaknesses. A self-assessment appears on the next page. (The student essay below contains some errors.)

The Wolf in the Junkyard

In a snowey forest, a wolf howls at the moon. What a wild sound! The funny thing is, you can hear the same sound in a city when a neighborhood German shepherd howls at an ambulance. A wolf and a German shepherd might live in different places, but they are similar.

Wolves look very much like German shepherds, with a few differences. Wolves have a wider head, longer legs, bigger feet, and a bushier tail. Most wolves also have coloring that is similar to a German shepherd, grayish brown with black. Wolves and German shepherds are even the same size, with males weighing around a hundred pounds and measuring about 2 1/2 feet tall at the shoulder.

If German shepherds were allowed to choose, they probably would eat the same thing their wolf cousins eat. Wolves eat mostly creatures with hooves, like deer and reindeer—and even moose. Since their prey is fast and strong, wolves hunt in packs. Most German shepherds eat dog food.

Of course, wolves and German shepherds have completely different places to live. Wolves live in the wild, weather on the artic tundra, a place without trees, or in the forests of Colorado. They have packs, with an alpha male as the leader. It's the opposite with German shepherds. They live wherever people live, sometimes as housepets and sometimes as junkyard dogs. Most German shepherds have a human family for a pack. Usually the person who feeds the dog most is its "alpha."

So, through they live in different places, wolves and German shepherds are pretty similar. The biggest difference is that a wolf is a wild creature and a German shepherd is a tame dog.

Student Self-Assessment

The assessment that follows includes the student's comments about his essay on page 196. The student mentions something positive first and then points out an area for possible improvement. (The writer used the rubric and number scale on pages 194–195 to complete this assessment.)

_5_ Ideas

1. *I've got a great topic and give a lot of interesting facts about it. Wolves rock!*
2. *I should have said more about what German shepherds eat.*

_4_ Organization

1. *I followed my planning chart from beginning to end.*
2. *My ending is weak.*

_4_ Voice

1. *Anybody can tell I like this topic.*
2. *My voice sounds a little stale in parts.*

_4_ Word Choice

1. *I defined "tundra."*
2. *I should have defined "alpha" and used more specific words.*

_4_ Sentence Fluency

1. *Most of my sentences are easy to read aloud.*
2. *A few spots are a little clunky.*

_3_ Conventions

1. *My subjects and verbs agree, and I used a comma to set off a definition.*
2. *I might have a few errors.*

Use the rubric. Assess your essay using the rubric on pages 194–195.

1 On your own paper, list the six traits. Leave room after each trait to write one positive comment and one thing that could be improved.

2 Then choose a number (from 1 to 6) that shows how well you used each trait.

Reflecting on Your Writing

Think about the essay you just finished. Then, on your own paper, finish each sentence starter below. Your thoughts will help you prepare for your next writing assignment.

My Comparison-Contrast Essay

1. The best part of my essay is . . .

2. The part that still needs work is . . .

3. The prewriting activity that worked best for me was . . .

4. The main thing I learned about writing an expository essay is . . .

5. In my next comparison-contrast essay, I would like to . . .

6. Here is one question I still have about writing a comparison-contrast essay:

Expository Writing

Cause-and-Effect Essay

Any big change can have many effects. For example, a dam on a river could destroy the habitat for certain animals, but could create new habitat for others. Put another way, a dam could be bad for some fish but good for the geese. Before people decide on a big change like building a dam, they should understand all the effects that the change will have.

In this chapter, you will write a cause-and-effect essay about a change in your school or community. As you write, you'll discover how one event can change the world around you in many ways.

Writing Guidelines

Subject:	**A change and its effects**
Form:	**Cause-and-effect essay**
Purpose:	**To explain**
Audience:	**Classmates**

Cause-and-Effect Essay

A cause-and-effect essay describes an event and what happens because of it. In the following essay, Rosalva writes about what happened when a dam was built on the river near her home.

Lower Forks Dam

After the big flood of 2001, Lower Forks built a dam on the Fox River. The dam stopped the flooding and created Fox Lake, but it had many other effects, too. Life in our town is completely different now. <u>The dam changed the landscape and the lives of people and animals in Lower Forks.</u>

First of all, the dam changed the landscape. When the dam was finished, water rose to swallow the riverbanks and the homes of animals that lived there. Trees along the south bank got flooded and died. A couple houses had to be torn down, too. One family even had their home hauled up the hillside. Still, Fox Lake was born. Cattails grew up among the dead trees, making a new wetland.

The dam changed the way people and animals use the water. People used to canoe from Upper Forks down to Kingston. After the dam was built, they stopped because of the long portage around the dam. Instead of canoes, the lake is full of motorboats and fishing boats. People catch different fish now, too. The river used to

Specific
details
make each
effect clear.

be full of catfish, but they're mostly gone, and the Department of Natural Resources stocks Fox Lake with walleye. Other new types of animals have shown up, too. Canada geese stop at Fox Lake when they migrate. Cranes have moved in on the south side of the lake, and a family of otters lives among the cattails.

Every season in Lower Forks feels different because of the dam. Before, when the snow melted, the river was fast and deep. It often flooded. As summer came on, the river calmed down to run only about a foot deep. Now, spring rarely brings any flooding. After a long dry summer, the river bed below the dam is sometimes only inches deep. Every winter, Fox Lake freezes over, which the river seldom did.

ENDING

The ending reflects thoughtfully on the cause and its effects.

After the 2001 flood, it was obvious that Lower Forks needed help. A dam on the Fox River got rid of the flooding, created Fox Lake, and made a new wetland habitat. Lower Forks used to be just a river town, but now it is also a lake town, and that fact affects every one of us.

EXPOSITORY

Respond to the reading. On your own paper, write answers to the following questions about the sample essay.

☐ **Ideas** **(1) What is the cause explained in the essay? (2) What are several of the effects?**

☐ **Organization** **(3) How did the writer organize the effects?**

☐ **Voice & Word Choice** **(4) What words and phrases show the writer's knowledge of this topic?**

Prewriting **Selecting a Topic**

Whether you live in a quiet town like Lower Forks or in a bustling city like Los Angeles, one change can cause many other changes. For this assignment, you'll need to find a change in your school or community that has had many effects. Rosalva used freewriting to think about changes around her.

> Well, here goes. Changes. I don't know any changes off the top of my head. Dad said there was going to be a superstore built in Kingston, only I guess that's in the future, so I don't know yet what will happen from that. He also said that before the highway bypass, State Street used to be filled with people. But I don't know enough about that since I wasn't even born yet! I wish I could just get out of here and go down to the lake. Hey, that's something. I remember when they built the dam, and how everything changed after that. . . .

Select your topic. Freewrite about changes in your school or community. Concentrate on changes that you know a lot about. Keep writing until you find a change that has had many effects.

Gathering Details

Once you have selected a change (cause), it's time to think about the effects it has had. One easy way to think about effects is to use a cause-effect chart. Rosalva used the following chart to gather details about her topic.

Cause-Effect Chart

Cause: Lower Forks Dam

Effects: wetlands / lake / dead trees \ cranes \ no canoeing

houses gone   otters   catfish gone   no spring floods

Gather details. Create your own cause-effect chart using the sample above as a guide. Write your cause at the top. Then write all the effects you can think of below it. Draw arrows to connect the cause to the effects.

Grouping Details

Next you need to organize the details you have gathered. Rosalva reviewed her cause-effect chart and noticed that the effects fell into three categories. She also added details as she worked.

Grouping Chart

The landscape	People and animals	How the seasons feel
lake	otters	no spring floods
wetlands	catfish gone	frozen lake in winter
dead trees	cranes	water low in summer
homes gone	no canoeing	

Group your details. Review your cause-effect chart. Notice how some details are related. Group your effects into two, three, or four different categories.

Creating an Organized List

In your cause-and-effect essay, each part has a different job. The opening paragraph introduces the cause. Each middle paragraph tells about one of the effects. The closing paragraph reflects on both the cause and effects. Rosalva used the following directions to create an organized list of ideas for her essay.

Directions

Organized List

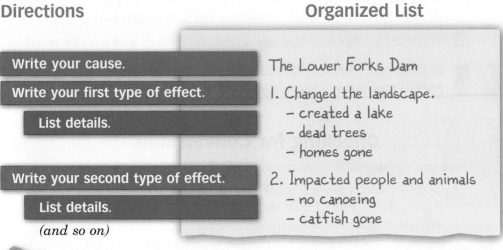

Write your cause.

Write your first type of effect.

List details.

Write your second type of effect.

List details.

(and so on)

The Lower Forks Dam

1. Changed the landscape.
   – created a lake
   – dead trees
   – homes gone

2. Impacted people and animals
   – no canoeing
   – catfish gone

Create an organized list. Use the directions above to make your own organized list of ideas. Include details from your cause-effect chart.

Writing Creating Your First Draft

Look over your organized list and the following tips before you write your essay.

- **BEGINNING** Capture your reader's interest. Then write a focus statement that names the cause and lists or summarizes its effects.
- **MIDDLE** Create a separate paragraph for each effect. Begin each paragraph with a topic sentence and support it with details.
- **ENDING** Write an ending that thoughtfully sums up your essay.

Write your first draft. Follow the tips above to create the first draft of your cause-and-effect essay.

Revising Improving Your Writing

Think about how you used the following traits in your first draft before you revise your essay.

- ☐ **Ideas** Do I clearly name the cause? Do I include enough details for each effect? Are all my details related to the effects?
- ☐ **Organization** Does my beginning contain a clear focus statement? Does each middle paragraph begin with a strong topic sentence? Does my ending reflect on the cause and its effects? Do I use transitions to connect my thoughts?
- ☐ **Voice** Do I show knowledge and interest in the topic?
- ☐ **Word Choice** Do I use specific nouns and action verbs?
- ☐ **Sentence Fluency** Are my sentences smooth and easy to read?

Revise your writing. Consider the questions above as you revise. Make any changes that will improve your essay.

Editing Checking for Conventions

Once you finish revising your essay, edit it by focusing on *conventions*.

- ☐ **Conventions** Have I checked spelling, capitalization, and punctuation? Have I also checked for usage errors (*to, too, two*) and other grammatical errors?

Edit your work. Edit your essay using the questions above. Have a trusted classmate edit your essay as well. Then make a final copy and proofread it.

Expository Writing
Across the Curriculum

Because expository writing shares information, you will use it throughout your school day, in just about every class.

This chapter gives you several examples of expository writing for different classes—an informative letter written for social studies, directions for a math procedure, a definition of a scientific process, and an e-mail that requests information. Finally, you will practice responding to an expository prompt.

Whatever the class, sharing your knowledge with a reader is often the key to communication and learning.

Mini Index

- **Social Studies**: Writing a Friendly Letter
- **Math**: Writing Explanations
- **Science**: Writing an Extended Definition
- **Practical Writing**: Writing an E-Mail Request
- **Writing for Assessment**

Social Studies:
Writing a Friendly Letter

Even though e-mail is fast and convenient, a friendly letter is still a wonderful way to send information to someone. The following letter was written by a student who was getting to know a pen pal from a different country.

The letter follows the friendly letter format.

The **beginning** gives a greeting.

The **body** includes the writer's thoughts and ideas.

The **closing** is polite and friendly.

100 Crabtree Way
Naples, FL 34100
January 12, 2004

Dear Soon-Li,

Thanks for the pictures and your letter about Seoul! I really like the photo of all the ships going in and out of the port. I can't even imagine what it would be like to be in a city with 9 million people!

I'd like to tell you about Naples, Florida, where I live. Naples is a lot smaller than Seoul. Our population is only about 24,000, though more people live here in the winter. Naples is farther south than most American cities, and it is beautiful. All along the west side run smooth, sandy beaches and the blue waters of the Gulf of Mexico. Often I can see dolphins from the beaches. The marinas hold thousands of boats, including some big yachts.

Naples is near the Everglades, a huge swamp with alligators, wild birds, and even deer and bears. Some alligators get to be six or eight feet long! My dad and I like to rent a canoe and spend hours paddling through the mangrove swamps. They are like a big green maze with twisty water paths. The roots of the trees stick up out of the water, which is really clear and warm.

Next time you write, could you tell me more about Korea? I hope that someday you can come and see my city, and that I can come and see yours!

Your friend,

Sam Johnson

Writing Tips

Use the following tips as a guide when you are asked to write an informative letter.

Before you write . . .

- **Choose a focus.**
  If you are writing to introduce yourself, you should share whatever information is appropriate. Be friendly and complete. If you are responding to a letter, review it. Try to answer whatever questions the writer may have asked.

- **Organize your thoughts.**
  Decide which details will be most interesting to your reader and plan your letter around those details.

During your writing . . .

- **Be specific.**
  Use clear details so that your reader will understand the information you are sharing.

- **Be enthusiastic.**
  Let your interest show in your voice and word choice.

After you've written a first draft . . .

- **Check for completeness.**
  Make sure you have provided whatever information your reader needs to understand your letter.

- **Check for correctness.**
  Read your letter, looking for errors. If possible, have someone else read it as well. Make sure your writing is free of errors in punctuation, capitalization, spelling, and grammar. Write or print a clean final copy.

EXPOSITORY

Imagine that Soon-Li is your pen pal. Write an unsent letter to her describing the place where you live. Try to explain what makes where you live different from other places.

Math: Writing Explanations

Once you can explain a math procedure to others, you know you have mastered it. Sharika wrote the following explanation to show how fractions are multiplied.

The beginning names the math procedure.

The middle explains the procedure.

The ending provides more advanced information.

Multiplying a Fraction by a Fraction

At first it might sound scary to multiply one fraction by another. But anyone who knows that $2 \times 4 = 8$ can multiply one fraction by another:

$$\frac{2}{1} \times \frac{4}{1} = \frac{8}{1}$$

What happened in the example above? The top numbers, or numerators, were multiplied together $(2 \times 4 = 8)$, and so were the bottom numbers, or denominators $(1 \times 1 = 1)$. The same technique works with other fractions.

$$\frac{1}{2} \times \frac{3}{4} = \frac{3}{8}$$

It might seem confusing that the product (3/8) is smaller than the two fractions that got multiplied. A way to make this less confusing is to replace the word "times" with the word "of." The equation above would read "one half of three quarters is three eighths."

There's one last thing to do when you multiply fractions: Remember to reduce the product to its simplest form.

$$\frac{3}{8} \times \frac{2}{3} = \frac{6}{24} \text{ simplified to } \frac{1}{4}$$

Writing Tips

Before you write . . .

- **Select a topic.**
  If your teacher has not given you a topic, search for one in your notes or math textbook.

- **Study the procedure.**
  Review the procedure that you will be writing about. Make sure you understand it thoroughly and have considered different ways of explaining it.

- **Think of examples.**
  Pick examples that will help you to clarify your explanation. A simple example can work as well as a more complex one, as long as it allows you to show every step of the process.

During your writing . . .

- **Think of your audience.**
  Imagine that the reader knows nothing about the math procedure you are explaining. Guide the reader step-by-step.

- **Organize your thoughts.**
  Decide on an order for presenting the information. Think of how your teacher or textbook first introduced the idea to you.

- **Focus on one step at a time.**
  Present the steps of the procedure in order. Write sentences that explain what you are doing in each example.

After you've written a first draft . . .

- **Check for completeness.**
  Make sure that you have included all the information a reader needs to understand the concept.

- **Check for correctness.**
  Edit and proofread your work to eliminate errors in spelling, punctuation, and other conventions.

EXPOSITORY

Write directions for a procedure that you are learning in math class. Use examples and clear steps.

Science: Writing an Extended Definition

A definition of a science term or process can be complicated. An essay that defines a term and includes examples, explanations, and many details is called an *extended definition*. The following student essay is an extended definition of a natural process.

What Is Metamorphosis?

The **beginning** provides a basic definition of the term.

Some animals grow by changing from one form to another. This process is called <u>metamorphosis</u>. A creature that goes through metamorphosis has one form as an infant and a completely different one as an adult. Differences can include shape, size, diet, and even habitat. Animals such as amphibians, crustaceans, and insects go through metamorphosis.

The **middle** provides examples and supporting details.

One example of metamorphosis occurs in frogs. They begin life as tadpoles, which are small, legless animals with long tails. Tadpoles live completely in the water, like fish. As tadpoles mature into frogs, they grow legs and gradually lose their tails. Frogs cannot live underwater. Instead, they must breathe air.

Butterflies also go through an amazing metamorphosis. They start out in a larva stage, in which they are caterpillars with many short legs. In the pupa stage, caterpillars wrap themselves in a chrysalis (a cocoon) and become dormant, which is like a very deep sleep. While dormant, they do not eat or move around, but they do change. When the butterfly finally breaks out of its chrysalis, it has wings, a different body, and six long legs.

The **ending** gives the reader something to think about.

People grow up, but they don't go through metamorphosis. Imagine what it would be like to roll out of bed one morning and discover you had grown wings!

Writing Tips

Before you write . . .

- **Choose a topic.**
  The glossary at the back of a science book would be a good starting point.
- **Do your research.**
  Make sure you thoroughly understand the term or process that you are going to define. Consult several sources if you have questions about a topic.
- **Organize your thoughts.**
  Write a statement that defines the term. Then plan how you will extend that definition with facts and examples.

During your writing . . .

- **Define your term.**
  Place your basic definition in the first paragraph.
- **Extend the definition.**
  Provide the reader with facts and examples that help explain the scientific term.
- **Use a comparison or a contrast.**
  Compare examples that fit the definition with those that don't. Note how the student writer compares the growth of animals that undergo metamorphosis with that of humans, who don't.

After you've written a first draft . . .

- **Get feedback.**
  Ask one of your classmates or someone from your family to read your definition. Listen carefully for any questions you could clear up or answer in a revision.
- **Proofread carefully.**
  Go over your essay to make sure that there are no mistakes in punctuation, capitalization, spelling, or grammar.

EXPOSITORY

 Write an extended definition about a scientific term related to nature or the environment.

Practical Writing:
Writing an E-Mail Request

E-mail allows quick communication between people across town—or across the world. The following e-mail was sent by a student to request information from a businessperson she had met on a field trip.

The **heading** includes sending information and a subject line.

The **beginning** shares a greeting and the purpose of the e-mail.

The **middle** lists questions.

The **closing** politely completes the e-mail.

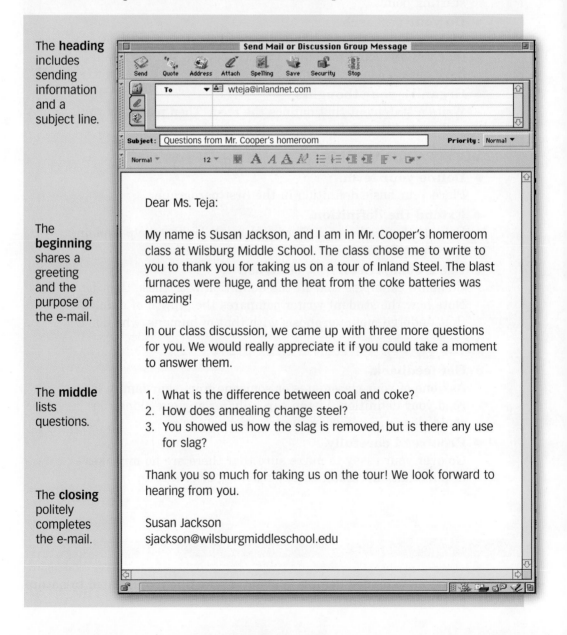

Send Mail or Discussion Group Message

Send Quote Address Attach Spelling Save Security Stop

To ▼ wteja@inlandnet.com

Subject: Questions from Mr. Cooper's homeroom   Priority: Normal ▼

Normal ▼   12 ▼

Dear Ms. Teja:

My name is Susan Jackson, and I am in Mr. Cooper's homeroom class at Wilsburg Middle School. The class chose me to write to you to thank you for taking us on a tour of Inland Steel. The blast furnaces were huge, and the heat from the coke batteries was amazing!

In our class discussion, we came up with three more questions for you. We would really appreciate it if you could take a moment to answer them.

1. What is the difference between coal and coke?
2. How does annealing change steel?
3. You showed us how the slag is removed, but is there any use for slag?

Thank you so much for taking us on the tour! We look forward to hearing from you.

Susan Jackson
sjackson@wilsburgmiddleschool.edu

Writing Tips

Before you write . . .

● **Know your goal.**
Think about what information you need. Then write a few questions for the person.

● **Think about your reader.**
Ask a reasonable number of questions that can be easily answered.

During your writing . . .

● **Fill in the heading.**
Complete the e-mail's heading. Then type in a subject line that tells your reader the topic at a glance.

● **Greet your reader and state your purpose.**
Identify yourself, be polite, and make sure your reason for writing is clear.

● **Give important facts.**
Provide any details that the reader needs to understand your request.

After you've written a first draft . . .

● **Check your facts.**
Double-check the information you include in your e-mail.

● **Tune up your questions.**
Make sure you've asked only necessary questions and have worded them in the best way.

● **Proofread carefully.**
Review your e-mail to make sure that there are no mistakes in punctuation, capitalization, spelling, or grammar.

EXPOSITORY

Remember a field trip you really enjoyed. Think of three questions you would like to ask about the place that you visited. Write an unsent e-mail to a person who works at the location and politely ask your questions.

Writing for Assessment

Many state and school writing tests ask you to respond to an expository prompt. An expository prompt will ask you to explain something or to share information. Study the sample prompt and the student response below.

Expository Prompt

No two people are exactly alike. Think of two people you know well. How are they similar, and how are they different? In an essay, compare and contrast two friends or two relatives. Include details about their appearance and personality as well as why each person is important to you.

The **beginning** introduces the focus of the writing (**underlined**).

The **middle** paragraphs each explain a different part of the focus.

We all need friends in our lives. I have two wonderful long-distance friends, Jayni and Berto. Jayni lives in Chicago in my grandmother's apartment building. Whenever I visit my grandmother, Jayni and I have a lot of fun together. I met Berto in chess camp, and I see him every summer. <u>Although these friends are very different, they are equally important to me.</u>

Jayni and Berto are the same age, but there are a lot of differences in their appearances. Of course, the main difference is that Jayni is a girl and Berto is a boy. Jayni has very dark skin and black, curly hair. Her eyes are light amber, almost golden. Berto has much lighter skin, but his eyes are so dark they are almost black. His hair is smooth and dark brown with red highlights. Jayni is as tiny as a little elf. She moves quickly and always seems to be running. Berto, on the other hand, is as tall and solid as a tree. He always takes his time, even when he should be in a hurry.

Each of my friends has a unique personality. Jayni is more serious and worries too much about everything from schoolwork to her basketball team. If she gets a poor mark, she panics. If she doesn't start or get to play a lot, she practices harder. Berto also gets good grades, but he never seems too concerned about his schoolwork. He could probably do even better if he'd just work a little harder. When he plays soccer, Berto doesn't seem to mind if he's not the star player. He has just as good a time sitting on the bench, cheering for the others.

Each of my long-distance friends is important to me, but for different reasons. When I'm feeling down about something, or when I have a problem, I know I can always count on both of them, but in different ways. Jayni is the one I e-mail for serious advice and help. But I know Berto can make me laugh, and his calm voice on the phone always helps me feel better.

I am lucky to have these great friends. I have other friends in school and in the neighborhood, but Jayni and Berto are special. I seem to have a connection with each of them that keeps our friendship close across the miles. They fill different spaces in my life, and each of them offers a special bond that isn't affected by distance.

The **ending** reinforces the focus.

EXPOSITORY

Respond to the reading. Answer the following questions to see how these traits were used in the sample response.

☐ **Ideas** (1) What is the focus of the writer's comparison and contrast? (2) What key words in the prompt also appear in the essay?

☐ **Organization** (3) How is the response organized—subject by subject or point by point?

☐ **Voice & Word Choice** (4) What words show the writer's feelings about these two friends?

Writing Tips

Use the following tips as a guide when responding to an expository writing prompt.

Before you write . . .

- **Understand the prompt.**
  Remember that an expository prompt asks you to explain.
- **Plan your time wisely.**
  Spend several minutes planning before starting to write. Use a graphic organizer (Venn diagram) to help you organize your ideas.

Venn Diagram

Subject A   Subject B

Similarities

Differences

During your writing . . .

- **Decide on a focus for your essay.**
  Keep your main idea or purpose in mind as you write.
- **Be selective.**
  Use examples and explanations that directly support your focus.
- **End in a meaningful way.**
  Remind the reader about the importance of the topic.

After you've written a first draft . . .

- **Check for completeness and correctness.**
  Present your details in a logical order and correct errors in capitalization, punctuation, spelling, and grammar.

Expository Prompts

- Few students enjoy doing homework, even though they know that it's important. Explain why homework is an important part of learning.
- Write an essay about something you learned recently that made you think. Explain what you learned and why it was important to you.

Plan and write a response. Respond to one of the prompts above. Complete your writing within the period of time your teacher gives you. Afterward, list one part that you like and one part that could have been better.

Expository Writing in Review

Purpose: In expository writing, you *explain something* to readers.

Topics: Explain . . . how to do or make something,
how things are similar or different,
the causes of something,
the kinds of something, or
the definition of something.

Prewriting

Select a topic that you know something about, or one that you want to learn about. (See page 166.)

Gather the important details and organize them according to time order, point-by-point, or in order of importance. (See pages 167–168 and 170.)

Write a focus statement, telling exactly what idea you plan to cover. (See page 169.)

Writing

In the beginning, introduce your topic, say something interesting about it, and state your focus. (See page 173.)

In the middle, use clear topic sentences and specific details to support the focus. (See pages 174–175.)

In the ending, summarize your writing and make a final comment about the topic. (See page 176.)

Revising

Review the ideas, organization, and voice first. Then review for **word choice** and **sentence fluency**. Make sure that you use terms that are clear and accurate. (See pages 178–188.)

Editing

Check your writing for conventions. Also have a trusted classmate edit your writing. (See pages 190–192.)

Make a final copy and proofread it for errors before sharing it. (See page 193.)

Assessing

Use the expository rubric to assess your finished writing. (See pages 194–195.)

EXPOSITORY

persuade

argue

Persuasive Writing

convince

reason

support

Persuasive Writing

Persuasive Paragraph

Are you too busy for breakfast? Try Go-Go-Cereal! Are you sick of unwanted e-mail? Try Mail Hound 3000! Need money? Send for *100 Ways to Get Rich*. Often, commercials try to persuade viewers by presenting a problem and proposing a solution. In 30 seconds, commercials like this can convince some viewers to buy a product or service.

Do you have the power to persuade someone in 30 seconds or less? In this chapter, you will write a persuasive paragraph. First, you'll briefly present a problem that you know about from personal experience. Then you will propose a solution to the problem. Think of your paragraph as a 30-second commercial and see if you can convince your reader to "buy into" your solution.

Writing Guidelines

Subject: A problem and a convincing solution

Form: Persuasive paragraph

Purpose: To propose a solution

Audience: Classmates, teachers, or parents

Persuasive Paragraph

A persuasive paragraph starts with a **topic sentence** that presents the problem. The **body** sentences explain the problem and convince the reader to agree with a proposed solution. The **closing sentence** sums up the solution. The persuasive paragraph below was written by Sarah, a student who wanted to convince her parents to change a family rule.

Topic sentence

Body

Closing sentence

Time Is Money

I have a big problem: I'm bored and broke. I have too much time and too little money. The problem is made worse because of a family rule. Until I turn 14, I can't get a job. Instead, I'm supposed to focus on my homework. The fact that I'm bored and broke won't change until we change the family rule. Why change it? For one thing, I make the A-B honor roll each semester and do my homework every night. A part-time job on Saturdays would not stop me from doing homework. For another thing, the family rule was made because my brother Frank's grades went down when he got a job, but I'm not Frank. I should have a chance to prove that I am responsible. All I want to do is turn my extra time into a little extra money, and changing the family rule is the best way to do it.

Respond to the reading. On your own paper, answer each of the following questions.

☐ **Ideas** (1) What problem does the writer present, and what solution does she propose?

☐ **Organization** (2) Where does the writer switch from talking about the problem to talking about the solution?

☐ **Voice & Word Choice** (3) What words or phrases show that the writer truly believes in the solution?

Prewriting **Selecting a Topic**

Your first step in writing a persuasive paragraph is to choose a problem to write about. For a paragraph, it's best to focus on a problem that you believe you can actually solve. Sarah used a cluster to think about possible topics.

Topics Cluster

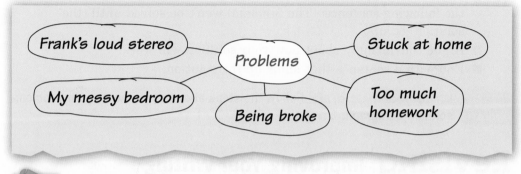

Frank's loud stereo

My messy bedroom

Problems

Being broke

Stuck at home

Too much homework

Prewrite

Create a cluster. Use the sample above as a guide to create your own cluster about problems you believe you can solve. Choose one problem to write about in a paragraph.

Defining the Problem and Solution

Once you have selected a problem, present it in a topic sentence. Beneath it, write a few sentences about possible solutions, just as Sarah did below.

Problem-Solution Chart

Topic Sentence: I have a big problem: I'm bored and broke.

Solution 1: Mom should raise my allowance.

Solution 2: I should find free things to do, such as going to the library.

Solution 3: Mom should change the family rule ✱ about getting a job.

Prewrite

Create a problem-solution chart. Write a sentence that names the problem you will be writing about. Then write three or four more sentences that propose solutions. Put a star next to the best solution for your paragraph.

Writing Creating the First Draft

Once you have written a sentence about the problem and a sentence about the solution, you are ready to write your first draft. Follow these guidelines.

- Start with your topic sentence, which tells about the problem.
- Provide details that convince the reader the problem needs to be solved.
- Write a sentence that introduces the solution. Model it after the following sentence: (The problem) won't be solved until (the solution) occurs.
- Argue convincingly about how your solution will work.
- End with a sentence that sums up the solution.

 Write your first draft. Follow the steps above as you write your problem-solution paragraph.

Revising Improving Your Writing

Read over your first draft. Consider how well you have handled the *ideas, organization, voice, word choice,* and *sentence fluency* in your paragraph.

 Revise your paragraph. Review and improve your paragraph as needed. Think about the following questions as you work on your writing.

1. Do I clearly present a problem and propose a solution?
2. Do I move logically from the problem to the solution?
3. Do I use a convincing, positive voice?
4. Do I use words that sound natural and sincere?
5. Have I written complete sentences that flow smoothly?

Editing Checking for Conventions

When you edit your paragraph, pay special attention to conventions.

 Edit your paragraph. Use the following questions to guide your editing.

1. Do I use correct end punctuation throughout my paragraph?
2. Have I checked for mistakes in spelling and grammar?

Proofread your paragraph. Before sharing your paragraph, make a final copy and proofread it one more time for errors.

Persuasive Writing

Proposing a Solution

It's easy to see problems. Maybe your city has a problem with litter or noise pollution or congestion. Maybe your school needs a new gymnasium or more computers or better wheelchair access. Everyone can see problems, but people who see solutions can make a real difference in the world around them.

In this chapter, you will be writing a persuasive problem-solution essay. First, you'll need to convince the reader the problem is serious. Then you must show that you have the best solution. With a well-written problem-solution essay, perhaps you can solve a problem in your school or community.

Writing Guidelines

Subject:	A problem in your school or community
Form:	Persuasive essay
Purpose:	To propose a solution
Audience:	Classmates and community members

Understanding Your Goal

Your goal in this chapter is to write a well-organized persuasive essay that proposes a solution to a problem. The traits listed in the chart below will help you plan and write your essay.

TRAITS OF PROBLEM-SOLUTION WRITING

Ideas

Convince the reader about a problem and propose your solution.

Organization

Develop an essay with a clear opinion statement and well-organized paragraphs.

Voice

Sound confident and convincing about the problem and your solution.

Word Choice

Use persuasive words that are appropriate for your audience.

Sentence Fluency

Use simple, compound, and complex sentences to create an essay that flows smoothly.

Conventions

Check your writing for errors in punctuation, capitalization, spelling, and grammar.

Get the big picture. Look at the rubric on pages 256–257. You can use that rubric to assess your progress as you write. Your goal is to write a persuasive essay that proposes a solution to a problem.

Problem-Solution Essay

A problem-solution essay is usually organized in two parts: (1) the writer convinces the reader that there is a problem, and (2) the writer persuades the reader to help with the solution. In the following essay, a student writes about a pollution problem at a local beach.

BEGINNING

The beginning introduces the problem and gives an opinion statement (**underlined**).

MIDDLE

The first middle paragraph convinces the reader the problem is serious.

The second middle paragraph proposes a solution.

Waterfront Rescue

If you visited City Beach last summer, you probably noticed the mess. Litter was scattered across the picnic area, and cans and bottles were all over the beach. The condition of City Beach has become a big community problem, and it won't be solved until we all get involved.

Mr. Sean Johnson of the city's maintenance department said the city can pay for just eight hours of work at the beach every week. This means that a worker comes to the park only one day each week. He or she empties the trash barrels but doesn't have time to gather all the trash left on the ground. When people leave their trash under the picnic tables or on the beach, it never gets picked up. Other people see how messy the area is, and they leave litter behind, too.

The big problem at City Beach needs a big solution. The kids from Lakeview School could be part of that solution. We could form a committee to keep the beach cleaner next summer. We might even start a tradition, and the kids from our school could do this every year.

PERSUASIVE

The other middle paragraphs persuade the reader to help solve the problem.

First, we would need to ask volunteers to spend Saturday morning at the beach just before it opens for the summer. Kids could wear protective gloves as they go around the park and pick up litter. They could put bottles and cans in recycling bins. Hot dogs, soda, and ice cream could be served to everyone who helps.

After the beach is cleaned up, we should add more garbage barrels and some "no littering" signs. Local organizations and businesses could sponsor the barrels. The signs could be bright and colorful, but they should also remind people that there is a fine for littering in the park.

ENDING

The ending answers a possible objection and calls the reader to action.

Some people might say it's not the job of Lakeview students to clean the beach, but if we make it our job, we can be the first ones to enjoy a clean beach. Also, once people see that the park is being cleaned, they may volunteer to help, too. So join the cleanup crew, and we'll all be proud of City Beach again!

Respond to the reading. Answer the following questions about the sample essay.

☐ **Ideas** (1) What details convince the reader to take the problem seriously? (2) What details persuade the reader to help solve the problem?

☐ **Organization** (3) Which paragraphs deal with the problem? (4) Which paragraphs deal with the solution?

☐ **Voice & Word Choice** (5) What words or phrases make the voice of the writer persuasive?

Prewriting

Before you begin to write, you'll need to select a topic, gather details, and organize your ideas. This process is called prewriting.

Keys to Effective Prewriting

1. Select a problem that you care about and that fits the assignment.

2. List possible solutions and choose one.

3. Gather details about the problem and the solution.

4. Write a clear opinion statement to guide you.

5. Create a list or an outline as a planning guide.

PERSUASIVE

Prewriting Selecting a Problem

The first step in writing a problem-solution essay is to select a problem. A cluster can help you think of the problems all around you.

Topics Cluster

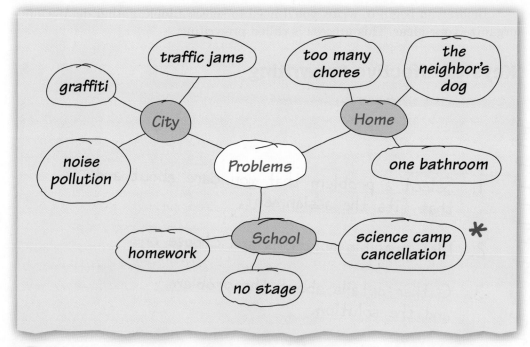

Create a cluster. Use the cluster above as a guide for creating your own topics cluster. Then use the questions below to help choose the best topic.

1 Which problem do I know a lot about?

2 Which problem could I help solve?

Focus on the Traits

Ideas The best writing always begins with strong ideas. In this case, the main idea of your essay is a problem that you can help solve. After you select your topic, you'll gather more details about the problem so that you can propose a realistic solution.

Gathering Details About the Problem

Your reader will have two questions about the problem: (1) why does this problem exist, and (2) why should the problem be solved? A chart like the one below can help you gather persuasive details such as facts, examples, and quotations.

Gathering Chart

Problem: **The school board might cancel science camp.**

Why does the problem exist?	Why should the problem be solved?
Science camp costs $30 per student.	Without science camp, we wouldn't get to do our outdoor projects. — mini-steam engines — solar panels
This year science camp would cost $3,000.	Nature is the place to learn about nature. — rock and plant identification — birds, animals, insects
The school budget has been cut.	Sixth graders want us to save the camp, too.
The economy has been bad.	
Everybody goes or nobody goes.	

Prewrite

Gather answers. Make your own chart like the one above. In one column, list reasons for the problem. In the other, list reasons why the problem should be solved.

Focus on the Traits

Organization A problem-solution essay has two parts. The first part will convince the reader that a problem exists. The second part will propose a solution that the reader can help with. By organizing your details carefully, you can make your essay both clear and persuasive.

Prewriting Proposing a Solution

A problem can have many possible solutions. Use a sentence starter like the one below and make a list of as many solutions as you can think of.

Sentence Starter

Science camp will be canceled unless . . .

    the economy gets better.

    the school board cuts something else.

    parents volunteer to run science camp at the school.

    students figure out how to raise $3,000 per year. ✷

    a miracle happens.

Write down solutions. Use a sentence starter that states your problem and ends with a word such as "unless" or "until." Write as many solutions as you can. Which solution could you and your reader help bring about? Put a star next to the best solution.

Gathering Details About the Solution

Now that you have chosen a solution, you need to figure out just how it would work. To persuade your reader to join in the solution, you need to answer every question the reader might have. The 5 W's and H can help.

5 W's and H Chart

Who? Principal Jeffries, the student council, and all Wadsworth Middle School students

What? Raise $3,000 per year to fill a "science camp fund"

Where? In the school district

When? Right away

Why? So that science camp won't be canceled

How? By holding fund-raisers like talent auctions and bake sales

Collect your details. Think about your solution. Then answer the 5 W's and H about it.

Avoiding Fuzzy Thinking

The details you have gathered will help you convince the reader that the problem needs to be solved and that your solution will work. However, when you present these details, you need to avoid errors in logic, or "fuzzy thinking."

Avoid jumping to conclusions.
The only reason that the school board would cut science camp is that they never experienced it themselves.
There could be many reasons the school board would cut science camp, not just this one.

Avoid bandwagoning.
Everybody thinks cutting science camp is a bad decision.
Many people thinking something is bad doesn't necessarily make it bad.

Avoid misleading comparisons.
Cutting science camp is like cutting down a tree.
Though both situations include "cutting," the similarities end there.

Avoid appealing only to emotion.
If science camp gets cut, the whole school will be in mourning.
Giving details about the negative effects is more convincing than talking about how sad everyone would be.

 Read the following statements. For each one, indicate what type of "fuzzy thinking" it shows.

1. Cutting science camp is like stealing from the seventh-grade class.
2. Everybody thinks science camp should be saved.
3. If Principal Jeffries wants the whole school to be completely depressed, he can go ahead and cancel science camp.
4. Without science camp, science grades will drop.

Focus on the Traits

Voice A persuasive voice needs to be logical and confident. By avoiding "fuzzy thinking," you can keep the reader on your side.

Prewriting Planning Your Essay

An opinion statement names the problem and proposes a solution.

the problem		the solution		an opinion statement
Science camp is in danger of being canceled.	**+**	*Students need to work together to raise money.*	**=**	*Science camp is in danger unless students raise money to save it.*

Prewrite

Write your opinion statement. Use the formula above to write your opinion statement. Name the problem and propose your solution.

Organizing Your Essay

The directions below can help you create an organized list for your essay.

Directions   **Organized List**

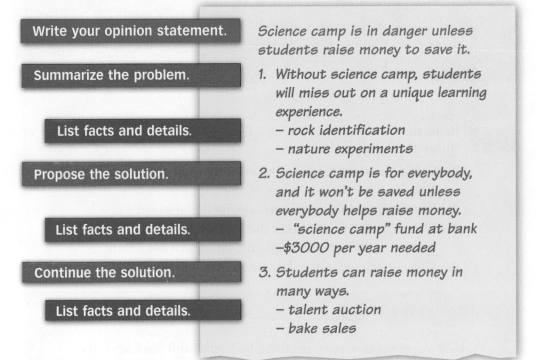

Directions	Organized List
Write your opinion statement.	Science camp is in danger unless students raise money to save it.
Summarize the problem.	1. Without science camp, students will miss out on a unique learning experience.
List facts and details.	– rock identification – nature experiments
Propose the solution.	2. Science camp is for everybody, and it won't be saved unless everybody helps raise money.
List facts and details.	– "science camp" fund at bank –$3000 per year needed
Continue the solution.	3. Students can raise money in many ways.
List facts and details.	– talent auction – bake sales

Prewrite

Make an organized list. To create your list, follow the "Directions" above. You will use this list as a guide when you write.

Writing

Once you finish creating a plan for your problem-solution essay, you are ready to put your ideas on paper.

Keys to Effective Writing

1. Use your organized list or an outline as a planning guide.

2. Get all your ideas on paper in your first draft.

3. Write on every other line to make room for changes later.

4. Write a clear opinion statement.

5. Use specific details to convince your reader that the problem is serious and your solution will work.

6. Use clear logic and avoid "fuzzy thinking."

PERSUASIVE

Writing Getting the Big Picture

Now that you have finished prewriting, you are ready to create a first draft of your problem-solution essay. The graphic that follows shows how the parts of your essay will fit together. (The examples are from the student essay on pages 235-238.)

BEGINNING

The **beginning** introduces the problem and provides the opinion statement.

Opinion Statement
Science camp is in danger unless students raise money to save it.

MIDDLE

The **first middle** paragraph summarizes the problem.

The **second middle** paragraph proposes a solution.

Other middle paragraphs contain details about the solution.

Topic Sentences

Without science camp, students will miss out on a unique learning experience.

Science camp is for everybody, and it won't be saved unless everybody helps raise money for it.

Students can raise money in many ways.

ENDING

The **ending** answers an objection and gives a call to action.

Answer to an Objection
Some people say it's too much work to save science camp, but the fact is that if we all help out, we can reach our goal easily.

Call to Action
Tell Principal Jeffries that you'll help raise money to save science camp.

Starting Your Essay

It's time to create your first draft. In the first paragraph of your persuasive essay, you will introduce the problem and provide your opinion statement. Before you do that, though, you need to get the reader's attention. Here are some strategies.

Beginning

Middle

Ending

- **Ask a question:** What do you think is the best thing about Wadsworth Middle School?
- **Quote someone:** "Nature is the best laboratory for learning about nature."
- **Share an experience:** When my brother saw a sandhill crane at science camp, he knew he wanted to go into wildlife management.
- **Give background information:** The state cut money to schools this year, which means that Wadsworth Middle School might have to cancel science camp.

Beginning Paragraph

The following essay captures the reader's attention by beginning with a quotation. The writer introduces the problem and gives an opinion statement.

A quotation gets the reader's attention.	"Nature is the best laboratory for learning about nature." Ms. Jacobson says this whenever she talks about science camp. For 10 years, every seventh grader at Wadsworth Middle School has
The problem is introduced.	attended the three-day camp in May. Sixth graders spend a whole year looking forward to "their turn," and eighth graders wish they could go again. Now
The opinion statement is given (underlined).	science camp might be canceled because of budget cuts. <u>Science camp is in danger unless students raise money to save it.</u>

PERSUASIVE

Write an opening. Write the beginning paragraph of your problem-solution essay. Use one of the four strategies above to get your reader's attention. Then introduce the problem and write your opinion statement.

Writing **Developing the Middle Part**

After you have written your opening paragraph, you need to develop the middle part, or the body, of your essay. As you write your middle paragraphs, use your organized list and the following tips.

Beginning
Middle
Ending

1 The **first middle paragraph** summarizes the problem.

2 The **second middle paragraph** proposes a solution.

3 The **other middle paragraphs** contain details that convince the reader your solution will work.

Middle Paragraphs

The topic sentence summarizes the problem.	*Without science camp, students will miss out on a unique learning experience.* In science class, we learn to identify rocks by picking them up out of a box. At science camp, we learn to identify rocks by finding them in cliff sides or riverbeds. Science
The body convinces the reader with details.	camp also lets students experiment with different forms of energy. For example, students get to build miniature steam engines that are powered by campfires. They also make solar panels that heat
The closing sentence tells why the problem needs a solution.	camp water. These experiences would be tough to create in a classroom. Science camp helps students understand nature while it teaches them to work with each other.

Topic sentence	*Science camp is for everybody, and it won't be saved unless everybody helps raise money for it.* To get started, Principal Jeffries and the student council could set up a "science camp fund" at a local bank. One student and an adult could be responsible for keeping the account. Every year, science camp costs $3,000. That sounds expensive, but if every student at Wadsworth raises just $10, the fund would be filled.
The second middle paragraph introuces a solution.	
Closing sentence	
Topic sentence	*Students can raise money in many ways.* For example, we could hold a talent auction. By raking lawns, cleaning gutters, baby-sitting, or using other talents, students can meet the goal. We could also arrange a rummage sale, or we could hold a bake sale. Students could even ask local businesses to sponsor them. If we all work together, we can easily raise the money.
This middle paragraph offers details about the solution.	
Closing sentence	

Write your middle paragraphs. Create middle paragraphs for your problem-solution essay. Follow the guidelines on page 236.

Drafting Tips

- **Follow the plan** in your organized list.
- **Use facts, examples, and quotations** to convince the reader to take the problem seriously and help solve it.
- **Avoid "fuzzy thinking."**
- **Use a convincing voice.**

Writing Ending Your Essay

Answering an Objection

In the ending, or conclusion, you should try to answer a main objection your reader might have. Use the formula below as a basic guide to answer an objection.

Beginning

Middle

Ending

> *Some people say* _____ ,
> (objection)
>
> *but the fact is* _____ .
> (answer)

Creating a Call to Action

A call to action is a command that tells the reader specifically how to help solve the problem. See the examples that follow.

- **Tell Principal Jeffries that you'll help raise money to save science camp.**
- **Sign Ms. Jacobson's petition to save science camp.**
- **Pledge your support for science camp at the student council meeting Monday.**

Ending Paragraph

An objection is answered.

A call to action asks the reader to help.

> *Some people say it's too much work to save science camp, but the fact is that if we all help out, we can reach our goal easily. Science camp is a terrific tradition that deserves to be saved. Tell Principal Jeffries that you'll help raise money to save science camp.*

Write your ending. Write the final paragraph of your essay. First answer any objection your reader might have. Then summarize the problem and solution and call your reader to action.

Form a complete first draft. Write a complete copy of your essay. Skip every other line if you write by hand, or double-space if you use a computer.

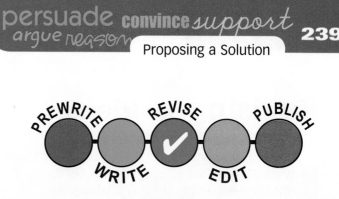

Revising

When you revise, you add or remove details, shift parts of the essay, and work on creating a more persuasive voice. You also check your word choice and refine your sentences.

Keys to Effective Revising

1. Read through your entire draft to get a feeling of how well your essay works.

2. Make sure your opinion statement names the problem and proposes a solution.

3. Check your paragraphs to make sure they follow your writing plan.

4. Revise your voice if it does not sound convincing.

5. Make sure your words and sentences are strong and clear.

6. Use the editing and proofreading marks inside the back cover of this book.

Revising **for** Ideas

6 I persuade my reader by using reasons and details and answering all the objections.

5 My details are persuasive, and I answer the reader's biggest objection.

4 My details are persuasive, but I did not answer an objection.

When you revise a problem-solution essay for *ideas*, you should check to make sure you have included enough persuasive details and have answered an objection. The rubric strip above can guide you.

How can I use details to persuade?

You can use details to convince your reader that the problem is serious and that your solution will work. During prewriting, you gathered details to answer the reader's questions about the problem and your solution. Now you will check to make sure these details appear in your essay.

Reviewing Details About the Problem

The details in your beginning paragraph and your first middle paragraph should provide clear answers to the following questions.

■ Why does this problem exist?
■ Why should the problem be solved?

Reviewing Details About the Solution

The details in your other middle paragraphs should provide clear answers to the following questions.

1. **Who** should help solve this problem?
2. **What** should they do to solve the problem?
3. **When** should they begin?
4. **Where** should they work?
5. **Why** should they help out?
6. **How** should they get involved?

Revise

Review your details. Read your first draft. Answer each of the questions above using details from your essay. If your essay is missing any important details, revise your writing to include them.

3 I need more details about the problem or solution, and I should answer an objection.

2 My essay lacks persuasive details and doesn't answer an objection.

1 I need to learn how to use details to persuade.

Have I answered a main objection?

You have answered an objection if you have mentioned a concern that a reader might have and then answered the concern in a satisfying way.

READER'S CONCERN

Some people say we don't need intramural sports,

SATISFYING ANSWER

but intramural teams help students keep physically fit.

 Read the following answers to objections. Indicate what is wrong with each: either the answer does not mention a concern, or the answer does not respond to the concern in a satisfying way.

1. Some people may think the crossing at Kane Street and Harper Avenue is safe, but those people are wrong.

2. The fact is that busywork wastes everybody's time.

3. Although most students like our school mascot, I don't.

 Revise your writing. Check to see that you have effectively answered an objection. Revise as needed.

Ideas
An answer to an objection is improved.

Some people say it's too much work to save
    if we all help out, we can reach our goal easily.
science camp, but the fact is that ~~those people~~
                    ^
~~have no idea what they're talking about,~~ Science. . .

Revising for Organization

6 My organization follows a well-developed plan, grabs the reader's attention, and has a clear call to action.	**5** My beginning gets the reader's attention, and my ending has a call to action.	**4** My beginning gets the reader's attention, but the call to action needs some work.

When you revise for *organization*, you check your essay to see that you have followed your organized list. Then you make sure that your beginning captures your reader's attention and that your ending gives a clear call to action. The rubric strip above can help.

Does my beginning capture my reader's attention?

Your first sentence is the most important one for capturing your reader's attention. To make sure you have the best first sentence, try several versions. On page 235, you were given four strategies: ask a question, quote someone, share an experience, or give background information. Here are four additional strategies for getting your reader's attention.

- **Sum up the problem.**

    The bill for science camp is $3,000 per year.

- **Make a shocking statement.**

    The seventh graders could lose the best part of the school year.

- **Begin with "if."**

    If we don't act, science camp might be canceled.

- **Describe a dramatic scene.**

    All the cabins stand empty, and all the campfires have burned out.

Try different beginnings. Review the strategies above and those on page 235. Then follow these instructions.

1 Choose two strategies you have not yet tried.

2 Write two new versions of your beginning sentence.

3 Share all three beginnings with a classmate and ask which beginning does the best job of capturing his or her attention.

4 Choose the best beginning.

3 I should improve both my beginning and my call to action.

2 The beginning, middle, and ending all run together and don't work well.

1 I need help organizing my essay.

Does my ending contain a clear call to action?

A clear call to action lets the reader know just what he or she should do to help with the solution. Your call to action needs to be

- specific,
- realistic, and
- stated as a polite command.

 Read the following *unclear* calls to action. On your own paper, indicate what the problem is with each call to action: not specific, not realistic, or not stated as a command. (There may be more than one problem.)

1. It would be nice if students donated money to the drama club.

2. Do everything you can to make our streets safe!

3. As a student of Lincoln Middle School, demand your rights to approve the school budget!

4. Clean up the planet!

5. It's time for all good students to help out with recycling.

 Check your call to action. Make sure that your call to action is specific, realistic, and stated as a polite command.

Organization
An unclear call to action is improved.

Science camp is a terrific tradition that deserves
to be saved. ~~Somebody ought to do~~
~~something about this problem.~~
Tell Principal Jeffries that you'll help raise money to save science camp.

PERSUASIVE

Revising **for** Voice

6 My voice is confident and persuasive and convinces my readers.

5 My voice is confident and persuasive throughout the essay.

4 My voice is confident, but I need to include more suggestions to be persuasive.

To revise for *voice*, check your writing to make sure it sounds confident and persuasive. The rubric strip above can help you.

How can my voice sound more confident?

One way to sound more confident is to make your point in the fewest words possible. Confident writing says a lot with a few words, and it is convincing. Writing that is not confident uses many words that say very little.

NOT CONFIDENT

It might be a useful solution to the problem of too many cars in front of the school if the school could have a different place marked out for people to come to drop off or pick up students.

CONFIDENT

New parking rules could solve the traffic jams before and after school.

Read the following sentences that lack a confident voice. Rewrite each in as few words as you can.

1. The problem that there are some rooms that are warm and stuffy could be helped if there were some sort of policy about adjusting the thermostat.

2. If people would slow down when they are driving along the road with the bike route, then maybe it wouldn't be quite so tough for cyclists to use the route to get places.

Revise your voice. Read your essay and look for places where you could say the same thing using fewer words. Revise your writing to make it sound more confident.

---

3 At times my voice sounds confident, but it never is persuasive.

2 I need to sound confident and persuasive throughout.

1 I need to understand how to create a confident and persuasive voice.

How can my voice sound more persuasive?

One way to make your voice sound more persuasive is to include a few suggestions. These are two types of suggestions: mild and strong.

■ **Suggestions:** A mild suggestion uses a verb such as *may, could, would;* a strong suggestion uses a verb such as *should, ought,* or *must.*

 Read the following statements. Turn each one into a mild or strong suggestion using one of the verbs listed above.

1. It is up to students to help with recycling day.

2. It is important that classmates know that teasing isn't allowed.

3. Students don't report accidents to teachers.

4. Seventh graders help sixth graders learn new skills.

5. It is a good idea for students to walk home in pairs instead of alone.

 Add suggestions or commands. Check your essay. If the voice needs to be more persuasive in parts, add suggestions.

Voice
A statement is turned into a suggestion, and an important point is said in fewer words.

> One student and an adult ^could be^ are responsible for
>   ~~Every year, science camp costs $3,000.~~
> keeping the account. ~~Taken on a yearly basis, the~~
> ^~~general expenses for science camp are round about~~^
> ~~in the range of $3,000 for the whole group of~~
> ~~seventh graders who go~~ That sounds expensive . . .

Revising for Word Choice

6 My words are engaging and positive, and they fit my audience and purpose.

5 I have avoided inflammatory words and am not too formal or too casual.

4 I use no inflammatory words, but some words might be too formal or casual.

When you check your essay for *word choice*, make sure you have avoided inflammatory words. Also make sure that you have used words that fit your audience and purpose. Use the rubric strip above to guide you.

What are inflammatory words and phrases?

Inflammatory words and phrases will upset or anger the reader. If you anger a reader, you'll have a hard time getting him or her to help with your solution. Inflammatory language includes insults, name-calling, and unrealistic exaggerations. If you feel a word or phrase in some way may upset the reader, make sure to change it.

Try It Read the following two paragraphs. Find at least five examples of inflammatory language and tell why each might upset the reader.

1   The town council must be crazy to suggest that the new
2 bypass be placed right next to the school. Truck traffic on the road
3 will rumble past until the school walls disintegrate. The only reason
4 this bypass route is suggested is to protect the fat-cat property
5 owners on the other side of the town.
6   People who would vote for the bypass must not believe in
7 education, or maybe they just dislike kids. How can students learn
8 anything with all that truck traffic rattling their skulls? We need to
9 speak up, or the school is doomed.

Check for inflammatory words. Read over your essay, imagining that you are a typical reader. Check each word (and phrase) to make sure you haven't said anything to insult your reader. Remove inflammatory words.

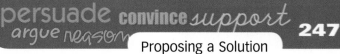

3 I have some inflammatory words and struggle with words that are too formal or casual.

2 I can't avoid inflammatory words and slang because of my strong feelings.

1 I need to learn about word choice for persuasive writing.

Do my words fit my audience and purpose?

To be persuasive, the words you choose should not be too formal or too casual. Words that are too formal sound stiff and unnatural. On the other hand, words that are too casual aren't very convincing. The following examples show how appropriate word choice makes writing more persuasive.

> **TOO FORMAL**
>
> The student council should address this concern with the utmost speed.
>
> **TOO CASUAL**
>
> The student council should hash out this deal A.S.A.P.
>
> **JUST RIGHT**
>
> The student council should discuss this problem right away.

Revise

Check for appropriate word choice. Read through your essay. Look for words that are too formal or too casual. Replace them with words that fit your audience and purpose.

Word Choice
Casual word choice is corrected, and an inflammatory word is removed.

> Without science camp, students will miss out
> on a ~~totally awesome~~ *unique* learning experience. In science
> class, we learn to identify rocks by picking them up
> out of a ~~stupid~~ box. At science camp, we learn to
> identify rocks by finding them in cliff sides or . . .

PERSUASIVE

Revising for Sentence Fluency

6 My sentences flow smoothly, and people will enjoy reading them.

5 I use compound sentences for equal ideas and complex sentences for unequal ideas.

4 I use a variety of sentences, but I need some complex sentences.

When you revise for *sentence fluency,* make sure you have used a variety of sentences—simple, compound, and complex. The rubric strip above will help to guide you.

Do I use compound sentences well?

Compound sentences can add variety and balance to your writing. When you have two ideas that are equally important, you can express them best in a compound sentence. A compound sentence consists of two simple sentences that are usually joined by a comma and a coordinating conjunction such as *and, but, or, nor, so, for,* or *yet.* (See page **516**.)

> **TWO EQUAL IDEAS**
>
> **The school will pay half the cost of the spring production.**
> **The drama club will need to raise money to pay for the rest.**
>
> **ONE COMPOUND SENTENCE**
>
> **The school will pay half the cost of the spring production**, but **the drama club will need to raise money to pay for the rest.**

 Combine each of the following pairs of simple sentences into one compound sentence. Use a different conjunction in each sentence.

1. The sports teams need new equipment. The band needs new sheet music.

2. Archery is offered in the summer recreation program. It is not offered in regular gym class.

3. The history class is planning a field trip to the museum next week. They might go to a historical site instead.

 Check your use of compound sentences. Read your essay and look for compound sentences. If you do not use many, look for short sentences that express equal ideas. Join them with a comma and a coordinating conjunction to form a compound sentence.

3 In some places, I use too many simple sentences. I need to combine some of them.

2 My writing has too many simple sentences. I need to combine many of them.

1 Most of my sentences need to be rewritten.

Do I use complex sentences well?

Complex sentences help to show the different kinds of connections between the ideas in your writing. Special transitions called *subordinating conjunctions* can be used to create these connections. (See page **517**.)

TIME		CAUSE-EFFECT		COMPARISON-CONTRAST	
after	until	because	so that	although	though
before	when	in order that	that	as though	where
till	while	provided that	unless	even though	whereas

For each complex sentence, tell what connection the subordinating conjunction makes: *time, cause-effect, comparison-contrast.*

1. Because the school building is old, some restrooms aren't accessible.

2. The student body must vote before the PTO can decide.

3. Though testing is important, learning is even more important.

4. When the annex is finished, everyone will have computer access.

5. Unless we act now, the marching band will be cut.

Create connections between ideas. Read your essay and look for complex sentences. If you do not use many, look for places where they could be used.

Sentence Fluency
Simple sentences are combined into a complex and a compound sentence.

Science camp helps students understand nature. ~~It~~ *while* It teaches them to work with each other.

Science camp is for everybody. *and* ~~It~~ It won't be saved unless everybody helps raise money for it.

Revising **Using a Checklist**

Check your revising. On a piece of paper, write the numbers 1 to 12. If you can answer "yes" to a question, put a check mark after that number. If not, continue to work with that part of your essay.

Ideas

_____ **1.** Do I focus on a clear problem and solution?

_____ **2.** Have I included persuasive details about the problem and the solution?

_____ **3.** Have I answered a reader's possible objection?

Organization

_____ **4.** Have I followed my organized list or outline?

_____ **5.** Does my beginning capture my reader's attention?

_____ **6.** Does my ending include a clear call to action?

Voice

_____ **7.** Does my voice sound confident?

_____ **8.** Does my voice sound persuasive?

Word Choice

_____ **9.** Have I avoided inflammatory words?

_____ **10.** Have I chosen words that are not too formal or too casual?

Sentence Fluency

_____ **11.** Do I use compound sentences well?

_____ **12.** Do I use complex sentences well?

Make a clean copy. When you've finished revising, make a clean copy before you edit. This makes checking for conventions easier.

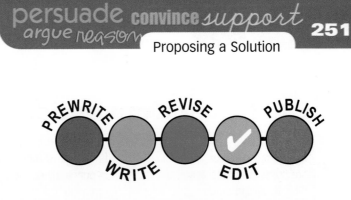

Editing

Once you are finished revising, you need to edit for punctuation, spelling, capitalization, and grammar. These rules are called *conventions*.

Keys to Effective Editing

1. Use a dictionary, a thesaurus, and the "Proofreader's Guide" in the back of this book.

2. Check for any words or phrases that may be confusing to the reader.

3. Check your writing for correct punctuation, capitalization, spelling, and grammar.

4. If you are using a computer, edit on a printed computer copy. Then enter your changes on the computer.

5. Use the editing and proofreading marks inside the back cover of this book.

PERSUASIVE

Editing for Conventions

6 My grammar and punctuation are correct, and the essay is free of spelling errors.

5 I have a few minor errors in punctuation, spelling, or grammar.

4 I need to correct some errors in punctuation, spelling, and grammar.

When you edit for *conventions*, you need to pay attention to spelling, punctuation, capitalization, and grammar. These two pages will help you check your compound and complex sentences for correct punctuation. The rubric strip above can also guide your editing.

Do I correctly punctuate compound sentences?

A correctly punctuated compound sentence will have a comma before the coordinating conjunction *(and, but, or, nor, for, so, yet)*. When you created the three compound sentences on page 248, you may have accidentally left out the comma or the conjunction. (See page **516**.)

> **MISSING COMMA**
>
> The school will pay for half the cost of the spring production but the drama club will need to raise money to pay for the rest.

> **MISSING CONJUNCTION (COMMA SPLICE)**
>
> The school will pay for half the cost of the spring production, the drama club will need to raise money to pay for the rest.

> **MISSING COMMA AND CONJUNCTION (RUN-ON)**
>
> The school will pay for half the cost of the spring production the drama club will need to raise money to pay for the rest.

 Rewrite each of the following compound sentences to correct the error.

1. Everybody has homework some of us also play sports after school.
2. Homework requires concentration and noise breaks concentration.
3. Study hall has become a problem, we need a solution.

 Check for errors in compound sentences. Check the compound sentences in your essay. Make sure each has a comma and a coordinating conjunction. Fix any errors you find.

I need to correct errors **3** that may confuse the reader.

I need to correct many **2** errors that make my essay difficult to read.

I need help making **1** corrections.

Do I correctly punctuate complex sentences?

Punctuating complex sentences can be a little tricky. If the dependent clause comes first in the sentence, a comma follows it. If the dependent clause comes at the end of the sentence, a comma is usually not needed.

After **the school board meets**, *(dependent clause)*
students will find out about the new school schedule. *(independent clause)*

We will have to elect a new student council president *(independent clause)*
before **the school year ends.** *(dependent clause)*

Try IT Rewrite each of the following sentences to correct the error.

1. When students don't respect the rules study hall becomes gab hall.
2. Often students can't finish their work, because study hall is too loud.
3. Until we fix this problem nobody will be able to work.

Edit

Check for errors in complex sentences. Check your complex sentences to make sure that you have correctly punctuated them.

Conventions
A comma splice is fixed, and a punctuation error is corrected in a complex sentence.

We could also arrange a rummage sale, or *we could hold a bake sale. Students could even ask local businesses to sponsor them. If we all work together,* *we can easily raise the money.*

Editing Using a Checklist

Edit

Check your editing. On a piece of paper, write the numbers 1 to 12. If you can answer "yes" to a question, put a check mark after that number. If not, continue to edit for that convention.

Conventions

PUNCTUATION

_____ **1.** Do I use end punctuation after all my sentences?

_____ **2.** Do I use commas before coordinating conjunctions in compound sentences?

_____ **3.** Do I use a comma after a dependent clause at the beginning of a complex sentence?

_____ **4.** Do I use quotation marks around any direct quotations?

CAPITALIZATION

_____ **5.** Do I start all my sentences with capital letters?

_____ **6.** Do I capitalize all proper nouns and proper adjectives?

SPELLING

_____ **7.** Have I spelled all words correctly?

_____ **8.** Have I double-checked the words my spell checker may have missed?

GRAMMAR

_____ **9.** Do I form comparative and superlative forms correctly?

_____ **10.** Do I use correct forms of verbs (*had gone,* not *had went*)?

_____ **11.** Do my subjects and verbs agree in number? (Jack and Jill *are* going, not Jack and Jill *is* going)?

_____ **12.** Do I use the right words (*to, too, two*)?

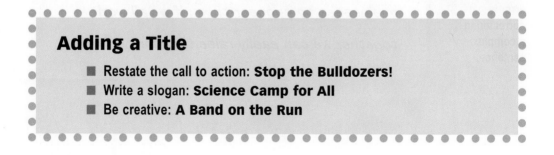

Adding a Title

- Restate the call to action: **Stop the Bulldozers!**
- Write a slogan: **Science Camp for All**
- Be creative: **A Band on the Run**

Publishing Sharing Your Essay

After all your work to write, revise, and edit your problem-solution essay, you'll want to make a neat final copy to share. You may also want to propose your solution to a group, submit it to a newsletter, or advertise it with a poster.

Publish

Make a final copy. Follow your teacher's instructions or use the guidelines below to format your essay. (If you are using a computer, see page 60.) Create a clean final copy of your essay and carefully proofread it.

Focus on Presentation

- ■ Use blue or black ink and write neatly.
- ■ Write your name in the upper left corner of page 1.
- ■ Skip a line and center your title; skip another line and start your writing.
- ■ Indent every paragraph and leave a one-inch margin on all four sides.
- ■ Write your last name and the page number in the upper right corner of every page after the first one.

Make an Oral Presentation

Decide what group could help with your solution—your class, the student council, a student club, the PTA or PTO, or some other group. Arrange to present your paper orally at the group's next meeting.

Submit to a School Newspaper or Web Site

Prepare your problem-solution essay for the school newspaper or Web site. Format your paper according to the submission guidelines and send it in.

Create a Poster

Develop a poster based on your essay. Decide what pictures, slogans, and details to include. Create your poster and put it up where it can make a difference.

PERSUASIVE

Rubric for Persuasive Writing

Use the following rubric as you assess and improve your persuasive writing using the six traits.

Ideas

6 **The clear reasoning informs and convinces the reader.**

5 The essay has a clear opinion statement. Persuasive details support the writer's opinion.

4 The opinion statement is clear, and most details support the writer's opinion.

Organization

6 **The organization presents a smooth flow of ideas from beginning to end.**

5 The beginning contains the opinion statement. The middle provides clear support. The ending reinforces the writer's opinion.

4 The beginning contains the opinion statement. The middle provides support. The ending needs work.

Voice

6 **The writer's voice is confident, positive, and completely convincing.**

5 The writer's voice is confident and helps persuade the reader.

4 The writer's voice is confident. It needs to persuade the reader.

Word Choice

6 **Precise words create a clear message to engage and persuade the audience.**

5 Precise words create a clear message and fit the purpose.

4 Accurate words create a message. More persuasive words are needed.

Sentence Fluency

6 **The sentences flow smoothly, and people will enjoy reading the variety of sentences.**

5 Variety is seen in both the types of sentences and their beginnings.

4 Varied sentence beginnings are used. Sentence variety would make the essay more interesting to read.

Conventions

6 **The grammar and punctuation are correct, and all the words are spelled correctly.**

5 Grammar and punctuation errors are few. The reader is not distracted by the errors.

4 Grammar and punctuation errors are seen in a few sentences. They distract the reader in those areas.

3 The opinion statement is clear. More persuasive details are needed.

2 The opinion statement is unclear. Persuasive details are needed.

1 An opinion statement, reasons, and details are needed.

3 The beginning has an opinion statement. The middle and ending need more work.

2 The beginning, middle, and ending run together.

1 The organization is unclear. The reader is easily lost.

3 The writer's voice needs to be more confident and persuade the reader.

2 The writer's voice rambles on without any confidence.

1 The writer's voice can't be heard.

3 More precise and accurate words are needed to create a clear message.

2 The words do not create a clear message.

1 Word choice has not been considered.

3 Varied sentence beginnings are needed. Sentence variety would make the essay more interesting.

2 Most of the sentences begin the same way. Most sentences are simple. Compound and complex sentences are needed.

1 Sentence fluency has not been established. Ideas do not flow smoothly.

3 There are a number of errors that may confuse the reader.

2 Frequent errors make the essay difficult to read.

1 Nearly every sentence contains errors.

PERSUASIVE

Evaluating a Persuasive Essay

As you read the problem-solution essay that follows, focus on the writer's strengths and weaknesses. Then read the student self-assessment on the next page. (The student essay below contains some errors.)

The Right Kind of B-Ball

Every Student Council needs money, and Ellingstad Middle school isn't any more different than others. In the past, student council fund raisers have included Candygrams and Car Washes. These fun activities not only get money but also get the school together. This year's activity, though, is turning into a big stupid problem. Some students may think donkey basketball is a funny sport, but others are worried about the affect on the donkeys.

In donkey basketball, a student team takes on a faculty team both sides have to ride donkeys as they play the game. Course, donkeys are stubborn. Maybe a rider is trying to move down court, the donkey might not want to go. What next? People start shouting at the donkeys, and sometimes they're even rougher to try to make the donkey move. I feel like that's when the game stops being funny and starts being a problem. Many Students at Ellingstad say so. Fifty of us have signed a petition.

The student Council needs a fund raiser that will get money and be also a blast. The kids that have signed the petition have a solution. Instead of donkey basketball, how about wheelchair basketball?

The Voree Volcanoes are a wheelchair basketball team that have won regional championships. They offer a fund raiser. They play against students and even loan them wheelchairs to use the Volcanoes even spot the student team 50 points! The money would get splitted between the student council and the Volcanoes. This game would be completely cool, would make tons of cash, and would help a great team.

The student council of Ellingstad Middle School may need money, but they also need a fund raiser everybody likes. Donkey basketball is a problem, but wheelchair basketball can be the solution!

Student Self-Assessment

The assessment that follows includes the student's comments about his essay on page 258. In each first comment, the student mentions something positive from the essay. In each second comment, the student points out an area for possible improvement. (The writer used the rubric and number scale on pages 256–257 to complete this assessment.)

5 Ideas
1. I included strong details about the problem and solution.
2. Some readers won't agree about donkey basketball.

4 Organization
1. I followed my plan for organization.
2. I forgot to include a call to action.

3 Voice
1. I tried to sound confident and persuasive.
2. I don't sound serious enough in places.

3 Word Choice
1. I cut out most inflammatory words—though "stupid" is still there.
2. In some places, my words seem weak.

3 Sentence Fluency
1. I used all kinds of sentences.
2. Some places don't flow well.

3 Conventions
1. I gave myself a 3 because I tried to fix convention problems.
2. I bet there are still some problems.

Use the rubric. Assess your essay using the rubric on pages 256–257.

1 On your own paper, list the six traits. Leave room after each trait to write at least one strength and one weakness.

2 Then choose a number (from 1 to 6) that shows how well you think you used each trait.

PERSUASIVE

Reflecting on Your Writing

Take some time to reflect on the problem-solution essay you have just completed. On your own paper, finish each starter sentence below. Your thoughts will help you prepare for your next writing assignment.

My Problem-Solution Essay

1. The best part of my essay is . . .

2. The part that still needs work is . . .

3. The prewriting activity that worked best for me was . . .

4. The main thing I learned about writing a persuasive essay is . . .

5. In my next problem-solution essay, I would like to . . .

6. Here is one question I still have about writing a problem-solution essay:

Persuasive Writing
Creating an Editorial

Every major newspaper has an "Op/Ed" page, which is short for "Opinion/Editorial." An editorial is a short essay that gives a writer's opinion about a timely event or issue. Many times during the history of our country, editorials have paved the way for great changes.

In this chapter, you will be writing an editorial of your own. Perhaps your school is having a crisis over the food choices in the vending machines. Or maybe some sports teams are arguing over who gets to use the gymnasium after school. In an editorial, you can give your opinion about the events happening around you.

Writing Guidelines

Subject:	A school issue
Form:	Editorial
Purpose:	To persuade the reader
Audience:	Classmates

Editorial

An editorial expresses an opinion about a timely event. The editorial that follows was written by Hassan and published in his local newspaper.

BEGINNING

The issue is introduced, and the opinion statement is given (**underlined**).

MIDDLE

The middle paragraphs support the writer's opinion.

Let the Kids Choose

A group of parents has asked the school board to remove the vending machines from Lincoln Middle School. They say that the soda and junk foods in the machines are creating bad eating habits among students. These parents are probably right, but removing vending machines won't solve the problem. Lincoln Middle School should keep its vending machines so that students have more food choices, not fewer.

A healthy diet is based on wise food choices. Removing the vending machines only removes the decisions students have to make about the foods they eat. The problem isn't the machines but what's in them. Machines that now hold only soda could just as easily hold juice, milk, and bottled water. Machines full of candy, cookies, and donuts could hold fruit snacks, nuts, and low-salt pretzels.

That doesn't mean that all the chips, cookies, donuts, and soda should be removed from the machines. If only healthy snacks are provided, students still won't learn anything about making smart choices. Instead, the vending machines should offer wholesome foods and other

foods side by side. Then students will have to learn how to choose for themselves.

ENDING

· · · · · · · · · · · · ·

The opinion is summed up in a thoughtful way.

Healthy eating habits begin with wise food choices. Removing the vending machines won't help students learn anything about healthy food choices, but stocking those machines with a mix of foods will.

Bridgewood Gazette

OPINION/EDITORIAL

City Voices: Let the Kids Choose

A group of parents has asked the school board to remove the vending machines from Lincoln Middle School. They say that the soda and junk foods in the machines are creating bad eating habits among students. These parents are probably right, but removing vending machines won't solve the problem. Lincoln Middle School should keep its vending machines so that students have more food choices, not fewer.

A healthy diet is based on wise food choices. Removing the vending machines only removes the decisions students have to make about the foods they eat. The problem isn't the machines but what's in them. Machines that now hold only soda could just as easily hold juice, milk, and bottled water. Machines full of candy, cookies, and donuts could hold fruit snacks, nuts, and low-salt pretzels.

That doesn't mean that all the chips, cookies, donuts, and soda should be removed from the machines. If only healthy snacks are provided, students still won't learn anything about making smart choices. Instead, the vending machines should offer wholesome foods and other foods side by side. Then students will have to learn how to choose for themselves.

Healthy eating habits begin with wise food choices. Removing the vending machines won't help students learn anything about healthy food choices, but stocking those machines with a mix of foods will.

Respond to the reading. On your own paper, write answers to the following questions about the editorial.

☐ **Ideas** **(1)** What is Hassan's opinion? **(2)** What details offer the strongest support? Name two.

☐ **Organization** **(3)** What purpose does the ending serve?

☐ **Voice & Word Choice** **(4)** How would you describe the writer's voice? **(5)** What words make it sound that way?

PERSUASIVE

Prewriting Selecting a Topic

An editorial gives an opinion about a current event or issue, so the best way to find a topic for an editorial is to focus on things happening around you. When Hassan received his assignment to write an editorial, he used sentence starters to make a list of all the current events he could think of.

Sentence Starters

At Lincoln Middle School,

the biggest problem is . . . the gym locker rooms are gross.
. . . that some homework is busywork.
the worst change is . . . removing the vending machines.
the one change I would make is . . . adding a study hall.
. . . starting school later!

Use sentence starters. Use the sentence starters above to think about issues or problems in your school. Finish each sentence with your opinion. Review your opinions and choose the one issue that will make the best editorial.

Supporting Your Opinion

Now that you have selected an opinion, it's time to come up with reasons to support it. Hassan used a table diagram. The "tabletop" gives his opinion, and the "table legs" are reasons that support it.

Table Diagram

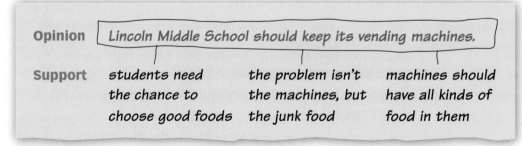

Opinion Lincoln Middle School should keep its vending machines.

Support students need   the problem isn't   machines should
the chance to   the machines, but   have all kinds of
choose good foods   the junk food   food in them

Create a table diagram. Use the sample above as a guide to create your own table diagram. Write your opinion in the top box and your supporting reasons underneath. Come up with at least three reasons.

Refining Your Opinion Statement

Now that you have selected an opinion and come up with reasons to support it, you are ready to write your opinion statement. An effective opinion statement gives your opinion and sums up the reasons for it.

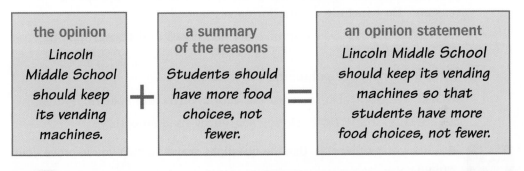

the opinion		a summary of the reasons		an opinion statement
Lincoln Middle School should keep its vending machines.	**+**	Students should have more food choices, not fewer.	**=**	Lincoln Middle School should keep its vending machines so that students have more food choices, not fewer.

Write an opinion statement. Create an opinion statement that combines your opinion with your reasons. Use the formula above as a guide.

Writing Creating Your First Draft

As you write your editorial, make sure each part does its job.

- **Beginning paragraph:** Introduce your topic and give your opinion statement.
- **Middle paragraphs:** Present your reasons in a logical order or in order of importance. (See page 551 for help.)
- **Closing paragraph:** Reflect on your opinion and reasons and give your reader something to think about.

Write your first draft. Let your table diagram list and the tips above guide you as you write your editorial.

Always think about your audience. In order to convince a reader to agree with you, avoid offending him or her. Therefore, don't blame or sharply criticize anyone in your editorial. Also avoid inflammatory words that are likely to make people angry. (See page 246.)

PERSUASIVE

Revising **Improving Your Writing**

Revise your first draft, by focusing on the following traits of writing.

- ☐ **Ideas** Do I clearly state my opinion? Do I provide supporting reasons? Do I include details for each reason?
- ☐ **Organization** Do I organize my sentences and paragraphs in the best order?
- ☐ **Voice** Is my voice polite and convincing?
- ☐ **Word Choice** Do I use strong action verbs and specific nouns?
- ☐ **Sentence Fluency** Do my sentences read smoothly?

 Revise your editorial. Use the questions above to help you improve your writing.

Editing **Checking for Conventions**

Once you finish revising your editorial, polish it by focusing on *conventions*.

- ☐ **Conventions** Have I checked for errors in punctuation, capitalization, spelling, and grammar?

 Edit your editorial. Check the conventions in your writing. Make a clean final draft and proofread it for any remaining errors.

Publishing **Sharing Your Editorial**

Because editorials share opinions about timely events or issues, this type of writing is made for publication. To find the right place to publish your editorial, ask yourself the following questions.

- ■ Who is my audience? (Classmates? Parents? People in the community? People who belong to a specific organization?)
- ■ What publication do these people read? (A local newspaper? A school paper or Web site? A PTO or PTA newsletter?)
- ■ How can I submit my editorial to this publication? (What are the guidelines? How should I send in my writing?)

 Publish your editorial. Use the questions above to help you find the right place to send your editorial for publication. Prepare your work according to the submission guidelines and send it in.

Persuasive Writing

Across the Curriculum

Some people think it's tough to be persuasive, but guinea pigs disagree. They use one sound to persuade their owners to feed them: "Reeeeeeeet!" They use another sound to persuade their owners to pet them: "Puuuuurrrrrr!" Imagine that! With two simple sounds, a guinea pig can persuade people to do just what it wants. You can be just as persuasive as a guinea pig—both in and out of school—by using convincing words and ideas.

In this chapter, you will see how persuasive writing is used in many settings. For example, in social studies, you may write a campaign speech. In math, you may compile data into a persuasive graph. For science, you may write a proposal for a science-fair project. And beyond the classroom, you may write a persuasive letter to convince someone to take action. Finally, you'll even learn how to be persuasive on a writing test.

Mini Index

- **Social Studies:**
  Writing a Campaign Speech
- **Math:** Creating a Graph
- **Science:** Writing a Proposal
- **Practical Writing:**
  Drafting a Business Letter
- **Writing for Assessment**

Social Studies: Writing a Campaign Speech

In a democracy, leaders are chosen by a vote, and candidates give speeches to persuade people to vote for them. The following speech was written by a middle school student running for student council president.

The beginning grabs the listeners' attention and presents the main issue.

The middle provides reasons for the main issue.

This paragraph lists the qualifications of the candidate.

The ending calls for listeners to vote.

Elect Suzie Ruiz!

Have you, or any of your friends, had to serve a detention at Garfield Middle School this year? Do you know someone who had to eat lunch in the office? Many students have felt the effects of the new policies here at Garfield. Even though the ideas behind these rules are good, we want to make sure the new policies are fair to everyone. If you elect me president of the student council, I will work with Principal MacKekkin and the school board to change the way these policies are applied.

I'm calling for a student court in which peers can advise the principal about a student who may have broken a rule. The student court can make sure all students receive reasonable punishments. It also can take the burden off Principal MacKekkin and the teachers of always being "the bad guys."

My opponents promise that they will make life here at Garfield better, but they are not offering any real suggestions about how they will do it. I am. In addition to my idea of a student court, I have plans for new fund-raisers and other activities. I am well qualified to represent students from across the student body. I play clarinet in band, write for the school paper, and run track. I'm a good student and a good listener.

So, if you want someone who will fight for student rights, elect Suzie Ruiz. Thank you for your time and for your votes!

Writing Tips

Before you write . . .

- **Decide on a main issue for your campaign speech.**
  Choose one main reason for your campaign. Make sure it is
  something students care about and can easily remember.

- **Organize your speech.**
  Think of an opening statement that will grab the listeners'
  attention. Plan the other points you will make and write down
  your qualifications.

During your writing . . .

- **Use details and examples.**
  Be specific about what you have to offer to voters and make
  your main reason a strong one.

- **Be concise.**
  Don't let your speech run on for very long. Make each sentence
  count and make sure each paragraph follows logically.

- **Be dramatic.**
  Show that you feel strongly about representing your listeners.

After you've written a first draft . . .

- **Review your beginning and ending.**
  Make sure you get the listeners' attention and leave them
  with a memorable call for votes.

- **Read the speech aloud and check its length.**
  Smooth out any places where you trip over the words. Time
  your performance to make sure it fits within the time allowed.
  If possible, tape your speech, or read it to a friend. Ask for
  comments. (See pages **423–430**.)

Try IT Imagine that you are running for student council. Write a short speech
to convince your classmates to elect you.

Math: Creating a Graph

Statistics can be very persuasive, especially when they appear in a graph. The following report was written by a student who wanted to show the health risks of smoking.

The **beginning** introduces the topic.

The **middle** introduces the graph and provides statistics.

The **ending** gives the source of the information.

Up in Smoke

When you see cigarette smoke in the air, do you know what you are seeing? You might know that nicotine and tar are in the smoke. Did you also know that cigarette smoke includes poison gases like carbon monoxide, ammonia, formaldehyde, and hydrogen cyanide?

As the chart below shows, you don't even have to be a smoker to die from cigarette smoke. Between 1995 and 2000, the number of Americans who died from secondhand smoke was more than a hundred thousand. Among smokers, there were nearly half a million deaths per year. The message is clear: smoking kills smokers and nonsmokers alike.

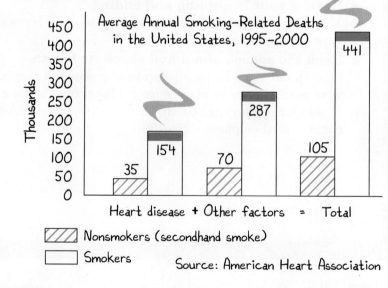

Average Annual Smoking-Related Deaths in the United States, 1995–2000

Thousands

450
400
350
300
250
200
150
100
50
0

35   154   70   287   105   441

Heart disease + Other factors = Total

Nonsmokers (secondhand smoke)

Smokers

Source: American Heart Association

Writing Tips

Before you write . . .

- **Decide what you are trying to prove.**
  State your opinion in a simple sentence, such as "Smoking kills smokers and nonsmokers alike." Keep your focus in mind as you create your graph.
- **Research thoroughly.**
  Look at several well-respected sources. Find statistics that help you prove your opinion.
- **Plan your graph.**
  Decide how to make the information most persuasive. Consider different kinds of graphs, such as pie, line, or bar graphs. (See page **575**.)

During your writing . . .

- **Quickly introduce your topic.**
  Give background information about your topic. Then write a few sentences that will help the reader understand what your graph shows.
- **Use colors and strong images.**
  Dress up your graph, but make sure that the reader will have no difficulty understanding exactly what you are trying to show.
- **Cite your sources.**
  List where you got the statistics for your graph.

After you've written a first draft . . .

- **Check your math.**
  Return to your sources to make sure your dates and numbers are correct.
- **Create a final version of your graph.**
  Make sure your graph is correct and clean. Proofread it a final time.

Think of a health or fitness issue. Write an opinion that you think you can prove with a graph. Then research the topic to find the numbers you want. Finally, create a persuasive graph.

PERSUASIVE

Science: Writing a Proposal

A well-written proposal can give you an advantage. In the proposal below, a student outlines a science-fair project and asks his teacher for approval.

The **beginning** describes the project.

The **middle** tells about the materials, the schedule, and the procedure.

The **ending** focuses on the expected results.

Traction and Four-Wheel Drive

Description: I'd like to test how well a motorized model truck climbs surfaces made of different materials and at different angles. I will create graphs to show how far and how fast the truck climbs in each situation.

Materials: I will use a radio-controlled four-wheel drive model truck, a plank, a protractor, a stopwatch, graph paper, and colored pencils. The different surface materials will include the following: water, aluminum foil, sandpaper, and loose sand.

Schedule: By March 7, I will have the materials collected and put together. By March 14, I will have run all my tests for different materials at different angles. By March 21, my display will be ready for the science fair.

Procedure:
- For each surface, the plank will be pitched at 10°, 20°, 30°, 40°, and 50°.
- First, I will test the plain wooden ramp at each pitch.
- Then I will repeat the experiment with the plank wet, with the plank coated with aluminum foil, coated with sandpaper, and finally coated with loose sand.
- I will create graphs displaying how far and how fast the truck climbed in each situation.

Conclusion: I believe this experiment will show different levels of traction. Please let me know if this proposal is accepted. Any suggestions are welcome.

Writing Tips

Before you write . . .

- **Select a topic.**
  Find a science topic that interests you.
- **Plan your project.**
  Think of how to demonstrate or test your topic. What
  materials will you need?
- **Organize the proposal.**
  Follow the proposal format your teacher gives you or use
  the sample on page 272 as a guide.

During your writing . . .

- **Be complete.**
  Give a quick overview of the project. Then list materials,
  provide a schedule, and talk about the procedure you will
  follow.
- **Be concise.**
  Get right to the point. Include only necessary information and
  important details.

After you've written a first draft . . .

- **Check for completeness.**
  Review your proposal as if you were the teacher and knew
  nothing about your idea. List any questions you might have.
  Then revise the proposal so that it answers those questions.
- **Edit your proposal.**
  Check your punctuation, capitalization, spelling, and
  grammar. Proofread your final copy.

PERSUASIVE

Imagine a science-fair project you would be interested in doing. Using
the tips above, write a proposal for it.

Practical Writing:
Drafting a Business Letter

In real-world situations, one of the best ways to get something done is to write a persuasive letter. The letter below was written by a student who wanted to convince a business owner to buy some guinea pigs from her.

The letter follows the correct format. (See pages 276–277.)

1212 Maple Park
Voree, IN 46300
March 24, 2004

Bruce Reynolds, Owner
Pet Project Pet Store
341 Jones Street
Voree, IN 46300

Dear Mr. Reynolds:

The **beginning** introduces the issue and asks a question.

Last year I bought two long-haired guinea pigs from your store, and this year we have five guinea pigs. Are you interested in buying the three babies? They are all female and six weeks old, and I have included pictures of them. We would like to sell them back to you if you are interested.

The **body** of the letter uses details to persuade the reader.

Our veterinarian checked the three babies, and they are in fine health. We also had the veterinarian neuter the father so that we won't have more pigs to care for.

The **closing** includes a polite call to action.

Please let me know if you are interested in buying our guinea pigs. You may call me at 555-9770 after 3:30 p.m. Otherwise, I will create fliers to sell them myself. Thanks for your time.

Sincerely,

Jessica Botticini

Jessica Botticini

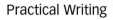

Writing Tips

Use the following tips as a guide when you are asked to write a persuasive letter.

Before you write . . .

- **Select a topic.**
  Think of something you would like another person to do—send you information, join a club, or come to your school.
- **Gather information.**
  Collect all the details your reader will need to know in order to be persuaded.

During your writing . . .

- **Get right to the point.**
  Identify yourself and tell the person why you are writing. Give only important details.
- **Be businesslike.**
  Write in a clear, businesslike voice. Be reasonable in any requests you make.
- **Provide an easy response.**
  Make sure there is an easy way that your reader can agree to help. For example, you could enclose a response postcard with your name and address filled in and postage paid.

After you've written a first draft . . .

- **Check for completeness.**
  Make sure you have given the reader all the information he or she needs.
- **Check for correctness.**
  Double-check names and addresses and all facts. Proofread your letter for errors in punctuation, capitalization, spelling, and grammar.

Try IT Think of a problem in your school or community. Come up with a solution and decide on a person who could help get the job done. Write a persuasive business letter to that person. (You may send the letter, or you may simply treat it as a school assignment.)

Parts of a Business Letter

1 The **heading** includes your address and the date. Write the heading at least one inch from the top of the page at the left-hand margin.

2 The **inside address** includes the name and address of the person or organization you are writing to.

- If the person has a title, be sure to include it. (If the title is short, write it on the same line as the name. If the title is long, write it on the next line.)

- If you are writing to an organization or a business—but not to a specific person—begin the inside address with the name of the organization or business.

3 The **salutation** is the greeting. Always put a colon after the salutation.

- If you know the person's name, use it in your greeting.

   Dear Mr. Christopher:

- If you don't know the name of the person who will read your letter, use a salutation like one of these:

   Dear Store Owner:

   Dear Sir or Madam:

   Dear Madison Soccer Club:

4 The **body** is the main part of the letter. Do not indent the paragraphs in your letter; instead, skip a line after each one.

5 The **closing** comes after the body. Use **Yours truly** or **Sincerely** to close a business letter. Capitalize only the first word of the closing and put a comma after the closing.

6 The **signature** ends the letter. If you are using a computer, leave four spaces after the closing; then type your name. Write your signature in the space between the closing and the typed name.

See page **577** for more about writing letters as well as a set of guidelines for addressing envelopes properly.

Business-Letter Format

1

2 ——— Four to Seven Spaces

——— Double Space

3 : ——— Double Space

——— Double Space

4

——— Double Space

——— Double Space

5 ,

6 ——— Four Spaces

Writing for Assessment

Many state and school writing tests ask you to respond to a persuasive prompt. A persuasive prompt asks you to state an opinion and support it with convincing reasons. Study the following sample prompt and student response.

Persuasive Prompt

The student council in your school has money to spend for something that will benefit all students. The suggestions include new computers, more assemblies, and a new scoreboard for the gymnasium. Students can suggest other choices, as well. Write a letter to the student council to persuade them to spend their money in the way that you think is best.

The **beginning** includes the opinion statement (**underlined**).

Dear Student Council President:

    My student council representative reported to our homeroom this morning that money is available for something that will benefit all students. <u>I think the money should be spent to buy laptop computers that students could check out of the media center.</u>

Each **middle** paragraph gives reasons that support the opinion.

    Students who don't have a computer at home could check out a laptop to do assignments. Papers look much better when they are done on a computer, and all students should have the chance to hand in work that will get them a good grade. Even students who already have a computer at home might need to use a school laptop because their brothers or sisters are always using the home computer.

    School laptops would also end all those problems with different formats. It's frustrating to get a disk from school that won't run on a home computer. It's worse to bring a disk from home and find out the school computer can't read the assignment. Also, Mrs. Jones in the media center is always complaining about students accidentally infecting school computers with viruses from their home computers. School laptops with virus protection would help end all those problems.

Finally, laptops would help with computer literacy. We each get to work in the media center once a week right now, but that's just not enough time. When big papers are due, the media center is overloaded. More computers— especially ones that could be checked out—would help more students become computer literate.

Buying laptops for the media center is something that can benefit all students. Please consider spending your funds on computers that all students can use.

Sincerely,
Olivia Lopez

The ending closes the essay with a call to action (underlined).

Respond to the reading. Answer the following questions about the sample response.

☐ **Ideas** (1) What is the writer's opinion? (2) How many supporting paragraphs are included in the essay?

☐ **Organization** (3) How is the essay organized—by time, location, or point by point?

☐ **Voice & Word Choice** (4) How would you describe the writer's voice in this essay (humorous, serious, angry)? (5) What words from the prompt also appear in the essay?

Writing Tips

Before you write . . .

- **Understand the prompt.**
  Remember that a persuasive prompt asks you to state and support an opinion.

- **Plan your time.**
  Spend a few minutes planning before you start to write. Use a graphic organizer (table diagram) as a guide.

Table Diagram

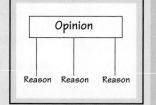

During your writing . . .

- **Form an opinion statement.**
  Think of an opinion that you can clearly support.

- **Build your argument.**
  Think of reasons that support your opinion.

- **End effectively.**
  Tell readers what you would like to see done.

After you've written a first draft . . .

- **Check for clear ideas.**
  Rewrite any ideas that sound confusing.

- **Check for conventions.**
  Correct errors in punctuation, spelling, capitalization, and grammar.

Persuasive Prompts

- Your parents are thinking about forbidding you to watch television during the school week. How do you feel about that? Write a letter to your parents expressing your opinion.

- What would the ideal lunch menu for the day look like? The food should be both good tasting and good for you. Write an essay to convince your school principal to adopt your menu.

 Plan and write a response. Respond to one of the prompts above. Complete your writing within the period of time your teacher gives you. Afterward, list one part that you like and one part that could have been better.

Persuasive Writing in Review

Purpose: In persuasive writing, you work to *convince people* to think the way you do about something.

Topics: Persuade readers . . . to agree with your opinion,
to take an action,
to support a cause, or
to solve a problem.

Prewriting

Select a topic that you care about, one that you can present confidently and that is appropriate for your audience. (See page **228**.)

Gather details about your topic. (See page **229**.)

Write an opinion statement that identifies the issue and proposes a solution. (See page **232**.)

Organize your ideas in a list or an outline. Put your opinion statement at the top, followed by topic sentences and supporting details. (See page **232**.)

Writing

In the beginning, give background information and clearly state your opinion. (See page **235**.)

In the middle, write a paragraph for each main point. Use supporting facts and examples to persuade your reader. (See pages **236–237**.)

In the ending, answer an objection, restate your opinion, and make a call to action. (See page **238**.)

Revising

Review the ideas, organization, and voice first. Next, check for **word choice** and **sentence fluency**. Avoid inflammatory words. Use a confident, persuasive voice and a variety of sentences. (See pages **240–250**.)

Editing

Check your writing for conventions. Ask a friend to edit the writing, too. (See pages **252–254**.)

Make a final copy and proofread it for errors before sharing it with your audience. (See page **255**.)

Assessing

Use the persuasive rubric as a guide to assess your finished writing. (See pages **256–257**.)

Writing About Literature

Response to Literature

Response Paragraph

A typical jar of spaghetti sauce holds ten tomatoes, two stalks of celery, an onion, a green pepper, four cloves of garlic, and five other spices. How can one jar hold so much? All the ingredients in spaghetti sauce get boiled down until only the best parts remain.

A typical novel contains more than a thousand paragraphs about the main character. Even so, you can capture that same character in just one paragraph. All you need to do is "boil down" the information.

On the next page, you will read a sample paragraph about Moon Shadow, a boy who leaves China to find a new home in America. Then you will write a paragraph response of your own.

Writing Guidelines

Subject: An important character in a book or short story

Form: Response paragraph

Purpose: To carefully examine a character

Audience: Classmates

Response Paragraph

When you write a paragraph about something you've read, you may be asked to focus on one character. The **topic sentence** of your paragraph identifies the title, the author, and the character. The **body** sentences tell about the character, and the **closing sentence** tells how the character changed. In the following response, Keira writes about a character named Moon Shadow.

Topic sentence
....

Body

Closing sentence
....

Moon Shadow

In the book *Dragonwings* by Laurence Yep, a young Chinese boy named Moon Shadow learns how to live in America. Moon Shadow is eight years old when he leaves his mother and grandmother in China and sails to America to be with his father, Wind Rider. Together the two of them work long, hard days at a laundry in San Francisco. They send money back to China. At first, Moon Shadow is suspicious of Americans with their strange language. He knows that his long braid of hair makes him a target for neighborhood bullies. Moon Shadow also faces many frightening situations, including an earthquake, but he bravely keeps going. Later, he makes two American friends, Miss Whitlaw and Robin. They help him overcome his fears and learn the ways of his new country. He learns how important family and friends are in pursuing lifelong dreams.

Respond to the reading. On your own paper, answer each of the following questions.

☐ **Ideas** (1) What main problem does the character face?
(2) What details about the problem does the writer include? Name two.

☐ **Organization** (3) Is this paragraph organized by time, by order of importance, or by logical order?

☐ **Voice & Word Choice** (4) What words or phrases near the end show how the writer feels about the character?

evaluate
react
PREVIEW
answer experience

285

Response Paragraph

Prewriting **Selecting a Topic**

Your first step in writing a response to literature is selecting a book or short story to write about. Keira began by listing books she had read. Then she wrote down the names and descriptions of characters that interested her.

Topics Chart

Books or Stories	Characters	Descriptions
Dragonwings	Moon Shadow	young boy from China
No More Dead Dogs	Wallace Wallace	eighth-grade football hero
"Flowers for Algernon"	Charlie Gordon	a mentally challenged man

Prewrite **Choose a book or short story.** Make a chart like the one above. Circle the character that interests you most.

Gathering Details About the Character

After you have chosen a character that you would like to write about, gather details about him or her. A cluster like the one below can help you.

Details Cluster

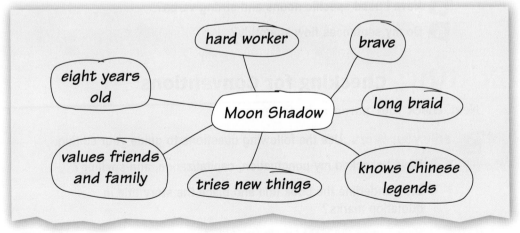

Prewrite **Create a cluster.** First write the name of the character and circle it. Around the name, write details about the character's appearance, personality, hopes, and fears.

Writing Creating Your First Draft

As you write your paragraph, make sure each of the parts does its job.

- **Topic sentence:** Write a sentence that names the book or short story, its author, and the character that you will describe.
- **Body:** Write sentences that describe the character and the important things that happen to him or her in the story.
- **Closing sentence:** End with a sentence that tells how the character changes by the end of the story.

 Write your first draft. Create a strong topic sentence, a body full of specific details, and a closing sentence that tells how the character changes.

Revising Improving Your Paragraph

Once you complete your first draft, it's time to revise your paragraph. Focus on *ideas, organization, voice, word choice,* and *sentence fluency.*

 Review your paragraph. Let the following questions guide your revision.

1 Have I written about one important character?

2 Are my sentences in the best order?

3 Does my voice show interest in the character and the story?

4 Have I used specific nouns and strong verbs?

5 Do my sentences flow smoothly?

Editing Checking for Conventions

Next, check your paragraphs for errors.

 Edit your work. Use the following questions to guide your editing.

1 Have I checked my punctuation, capitalization, and spelling?

2 Did I underline the book title and place the story title in quotation marks?

3 Have I used the right words (*to, two, too*)?

 Proofread your paragraph. After making a copy of your final paragraph, check it one more time for errors.

Response to Literature

Interpreting a Story

Often the events in a story change the main character. For example, in this chapter you will read about Adam Zebrin, a boy whose life changes when he becomes fascinated with zebras. The way Adam changes gives clues to the theme of the story.

Writing about literature is a good way to connect characters and themes. In this chapter, you will write about a main character in a piece of literature and tell how the character contributes to the theme of the novel or story.

Writing Guidelines

Subject:	**A book or a story**
Form:	**An essay**
Purpose:	**To interpret a story**
Audience:	**Classmates**

Understanding Your Goals

What should you include in your response to literature? You should include a clear interpretation of the story's meaning, or theme. Your interpretation will be based on your study of a character. The chart below lists the key traits in a response to literature, with specific suggestions for this assignment.

TRAITS OF A RESPONSE TO LITERATURE

Ideas

Write a statement that explains the focus of your response and select details that support it.

Organization

Organize your response using one of the patterns of organization and write an ending that explains and strengthens the theme.

Voice

Use a voice that shows interest in the book or story and reflects the overall feeling.

Word Choice

Use specific nouns and strong verbs.

Sentence Fluency

Write sentences that flow smoothly and are easy to understand.

Conventions

Correct all grammar, capitalization, spelling, and punctuation errors.

Get the big picture. Look at the rubric on pages 318–319. You can use this rubric to assess your progress. Your goal is to write an essay that interprets the theme of a book or story.

Response Essay

The novel *Esperanza Rising* tells the story of a group of migrant workers in California during the 1930s. A student who read the book wrote this interpretation of the story and its main character, Esperanza Ortega.

Her Name Means Hope

BEGINNING

The beginning introduces the book and states the focus (**underlined**).

Esperanza Rising, by Pam Muñoz Ryan, is the story of a Mexican girl who becomes a migrant worker in California. Making such a big move in life is never easy, but Esperanza must rise above even more problems than most immigrants do. In one year, she faces many difficulties that change her and make her a better person. Although she is only 14 years old when the story ends, it is clear that these challenges have taught Esperanza to be strong.

Migrants often come to the United States because they have been poor all of their lives, but that is not the case with Esperanza. She grows up on a big ranch in Mexico, and her family is rich and important. Esperanza spends her time going to school, learning to love the ranch, and being spoiled by "Papi," her father. Her main worry is what kind of dress she will wear to the next fancy party. When Papi dies the day before her 13th birthday, Esperanza and her mother find themselves without a home or a way to make money in Mexico. They decide to move to the United States.

MIDDLE

Each middle paragraph explains an important event in Esperanza's experience.

In the beginning of their journey to California, Esperanza looks down on the other migrants. She is shocked by the living conditions in the migrant camps and believes that the other workers are not as intelligent as she is. Esperanza quickly learns that the peasants are smart, even smarter than she is in many ways. They know how to survive and support each other. She soon realizes that

LITERATURE

dignity and honor come from the way that someone lives life, not from family status.

Esperanza now faces the same problems that other Mexican immigrants do. She learns that immigrants have to deal with prejudice, poverty, and bosses who cheat them. Esperanza misses her old life. Still, like the other immigrants, she hopes that in America she will never run out of chances.

MIDDLE

This middle paragraph discusses a key event.

But Esperanza's problems soon get worse instead of better. Her mother is very sick and has to go to the hospital for many weeks, leaving Esperanza alone. Mama has always been a loving woman who faces her troubles with great strength, and Esperanza has always depended on her for support. Now Esperanza must be strong, and her mother's example helps her survive.

ENDING

The ending paragraph summarizes the theme.

In the end, Esperanza learns to make the best of what she has. She has learned to love her new land and now realizes that worrying about dresses is not the most important thing. Esperanza, whose name means "hope" in Spanish, says, "Do not ever be afraid to start over." That's good advice for everyone.

Respond to the reading. Answer the following questions about the sample response to literature.

☐ **Ideas** **(1)** According to the second paragraph, what tragic experience does Esperanza go through? **(2)** How does Esperanza react to her difficulties?

☐ **Organization** **(3)** Are the middle paragraphs organized by time, order of location, or by some other logical order? **(4)** How is the theme stated in the book's ending?

☐ **Voice & Word Choice** **(5)** Find two sentences that show the writer's understanding of the story.

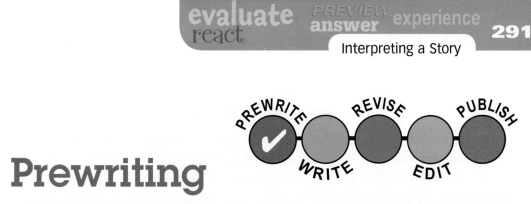

Prewriting

The writing process starts with prewriting. Begin by thinking about an interesting book or story you've read recently. Then gather details to include in your interpretation and plan your paragraphs.

Keys to Effective Prewriting

1. Select an interesting book or short story that you have read recently.

2. Identify the main character and theme in the story.

3. Gather details about the character and theme.

4. Write a clear focus statement for your essay.

5. Decide on a pattern of organization for your middle paragraphs.

6. Write a topic sentence for each of the middle paragraphs.

Prewriting Selecting a Topic

Think about books and stories that you have read recently. What main characters are the most interesting? What do these characters learn during the story? A chart can help you think about main characters and what they learn.

Character Chart

Main Character	What the Character Learns
Crispin (from *Crispin* by Avi)	Crispin learns that the most important things in life are friendships and courage—things nobody can take away.
Adam Zebrin (from "Zebra" by Chaim Potok)	Adam learns that art can help heal his body and his mind.
Phoebe (from <u>Walk Two Moons</u> by Sharon Creech)	Phoebe learns that every person she meets, no matter how odd, has value.

Prewrite

Create a character chart. Use the chart above as a model and follow these directions.

1 In the first column, list the main character from books and stories you have read recently.

2 In the second column, write down what the character learns in the story.

3 Then choose one character to write about. Write one sentence telling why you chose this character.

I chose Adam because art is my favorite class.

Focus on the Traits

Ideas When people talk about the theme of a book or short story, they are talking about the message the story tells about life. One way to discover the theme in a book or story is to ask yourself what the main character learns.

Gathering Details

Once you select a character, the next step is to identify the key events that teach the character something about life (the theme). You will want to choose events that change the character in some way. A gathering chart can help you list key events.

Gathering Chart

Event 1	Event 2	Event 3
Adam runs into a car and is injured. – hurts his legs and left hand – can't run anymore – left hand doesn't heal well and is useless – feels like a loner because of his hand	Adam gets drawing lessons from John Wilson. – surprised that John knows he is a loner – learns not to look directly at things he's drawing – finds out he is as good at drawing as he once was at running	Adam makes a helicopter sculpture from junk. – knows John lost an arm in Vietnam – gets so involved in making a helicopter that he uses left hand without thinking – begins to return to normal

Chart the key events. Create a chart like the one above. List key events
that show important changes in the character. Under each event, list specific
details that you might include in your interpretation.

Prewrite

Focus on the Traits

Voice Your interest in the character and the theme should come
through in your essay. Be sure to select details that show you care
about this story.

Prewriting **Writing a Focus Statement**

Now that you have identified the main character and theme (what the main character learns), you are ready to write your focus statement.

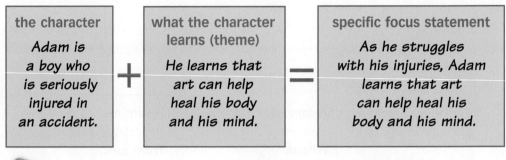

the character		what the character learns (theme)		specific focus statement
Adam is a boy who is seriously injured in an accident.	**+**	He learns that art can help heal his body and his mind.	**=**	As he struggles with his injuries, Adam learns that art can help heal his body and his mind.

Form a focus. Write a focus statement for your interpretation using the formula above.

Planning the Middle Part of Your Essay

After you write a focus statement, the next step is to plan the middle paragraphs of your essay. Each middle paragraph should include a topic sentence and deal with one key event.

Below is the plan the writer of the sample essay made for the order of the key events. However, he later realized that he needed another event. He placed it between events 2 and 3.

Event 1 – Adam's problems begin with his accident.

Event 2 – He decides to take art classes.

Event 3 – He discovers he enjoys building rather than drawing.
    4

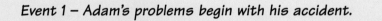

Event 3: Adam becomes good at drawing.

Plan your middle paragraphs. Review your gathering chart.

1 Decide on the best order for your events.

2 Add any events that you feel are necessary to explain your interpretation.

3 Using your events, write a topic sentence for each of your middle paragraphs.

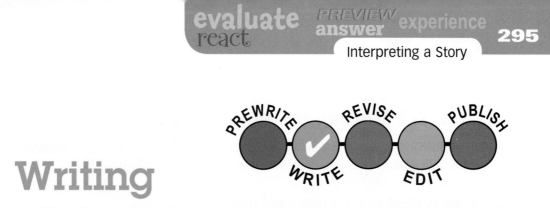

Writing

Now that you have done your prewriting, you need to write your essay. You can use your gathering chart, focus statement, and topic sentences as a guide.

Keys to Effective Writing

1. Write on every other line so that you can make changes later.

2. Organize your paragraphs using your focus statement and topic sentences.

3. Support your topic sentences with specific details.

4. Use the ideas from your gathering chart.

5. Get all of your thoughts on paper.

6. Tie your thoughts together with transitions.

Writing Getting the Big Picture

The following chart shows how the three parts of a response to literature fit together. (The examples are from the essay on pages 297–300.) You're ready to write your response if you have . . .

- thought about your character and theme,
- written a clear focus statement, and
- planned your paragraphs.

BEGINNING

The **beginning** paragraph introduces an important character and states the focus of your interpretation.

Focus Statement
As he struggles with his injuries, Adam learns that art can help heal his body and his mind.

MIDDLE

The **middle** paragraphs show the key events in the development of the story's theme.

Four Topic Sentences
Adam's problems start when he hits the car, injuring his legs and his left hand.

One day during the next spring, Adam's life begins to change.

The art class teaches Adam about drawing and about life.

At the end of the summer, Adam suddenly shifts his focus from drawing to building.

ENDING

The **ending** paragraph explains and summarizes the theme.

Closing Sentence
In the end, Andrea playfully tells him, "You are becoming a pleasant life-form."

Starting Your Interpretation

The beginning of a response to literature should introduce the focus of your essay as well as any important background information. Be sure that your opening includes . . .

- background about the character,
- the title and author of the work, and
- your focus statement.

Beginning Paragraph

The beginning paragraph below starts with background information about the character and ends with the focus statement.

> **Background information begins the paragraph.**
>
> **The last sentence forms the essay's focus (underlined).**
>
> In "Zebra" by Chaim Potok, Adam Zebrin sees a movie about zebras running in Africa. When he gets home, he runs around the neighborhood, trying to be as graceful as a zebra. Sometimes Adam runs so fast that he feels like he is flying. Racing along one day, he closes his eyes and seems to take off—right into the side of a car. As he struggles with his injuries, Adam learns that art can help heal his body and his mind.

Write **Write your beginning.** Write the beginning paragraph of your essay. Include background information, the title and author, and your focus statement.

Drafting Tips

- **Review the story** to make sure that you are clear about the main character, the key events, and the theme.
- **Include enough details** to help the reader understand the importance of each event.
- **Write as freely as you can**, getting all of your thoughts and ideas on paper.

Writing **Developing the Middle Part**

Each middle paragraph tells about one key event in your interpretation of the theme. Every middle paragraph should contain a topic sentence.

Beginning

Middle

Ending

Middle Paragraphs

The first paragraph below gives reasons for Adam's problems. The second covers another important event, and so on. Each topic sentence is underlined.

The first middle paragraph covers the first event, the accident.

Transitions (in blue) connect the events.

The second middle paragraph covers the start of Adam's recovery.

<u>Adam's problems start when he hits the car, injuring his legs and his left hand.</u> In a short time his legs recover, although he can't run anymore. His left hand doesn't heal as quickly, and it stays painful and stiff long after the accident. The useless hand makes him feel like he doesn't belong. Soon he becomes a loner, standing off on the side while everyone else plays. Finally, this inner conflict makes his only friend, Andrea, call him a "gloomy life-form."

<u>One day during the next spring, Adam's life begins to change.</u> He stands by himself near the playground when he notices a one-armed man coming toward him. The man pauses at a trash can, plucks something out, and places it in a plastic bag. When he gets to Adam, the man asks him for directions to the school office, and Adam tells him how to get there. It turns out that the one-armed man is John Wilson, a Vietnam veteran who plans to teach a summer art class. Adam and Andrea sign up for the class.

evaluate
react
PREVIEW
answer experience

299

Interpreting a Story

The third middle paragaph covers another step in Adam's recovery.

<u>The art class teaches Adam about drawing and about life.</u> John Wilson understands the problems Adam is experiencing. One day, John draws a picture of Adam and a zebra. The zebra seems to be moving mysteriously off the edge of the paper. Then John teaches Adam to draw, telling him not to look directly at the thing he is drawing. John instructs him to look at the space around the object. Adam takes the advice and discovers that he is as good at drawing as he once was at running. His left hand still hasn't healed, though.

The last middle paragraph covers the last stage in the recovery.

<u>At the end of the summer, Adam suddenly shifts his focus from drawing to building.</u> He builds a sculpture of a helicopter from some of the junk, mostly wire and paper, that John has collected from trash cans. As Adam builds the sculpture, he begins to use his left hand without thinking about it. Soon Adam's left hand recovers, and so does Adam. The conflict he has been having with himself slowly comes to an end.

Write the middle paragraphs of your essay. Use the gathering chart and the guidelines below.

1 Begin each middle paragraph with a topic sentence about the key event in the paragraph.

2 Add details that support the topic sentence. Refer to your gathering chart (page 293).

3 Connect your ideas with transitions.

LITERATURE

Writing Ending Your Interpretation

Your essay should focus on what the main character learns. This is the theme of the story. The following questions can help you summarize the theme.

Beginning

Middle

Ending

- What does the main character learn from the key events?
- What did I learn from reading the book or story?

 A theme is a general statement about life. As you interpret the theme of your book or story, remember to relate what the character learns to life in general.

Ending Paragraph

The ending paragraph below summarizes and further explains the theme by showing what Adam has learned.

> The conclusion explains the theme (underlined).
>
> *John teaches Adam to pay attention to the space around an object.* <u>*In the same way, art trains Adam to think about what is around him rather than thinking only about himself.*</u> *Art gives him a new focus. Like many people, Adam has been trapped inside himself, but art helps him escape. Adam's days as a loner are over. In the end, Andrea playfully tells him, "You are becoming a pleasant life-form."*

 Write your ending. Write the last paragraph of your interpretation. Be sure to sum up the theme by showing what the main character learned.

Form a complete first draft. Make a complete copy of your essay. Write on every other line (or double-space if you are using a computer) so that you have room for revising.

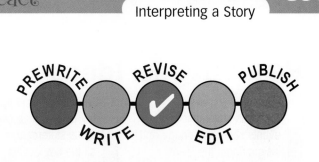

Revising

After you finish your first draft, you can begin revising. By focusing on ideas, organization, and other traits, you can make changes that will improve your writing.

Keys to Effective Revising

1. Read your entire essay aloud so that you get a feel for how well it works.

2. Check your focus statement to see if it includes the topic of the essay.

3. Be sure that the details in your paragraphs support the topic sentences.

4. Check your voice for enthusiasm and confidence.

5. Review your word choice and sentence fluency.

6. Use the editing and proofreading marks inside the back cover of this book.

Revising for Ideas

6 My focus statement and key events show knowledge and insight about the reading.

5 My essay has a clear focus statement, and all the key events support the focus.

4 My essay has a focus statement, but I need to cut a few unnecessary events.

Ideas are the basic ingredients of an essay. Write a clear focus statement and add key events to support your focus. Use the rubric above as a guide when revising the thoughts and details in your interpretation.

Have I written a clear focus statement?

Your focus statement is clear if it names the main character and tells what the person learns (the theme). (See page **294**.)

> **CLEAR FOCUS STATEMENT**
>
> **As Huckleberry and Jim travel the Mississippi, Huckleberry** (*main character*) **learns that friendship is the most important thing in the world** (*the theme*).

Read the following focus statements. Decide which statements clearly name the main character and tell what the person learns. If a focus statement is unclear, tell what is wrong with it.

1. In "Casey at the Bat," the "mighty Casey" learns that even big stars can't ignore the basics of baseball.

2. Branch Rickey is someone that few people know about.

3. In *Diary of a Young Girl*, Anne Frank is the main character.

4. Mrs. Luella Bates Washington Jones teaches a boy named Roger an important lesson about respect.

5. Mr. Pignati is an older man in *The Pigman*.

Review your focus statement. Make sure it names the main character and tells what he or she learns during the story. If your focus statement is unclear, revise it.

3 My focus statement is incomplete. I also need to cut a few unnecessary events.

2 I need a clear focus statement and more key events.

1 I need to learn how to write a focus statement and select key events.

Have I included key events that support the focus?

Key events are those that affect the way a character acts, thinks, or feels. One way to check whether you have included only key events is to create a cause-effect chart.

Cause-Effect Chart

Key Event (Cause)	Change to the Character (Effect)
Esperanza's father dies.	She is left poor and homeless.
Esperanza has to deal with prejudice and injustice.	She discovers that she is tougher than she thought.
Esperanza's mom gets sick.	She has to "grow up" quickly.

Revise

Check your key events. Make a chart like the one above. List key events and the ways they change the character. If any one of your body paragraphs doesn't show how the event changed your character, revise the paragraph to make the change clear.

Ideas
The focus statement is clarified.

Racing along one day, he closes his eyes and

seems to take off—right into the side of a car.

learns that art can help heal his body and his mind.
As he struggles with his injuries, Adam ~~learns to~~

∧

~~like art~~

LITERATURE

Revising for Organization

6 My organization and transitions lead the reader smoothly through my essay from start to finish.

5 I use a variety of transitions in my essay, and my ending works very well.

4 I use some transitions, and my ending works pretty well.

When you revise for *organization*, make sure you have used a variety of transitions to connect your ideas. Also, check to see if your ending summarizes the theme. The rubric above can help you review your organization.

Why should I use a variety of transitions?

When you respond to literature, you might use only transitions that show time: *First* one thing happened. *Then* another thing happened. *Afterward* a third thing happened. You can improve the organization of your essay by using some transitions that show other types of connections. Here are two types.

IMPORTANCE

For this reason	Truly
Especially	To emphasize
In fact	To repeat

CAUSE AND EFFECT

Because of	Therefore
As a result	Since
Due to	If . . . then

Read the paragraph below. Write down each underlined transition and indicate whether it shows *time*, *importance*, or *cause and effect*.

1 <u>After</u> Meg, Charles Wallace, and Calvin arrive on the planet,
2 they notice strange behavior. Every girl jumps rope at the same
3 time, and every boy bounces a ball in the same rhythm. <u>In fact</u>,
4 <u>when</u> one boy gets out of rhythm, his mother fearfully pulls him
5 from the street. Meg <u>soon</u> finds out that the ruler of the planet is
6 IT. <u>If</u> IT can control people's lives so completely, <u>then</u> Meg knows
7 she can't overpower IT. <u>As a result</u>, she chooses a weapon that IT
8 can never defeat. . . .

Check the variety of your transitions. Read your essay, looking for transitions. Do you use a variety, some to show time and others to show importance or cause and effect? If not, consider adding some new transitions.

3 I need more transitions, and I need to work on my ending.

2 I need to use transitions in my essay and write a new ending.

1 I need to learn how to use transitions and write an ending.

Does my ending summarize the theme?

Showing what your character learned is often the best way to summarize the theme. Your summary should give your reader an insight about how the theme relates to life.

Try IT Read the following ending. Find the sentences that indicate that the character learns something from her experience.

1   At the end of the novel, Sal and her father have returned
2 to Bybanks, Kentucky. Gramps comes to live with them. His
3 presence helps Sal remember what she has learned. She knows
4 that after walking in other people's shoes, it's better to accept
5 people than it is to judge them. Walking in another person's
6 shoes helps us be better human beings.

Revise **Review your first draft.** Check to make sure that your ending summarizes the theme and relates it to life.

Organization
Changes help relate the theme to life.

Like many people,
Art gives him a new focus. Adam has been
but art helps him escape. Adam's
trapped inside himself. His days as a loner are

over. In the end, Andrea playfully tells him, "You

are becoming a pleasant life-form."

Revising **for Voice**

6 My voice expresses great interest and matches the feeling of the story.

5 My voice expresses interest and matches the feeling of the story.

4 My voice shows interest, but I need to match the feeling better.

Voice is the way that your writing "sounds" to your readers. The rubric above and the information that follows will help you revise your interpretation for voice.

Does my voice show that I am interested in the character and the theme?

Your voice will sound interesting if you show that you really understand and care about the character and the theme. The voice in the first paragraph below is too flat. The writer does not sound interested.

NOT INTERESTED

> Pony and Johnny go to an old church. That's where they hide. They read an old book. Pony recites a poem.

The voice in the next paragraph shows that the writer really cares about the situation in the novel.

INTERESTED

> Pony and Johnny cut their long "greaser" hair and hide out in an abandoned church in Windrixville. There's nothing to do but think about the terrible fight and Bob's death. To pass the time, They read *Gone with the Wind* to each other, and Pony recites "Nothing Gold Can Stay" by Robert Frost. Even then, Pony seems to know the poem is about his own life.

Revise

Check for an interested voice. Review your essay to see whether you sound interested in the character and the theme. Reading your writing out loud is a good way to get a feel for how your voice sounds. Revise any paragraphs that sound flat.

3 My voice needs to show more interest and match the feeling better.

2 My voice does not show interest or match the feeling of the story.

1 I need to understand how to create a voice.

Is my voice too formal or informal?

A light, informal voice is a good choice when you write about a humorous story, but you need a more formal voice for a serious subject. The essay about Adam Zebrin is written in a more formal voice because the subject is serious.

Try IT Read the following focus sentences. For each one, decide whether the writer's voice should be formal and serious or informal and humorous.

1. "Rikki-tikki-tavi" is the story of a mongoose that fights a deadly cobra and saves a family.

2. Mrs. Schukin screams, cries, and pulls out her hair so that a bank manager who doesn't like loud noises will give her money that he doesn't owe her.

3. Ernest Hemingway tells the story of a boy named Schatz who catches the flu and is afraid to fall asleep because he believes he will never wake up.

 Revise

Check the voice of your essay. Make sure that your voice matches the language and feeling of the story. After thinking about the story that you are interpreting, change the voice of your essay as necessary.

Voice
The voice is made more formal.

Adam's problems start when he hits the car,

injuring his legs and his left hand. In a short

time his legs recover, although he can't run

~~in his goofy way~~ anymore. His left hand . . .

Revising for Word Choice

6 My words are clear and concise and create a response that engages the reader.

5 I use clear, concise words that express the right feeling.

4 I use clear, concise words most of the time, and most words express the right feeling.

When you revise your writing for *word choice,* check to be sure that you use specific nouns and verbs. Also review the words that help you create your voice. Use the rubric above as a guide.

How can I improve my word choice?

When writing about literature, you often need a special vocabulary. Words such as *plot, theme, conflict,* and others can help make responses to literature clear and effective. (See pages **351–352** for the many terms you can use to write about novels and stories.)

 Use the words below to complete the sentences that follow. Turn to pages 351–352 if you need to review these terms as well as other terms in your literary vocabulary.

protagonist   theme   setting   plot line
antagonist   dialogue   high point

1. An _____ is the person who works against the hero of a story.

2. The _____ is the moment when the conflict is strongest.

3. The series of events in a novel or story is called a _____ .

4. The _____ is the message in the story about life or human nature.

5. The hero or heroine is often called the _____ .

6. _____ is the words that characters speak to each other.

7. The place where a story happens is part of the _____ .

 Revise for literary terms. Underline the literary words you use in your response to literature. Will the use of additional literary terms help you write a clearer, more effective essay?

I need to make a few words
clearer and use words with
better feeling.

2 I need to choose words
with better feeling.

1 I need help choosing
better words.

Do my words have the right feeling?

Your words should be specific and also have the right feeling, or *connotation*. Connotation involves something more than a simple dictionary definition. It includes the word's emotional impact. Read the paragraph below, noticing how the underlined words suggest the strong emotions of the character.

> Esperanza <u>cringes</u> as she thinks of the day that her father died. She had awakened in a <u>cheerful</u> mood, excited about her 13th birthday party, a <u>feast</u> that was scheduled for the next day. Then she learned the <u>terrible</u> news, and her world seemed to <u>shatter</u>.

tip Use a thesaurus to find a list of synonyms for a word in your essay. Choose the synonym that best fits the feeling you're looking for.

 Revise for word choice. Look back at the way you use words in your response to literature. Replace words that should be more specific or that need a more exact feeling or connotation.

Word Choice
More specific words are inserted.

Connotation is improved.

> *Racing*
> ∧Running along one day, he closes his eyes and
>
> seems to take off—right into the side of a car. As
>
> *struggles*
> he has trouble with his injuries, Adam learns that
> ∧
> art can help heal his body and his mind.

Revising **for** Sentence Fluency

6 My sentences are skillfully written and keep the reader's interest.

5 I avoid short, choppy sentences and run-on sentences.

4 I avoid run-on sentences, but some short, choppy sentences need to be combined.

To revise for *sentence fluency*, check the clarity, flow, and smoothness of your sentences. The rubric above and the information below will help you.

How do I combine short, choppy sentences?

One way to combine short sentences is to make one of the sentences into an appositive. An appositive is a group of words that follows a noun, renaming or explaining it. The following example shows how two short sentences are combined with an appositive. (See pages **512–514** for other ways to combine sentences.)

> **TWO SHORT SENTENCES**
>
> **Branch Rickey worked to integrate sports.**
> **He was the general manager of the Dodgers in 1947.**
>
> **COMBINED SENTENCE WITH APPOSITIVE**
>
> **Branch Rickey, the general manager of the Dodgers in 1947, worked to integrate sports.**

 Rewrite the following paragraph, using appositives to make the four short sentences into two longer ones.

Jackie Robinson is an inspiration to many people. He was the first black player in the major leagues. In his book, Robinson gives much of the credit for his career to Branch Rickey. Rickey is an important man in professional sports.

 Combine choppy sentences. Read your essay. Look for sentences you could combine using an appositive.

3 I need to fix a few run-on sentences and combine some short, choppy sentences.

2 I need to fix many run-on sentences and combine many short, choppy sentences.

1 My sentences show a number of problems. I need to learn more about sentences.

How do I fix run-on sentences?

A run-on is two sentences joined without proper punctuation or a connecting word. Run-ons can be repaired by separating them with a period and a capital letter or by inserting a comma and a coordinating conjunction (*and, but, or, nor, so, yet*). They can also be corrected by using a semicolon.

Run-on: **Roger meets Mrs. Washington he doesn't know what to think.**

Corrected: Roger meets Mrs. Washington. He doesn't know what to think.

Corrected: Roger meets Mrs. Washington, and he doesn't know what to think.

Corrected: Roger meets Mrs. Washington; he doesn't know what to think.

 Rewrite the paragraph below, fixing the three run-on sentences.

> **The first thing Mrs. Washington makes Roger do is wash his face then she says she will make him supper. No one at his house cooks for him he hasn't eaten for three days. Roger is grateful for Mrs. Washington's help he doesn't know how to thank her.**

Revise for sentence fluency. Check your essay for short, choppy sentences and for run-ons. Make necessary sentence revisions.

Sentence Fluency
Choppy sentences are combined with an appositive, and a run-on is fixed.

It turns out that the one-armed man is John Wilson. He is a Vietnam veteran. John who plans to teach a summer art class. Adam and Andrea sign up for the class.

Revising Using a Checklist

Check your revising. On a piece of paper, write the numbers 1 to 12. If you can answer "yes" to a question, put a check mark after that number. If not, continue to work with that part of your essay.

Ideas

_____ **1.** Have I included a good focus statement?

_____ **2.** Do my key events support the focus?

_____ **3.** Do I need to cut any unnecessary events?

Organization

_____ **4.** Have I included a beginning, a middle, and an ending?

_____ **5.** Do I use a variety of transitions?

_____ **6.** Does my ending explain and strengthen the theme?

Voice

_____ **7.** Does my voice show interest in the character and the theme?

_____ **8.** Does my voice reflect the feeling of the story?

Word Choice

_____ **9.** Are my words clear and concise?

_____ **10.** Do my words have the right feeling, or connotation?

Sentence Fluency

_____ **11.** Have I combined short, choppy sentences?

_____ **12.** Have I corrected run-on sentences?

Make a clean copy. When you've finished revising your essay, make a clean copy before you begin to edit.

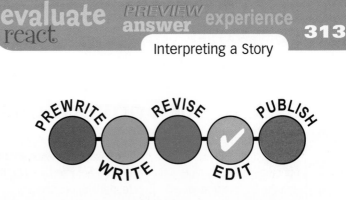

Editing

After you've finished revising your essay, it's time to edit for the following conventions: punctuation, capitalization, spelling, and grammar.

Keys to Effective Editing

1. Use a dictionary, a thesaurus, and the "Proofreader's Guide" in the back of this book.

2. Check for consistency of verb tenses.

3. Check your writing for correctness of punctuation, capitalization, spelling, and grammar.

4. If you use a computer, edit on a printed copy and enter your changes on the computer.

5. Use the editing and proofreading marks inside the back cover of this book.

Editing for Conventions

6 My grammar and punctuation are correct, and the copy is free of spelling errors.

5 My essay has minor errors that do not interfere with the reader's understanding.

4 I need to correct some errors in punctuation, spelling, or grammar.

The accepted rules for grammar, punctuation, capitalization, and spelling are called *conventions*. To edit for conventions, use the rubric above and the information below as guides.

How do I avoid shifts in verb tense?

When you write, make sure that your verb tenses are consistent. If you start telling about something in the present tense, don't shift to the past tense unless you have a good reason. (See page **483**.)

INCONSISTENT VERB TENSES

Esperanza now faces the same problems that other Mexican immigrants do. She was shocked to learn that immigrants had to deal with prejudice, poverty, and bosses who cheat them.

CONSISTENT VERB TENSES

Esperanza now faces the same problems that other Mexican immigrants do. She is shocked to learn that immigrants have to deal with prejudice, poverty, and bosses who cheat them.

Try It The following sentences should be written in the present tense. Correct any verbs that are not in this tense. The key verbs are in bold type.

1. Henry **did** not **have** any money, so he **is looking** for a job.
2. Tom **forgot** his old friends and **makes** new ones every month.
3. Before long, his new friends **learn** the same thing about him and **felt** the same way about him.
4. Willa Mae **continued** to take piano lessons even though they **are getting** more difficult.
5. Anne **writes** about her life in hiding and **dreamed** of a time when she and the others **can be** free.

3 I need to correct errors that may confuse the reader.

2 I need to correct many errors that make my essay confusing and hard to read.

1 I need help making corrections.

Have I punctuated my appositives correctly?

An appositive is an explanatory word or phrase that identifies or renames a noun. An appositive should be set off from the rest of the sentence with commas. (An appositive that comes at the end of a sentence should be set off with just one comma.)

Herman Calloway, the leader of a jazz band, **doesn't have time for Buddy.**

Buddy is afraid of Herman Calloway, a grumpy band leader.

 Copy the following paragraph. Then insert commas to set off three appositives.

Bud a ten-year-old boy thinks he can take care of himself. His mother has died, and he has been living in an orphanage. One night he packs his suitcase and heads down the road to Grand Rapids a big city to the east. The whole time he wonders about Herman Calloway the man on the poster.

 Edit for conventions. Pay special attention to inconsistent verb tense and to appositives that need to be set off with commas.

Conventions
A comma error is corrected, and a verb tense is fixed.

He builds a sculpture of a helicopter from some of the junk, mostly wire and paper, that John has collected from trash cans. As Adam built _builds_ the sculpture, he begins to use his left hand without thinking about it. Soon Adam's left hand . . .

Editing **Using a Checklist**

Check your editing. On a piece of paper, write the numbers 1 to 14. If you can answer "yes" to a question, put a check mark after that number. If not, continue to edit for that convention.

Conventions

PUNCTUATION

_____ **1.** Do I punctuate titles correctly?

_____ **2.** Does each sentence have end punctuation?

_____ **3.** Do I use commas after introductory word groups?

_____ **4.** Do I use commas between items in a series?

_____ **5.** Are my appositives set off with commas?

_____ **6.** Do I use apostrophes to show possession?

CAPITALIZATION

_____ **7.** Do I start all my sentences with capital letters?

_____ **8.** Have I capitalized all proper nouns?

SPELLING

_____ **9.** Have I spelled all my words correctly?

_____ **10.** Have I double-checked the words my spell checker may have missed?

GRAMMAR

_____ **11.** Do I use correct forms of verbs (*had come*, not *had came*)?

_____ **12.** Do my subjects and verbs agree in number?

_____ **13.** Have I used the right words (*there, their, they're*)?

_____ **14.** Have I avoided shifts in verb tense?

Adding a Title

■ Use the title of the book or story: **Zebra**

■ Refer to the character: **Adam's Recovery**

■ Be creative: **Drawing on Inner Strength**

Publishing **Sharing Your Essay**

After doing all of this work on your essay, you'll want to make it look good so that others can enjoy it. You may also decide to present your essay in some other form: a drawing, an introduction, or a submission to a writers' conference. (See the suggestions in the boxes below.)

Make a final copy. Follow your teacher's instructions or use the guidelines below to format your paper. (If you are using a computer, see pages 60–62.) Write a final copy of your essay and proofread it for errors.

Focus on **Presentation**

- Use blue or black ink and write neatly.
- Write your name in the upper left corner of page 1.
- Skip a line and center your title; skip another line and start your writing.
- Indent every paragraph and leave a 1-inch margin on all four sides.
- Write your last name and the page number in the upper right corner of every page after the first one.

Introduce It

Write a short introduction about your character and read it to the class. Try to convince your classmates to read the book or story by getting them interested in this person.

Submit Your Essay to a Young Writers' Conference

Check the Web for young writers' conferences. Submit your interpretation to one or more of them to see if they will publish it in their annual collection.

Make a Drawing

Draw a picture of an important stage in your character's life. Post your essay and the illustration in your classroom.

LITERATURE

Rubric for Writing About Literature

Use this rubric for guiding and assessing your writing. Refer to it whenever you want to improve your writing by using the six traits.

Ideas

6 The focus statement and the meaningful details show knowledge of the reading.

5 The essay has a clear focus statement and all the necessary details.

4 The essay has a clear focus statement. Unnecessary details need to be cut.

Organization

6 The opening, middle, and ending lead the reader smoothly through the essay.

5 The organization pattern fits the topic and purpose. All parts of the essay are well developed.

4 The organization pattern fits the topic and purpose. A part of the essay needs better development.

Voice

6 The voice expresses interest and complete understanding. It engages the reader.

5 The voice expresses interest and complete understanding.

4 The voice expresses interest, but needs to show more understanding.

Word Choice

6 Clear word choice creates a response that engages the reader.

5 Connotative words and literary terms create a clear message.

4 Literary terms create a clear message, but connotative words would add feeling.

Sentence Fluency

6 All sentences are skillfully written and keep the reader's interest.

5 No sentence problems exist. Sentence variety is evident.

4 No sentence problems exist. More sentence variety is needed.

Conventions

6 Grammar and punctuation are correct, and words are spelled correctly.

5 The essay has minor errors that do not interfere with the reader's understanding.

4 The essay has some errors in punctuation, spelling, or grammar.

3 The focus statement is too broad. Unnecessary details need to be cut.

2 The focus statement is unclear. More details are needed.

1 The essay needs a focus statement and details.

3 The organization fits the essay's purpose. All the parts need more development.

2 The organization doesn't fit the purpose.

1 A plan needs to be followed.

3 The voice needs to be interesting and express an understanding.

2 The voice is uninteresting and does not express an understanding.

1 The writer needs to understand how to create voice.

3 Too many general words are used. More clear, concise words are needed.

2 General or overused words make this essay hard to understand.

1 The writer needs help finding specific words.

3 Sentence problems are found in a few places.

2 The essay has many sentence problems.

1 The writer needs to learn how to construct sentences.

3 The essay has errors that may confuse the reader.

2 The number of errors confuses the reader and makes the essay hard to read.

1 Help is needed to make corrections.

LITERATURE

Evaluating an Interpretation

Read through the following essay, focusing on its strengths and weaknesses. Then read the student's self-evaluation on the next page. (There may be errors in the essay below.)

The Man Behind the Hero

In *I Never Had It Made,* Jackie Robinson tells about being the first black player in major league baseball. He does not take all of the credit for his success, though. Branch Rickey, the boss of the Dodgers when Robinson joins the team in 1947, has been working for years to integrate sports. When Rickey finds Robinson, he learns that one man really can change the world.

Long before Robinson was born, Rickey had been trying to open college and professional teams to athletes of all races. After all of those years, Rickey knows exactly what he is looking for. He needs a black man who is an excellent player. He also needs someone who can face the people who do not want to see baseball change. Rickey quietly sends scouts all over the United States and foreign countries to search the Negro leagues for such a player.

Rickey really understands what makes people successful. He hears about Robinson, an excellent player in the Negro leagues. Robinson had been called a troublemaker at UCLA because he spoke out against segregation in sports. Rickey doesn't think that is a problem. He thinks that it is the sign of a great competitor.

When Robinson meets Rickey, he sees a man who has "a way of cutting through red tape and getting down to the basics." Robinson thinks at first that Rickey wants someone who won't fight back. Rickey tells him that he doesn't want a coward, but someone "with guts enough not to fight back." In 1947, the Brooklyn Dodgers give Robinson a baseball contract, and the color barrier in baseball falls.

Successful people owe a lot to those who help them. Jackie Robinson is a legend in baseball, one of the best players ever. Branch Rickey is the man who made that great career possible and Robinson never forgot that.

Student Self-Assessment

The assessment below is the student's evaluation of his essay, including his comments. The first comment is something positive. The second comment is something he could improve. (The writer used the rubric and number scale on pages 318–319 to complete this assessment.)

5 **Ideas**
1. My focus states the theme and tells why Branch Rickey is important.
2. I could have given more details about Branch Rickey.

4 **Organization**
1. My essay contains a beginning, a middle, and an ending.
2. One of my paragraphs may be out of order.

5 **Voice**
1. I admire the character and agree with the theme, and my voice shows it.
2. Maybe I need a lighter voice in the last paragraph.

5 **Word Choice**
1. Most of my words have correct connotations.
2. Some of my words are not clear and specific.

4 **Sentence Fluency**
1. I don't have any choppy sentences or run-ons.
2. I could vary more of my sentence beginnings.

6 **Conventions**
1. My paper is free of careless errors.
2. I may need a comma in the last sentence.

Use the rubric. Assess your essay using the rubric on pages 318–319.

1 On your own paper, list the six traits. Leave room after each trait to write one strength and one weakness.

2 Then choose a number (from 1 to 6) that shows how well you used each trait.

Reflecting on Your Writing

Now that your interpretation is finished, you can think about it by completing each starter sentence below. These reflections will help you see how you are growing as a writer.

My Interpretation

1. The best part of my essay is . . .

2. The part that most needs change is . . .

3. The main thing I learned about writing an interpretation is . . .

4. In my next interpretation, I would like to . . .

5. Here is one question I still have about writing an interpretation:

6. Right now I would describe my writing ability as . . . (excellent, good, fair, poor)

Response to Literature
Poetry Review

Poetry uses sounds and images to reach beyond your mind and grab your heart. Other forms of writing may inform or entertain, but a poem's purpose is to make you feel and respond—and sometimes even soar!

One great way to respond to a poem is to write a poetry review. Like a book review, a poetry review tells what the poem is about. It also explains what makes the poem work so well. In this chapter, you will learn how to write your own poetry review.

Writing Guidelines

Subject:	**A poem that you enjoy**
Form:	**A review**
Purpose:	**To analyze and explain what is good about the poem**
Audience:	**Family and classmates**

Poetry Review

For her response to poetry, Teresha chose to write a review of the following poem about a hawk. You will find Teresha's review on the next page.

The Hawk

Keen yellow eyes
fly high. Sharp shrieks
pierce the clouds.

He is lord of height and
    gusting wind,
master of green valleys
    and harvest fields.

A songbird trembles.
A mouse
hides as the winged
shadow passes.

The hungry hunter glides
    alone
through autumn's
cloudy gray sky.

—Doug Niles

Writing the Review

When Teresha wrote her review of "The Hawk," she focused on the following elements of poetry:

- **Meaning:** The first paragraph describes the topic of the poem.
- **Imagery:** The second paragraph focuses on images, or word pictures.
- **Sound:** The third paragraph deals with the sounds in the poem.
- **Thoughts:** The final paragraph tells what Teresha thought of the poem.

See pages **360–361** for poetry terms you may want to use in your review. Each term has a definition and an example to make it easy to understand.

BEGINNING

The beginning identifies the poet and tells about the **meaning** of the poem.

MIDDLE

The middle paragraphs focus on **imagery** and **sound**.

ENDING

The ending reflects on the reviewer's **thoughts**.

Flying with "The Hawk"

Doug Niles's poem, "The Hawk," is about a hawk flying high on a fall day. The poem describes the bird as a hunter, gliding far above the ground as it watches for prey. The poem does a good job of making me feel the greatness of this hunting bird.

One way the poet expresses this greatness is with exciting imagery. He includes sights like the hawk's yellow eyes, its passing shadow, the green land below, and the cloudy gray sky. The poem also mentions the trembling of a songbird as the hawk passes overhead.

The poem includes some interesting sounds as well. There's a little alliteration in the poem, in "sharp shriek" and "hungry hunter." The poem also uses words that make interesting sounds. The cry of a hawk is a "shriek," the word "gusting" sounds like a blustery wind, and the word "trembles" seems to shake with fear.

This poem definitely captures the feeling of watching a hawk flying high in the air. Whenever I read it, I feel as if I were actually gliding with the hawk, trembling with the songbird, and hiding with the mouse.

Respond to the reading. Think about how Teresha uses the following traits in her review; then answer the questions that follow each trait.

- ☐ Ideas **(1)** Did Teresha notice anything about the poem that you did not? Explain.

- ☐ Organization **(2)** What is the main purpose for each of the paragraphs in Teresha's review?

- ☐ Voice & Word Choice **(3)** What words show Teresha's feelings about this poem?

Prewriting Understanding a Poem

The first step to understanding a poem is reading it—several times. Read the following poem and then consider the questions below.

Meaning: Poems are full of meaning. To understand the meaning of a poem, ask yourself three questions.

- What is the poem's subject?
- How does the writer feel about the subject?
- How do I feel about the writer's ideas?

Imagery: Poems contain images, or word pictures. Ask yourself the following questions to focus on imagery.

- What sensory details (things you can see, hear, smell, taste, or touch) does the writer include?
- What feelings do those sensory details create?

Sound: Poems play with the way words sound. Focus on the sound of the poem by asking yourself the following questions. (See pages 360–361.)

Never Out of Mind

My favorite place
    is not far away,
    is never out of mind—
    a waterfall above a quiet pool.
I look for my waterfall
    in rain on bus windows
    and parking lot puddles
    and foam in storm drains.
I listen for my waterfall
    in clock-radio static
    and hissing strips of bacon
    and distant moans of traffic.
I reach for my waterfall
    in steam from the shower
    or spray from a hydrant
    or the slick handle on my front door.
My favorite place
    is not far away
    is never out of mind—
    as long as I look and listen and reach.

—Luke Regan

- Does the poem include words that sound alike *(rhyme)* or words that repeat beginning consonant sounds *(alliteration)*?
- Does the poem include words that sound like the noise they name *(onomatopoeia)*?

Review the poem. Reread "Never Out of Mind." Ask yourself the questions above and think about the meaning, imagery, sound, and overall thoughts and feelings about the poem.

Gathering Details

Teresha used a chart to help her gather answers about the meaning, imagery, and sound of the poem she reviewed—"The Hawk."

Gathering Chart

Meaning	Imagery	Sound
The hawk is	Word pictures	Rhymes
–alone	–yellow eyes	–hides/glides
–feared	–green valleys	Alliteration
–a hunter	–harvest fields	–sharp shrieks
	–winged shadow	–hungry hunter
	–gray sky	Onomatopoeia
		–"shriek"
		–"gusting"

Create a poem chart. Use the chart above as a guide to gather details about your poem. Fill in information about your poem's meaning, imagery, and sound.

Writing Creating Your First Draft

With your chart in hand, you are ready to write the first draft of your poetry review. Take it one paragraph at a time.

- **BEGINNING PARAGRAPH** In your first paragraph, name the poem (in quotation marks) and the poet. Then summarize the poem's *meaning* by using information from your gathering chart. End with a focus statement that sums up how you feel about the poem.

- **MIDDLE PARAGRAPHS** Use the second and third columns of your chart to write the middle paragraphs of your review. In the first middle paragraph, describe the *imagery* of the poem. In the second middle paragraph, focus on the *sound*.

- **ENDING PARAGRAPH** In your last paragraph, explain your *feelings* about the poem. Leave the reader with a final thought about it.

Create your first draft. Write the beginning, middle, and ending of your poetry review. Follow the guidelines above.

LITERATURE

Revising **Improving Your Writing**

Once you finish the first draft of your poetry review, set the draft aside for a while. Then return to it and revise it by looking at the first five traits.

- ☐ **Ideas** Have I summed up the meaning of the poem? Have I included specific details about the imagery and sound?
- ☐ **Organization** Do I follow the plan from page 327 for my beginning, middle, and ending?
- ☐ **Voice** Does my interest show? Is my review enjoyable to read?
- ☐ **Word Choice** Are my words clear and accurate?
- ☐ **Sentence Fluency** Do my sentences flow smoothly?

Assess your review. Using the questions above as a guide, revise your work until it flows smoothly and is clear and interesting throughout.

Editing **Checking for Conventions**

Now that you have revised your work, it's time to check it for any errors in conventions.

- ☐ **Conventions** Is my review free of errors in spelling, punctuation, capitalization, and grammar?

Edit your work. Check your review carefully and correct any errors you may find in spelling, punctuation, and so on.

Publishing **Sharing Your Writing**

By letting other people read your review, you encourage them to read and think about the poem. Here are some ideas for publishing your review.

- ■ Submit your review to the school paper.
- ■ Post your review on a bulletin board where classmates can read it.
- ■ Mail a copy of the poem and your review to a relative. Ask the person to respond with an opinion of the poem and of your review.
- ■ Send your review to the poet (perhaps in care of the publisher). Let him or her know why you enjoyed the poem.

Share your opinion. Let other people see your review. Their responses may give you new insights into the poem, and they may recommend other poems for you to read.

Response to Literature
Across the Curriculum

Imagine that you could travel back in time and interview a historical figure. Whom would you choose? Joan of Arc? Galileo? King Arthur? Imagine that you could travel to another planet. Where would you go? Mars, Neptune, or some undiscovered world? Literature allows you to make these journeys.

This chapter shows you how you might respond to literature in a number of classes. For example, you will learn how to interview a historical figure and summarize a scientific article. The chapter will also help you prepare for a writing assessment.

Mini Index

- **Social Studies:** Interviewing a Person from History
- **Science:** Summarizing a Science Article
- **Practical Writing:** Evaluating a Book
- **Writing for Assessment**

Social Studies:
Interviewing a Person from History

One way to bring the past to life is to imagine interviewing an important person you have read about. In the following interview, one student asks Queen Elizabeth I of England about her reign.

The Interview of a Lifetime

The **beginning** answers the questions *when, where,* and *who.*

JB: This is Johnny Babcock, time-traveling reporter for Time Travel Network News. I'm in Windsor, England. It's 1590, and I have been granted an interview with Queen Elizabeth herself. Your Majesty, would you mind answering a few questions?

QE: It would be our pleasure. What do you want to know?

JB: Well, I'm interested in your place in history. Some would say that you are one of the greatest rulers in English history. Do you think so?

QE: We certainly would never state it quite so bluntly, but our reign has been long, and it has been marked by significant achievements.

JB: Your Majesty, why do you say "our" instead of "my" reign? You don't have a king, do you?

The **middle** includes important facts about the person.

QE: No, we have never married. But since we represent the people and the land of England, as well as ourselves—the person named Elizabeth—it is common for the monarch to use "we," not "I."

JB: I see. What do you think is the greatest accomplishment of England under your rule?

QE: It has to be the destruction of the Spanish Armada. If our fleet had failed to defeat the ships of Phillip II, England would have lost the war with Spain. The English people's freedom would have ended then and there. Instead, our lands prospered, and we became a great world power.

The **ending** shows the person in her time in history.

JB: What do you do for fun?

QE: We are very interested in the plays of that Shakespeare fellow. In fact, we are going to one now, and we must not be late.

JB: You've been very generous with your time, Your Majesty. Thank you, and enjoy the play!

Writing Tips

Before you write . . .

- **Do your research.**
  Learn a lot about the person you are going to interview. Check several different sources: an encyclopedia, a book, Web sites, and perhaps even a historically accurate movie.

- **Take notes.**
  Jot down plenty of facts that you can use to write questions for the interview.

- **Organize your thoughts.**
  Plan how you will begin your interview. Then think about your purpose and consider which facts you will use in the middle. Finally, decide on a dramatic detail that you can use in your conclusion.

During your writing . . .

- **Let your questions guide you.**
  Ask questions that require more than a *yes* or *no* answer. Ask about the person's place in history, as well as his or her successes and failures.

- **Let the character speak in his or her true voice.**
  Learn a little about the manner of speech the person might have used and let that show in the interview.

After you've written a first draft . . .

- **Get feedback.**
  Ask one of your classmates or someone from your family to read your interview. See if the reader has any suggestions for revision.

- **Proofread carefully.**
  Go over your interview to make sure that there are no mistakes in spelling, punctuation, or other conventions.

Try **IT** Choose a real person from history and imagine a fictional interview with him or her. Research your subject and write an imaginary conversation with that person. Then share your interview with your teacher and classmates.

Science: Summarizing a Science Article

A summary paragraph "boils down" the information in a longer piece of writing. The article on this page describes the excitement in the scientific community as new discoveries are made about the planet Mars. The paragraph is a student's summary of the article.

A New Era of Planetary Exploration

Mars, named for the Roman god of war, has always been an intriguing spark of color in the night sky. With its faint reddish hue and unusual brightness, it stands out among the field of stars. Mars is the planet most similar to Earth in the solar system. For thousands of years, humans have studied and pondered the Red Planet. Beginning with crude probes that reached the planet in the 1970s, scientists have progressed until we now have three satellites—two American and one from the European Union—in orbit around Mars.

By far the most detailed information on Mars has reached us through the Martian rover project. Two robots, named *Spirit* and *Opportunity*, were launched in 2003 and landed on the Red Planet early in 2004. Unlike some earlier probes, these robots landed perfectly and went to work studying the planetary surface. Their primary mission was to look for signs of water, and they recorded much data from each of the landing sites, which were on opposite sides of Mars.

Spirit landed in Gusev Crater, an area about the size of Connecticut. *Spirit* soon began to move around, dig in the sandy ground, and grind away at nearby rocks. On the other side of the planet, *Opportunity* rolled right into a small crater—a cosmic "hole in one." It went to work studying bedrock that was exposed when the crater was formed. Both rovers have added much new evidence to support the hypothesis that Mars was once a much wetter, warmer place than it is today. No doubt the future will reveal even greater secrets, especially when the first human astronauts arrive, perhaps as soon as 20 years from now.

Topic sentence

Body

Closing sentence

A Good Year for Mars

Mars has been watched throughout history and is being closely studied today. It is the planet most like Earth and was named for the Roman god of war. Humans have launched satellites that are in orbit around Mars. In 2004, two rovers, named <u>Spirit</u> and <u>Opportunity</u>, found out a lot about Mars. The rovers landed on two different sides of the planet. Their main mission was to look for signs of water, and both rovers found evidence that water was once there. Together, the rovers have sent much useful information back to Earth. Someday, humans themselves may go to Mars.

Writing Tips

Before you write . . .

- **Read the article carefully.**
  Review the material to make sure you know it well. Use a dictionary to look up any words you don't understand.

- **Take notes.**
  Write down the main point of the article. Then write down important details you will want to use in the summary. For example, the main point of the article on page 332 is the history of Mars exploration. The names of the two rovers are important details that support the main point.

- **Organize your thoughts.**
  Plan a good topic sentence to begin your paragraph. Then consider which facts you will use in the body. Finally, decide on a strong concluding sentence.

During your writing . . .

- **Stick to important facts.**
  Try to write a summary that is about one third the length of the original—or shorter. Focus on the main point of the article and the most important details to support the point.

- **Use your own words.**
  Think of ways to paraphrase or summarize information. Avoid copying phrases and sentences from the article.

After you've written a first draft . . .

- **Review your paragraph.**
  Make sure that you have captured the main point of the article. Check to see that you have included the most important details.

- **Proofread carefully.**
  Check your paragraph to make sure that there are no mistakes in spelling, punctuation, or other conventions.

 Read a brief article that you find (in a newspaper or magazine) or one that your teacher hands out to you. Using the tips above, write a single paragraph that summarizes the article.

LITERATURE

Practical Writing: Evaluating a Book

A book evaluation form gives readers a quick way to write about literature. It also allows other students to decide if they would like to read the book. The following evaluation was filled out by a student who had just finished reading *The Black Cauldron*.

Talk Back to Books: Reader Reaction Form

Please answer the questions below by circling the appropriate number or writing a brief response.

Book and Author ___*The Black Cauldron* by Lloyd Alexander___

Rate your reaction to the following:

Setting	1	2	③
	Dull	Interesting	Exciting

Plot	1	②	3
	Boring	Engaging	Thrilling

Characters	1	②	3
	Shallow	Believable	Fascinating

Author's Voice	1	2	③
	Hard to recall	Interesting	Unforgettable

What was the best part of the book? *I liked the part where Taran and his friends were arguing with Orwen, Orgoch, and Orddu about the Black Cauldron.*

Who was your favorite character, and why? *I liked Taran because he was confused about what to do but really tried to do the right thing. I think it was funny that he was called an "Assistant Pig-Keeper."*

List any criticisms of the book. *I didn't like the way Prince Ellidyr was unkind to Taran and that Taran could never fight back.*

Writing Tips

Before you write . . .

- **Consider the questions you will need to answer.**
  Review the evaluation form before you read the book, if
  possible. Pay special attention to the items on the form.

- **Read the book carefully.**
  Take your time as you read. Notice how the story is
  developing, what the characters are like, and how the
  writer chooses words and puts them together.

- **Take notes.**
  Jot down any reactions that strike you as important. If
  you really like something, are puzzled by something, or dislike
  something about the book, make a note of your reaction so
  you'll remember it later.

During your writing . . .

- **Be honest.**
  Share what you liked and didn't like about the book.
  Provide reasons for your opinions.

- **Use complete sentences.**
  If a question requires more than a short answer, write out
  your response as a complete sentence.

After you've written a first draft . . .

- **Check all the questions.**
  Make sure you haven't misread a question. Double-check your
  answers to make sure they represent your true opinions.

- **Proofread carefully.**
  Review your evaluation form to make sure that there are
  no mistakes in spelling, punctuation, or other conventions.

Think of a book you have recently read. Then, on your own paper,
re-create and complete the form on the bottom of page 334.

Writing for Assessment

On some state and school tests, you may be asked to read a story and write a response to it. The next two pages give you an example of such a test. Read the directions, the story, and notice the student's underlining and comments (**in blue**). Then read the student's response on pages 338–339.

Response to Literature Prompt

DIRECTIONS:

- Read the following story.
- As you read, make notes. (Your notes will not be graded.)
- After reading the story, write an essay. You have 40 minutes to read, plan, write, and proofread your work.

When you write, focus on the main characters in the story. Show your insight into how the characters change as they interact with each other. Use clear organization, and support your focus with examples from the text.

Acquiring the Taste

When Maria and Janelle became seventh graders, they thought they were pretty grown-up. They had graduated from Franklin Elementary and now attended Westmore Junior High. The old posters of cats and koalas had come down from their bedroom walls, and new posters of rock stars had gone up. Maria and Janelle decided they even "needed to learn how to drink coffee." One Saturday morning, they met at Chiara's Coffee Shop and ordered cappuccinos.

"Bleck!" Maria said, letting the coffee dribble out of her mouth and back into the cup. "How can adults drink this stuff?"

Janelle laughed. "Cappuccino is an acquired taste." She took a sip and winced.

"If *acquired* means *awful*, I have to agree," Maria said. She took another taste. The stuff was bitter and burning. She gasped and started to choke.

Janelle leaned toward her and patted her back. "Maria, pull yourself together. Somebody's staring at us."

Maria looked across the coffee shop and saw an elderly lady sitting at another table. Her big brown eyes didn't blink as she stared at the two girls. The woman seemed to scowl.

Maria looked away and coughed into a napkin. "I wish she'd leave."

The woman pushed herself up with her stainless steel cane and shuffled away from the table. Instead of walking out the door, though, she walked to the counter and ordered. "A cappuccino and six biscotti."

"She must have worked up an appetite from all that staring," Maria whispered to Janelle, and they laughed quietly.

The woman turned around. In one hand, she held a tray with coffee and six slices of crunchy pastry. She stared at the girls. Then, ambling with her cane, the woman came right up to their table.

"Those cappuccinos are the best in the city," she said with a thick Italian accent. "But these biscotti are the best in the world. I should know. I brought this recipe with me from Rome."

The girls stared at her. Maria said, "You must be Chiara." *

"I must be," she said, pulling up a chair and sitting down. She lifted a piece of biscotti, dunked it into her coffee, and then raised it slowly to her mouth. "Here's how you learn to like cappuccino." She crunched on the pastry and slid the other biscotti toward the girls.

Each of them took a piece and dunked it into the coffee. Nervously, they bit in. The bitterness of the coffee somehow tasted right with the mild sweetness and crunch of the biscotti.

"Did you grow up in Rome?" Maria asked. "My great-grandma came from Italy."

"Yes. I even had children there—two daughters. They were *
your age when we moved to America." As Chiara spoke, Maria could picture the places she described: the Colosseum, the Pantheon, and the fountains of Rome. The woman's voice carried Maria back 60 years, back to when Chiara had been her age. They connect.

Half an hour later," the girls' coffee cups were empty, and their minds were full."

"Is there always biscotti?" Maria asked as Janelle got up to go. "I mean, every Saturday?"

Chiara said, "Sure. Always biscotti and cappuccino and stories."

"Then we'll be back," Maria pledged, and Janelle agreed. They'd acquired the taste. not just for coffee

Student Response

The following essay is a student's response to the story "Acquiring the Taste." Notice how the student uses details from the story to support the focus.

BEGINNING

The first paragraph states the focus of the essay.

The story "Acquiring the Taste" is about two seventh-grade girls who want to be grown-up. Maria and Janelle think that changing the posters on their walls and learning to drink coffee will make them more grown-up. These changes are just on the surface, though. When the girls meet a woman named Chiara, they find out that there's a lot more to growing up than just coffee.

Maria and Janelle go to Chiara's Coffee Shop because they feel like they need "to learn how to drink coffee." They order cappuccinos and get drinks that are bitter. Maria even starts to choke.

MIDDLE

The middle paragraphs support the focus with examples from the story.

The girls are acting pretty immature at this point. Then Chiara comes to their table, gives them biscotti, and shows them how to dunk the pastry in their coffee. The sweet biscotti and the bitter coffee taste good together. Chiara also tells the girls stories about her life. She grew up in Rome and had daughters like Maria and Janelle before she moved to America. The girls like Chiara's stories more than they like the coffee. In the end, "the girls' coffee cups were empty, and their minds were full."

ENDING

The final paragraph explains how the characters have changed. It also discusses the overall meaning of the story.

By the end of the story, Maria and Janelle are more grown-up than when the story started. They've gone from having posters of rock stars in their bedrooms to actually meeting a person from Rome and learning about her life. The story "Acquiring the Taste" is about learning to like coffee, but it is also about developing an appreciation for the lives of other people and the stories they have to tell.

Respond to the reading. Answer the following questions about the sample prompt and student response.

☐ **Ideas** **(1)** What is the focus of the student's response? **(2)** What changes in the characters does the student note?

☐ **Organization** **(3)** How did the underlining and comments on pages 336–337 help the student organize the response?

☐ **Voice & Word Choice** **(4)** Is the student's voice objective or personal? **(5)** What words tell you so?

Practice Writing Prompt

Practice a response to literature. Carefully read the directions to the practice writing prompt on the next two pages. Use about 10 minutes at the beginning to read the story, make notes, and plan your writing. Also leave time at the end to proofread your work.

DIRECTIONS:
- Read the following story.
- As you read, make notes on your own paper.
- After reading the story, write an essay. You have 40 minutes to read, plan, write, and proofread your work.

When you write, focus on the main character. Show your insight into how he changes over the course of the story. Use clear organization, and support your focus with examples from the text.

The Mute King

From February through April, the school auditorium became Yan's second home. It wasn't that he liked drama. He hadn't even tried out for the spring production of *Once Upon a Mattress* because he was terrified of being onstage. Yan didn't like drama, but his girlfriend Kallie did. So he camped in the school auditorium every afternoon, his glossy black hair hanging over his face as he bent above algebra homework. Yan sat and worked, waiting for the times when Kallie came onstage and started to sing.

And could she sing! Kallie was playing Princess Winnifred the Woebegone, and whenever she came onstage, she owned the whole auditorium. Everybody stopped and just stared in amazement. Yan would lift his eyes from his algebra paper and let his pencil drop to the page and just soak in the sound of her voice. Those moments made all the waiting worthwhile. But the best moment of all was when play practice was done and Yan got to walk Kallie home.

"You should have tried out, you know," Kallie said to him

one day as they strolled past the park.

Yan looked at her and shrugged. "You know I couldn't talk in front of all those people."

"I know, but you could've tried out for the part of the mute king," Kallie shot back with a laugh.

Kallie hadn't meant anything by it, but the comment stung Yan. The king in the play was under a spell that kept him from talking. Yan felt like he was under a spell, too. He knew this play as well as anybody. He'd watched it a hundred times. He could have recited the lines and sung every song. Instead, stage fright kept him where he was, in the seats instead of onstage. He was like the mute king, just waiting for his chance to speak.

Dress rehearsal came. Kallie looked great in her princess getup, and everybody buzzed with excitement. Still, by 3:15, the rehearsal hadn't begun.

Suddenly, Kallie burst onstage and shuffled down the aisle. Behind her walked Mrs. Spejewski, who was in charge of music. Kallie approached Yan and pointed at him. "He can do it. He's our only hope. He knows the whole play."

"What? What?" Yan asked, standing up to protest.

"Our drummer Tony's got the flu," Mrs. Spejewski explained, "and Kallie says you know how to play drums."

"Yeah, I do, but—"

"You're hired," Kallie said, grabbing Yan's hand and pulling him toward the stage.

A moment later, Yan sat in the pit with the other musicians. He held drumsticks in his hand and stared at the printed music—but he knew every song by ear. Mrs. Spejewski lifted her baton, and the overture began. Yan played as if he'd always been behind those drums.

Out came the actors, and they sang, and Yan kept up the beat. Even when Kallie appeared to belt out her first solo, Yan didn't give in to the old spell.

He smiled. At last, he had found his place in the play, and the mute king had found his voice.

Creative Writing

Creative Writing
Writing Stories

Have you ever seen a movie with amazing special effects but no story? What a disappointment! On the other hand, a movie with an amazing story may not need special effects.

What makes a story amazing or wonderful? Usually, it has *people* in a *place* where a *conflict* occurs. If readers or viewers care about the people and the conflict, they will care about the story.

In this chapter, you will read a sample story about a tough decision at a school dance. Then you will develop a decision story of your own to share.

Writing Guidelines

Subject:	**A decision**
Form:	**Short story**
Purpose:	**To entertain**
Audience:	**Classmates**

Short Story

One type of story is based on a tough decision that the main character must make. In the beginning, the character wonders what to do. Tension builds until he or she makes the decision, and the ending tells how that decision changes the character. The following story is about a girl named Celia who faces a tough decision at a school dance.

BEGINNING

The beginning introduces the characters, the setting, and the decision.

RISING ACTION

The rising action adds a conflict for the characters.

Just Keep Going . . .

"Why don't you take a break, Celia?" Shaundra shouted above the pounding beat of the dance music. "You've been serving punch all night. Aren't you going to dance?"

"No," Celia shot back. "I mean, sure. Of course I'm going to dance." She ran her thumb up the stack of party napkins. "But we've been really busy. People get thirsty, dancing."

"Yeah, and people who aren't dancing need something to do."

Celia watched the ice bob in the bowl. "Nobody's asked me."

"Girl, you think this is the '90s? You've got to do the asking." Shaundra took the ladle from Celia's hand and nodded across the gym. "Jerome's been waiting for you all night."

Celia's eyes grew wide. "You better not have told him I like him!"

"Maybe I did. Maybe I didn't. If you don't ask him, you'll never know."

Drawing a deep breath, Celia clenched her fists beside her hips. How could she bear to ask Jerome to dance? She stared out across the crowded basketball court to see him leaning against the folded bleachers.

CREATIVE

Jerome's hair was shaved short, and he wore a button-down shirt with khaki pants. He was more dressed up than Celia had ever seen him.

"Well," Shaundra said, "what's your decision?"

Celia began to walk. The first step was the hardest. She felt like she was teetering on a tightrope. The music pounded in her chest. Halfway there, she wondered if she should veer off to the restroom, but something inside her said, "Just keep going." Suddenly, she stood in front of Jerome.

He looked up, saw her, and smiled. "What's up, Celia?" He was wearing cologne.

Celia shrugged, and she couldn't think of a single thing to say. How was she going to get out of this one? Taking a deep breath, she blurted, "You don't want to dance, do you?"

Jerome's smile grew broader. "Sure." They walked together out to the free-throw line. Then the beat stopped. Celia and Jerome were left standing there, facing each other in dead silence. She wanted to sink into the floor. At last, the DJ started a slow song.

Jerome murmured, "So, I guess Shaundra told you I like you."

Celia relaxed and smiled. "Maybe she did, and maybe she didn't."

HIGH POINT
. . . .

The high point is when the main character makes her decision.

ENDING
. . . .

The ending suggests that the main character changes.

Respond to the reading. Review the story and answer the following questions.

☐ **Ideas** **(1) How are Celia and Shaundra different? (2) What decision is Celia struggling to make?**

☐ **Organization** **(3) How does the writer build the suspense that leads up to Celia's decision?**

☐ **Voice & Word Choice** **(4) What words or phrases keep your interest? List at least three.**

Prewriting Selecting a Topic

A strong decision story starts with an interesting character. One way to create a character that readers will care about is to give the person one main strength and one main weakness. The strength makes the character admirable, and the weakness primes the character for a tough decision. A table diagram like the one below can help.

Table Diagram

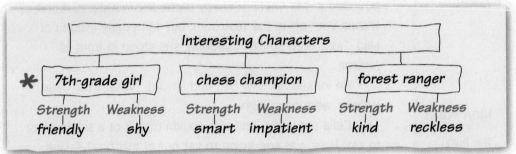

 Create a table diagram. List three characters you find interesting. Under each, list one strength to make your character likable and a weakness to challenge him or her. Choose one character to write about in a story.

Creating a Conflict

The difficult decision your character will face will create the conflict in your story. The reason the decision is difficult is that the character must overcome his or her weakness to make the right choice. The writer of the sample story listed decisions that would be tough for her character.

Character weakness:
 —Celia is shy.
Tough decisions:
 —Whether to throw a surprise party for her best friend.
 —Whether to make friends with a new girl from Japan.
 —Whether to talk to a boy she likes.

 Choose a conflict. Think about the character you chose and his or her weakness. List decisions that would be tough for the person to make. Choose one decision for your story.

Setting the Scene and Gathering Details

You have discovered the character and the conflict for your story. Now it's time to think about the place, or setting, where your story happens. Think of a place that would make the decision especially difficult.

For the main character of the sample story, the setting is a school dance. The author used a sensory chart to gather details about the setting.

Sensory Chart

Setting: *School dance in a gymnasium*

See	Hear	Smell	Taste	Touch/Feel
punch bowl	hip-hop	cologne	punch	cold ice
khaki pants	advice	cookies	pretzels	pounding beat
shaved hair	awkward			dizzy
	silence			shaky

Prewrite **Set the scene.** Choose the place where your story will occur. Then use a sensory chart to gather details about the place. Try to come up with at least two details for each sense.

Focus on the Traits

Organization

The actions that take place during a story make up the plot line. Each part of the plot plays an important role in the story.

- The **beginning** introduces the characters and setting.
- The **rising action** adds a conflict—a problem for the characters.
- The **high point** is the moment when the conflict is strongest, and a decision is made.
- The **ending** tells how the main character has changed.

Writing Developing Your First Draft

Now that you have created a character, a conflict, and a setting, you are ready to write your story. As you write, use the following tips.

1. Start strong. In your first sentence, focus on the character, the conflict, or the setting.

Character: Celia smiled shyly as she ladled more punch from the bowl.

Conflict: Celia had watched Jerome all evening, but he didn't seem to know she even existed.

Setting: The gymnasium of Cleveland Junior High was hopping.

2. Describe the action. Describe the action using a variety of specific details.

Celia began to walk. The first step was the hardest. She felt like she was teetering on a tightrope. The music pounded in her chest.

3. Include dialogue. Let your characters speak in their natural voices.

Jerome murmured, "So, I guess Shaundra told you I like you."
Celia relaxed and smiled. "Maybe she did, and maybe she didn't."

 Write your first draft. Tell the story of your character's big decision. Start strong and then include action and dialogue to build up to the decision point. Remember to think about the strength and weakness of your main character as you end the story.

Revising Improving Your Writing

Once you complete your first draft, take a break. Later, you can return to your story and revise it by looking at the following traits.

☐ **Ideas** Do I tell about a tough decision for my main character? Do I include sensory details, action, and dialogue?

☐ **Organization** Do I start strong? Do I build to the decision point? Do I resolve, or end, the story quickly after the high point?

☐ **Voice** Does my voice (including dialogue) keep the reader's interest?

☐ **Word Choice** Have I chosen words that capture the character, conflict, and setting?

☐ **Sentence Fluency** Do my sentences flow well?

 Revise your story. Use the questions above as a guide when you revise your first draft.

Editing **Checking for Conventions**

After you finish revising your story, you should edit it for *conventions*.

☐ **Conventions** Have I punctuated dialogue correctly? Have I checked my spelling and grammar?

Edit your story. Use the questions above to guide your editing. When you finish, use the tips below to write a title. Then create a clean final copy and proofread it.

Creating a Title

Your title is your first opportunity to hook the reader, so make it memorable. Here are some tips for writing a strong title.

- Use a metaphor: **Teetering on a Tightrope**
- Borrow a line from the story: **Just Keep Going . . .**
- Be creative: **The Punch-Bowl Predicament**

Publishing **Sharing Your Story**

Stories are meant to be shared. Here are three publication ideas.

- **Recite your story.**
  Read your story out loud to friends or family, or recite it from memory. Be dramatic with your voice, your facial expressions, and your gestures.

- **Create a skit.**
  Ask classmates to help you act out your story. If you can, gather costumes and props. Then perform the story for your class.

- **Submit your story.**
  Check the library for youth publications that accept stories. Format your work according to the submission guidelines and send your story in.

Present your story. Choose one of the ideas above or make up one of your own. Then share your story with the world.

Story Patterns

You just finished writing a decision story, but there are many other story patterns to choose from.

The Initiation

In an *initiation* story, a young person has to overcome a test of his or her abilities or beliefs. The way the person deals with the test will influence the rest of his or her life.

Sarah struggles to adjust to a new school.

The Surprise

In a *surprise* story, the main character and the reader misunderstand what is happening around them. The high point reveals a surprise that explains everything.

Jack thinks his friends are gossiping about him, but really they are planning a party for him.

The Union

The *union* pattern features two main characters who are attracted to each other. Usually, they have to overcome obstacles to be together.

Haleh meets a handsome young runner from a rival school's track team.

The Quest

In the *quest* pattern, the main character goes on a journey into the unknown, often to search for an object or reach a goal. The person usually gains the prize—or learns something in the process of losing it.

Drew journeys into the rain forest to find his father, who has been lost there for three weeks.

The Mystery

In a *mystery* story, the main character must follow a series of tantalizing clues to discover a secret.

Jessica stays up one night to discover who is leaving flowers on her front step.

 Choose one of the story patterns above. Think of a story that would fit that pattern. Write a single sentence that sums up the story.

Elements of Fiction

The following list includes many terms used to describe the elements or parts of literature. This information will help you discuss and write about the novels, poetry, essays, and other literary works you read.

Action: Everything that happens in a story

Antagonist: The person or force that works against the hero of the story (See *protagonist.*)

Character: A person or an animal in a story

Characterization: The way in which a writer develops a character, making him or her seem believable
Here are three methods:

- Sharing the character's thoughts, actions, and dialogue
- Describing his or her appearance
- Revealing what others in the story think or say about this character

Conflict: A problem or clash between two forces in a story
There are five basic conflicts:

- **Person Against Person** A problem between characters
- **Person Against Himself or Herself** A problem within a character's own mind
- **Person Against Society** A problem between a character and society, the law, or some tradition
- **Person Against Nature** A problem with some element of nature, such as a blizzard or a hurricane
- **Person Against Destiny** A problem or struggle that appears to be beyond a character's control

Dialogue: The words spoken between two or more characters

Foil: The character who acts as a villain or challenges the main character

Mood: The feeling or emotion a piece of literature or writing creates in a reader

Moral: The lesson a story teaches

Narrator: The person or character who actually tells the story, giving background information and filling in details between portions of dialogue

Plot: The action that makes up the story, following a plan called the plot line

Plot Line: The planned action or series of events in a story (The basic parts of the plot line are the beginning, the rising action, the high point, and the ending.)

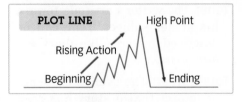

- The **beginning** introduces the characters and the setting.
- The **rising action** adds a conflict— a problem for the characters.
- The **high point** is the moment when the conflict is strongest.
- The **ending** tells how the main characters have changed.

Point of View: The angle from which a story is told (The angle depends upon the narrator, or person telling the story.)

- **First-Person Point of View**
  This means that one of the characters is telling the story: "We're just friends—that's all—but that means everything to us."

- **Third-Person Point of View**
  In third person, someone from outside the story is telling it: "They're just friends—that's all—but that means everything to them." There are three third-person points of view: *omniscient, limited omniscient,* and *camera view.* (See the illustrations on the right.)

Protagonist: The main character or hero in a story (See *antagonist.*)

Setting: The place and the time period in which a story takes place

Theme: The message about life or human nature that is "hidden" in the story that the writer tells

Tone: The writer's attitude toward his or her subject. Tone can be described by words like *angry* and *humorous.*

Total Effect: The overall influence or impact that a story has on a reader

Third-Person Points of View

Omniscient point of view allows the narrator to tell the thoughts and feelings of all the characters.

Limited omniscient point of view allows the narrator to tell the thoughts and feelings of only one character at a time.

Camera view (objective view) allows the story's narrator to record the action from his or her own point of view without telling any of the characters' thoughts or feelings.

 Select a story that you have read that fits one of the five basic conflicts on page 351. In one sentence, describe its conflict. In another sentence, describe the setting for this story. Add a sentence that describes the protagonist.

Creative Writing

Writing Poems

"A poem begins with a lump in the throat," says Robert Frost, but that's not where poetry ends. Poetry doesn't tell readers what they should feel. It leads them to discover the feeling for themselves. Along the way, a poem also entertains them with carefully chosen words, phrases, and rhythms.

Most modern poems are written in free-verse style, which means they do not have to rhyme. In this chapter, you will write your own free-verse poem about a weather event. If all turns out well, people will be able to hear raindrops on their windows or feel the wind whirling around them when they read your poem.

Writing Guidelines

Subject:	**A type of weather**
Form:	**Free-verse poem**
Purpose:	**To entertain**
Audience:	**Family and classmates**

Free-Verse Poem

Traditional poems follow a strict pattern of rhythm and rhyme, but each free-verse poem creates its own form. Even so, when poets write free-verse poetry, they carefully consider each word and line. They want to make sure their poems sound good and create effective images (word pictures) in the reader's mind. Hector wrote this free-verse poem to convey his feelings about lightning.

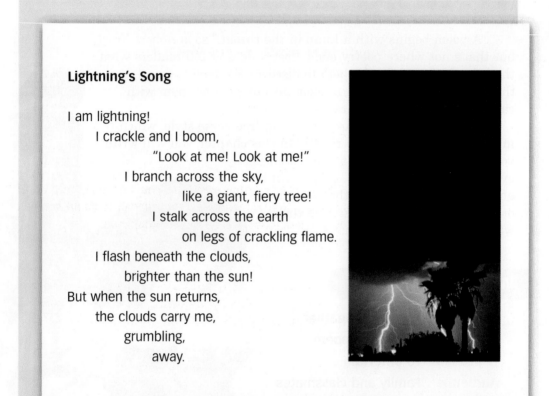

Lightning's Song

I am lightning!
   I crackle and I boom,
      "Look at me! Look at me!"
   I branch across the sky,
      like a giant, fiery tree!
   I stalk across the earth
      on legs of crackling flame.
I flash beneath the clouds,
   brighter than the sun!
But when the sun returns,
   the clouds carry me,
      grumbling,
         away.

Respond to the reading. Reflect on the traits in the free-verse poem above.

☐ **Ideas** (1) What sounds and sights does the writer include? List two of each.

☐ **Organization** (2) Why are the lines of the poem staggered on the page?

☐ **Voice & Word Choice** (3) What words show the personality of the lightning?

Prewriting Selecting a Topic

Like Hector, you will be writing a poem about a memory of some type of weather. To generate possible topics, Hector made a list of weather memories.

Listing

> *Weather Memories*
> – *Riding home in my uncle's car during a lightning storm*
> – *Wind rattling the windows of our apartment*
> – *My bare feet on hot sand at the beach*
> – *Rain from one little cloud on a sunny day*
> – *Wading through deep snow in the park*
> – *Feeling fog's mist on my face on the way to school*

Make a list. Write the words "weather memories" as a heading on a blank piece of paper. Then start listing experiences you remember about weather until you have at least six memories. Select one as your topic.

Gathering Details

An encyclopedia explains; a poem usually describes. Hector created the following sensory chart to gather details about a lightning storm before writing his poem. These details helped him create effective images in his poem.

Sensory Chart

See	Hear	Smell	Taste	Touch/Feel
bright flashes	crackle	dampness	moist air	mist or rain
jagged lines	rumble	ozone		heart
branching fingers	boom			thumping
dark clouds				
sun breaking through				

Create a sensory chart. Gather sensory details about your own weather memory, using the chart above as a guide. Include specific details from the image in your mind.

Prewriting Using Poetry Techniques

Poets play with the sounds of words. **Onomatopoeia** (ŏn´ə-mat´ə-pē´ə) is one example. It means using words that sound like the noises they name.

> **I crackle and I boom.**

Sometimes poets use **personification** (pər-sŏn´ə-fĭ-kā´shən), which means treating a nonhuman subject as if it were human. Hector's lightning poem personifies lightning as a bold personality who speaks directly to the reader.

> **"Look at me! Look at me!"**

Use special techniques. On your sensory chart, underline words that sound like noises. Circle words or details that could be used as personification. (For a list of other special poetry techniques, turn to pages 360–361.)

Writing Developing Your First Draft

The following tips will help you as you write your first draft.

- **Think** about the weather memory you have chosen. Scan your sensory chart again for details about it.
- **Recall** your feelings as you think about that memory.
- **Write** the first sentence or phrase that comes to mind. Don't worry about getting it perfect. Just get the words flowing. Hector started by writing, "I am lightning."
- **Keep writing** until you run out of ideas and sensory details.

Shaping Poetry

Poets also play with the way words are placed on the page. **Line breaks,** for instance, help control the rhythm of a poem. In the following example, line breaks cause pauses that emphasize the word "grumbling" and represent the storm fading in the distance.

> **The clouds carry me,**
> **grumbling,**
> **away.**

Write your first draft. Use the tips above to guide your writing. Experiment with onomatopoeia, personification, and line breaks.

CREATIVE

Revising Improving Your Poem

An expert gymnast makes a handstand look easy, even though it is not. A great poem may look simple, too, but it takes more than one draft to get there. Consider these traits when revising your poem.

- [ ] **Ideas** Do I use sensory details? Does my poem convey my true thoughts and feelings?
- [ ] **Organization** Are my ideas in the best order? Do my line breaks and indents help the poem make sense?
- [ ] **Voice** Does my poem show my personality?
- [ ] **Word Choice** Do I use creative poetic techniques like onomatopoeia, personification, and line breaks?
- [ ] **Sentence Fluency** Does the rhythm of my poem fit my topic?

Revise your poem. Using the questions above as a guide, keep revising until you are happy with your poem.

Editing Fine-Tuning Your Poem

Poems are shorter than most other types of writing, so every word and punctuation mark is important.

- [ ] **Conventions** Do my capitalization and punctuation make my poem clear? Do I avoid errors in spelling or grammar? Have I checked for any other errors that could distract the reader?

Edit your poem. Check your poem for conventions. Remember, poems sometimes break the rules for a reason, but never by accident.

Publishing Sharing Your Poem

When your poem is finished, share it with other people. Here are some good ways to do that. (See pages **57–64** for other publishing ideas.)

- **Post it.** Put it on a bulletin board, a Web site, or your refrigerator.
- **Submit it.** Send your poem to a contest or magazine.
- **Perform it.** Read your poem aloud to friends and family.

Publish your work. Poems are made to be shared. So make yours look its best, and then make it public.

Writing a Parts of Speech Poem

Writing special forms of poetry can stretch your imagination. One simple form is a "parts of speech" poem. The examples below follow this pattern.

Each poem has five lines.

- **Line 1** is one article and one noun.
- **Line 2** is an adjective, a conjunction, and another adjective.
- **Line 3** is one verb, one conjunction, and one verb.
- **Line 4** is one adverb.
- **Line 5** is one article and one noun that completes the thought.

```
1   The wind
2   howling and sighing
3   shakes and rattles
4   rudely
5   the window
```

A snowflake
shy and hesitant
pauses and hovers
briefly
a butterfly

A puddle
dark and chill
splashes and soaks
thoroughly
a sock

Writing Tips

- **Select a topic.** Think of a weather-related noun that you would like to write a poem about.
- **Gather details.** Jot down details about that topic and choose a few to include in your poem.
- **Follow the form.** Review the pattern above and choose words to match it.

Create your parts of speech poem. Following the writing tips above, write your own parts of speech poem.

Writing Other Forms of Poetry

There are many additional forms of poetry. The following are three types of free-verse forms that work well for weather poems.

Concrete Poem

The words of a concrete poem are arranged in the shape of the subject. For example, Hector's verse about lightning (see page **354**) has a jagged shape like a lightning bolt. Here's a much shorter concrete poem:

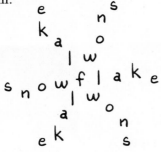

Acrostic Poem

In an acrostic poem, the first letter of each line together spell the subject. Sometimes acrostic poems are called "name poems."

See it glitter on the water's back!
Underneath, it glows through the belly of the wave.
Now it makes a rainbow in the spray.

5 W's Poem

Each line in a 5 W's poem answers *who? what? when? where?* and *why?*

My warmly bundled brother
steps down slowly
these frosty mornings
on frozen puddles
to hear the ice crack.

Write a poem. Choose one of the three forms above and write your own weather poem. (For fun, try all three!)

Using Special Poetry Techniques

Poets use a variety of special techniques in their work. This page and the next define some of the most important ones.

Figures of Speech

■ A **simile** (*sĭm′ə-lē*) compares two unlike things with the word *like* or *as*.

Dry earth cracked like a jigsaw puzzle.

■ A **metaphor** (*mĕt′ə-fôr*) compares two unlike things without using a comparison word (such as *like* or *as*), as in this line that uses a cattle stampede to represent a flooded river.

The swollen river stampedes past.

■ **Personification** (*pər-sŏn′ə-fĭ-kā′shən*) treats a nonhuman subject as if it were a person.

Puddles beg me to stop and play.

■ **Hyperbole** (*hī-pûr′bə-lē*) uses exaggeration for a special, often humorous, effect.

A million degrees on the thermometer, and I still can't go swimming.

Sounds of Poetry

■ **Alliteration** (*ə-lĭt′ə-rā′shən*) is the repetition of consonant sounds at the beginning of words.

The wicked wind laughs long and loud.

■ **Assonance** (*ăs′ə-nəns*) is the repetition of vowel sounds anywhere in words.

Blustery autumn drums our door.

CREATIVE

- **Consonance** (kŏn´sə-nəns) is the repetition of consonant sounds anywhere in words.

  Stark stones caressed by mist.

- **Line breaks** help to control the rhythm of a poem as it is read. Readers tend to pause slightly at the end of a line.

  We crest the rise and then
  plummet!

- **Onomatopoeia** (ŏn´ə-mat´ə-pē´ə) is the use of words that sound like what they name.

  Plop! Splat!
  Raindrops clap
  the roof and tap
  the skylight.

- **Repetition** (rĕp´ĭ-tĭsh´ən) uses the same word or phrase more than once, for emphasis or for rhythm.

  Hot today, so very.
  Hot as a coal stove.
  Hot as a steam iron.
  Hot as hot can be.

- **Rhyme** means using words whose endings sound alike. *End rhyme* happens at the end of lines.

  The dumpster lids are loaded down
  with white snow; in the street, it's brown.

  Internal rhyme happens within lines.

  Cold waves rolled beneath gray sky.

- **Rhythm** (rĭth´əm) is the pattern of accented and unaccented syllables in a poem. The rhythm of free-verse poetry tends to flow naturally, like speaking. Traditional poetry follows a more regular pattern, as in the following example.

  Ăn éarthwŏrm wrígglĕs áftĕr raín.

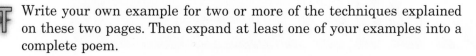

Try IT Write your own example for two or more of the techniques explained on these two pages. Then expand at least one of your examples into a complete poem.

organize

NOTE

Research Writing

summarize

RESEARCH

cite

Research Writing
Building Skills

When your parents were your age, doing research meant using magazines and books. Nowadays, researchers can surf the Internet, explore CD-ROM's, check out documentaries on DVD, watch live Web-casts, and even e-mail experts on the other side of the world! Of course, no report would be complete without magazines and books, but even these resources are easier to use than ever before.

In this chapter, you'll learn about research in today's world. You might even learn a few tips that you can pass on to your parents!

Mini Index

- **Primary vs. Secondary Sources**
- **Using the Internet**
- **Using the Library**
- **Using Reference Materials**
- **Evaluating Sources**

Primary vs. Secondary Sources

Primary sources of information are original sources. They give you first-hand information. Secondary sources contain information that has been gathered by someone else. Most nonfiction books, newspapers, magazines, and Web sites are secondary sources.

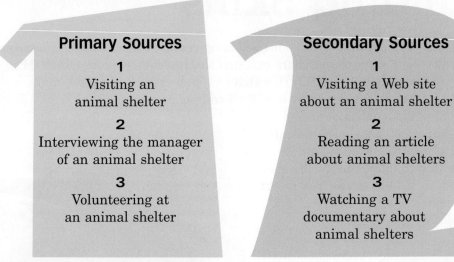

Primary Sources	Secondary Sources
1 Visiting an animal shelter	**1** Visiting a Web site about an animal shelter
2 Interviewing the manager of an animal shelter	**2** Reading an article about animal shelters
3 Volunteering at an animal shelter	**3** Watching a TV documentary about animal shelters

Types of Primary Sources

- **Diaries, Journals, and Letters** You can find these sorts of primary sources in libraries and museums.
- **Presentations** Historical sites, museums, guest speakers, and live demonstrations can give you firsthand information.
- **Interviews** You can interview an expert in person, by phone, by e-mail, or through the mail.
- **Surveys and Questionnaires** To gain information from many people at once, have them answer a list of questions. Then study the results.
- **Observation and Participation** You can observe a person, place, or thing or participate in an event yourself as a method of gathering firsthand information.

 Decide whether each of the following is a primary or a secondary source of information.

> Listening to a radio program about animal shelters
>
> Talking with someone who works at an animal shelter

Using the Internet

People all around the world publish information on the Internet. That makes it a great place to do research. By using the Net, you can quickly find basic information about your topic in online encyclopedias. You can also use a search site to help you find other sources on the Net. Just remember, because information on the Net comes from a variety of people and places, you need to evaluate each source carefully. (For guidelines, see page **376**.)

Using a Browser

A browser is a program for exploring (or surfing) the Net. A browser window has controls to help you travel the Net from page to page. See the diagram below, which shows a browser window displaying a search site's page.

REPORT

Address bar — `◄ ► C +` http://www.student-search.com

Navigation buttons

Student Search!

Search box — [   ] Search

Directory

Index heading — 🌐 **About Our World**
Continents, Countries, States, . . .

🎨 **Art & Entertainment**
Links — Books, Movies, Music, . . .

🎹 **Computers & Games**
Games, News, Themes, . . .

🏫 **Schoolhouse**
Clubs, Homework Help, News, . . .

🧪 **Science Lab**
Animals, Ocean, Space, . . .

⚾ **Sports & Recreation**
Baseball, Basketball, Soccer, . . .

If you know the Web address of a page on the Net, you can type it into the address bar and use your "Return" or "Enter" key to go there. By clicking the links on a page, you can go directly to related pages. The navigation arrows at the top of the browser window let you return to pages you have visited.

Open your browser. Then type the following address into the address bar—www.thewritesource.com. Use a link there to visit a page that interests you. Use the browser's navigation buttons to move backward and forward through the pages you have visited.

Using a Search Site

A search site is like a computer catalog for the Internet. When you type a subject into the search box and use your "Return" or "Enter" key, the search site gives you a list of all the pages it knows that contain your subject. You can also explore subjects by clicking directory headings.

Points to Remember

- **Use the Web carefully.**
  Look for sites that have *.edu, .org,* or *.gov* in the address. These are educational, nonprofit, or government Web sites and will offer the most reliable information. If you are not sure about a site, check with your teacher or librarian. (Also see page **376**.)

- **Use a search site.**
  A search site such as www.google.com or www.yahoo.com is like a computer catalog for the Internet. You can enter keywords to find Web pages about your subject.

- **Look for links.**
  Often, a Web page includes links to other pages dealing with your topic. Take advantage of these links.

- **Be patient.**
  The Web is huge and searches can get complicated. New pages are added all the time, and old ones may change addresses or even disappear completely.

- **Know your school's Internet policy.**
  To avoid trouble, be sure to follow your school's Internet policy. Also follow whatever guidelines your parents may have set up for you.

 Visit www.thewritesource.com/research.htm and choose one of the search sites listed there. Then use one of these two search strategies: (1) use the search bar to look for the words "animal shelter" on the Net, or (2) look for topic headings on the site and use them to search for animal shelters. What interesting links do you find?

Using the Library

Libraries hold a wide range of resources for your research. Besides books, you'll find periodicals (like magazines and newspapers), CD's, and a lot more. Check your school's library and the local public library to see what sorts of things are available there.

 1 **Books** are usually divided into three sections.

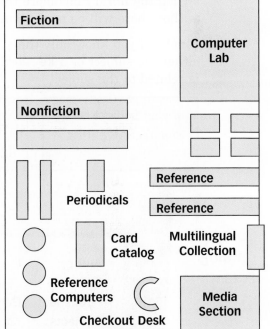

- The **fiction** section includes stories and novels. These books are arranged in alphabetical order by the authors' last names.

- The **nonfiction** section contains books that are based on fact. They are usually arranged according to the Dewey decimal system. (See page **370**.)

- The **reference** section has encyclopedias, atlases, dictionaries, directories, and almanacs.

2 The **periodicals** section includes magazines and newspapers.

3 The **computer lab** has computers, often connected to the Internet. You usually sign up to use a computer.

4 The **media section** includes music CD's, cassettes, DVD's, videotapes, and CD-ROM's. Computer software (encyclopedias, games, and so on) may be found in this section as well.

Try IT Write the following list of words down the left side of a piece of paper: *fiction books, nonfiction books, reference section, periodicals section, computer lab, media section.* Then visit your school library and look for each of these sections. When you find a section, write a short description of what is there.

Searching a Computer Catalog

Every computer catalog is a little different. Therefore, the first time you use a particular computer catalog, it's a good idea to check the instructions for using it or to ask a librarian for help. With a computer catalog, you can find information on the same book in three ways:

1 If you know the book's **title**, enter the title.

2 If you know the book's **author**, enter the author's name. (When the library has more than one book by the same author, there will be more than one entry.)

3 Finally, if you know only the **subject** you want to learn about, enter either the subject or a keyword. (A *keyword* is a word or phrase that is related to the subject.)

If your subject is . . .	your keywords might be . . .
constructing kites,	kite design, kite history, kite festivals and exhibitions.

Computer Catalog Screen

Author:	Hunt, Leslie L.
Title:	25 Kites That Fly
Published:	Dover Publications, 1996
Subjects:	Kites, kite design and construction, kite design and plans, kite exhibitions, kite festivals, kite folklore, kite history

STATUS:	**CALL NUMBER:**
Available	629.133Hun

LOCATION:
Nonfiction

 Create a computer catalog screen like the one above for a book you have read or one you are reading.

Searching a Card Catalog

If your library has a card catalog, it will most likely be located in a cabinet full of drawers. The drawers contain title, author, and subject cards, which are arranged in alphabetical order.

1 To find a book's **title card**, ignore a beginning *A, An,* or *The* and look under the next word of the title.

2 To find a book's **author card**, look under the author's last name. Then find the author card with the title of the book you want.

3 To find a book's **subject card**, look up an appropriate subject.

All three cards will contain important information about your book—most importantly, its call number. This number will help you find the book on the library's shelves.

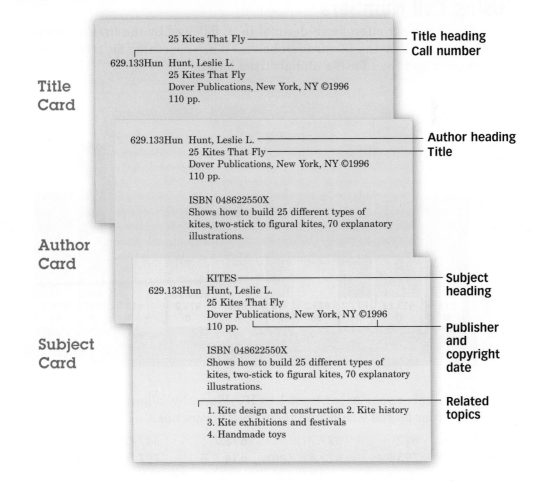

Title Card

25 Kites That Fly —————————————— **Title heading**
—————————————— **Call number**
629.133Hun Hunt, Leslie L.
25 Kites That Fly
Dover Publications, New York, NY ©1996
110 pp.

Author Card

629.133Hun Hunt, Leslie L. ———————— **Author heading**
25 Kites That Fly ———————— **Title**
Dover Publications, New York, NY ©1996
110 pp.

ISBN 048622550X
Shows how to build 25 different types of
kites, two-stick to figural kites, 70 explanatory
illustrations.

Subject Card

KITES ———————— **Subject heading**
629.133Hun Hunt, Leslie L.
25 Kites That Fly
Dover Publications, New York, NY ©1996
110 pp. ———————— **Publisher and copyright date**

ISBN 048622550X
Shows how to build 25 different types of
kites, two-stick to figural kites, 70 explanatory
illustrations.

1. Kite design and construction 2. Kite history ———————— **Related topics**
3. Kite exhibitions and festivals
4. Handmade toys

Finding Books

Each catalog entry for a book includes a **call number**. You can use this number to find the book you are looking for. Most libraries use the Dewey decimal classification system to arrange books. This system divides nonfiction books into 10 subject categories.

000-099 **General Works**	500-599 **Sciences**
100-199 **Philosophy**	600-699 **Technology**
200-299 **Religion**	700-799 **Arts and Recreation**
300-399 **Social Sciences**	800-899 **Literature**
400-499 **Languages**	900-999 **History and Geography**

Using Call Numbers

A call number often has a decimal in it, followed by the first letters of the author's name. (See the illustration below.) When searching for a book, look for the number and then for the alphabetized letters.

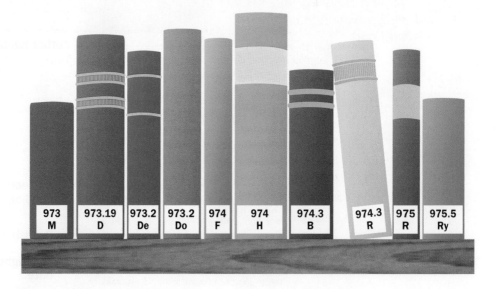

973 M	973.19 D	973.2 De	973.2 Do	974 F	974 H	974.3 B	974.3 R	975 R	975.5 Ry

Try IT Number your paper from 1 to 10. Place the following call numbers in order as you would find them on a library shelf.

812	637.7	636.7	347 Gil	797.52
793 Ka	822.82 Kam	636.7 B	797.5	546.44 C

Understanding the Parts of a Book

Understanding the parts of a nonfiction book can help you to use that book efficiently.

- The title page is usually the first page. It tells the title of the book, the author's name, the illustrator's name, and the publisher's name and city.

- The copyright page comes next. It tells the year the book was published. This can be important because some information in an old book may no longer be correct.

- A preface, a foreword, or an introduction may follow. It may tell what the book is about, why it was written, and how to use it.

- The table of contents shows how the book is organized. It gives the names and page numbers of the sections, chapters, and major topics. (See illustration.)

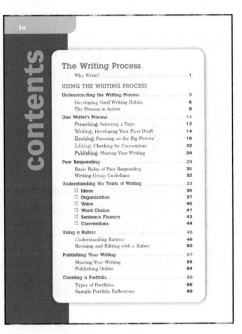

- A cross-reference sends the reader to another page for more information. *Example:* (See page 372.)

- An appendix has extra information, such as maps, tables, lists, and so on.

- A glossary explains special words used in the book. It's like a mini-dictionary.

- A bibliography lists books, articles, and other sources that the author used while writing the book. To learn more about the topic, read the materials listed in the bibliography.

- The index is an alphabetical list of all the topics in the book. It gives the page numbers where each topic is located.

Try It Find the following information in this book.

  1. Who is the illustrator of the book?

  2. What are the page numbers of the table of contents?

  3. What is the first entry under H in the index?

Using Reference Materials

The reference section in a library contains materials such as encyclopedias, atlases, and dictionaries.

Using Encyclopedias

An **encyclopedia** is a set of books, a CD, or a Web site with articles on almost every topic you can imagine. The topics are arranged alphabetically. The tips below can guide your use of encyclopedias.

- If the article is long, skim any subheadings to find specific information.
- Encyclopedia articles are written with the most basic information first, followed by more detailed information.
- At the end of an article, you may find a list of related topics. Use them to learn more about your topic.
- The index lists all the places in the encyclopedia where you will find more information about your topic. (See the sample below.) The index is usually in the back of the last volume of a printed set.

Encyclopedia Index

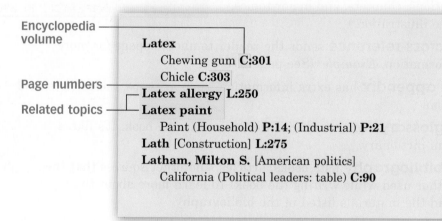

Encyclopedia volume

Page numbers

Related topics

Latex
    Chewing gum **C:301**
    Chicle **C:303**
Latex allergy L:250
Latex paint
    Paint (Household) **P:14**; (Industrial) **P:21**
Lath [Construction] **L:275**
Latham, Milton S. [American politics]
    California (Political leaders: table) **C:90**

 Using the index entries above, list the volume and page or pages where you might find the following information.

1. A description of chewing gum.

2. An explanation of the difference between house paint and industrial paint.

3. A list of political leaders of California.

Finding Magazine Articles

Periodical guides are found in the reference section of the library and list magazine articles about many different topics.

- **Locate the right edition** of the *Readers' Guide to Periodical Literature* (or a similar guide). The latest edition will have the newest information, but you may need information from an older edition.

- **Look up your subject**. Subjects are listed alphabetically. If your subject is not listed, try another word related to it.

- **Write down the information** about the article. Include the name of the magazine, the issue date, the name of the article, and its page numbers.

- **Find the magazine**. Ask the librarian for help if necessary.

Readers' Guide Format

Entry	Label
	Subject Entry
PEROXIDES	
Cosmetic and skin protective compositions. *Soap, Perfumery & Cosmetics* v77 no2 p57 F 2004.	**Title of Article**
See also	**Cross-Reference**
Hydrogen peroxide	
PEROXISOMES	
Treating a mystery malady. M. Egan. *Forbes* v173 no2 p38–39 F 2 2004.	**Name, Volume, and Number of Magazine**
Unloading dock. G. Chin. *Science* v303 no5666 p1947–1948 Mr 26 2004.	
PERPETUAL MOTION	
McKeon, 73, continues to be one for the ages. H. Bodley. *USA Today* Ja 16 2004.	**Name of Author**
Perpetual motion, almost. K. Smith. *Motor Trend* v56 no1 p24 Ja 2004.	**Page Number/Date**
PERRIN, PAT	
What happened next? P. Perrin. *Appleseeds* v6 no6 p24–27 F 2004.	**Author Entry**

Internet-based databases are online subscription services that allow you to search for and read periodicals on the Internet.

 Using the sample entries above, write answers to these questions.

1. Under what additional heading can you find more articles about peroxides?

2. Who wrote the article "Unloading Dock"?

3. What month is listed most often in the entries above?

Checking a Dictionary

A dictionary is the most reliable source for learning the meanings of words. It offers the following aids and information.

- **Guide words** are located at the top of every page. They show the first and last entry words on a page, so you can tell whether the word you're looking up is listed on that page.

- **Entry words** are the words that are defined on the dictionary page. They are listed in alphabetical order for easy searching.

- **Parts of speech** labels tell you the different ways a word can be used. For example, the word *Carboniferous* can be used as a noun or as an adjective.

- **Syllable divisions** show where you can divide a word into syllables.

- **Spelling and capitalization** (if appropriate) are given for every entry word. If an entry is capitalized, capitalize it in your writing, too.

- **Spelling of verb forms** is shown. Watch for irregular forms of verbs because the spelling can be a whole new word.

- **Illustrations** are often provided to make a definition clearer.

- **Accent marks** show which syllable or syllables should be stressed when you say a word.

- **Pronunciations** are special spellings of a word to help you say the word correctly.

- **Pronunciation keys** give symbols to help you pronounce the entry word correctly.

- **Etymology** gives the history of a word [in brackets]. Knowing a little about a word's history can make the definition easier to remember.

Remember: Each word may have several definitions. It's important to read all of the meanings to determine if you're using it accurately.

 Open a dictionary to any page and find the following information.

1. Write down the guide words on that page.
2. Find a multisyllable word and write it out by syllables. Jot down the word's part of speech. (There may be more than one.)
3. Find an entry that includes spelling of verb forms and write them down.

Dictionary Page

Guide words —————— **carbon dioxide | carburetor**   150

Entry word —————

carbon dioxide *n.* A colorless, odorless gas that does not burn, composed of carbon and oxygen in the proportion CO_2 and present in the atmosphere or formed when any fuel containing carbon is burned. It is exhaled from an animal's lungs during respiration and is used by plants in photosynthesis. Carbon dioxide is used in refrigeration, in fire extinguishers, and in carbonated drinks.

Part of speech —————

carbonic acid *n.* A weak acid having the formula H_2CO_3. It exists only in solution and decomposes readily into carbon dioxide and water.

Syllable division —————

car·bon·if·er·ous (kär'bə-**nif**'ər-əs) *adj.* Producing or containing carbon or coal.

Spelling and capitalization —————

Carboniferous *n.* The geologic time comprising the Mississippian (or Lower Carboniferous) and Pennsylvanian (or Upper Carboniferous) Periods of the Paleozoic Era, from about 360 to 286 million years ago. During the Carboniferous, widespread swamps formed in which plant remains accumulated and later hardened into coal. See table at **geologic time.—Carboniferous** *adj.*

Spelling of verb forms —————

car·bon·ize (kär'bə-nīz') *tr. v.* **car·bon·ized, car·bon·iz·ing, car·bon·iz·es 1.** To change an organic compound into carbon by heating. **2.** To treat, coat, or combine with carbon.—**car·bon·i·za·tion** (kär'bə-ni-zā'shən) *n.*

Illustration —————

air
air filter
choke valve
gas
gas and air mixture
float
venturi
throttle valve
float chamber
carburetor
cross section of a carburetor

carbon monoxide *n.* A colorless, odorless gas that is extremely poisonous and has the formula CO. Carbon monoxide is formed when carbon or a compound that contains carbon burns incompletely. It is present in the exhaust gases of automobile engines.

carbon paper *n.* A paper coated on one side with a dark coloring matter, placed between two sheets of blank paper so that the bottom sheet will receive a copy of what is typed or written on the top sheet.

Accent marks —————

carbon tet·ra·chlor·ide (tĕt'rə-**klôr**'īd') *n.* A colorless, poisonous liquid that is composed of carbon and chlorine, has the formula CCl_4, and does not burn although it vaporizes easily. It is used in fire extinguishers and as a dry-cleaning fluid.

Pronunciation —————

Car·bo·run·dum (kär'bə-**run**'dəm) A trademark for an abrasive made of silicon carbide, used to cut, grind, and polish.

Pronunciation key —————

ă	pat	ôr	core
ā	pay	oi	boy
âr	care	ou	out
ä	father	ŏŏ	took
ĕ	pet	ōōr	lure
ē	be	ōō	boot
ĭ	pit	ŭ	cut
ī	bite	ûr	urge
îr	pier	th	thin
ŏ	pot	*th*	this
ō	toe	zh	vision
ô	paw	ə	about

car·bun·cle (kär'**bung**'kəl) *n.* **1.** A painful inflammation in the tissue under the skin that is somewhat like a boil but releases pus from several openings. **2.** A deep-red garnet.

car·bu·re·tor (kär'bə-rā'tər *or* kär'byə-rā'tər) *n.* A device in a gasoline engine that vaporizes the gasoline with air to form an explosive mixture. [First written down in 1866 in English, from *carburet*, carbide, from Latin *carbō*, carbon.]

Etymology —————

Evaluating Sources

Before you use any information in your writing, you must decide if it is trustworthy. Ask yourself the following questions to help judge the value of your sources.

Is the source a primary or a secondary source?

Firsthand facts are often more trustworthy than secondhand facts. However, many secondary sources are also trustworthy. (See page **364**.)

Is the source an expert?

An expert is an authority on a certain subject. You may need to ask a teacher, parent, or librarian for help when deciding how experienced a particular expert is.

Is the information accurate?

Sources that are well respected are more likely to be accurate. For example, a large city newspaper is much more reliable than a supermarket tabloid.

Is the information complete?

If a source of information provides some facts about a subject, but you still have questions, find an additional source.

Is the information current?

Be sure you have the most up-to-date information on a subject. Check for copyright dates of books and articles and for posting dates of online information.

Is the source biased?

A source is biased when it presents information that is one-sided. Some organizations, for example, have something to gain by using only some of the facts. Avoid such one-sided sources.

Research Writing

Summary Paragraph

After you see a movie, someone may ask, "What was it about?" You don't tell them the whole thing. Instead, you share with them the main idea and a few important facts.

When you write a summary paragraph of an article, you also share the main idea and some key facts. You want the reader to get an overview of the article. You will find that summary writing is a useful skill whenever you are asked to do research or report writing.

In this chapter, you'll learn how to find the main idea and most important information in an article. Then you'll learn to write a summary paragraph that clearly presents that information.

Main Ideas + Key Facts
SUMMARY

Writing Guidelines

Subject: **A research article**

Form: **Summary paragraph**

Purpose: **To express the main idea**

Audience: **Classmates**

Summary Paragraph

The following article, "Portugal's 'Triangle Trade,'" explains how and why Portugal set up trade routes between Brazil, Africa, and Portugal. The paragraph "The Trade Triangle" summarizes that article.

Portugal's "Triangle Trade"

During the 1400s, Portugal was looking for an ocean route to the East Indies. The Portuguese were tired of the Italian merchants controlling the trade of cinnamon, peppercorn, and cloves from the East. To compete with the Italians, they sent ships south along the coast of Africa, seeking a route to India. Along the way, they began to trade with African nations, giving cloth, knives, and guns in exchange for gold and ivory. In 1498, they finally reached India.

At about the same time, Portuguese ships also landed in Brazil and started a colony there. The colonists set up sugar, cotton, and tobacco plantations, using local people as workers.

However, the native workers soon came down with smallpox and measles, diseases that the Portuguese brought with them. Many of the workers died. As a result, the plantation owners needed new workers to harvest the sugarcane.

Portuguese merchants began to trade for slaves from Africa to work in the sugarcane fields. Ships would sail from Portugal to Africa with cloth, knives, and guns to trade for slaves. Then they would sail from Africa to Brazil with slaves. Finally, they would sail back to Portugal with sugar, cotton, and tobacco. Their trade routes formed a triangle in the Atlantic Ocean, often referred to as the "Triangle Trade."

The Trade Triangle

Topic sentence (main idea)

Portugal's "Trade Triangle" began with Africa and Brazil around the beginning of the 1500s. Up until that time, the Portuguese traded with African nations for gold and ivory. After they colonized Brazil, however, they soon found that they needed more workers. The natives they had been using were dying from smallpox and measles, diseases that were brought in by the Portuguese. They decided to use Africans as replacements and began trading cloth, knives, and guns for human beings. The Portuguese then took the Africans to Brazil to work as slaves. *From Brazil, the traders completed the triangle when they returned to Portugal on ships loaded down with sugar, cotton, and tobacco.*

Body

Closing sentence

Respond to the reading. Answer the following questions.

☐ **Ideas** (1) What is the main idea of the summary?

☐ **Organization** (2) How is the paragraph organized?

☐ **Word Choice** (3) What two sentences from the original selection are paraphrased in the fourth summary sentence?

Prewriting Selecting an Article

For this assignment, you must find an article to summarize. Choose an article that . . .

- relates to a subject you are studying,
- discusses an interesting topic, and
- is fairly short (between three and six paragraphs).

Choose an article. Look through magazines and newspapers for an article to summarize. Choose one that has the three features listed above. Ask your teacher if the article will work for your summary paragraph.

Reading the Article

If possible, make a photocopy of your article so that you can underline important facts as you read. Otherwise, take brief notes on the article. The writer of the sample summary underlined the key facts.

> Portuguese merchants began to trade for slaves from Africa to work in the sugarcane fields. Ships would sail from Portugal to Africa with cloth, knives, and guns to trade for slaves. Then they would sail from Africa to Brazil with slaves. Finally, they would sail back to Portugal with sugar, cotton, and tobacco. Their trade routes formed a triangle in the Atlantic Ocean, often referred to as the "Triangle Trade."

Read your article. First, read through the article. Then reread it and take notes or underline the important facts.

Finding the Main Idea

A summary focuses on the main idea of an article. Look over the facts you noted or underlined. What main idea do those facts present? The writer of the sample summary wrote this main idea: *Portugal's "Trade Triangle" began with Africa and Brazil around the beginning of the 1500s.*

Write the main idea. Review the facts you identified. What main idea do they suggest? Write the main idea as a single sentence. This sentence (or a version of it) will be the topic sentence for your paragraph.

Writing Developing the First Draft

A summary paragraph includes a topic sentence, a body, and a closing sentence. As you write each part, follow these tips.

- **Topic sentence:** Introduce the main idea of the article.
- **Body:** Include just enough important facts to support or explain the main idea. As much as possible, use your own words and phrases to share these facts.
- **Closing sentence:** Restate the main idea of the summary in a different way.

Write the first draft of your summary paragraph. Complete your topic sentence based on the main idea of the article. Add facts that support the main idea. Then end your paragraph with a closing sentence.

Revising Reviewing Your Writing

As you revise, check your first draft for the following traits.

- ☐ **Ideas** Does the topic sentence correctly identify the main idea? Do I include only the most important facts to support it?

- ☐ **Organization** Is all of the information in a logical order?

- ☐ **Voice** Does my voice sound confident and informative?

- ☐ **Word Choice** Do I use my own words? Do I define any difficult terms?

- ☐ **Sentence Fluency** Do I use a variety of sentence types and lengths?

Revise your paragraph. First, reread the article and your summary. Then use the questions above as a guide for your revising.

Editing Checking for Conventions

Focus on conventions as you edit your summary.

- ☐ **Conventions** Have I checked the facts against the article? Have I checked for errors in punctuation, spelling, and grammar?

Edit your work. Use the questions above as your editing guide. Make your corrections, write a neat final copy, and proofread it for errors.

Research Writing

Research Report

History is full of stories of amazing people—whether ancient kings and queens who lived long ago or heroes who are still living today. We can learn a lot by finding out how these people grew from childhood to adulthood, what obstacles they faced along the way, and how they overcame them. Their stories can inspire us to accomplish great things ourselves.

In this chapter, you will write a report about a person who inspires you. You will use the research skills you learned about in "Building Skills" (pages 363–376) to uncover important information about this person. You will then compile the information in a research report to share with your classmates. Along the way, you're sure to learn a lot about your subject— and about yourself.

Writing Guidelines

Subject:	A person who inspires you
Form:	Research report
Purpose:	To present research about a person's accomplishments
Audience:	Classmates

Research Report

Miri Mocelin wrote this research report about an important figure in African history. Notice how the information in the report is organized. The side notes point out key features in the report.

↑ 1" ↓

1/2" ↓

Mocelin 1 ← 1" →

← 1" → Miri Mocelin

Mr. Sanchez

Language Arts

May 4, 2005

The entire report is double-spaced.

An Ideal "King"

BEGINNING

· · · · · · · · · · · · · ·

The opening shares an interesting fact to gain the reader's attention.

The United States has had more than 40 different presidents, all of them men. Some Americans have a hard time imagining a woman as their president. However, history gives many examples of women leading nations, such as Indira Gandhi of India and Golda Meir of Israel. Another example is the seventeenth-century African ruler Nzinga Mbande (Geen-gah Em-bahn-day), often just called "Ginga." <u>By protecting her people from a takeover by the Portuguese, Ginga showed that a woman can be a great leader.</u>

· · · · · · · · · · · · · ·

The thesis (focus) statement identifies the topic (underlined).

Ginga's Background

Ginga lived from about 1583 to 1663 in western Africa, where Angola is now located. Her father was the king of Ndongo, near the coast. He fought three

↑ 1" ↓

REPORT

Mocelin 2

wars against the Portuguese, who were invading the region and capturing people for slavery. He won the first two wars, but he lost the third. Her father died in 1617, and Ginga's younger brother became king. Her brother was not a strong king, so Ginga began to take on his responsibilities (Grayson 47). Through negotiation, leadership, warfare, and alliances with other nations, Ginga worked to protect her people from the Portuguese.

Portugal & Angola 1500–1800

EUROPE

Portugal

AFRICA

Angola

Ginga's Accomplishments

Ginga showed her skill for negotiation when her brother first became king. Because he knew she was a good negotiator, he sent her in his place to make a treaty with the Portuguese. Ginga went to meet the Portuguese governor in the city of Luanda, where he ruled. The governor met Ginga in a room with only one chair, his official seat, to make her feel like his subject. To show that she was his equal, Ginga gestured to one of her followers. That follower knelt on the ground to become a seat for her. Having shown

MIDDLE
The first middle paragraph gives background about the person's family and homeland.

Headings help the reader to understand the paper's organization.

Each of the next four middle paragraphs starts with a topic sentence that covers one main accomplishment.

A source and page numbers are identified in parentheses.

her authority, Ginga was then able to negotiate a good treaty for her people (Diouf 18–20).

In 1624, when Ginga's brother died, she took the throne and proved her leadership skills. To get her people's respect, she insisted on being called King instead of Queen. To show that women could be strong, she gathered bodyguards who were all women, and she formed three regiments of women in her army. She and her two sisters each led one of these regiments whenever her army went to war (Grayson 49).

When the Portuguese broke their treaty a few years later, Ginga showed her skill as a war leader. She personally led troops into battle against the invaders. Author Emma Hahn explains some of Ginga's tactics. She says that because the Portuguese had gunpowder and Ginga's people did not, Ginga learned to ambush the invaders on rainy days when their weapons would

When the source or author is mentioned in the text, only the page number is listed in parentheses.

not fire well. Ginga also used the jungle to hide her warriors from the enemy. Sometimes she would attack and then retreat to lead the enemy into a trap (77). Ginga's warriors respected her leadership and fought fiercely for her.

Mocelin 4

The writer's last name and page number go on every page.

As the Portuguese gained power in the region, Ginga made deals with other African nations and with the Dutch for help. She even married the chief of a neighboring tribe to gain their aid. Eventually, Ginga moved her people, "every man, woman, and child— including the elderly, sick, and wounded—and their cattle," to the highlands of Matamba in order to save them from the Portuguese (Diouf 22). That long march took five years, but it kept her people from being enslaved.

The exact words of the author are placed in quotation marks.

Ginga's Legacy

ENDING

The final paragraph sums up the paper and tells the reader one last interesting fact.

Ginga continued to rule her people until she died at the age of 81. Because of her, the nation remained strong long afterward, and it had many women rulers as well as men. Eventually, it became part of modern Angola. Ginga's struggle against the Portuguese kept them from conquering all of western Africa. Because of that, today she is remembered as a hero in Africa. She is also respected throughout Europe, even in Portugal. People remember her as a great diplomat, a fierce war leader, and a strong ruler ("Kingdom"). By being a great "king," Ginga showed that in a leader, being male or female really doesn't matter.

REPORT

Mocelin 5

Works Cited

Diouf, Sylviane Anna. Kings and Queens of

Southern Africa. New York: Franklin Watts,

2000.

Grayson, John. "Nzinga of Ndongo and Matamba."

Legendary Figures 28 Dec. 2003: 47-50.

Hahn, Emma. Unlikely Heroes: Historic and

Contemporary Figures. Portland, ME:

J. Weston Walch, 1997.

"Kingdom of Ndongo." About Angola. Republic of

Angola's Embassy in Stockholm and to the

Nordic Countries. 1 May 2004 <http://

www.angolaemb.se/angola/nzinga.htm>.

A separate page alphabetically lists sources cited in the paper.

Respond to the reading. After you have finished reading the sample research report, answer the following questions about the traits of writing.

☐ **Ideas** (1) What is the main idea of the report? (2) What four aspects of leadership does the writer talk about?

☐ **Organization** (3) What is the main idea in each middle paragraph? Make a list.

☐ **Voice** (4) How does the author show her admiration for her subject? Choose two sentences from the final paragraphs that show this.

Prewriting

Prewriting is to writing what packing your gear is to traveling. The more prepared you are for the "journey," the more successful you will be. Keep the following points in mind as you prepare.

Keys to Effective Prewriting

1. As a topic, choose an important person who interests you.

2. Make a list of questions you want to have answered about the person.

3. Make sure that there is enough to say about your topic; you need background information and at least three important ideas about the person.

4. Use a gathering grid to organize your research questions and the answers you find. Use note cards to keep track of longer answers.

5. Be careful to credit your sources when paraphrasing ideas or quoting words.

6. Keep track of the publication details for all your sources so you can use them in a works-cited page later.

PROD. NO. TAKE ROLL
SCENE
SOUND

Prewriting Selecting a Topic

To find a topic, make a list of important people who interest you. Start by answering the following questions. (Also read the list of possible topics below that Miri made for her report on "An Ideal 'King.'")

● What famous or historical people would I like to know more about?
● What events would I like to research, and who was involved?
● What interesting people does my social studies textbook mention?

TOPICS LIST

I'd like to know more about these people . . .
 – George Lucas
 – J. K. Rowling
 – Genghis Khan
 – Albert Schweitzer
 – Helen Keller

I'd like to learn about the people involved in these events . . .
 – finding the Titanic
 – building the Great Wall of China
 – landing on the moon

My textbook mentions these historical figures . . .
 – Nzinga Mbande, 1583–1663 C.E., African hero
 – Xuanzang, 600–664 C.E., Chinese traveler
 – Timur the Lame, 1336–1405 C.E., Mongol leader

Make your topics list. Try to list at least five people as possible topics.
Prewrite Then choose the one that interests you the most.

REPORT

Sizing Up Your Topic

A good research report about an important person should include detailed information about the person's background and three or four major points about the person's accomplishments.

Miri decided to write about Nzinga ("Ginga") Mbande, an African leader mentioned in her social studies textbook.

Research Notes About Ginga

Background
* She lived during the late 1500s and middle 1600s near the western coast of Africa, and she became "King" of her people. (She refused to be called "Queen.")

Major Accomplishments
* She was famous as a negotiator.
* She was also a skilled war leader.
* Her people respected her strength as a ruler.
* She fought against the Portuguese invasion of Africa and against the slave trade.

Legacy
* She kept the Portuguese from conquering western Africa.
* She is a hero for African people today.

From this information, Miri felt confident that she would be able to write a good research paper about Ginga.

Size up your topic. Look up your chosen topic in an encyclopedia and on the Internet. List background information and the most important points about the person. Are there enough details to write a good research report?

Prewriting Gathering Details

A gathering grid can help you organize the information from your research. Miri made the following grid during her research about Ginga. Down the left-hand side, she listed her questions. Across the top, she listed sources she found. For answers too long to fit in the grid, Miri used note cards. (See page 391.)

Gathering Grid

"Ginga" Mbande	Kings and Queens of Southern Africa	Unlikely Heroes	Grayson article	Angola Web site
What is her background?		Lived 1583 to 1663 in what is now Angola	See note card number 1.	Daughter of an African king
How was she great?	Protected her people from Portuguese invasion			
What were her major deeds?	Negotiated a treaty with the Portuguese governor	Led troops into battle See note card number 2.	Took over as "King" when her brother died	
What has been her effect on the world?				Kept Portuguese from conquering western Africa

Create a gathering grid. Make a list of questions in the left-hand column of your grid. Across the top, list the sources you will use. Fill in the squares with answers you find. Use note cards for longer, more detailed answers.

Creating Note Cards

While a gathering grid is a great way to see all your research at one glance, sometimes you need more space for an answer. You can use note cards to keep track of longer answers and the details from your research.

When using note cards, number each card and write a question at the top. Then answer the question by writing a paraphrase (see page **392**), a list, or a quotation. At the bottom, identify the source of the information (including a page number if appropriate). Here are three sample cards Miri made for her report on Ginga.

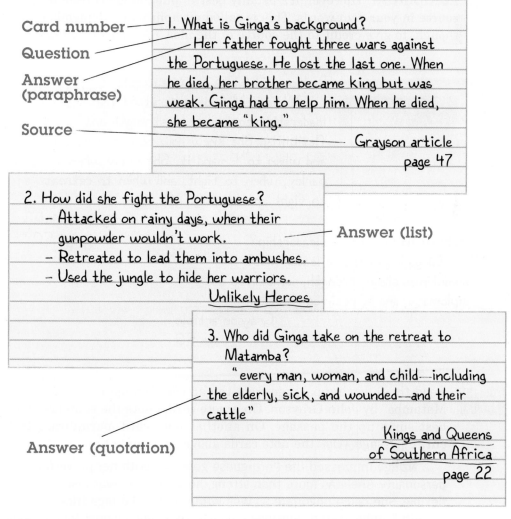

Card number

Question

Answer
(paraphrase)

Source

1. What is Ginga's background?
Her father fought three wars against the Portuguese. He lost the last one. When he died, her brother became king but was weak. Ginga had to help him. When he died, she became "king."
Grayson article
page 47

2. How did she fight the Portuguese?
 - Attacked on rainy days, when their gunpowder wouldn't work.   Answer (list)
 - Retreated to lead them into ambushes.
 - Used the jungle to hide her warriors.
Unlikely Heroes

3. Who did Ginga take on the retreat to Matamba?
"every man, woman, and child—including the elderly, sick, and wounded—and their cattle"
Kings and Queens
of Southern Africa
page 22

Answer (quotation)

Prewrite

Create note cards. Make note cards like the examples above whenever your answers are too long to fit on your gathering grid.

Prewriting Avoiding Plagiarism

You must be careful to give credit for the facts and ideas you find in your sources. Using other people's words and ideas without giving them credit is called **plagiarism**, and it is stealing. Here are two ways to avoid plagiarism.

- **Quote exact words:** When a source states something so perfectly that it makes sense to use those exact words, you may include them in quotation marks and give credit to the source. (See page **385**.)

- **Paraphrase:** However, it's usually best to put the ideas from a source in your own words. This is called paraphrasing. Remember, though, to give credit to the source of the idea. (See pages **383–384**.)

> **QUOTING EXACT WORDS**
>
> 4. How did Ginga show leadership?
>   "Nzinga Mbande understood that leadership required both strength and flexibility. She knew how to earn respect and when to demand it. She knew when to parley, when to fight, and when to retreat to fight another day."
>   Grayson article
>   page 50

> **PARAPHRASING**
>
> 4. How did Ginga show leadership?
>   Ginga knew that a leader must sometimes show strength, sometimes use diplomacy, and sometimes retreat.
>   Grayson article
>   page 50

 Read the following passage from the article "Nzinga of Ndongo and Matamba" by John Grayson. On a note card, quote the sentence that best sums up the passage. On another note card, paraphrase the entire passage. (Use the note cards above as a guide.)

> Nzinga impressed the Portuguese governor with her powerful personality. She was more than strong, however; she was also flexible. She could negotiate as well with the warlike Jaga tribes as with "sophisticated" European leaders. In allying against the Portuguese with both the Jaga and the Dutch, Nzinga showed strength and flexibility.

Keeping Track of Your Sources

As you research, keep careful track of your sources so that you can cite them correctly in your final report. You'll need to write down the following information.

- **Encyclopedia entry:** Author's name (if listed). Entry title. Encyclopedia title. Edition (if given). Publication date.
- **Book:** Author's name. Title. Publisher and city. Copyright date.
- **Magazine:** Author's name. Article title. Magazine title. Date published. Page numbers.
- **Internet:** Author's name (if listed). Page title. Site title. Date posted or copyright date (if listed). Date found. Electronic address.

REPORT

My Source Notes

ENCYCLOPEDIA

"Angola." Columbia Encyclopedia. 2001.

BOOK

Sylviane Anna Diouf. Kings and Queens of Southern Africa. Franklin Watts. New York. 2000.

MAGAZINE

John Grayson. "Nzinga of Ndongo and Matamba." Legendary Figures December 28, 2003. Pages 47-50.

INTERNET

No author. "Kingdom of Ndongo." About Angola. Republic of Angola's Embassy in Stockholm and to the Nordic Countries. No posting date. May 1, 2004. <www.angolaemb.se/angola/nzinga.htm>.

List sources. Keep a list of all your sources, recording the information listed
above. Whenever you find a new source, add it to the list.

Prewrite

Prewriting Writing Your Thesis Statement

After your research is done, you need to develop a thesis (focus) statement to guide your writing. The thesis is the main point or idea you want to emphasize. It serves as the focus for your report so that all the parts work together. Use the following formula to help you write your thesis statement.

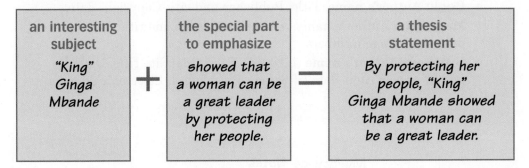

an interesting subject		the special part to emphasize		a thesis statement
"King" Ginga Mbande	+	showed that a woman can be a great leader by protecting her people.	=	By protecting her people, "King" Ginga Mbande showed that a woman can be a great leader.

Example Thesis Statements

Ginga Mbande, a seventeenth-century African ruler (an interesting topic), protected her people from the Portuguese invasion (the part to emphasize).

Robert Ballard, the man who found the Titanic (an interesting topic), is both an ocean scientist and an explorer (the part to emphasize).

Donna Shirley, who had been told, "Girls can't be engineers," (an interesting topic) went on to lead NASA's Mars exploration program (the part to emphasize).

Prewrite

Form your thesis statement. Review your research notes on page 389 and choose one main point you could make about your topic. Using the formula above, write a thesis statement.

Outlining Your Ideas

An outline is one way to organize your thinking and plan your report. You can use either a topic outline or a sentence outline to list the main ideas of your report. A **topic outline** lists ideas as words or phrases; a **sentence outline** lists them as full sentences. (Also see page 550.)

Sentence Outline

Below is the first part of a sentence outline for the report on pages 382–386. Notice that the outline begins with the thesis statement and then organizes ideas below it. Compare this partial outline with the opening paragraph and first middle paragraph of the report.

Thesis statement	*THESIS STATEMENT: By protecting her people from a takeover by the Portuguese, Ginga showed that a woman can be a great leader.*
I. Topic sentence for first middle paragraph	*I. Ginga lived from about 1583 to 1663 in western Africa, where Angola is now located.*
A. B. C. D. Supporting ideas	*A. Her father was the king of Ndongo.* *B. He fought three wars against the Portuguese slave trade, winning two but losing the third.* *C. When he died, Ginga's brother became king, and she carried some of his responsibilities.* *D. Ginga used negotiation, warfare, and alliances with other nations to protect her people.*
II. Topic sentence for second middle paragraph	*II. Ginga showed her skill for negotiation when her brother first became king.* *A. . . .* *B. . . .*

Remember: In an outline, if you have a I, you must have at least a II. If you have an A, you must have at least a B.

Create your outline. Write a sentence outline for your report, using the details from your research. Be sure that each topic sentence (I, II, III, . . .) supports the thesis statement and that each detail (A, B, C, . . .) supports the topic sentence above it. Use your outline as a guide when you write the first draft of your report.

Writing

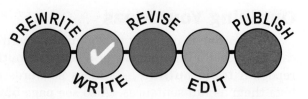

PREWRITE · WRITE · REVISE · EDIT · PUBLISH

With your research and planning finished, it's time to write the first draft of your paper. This is your chance to share your information and thoughts with other people. As you write, keep the following points in mind.

Keys to Effective Writing

1. Use your first paragraph to grab your reader's attention, introduce your topic, and present your thesis statement.

2. In the second paragraph, give the background for the person's accomplishments.

3. In the next several paragraphs, give details about those accomplishments. Start each paragraph with a topic sentence.

4. In your ending paragraph, explain how the person has contributed to history.

5. Remember to cite the sources of any ideas you paraphrase or quote. List your sources alphabetically on a works-cited page.

Citing Sources in Your Report

As you write, remember to give credit to the sources you quote directly or paraphrase in your report.

WHEN YOU HAVE ALL THE INFORMATION

■ The most common type of credit (citation) lists the author's last name and the page number in parentheses.

She and her two sisters each led one of these regiments whenever her army went to war (Grayson 49).

■ If you already name the author in your report, just include the page number in parentheses.

Author Emma Hahn explains . . . Sometimes she would attack and then retreat to lead the enemy into a trap (77).

WHEN SOME INFORMATION IS MISSING

■ Some sources do not list an author. In those cases, use the title and page number. (If the title is long, use only the first word or two.)

The Sahara Desert made it difficult for people in North Africa to communicate with people in South Africa ("History" 39).

■ Some sources (especially Internet sites) do not use page numbers. In those cases, list just the author.

In 1635, Ginga formed an alliance with the kingdoms of Kongo and Kassange (O'Shaughnessy).

■ If a source does not list the author or page number, use the title.

People remember her as a great diplomat, a fierce war leader, and a strong ruler ("Kingdom").

(Notice that in each of the examples above, the period comes after the parentheses that include the title or author credit.)

Try IT Copy the following sentence by Rachel Buchholz from page 31 of *Legendary Figures,* and then cite the source.

The Portuguese encouraged the Jaga people to war upon their peaceful neighbors.

Writing Starting Your Research Report

The opening paragraph of your report should grab the reader's attention, introduce your topic, and present your thesis statement. To start your opening paragraph, try one of these three approaches.

Beginning

Middle

Ending

- **Start with an interesting fact.**

  The United States has had more than 40 different presidents, all of them men.

- **Ask an interesting question.**

  Did you know that one of the most powerful leaders in African history was a woman?

- **Start with a quotation.**

  "Sometimes the best man for the job is a woman," it has been said.

Miri decided to begin her opening paragraph with an interesting fact.

Beginning Paragraph

The beginning paragraph starts with an interesting fact and ends with the thesis (focus) statement (underlined).

> The United States has had more than 40 different presidents, all of them men. Some Americans have a hard time imagining a woman as their president. However, history gives many examples of women leading nations, such as Indira Gandhi of India and Golda Meir of Israel. Another example is the seventeenth-century African ruler Nzinga Mbande (Geen-gah Em-bahn-day), often just called "Ginga." By protecting her people from a takeover by the Portuguese, Ginga showed that a woman can be a great leader.

Write

Write your opening paragraph. Use one of the three strategies listed above to start your paragraph. After you grab the reader's attention, be sure to introduce your topic. End your paragraph with a clear thesis statement.

Developing the Middle Part

Begin the middle part of your report with background information, starting with where and when your subject lived, and how that person became involved in his or her work. After that, provide details about the work and its importance to the world.

Start each middle paragraph with a topic sentence that covers one main idea. The other sentences in each paragraph should support that main idea. Remember to use your sentence outline as a guide when writing.

Beginning

Middle

Ending

Middle Paragraphs

The first middle paragraph explains the subject's background.

All the details support the topic sentence (underlined).

Ginga's Background

Ginga lived from about 1583 to 1663 in western Africa, where Angola is now located. Her father was the king of Ndongo, near the coast. He fought three wars against the Portuguese, who were invading the region and capturing people for slavery. He won the first two wars, but he lost the third. Her father died in 1617, and Ginga's younger brother became king. Her brother was not a strong king, so Ginga began to take on his responsibilities (Grayson 47). Through negotiation, leadership, warfare, and alliances with other nations, Ginga worked to protect her people from the Portuguese.

Portugal

Europe

Africa

Angola

Ginga's Accomplishments

Ginga showed her skill for negotiation when her brother first became king. Because he knew she was a good negotiator, he sent her in his place to make a treaty with the Portuguese. Ginga went to meet the Portuguese governor in the city of Luanda, where he ruled. The governor met Ginga in a room with only one chair, his official seat, to make her feel like his subject. To show that she was his equal, Ginga gestured to one of her followers. That follower knelt on the ground to become a seat for her. Having shown her authority, Ginga was then able to negotiate a good treaty for her people (Diouf 18–20).

In 1624, when Ginga's brother died, she took the throne and proved her leadership skills. To get her people's respect, she insisted on being called King instead of Queen. To show that women could be strong, she gathered bodyguards who were all women, and she formed three regiments of women in her army. She and her two sisters each led one of these regiments whenever her army went to war (Grayson 49).

When the Portuguese broke their treaty a few years later, Ginga showed her skill as a war leader.

The second middle paragraph reveals an interesting event that illustrates Ginga's negotiation skills.

In the third middle paragraph, the writer tells of Ginga's leadership skills.

REPORT

The fourth middle paragraph describes Ginga as a skilled leader.

She personally led troops into battle against the invaders. Author Emma Hahn explains some of Ginga's tactics. She says that because the Portuguese had gunpowder and Ginga's people did not, Ginga learned to ambush the invaders on rainy days when their weapons would not fire well. Ginga also used the jungle to hide her warriors from the enemy. Sometimes she would attack and then retreat to lead the enemy into a trap (77). Ginga's warriors respected her leadership and fought fiercely for her.

In the fifth middle paragraph, Ginga's alliances with others are explained.

As the Portuguese gained power in the region, Ginga made deals with other African nations and with the Dutch for help. She even married the chief of a neighboring tribe to gain their aid. Eventually, Ginga moved her people, "every man, woman, and child—including the elderly, sick, and wounded—and their cattle," to the highlands of Matamba in order to save them from the Portuguese (Diouf 22). That long march took five years, but it kept her people from being enslaved.

Write your middle paragraphs. Keep these tips in mind as you write.

1 Support the topic sentence for each paragraph with details.

2 Refer to your outline for help with your organization. (See page 395.)

3 Give credit to your sources in your paper. (See page 397.)

Writing Ending Your Research Report

Your ending paragraph should bring your report to a thoughtful close. Try one or more of the following ideas in your closing paragraph.

- **Remind the reader about the overall point or thesis of the report.**
- **Tell one last interesting fact about the topic.**
- **Explain the person's contribution to history.**

Ending Paragraph

The ending paragraph explains the person's contribution to history.

Ginga's Legacy

Ginga continued to rule her people until she died, when she was 81 years old. Because of her, the nation remained strong long afterward, and it had many women rulers as well as men. Eventually, it became part of modern Angola. Ginga's struggle against the Portuguese kept them from conquering all of western Africa. Because of that, today she is remembered as a hero in Africa. She is also respected throughout Europe, even in Portugal. People remember her as a great diplomat, a fierce war leader, and a strong ruler ("Kingdom"). <u>By being a great "king," Ginga showed that in a leader, being male or female really doesn't matter.</u>

The thesis statement is repeated (underlined).

Write your final paragraph. Draft your final paragraph using one or more of the strategies listed above.

Look over your report. Read your report, looking over your notes and outline to see whether you have included all the necessary details. Make notes about possible changes.

Creating Your Works-Cited Page

The first step in creating a works-cited page is to set up or "format" your sources. The following two pages show the proper format for common types of sources. Notice that the second line and additional lines for each source are indented five letters or spaces. (See the following examples.)

ENCYCLOPEDIA

Author (if available). Article title (in quotation marks). Title of the encyclopedia (underlined). Edition (if available). Date published.

> "Angola." Columbia Encyclopedia. 2001.

BOOKS

Author or editor (last name first). Title (underlined). City where the book was published: Publisher, copyright date.

> Diouf, Sylviane Anna. Kings and Queens of Southern Africa. New York: Franklin Watts, 2000.

NOTE Include a state abbreviation (or country) after the city if needed for clarity.

MAGAZINES

Author (last name first). Article title (in quotation marks). Title of the magazine (underlined) Date (day, month, year): Page numbers of the article.

> Grayson, John. "Nzinga of Ndongo and Matamba." Legendary Figures 28 Dec. 2003: 47-50.

INTERNET

Author (if available). Page title (if available, in quotation marks). Site title (underlined). Name of sponsor (if available). Date published (if available). Date found <electronic address>.

> "Kingdom of Ndongo." <u>About Angola.</u>
>   Republic of Angola's Embassy
>   in Stockholm and to the Nordic
>   Countries. 1 May 2004 <http://
>   www.angolaemb.se/angola/nzinga.htm>.

 Format your sources. Check your report and your list of sources (from page 393) to see which sources you actually used. Then follow these directions.

1 Write your sources using the guidelines above and on the previous page. You can write them on a sheet of paper or on note cards.

2 Alphabetize your sources.

3 Create your works-cited page. (See the example below.)

Works Cited

Diouf, Sylviane Anna. <u>Kings and Queens of Southern</u>
   <u>Africa.</u> New York: Franklin Watts, 2000.
Grayson, John. "Nzinga of Ndongo and Matamba."
   <u>Legendary Figures</u> 28 Dec. 2003: 47–50.
Hahn, Emma. <u>Unlikely Heroes: Historic and Contemporary</u>
   <u>Figures.</u> Portland, ME: J. Weston Walch, 1997.
"Kingdom of Ndongo." <u>About Angola.</u> Republic of Angola's
   Embassy in Stockholm and to the Nordic Countries.
   1 May 2004 <http://www.angolaemb.se/angola/
   nzinga.htm>.

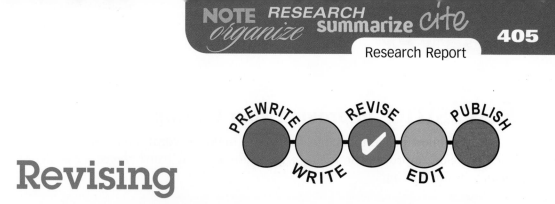

PREWRITE · REVISE · PUBLISH · WRITE · EDIT

Revising

A good research report needs more than one draft. The first time through, you work mainly with organization and ideas. In the second draft, you fill in missing information, rearrange ideas for clarity, and polish your word choice. Take the time to make your report as good as it can be.

Keys to Effective Revising

1. Read your entire draft to get an overall sense of your report.

2. Review your thesis statement to be sure that it clearly states your main point about the topic.

3. Make sure your beginning draws readers in. Then check that your ending brings your report to an interesting close.

4. Make sure you sound knowledgeable and interested in the topic.

5. Check for correct, specific words and complete sentences.

6. Use the editing and proofreading marks inside the back cover of this book.

Revising Improving Your Writing

In the following sample page, the writer makes several important revisions. Each revision improves the *ideas, organization, voice, word choice,* or *sentence fluency* in the writing.

A phrase is reworded for better voice.

The United States has had more than 40 different presidents, all of them men. Some Americans ~~think~~ *have a hard time imagining* ~~it would be crazy to have~~ a woman as their president. However, history gives many examples of women leading nations, such as Indira Gandhi of India and Golda

A helpful pronunciation is added.

Meir of Israel. Another example is the seventeenth-century African ruler Nzinga Mbande, *(Geen-gah Em-bahn-day)* often just called "Ginga." By protecting her people from a takeover by the Portuguese, Ginga showed that a woman can be a great

Details are added for clarity.

leader.

Ginga's Background

Ginga lived from about 1583 to 1663 in western

A sentence is moved for better organization.

Africa. ~~The Portuguese~~ *where Angola is now located.* were invading the region and capturing people for slavery. Her father was the king of Ndongo, near the coast. He fought three wars against the Portuguese. *who* He won the first two wars, but he

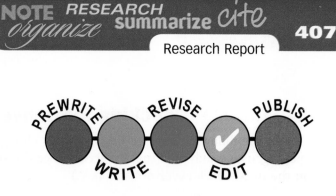

Editing

Once you have finished revising your report, edit your work for conventions like spelling, punctuation, capitalization, and grammar.

Keys to Effective Editing

1. Use a dictionary, a thesaurus, your computer's spell checker, and the "Proofreader's Guide."

2. Read your essay out loud and listen for words or phrases that may be incorrect.

3. Look for errors in punctuation, capitalization, spelling, and grammar.

4. Check your report for proper formatting. (See pages 382–386 and 403–404.)

5. If you use a computer, edit on a printed computer copy. Then enter your changes on the computer.

6. Use the editing and proofeading marks inside the back cover of this book.

REPORT

Editing **Checking for Conventions**

In the following sample page, editing changes have been made to correct spelling, usage, and punctuation errors. (See the editing and proofreading marks on the inside back cover of this book.)

<u>Ginga's Accomplishments</u>

Ginga showed her skill for negotiation when her brother first became king. Because he knew she was a good negotiator, he sent her in his place to make a treaty with the Portuguese. Ginga went to meet the Portuguese ~~governer~~ *governor* in the city of Luanda, where he ruled. The ~~govener~~ *governor* met Ginga in a room with only one chair, his official seat, to make her feel like his subject. To show that she was his equal, Ginga gestured to one of her followers; that follower knelt on the ground to become a seat for her. Having shown her authority, Ginga was then able to negotiate a good treaty for her people. (Diouf 18–20)

In 1624, when ginga's brother died, she took the throne and proved her leadership skills. To get her people's respect, she insisted on being called King instead of Queen. To show that women could be . . .

A spelling error is corrected.

A run-on sentence is corrected.

A period is moved to its proper place.

Capitalization errors are corrected.

Publishing **Sharing Your Report**

After you have worked so hard to write and improve your report, you'll want to make a neat-looking final copy to share. You may also decide to prepare your report as an electronic presentation, an online essay, or an illustrated report.

Make a final copy. Use the following guidelines to format your report. (If you are using a computer, see page 60.) Create a clean final copy and carefully proofread it.

Focus on Presentation

- Use blue or black ink and double-space the entire paper.
- Write your name, your teacher's name, the class, and the date in the upper left corner of page 1.
- Skip a line and center your title; skip another line and start your writing.
- Indent every paragraph and leave a one-inch margin on all four sides.
- For a research paper, you should write your last name and the page number in the upper right corner of every page of your report.

Creating a Title Page

If your teacher requires a title page, follow his or her requirements. Usually you center the title one-third of the way down from the top of the page. Then go two-thirds of the way down and center your name, your teacher's name, the name of the class, and the date. Put each piece of information on a separate line.

An Ideal "King"

Miri Mocelin
Mr. Sanchez
Language Arts
May 4, 2005

Research Paper Checklist

Use the following checklist for your research paper. When you can answer all of the questions with a "yes," your paper is ready to hand in.

Ideas

_____ **1.** Is my research paper interesting and informative?

_____ **2.** Are my sources current and trustworthy?

Organization

_____ **3.** Does my paper have a thesis statement in the opening paragraph and a topic sentence in each middle paragraph?

_____ **4.** Does my ending paragraph bring my paper to an interesting close?

Voice

_____ **5.** Do I sound knowledgeable and interested in my topic?

Word Choice

_____ **6.** Have I explained any technical terms or unfamiliar words?

_____ **7.** Do I use quotations and paraphrasing effectively?

Sentence Fluency

_____ **8.** Do my sentences flow smoothly from one to another?

Conventions

_____ **9.** Does my first page include my name, my teacher's name, the name of the class, the date, and a title? (See page 382.)

_____ **10.** Do I correctly cite my sources? (See pages 383–385 and 397.)

_____ **11.** Is my works-cited page set up correctly? Are the sources listed in alphabetical order? (See pages 386 and 403–404.)

_____ **12.** If my teacher requires a title page, is mine done correctly? (See page 409.)

Research Writing

Multimedia Presentations

If you've just written your best report or essay ever, you may want to share it with a larger audience. To reach a larger audience, you may have to shift from being the writer to being the director. As director, you can write a multimedia presentation complete with special effects, which a wide range of viewers can enjoy.

There are several kinds of software that you can use to produce multimedia presentations. Just add a little imagination, and you'll be connecting with your audience in a new, dynamic way.

Mini Index

- **Creating Interactive Reports**
- **Interactive Report Checklist**

Creating Interactive Reports

With the help of a computer, you can design a report that others can interact with. Your computer-generated slides, graphics, and sound effects will make the important parts of your report clearer and more interesting.

Prewriting **Selecting a Topic and Details**

For your interactive report, you will want to use something you've already written, something that interests both you and your audience. After you've chosen your piece of writing, make a list of its main ideas. Then find or create one or more of the following graphics or sound effects:

- **Pictures** such as photos or "clip art"
- **Animations** that show a process or tell a story
- **Videos** of something you've filmed yourself
- **Sounds and music** to use as background or to make a point

Try IT Make a plan and organize your ideas by creating a list or media grid like the one below.

Media Grid

Main Ideas	Pictures or Videos	Animations or Music	Sounds
1. Ginga was a great African leader in the seventeenth century.	portrait of Ginga	background music	
2. She took her brother's throne when he died.	picture of a throne		cheers of a crowd

Prewrite **Gather details.** Select ideas from your list or media grid for graphics and sounds to include with each slide. Create the graphics or sounds yourself or find them on the Internet. Save the images (credit the source if necessary) and sounds on your computer in a special folder created for this report.

Writing **Preparing the Report**

Before you record your report, you need to make a *storyboard*. A storyboard is a "map" of the slides you plan to use in your report. (See the sample storyboard on the next page.) Using your list or media grid as a guide, include one box in the storyboard for each main idea. Then add links from these boxes to additional information.

Use your computer software to design the slides. Choose a typestyle that is easy to read. Use the graphics and sounds you found earlier, and consider using bulleted lists and graphs to organize your information. Show the user how to get around in the report using easily recognized navigation buttons, such as arrows or the words "next" and "back."

Create a storyboard. Refer to your list or media grid to help you map out your storyboard. Include ideas for what your audience will see and hear. This kind of preparation will give you an idea of how the slides should look before you actually make them on the computer.

Revising **Improving Your Report**

Since your audience is on their own with this type of report, it's important to double-check to make sure that it works as it should. Have several friends or family members test it for you. Ask them to tell you if it is clear, interesting, and easy to get around.

Get feedback. If your "testers" have good suggestions, revise the text and design of your report where necessary.

Editing **Checking for Conventions**

Check the text on each slide for spelling, punctuation, grammar, and capitalization errors. Consider asking an adult or a classmate to check your slides, too.

Make corrections. After you've made corrections, go through the report once more to make sure it works well.

You can save your report on a disk or CD to share with others. Make sure you copy all the necessary files.

Multimedia Presentation Storyboard

Here is the map, or storyboard, for an interactive report based on the student research report "An Ideal 'King.'" (See pages **382–386**.) Since a computer user accesses the report on his or her own, the report needs to share the essay's information as completely as possible. (The gold boxes are added links for the interactive report.)

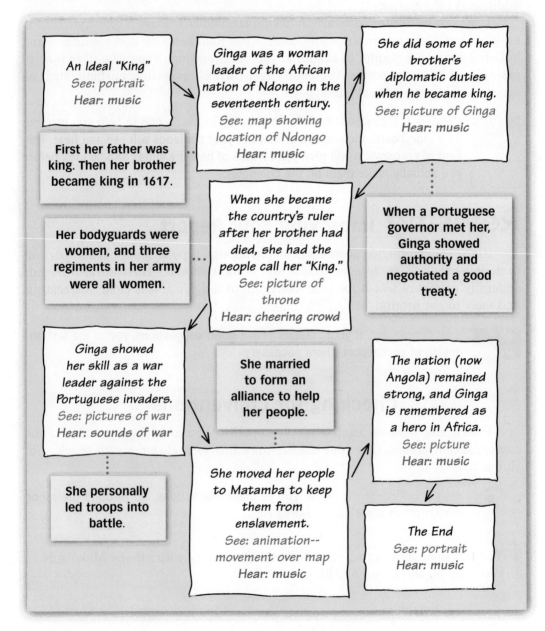

Interactive Report Checklist

Use the following checklist to make sure your report is the best it can be. When you can answer all of the questions with a "yes," it's ready!

Ideas

_____ **1.** Did I choose a strong essay or report for my interactive report?

_____ **2.** Do my graphics help communicate my ideas clearly?

_____ **3.** Does each slide fit the audience and the purpose of the report?

Organization

_____ **4.** Did I introduce my topic clearly in the beginning?

_____ **5.** Did I include the important main points in the middle part?

_____ **6.** Did I end with a summary or wrap-up thought?

Voice

_____ **7.** Did I use an interesting, somewhat formal voice?

_____ **8.** Does my voice fit my audience and topic?

Word and Multimedia Choices

_____ **9.** Are the words on my slides easy to read?

_____ **10.** Did I choose the best pictures and sounds for my ideas?

Presentation Fluency

_____ **11.** Does my report flow smoothly from slide to slide?

Conventions

_____ **12.** Is my report free of grammar, spelling, and punctuation errors?

LISTEN
respect
clarify

Speaking and Writing to Learn

revise
speak

Listening and Speaking

"Didn't you hear what I told you?"

"I'm sorry. I heard you, but I wasn't listening."

That statement shows the difference between hearing and listening. Simply hearing what your teachers, coaches, parents, and classmates say is not the same as listening to them. When you listen, you think about what you hear, and that's what makes listening an important learning skill.

Speaking well is also important. In fact, listening and speaking skills are so closely related that *good listeners* are likely to be *good speakers*. Improving these skills will make you more confident and successful in school—and beyond!

Mini Index

- **Listening in Class**
- **Participating in a Group**
- **Speaking in Class**

Listening in Class

Listening takes more effort than hearing. Good listening habits include paying attention, staying focused, and thinking about the speaker's ideas. The following tips will help you become a better listener—in and out of school.

1 **Figure out your purpose for listening.** Is the speaker introducing a new idea, explaining a key example, or reviewing for a test?

2 **Listen carefully.** Think about what you hear. Use your mind to help you understand what your ears are hearing.

3 **Listen for the main ideas and take notes.** Writing down a speaker's main ideas will help you focus on what is essential. When you don't understand something you've written, make a note to yourself or simply put a question mark in the margin of your notebook.

4 **Condense information.** Use lists, abbreviations, and phrases to keep information brief, organized, and easy to understand. Skip the small, unnecessary words such as articles and modifiers. Shorten some words—*intro* for introduction, *chap* for chapter, and so on.

Condense information. The next time you take notes in class, practice condensing or summarizing information. Use lists and abbreviations and avoid unnecessary wording. The example below can guide you.

LUNGS   –remove carbon dioxide from blood
          –supply blood with oxygen

Blood with carb diox pumped to lungs by heart
          ↓
Bld with oxy returns to heart
          ↓
Bld with oxy pumped through arteries
          ↓
Bld with carb diox back to heart through veins

A Closer Look at Listening and Speaking

Improving your listening and speaking skills will help you become a better learner. Good listeners and good speakers follow these basic guidelines.

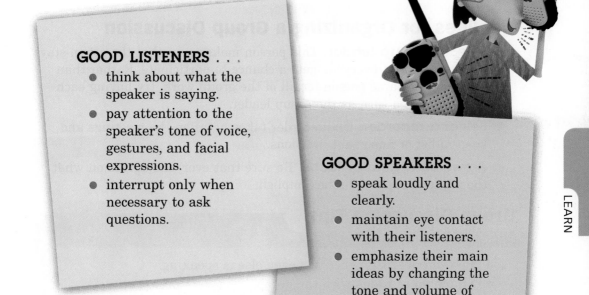

GOOD LISTENERS . . .

- think about what the speaker is saying.
- pay attention to the speaker's tone of voice, gestures, and facial expressions.
- interrupt only when necessary to ask questions.

GOOD SPEAKERS . . .

- speak loudly and clearly.
- maintain eye contact with their listeners.
- emphasize their main ideas by changing the tone and volume of their voice.

LEARN

 Focus on speaking and listening skills by trying this activity. One person in your class will be the speaker, and the rest will be listeners. Each listener will need a full sheet of paper and a pencil or pen. The speaker will read the following instructions.

1. Write your name at the top of your paper.

2. Fold your paper in half.

3. Draw a star in the middle of your paper.

4. Tear off the corner of your paper.
All listeners now compare their papers. Are they all the same? If they are not, discuss these two questions:

- What information did the speaker leave out?
- What questions did the listeners have about the directions?

Participating in a Group

When you participate in a group, you work together with others. That means you need to (1) listen to what the other members of the group say, (2) add to their thoughts, and (3) ask for their comments about your ideas. By following some basic guidelines and tips, you will be able to work smoothly within a group.

Guidelines for Organizing a Group Discussion

- **Select a group leader.** This person makes sure that the group stays focused and that everyone gets a chance to participate. Rather than selecting the same person for all of the group work, try having each member take a turn as the group leader.

- **Select a recorder.** The recorder takes notes on the meetings and keeps a list of important decisions.

- **Agree on a goal or focus.** Be sure that everyone agrees on what the group is supposed to accomplish.

Group Discussion Tips

- **Listen carefully** when someone else is speaking.
- **Share your ideas** with the group.
- **Be respectful at all times,** especially when you disagree with someone's ideas. ("I understand your point, but I think . . . ")
- **Stick to the topic** and keep your goal in mind.

 What would you do if . . . ? Imagine yourself in the situations below. Keeping in mind the guidelines and tips above, write a few sentences telling what you would do in each case.

SITUATION 1

You are assigned to be part of an English class discussion group, but everyone in the group talks all at once. What should you do?

SITUATION 2

You are the chairperson of a discussion group. One member keeps criticizing other members when they try to give their opinions. What should you do?

Group Skills

It's a pleasure to work in a group when the members respect each other, because the group will get more done. A few specific skills will improve a group's effectiveness: observing, cooperating, encouraging, and clarifying.

Observe the speaker by . . .

- watching body language, including facial expressions, gestures, and posture.
- listening to the tone of voice—excited, nervous, or shy.

Cooperate by . . .

- staying positive and waiting your turn.
- avoiding put-downs.
- being respectful when you disagree.

Encourage others by . . .

- complimenting them on their ideas.
- asking them for their opinions.

Clarify by . . .

- asking if there are any questions you can answer.
- restating a speaker's idea to be sure you understand it.

LEARN

Try IT Observe, cooperate, encourage, and clarify. Read the situations and questions below and discuss your answers with a classmate.

1. When Jim speaks, he talks too fast and looks out the window of the classroom.
   What impression will Jim's listeners get from the way he speaks?
2. Juana is shy about speaking in the group.
   What can group members do to encourage Juana to participate?
3. Yolanda notices that group members sometimes seem confused about what she is saying.
   What should Yolanda do when her listeners appear to be puzzled?

Speaking in Class

Speaking in class is sometimes like playing a sport—it's a team effort. You can only speak effectively in the classroom or have a good discussion when the group is working well together. These basic strategies will help you and your classmates become better speakers.

Before you speak . . .

- listen and take notes.
- think about what others are saying.
- wait until it's your turn to speak.
- plan how you can add something positive to the discussion.

When you speak . . .

- speak loudly and clearly.
- stick to the topic.
- avoid repeating what's already been said.
- support your ideas with examples.
- look at others in the group or class.

Play "Twenty-Question Who Am I?" In your group or class, select one person to play the part of the mystery guest. The mystery guest is a famous person whose identity everyone else has to guess by asking "yes" or "no" questions. As you play this game, practice using the strategies listed above.

1 Each player takes a turn asking one question until someone guesses who the famous person is.

2 The player who guesses correctly becomes the next mystery guest.

3 If no one guesses correctly within 20 questions, the mystery guest reveals his or her identity and becomes a new famous person.

Making Oral Presentations

"The world famous Flying Ling has just crawled into the loudspeaker. He gives the signal. The fuse is lit. This is one oral presentation that should start off with a bang. . . . "

Luckily, when you make an oral presentation, you won't have to crawl into a loudspeaker, but you might feel like crawling under a rock. "Stage fright" happens to everyone. Careful preparation is the key to overcoming this feeling and creating an effective oral presentation.
This chapter will lead you through the process.
With a little work, your presentation
will be a big hit!

Mini Index

- **Preparing Your Presentation**
- **Using Visual Aids**
- **Organizing an Informative Speech**
- **Delivering Your Speech**
- **Overcoming Stage Fright**

Preparing Your Presentation

Preparing an informative speech from a research report is different than writing a speech from scratch. You already have a topic, you've gathered lots of information, and you know the type of speech you will make. Here are some tips to help you shape the information from your report into a good speech.

- Grab your listeners' attention with an opening question or a surprising fact.
- Know how much time you have to give your presentation.
- Emphasize your most important points and cut unneeded information.
- Mark your paper for visual aids or gestures.

Rewriting in Action

Below is the opening of the research report on pages 382–386. Notice that the new beginning (on gold paper) has been revised to better fit the requirements of an oral presentation and get the listeners' attention.

An Ideal "King"

The United States has had more than 40 different presidents, all of them men. Some Americans have a hard time imagining a woman as their president. However, history gives many examples of women leading nations, such as Indira Gandhi of India and Golda Meir of Israel. Another example is the seventeenth-century African ruler Nzinga Mbande (Geen-gah Em-bahn-day), often just called "Ginga." By protecting her people from a takeover

Do you ever wonder why the United States has never elected a woman president? Although some Americans have a hard time imagining a woman as their leader, history gives many examples of women leading nations. An excellent example is Nzinga Mbande, a seventeenth-century African woman who protected her people from being taken over by another country.

Rework your beginning and think about the main points. Choose a research report you would like to present orally. Rewrite your opening so that it grabs your audience's attention. Then think about which important details you want to emphasize in your report.

Using Visual Aids

After you finish rewriting the beginning of your informative speech and choosing the most important details, it's time to gather visual aids for your presentation. Visual aids like those listed below are informative and will hold your listeners' interest.

Posters	show words, pictures, or both.
Photographs	help your audience "see" who or what you are talking about.
Charts	compare ideas or explain main points.
Transparencies	highlight key words, ideas, or graphics.
Maps	show specific places being discussed.
Objects	allow your audience to see the real thing.

Here are some tips for preparing your visual aids.

1 **Bigger is better.** Be sure your visual aids can be seen by the people in the back row.

2 **Keep the wording simple.** Sentences and paragraphs are out. Labels are in.

3 **Make your visual aids eye-catching.** Colorful and attractive designs are the key.

List visual aids. List a number of possible visual aids you could use in your presentation. Then select two that you think will work best. Jot down notes about how you will use them.

	Map	show a map of Africa and Europe
	Photograph	show a picture of Ginga

Organizing an Informative Speech

Now that you've written an exciting beginning and have gathered visual aids, you're ready to organize your speech. *Remember:* An informative speech is meant to teach your audience something. Clear organization is the key. Use the following tips.

1 **Start strong.** Grab the listeners' attention and keep it.

2 **Organize your details logically.** Put your details in the best order and use transitions to guide listeners from one idea to another.

3 **End even stronger.** Make sure that the last thing your audience hears is memorable.

Using Note Cards

Putting information on note cards is a simple and an effective way to organize your speech. The cards can contain your main points and are easier to handle during a presentation than sheets of notepaper. By using note cards, you also have more opportunity for eye contact.

For example, the student who developed an informative speech from her research report on pages 382–386 put her main ideas and details on note cards. She gave her speech using the note cards as a guide.

Note-Card Guidelines

- Write out your entire introduction on the first note card.
- Use a separate card for each of the main ideas that follow.
- Number each card and write the main idea at the top. Add specific details for that idea underneath.
- Note your visual aids on appropriate cards, with instructions for what to do with each one.
- Write out your entire ending on the last note card.

Create your note cards. Look over the note cards on the next page. Then create a note card for each step in your presentation. Be sure to add notes to yourself about visual aids. Also write a memorable ending.

1

Introduction

Do you ever wonder why the United States has never elected a woman president? Although some Americans have a hard time imagining a woman as their leader, history gives many examples of women leading nations. An excellent example is Nzinga Mbande, a seventeenth-century African woman who protected her people from

2

When and where Ginga lived.

(Use map visual aid.)

– Lived from about 1583 to 1663.

– Lived in Western Africa

– Angola

3

Troubles with Portuguese.

(Use map—visual aid.)

– Ginga's father was king and fought three wars against Portuguese.

– After her father died, her brother became king,

4

Diplomacy Skills

– Ginga sent by her brother to make treaty with

5

Ending

Today, Ginga is still remembered as a hero in Africa. She is also respected in Europe, even in Portugal. She was a great diplomat, a fierce war leader, and a strong ruler. Ginga, the queen who called herself "King," showed that a good leader could be either a male or a female.

LEARN

Delivering Your Speech

Both your voice and your body communicate your message. At times, your movements, facial expressions, and gestures have as much meaning as your words. This is especially true during an informative speech. The following suggestions can help.

Using Body Language

1 **Keep your shoulders back** but stay relaxed. If you look at ease, your audience can concentrate on your presentation.

2 **Breathe deeply** and give yourself a moment to think about what you will say.

3 **Make eye contact,** but if looking at your audience is hard for you, look slightly above their heads.

4 **Be yourself** and let your facial expressions reflect what you're saying. Artificial expressions and gestures will distract your listeners.

5 **Use simple hand gestures,** such as pointing to a visual aid, to add emphasis and interest.

Using Your Voice

The way that you use your voice can add to the meaning of your words. The three most important characteristics of your speaking voice are *volume, tone,* and *speed*.

Volume	Speak loudly enough so that the people at the back of the room can hear you.
Tone	Stress important words to help listeners focus on your most important ideas.
Speed	Speak at a relaxed pace. Rushing is one of the most common faults in making oral presentations.

Practice and present. Using the tips above, practice delivering your presentation. If you practice in front of friends or family members, consider their suggestions.

Overcoming Stage Fright

If you think you're the only one who feels nervous speaking in front of a group, you're wrong. Everyone feels that way at one time or another. There are things that you can do to relax and reduce "stage fright."

1 **Practice, practice, practice.**

Preparation is the key. The more often you rehearse your speech, the more relaxed you will be. Practicing in front of friends or family will also help you get used to having an audience.

2 **Take a deep breath.**

Arrange your notes. Look around before you begin. Don't rush into your speech.

3 **Focus.**

Concentrate on what you are doing and on what comes next. Visualize the steps in your presentation.

Using a Checklist

Practice your presentation using the checklist below. If possible, videotape yourself so that you can see what you do well and what you can improve. Also consider having someone else watch your presentation and make suggestions.

_____ **1.** I stand up straight, and I look relaxed.

_____ **2.** I maintain eye contact with my audience instead of staring at my notes.

_____ **3.** My voice is loud and clear.

_____ **4.** My voice and appearance show that I am interested in my topic.

_____ **5.** I speak at a natural pace (not too fast or too slow).

_____ **6.** I avoid "stalling" words like *um, er,* and *like.*

_____ **7.** My visual aids are large and easy to understand.

_____ **8.** I make gestures for emphasis, and I point out my visual aids.

LEARN

Presentation Tips

Before your presentation . . .

- **Get everything organized.**
  Put the main points of your speech on note cards and make your visual aids.

- **Time your speech.**
  If it's too long or too short, adjust the length by adding or removing note cards.

- **Practice.**
  The more you remember without looking at your notes, the easier it will be to give the presentation.

During your presentation . . .

- **Project your voice.**
  Be sure everyone can hear you.

- **Speak clearly and slowly.**
  Don't rush through your speech.

- **Maintain eye contact.**
  Make a connection with your audience.

- **Hold visual aids so that everyone can see them.**
  Point out the things that you are talking about.

After your presentation . . .

- **Answer questions.**
  Clarify any information that your listeners ask about.

- **Make closing comments.**
  Summarize the listeners' questions and concerns.

Practice and present. Have a final practice with a friend or someone at home. After you make your speech in the classroom, listen for suggestions from your teacher and classmates. You can try out these ideas in your next speech.

Keeping Journals and Learning Logs

Every day, amazing thoughts go through your mind. Journals and learning logs can capture and organize these thoughts and can also help you to become a better writer and thinker.

A journal lets you reflect on your daily experiences. In the same way, a learning log lets you reflect on classroom experiences. When you write learning-log entries, you think about what you are learning and gain a deeper understanding of the material.

This chapter will teach you more about journals, learning logs, and other writing-to-learn activities.

Mini Index

- **Writing in a Travel Journal**
- **Writing in Other Journals**
- **Writing in a Learning Log**
- **Writing-to-Learn Activities**

Writing in a Travel Journal

When you travel, you have new experiences. Perhaps you sleep in a tent in the woods, touch a porpoise at an aquarium, or see trees that have turned to stone. A travel journal can help you think about such experiences. You don't have to organize your thoughts into an essay—you just record them.

Getting Started

To get started on your own travel journal, follow these steps:

1 Gather the proper tools.

All you need is some paper and your favorite pen or pencil. You can buy a special journal or a blank book, or an ordinary school notebook—whatever you wish. You can even use a portable computer if you have one available.

2 Establish a regular routine.

Choose a time of day for journaling. Maybe you'll write at night, just before going to sleep, or first thing in the morning. When you write, find a comfortable place where you won't be interrupted.

3 Write for at least 5 to 10 minutes at a time.

Write freely. This may seem hard at first, but you'll relax as time goes on. After several days, look back at your earlier efforts. You'll probably notice a big improvement in the length and quality of your writing.

4 Write about things that are important to you.

Here are some topic ideas to consider:
- interesting things you see and hear,
- personal thoughts and feelings,
- daily happenings, or
- funny or surprising stories

5 Return to your writing.

Go back and read your travel journal from time to time. Mark ideas and entries that you would like to write more about in the future. Watch for possible story or poem ideas.

Start your journal writing. Write in a journal the next time you go somewhere. Review your entries a week or two later and explain how you might develop one of them into a longer piece.

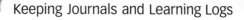

Travel Journal Entry

In the journal entry below, a student writes about her first airplane trip. She went to her cousin's wedding in Los Angeles with her parents and her brother Eric.

June 16

When we got on the plane to Los Angeles this morning, I couldn't believe how big it was! I was worried that the pilots wouldn't get the thing off the ground with the hundreds of people in it, but at 9:00 we took off with no problems. Later, the flight attendants brought us a snack. Eric complained there wasn't enough to eat, but he always says that at home, too. I liked the little bags of pretzels.

I fell asleep, and later I woke up when a pilot announced we were over the Pacific Ocean. Eric told me they had missed LA and we were flying to Japan, but pretty soon the plane swung around and we headed down to our landing at Los Angeles International Airport.

We waited at the baggage claim for a long time, because Eric's bag didn't show up. After about a half hour, we went to the office where you report lost luggage. When the man in the office asked Eric what his bag looked like, Eric got a blank look on his face. He finally told Mom and Dad that he thought his bag was still sitting in his bedroom in Chicago. I told him I thought that it was probably on its way to Japan. I didn't know that flying could be so funny.

LEARN

When you write a journal entry about an experience, focus on the most important details. The following two questions will help you.

What was most surprising or interesting about the experience?

What did I learn from the experience?

Writing in Other Journals

Travel journals can help you reflect on school trips, vacations, and other journeys. Here are some other types of journals for you to try.

Personal Journal

A personal journal contains thoughts and observations about your life and experiences. Certain entries may inspire you to create longer pieces of writing. Sometimes personal journals contain poems, stories, and jokes.

Diary

A diary is like a personal journal, but a diary focuses more on daily events and experiences. The entries are often shorter, and the details are more specific. A diary is a history of your day-to-day life.

Specialized Journal

A specialized journal focuses on an ongoing activity or experience. It can be a separate journal or a section set aside in your regular journal or diary. You may want to use a specialized journal to explore your thoughts while practicing for a school play, participating in a team sport, or working on a group project.

Reader-Response Journal

A reader-response journal is an excellent way for you to reflect about the content of a book, magazine, or textbook chapter you're reading. Here are some questions that will help you write about what you read.

1 What were my main impressions after reading the opening? After reading half of the selection? After finishing?

2 Did the reading change my understanding or feelings about anything? In what way?

3 Does the reading connect with my life?

4 What is most important about the reading? An idea? A theme? A character?

5 Would I recommend this reading to others? Why?

Write in a specialized journal. The next time you are involved in an ongoing activity or experience, set aside a section of your notebook to write about your thoughts. Use the explanation above to help you get started with your specialized journal.

Writing in a Learning Log

Learning logs are outstanding tools for students. They can be made to fit any school subject and are especially useful for making sense out of new or difficult material.

 Create a learning log for any subject.
Difficult subjects are made easier when you write about them.

 Keep your learning log in good order.
Either keep a separate notebook or make a learning-log entry after each day's class notes in your regular notebook. Date each entry and leave margins to add information later.

3 **Make charts and drawings.**
Illustrations and graphic organizers can help you understand difficult concepts.

4 **Write freely about any of the following:**
- the key idea from a reading assignment or lecture,
- your questions, or
- how the material relates to your experience.

LEARN

English Class   Mar. 7

high point

Key words about plot: rising action
beginning = The setting,
characters, and conflict   beginning   ending
are introduced.
rising action = A character
struggles to try to solve a problem.
high point = The most important or exciting part of
the story—the turning point.
ending = The problem is solved, and the story ends.

   In the beginning of Langston Hughes's story
"Thank You, Ma'am," I thought Roger's treatment
of Mrs. Washington was very rude. This was not a
conflict that I would have handled well. Then she

Science Log

The learning-log entry below was written after a science class discussion about how heat flows from one object to another. Learning logs work best if you put ideas into your own words and include drawings and other graphic aids.

Science Class   Feb. 5

Heat Transfer (The flow of heat)

Key words:
conduction, convection, radiation

   I never thought much about how heat moves from one place to another. Now I know that hot and cold air move in different directions. I also know that metal and cloth can be the same temperature, but metal will feel hotter or colder because of conduction. Also, the bank thermometer on the corner is often wrong because it sits in the sun and heats up from radiation.

Convection is the reason that my bedroom is hot in the summer.

Hot air rises.

Log on in science. On your own paper, write down the subject of the science unit you are currently studying. Then write a learning-log entry about something in the unit that you find interesting, surprising, or confusing.

Math Log

Keeping a math log is a good way to focus on the concepts taught in your math class. One way to set up a math log is to use a question-answer pattern. Write a question related to the day's lesson and then answer that question. Two examples are shown below.

Math Class   Sept. 13
Question: Who invented zero?
Answer: I couldn't understand why somebody had to invent zero. Wasn't it always there? It all became clear when Ms. Jackson told us that Hindus in India worked out a number system based on ten places. In about 200 C.E., they used a dot that meant "empty" as the tenth numeral. Later, the dot became a small circle—zero.

                                                    Sept. 14
Question: How does zero work together with the other numerals?
Answer:
   Any number + or − 0 = the original number.
   If I have five cookies and add none or take none away, I still have five cookies. Simple.

   Any number x 0 = 0. I think of multiplying by 0 as the opposite of adding 0. I end up with 0 instead of the number. I can't multiply or divide something that's not there in the first place, right?

LEARN

Log on in math. On your own paper, write a learning-log entry for math. First write down a question about a math concept you are studying. Then answer that question. (Use the samples above as a guide.)

Social Studies Log

In the following sample, the student writes about a period of history that was introduced in her social studies class. She reflects on how her life might be different today if events had happened differently back then.

Social Studies   Nov. 17

Magna Carta

Mr. Simpson was telling us about how the feudal lords in England forced bad King John to sign the Magna Carta in 1215. Mr. S. said that the Magna Carta was the basis for our Constitution and Declaration of Independence. What really hit me was that the king basically agreed to obey the same laws as everyone else.

More than 500 years later, Americans rebelled because they were being treated poorly under different laws than the people in England had. So here's the part I think is amazing. If John had been a better king, he might not have been forced to sign the Magna Carta. If George III had been a better king, there might not have been an American Revolution. It's hard for me to believe we have all this freedom because of two bad kings. The M.C. was really important to us and to everybody in the world who has a government like ours.

Last summer, Uncle Bill was in England and visited the place where King John signed the Magna Carta.

Log on in social studies. On your own paper, write the subject of the unit you are now studying in social studies. Then write an entry about something in the unit that you can relate to in a personal way.

Writing-to-Learn Activities

There are many different ways to write in a learning log. Three basic ways are described below, and five additional approaches are discussed on the next page.

The Basic Three

1 **Freewriting** When you freewrite in a learning log, you write quickly about a subject you are studying. Writing freely and rapidly allows you to explore a subject from many different angles. Don't stop to correct your writing—just keep writing. Try to write for at least 5 to 10 minutes at a time.

2 **Clustering** Clustering works well in a learning log because the cluster actually gives you a picture of how ideas fit together. Place the subject you are studying in the center of the page and circle it. Then write words and phrases about the subject. Circle each one and draw a line connecting it to the closest related word. (See page **544**.)

3 **Listing** Listing is another way to discover how ideas relate to each other. As you think about a subject, make a list of ideas, feelings, and questions that come to mind.

LEARN

Stopping the Use of Tobacco

—nicotine and carbon monoxide in blood drop the first day
—heart rate and blood pressure get lower the first week
—heart disease and cancer risk lower within a few years
—stop wasting money on bad habit
— Why is it so hard to quit smoking?
—Which method of stopping is the most successful?
  (Nicotine patch, hypnosis, and so on)

After listing for 3 or 4 minutes, you may find it helpful to freewrite about the subject using one or more of the ideas in your list.

Try IT Make a list like the one above for a subject you are studying in one of your classes. *Remember:* Write the subject at the top of your list. Keep listing until you run out of ideas.

Special Writing Activities

The learning-log activities on this page are quite different from each other and can be used for special purposes. As you read about them, try to think of a class in which each one would help you.

First Thoughts When you begin a new unit in one of your classes, write about your first impressions. Does the new material sound difficult or easy? Can you connect it with something you've learned before?

Stop 'n' Write After you get into the middle of new material, stop and write down what you are thinking, including any questions that you may have. This will help you understand what you are studying.

Picture Outlining A picture can help you "see" what you're learning. Make a drawing to help you understand and remember a set of ideas. Your drawing can be a diagram that the teacher has put on the board, or your drawing can be of your own "mental picture."

Role-Playing Imagine yourself as an eyewitness to some important event. Write about what happened as if you were a reporter or bystander at the time of the event.

Personal Summary Summarize a reading assignment or a lecture and put the information in your own words. Adding your own thoughts and experiences will help you understand and remember the material. The sample below is about a biology lesson.

> Mr. Petrie's leaf diagram looks like a big layer cake. In the middle of the leaf "cake" are plastids—little structures that have lots of green chlorophyll in them. They also contain yellow and orange, but in summer the chlorophyll blocks those colors. The sap has reds and purples, which are also blocked by the green.
>
> I think the leaf is like a big glass jar filled with yellow, red, orange, and purple marbles. But you can't see the marbles because someone has put dark green food coloring in water and then poured it into the jar.

 Write a personal summary of a recent class lesson. Try to recall the main points from memory rather than looking at your class notes.

Taking Notes

Have you ever thought about how many ideas fly around a classroom in a day? One of the best ways to catch new ideas is to write them down. Note taking is a simple form of classroom writing. Taking good notes can help you organize your thoughts and increase your understanding of new ideas.

Taking notes also helps you remember. People who forget their grocery lists at home often manage to buy everything they need anyway. Just having written the items down boosts a shopper's memory. Likewise, if you take good notes, you're more likely to remember the information your teachers share.

Taking notes is one of the most valuable writing skills you can develop. There aren't a lot of rules for note taking—just a few guidelines that will make this specialized form of writing one of your most important learning tools.

Mini Index

- **Taking Classroom Notes**
- **Taking Reading Notes**

page 11
How Hot-Air Balloons Fly
Scientific Principles
* Warm air rises in cooler air.
* Wind blows in different directions
  at different altitudes.
Three Parts of a Balloon (3 B's)
Burner—heats the air
envelope—holds the air
pilot

Taking Classroom Notes

Taking notes can help you learn new material and prepare for tests. Note taking helps you . . .

- pay attention,
- understand, and
- remember.

Guidelines for Note Taking

1 **Write the topic and date at the top of each page.**
Also number your pages. If a page gets out of order, you'll know where it belongs.

2 **When the teacher introduces the topic, listen for the main ideas.**
For example, if your teacher says, "The cerebrum and cerebellum have different functions," you can be prepared to list those functions under one of the main parts—the cerebrum or the cerebellum.

3 **Be alert for signal words.**
Signal words include *most important, as a result, finally,* and so on.

4 **Put the main ideas in your own words.**
Saying things your own way can help you understand new ideas.

5 **Organize your notes with numbers, words, or symbols.**
For example, you can identify the steps in a process using *first, second, third,* and so on, or you can use an asterisk (*) to indicate a main idea.

6 **Write down new or important terms and their meanings.**
Be sure to make a note if there's something you don't understand. Then ask your teacher or look for more information later.

7 **Pay attention to what the teacher writes on the board.**
What's on the board is often the most important information.

[
Don't get so involved in trying to write down every word that you miss the main ideas. If you listen carefully, you will be able to fill in details later.
]

Compare some of your recent class notes with the guidelines above to see if there are areas where you can improve.

Setting Up Your Notes

Keep your notes in a notebook, preferably one for each subject. (Follow your teacher's instructions for the type and size of each notebook.) Keep your notes neat and leave wide margins. This makes your notes easier to read and illustrate. The side notes below give additional tips.

LEARN

page 11

How Hot-Air Balloons Fly   Oct. 17

Scientific Principles
 * Warm air rises in cooler air.
 * Wind blows in different directions
    at different altitudes.

Leave wide margins.

Three Parts of a Balloon (3 B's)
 1. Burner—heats the air
 2. Balloon envelope—holds the air
 3. Basket—carries pilot

Make sketches.

Steps in Launching a Balloon
 1. Attach propane burner to basket
    and then attach basket to balloon.
 2. Unroll balloon.
 3. Inflate balloon with huge fan.
 4. Ignite burner flame to heat air in balloon.
 5. Climb into basket.
 6. Ground crew lets the balloon go.

Skip a line between ideas.

Flying the Balloon
 1. Blast large flame to heat air and ascend.
 2. Open parachute valve at top of balloon
    to let hot air out and descend.

Reviewing Your Notes

Review your notes each day.

- **In the margins, briefly note any questions that you have.** Ask your teacher or a classmate to help you understand any difficult concepts; then add the explanation to your notes.

- **Follow up on any words you don't understand.** Look up unfamiliar terms in a dictionary and add the correct spelling and meaning to your notes.

- **Rewrite your notes if they are confusing or unreadable.** Keep your notes organized so that you will be able to understand them later.

- **Read your notes before the next class.** Then you'll be ready for a class discussion or a test.

page 11

How Hot-Air Balloons Fly   Oct. 17

Scientific Principles
  * Warm air rises in cooler air.
  * Wind blows in different directions
      at different altitudes.

envelope:
the balloon
before   Three Parts of a Balloon (3 B's)
it is   1. Burner—heats the air
filled   2. Balloon envelope—holds the air
with   3. Basket—carries pilot
hot air

Steps in Launching a Balloon
  1. Attach propane burner to basket   Find out
      and then attach basket to balloon. if this is
  2. Unroll balloon.   dangerous. Does balloon ever
  3. Inflate balloon with huge fan. catch on fire?
  4. Ignite burner flame to heat air in balloon.
  5. Climb into basket.
  6. Ground crew lets the balloon go.

Review your work. How well does your note taking compare with the suggestions on this page? Which suggestion would improve your notes the most?

Taking Reading Notes

If you take notes when you read, you will understand and remember the information better. As you read, pause to jot down important ideas. Here are some tips for taking reading notes.

1   Skim an assignment before reading it.

Preview the title, introduction, headings, and chapter summaries. Study the pictures, charts, or other graphics. These steps can give you many of the main ideas before you start reading.

2   Take notes while you read.

Concentrate on what you are reading and write down only what is important.

- **Note each heading or subtopic.** Write down the heading and all the important facts you find there.
- **Write your notes in your own words.** Rewording the text will help you to understand and remember the material.
- **Summarize the information in pictures, charts, or maps.** Making your own drawings is another option.
- **Read challenging material out loud.** *Hearing* what you are reading will help you understand the information better.
- **List words that are new to you.** Find definitions in a dictionary or glossary and write them down. Be sure you understand how the words fit into the reading before you move on.
- **Go through your notes.** Review your notes and write down any questions you have.

3   Add graphic organizers to your notes.

Use any of the helpful organizers on the next three pages for taking notes.

 The next time you have a reading assignment, take reading notes. Use the tips from this page.

Using a Cause-Effect Organizer

Cause-and-effect writing shows how or why things happen. It may be one cause that has many effects, several causes and several effects, or lots of causes for one effect. The article "Northward Ho!" below tells about one effect that has several causes. The **cause-effect organizer** to the right of the article is an example of a good way to chart this type of writing.

Northward Ho!

For many reasons, the people of the Middle Americas were urged to move to the north. Some Spaniards moved north because they wanted more land or gold, and some wanted to spread Christianity. The Spanish also ventured north because there was not much food in the south.

In less than 50 years, the land that is now the south-western part of the United States had changed hands three times. This all began when the Spanish moved.

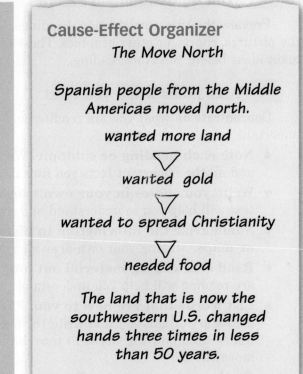

Cause-Effect Organizer
The Move North

Spanish people from the Middle Americas moved north.

wanted more land

▽

wanted gold

▽

wanted to spread Christianity

▽

needed food

The land that is now the southwestern U.S. changed hands three times in less than 50 years.

Try IT Read the following paragraph about Spanish claims to the Southwest. Then create an organizer that shows the causes and their effect.

1 The Spanish felt they could claim part of the southwestern
2 United States because Coronado had explored it. He was
3 looking for the golden city of Cibola. First Coronado went to
4 New Mexico looking for the golden city but found only a Zuni
5 pueblo. He sent men east and west, but they found only the
6 Rio Grande and the Grand Canyon. Then Coronado went north
7 to Kansas, but he didn't find the city of gold there, either.
8 He returned to Mexico a failure, but his travels allowed the
9 Spanish to claim the desert Southwest.

Using a Table Organizer

Some types of writing are organized around a main idea. Each main idea is supported by details, the way a tabletop is supported by legs. Essays, articles, feature stories, and textbook chapters are usually organized in this way.

Read the following paragraph, "Don't Hold Your Breath." Then look at the **table organizer** to see how one student took notes on this reading.

Don't Hold Your Breath

Marine mammals can stay under the water longer than we can because their bodies are built differently. When a marine mammal dives, its heart rate drops dramatically—to as low as four to six beats per minute! In addition, marine mammals such as seals and whales have more oxygen-carrying cells in their blood than humans do. Finally, they have more blood. For example, a seal can have two to three times more blood than a man. It can even store oxygen-rich blood in its huge spleen.

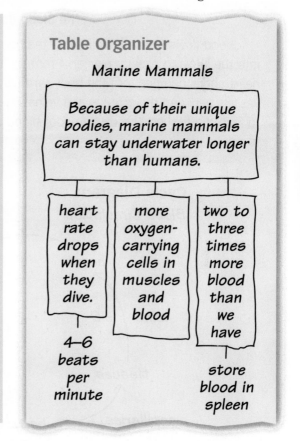

Table Organizer

Marine Mammals

Because of their unique bodies, marine mammals can stay underwater longer than humans.

| heart rate drops when they dive. | more oxygen-carrying cells in muscles and blood | two to three times more blood than we have |

4–6 beats per minute

store blood in spleen

LEARN

Try IT Read the following paragraph about marine mammals. Then take notes on it using a table organizer. Put the main idea in the top box (the tabletop). Under it, put supporting details (the table legs).

1   There are three main orders of marine mammals: carnivora,
2 cetacea, and sirenia. Carnivora are meat eaters that live on land
3 or in the sea. This group includes seals, sea lions, otters, and
4 even polar bears! Cetacea are meat eaters that live in the open
5 ocean. This group includes whales, dolphins, and porpoises.
6 Finally, sirenia are plant eaters that live in warm tropical waters
7 near shorelines. This group includes dugongs and manatees.

Using a Cycle Diagram

Science writing often describes various processes that are repeated. A **cycle diagram** is an effective way to record the steps or details in such a process. Read the paragraph below. Then look at the cycle diagram one student made to remember the details.

The Blood Circle

Blood flows from the veins into the heart. The heart pumps the blood into the lungs to pick up oxygen. From the lungs, the blood returns to the heart and is pumped into the body through the arteries. Capillaries are little vessels between the arteries and veins where the oxygen leaves the blood to feed the tissues. The oxygen-poor blood collects in the veins and returns to the heart.

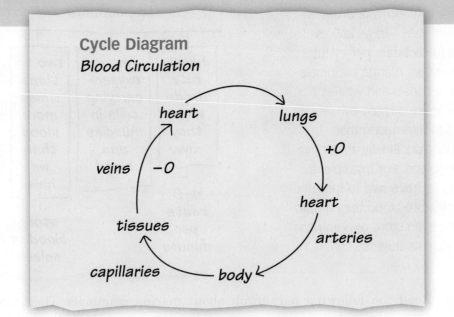

Cycle Diagram
Blood Circulation

 Read the following brief paragraph about the birth of the stars. Then create a cycle diagram that shows the process.

1 Some stars eventually produce more stars. A nebula of gas
2 and dust is pulled together by gravity. It gets very hot and forms
3 a star that gives off heat and light. The star gradually runs out of
4 fuel and turns into a red giant. The red giant may explode into a
5 supernova. Gas and dust fly away from the supernova and form a
6 nebula, which can form a new star.

Completing Writing Assignments

Have you ever gotten lost in a writing assignment? You thought you knew where you were going, but you reached the second paragraph and hit "the wall." You couldn't move forward, you couldn't move backward, and there was no end in sight. What a frustrating "place" to be!

This chapter is your writing compass, and it will help you navigate through even the most difficult writing assignments. By plotting your course before you head out and by checking for milestones along the way, you'll soon reach your writing goal.

Mini Index

- **Understanding the Assignment**
- **Thinking Through Each Assignment**
- **Setting Up an Assignment Schedule**

Understanding the Assignment

There are three basic kinds of writing assignments.

OPEN-ENDED

An open-ended assignment allows you to select your own topic. (Write a story about your most embarrassing moment.)

SPECIFIC

A specific assignment provides the topic for you. (Explain why the sky is blue.)

COMBINATION

A combination assignment gives one part of the topic but allows you to select another part. (Compare today's teen fashion with teen fashion from another era.)

Try IT Decide if each of the assignments below is open-ended, specific, or a combination. Write your answers on your own paper.

1. *Tell how a cell phone works.*
2. *Persuade others to watch your favorite TV show.*
3. *Compare jogging with some other form of exercise.*

Assignment Checklist

Make sure that you understand everything about your writing assignment before you begin. Use the following checklist as a guide.

_____ 1. **Plan ahead** so that you have enough time to do a good job.

_____ 2. **Know what is expected** in the assignment.

_____ 3. **Follow the directions** and ask questions.

_____ 4. **Focus on key words**—*persuade, explain, recall*—so you know exactly what your writing should do.

_____ 5. **Revise and improve** your writing.

Thinking Through Each Assignment

Your brain thinks in a lot of different ways, including *recalling, understanding, applying, analyzing, synthesizing,* and *evaluating.* Different writing assignments ask you to use different kinds of thinking. The chart below briefly describes these thinking tasks, and the next six pages give you a closer look at each one.

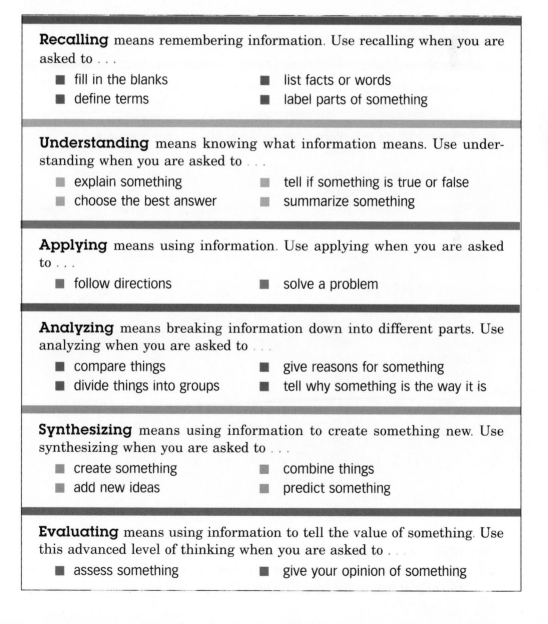

Recalling means remembering information. Use recalling when you are asked to . . .

- fill in the blanks
- define terms
- list facts or words
- label parts of something

Understanding means knowing what information means. Use understanding when you are asked to . . .

- explain something
- choose the best answer
- tell if something is true or false
- summarize something

Applying means using information. Use applying when you are asked to . . .

- follow directions
- solve a problem

Analyzing means breaking information down into different parts. Use analyzing when you are asked to . . .

- compare things
- divide things into groups
- give reasons for something
- tell why something is the way it is

Synthesizing means using information to create something new. Use synthesizing when you are asked to . . .

- create something
- add new ideas
- combine things
- predict something

Evaluating means using information to tell the value of something. Use this advanced level of thinking when you are asked to . . .

- assess something
- give your opinion of something

LEARN

Recalling

Recalling is remembering what you have learned. To prepare for this type of thinking, listen carefully in class, read your assignments, and take careful notes.

You recall when you . . .

- study the information until you can remember it.
- write down facts, terms, and definitions.

The following test questions ask the student to recall.

DIRECTIONS: Fill in the blanks below with the correct answers.

1. The Middle Ages in Europe lasted about _____ (number) years.

2. Kings awarded land to their nobles under the _____ system.

DIRECTIONS: Define each term by completing the sentence.

1. A lord's *manor* was his _____

_____ .

2. *Guilds* were _____

_____ .

recall

Try IT   Work with a classmate to review your notes on a topic that you are studying. Then ask each other questions to see how many details the two of you can *recall* from the notes.

Understanding

Understanding information is knowing what it means. If you are able to accurately put the information in your own words, then you clearly understand it.

You understand when you . . .

- **explain something in your own words.**
- **tell how something works.**
- **summarize information.**

The following question asks the student to show understanding, and the answer does that.

LEARN

DIRECTIONS: Explain how the feudal system worked in the European Middle Ages.

During the Middle Ages, a king gave land to his nobles. In return, the nobles supplied soldiers for the king's army. Peasants worked the land in return for protection from thieves and invading armies. The peasants had to give most of what they produced to the noble and got to keep only as much as they needed to survive. The lives of the peasants, also known as serfs, were controlled by the noble. That noble, lord of the manor, even made the laws and enforced them.

understand

 Try It Write a paragraph explaining your *understanding* of something you've recently learned in social studies class.

Applying

When you *apply* information, you understand it well enough to use it.

You apply when you . . .

- use information to solve problems.
- select the most important facts or details.

In this assignment, the writer reviews information and chooses the most important details.

ASSIGNMENT: Why did the feudal system last so long in medieval Europe? Give the most important reason.

The feudal system lasted for a long time in medieval Europe because the family was its basic unit. These were not the families of the peasants, but of the nobles who controlled the land. Huge estates remained in these upper-class families for hundreds of years. The reason for this was that all across Europe, laws were passed so that only the oldest son in the family could inherit the property. Under these laws, the property was never broken up, and the original families continued the feudal system.

apply

 Write a journal entry about an important reason for a problem in today's world or in your school.

Analyzing

Analyzing information is breaking it down into parts. There are many different ways to analyze information.

You analyze when you . . .

- tell how things are alike or different.
- tell which parts are most important.
- divide things into different groups.
- give reasons for something.

In this assignment, the writer tells how two periods of time are alike and different.

ASSIGNMENT: How is life today both better and worse than it was for a serf in the Middle Ages?

Life today is better than the life of a serf in the Middle Ages. We have more freedoms. No one controls our lives like the nobles did back then. We can own property, change jobs, and move to new places. Also, we have the right to a fair trial, unlike the peasants.

In one way, the serfs seemed to have it better than we do. Their lives were simpler than ours. They knew what they were supposed to do, and they knew that someone would take care of them. Knowing that they would be protected must have been a good feeling.

analyze

LEARN

Try IT Give reasons why cell phones or some other recent technology have become so popular.

Synthesizing

When you *synthesize*, you create something new using information you have already learned.

You synthesize when you . . .

- add some new ideas to existing information.
- use information to make up a story or other creative writing.
- predict the future based on this information.

In this assignment, the writer uses information to imagine living in medieval times.

ASSIGNMENT: Imagine that you and a friend live in another time and place. Write a short narrative that describes how you each would live.

My friend Hob leaves today. He is the squire to Sir Nicolet. Lord Halfdome promised Sir Nicolet to the king for his wars against France, so Hob has to leave, too. I will probably never see him again because these French wars seem to go on forever. Hob will ride away wearing a shirt embroidered with spring flowers. I wear the plain-colored tunic of the household. That's only the beginning of how different our lives will be. I will be trained to be the next bailiff of the manor. Hob will visit foreign lands and see wonders, while I will spend my life on the lord's estate. Oh well, we must do as we are told.

synthesize

 Write your own narrative about how you and a friend would live in a time or place you are studying in social studies.

recall *apply* UNDERSTAND
analyze synthesize evaluate **457**
Completing Writing Assignments

Evaluating

When you *evaluate*, you tell the value of something. Before you can evaluate something, you must know a lot about it.

You evaluate when you . . .

- ● tell your opinion about something.
- ● tell the good points and bad points about something.

In this assignment, the writer gives her opinion about a historical event.

ASSIGNMENT: What is your opinion about the importance of the Black Death in the medieval world?

I think that the spread of the Black Death (bubonic plague) was the most important event of the medieval period. It killed about one out of three people in Europe and Asia. It was a horrible, disgusting way to die, and whole cities fell apart in fear. The Church couldn't explain it, so people lost faith. There weren't enough peasants and laborers alive to work the fields, so the feudal system fell apart. Today we worry about cancer, AIDS, and diseases we will probably never get, like Ebola virus. If we had a plague like the Black Death, it would change our world.

evaluate

Try IT Write a paragraph that explains your opinion about country music, whole-grain bread, or exercise.

Setting Up an Assignment Schedule

Your teacher may give you a schedule to follow for completing your writing assignments. If not, you can set up your own. Let's say that you have been asked to write a persuasive essay, and it is due in two weeks. Here's a suggested schedule.

Day	Week 1	Day	Week 2
1	**PREWRITING:** • Review the assignment and the assessment rubric. • Begin a topic search.	1	**REVISING:** • Revise the completed draft for ideas and organization.
2	**PREWRITING:** • Choose a writing topic. • Start gathering details.	2	**REVISING:** • Revise the draft for voice. • Ask a peer to review it.
3	**PREWRITING:** • Gather and organize details. • Find a focus for the writing.	3	**REVISING:** • Check for word choice and sentence fluency.
4	**WRITING:** • Begin the first draft.	4	**EDITING:** • Check for conventions. • Write and proofread the final copy.
5	**WRITING:** • Complete the first draft.	5	**PUBLISHING:** • Share the final copy.

✱ Change this schedule to fit your assignment. For example, if you have a week to do your work, you could focus on one step in the writing process per day.

Scheduling a Timed Writing

If you must complete a piece of writing in a single class period (for example, 45 minutes), it is very important to plan your work. Try to set aside 5 to 10 minutes at the beginning of the period to plan your writing, 25 to 30 minutes for drafting, and about 5 to 10 minutes at the end to make any necessary changes.

Taking Classroom Tests

Everyone gets a little nervous about tests. They're hardly ever fun, but they are a fact of life in school. Teachers use tests to find out how well you are learning the material in their classes, and your grades, in some part, depend on how well you do on tests.

Although tests are unavoidable, you can make your life easier by preparing well for them. You need to keep up with your daily work, pay attention in class, and take good notes. After you take care of these basics, this chapter will help you understand how tests work and what you can do to get ready for them.

Mini Index

- **Preparing for a Test**
- **Taking Objective Tests**
- **Taking Essay Tests**

ience Test: The Weather

thunderstorm forms,

Preparing for a Test

Getting ready for a test isn't a one-night effort. It's a cycle that begins the moment the teacher introduces new material. The chart below will help you understand the cycle of test preparation.

Take good notes.
- Take notes in class.
- Finish assignments on time.
- Review your notes once a week.

Learn from the test.
- Notice what you do well and think about how you can improve.
- If there's something you don't understand, ask a question.

Ask questions.
- Ask what the test will cover.
- Ask what types of questions will be on the test (multiple-choice, essay, and so on).

Study for the test.
- Transfer key information to note cards.
- Read your note cards aloud.
- Picture the information in your mind.
- Explain the information to someone else.

Test-Taking Tips

Before you begin . . .

- **Listen** carefully to the instructions.
- **Write** your name on your paper.
- **Check the clock** to see how much time you have.

During the test . . .

- **Skim the whole test quickly** so that you can plan your time.
- **Read and answer each question carefully.**
- **Skip difficult questions** and come back to them later.
- **Watch the time** so that you can finish the whole test.

After you've finished the test . . .

- **Go back and check your answers,** if you have time.
- **Be sure that you have put your name on the test.**

One of the most important ways to prepare for a test is to get a good night's sleep beforehand. Also make sure to eat a good breakfast. If your body is rested and fed, your mind is free to work.

 Write a paragraph about an upcoming test. In your paragraph, answer the following questions.

1. What information will the test cover, and what types of questions will appear on the test?

2. What will be the most difficult area for you?

3. Would it be helpful to study with someone else for this test? Why or why not?

LEARN

Taking Objective Tests

Objective tests have four common types of questions: true/false, matching, multiple-choice, and fill-in-the-blanks. Depending upon what type of question you're answering, you'll want to keep certain tips in mind.

True/False

On this type of test, you decide whether a statement is true or false.

■ Remember that if *any* part of the statement is false, the answer is "false."

False **A barometer measures humidity in the air.**
(A barometer measures air pressure.)

■ Look carefully at words like *always, all, every, never, none,* or *no.* Few things are always or never true.

False **Lightning never strikes twice in the same place.**
(The word "never" makes this statement false.)

■ Be aware of words containing the contraction for "not": *doesn't, don't, isn't, wasn't.* Make sure that you understand what the statement means.

True **Precipitation isn't always rain.**

Matching

Matching is connecting an item in one list to an item in another.

■ Read both lists and then match the items you are sure of. Next, match the more difficult items using the process of elimination. Cross out the answers as you use them.

B **1. Some people are allergic to this.**	A.	bacteria
A **2. Antibiotics kill them.**	B.	pollen
C **3. They cause the common cold.**	C.	viruses

■ Think carefully about items in a list that seem to mean about the same thing. They can be the hardest to match.

Try IT On your own paper, answer each of the following questions.

1. Are questions containing words like "never" always false?
2. How do you use the process of elimination in matching tests?

Multiple-Choice

Multiple-choice questions ask you to choose from several possible answers. Follow the tips below.

- Check the directions carefully to see if you are allowed to choose just one answer or more than one.

   1. Which of the following were important during the Renaissance?
   A. Mark Twain   **C. Julius Caesar**
   (B.) Michelangelo   **(D.) Shakespeare**

- Pay special attention to words like *never, except,* and *unless.*

   2. All of the following were important during the Renaissance except
   A. art   **(C.) the steam engine**
   B. literature   **D. the printing press**

- The hardest questions often include possible answers like "both A and B" or "None of the above."

   3. Renaissance writers wrote about
   A. philosophy   **C. patriotism**
   B. the Civil Rights   **(D.) both A and C**
   Movement   **E. none of the above**

Narrow your choices by eliminating answers you know are incorrect. Then focus on the remaining answers.

Fill-in-the-Blanks

On a fill-in-the-blanks test, you supply key terms that are missing.

- A blank usually stands for one missing answer. Therefore, three blanks would mean you will be filling in three answers.

   1. All cells have a
   _____membrane_____, _____cytoplasm_____, **and a** _____nucleus_____.

- Sentences sometimes give you clues about answers. If the word before a blank is *an,* the word you have to fill in will begin with a vowel sound.

   2. An _____extinct_____ **species no longer exists.**

 Discuss the following statement with a classmate: Some students say that multiple-choice questions are easier than fill-in-the-blank questions. Do you agree? How would you study differently for the two kinds of questions?

LEARN

Taking Essay Tests

An essay-test question asks you to give a written response. Your response may be one paragraph or longer, and your time is usually limited. The information below will help you write effective essay-test answers.

1 Understand the Question

- Read the question very carefully.
- Identify the key word that explains what you have to do. Here are some key words and an explanation of what each asks you to do.

Compare . . .	tell how things are alike.
Contrast . . .	tell how things are different.
Define . . .	give a clear, specific meaning of a word or an idea.
Describe . . .	tell how something looks, sounds, and feels.
Diagram . . .	explain using lines, a web, or other graphic organizer.
Evaluate . . .	give your opinion about the value of something.
Explain . . .	tell what something means or how something works.
Identify . . .	answer the 5 W's about a topic.
Illustrate . . .	show how something works by using examples.
Prove . . .	present facts that show something is true.
Review . . .	give an overall picture of a topic.
Summarize . . .	tell just the key information about a topic.

 Read the following essay questions. For each one, identify the key word. Write your answers on your own paper.

1. Explain how a thunderstorm forms.
2. Write a paragraph that illustrates condensation.
3. In a paragraph, define the term "super cell."
4. Write an essay that contrasts cumulonimbus clouds with cirrus clouds.
5. Draw a meteorological map that diagrams a cold front and a warm front.

2 Plan a One-Paragraph Answer

Some essay-test questions require a one-paragraph answer. The following guidelines will help you with this type of question.

- Study the essay-test question and the key word used.
- Write a focus (topic sentence) to start your answer.
- Use a list, an outline, or a graphic organizer to arrange your details.

Science Test: Explain how a thunderstorm forms.

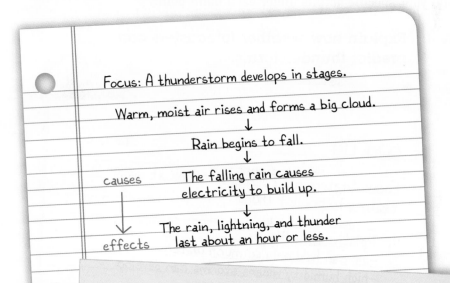

Focus: A thunderstorm develops in stages.

Warm, moist air rises and forms a big cloud.
↓
Rain begins to fall.
↓
causes   The falling rain causes electricity to build up.
↓
↓
effects   The rain, lightning, and thunder last about an hour or less.

How a Thunderstorm Forms

A thunderstorm develops in stages. It all begins when warm air and moisture come together. Then the warm air rises rapidly and carries the moisture up into colder air. If there is enough moisture, a huge cloud forms. As the cloud gets full, rain begins to fall. This movement causes electricity to build up in the air, and lightning jumps from one place to another, making thundering noises. The whole process is usually over in less than an hour because the cloud runs out of moisture.

LEARN

3 **Plan an Essay Answer**

Some essay-test questions require you to write an answer longer than one paragraph. For example, the question below asks you to explain how weather forecasters predict thunderstorms. The question needs an essay-length answer, not just one paragraph.

● Study the essay-test question and write a focus statement.

● Make a "quick list" of the main points of your essay, leaving room under each point for details.

● Add your specific details under each main point.

Science Test: **Explain how weather forecasters can predict thunderstorms.**

Quick List

Focus Statement: Forecasters look at many factors to predict thunderstorms.

1. Relative humidity
   –air can hold only so much water
   –high humidity means storms can develop

2. Temperature
   –hotter air holds more water
   –hot air rises and cools
   –loses water and forms storms

3. Wind
   –carries moisture and heat
   –direction tells where a storm will hit

 Think of a scientific process that you can explain. Make a quick list of main points and details for your explanation.

Essay Answer

The essay below uses the main points and details from the quick list on page 466.

Wind, the movement of air that carries moisture and heat, is important in forecasting A big nd, radar ire, long ver. , the lessen. longer, ithin

Science Test: The Weather

Explain how weather forecasters can predict thunderstorms.

Forecasters look at lots of factors to predict thunderstorms. Moisture, temperature, and air movement are a few of these factors. Each one plays an important part in severe weather.

We hear about "relative humidity" quite often in weather reports. Relative humidity tells us how much water vapor the air has in it. Air can hold only a certain amount of water vapor, so 50 percent humidity tells us that the air contains half as much water as it can hold. Weather forecasters know that high humidity can mean that it may rain and that thunderstorms can develop.

Temperature is the amount of heat in the air. Hot air can hold more water vapor than cold air can. Hot air also rises, carrying water vapor up into the colder air. Forecasters know that when warm air full of water vapor rises and is suddenly cooled, violent storms can happen.

agree vary

CONNECT organize model

The Basic Elements of Writing

Working with Words

Writing is like cooking. You have eight basic ingredients, called the parts of speech. Take a cupful of specific nouns and add a tablespoon of comparative adjectives. Then blend in a pint of action verbs, seasoned with superlative adverbs. Finally, mix in the pronouns, interjections, prepositions, and conjunctions, and you'll be cooking with words!

This section provides some basic information about each part of speech and answers the question,

"How can I use words effectively in my own writing?"

Mini Index

- **Using Nouns**
- **Using Pronouns**
- **Choosing Verbs**
- **Describing with Adjectives**
- **Describing with Adverbs**
- **Connecting with Prepositions**
- **Connecting with Conjunctions**

DICTIONARY

Using Nouns

A noun is a word that names a person, a place, a thing, or an idea in your writing. (See page **702**.)

PERSON	athlete, Bonnie Blair, students, President Taft
PLACE	country, Canada, gymnasium, Tampa, middle school
THING	dog, Irish setter, kayaks, stopwatch
IDEA	holiday, Fourth of July, strength, freedom

 Number from 1 to 10 on a piece of paper. For each of the 10 underlined nouns in the paragraph below, write whether it is a person, a place, a thing, or an idea.

Volleyball is one of the fastest-growing team **(1)** sports. Team **(2)** members play the **(3)** game on a **(4)** court divided by a net. To get started, the **(5)** players on team A serve the ball over the **(6)** net to team B. Players on team B can then hit the ball three **(7)** times on their **(8)** side of the net before returning the ball to team A's side. If team B is not able to return the **(9)** ball, team A scores a **(10)** point.

Concrete, Abstract, and Collective Nouns

Concrete nouns name things that can be seen or touched.
Abstract nouns name things that you can think about but cannot see or touch.

Concrete	food	snow	storm	heart
Abstract	hope	December	fear	love

 On your own paper, write three more concrete nouns and three more abstract nouns. Use each pair of nouns in a separate sentence.

Collective nouns name a collection of persons, animals, or things.

Persons	class	team	family	troop	crew
Animals	herd	flock	pack	pod	school

 List at least five additional collective nouns of your own. Use each of these nouns in a separate sentence.

Proper and Common Nouns

Proper nouns name specific people, places, things, or ideas. Proper nouns are always capitalized. A **common noun** is any noun that is not a proper noun.

Common	catcher	stadium	bat	league
Proper	Rachel	Yankee Stadium	Louisville Slugger	American League

Common nouns   The man **toured** the stadium **on** the holiday.

Proper nouns   Randy Williams **toured** Yankee Stadium **on** Labor Day.

Try IT   Make a chart like the one above. Add four of your own common and four of your own proper nouns. Be sure to capitalize the proper nouns.

General and Specific Nouns

When you use specific nouns in your writing, you give the reader a clear picture of people, places, things, and ideas. The following chart shows the difference between **general nouns** and **specific nouns**.

General	coach	field	hat	principle
Specific	Frank Bender	Wrigley Field	baseball cap	fairness

Try IT   Read the facts below about Sammy Sosa. Then write a brief paragraph about him, using as many specific nouns as possible.

Full Name:	Samuel Sosa
Born:	November 12, 1968
Birthplace:	San Pedro de Macoris, Dominican Republic
Family:	wife Sonia, children Keysha, Kenia, Sam, and Michael
Employed by:	Chicago Cubs
Position:	right field
Accomplishments:	has hit more than 500 home runs; in 1998 named Most Valuable Player by the National Baseball League

BASIC ELEMENTS

What can I do with nouns in my writing?

Show Possession

You can make your writing more specific by naming who (or what) possesses something. See the guidelines below. (Also see **604.4** and **606.1**.)

Forming the Singular Possessive

- Add an apostrophe and an *s* to a singular noun: Pat's **ball**.
- For multi-syllable nouns ending in an *s* or a *z* sound, the possessive may be formed in two ways: Cletus' **glove or** Cletus's **glove**.

Forming the Plural Possessive

- Add an apostrophe for most plural nouns ending in *s*: **the** boys' **bats**.
- Add an apostrophe and an *s* for plural nouns not ending in *s*: **the** men's **lockers**.

 List five singular nouns in one column and five plural nouns in another column. (Include at least one or two singular nouns that end in an *s* or a *z* sound.) Then exchange papers with a classmate and write a sentence for each noun, using the possessive form of the word. Discuss the results with your partner.

Rename the Subject

Whenever you use a noun after a linking verb (*am, is, are, was, were, be, been, being*), the noun renames the subject and is called a **predicate noun**.

Dad was a pitcher for his high school team, but he was never a catcher.

 List the 10 predicate nouns in the paragraph below.

1 Gita is not just any soccer player; she is the best scorer in the
2 league. When she was a young girl, her mother was the coach of the
3 local soccer team. Gita often tagged along with her mother to the
4 matches. She must have been a keen observer because she learned
5 very quickly when she started playing. Although her teammates were
6 good players, Gita was a standout. She has been a top-rated player
7 for the last three years. Gita has also been an excellent role model for
8 youngsters, and someday she may be an excellent coach.

Make the Meaning of the Verb Complete

Some sentences are not complete with just a subject and a verb.

Reggie threw. (*What* did Reggie throw?)

Nell trusts. (*Whom* does Nell trust?)

When you use a transitive verb like "threw" or "trusts" in a sentence, you need to include a **direct object** to make the meaning of the verb complete. The direct object is a noun (or pronoun) that answers the question *what* or *whom*.

Reggie threw the football.   **Nell trusts her teammates.**

To add further information, you might include a noun (or pronoun) that answers the question *to whom* or *for whom*. This type of noun is called an **indirect object**. In order for a sentence to have an indirect object, it must also have a direct object.

Wayne tossed Raj the ball. (Wayne tossed the ball *to Raj*.)

I made my sister a pom-pom. (I made a pom-pom *for my sister*.)

 Write the direct object in each of the following sentences. If there is an indirect object as well, write it and underline it.

1. Tennis can give you a strong body.

   1. body, <u>you</u>

2. This sport burns calories, too.

3. Aunt Sheryl gave me a racquet.

4. I play tennis regularly.

5. Yesterday, I sent Ruth a powerful serve.

Add Specific Information

Another kind of object noun is the **object of a preposition** (see **704.7**). A prepositional phrase begins with a preposition and ends with an object. You can use prepositional phrases to add specific information to sentences. The object of each prepositional phrase below is highlighted in blue. (Also see pages **494–495**.)

I do some stretches <u>before a game</u> <u>of tennis</u>.

I also drink lots <u>of water</u> <u>during a game</u>.

 Write a brief sports-related paragraph that includes at least five prepositional phrases. Underline the object of each prepositional phrase. Here are some prepositions to choose from: *over, under, before, after, during,* and *against.* (See page **742** for more.)

Using Pronouns

A pronoun is a word used in place of a noun. The noun replaced, or referred to, by the pronoun is called the pronoun's **antecedent**. The arrows below point to each pronoun's antecedent. (Also see **706.1**.)

The volleyball team was determined, so it won the match.

Coach Johnson said that she never saw a team work so hard.

The **personal pronouns** listed below are the most common pronouns used by writers. (For a complete list of personal pronouns, see page **710**.)

PERSONAL PRONOUNS						
I	you	he	she	it	we	they
me		him	her		us	them

Person and Number of a Pronoun

Pronouns show "person" and "number" in writing. The following chart shows which pronouns are used for the three different persons (*first, second, third*) and the two different numbers (*singular* or *plural*).

		Singular	Plural
FIRST PERSON	(The person speaking)	I called.	We called.
SECOND PERSON	(The person spoken to)	You called.	You called.
THIRD PERSON	(The person spoken about)	He called. She called. It called.	They called.

 Number your paper from 2 to 5. Write sentences that use the pronouns described below as subjects.

1. first-person singular pronoun (*I*)
   1. I want to join the basketball team.

2. third-person singular pronoun

3. third-person plural pronoun

4. second-person singular pronoun

5. first-person plural pronoun

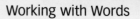
Indefinite Pronouns

An **indefinite pronoun** refers to people or things that are not named or known. The chart below lists which indefinite pronouns are singular, which are plural, and which can be singular or plural.

INDEFINITE PRONOUNS				Plural	Singular or Plural
Singular					
another	either	nobody	someone	both	all
anybody	everybody	no one	something	few	any
anyone	everyone	nothing		many	most
anything	everything	one		several	none
each	neither	somebody			

When you use a singular indefinite pronoun as a subject, the verbs and the other pronouns that refer to the subject all must be singular. If the indefinite pronoun is plural, the verbs and other pronouns that refer to the subject must all be plural.

Singular
Everybody does his or her **stretches before practice.**

Plural
Several of the boys do their **sit-ups after warming up.**

Singular or Plural
Most of the time is spent **on drills.** (singular)
Most of the players are looking **forward to the match.** (plural)

Try IT Number your paper from 1 to 5. Choose the correct pronoun to complete each of the following sentences. (See page **714**.)

1. Someone left *(their, his or her)* racquet on the tennis court.
2. None of the girls were happy about losing *(their, her)* match.
3. Most of the match would be remembered for *(their, its)* intensity.
4. Has everyone turned in *(their, his or her)* gear?
5. Several of the coaches will drive *(their, his or her)* own cars.

If using *his or her* is clumsy, try changing the singular pronoun to a plural pronoun. For example, the first sample sentence above could be rewritten like this: **All** *of the players* **do their** *stretches before practice.*

How can pronouns improve my writing?

Avoid Repeating Nouns

You can use pronouns in your writing to avoid repeating the same nouns over and over again. (See pages **706–714**.) Read the sample paragraph below. How many times did the writer use "Lance Armstrong"?

> **WITHOUT PRONOUNS**
>
> Lance Armstrong, a champion cyclist, was born in 1971. Lance Armstrong's competitive nature led Lance Armstrong to win the Iron Kids Triathlon when Lance Armstrong was only 13 years old. Armstrong became a member of the United States Olympic Team in 1992. Despite getting cancer at age 25, Lance Armstrong went on to win the Tour de France five times by 2004.

Now read the revised sample below. The writer has replaced some of the nouns with pronouns. Which pronouns refer to Lance Armstrong?

> **WITH PRONOUNS**
>
> Lance Armstrong, a champion cyclist, was born in 1971. His competitive nature led him to win the Iron Kids Triathlon when he was only 13 years old. Armstrong became a member of the United States Olympic Team in 1992. Despite getting cancer at age 25, he went on to win the Tour de France five times by 2004.

Try It On your own paper, rewrite the following paragraph, changing some of the underlined nouns to pronouns so that the paragraph reads more smoothly.

> At the start of <u>Lance Armstrong's</u> professional career, <u>Lance Armstrong</u> spent eight months a year racing in Europe. <u>Lance Armstrong</u> became very popular with European <u>fans</u>, and <u>Lance Armstrong</u> had to learn how to deal with the <u>fans</u>. Very quickly, <u>Lance Armstrong</u> gained recognition as a world-class cyclist. In many events, <u>Lance Armstrong</u> was the only American racer. During <u>Lance Armstrong's</u> first professional year, <u>Lance Armstrong</u> won 10 races.

How can I use pronouns properly?

Avoid Agreement Problems

You can make your writing clear by using pronouns properly. You must use pronouns that agree with their antecedents. (An antecedent is the noun or pronoun that a pronoun replaces or refers to.) Pronouns must agree with their antecedents in number, person, and gender. (See **712.1–712.4**.)

When Mom and Dad go golfing, they usually rent a golf cart.

Uncle Carl didn't know how to golf, so Dad taught him.

Agreement in Number

The **number** of a pronoun is either singular or plural. The pronoun must match the antecedent in number.

■ A singular pronoun refers to a singular antecedent.

Dad has had his own golf clubs since he was 18 years old.

■ A plural pronoun refers to a plural antecedent.

All of the woods have their own protective covers.

 Select the correct pronouns from the following list to complete the sentences below.

his	its	their	he	them	her	they	it

1. Dad plays golf whenever _____ gets a chance.
   1. he

2. Golfers try to keep _____ scores as low as possible.

3. The pitted surface of a golf ball helps _____ fly more smoothly.

4. A putting green is different from the rest of the golf course because _____ grass is very short.

5. Some people lose their golf balls forever when _____ hit _____ into the water.

6. Golfers usually bring an umbrella along with _____.

7. Babe Didrikson Zaharias, one of the most famous female golfers, did not let fame go to _____ head.

Agreement in Person

When you use pronouns, you must choose either first, second, or third **person** pronouns. If you start a sentence in one "person," don't shift to another "person" later in the sentence.

Pronoun shift: I **have learned a lot about Babe, and with all that knowledge** you **can write an interesting report.**

Correct: I **have learned a lot about Babe, and with all that knowledge** I **can write an interesting report.**

 For each sentence below, change the underlined pronoun so it doesn't cause a shift in person.

1. We are studying famous athletes in <u>their</u> social studies class.
2. If golfers knew how many sports Babe shined in, <u>you</u> would be amazed.
3. She was an incredible athlete, and <u>we</u> won 13 straight golf tournaments in 1946.
4. Babe won 82 golf tournaments in all, and <u>you</u> became famous on both sides of the Atlantic.
5. Babe qualified for five Olympic events in 1932, but, as a woman, <u>you</u> could compete in only three.

Agreement in Gender

The **gender** of a pronoun *(her, his, its)* must be the same as the gender of its antecedent. Pronouns can be feminine (female), masculine (male), or neuter (neither male nor female).

Babe Didrikson's father required his **children to take part in a sport.**

Babe Didrikson excelled in nearly every sport she **tried.**

 Number your paper from 1 to 5. Correct each underlined pronoun so that it agrees with its antecedent in gender.

Babe challenged some old-fashioned ideas about <u>his</u> role in sports. Although best known for golf, she did not limit <u>himself</u> to that sport. <u>He</u> played basketball, tennis, and softball. <u>Its</u> participation in the 1932 Olympics led to three medals in track and field. The Associated Press named <u>him</u> Athlete of the Year six times.

What else should I know about pronouns?

Make Your References Clear

When you use a pronoun, don't confuse your reader by making its antecedent unclear. Make sure that the word your pronoun refers to is obvious; it should plainly refer to only one noun.

Confusing Pronoun Reference

Ancient Egyptian drawings show some people playing handball. They were found in tombs.
(Which noun—*drawings* or *people*—does the pronoun *they* refer to?)

There are two ways to fix this error. The first way is to reword the sentences to clarify your meaning.

In ancient Egyptian tombs, drawings were found. They show some people playing handball.

The second way to fix the error is to reword the sentences without using a pronoun.

Ancient Egyptian drawings show some people playing handball. The drawings were found in tombs. (or)

Ancient Egyptian drawings found in tombs show some people playing handball.

Try IT Correctly rewrite the passages below that contain confusing pronoun references. (There are five.)

People played many games long before they were included in the Olympics. Field hockey, for example, is one of the oldest competitive sports in the world. It began with the ancient civilizations of Egypt, Greece, and Rome.

Today, players use field hockey rules that were developed in the mid-1800s in England. They say that there are 11 people per team. Each team tries to advance the ball down the field to the other team's goal cage. Players can hit it only with the flat side of their sticks. Players can shoot at the goal only from within the "striking circle," which extends 16 feet from the goal.

Now, every four years, field hockey teams vie for the World Cup. When the 2002 World Cup competition was held in Perth, Australia, more people became aware of it. In fact, field hockey has gained in popularity every year.

BASIC ELEMENTS

Choosing Verbs

Writers must constantly make choices, and one of their most important choices is which verb to use to express their thoughts clearly.

Action Verbs

An **action verb** tells what the subject is doing. Action verbs help bring your writing to life.

A luge zooms down ice-covered canals.

Lugers race at high speeds through the frozen canals.

Linking Verbs

A **linking verb** connects (links) a subject to a noun or an adjective in the predicate.

COMMON LINKING VERBS	
Forms of "be"	be, is, are, was, were, am, been, being
Other linking verbs	appear, become, feel, grow, look, remain, seem, smell, sound, taste

A luge is a type of sled.

(The linking verb *is* connects the subject *luge* to the noun *type*. *Type* is a **predicate noun**.)

The rider must be brave.

(The linking verb *be* connects the subject *rider* to the adjective *brave*. *Brave* is a **predicate adjective**.)

 For the sentences below, write the subject, the linking verb, and the predicate noun or predicate adjective that follows the verb. (One of the sentences does not include a linking verb.)

1 One kind of luge track is natural, following the contours of a

2 snowy mountain. The other kind (used in the Olympics) is a frozen

3 ice canal built for speed. The luger lies on the luge, faceup and

4 feetfirst. During a run, he or she remains still to increase speed.

5 Obviously, speed is very important. The luger with the fastest run

6 becomes the leader in a competition.

Helping Verbs

The simple predicate may include a **helping verb** plus the main verb. The helping verb makes the verb more specific.

Valerie will attempt a luge run.
(The helping verb *will* helps express future tense.)

She may need special clothing. (*May* helps express a possibility.)

The track, which was destroyed, had been built for the 1984 Olympics in Sarajevo. (*Had been* helps express past perfect tense and passive voice.)

Try IT Select a helping verb from the following list to complete each sentence in the paragraph below.

| would does will could should |

I **(1)** _____ like to ride a luge, but Mom **(2)** _____ not think that's a good idea. Dad thinks that I **(3)** _____ learn more about luges first. Are there any luge schools that I **(4)** _____ attend? I **(5)** _____ research that on the Internet, and perhaps I **(6)** _____ find an instructor nearby.

Irregular Verbs

Most verbs in the English language are regular. A writer adds *ed* to regular verbs to show a past action. A writer can also use *has, have,* or *had* with the past participle to make other verb tenses. **Irregular verbs** do not follow the *ed* rule. Instead of adding *ed* to show past tense, the word might change. (See the list of irregular verbs on page **722**.)

PRESENT	PAST	PAST PARTICIPLE
I speak.	Yesterday I spoke.	I have spoken.
She runs.	Yesterday she ran.	She has run.

Try IT On your own paper, write five sentences using the irregular verbs listed below.

1. took
2. make
3. has seen
4. went
5. ride

How can I use verbs effectively?

Show Powerful Action

You can use **action verbs** to show the reader exactly what is happening (or has happened).

> **ORDINARY ACTION VERBS**
>
> Vashon shot the basketball through the hoop.
>
> Dave got the rebound and ran up the court.
>
> **POWERFUL ACTION VERBS**
>
> Vashon flipped the basketball through the hoop.
>
> Dave grabbed the rebound and dashed up the court.

Try to avoid using linking verbs *(is, are, was, were)* too much. Often, a stronger (action) verb can be made from another word in the same sentence.

> Kristy is a good basketball player. (linking verb)
>
> Kristy plays basketball well.
>
> (The action verb *plays* is made from the word *player*.)

Create Active Voice

A verb is in the **active voice** if the subject in the sentence is doing the action. (See page **726**.) A verb is passive if the subject is not doing the action. Try to use active verbs as much as possible because they make your writing sound more direct and action packed.

> The ball was passed from Kristy to Tamika. (passive)
>
> Kristy passed the ball to Tamika. (active)

 Rewrite each of the following sentences so that the verb is in the active voice rather than the passive voice.

1. A basket was made by Will.

   1. Will made a basket.

2. Thirteen points were scored by Yao in the first half.

3. A layup was attempted by me, but I missed the basket.

4. Most of the fouls were called by one referee.

5. A zone defense was played by the opposing team.

6. Basketball games at my school are attended by many people.

Show When Something Happens

You can use different verb tenses to "tell time" in sentences. The three **simple tenses** are *present, past,* and *future.* (See page **720.**)

At times, you might need to use different tenses in the same sentence to show that one action happened before another action.

The Harlem Globetrotters is a basketball team that began in the 1920s.

Both a present tense verb and a past tense verb appear in the sentence, and it makes sense. However, you need to avoid a shift in verb tense if it is unnecessary.

Shift in tense:

They tour the country and played any team that will take them on.
(The verb tense shifts from *present* to *past,* confusing the reader.)

Corrected:

They tour the country and play any team that will take them on.

Try IT For each blank in the sentences below, write a verb that is the same tense as the first verb in the sentence.

1. When the Globetrotters play another team for the first time, their opponents _____ surprised.

2. Early on, the Globetrotters recruited players from many places, and they _____ a long time to play together as a team.

3. One cannot deny the skill of these team members; they _____ superior athletes.

4. The Globetrotters will play at the arena next week, and I _____ there.

Try IT Rewrite each sentence below that has an unnecessary shift in verb tense. (You should find three tense-shift errors.)

(1) Players for the Harlem Globetrotters have always been truly talented athletes. **(2)** In a 1939 game, however, the Globetrotters led by more than 100 points, so they start clowning around. **(3)** From then on, the team included comedy routines in their games.

(4) Since the Globetrotters regularly entertain sold-out crowds around the world, they were the most-recognized team on earth. **(5)** The team's 76-year record for 21,236 games includes only 336 losses, and there was no doubt that they will continue to win. **(6)** The Globetrotters will delight fans around the globe for years to come.

BASIC ELEMENTS

How else can I use verbs?

Show Special Types of Action

You need **perfect tense verbs** to express certain types of action. (See page **724** in the "Proofreader's Guide.") There are three perfect tenses.

play, played	Singular	Plural
Present perfect tense states an action that *began in the past but continues or is completed in the present.*		
Present perfect (use *has* or *have* + past participle)	I have played. You have played. He or she has played.	We have played. You have played. They have played.
Past perfect tense states an action that *began in the past and was completed in the past.*		
Past perfect (use *had* + past participle)	I had played. You had played. He or she had played.	We had played. You had played. They had played.
Future perfect tense states an action that *will begin in the future and will be completed by a specific time in the future.*		
Future perfect (use *will have* + past participle)	I will have played. You will have played. He or she will have played.	We will have played. You will have played. They will have played.

Try IT Identify the tense of each underlined verb in the following paragraphs. The first one has been done for you.

1. past perfect

At the end of last summer, our local bowling alley **(1)** had burned down. Since then our bowling league **(2)** has moved to another bowling alley across town. I hope the owners of the old alley **(3)** will have rebuilt our bowling alley by the start of the next season. We **(4)** have missed bowling there.

I **(5)** have owned my bowling ball for one year. Up until three months ago, my fingers **(6)** had fit the holes perfectly. Now the thumb hole is getting a bit tight because I **(7)** have grown so much. By the end of the season, I'm sure the local sports store **(8)** will have redrilled the holes for me.

Form Verbals

Verbals are words that are made from verbs but are used as other parts of speech. Verbals are used as nouns, adjectives, and adverbs, and they are often used in phrases. (See **730.2–730.4**.)

Gerunds

A **gerund** is a verb form that ends in *ing* and is used as a noun.

Bowling **is an enjoyable activity.**
(The gerund *bowling* acts as a subject noun.)

You should try bowling in our league.
(The gerund phrase *bowling in our league* acts as a direct object.)

Participles

A **participle** is a verb form used as an adjective. A participle ends in *ing* or *ed*.

Regina had a bowling **party on her birthday.**
(The participle *bowling* describes what kind of party;
bowling acts as an adjective.)

A ball spinning down the next alley **hit the pocket perfectly.**
(The participial phrase acts as an adjective describing *ball*.)

Infinitives

An **infinitive** is a verb with "to" before it. An infinitive can be used as a noun, an adjective, or an adverb.

My goal for today is to get three strikes.
(The infinitive phrase *to get three strikes* acts as a predicate noun.)

Our plan to go bowling **is still a "go."**
(*To go bowling* acts as an adjective modifying the noun *plan*.)

Please watch me carefully to evaluate my form.
(*To evaluate my form* acts as an adverb modifying the verb *watch*.)

 Write a sentence for each of the verbals listed below.

1. knocking down the pins *(gerund phrase)*

2. to earn a good score *(infinitive phrase)*

3. spinning *(participle)*

4. taking a few long strides *(participial phrase)*

5. to make a spare *(infinitive phrase)*

BASIC ELEMENTS

Describing with Adjectives

Adjectives are words that describe or modify nouns or pronouns. Sensory adjectives help the reader see, hear, feel, smell, and taste what writers are describing. (Also see pages **732** and **734**.)

WITHOUT ADJECTIVES

LeRoy dived into the water. He swam along the lane markers to the end of the pool. His coach held up a stopwatch.

WITH ADJECTIVES

Leroy dived into the cold, blue water. He swam along the red, white, and blue lane markers to the end of the Olympic-sized pool. His cheering coach held up an oversized stopwatch.

Adjectives answer four questions: *what kind? how much? how many?* or *which one? Remember:* Proper adjectives can be made from proper nouns (England, *English;* Italy, *Italian*) and are capitalized.

WHAT KIND?	French **bread**	sour **lemon**	black **cat**
HOW MUCH? HOW MANY?	few **friends**	two **puppies**	some **milk**
WHICH ONE?	this **chair**	these **students**	those **caps**

Try IT For each blank in the sentences below, write an adjective of the type called for in parentheses.

1. There are _(how many?)_ students on the swim team.

2. Marla just got a _(what kind?)_ swimsuit.

3. She has swum on the team for _(how many?)_ years.

4. Marla always swallowed _(how much?)_ water during practice.

5. Last year, she injured her _(which one?)_ elbow during a race.

6. During the conference meet, Marla's relay team won a _(what kind?)_ medal.

7. Altogether, Marla won _(how many?)_ medals during the meet.

8. The _(which one?)_ meet was the highlight of last season.

9. This year's _(what kind?)_ swim team will be as good as last year's.

10. Marla accepts _(how much?)_ responsibility for her performances.

Comparative and Superlative Forms

You can use comparative adjectives to compare two things. For most one-syllable adjectives, add *er* to make the **comparative form**. To compare three or more things, add *est* to make the **superlative form**.

POSITIVE	COMPARATIVE	SUPERLATIVE
large	larger	largest

Comparative: **A volleyball is** larger **than a baseball.**

Superlative: **The** largest **ball in professional team sports is a basketball.**

Add *er* and *est* to some two-syllable words and use *more* or *most* (or *less* or *least*) with others. Always use *more* or *most* with three-syllable adjectives.

POSITIVE	COMPARATIVE	SUPERLATIVE
joyful	more joyful	most joyful

Comparative: **Swimming is a** more strenuous **sport than golf is.**

Superlative: **I think that gymnastics is the** most strenuous **of all sports.**

NOTE Some adjectives use completely different words to express comparison—for example, *bad, worse, worst.* (See **734.6**.)

Try IT Write the positive, comparative, or superlative form of the underlined adjective to fill in the blanks in each of the following sentences.

1. You will see some <u>fast</u> balls in baseball, but a golf ball hit from a tee is a _____ ball. The _____ of all balls in sports is a jai-alai ball.

2. The soccer practices are _____, but the games are <u>more difficult</u> than the practices are. I had the _____ of all my games when I was sick.

3. Student athletes do some <u>amazing</u> feats. Of course, professional athletes can do things that are _____ than what the students can do. However, participants in extreme sports can do the _____ feats of all.

4. While Angela is a _____ runner, Lee is a <u>better</u> runner, and Takeisha is the _____ runner of all.

5. For a few players, spiking a volleyball is <u>easy</u>. For many other players, serving is _____ than spiking the ball. Then there are those who find setting up the _____ part of the game.

How can I strengthen my writing with adjectives?

Use Sensory Details

Writers use adjectives to help create **sensory details**. Sensory details help readers experience something with all their senses. Note how the sensory adjectives add effective details in the following paragraph.

The sweet aroma of fresh-mown grass floated off the baseball diamond. Bright white lines had been carefully painted on it. The buzzing crowd waited in anticipation. Food and drink vendors began hawking their mouth-watering treats as the first blaring notes of "The Star-Spangled Banner" tumbled out of the band's shiny instruments.

 Draw a chart like the one below and list two or three adjectives for each sense.

sight	sound	smell	taste	feeling (texture)
golden	humming	rich	salty	smooth

Form Extra-Strength Modifiers

Compound adjectives are made of two or more words. Some are spelled as one word; others are hyphenated. (Use a dictionary to check spelling.)

Some baseball fields feature man-made grass.

 For each of the following sentences, write a compound adjective to fill in the blank. Make your compound adjectives by combining words from the following list. (All of them should be hyphenated.)

| front | high | filled | row | flying | third | fan | base |

1. We entered the noisy, _____ stadium just as the game started.
   1. fan-filled

2. Our tickets were for _____ seats.

3. Santiago hit a _____ ball toward the bleachers.

4. The _____ umpire shouted, "Foul ball!"

Include Adjectives in the Predicate

Most adjectives are placed before the nouns they describe. A **predicate adjective** comes after a linking verb and describes the noun or pronoun before it.

The worn mitt is ancient, **and it smells** musty.

Darnell remains confident **about the mitt's supposed "luck."**

Try IT Write a predicate adjective to fill in each blank in the paragraph below. The linking verbs are underlined.

> When Mom dropped me off at baseball practice, I <u>was</u> **(1)** _____.
> Our opening game was only three days away. The whole team <u>seemed</u>
> **(2)** _____. Our fielders <u>were</u> **(3)** _____, and some of the batters
> <u>were</u> really **(4)** _____. Carl, our main pitcher, <u>looked</u> **(5)** _____. We
> didn't know how the other team would play, but we <u>felt</u> **(6)** _____.
> We couldn't wait!

Try IT Write a brief paragraph about a personal experience related to your favorite sport. In your paragraph, use at least five linking verbs, such as *become, feel, seem, appear,* and *sound,* that link to predicate adjectives.

Be General or Specific

You can use **indefinite adjectives**, such as *few, many, more,* and *some,* to give the reader approximate information. (*Approximate* means "general" rather than "specific.")

Some **neighborhood kids picked teams for baseball.**

Gina and Sandy decided to play another **game.**

A **demonstrative adjective** points to a specific noun. The demonstrative adjectives are *this, that, these,* and *those.*

Those **kids over there want to play, too.**

I want to use this **bat when it's my turn.**

Note that both indefinite and demonstrative adjectives must come before the nouns they modify. If they appear alone, they are pronouns.

Try IT Write two sentences that use indefinite adjectives and two that use demonstrative adjectives. Exchange papers with a classmate and underline each other's indefinite and demonstrative adjectives.

BASIC ELEMENTS

Describing with Adverbs

Adverbs describe or modify verbs, adjectives, or other adverbs. You can use adverbs to answer *how? when? where?* or *how much?* (See pages 736 and 738.)

How?	gracefully	Deena did a back flip gracefully on the beam.
When?	yesterday	She was in the semifinals yesterday.
Where?	indoors	The events were all held indoors.
How much?	barely	Mark barely met the time limit on his routine.

Try IT For each of the following paragraphs, write the adverbs you find. (The number of adverbs in each paragraph is shown in parentheses.)

I.   I went with Darla to a gymnastics competition today. She told me about the men who perform gymnastic routines on a pommel horse. These athletes must practice regularly. The most basic skills are extremely difficult to master because only the hands can touch the horse. The athlete spends most of the time carefully balancing on one arm as his free hand reaches to begin the next skill. There are no stops or pauses allowed. At the end of his routine, the gymnast's dismount is a landing without any steps or hops afterward. That's a challenge! (5)

II.   Although Darla really liked the uneven bars when she started gymnastics, her favorite event now has become the balance beam. She fearlessly leaps, jumps, and does handsprings on a four-foot high, four-inch-wide beam! The hard ground lies below. Her dance moves are expertly completed. Of course, she is very flexible, but she must concentrate totally for the 90 seconds of her routine. (7)

Comparative and Superlative Adverbs

You can use adverbs to compare two things. The **comparative form** of an adverb compares two people, places, things, or ideas. The **superlative form** of an adverb compares three or more people, places, things, or ideas.

 For most one-syllable adverbs, add *er* to make the comparative form and *est* to make the superlative form.

POSITIVE	COMPARATIVE	SUPERLATIVE
soon	sooner	soonest

While you add *er* and *est* to some two-syllable adverbs, you need to use *more* or *most* (or *less* or *least*) with others. Always use *more* or *most* with adverbs of three or more syllables.

POSITIVE	COMPARATIVE	SUPERLATIVE
quickly	more quickly	most quickly
importantly	more importantly	most importantly

Comparative: **I ran** faster **than my guard did.**

Ed plays basketball more frequently **than I do.**

Superlative: **Kayla ran** fastest **of all and grabbed the jump ball.**

Of all of us, Ed plays basketball most frequently.

 Make sure that you write a complete comparison: *I ran faster than my guard did* rather than *I ran faster than my guard.*

 In each sentence below, change the adverb (underlined) twice: first to compare two things and then to compare three (or more) things. Reword the sentences as needed.

1. Delia <u>quickly</u> put on her uniform.

1. I put my uniform on more quickly than Delia did.
Of the three of us, Beryl put hers on most quickly.

2. She would be on the soccer field <u>soon</u>.

3. Rolando kicked the ball <u>powerfully</u>.

4. Joe <u>skillfully</u> set up his teammates.

How can I use adverbs effectively?

Describe Actions

You can make your writing more descriptive by using adverbs. Since they can appear just about anywhere in a sentence, experiment to find the best place to include them. *Remember:* Changing an adverb's location may slightly change the meaning of the sentence.

> **Greg** smoothly **rowed his kayak through the water.**
> **Greg rowed his kayak** smoothly **through the water.**
> **Greg rowed his kayak through the water** smoothly.
> Smoothly, **Greg rowed his kayak through the water.**

 Rewrite the following sentences, placing the adverb (in parentheses) where you think it fits best.

1. I decided to try kayaking myself. *(finally)*
2. I will have to practice. *(definitely)*
3. I don't want to go where the current is fast. *(really)*
4. A kayak has a low probability of capsizing. *(surprisingly)*
5. Kayakers should learn how to flip themselves back up again if they do capsize. *(actually)*

Add Emphasis

You can stress the importance of something with adverbs. Generally, use adverbs of degree (those that answer *how much?*) for this job. (See **736.4.**)

> **We paddled** extremely **fast in the river rapids.**
> **Rapids can be** awfully **dangerous.**

 Write a short paragraph about this picture that shows kayakers in calm water. Use a few adverbs to add emphasis.

Express Frequency

With adverbs, you can describe how often something happens or how often something is done in a certain way. Adverbs that tell how often include *often, sometimes, usually, occasionally, always,* and so on.

Dwight has always enjoyed track-and-field events.

He is rarely disappointed in the athletes' performances.

Try It Use three of the following "how often" adverbs in sentences about your attitude toward a specific sport.

| regularly | never | occasionally | always | seldom | frequently |

When you use a negative adverb such as *hardly, barely,* or *scarcely* in a sentence, avoid using another negative term *(no, not, neither)* to express the same idea. Using two negative words together results in a **double negative**, which is an error.

I can't hardly fit this skateboard in my backpack.

To correct a double negative, remove one of the negative terms:

I can't fit this skateboard in my backpack.

I can hardly fit this skateboard in my backpack.

Be Precise

With adverbs, you can tell the readers exactly when *(then, yesterday, now, right away)* or where *(here, there, nearby, inside)* something happens.

Leila then invited me to jump on her trampoline.

"Will you stay close while I jump?" I asked.

Try It For each blank, write an adverb that tells "when" or "where."

When I went to Leila's house **(1)** _____, I saw her trampoline. Other families who lived **(2)** _____ also had trampolines. I asked Leila if we could try out her tramp **(3)** _____. **(4)** _____ we jumped for a long time. Leila's friend next door called to us. "Come **(5)** _____ and jump on our tramp, too!" she said.

BASIC ELEMENTS

Connecting with Prepositions

A preposition is a word (or words) that show how one word or idea is related to another. A preposition is the first word of a prepositional phrase, a phrase that acts as an adjective or an adverb in a sentence. (See page **742** for a complete list of prepositions.)

The Astrodome is located in Houston, Texas.

(The preposition *in* shows the relationship between the verb *is located* and the object of the preposition *Houston, Texas*. The prepositional phrase acts as an adverb telling "where.")

When the panels in the roof **were painted, the grass died.**

(The preposition *in* shows the relationship between the noun *panels* and the object of the preposition *roof*. The prepositional phrase acts as an adjective telling "which ones.")

■ **The same word may be a preposition or an adverb.** If a word that sometimes is used as a preposition appears alone in a sentence, that word is probably an adverb, not a preposition.

Two students lagged behind the group.

(*Behind the group* is a prepositional phrase.)

Two students lagged behind, **so we waited.**

(*Behind* is an adverb that modifies the verb *lagged*.)

■ **The word *to* may be a preposition or part of an infinitive phrase.** If the words that follow *to* do not include the object of the preposition (a noun or pronoun), then *to* is not a preposition. When a verb or verb phrase follows *to*, *to* is considered an infinitive, a kind of verbal. (See page **485**.)

We are going to the stadium.

(*To the stadium* is a prepositional phrase.)

We are going to watch **a football game.**

(*To watch* is an infinitive.)

 Write four sentences about a place where people play a sport. Use the word *around* as a preposition in one sentence and as an adverb in another. Use the word *to* as a preposition in one sentence and as part of an infinitive in another.

How can I use prepositional phrases?

Add Information

You can use a prepositional phrase as an adjective to describe either a noun or a pronoun. Adjectives answer *what kind? how many?* or *which one?*

Which one?

The Major League Baseball park on Chicago's north side, Wrigley Field, is a

What kind?

stadium just for baseball.

Try It Write a prepositional phrase that could modify each of the subjects below. Your phrases should answer *what kind? how many?* or *which one?* Use a variety of prepositions to introduce your prepositional phrases.

1. the players
   the players on our team
2. the most exciting game
3. the sports arena
4. the locker room
5. several days

6. that camera
7. the referee
8. those basketballs
9. a shrill whistle
10. spectators
11. the scoreboard

You can also use a prepositional phrase as an adverb to describe a verb, an adjective, or another adverb. Adverbs answer *how? when? where? how long? how often?* or *how much?*

Where?   *When?*

The team will play at Green Field on Tuesday afternoon.

Try It On a piece of paper, list each prepositional phrase that is used as an adverb in the following paragraph. (You should find nine.) Tell what question each one answers.

1 Team Members:

2   We will be going to a tournament on Saturday. If you can attend,

3 let me know before Friday. We will meet in the school parking lot at

4 8:00 a.m., and we'll get there by bus. We will return between 8:00 and

5 9:00 p.m., and the bus will drop us at the school. Please note: All team

6 members must wear uniforms during the tournament.

7   Coach Marty

BASIC ELEMENTS

Connecting with Conjunctions

Conjunctions connect words, groups of words, and sentences. There are three kinds of conjunctions: *coordinating, subordinating,* and *correlative*. The following sentences show some of the ways to use conjunctions. (See page **744** for a list of common conjunctions.)

COORDINATING CONJUNCTIONS CONNECT WORDS

Should I play basketball or volleyball this winter?

I am good at dribbling and shooting the ball.

CONNECT COMPOUND SUBJECTS AND PREDICATES

All the coaches and current team members attend tryouts.

The coaches will test our skills and make the final decisions.

CONNECT SENTENCES

I hope I make the team, but I am not worried about it.

The team has practice every day, and that's a big commitment.

SUBORDINATING CONJUNCTIONS CONNECT DEPENDENT CLAUSES TO INDEPENDENT CLAUSES

Players remain on the team as long as their grades are satisfactory.

When the team goes to the playoffs, students seem to have more school spirit.

CORRELATIVE CONJUNCTIONS CONNECT NOUN PHRASES AND VERB PHRASES

Our team neither wins all the time nor loses all the time.

Being part of a team can help you improve not only your physical abilities but also your mental skills.

 Choose three of the sentences above to use as models. Write three sentences of your own imitating the three you've chosen. (Make sure to use your own words.) Underline the conjunctions you use.

How can I use conjunctions?

Connect a Series of Ideas

You can use a conjunction to connect a series of three or more words or phrases in a row. Place commas between the words or phrases and place a conjunction before the final item.

Blind athletes compete in skiing, swimming, and football.
(The conjunction *and* connects three nouns.)

They also ride bikes, lift weights, or shoot targets.
(The conjunction *or* connects three verb phrases.)

Try IT Copy the following sentence beginnings. Include a series of three or more ideas to finish each one.

1. My favorite sports are . . .

2. I admire how the players . . .

3. A few sports I'd like to try include . . .

Expand Sentences (with Coordinating Conjunctions)

You can use **coordinating conjunctions** (*and, but, or, nor, for, so, yet*) to make compound subjects and predicates and to write compound sentences.

Blind individuals and visually impaired people are able to participate in sports, but they don't always have the necessary equipment.
(The conjunction *and* creates a compound subject, and *but* creates a compound sentence.)

Try IT For each blank below, write a coordinating conjunction. Tell whether it connects a compound subject, a compound predicate, or a compound sentence.

An athlete may be blind, **(1)** _____ that doesn't mean he or she is less talented than any other athlete. In fact, some blind athletes have competed against sighted individuals **(2)** _____ won medals. The International Blind Sports Association conducts sports programs for blind people, **(3)** _____ it changes negative ideas about them in the process. The organization wants to spread its message, **(4)** _____ it runs public service campaigns. A blind person **(5)** _____ a sighted individual can be a successful athlete.

BASIC ELEMENTS

Expand Sentences (with Subordinating Conjunctions)

You can use a **subordinating conjunction** to connect a dependent clause to another sentence. A dependent clause (one that *cannot* stand alone as a sentence) must be connected to an independent clause (one that *can* stand alone as a sentence). In the expanded sentences below, the dependent clause is underlined, and the subordinating conjunction is in blue.

> Although martial arts teach self-defense, they also provide benefits to the body, mind, and spirit. Students improve themselves as they make progress in these three areas.

Choose a subordinating conjunction from the following list to fill in each blank below: *until, because, when, since, even though.* Try to fill in each blank with a different conjunction.

> Many martial arts are linked to the Far East **(1)** _____ that is where they were first practiced. *Martial arts* means "arts of war" **(2)** _____ people used them in actual combat. **(3)** _____ the martial arts are considered sports, people have discovered the health benefits they offer. Students still learn self-defense **(4)** _____ they learn a chosen "art." **(5)** _____ a person becomes really skilled, he or she stays out of competitions.

Show a Relationship

You can use **correlative conjunctions** to show a relationship between two words, phrases, or clauses. Correlative conjunctions are always used in pairs: *both / and, not only / but also, neither / nor, either / or, whether / or.*

> While performing martial arts, people use not only their bodies, but also their minds.

> Both tai chi and jujitsu are forms of martial art.

For each of the blanks in the sentences below, write the correlative conjunctions that make the most sense. (More than one answer may be correct.)

1. The martial arts stress _____ aggression _____ domination.

2. Practicing martial arts can help improve _____ your health _____ your self-esteem.

3. A bow to an instructor can express _____ gratitude _____ respect.

Building Effective Sentences

Imagine eating the same thing every day, at every meal. Eventually, you would dislike even the cheesiest pizza or the most scrumptious ice cream. People just naturally like variety.

The same is true with writing. A story with one long sentence after another, or one short sentence after another, would soon become boring. Sometimes a short sentence expresses feeling in a way that a long sentence cannot, and a long sentence does a better job of explaining a complicated idea. One key to clear writing is sentence variety.

Mini Index

You will learn about . . .

- writing complete sentences.
- fixing sentence problems.
- improving your sentence style.
- combining sentences.
- adding variety to your sentences.
- using different types of sentences.
- expanding and modeling sentences.

Writing Complete Sentences

A sentence is a group of words that forms a complete thought. Writers use complete sentences in order to communicate clearly. The following group of words does not form a complete thought:

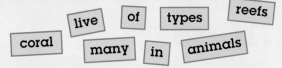

The jumble of words above does not make sense. When these same words are rearranged into a sentence, however, they do make sense. They communicate a clear, complete thought:

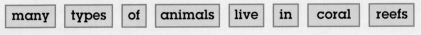

 On your own paper, unscramble the word groups below to create complete sentences. (See the helpful clues in parentheses.) Remember to capitalize and punctuate each sentence correctly.

1. in corals clear live shallow water (*equal adjectives*)

    1. Corals live in clear, shallow water.

2. they simple creatures without are eyes (*pronoun subject*)

3. tiny animals corals the in eat floating ocean (*prepositional phrase*)

4. form limestone reefs huge of coral ridges under water (*appositive*)

5. fish sharks and eat seals (*compound direct objects*)

6. some hundreds grow very slowly for corals and live of years (*compound verb*)

7. the Reef is about Barrier 1,250 Great long miles (*prepositional phrase*)

8. shrimp and on live fish coral reefs (*compound subject*)

9. purple can red be yellow coral green or (*a series*)

10. pollution can and hurt garbage coral oil (*appositive*)

Write **NOW** Write three sentences about the animals living on a coral reef. On another sheet, mix up the words and leave out punctuation and capitalization. Ask a classmate to rearrange the words so they form complete sentences.

Basic Parts of a Sentence

Every sentence has two basic parts: a complete subject (which tells who or what is doing something) and a complete predicate (which tells what the subject is doing).

COMPLETE SUBJECT	COMPLETE PREDICATE
Who or what did something?	*What did the subject do?*
Jacques Cousteau and Emile Gagnan	invented modern scuba gear.
Cousteau, a famous ocean explorer,	was also a film producer.

Try It Divide a piece of paper into two columns. For each of the sentences below, write the complete subject in the left column and write the complete predicate in the right column.

> In the following sentences, the words that come before the verb are the *complete subject*. The verb and all the words that follow it are the *complete predicate*.

1. People have always explored under the sea.

1. People | have always explored under the sea.

2. The first piece of diving equipment was a snorkel made of a hollow reed.

3. The ancient Greeks used diving bells to walk underwater.

4. The English astronomer Edmond Halley discovered a comet and invented a diving bell.

5. *Scuba* stands for self-contained underwater breathing apparatus.

6. Diving suits with heavy helmets appeared for the first time in the 1800s.

7. Harry Houdini, the famous magician, invented a diving suit.

8. Plastic or rubber swim fins help a diver swim through the water.

9. The first team of women divers to live underwater for weeks was led by Sylvia Earle.

10. Earle, who spent more than 6,000 hours underwater, continues to work on saving oceans.

BASIC ELEMENTS

Subjects and Predicates

Every sentence has a subject and a predicate. A simple subject consists of the subject without the words that modify it. A simple predicate is the verb without the words that modify it or complete the thought. In the sentences below, the simple subjects are orange and the simple predicates are blue.

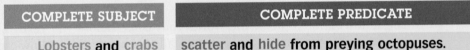

COMPLETE SUBJECT	COMPLETE PREDICATE
Octopuses	have the most complex brain of all invertebrates.
Their acute sense of touch	also aids in their survival.

A compound subject includes two or more subjects that share the same predicate (or predicates). A compound predicate includes two or more predicates that share the same subject (or subjects).

COMPLETE SUBJECT	COMPLETE PREDICATE
Lobsters and crabs	scatter and hide from preying octopuses.

Try It Number a piece of paper from 2 to 6, skipping a line between numbers. For each sentence below, write the simple subject on one line and the simple predicate on the next line. (Remember to look for compound subjects and predicates.)

1. A female octopus lays between 200,000 and 400,000 eggs at one time and dies shortly after laying her eggs.
   1. octopus
   lays, dies

2. Newborn octopuses float to the surface for about a month and then sink to live on the bottom of the ocean.

3. Crustaceans and mollusks are the main sources of food for newborn octopuses.

4. Moray eels eat octopuses.

5. Octopuses change color and squirt ink to protect themselves.

6. Sometimes, in calm water, the cloud of ink harms or kills the octopus.

 Write NOW Write one sentence with a single subject and a compound predicate. Then write another sentence with a compound subject and a compound predicate. Ask a classmate to underline the simple subjects once and the simple predicates twice in each sentence.

How can I make sure my sentences are complete?

Check Your Subjects and Predicates

Incomplete thoughts are called fragments. Fragments may be missing a subject, a predicate, or both. Study the fragments below. Then read the complete sentences made from them. Notice that a subject, a predicate, or both have been added to make the corrections.

FRAGMENT	SENTENCE
Are lurking in Monterey Bay.	**Strange creatures are lurking in Monterey Bay.** (A subject is added.)
Battery-powered robots deep to gather data.	**Battery-powered robots dive deep to gather data.** (A simple predicate is added.)
Part of a $10 million study of the ocean's climate.	**Underwater robots are part of a $10 million study of the ocean's climate.** (A subject and a simple predicate are added.)

Try It Number your paper from 2 to 6. Read each group of words below. If the group of words is a complete sentence, write "C" next to the number. If it is a fragment, write "F" and tell if you need to add a subject, a predicate, or both to make it a complete sentence.

1. Can operate for days or weeks on lithium flashlight batteries.

   1. F—subject

2. They can gather ocean data cheaper than research ships can.

3. According to scientist Francisco Chavez, "We to predict undersea weather."

4. Can affect surface weather, shoreline recreation, and fishing.

5. Monterey Bay once the largest sardine fishery in the world.

6. Scientists think many sardines may have died because of a change in underwater weather.

 Write NOW Correct any fragments above by adding the missing parts to form complete sentences. Exchange papers with a classmate and check each other's sentences.

Edit Your Writing Carefully

A sentence must express a complete thought. A sentence fragment does not do this even though it may look like a sentence with a capital letter and end punctuation. Reading a sentence out loud, however, can help a writer figure out whether a sentence is expressing a complete thought.

In the example below, the writer found and underlined a number of fragments. Then she turned the fragments into complete sentences by adding information to finish each thought.

SOME FRAGMENTS	ALL SENTENCES
<u>Before a newly hatched lobster looks like a real lobster.</u> The newborn must shed its shell three times. <u>When baby lobsters are 15 days old.</u> They live within three feet of the surface of the ocean. <u>Called "bugs" during this stage.</u>	Before a newly hatched lobster looks like a real lobster, the newborn must shed its shell three times. When baby lobsters are 15 days old, they live within three feet of the surface of the ocean. They are called "bugs" during this stage.

Try It Read the following paragraph and check for fragments. Then, on your own paper, tell how many fragments you found. Rewrite the paragraph, correcting each of the fragments.

1   Before lobsters become a favorite food of many people. The
2   animals begin life as tiny creatures swimming near the surface
3   of the ocean. When the baby lobsters are about a month
4   old. They begin looking for a hiding place on the ocean's
5   floor. After they settle into this spot or find another safe
6   habitat. They spend their first year hiding in small tunnels.
7   Because they have so many enemies. The young lobsters
8   usually eat just the food that floats through their little tunnels.

Write NOW Write a short paragraph about lobsters or another sea creature you know about. Have a classmate check your writing for fragments.

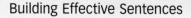

Move Misplaced Modifiers

A misplaced modifier can make a sentence very confusing. You can avoid this problem by making sure that modifiers are placed next to the words they modify. This is especially important when using descriptive phrases.

MISPLACED MODIFIERS	CORRECTED SENTENCES
Looking like a balloon with fins, the predator lets the puffer fish escape. (It sounds as though the predator looks like a balloon.)	**Looking like a balloon with fins, the puffer fish escapes from the predator.** (or) **The puffer fish, looking like a balloon with fins, escapes from the predator.** (Move the word being modified closer to its modifying phrase.)
We set out to observe fish in a glass-bottom boat. (It sounds like the fish are in a glass-bottom boat.)	**We set out in a glass-bottom boat to observe fish.** (or) **To observe fish, we set out in a glass-bottom boat.**

 Rewrite each of the sentences below so that the proper word is modified.

1. Hiding in deep sea grasses, you can find the puffer fish.
1. You can find the puffer fish hiding in deep sea grasses.

2. Camouflaged by the seaweed, predators can't always see the fish.

3. Prized for superb flavor, many people want a puffer fish for dinner.

4. Although it is tasty, poison makes the puffer fish dangerous to eat.

5. When properly trained, puffer fish can be prepared by careful chefs.

6. Swimming in an aquarium, I saw a puffer fish and its cousin, a porcupine fish.

Write **NOW** Using the facts below, write two sentences containing misplaced modifiers. (Hint: Separate your modifying phrase from the thing it is describing.) Then exchange sentences with a classmate and correct each other's work.

A Porcupine Fish

– normally swims around with spikes lying flat
– when threatened, spikes stick out and body inflates
– inflates by taking in tiny gulps of water
– feeds at night
– sends a jet spray into sand, looking for mollusks
– has large teeth

BASIC ELEMENTS

Fixing Sentence Problems

Avoid Run-On Sentences

Sometimes you may accidentally write a run-on sentence by putting together two or more sentences. One type of run-on is called a *comma splice,* in which the sentences are connected with a comma only. Another type of run-on has no punctuation at all.

One way to fix run-on sentences is to add a comma and a coordinating conjunction (*and, so, or, for, but, yet,* and *nor*). Another way is to connect the two sentences with a semicolon.

RUN-ON SENTENCE	CORRECTED SENTENCES
Manta rays are similar to sharks they both have skeletons made of cartilage.	Manta rays are similar to sharks, for they both have skeletons made of cartilage.
	Manta rays are similar to sharks; they both have skeletons made of cartilage.

On your own paper, correct the run-on sentences below by adding a comma and a coordinating conjunction.

1. Manta rays live in warm oceans these fish have fins that look like giant wings.

   1. Manta rays live in warm oceans, and these fish have fins that look like giant wings.

2. These huge creatures look ferocious they are really quite gentle.

3. Mantas use their wings to "fly" through the water they look like great floating triangles.

4. Manta rays that weigh more than 3,000 pounds can leap out of the water they can also gracefully avoid divers underwater.

5. Manta rays do not have a stinging barb they do not have sharp teeth.

6. These unique fish often swim near the surface they sometimes swim in deeper lagoon water, too.

Write NOW Now rewrite each run-on sentence above, correcting each with a semicolon.

Eliminate Rambling Sentences

A rambling sentence occurs when you use too many *and*'s to combine your ideas. You can eliminate rambling sentences by checking for extra *and*'s. Here are two ways to correct the same rambling sentence.

RAMBLING SENTENCE	CORRECTED SENTENCES
The number of North Atlantic right whales has been reduced by heavy whaling and only about 300 whales are left and efforts to increase their numbers are starting to bring results.	**The number of North Atlantic right whales has been reduced by heavy whaling; therefore, only about 300 whales are left. Efforts to increase their numbers are starting to bring results.** (Replace the first *and* with a semicolon and a conjunctive adverb to connect two related thoughts. Drop the second *and* to make two sentences.)
	The number of North Atlantic right whales has been reduced by heavy whaling. There are only about 300 whales left, although efforts to increase their numbers are starting to bring results. (Drop the first *and* to make two sentences. Combine thoughts by using a subordinating conjunction to create a subordinate clause.)

tip Some *and*'s are needed in sentences to connect compound subjects, compound predicates, items in a list, and so on.

Try It Correct the following rambling sentences on your own paper. Try using a subordinating conjunction where possible. (See **746.1**.)

1. Right whales were prized by whalers and they were easy to hunt and the whales were almost hunted to extinction and then, 100 years ago, laws were made to protect them.

2. Female whales give birth and they nurse their babies, called calves, for 13 months, sometimes carrying them on their backs, and then the mothers keep the babies close to them for another year and a female may have a calf every three to five years.

3. The northern right whale was almost extinct and the species is now making a comeback and scientists are finding that more babies are being born each year and last year 14 whale calves were born and that was the most calves born in one year recently.

BASIC ELEMENTS

What can I do to write clear sentences?

Make Subjects and Verbs Agree

Writers must be careful to make the subjects and verbs in each of their sentences agree. That means a singular subject needs a singular verb, and a plural subject needs a plural verb. (Also see **728.1**.) Indefinite pronouns used as subjects can be tricky because some of them can be singular or plural. (See the chart on page **475**.)

SINGULAR OR PLURAL SUBJECTS

A verb must agree with its subject in number.

■ If a subject is singular, the verb must be singular, too.
   A pod **is a group of dolphins**.

■ If a subject is plural, the verb must be plural.
   Bottleneck dolphins live **in pods**.

(Don't forget that most nouns ending in *s* or *es* are plural, and most verbs ending in *s* are singular.)

■ If an indefinite pronoun is singular, its verb must be singular, too.
   Nobody **wants to be left behind for the dolphin tour**.

■ If an indefinite pronoun is plural, its verb must be plural also.
   Many like **watching the playful dolphins**.

 Number your paper from 2 to 8. For each of these sentences, write the form of the verb (or verbs) that agrees with its subject.

1. Bottlenose dolphins sometimes swims with whales.
   1. swim

2. Like humans, both is mammals.

3. A dolphin are not a porpoise.

4. Dolphins hunts and plays together.

5. Everybody know that dolphins does not chew their food.

6. Using its tail, a dolphin often flip a fish out of the water and then eat it.

7. Dolphins fears sharks.

8. Many people swims with and feeds dolphins.

Write NOW Write one sentence using the subject "dolphins" and another using the subject "all." Make sure your subjects and verbs agree.

COMPOUND SUBJECTS CONNECTED BY "AND"

A compound subject connected by the word *and* usually needs a plural verb.

> **Our** guide **and our** chaperones take **us on a tour.**

COMPOUND SUBJECTS CONNECTED BY "OR"

A compound subject connected by the word *or* needs a verb that agrees in number with the subject nearest to the verb.

> **Tour** guides **or the boat's** captain talks **about the dolphins.**
> (*Captain*, the subject nearer the verb, is singular, so the singular verb *talks* is used.)

 Number your paper from 2 to 9. Write the correct verb choice for each of these sentences.

1. Manatees and a dolphin pod (*is, are*) fun to watch.

   1. are

2. Large tours or small private boats (*let, lets*) people view dolphins in harbor areas.

3. A telescope and an observation deck (*offer, offers*) clear views of the marine life.

4. Passengers or a crew member (*report, reports*) interesting sights.

5. Electronic games and cell phones (*is, are*) not affected by the ship's magnetic navigation equipment.

6. Either a dolphin or manatees (*like, likes*) to swim in a boat's wake.

7. Sometimes, dark skies or rain (*spoil, spoils*) the outings.

8. My brothers and Mom (*enjoy, enjoys*) boat rides more than I do.

9. Dockside shopkeepers and restaurant owners (*wait, waits*) impatiently for the tour to be over.

Write NOW Rewrite sentence 6 above so that a singular verb is correct. Rewrite sentence 7 so that a plural verb is correct. (Do not add or change anything—except the word order.)

What should I do to avoid nonstandard sentences?

Avoid Double Negatives

Two negative words used together in the same sentence form a double negative (*not no, barely nothing, not never*). Double negatives also happen if you use contractions ending in *n't* with a negative word (*can't hardly, didn't never*). Your writing will not be accurate if you use double negatives.

NEGATIVE WORDS								
nothing	nowhere	never	not	barely	hardly	nobody	none	no

NEGATIVE CONTRACTIONS							
don't	can't	won't	shouldn't	wouldn't	couldn't	didn't	hadn't

Number your paper from 2 to 6. List the double negatives you find in the sentences below and then correctly rewrite each sentence. *Remember:* There is usually more than one way to correct a double negative.

1. My family never has no time to go to the ocean.

> *1. never has no*
> *My family never has any time to go to the ocean.*

2. Just yesterday, Dad said, "I can't hardly find time to watch TV."

3. I wonder why we aren't going nowhere for a vacation this year.

4. Maybe it's because Mom and Dad don't barely get any time off.

5. Or maybe it's because my brother and I wouldn't hardly want to miss any baseball games.

6. I don't want nothing to keep us from taking an ocean-side vacation.

Avoid Using "Of" for "Have"

Do not use "of" in a sentence when you mean "have." When *have* is said quickly it can sound like *of*.

Incorrect: We could of gone to the beach together.

Corrected: We could have gone to the beach together.
We could've gone to the beach together.

Write four sentences. In two of them use double negatives. In the other two use "of" when you really mean "have." Exchange papers with a classmate, rewrite each other's sentences correctly, and then check each other's work.

Improving Your Sentence Style

There are a number of ways to add variety to your sentences and improve your writing style. Here are four of the most common ways.

1 Combine short sentences.

2 Use different types of sentences.

3 Expand sentences by adding words and phrases.

4 Model sentences of other writers.

What happens when too many sentences in a paragraph are the same length or follow the same pattern? Read the following paragraph to find out.

LITTLE VARIETY

> Eelgrass is a flowering saltwater plant. It grows along the coasts of the Atlantic, Pacific, and Indian Oceans. Eelgrass helps the environment in two ways. It uses photosynthesis and puts oxygen into our water and air. Many fish and marine animals live at least part of their lives in eelgrass. Eelgrass is home to crustaceans, sea stars, clams, and young salmon.

Using different types of sentences would keep this paragraph from sounding choppy. Read the following version, which has a better variety of sentences.

GOOD VARIETY

> Eelgrass, a flowering saltwater plant, grows along the coasts of the Atlantic, Pacific, and Indian Oceans. Eelgrass helps the environment in two ways. First, through photosynthesis, eelgrass puts oxygen into our water and air. Second, eelgrass is "home" to many fish and marine animals. Crustaceans, sea stars, clams, and young salmon live at least part of their lives in eelgrass.

 Read the paragraph below. Then, on your own paper, rewrite the paragraph by creating more sentence variety.

1   Eelgrass along the Atlantic coast was almost destroyed during
2 the hot weather in 1930–1931. The water temperature rose. The
3 eelgrass died out. Fish and animals that lived in the eelgrass died. Then
4 the fishing industry ran into trouble. There were fewer fish. This made
5 a bad economy worse. It took nearly 20 years for the eelgrass to grow
6 back. Today, boat engines destroy eelgrass. Coastal construction and oil
7 spills also kill eelgrass. People need to protect this valuable plant.

How can I make my sentences flow more smoothly?

Writers often combine sentences to help their writing flow more smoothly. Too many short sentences can make writing sound choppy. Combining some of the sentences will add variety to your writing and improve your overall writing style.

Combine with Phrases

COMBINE USING TWO OR MORE PHRASES	
Short Sentences	*Combined Sentences*
Seals don't have hands. Seals have short front flippers.	**Seals have short front flippers** instead of hands.

COMBINE USING AN APPOSITIVE PHRASE	
Elephant seals sometimes weigh more than 5,000 pounds. Elephant seals are the largest seal species.	**Elephant seals,** the largest seal species, **sometimes weigh more than 5,000 pounds.**

COMBINE USING A PREPOSITIONAL PHRASE	
Seals are able to stay submerged at great depths. Seals can do this for long periods of time.	For long periods of time, **seals are able to stay submerged at great depths.**

 Combine each of the following sets of sentences by using the method given in parentheses.

1. Seals can lift their bodies off the ground. Seals do this with their flippers. (*prepositional phrase*)

2. Sea lions can swim at the top speed of 25 mph. Sea lions are the fastest seals. (*appositive phrase*)

3. Antarctic seals eat krill. These are tiny shrimp-like creatures. (*appositive phrase*)

4. Baby harp seals are born with white fur. The white fur is a natural camouflage. (*appositive phrase*)

5. The stout-bodied walrus is a unique-looking mammal. It has wrinkled skin and long tusks. (*prepositional phrase*)

 Write a pair of sentences for a classmate to combine. Model your sentences after one of the sentence pairs above.

Combine with a Series of Words

You can combine sentences using a series of words, phrases, or clauses.

COMBINE WITH A SERIES	
Short Sentences	*Combined Using a Series of Words*
Moray eels eat shrimp and small fish. They also eat crabs and octopuses.	**Moray eels eat** shrimp, small fish, crabs, **and** octopuses.
Short Sentences	*Combined Using a Series of Phrases*
Eels make good aquarium pets if they have plenty of room to swim. They also need a place to hide. They need plenty of food to eat, too.	**Eels make good aquarium pets if they have** plenty of room to swim, a place to hide, **and** plenty of food to eat.

The items in any series must be alike (or parallel). For example, if the first item is a phrase, all the items must be phrases. The same is true for series containing words or clauses. (See **582.1**.)

Try It Using a series of parallel words or phrases, combine each of the following groups of sentences. (You may change some words to make the sentences work.)

1. Moray eels are related to American eels and conger eels. Worm eels and wolf eels are also related to moray eels.

　　1. American, conger, worm, and wolf eels are all related to moray eels.

2. Eels have long, thin bodies. They have snake-like heads. They have large mouths.

3. Some moray eels can weigh up to 100 pounds. Some can grow to 10 feet long. They can look like prehistoric monsters.

4. Moray eels live in caves. They live in coral reefs. Some also live in shallow waters.

5. Would you like to keep an eel for a pet? Would you like to see an eel in the wild? Would you like to eat "eel surprise" for dinner?

 Write NOW Write one sentence about another animal in which you use three or more words in a series. Then write another sentence about the same or a different animal in which you use three or more phrases in a series.

BASIC ELEMENTS

Combine with Relative Pronouns

You can combine two short sentences by using a relative pronoun to make a complex sentence. A complex sentence contains one independent, or main, clause and one dependent clause. (See 698.2–698.3 for more information.)

Relative pronouns include words such as *who, which, that, whose, whom,* and so on.

COMBINE WITH RELATIVE PRONOUNS	
Two Short Sentences	*Combined Using a Relative Pronoun*
The Bay of Fundy has the world's highest tides. The bay is in Nova Scotia.	**The Bay of Fundy, which is in Nova Scotia, has the world's highest tides.** or **The Bay of Fundy, which has the world's highest tides, is in Nova Scotia.**

 Combine each set of sentences below by using the relative pronoun in parentheses. (A dependent clause beginning with the relative pronoun "which" is always set off by commas.)

1. At high tide, the water rises as much as 53 feet. This is as high as a four-story building. *(which)*

   1. At high tide, the water rises as much as 53 feet, which is as high as a four-story building.

2. Many people love exploring tidal pools. These people enjoy viewing sea creatures close-up. *(who)*

3. Tide-pool creatures can survive the varying temperatures of water and air. These temperatures may be as hot as 86 degrees Fahrenheit in summer or −22 degrees Fahrenheit in winter. *(which)*

4. Many animals and plants thrive in tidal zones. These animals and plants need constant moisture. *(that)*

5. At around mid-tide, you can hear what is called the "voice of the moon." This "voice" is actually the roar of the tidal currents. *(which)*

 Write freely for 5 minutes about a water-related experience. Afterward, underline any sentences containing relative pronouns. Also find two shorter sentences in your writing that you can combine using a relative pronoun.

What can I do to add variety to my writing?

Writers use different types of sentences to add variety to their writing and make it sound interesting. The three common types of sentences are **simple**, **compound**, and **complex**. By learning to write these three types of sentences effectively, you can create sentence variety in your writing.

Write Simple Sentences

A **simple sentence** is one independent clause. (An independent clause is a group of words that can stand alone as one sentence.) A simple sentence may contain a single or compound subject and a single or compound predicate.

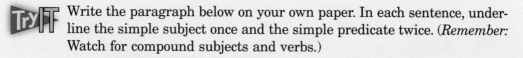

SIMPLE SENTENCE = ONE INDEPENDENT CLAUSE

Single Subject with a Single Predicate
Icebergs are a hazard to shipping.

Single Subject with a Compound Predicate
Usually ships avoid icebergs but sometimes collide with one.

Compound Subject with a Single Predicate
"Growlers" and "bergy bits" are two names for small Arctic icebergs.

 Write the paragraph below on your own paper. In each sentence, underline the simple subject once and the simple predicate twice. (*Remember:* Watch for compound subjects and verbs.)

1   Icebergs come from glaciers and float in the ocean. Antarctic
2   icebergs are the largest type of iceberg. Antarctic icebergs and
3   Arctic icebergs have only a small portion showing above the
4   water. Most of an iceberg remains below the water. Tall castle
5   bergs and pinnacle icebergs are found in the Arctic. Huge tabular
6   icebergs with vertical sides and flat tops form in the Antarctic.

Write **NOW** Write three simple sentences about something in nature that interests you. Give the first sentence a single subject and predicate, the second one a compound subject, and the third one a compound predicate.

BASIC ELEMENTS

Create Compound Sentences

A **compound sentence** is made up of two or more simple sentences (independent clauses) joined by a comma and a coordinating conjunction (*and, for, but, or, so, nor,* and *yet*) or by a semicolon.

COMPOUND SENTENCE = TWO INDEPENDENT CLAUSES

Pacific manta rays are the largest in the ray family, and some of them have wingspans of 20 feet. (A comma and the conjunction *and* join the two independent clauses.)

Mobilla rays are smaller than the Pacific rays; Mobilla rays seem to enjoy swimming with and being touched by humans. (Here, the two independent clauses are joined by a semicolon.)

Try IT On your own paper, join the following sets of independent clauses (simple sentences) using either a semicolon or a comma and a coordinating conjunction.

1. Stingrays are known as "birds" of the sea. Manta rays are called the "gigantic birds" of the sea.

   1. Stingrays are known as "birds" of the sea, but manta rays are called the "gigantic birds" of the sea.

2. Manta rays sometimes swim in tropical waters close to shore. They really prefer to roam in the open sea.

3. A manta ray is one of the gentlest creatures in the sea. For many years, the manta ray was known as a "devil fish."

4. Growths on either side of the manta's head look like horns. These "horns" help the ray to herd plankton into its mouth.

5. Female rays give birth to one or two babies at a time. Each "pup" may weigh as much as 25 pounds.

6. Baby manta rays learn to avoid predators. The babies spend much of their time on the sea floor, flapping their fins to throw sand over their bodies.

 Write NOW Write two compound sentences explaining how you would feel about swimming with a giant manta ray. Make sure to punctuate your sentences correctly.

Develop Complex Sentences

When you join a dependent clause to an independent clause, you form a **complex sentence**. Complex sentences may contain a relative pronoun such as *that, which,* and *who*. (See page **710** for more information.) They may also contain a subordinating conjunction such as *after, although, because, before, until, when,* and *while*. (See page **744** for more subordinating conjunctions.)

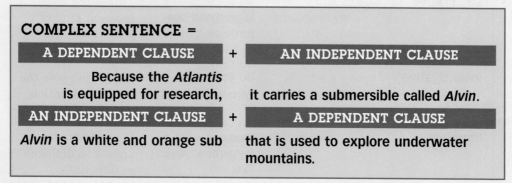

COMPLEX SENTENCE =

A DEPENDENT CLAUSE	+	AN INDEPENDENT CLAUSE
Because the *Atlantis* is equipped for research,		it carries a submersible called *Alvin*.

AN INDEPENDENT CLAUSE	+	A DEPENDENT CLAUSE
Alvin is a white and orange sub		that is used to explore underwater mountains.

 Number your paper from 2 to 6. Then write the dependent clause in each of the following complex sentences.

1. Because scientists were exploring undersea mountains south of Kodiak Island in Alaska, *National Geographic Today* sent a reporter along on the expedition.

   1. Because scientists were exploring undersea mountains south of Kodiak Island in Alaska

2. Chad Cohen, a reporter, joined the crew researching a world that contains bizarre spider crabs, exotic corals, and squiggly rockfish.

3. *Alvin* is launched by a giant A-frame, which first lifts the sub off of *Atlantis'* deck and then sets the sub into the water.

4. When the sub is cut loose, it falls below the ocean's surface and starts to descend into the darkness.

5. As soon as the sub reaches the ocean floor, *Alvin's* lights reveal millions of tiny jellyfish and bacteria glowing like stars.

6. *Alvin* maneuvers around on the lunar-like seafloor and gathers crabs and coral until the engine runs out of power and has to resurface.

Write **NOW** Write a short paragraph about some undersea exploring that you would like to do. Underline any complex sentences that you used. Also try to find two shorter sentences that you could combine into a complex sentence.

BASIC ELEMENTS

Use Questions and Commands

Writers use a variety of sentences to make statements, ask questions, give commands, or show strong emotion. See the chart below.

KINDS OF SENTENCES			
Declarative ▪	Makes a statement about a person, a place, a thing, or an idea	An adult loggerhead sea turtle weighs 200 to 350 pounds.	This is the most common kind of sentence.
Interrogative **?**	Asks a question	Do you know where they nest?	A question gets the reader's attention.
Imperative ▪	Gives a command	Find out what a loggerhead looks like.	Commands often appear in dialogue or directions.
Exclamatory **!**	Shows strong emotion or feeling	Wow, its head is 10 inches wide!	Use these sentences for occasional emphasis.

 On a piece of paper, write the numbers 1 to 5. Identify each of the sentences below by writing "D" for declarative, "INT" for interrogative, "IMP" for imperative, or "EX" for exclamatory.

1. Can you imagine not living to be 12 years old?

2. Only one in ten thousand loggerhead sea turtles lives that long!

3. Every year, on certain beaches from the eastern coast of the United States through Central and South America, female loggerheads lay their eggs.

4. Using their rear flippers, the turtles dig egg chambers that are about 20 inches deep.

5. Count the number of threats they have to face: humans, raccoons, skunks, shorebirds, sharks, fishing nets, and motorboats.

 Write four sentences—one of each kind—about a sea creature you find interesting.

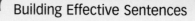
What can I do to add details to my sentences?

Expand with Prepositional Phrases

Writers use prepositional phrases to add details and information to their sentences. The chart below shows how this is done. Prepositional phrases function as adjectives or adverbs. *Remember:* A prepositional phrase includes a preposition, the object of a preposition, and the modifiers of the object. (See page **742** for a list of prepositions.)

PREPOSITIONAL PHRASE	USE IN SENTENCE
Some fish have beaklike mouths of fused teeth.	The phrase acts as an **adjective** to describe the noun *mouths*.
Parrot fish live on coral reefs.	The phrase acts as an **adverb** to modify the verb *live*.

■ Prepositional phrases used as adjectives answer the questions *How many? Which one? What kind?*

■ Prepositional phrases used as adverbs answer the questions *When? How? How often? How long? Where? How much?*

 Write the prepositional phrases that you find in the following sentences. (There are 10 phrases in sentences 2 through 6.)

1. Parrot fish can be a variety of colors and patterns.
   1. of colors and patterns
2. These fish swim between coral formations.
3. Their beaklike teeth scrape algae-covered coral from the reef.
4. After swallowing pieces of algae-covered coral, the parrot fish spits out the bits of coral.
5. At night, parrot fish sleep along the bottom of the reef.
6. Some types of parrot fish bury themselves in the sand until morning.

Write **NOW** Use one or two prepositional phrases to add information to each of the sentences below.

1 City aquariums have huge tanks of water.

2 One of my favorite tanks contains freshwater fish.

3 A new exhibit presents tropical fish.

BASIC ELEMENTS

Expand with Participial Phrases

Writers sometimes make their sentences more interesting by adding participial phrases. A participial phrase includes a participle and its modifiers. (A participle is a verb form usually ending in *ed* or *ing*.) A participial phrase serves as an adjective in a sentence.

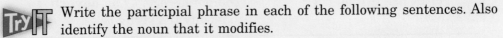

PARTICIPIAL PHRASES

Sea horses have a body encased in hard armor.
(This participial phrase modifies the noun *body*.)

Drifting from one coral to another, **sea horses are beautiful to watch.**
(The participial phrase modifies the noun *sea horses*.)

Write the participial phrase in each of the following sentences. Also identify the noun that it modifies.

1. Adapting their color to their surroundings, some sea horses depend on camouflage for protection.

   1. adapting their color to their surroundings, sea horses

2. Reaching the length of 10 inches, sea horses swim slowly among seaweed.

3. Depending on the size of its brooding pouch, a sea horse hatches between 10 and 100 eggs.

4. The bottom of a large aquarium or reef tank covered in a layer of sand is a good home for sea horses.

5. A sea horse likes certain types of structures, including colorful coral branches.

6. An adult sea horse maintained in good health may live more than three years.

Write **NOW** Write a brief paragraph about the sand dollar or another interesting sea creature of your own choosing. Include at least two participial phrases in your writing.

A Sand Dollar

- missing its cover of little spines when washed up on a beach
- related to sea lilies and starfish
- pores, or little holes, used to move seawater for movement
- lives on top or just beneath the surface of sandy or muddy areas
- eats organic particles
- no real predators
- when alive, often found with other sand dollars

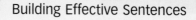
How can I make my sentences more interesting?

Model Sentences

You can learn a great deal about writing by studying the sentences of other writers. When you come across sentences that you like, practice writing some of your own that use the same pattern. This process is called *modeling*.

PROFESSIONAL MODELS	STUDENT MODELS
I walked along the sandy beach, inhaling the smell of salty surf and dried seaweed.	I ate at the carnival, devouring the huge sour pickles and salty French fries.
Manatees have blimpy bodies, giant beaver tails, and rubbery faces bristling with whiskers. —*Muse*	My tabby cat has a fat tummy, huge tiger paws, and soft fur marked by dark orange stripes.

Guidelines for Modeling

- Find a sentence or a short passage that you like and write it down.
- Think of a topic for your practice writing.
- Follow the pattern of the sentence or passage as you write about your own subject. (You do not have to follow the model exactly.)
- Build each sentence one part at a time and check your work when you are finished. (Take your time.)
- Review your work and change any parts that seem confusing or unclear.
- Share your new sentences with your classmates.
- Find other sentences to model and keep practicing.

Write **NOW** On your own paper, model the following sentences. *Remember:* You do not have to follow the model sentence exactly.

1 The sun was dropping into the dark ocean, but I kept wandering down the beach.

2 Ocean waves pounded the beach, washing away Tegan's sand castle.

3 I wanted to dive into the water, swim out to the nearest island, and hide away for a day or two.

Develop a Sentence Style

Modeling sentences can help you make your writing more exciting, lively, and appealing. The following writing techniques will also help you improve your style. (Also see page 42.)

Varying Sentence Beginnings

To add variety to the common subject-verb pattern, try beginning a sentence with a phrase or a dependent clause.

In his hand he held a whip.
—*Black Stallion* by Walter Farley

As winter drew on, Mollie became more and more troublesome.
—*Animal Farm* by George Orwell

Moving Adjectives

Usually, you write adjectives before the nouns they modify. You can also emphasize adjectives by placing them after the nouns.

I would come in from a day of progging for crab, sweating and filthy.
—*Jacob Have I Loved* by Katherine Paterson

Repeating a Word

You can repeat a word to emphasize a particular idea or feeling.

Little by little, the wind died down.
—*The Count of Monte Cristo* by Alexandre Dumas

Creating a Balanced Sentence

You can write a sentence that uses parallel words, phrases, or clauses for emphasis.

The wind in our ears drove us crazy and pushed us on.
—*Rogues to Riches* by Rob King

 Write NOW Study the sample sentences above. Then write your own sentences that follow each sample pattern. Share your sentences with your classmates.

Constructing Strong Paragraphs

One thing that can help you gain control of your writing is learning to write a good paragraph. Think of the paragraph as an important building block for all of your writing. If you can create strong, well-organized paragraphs, you can also create effective essays, book reviews, and reports.

A paragraph is made up of a group of sentences focused on one topic. Each sentence should add something to the overall picture. A paragraph can be developed to explain a process, share an opinion, describe something, or tell a story.

Mini Index

You will learn about . . .

- **the parts of a paragraph.**
- **types of paragraphs.**
- **writing effective paragraphs.**
- **adding details to paragraphs.**
- **gathering details.**
- **organizing your details.**
- **refining your details.**
- **turning paragraphs into essays.**

The Parts of a Paragraph

Most paragraphs have three main parts: a topic sentence, a body, and a closing sentence. Paragraphs usually begin with a **topic sentence** that tells what the paragraph is about. The sentences in the **body** share details about the topic, and the **closing sentence** brings the paragraph to a close.

Topic sentence

Body

Closing sentence

Adventure Sports

Many outdoor enthusiasts are looking for more adventure in their sports. Why else would a sane person jump out of an airplane, do some acrobatic tricks on a skyboard, and then parachute to the ground? People seek adventure by water, too. They navigate the same rivers and shoot the same rapids that early Native Americans, fur traders, and explorers did. They travel by canoe, kayak, or raft. On land, adventurers backpack and camp in the wilderness, in areas where they might meet bear, moose, and mountain lions. After climbing mountains, some outdoor enthusiasts ski, snowboard, or even bike down to the bottom. Today, an adventure sport is out there for just about anyone, and more sports are being invented all the time.

Respond to the reading. How many types of adventure sports are mentioned? What do they all have in common?

A Closer Look at the Parts

The Topic Sentence

The topic sentence tells the reader what a paragraph is going to be about. A good topic sentence (1) names the topic and (2) states a specific detail or a feeling about it. Here is a simple formula for writing a topic sentence.

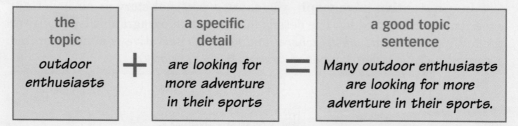

the topic		a specific detail		a good topic sentence
outdoor enthusiasts	**+**	*are looking for more adventure in their sports*	**=**	*Many outdoor enthusiasts are looking for more adventure in their sports.*

The topic sentence is usually the first sentence in a paragraph, although sometimes it comes later. It guides the direction of the sentences in the rest of the paragraph.

> *Many outdoor enthusiasts are looking for more adventure in their sports.*

The Body

The sentences in the body of the paragraph include the details needed to understand the topic.

- **Use specific details to make your paragraph interesting.**
  The specific details below are shown in red.

  > *People seek adventure by water, too. They navigate the same rivers and shoot the same rapids that early Native Americans, fur traders, and explorers did.*

- **Organize your sentences in the best possible order.**
  Five common ways to organize sentences are chronological (time) order, order of location, order of importance, comparison, and logical order. (See page 551.)

The Closing Sentence

The closing sentence comes after all the details in the body. It will often restate the topic, give the reader something to think about, or provide a transition into a following paragraph.

> *Today, an adventure sport is out there for just about anyone, and more sports are being invented all the time.*

Types of Paragraphs

There are four basic types of paragraphs: *narrative, descriptive, expository,* and *persuasive.* Each type requires a different way of thinking and planning.

Write Narrative Paragraphs

In a **narrative paragraph**, you share a personal story or an important experience with the reader. The details in a narrative paragraph should answer the 5 W's *(who? what? when? where?* and *why?).* A narrative is often organized according to time (what happened *first, next, then, finally).*

Topic sentence
· · · · · · · · · · · ·

Body

Closing sentence
· · · · · · · · · · ·

My Camping Adventure

Camping in the wilderness can be a real adventure, especially if you have a close encounter with a bear. One night while camping, my mom, dad, and younger sister were sound asleep in the tent, but I was wide-awake. Suddenly, I heard snorting noises coming from our campsite. I crept to the door and peered out cautiously. By the light of the moon, I saw a big brown bear munching on a bag of our marshmallows. I wanted to shout a warning, but I was so scared that I couldn't get out one sound. As I crawled across the tent to wake my dad, I must have bumped my sister. She sat up and screamed. Her scream startled me, and I yelled, "It's a bear!" Our shouts must have scared the bear because when we opened the tent, there was no bear. My family said I must have been dreaming about a bear, but they couldn't explain how that bag of marshmallows disappeared.

Respond to the reading. Find the key word repeated in the topic sentence and the closing sentence. Does this paragraph answer the 5 W's?

Write your own paragraph. Write a paragraph that tells about a memorable experience you've had. Include the 5 W's and whatever details are needed.

Develop Descriptive Paragraphs

When you write a **descriptive paragraph**, you give a detailed picture of a person, a place, an object, or an event. Descriptive paragraphs include many sensory details (sight, sound, smell, taste, touch).

Topic sentence
· · · · · · · · · ·

Rainbow Rock

Rainbow Rock, a huge man-made wall, helps people learn rock-climbing techniques. Rainbow Rock rises 30 feet above the ground and is covered with purple, green, and red climbing paths. Each path contains a variety of odd-shaped footholds, rough outcroppings, and challenging overhangs. The purple path offers a low-key climbing experience that just about anybody can scratch and scramble up. The green path

Body

is more advanced and ends with a very tricky, smooth overhang right at the top. The difficult red path has tiny, slippery toeholds that are only about one inch in diameter. It almost takes a mountain goat to maneuver on this path. If someone missteps and falls, a harness snaps into

Closing sentence
· · · · · · · · · ·

action and catches the climber. He or she is left groaning and swinging in midair. Rainbow Rock may be just an artificial training ground, but it provides a real test of a rock climber's balance, strength, and courage.

BASIC ELEMENTS

Respond to the reading. Which of the five senses are covered in the paragraph? Which two or three details are especially descriptive?

Write

Write your own paragraph. Write a paragraph that describes a place. Use lots of sights, sounds, and other sensory details in your description.

Construct Expository Paragraphs

In an **expository paragraph**, you share information. You can explain a subject, give directions, or show how to do something. Transition words like *first, next, then,* and *finally* are often used in expository writing.

Topic sentence
∙∙∙∙∙∙∙∙∙∙∙∙∙

Body

Closing sentence
∙∙∙∙∙∙∙∙∙∙∙∙∙

Snowboarding

Today, snowboarding is one of the most popular and exciting winter sports in America. While people have been skiing and ice-skating for centuries, snowboarding has been around for only about 40 years. In 1998, snowboarding became an Olympic sport in Nagano, Japan. By the year 2000, 7.2 million snowboarders, also known as "shredders," were hitting the slopes. Now, both children and adults seem to love snowboarding. Freestyle snowboarders do all sorts of jumps and tricks. These people use a soft boot and a fairly short board. On the other hand, Alpine snowboarders focus on carving turns down the slopes and on racing. Their boots are hard, and their boards are longer and narrower. Snowboarding will probably continue to take the winter sports scene by storm.

Respond to the reading. List the transitions used between sentences in the paragraph above. (See pages 572–573 for a list of transitions.)

Write an expository paragraph. Write a paragraph that explains a sport that you know very well. Be sure to use transitions to connect your ideas.

Build Persuasive Paragraphs

In a **persuasive paragraph**, you share your opinion (or strong feeling) about a topic. To be persuasive, you must include plenty of reasons, facts, and details to support your opinion. Persuasive writing is usually organized by order of importance or by logical order (as in the paragraph below).

Topic sentence

Body

Closing sentence

High Ropes Course

The high ropes course is waiting to help you and your friends build confidence and group cooperation. It's also a lot of fun. Many courses, indoor and outdoor, are available in camps, clubs, and schools across America. You may think that climbing the high ropes is dangerous, but it isn't. Safety ropes and harnesses are carefully managed by course experts and members of your group to give you lots of support. When you attempt to cross a suspended log or move by rope across an expanse that seems scary, your teammates will encourage you. You'll also feel great when you can encourage someone else to succeed. Even if you cannot complete the course, you'll feel supported and know the accomplishment of having faced the challenge. Why not join a group this summer and experience the true team spirit and the confidence that a high ropes course offers?

BASIC ELEMENTS

Respond to the reading. What is the writer's opinion in the paragraph? Name reasons that support her opinion. When is the most important reason given?

Prewrite

Write an opinion paragraph. Write an opinion about an outdoor activity. Include at least three strong reasons that support your opinion.

Writing Effective Paragraphs

Use the following general guidelines whenever you write paragraphs.

Prewriting Selecting a Topic and Details

- Select a specific topic.
- Collect facts, examples, and details about your topic.
- Write a topic sentence that states what your paragraph is going to be about. (See page **525** for help.)
- Decide on the best way to arrange your details.

Writing Creating the First Draft

- Start your paragraph with the topic sentence.
- Write sentences in the body that support your topic. Use the details you collected as a guide.
- Connect your ideas and sentences with transitions.
- End with a sentence that restates your topic, leaves the reader with a final thought, or (in an essay) leads into the next paragraph.

Revising Improving Your Writing

- Add information if you need to say more about your topic.
- Move sentences that aren't in the correct order.
- Delete sentences that do not support the topic.
- Rewrite any sentences that are not clear.

Editing Checking for Conventions

- Check the revised version of your writing for capitalization, punctuation, grammar, and spelling errors.
- Then write a neat final copy and proofread it.

 When you write a paragraph, remember that readers want . . .
- original ideas. *(They want to learn something new and interesting.)*
- personality. *(They want to hear the writer's voice.)*

How can I find interesting details?

Every paragraph needs good supporting details. Here are several types of details you can use in expository and persuasive paragraphs: facts, explanations, definitions, reasons, examples, and comparisons. You might get these details from personal knowledge and memories or from other sources of information.

Use Personal Details

For narrative and descriptive writing, personal details can add interest. Personal details may include sensory, memory, and reflective details.

- **Sensory details** are things that you see, hear, smell, taste, and touch. (These details are important in descriptive paragraphs.)

    He or she is left groaning and swinging in midair.

- **Memory details** are things you remember from experience. (These details are important in narrative paragraphs.)

    Her scream startled me, and I yelled, "It's a bear!"

- **Reflective details** are things you think about or hope for. (These details are often used in narrative and descriptive paragraphs.)

    Rainbow Rock may be just an artificial training ground, but it provides a real test of a rock climber's balance, strength, and courage.

Use Other Sources of Details

To collect details from other sources, use the following tips.

1. **Talk with someone you know.** Parents, neighbors, friends, or teachers may know a lot about your topic.

2. **Write for information.** If you think a museum, a business, or a government office has information you need, send for it.

3. **Read about your topic.** Gather details from books, magazines, and newspapers.

4. **Use the Internet.** The quickest source of information is the Internet. Remember to check Internet sources carefully for reliability. (See page 376.)

BASIC ELEMENTS

How do I know what kinds of details to gather?

Here are tips that will help you collect the right kinds of details when you write paragraphs about people, places, objects, and events, and when you write definitions.

Writing About a Person

When writing about or describing a person, make sure you collect plenty of information. The following guidelines will help.

Observe ■ If possible, carefully watch the person. Maybe the person laughs in a special way or wears a certain type of clothing.

Interview ■ Talk with your subject. Write down words and phrases that the person uses.

Research ■ Use whatever sources are necessary—books, articles, the Internet—to find out more about this person.

Compare ■ Can your subject be compared to some other person?

Describe ■ List any physical characteristics and personality traits.

Writing About a Place

When describing or writing about a place, use details that help the reader understand why the place is important to you.

Observe ■ Study the place you plan to write about. Use photos, postcards, or videos if you can't observe the place in person.

Remember ■ Think of a story (or an anecdote) about this place.

Describe ■ Include the sights, sounds, and smells of the place.

Compare ■ Compare your place to other places.

Writing About an Object

When writing about an object, tell your reader what kind of object it is, what it looks like, how it is used, and why this object is important to you.

Observe ■ Think about these questions: How is it used? Who uses it? How does it work? What does the object look like?

Research ■ Learn about the object. Try to find out when it was first made and used. Ask other people about it.

Define ■ What class or category does this object fit into? (See "Writing a Definition" on the next page.)

Remember ■ Recall interesting stories about this object.

Writing About an Event

When writing about or describing an event, focus on the important actions or on one interesting part. Also include sensory details and answer the 5 W's. The following guidelines will help.

Observe ■ Study the event carefully. What sights, sounds, tastes, and smells come to mind? Listen to what people around you are saying.

Remember ■ When you write about something that has happened to you, recall as many details connected with the event as you can.

List ■ Answer the *who? what? when? where?* and *why?* questions for facts about the event.

Investigate ■ Read about the event and ask other people what they know about it.

Evaluate ■ Decide why the event is important to you.

Writing a Definition

When you write a definition, you need to think about three things.

● First put the **term** you are defining *(coyote)* into a **class** or category of similar things *(wild member of the dog family)*.

● Then list special **characteristics** that make this individual different from others in that class *(like a wolf, only smaller)*.

Term—*A coyote*

Class—*is a wild member of the dog family and is*

Characteristic— *like a wolf, only smaller.*

What can I do to organize my details effectively?

After you've gathered your details, you need to organize them in the best possible way. You can organize a paragraph by *time, location, importance, comparison*, or *logical order*. Graphic organizers can help you keep your details in order.

Use Chronological Order

Chronological means "according to time." Transition words and phrases (*first, second, then,* and *finally*) are often used in narrative and expository paragraphs. A time line can help you organize your details.

Bill-to-Law Time Line					
Bill introduced by senator in Senate	Goes to committee for study	Voted on by Senate (passed)	Voted on by House (passed)	Goes to president to sign into law	If vetoed, back to House and Senate (needs 2/3 vote each)

Topic sentence

Body

Closing sentence

Making a Law

Turning a bill into a law at the federal level is a complicated process. First, a senator or House representative introduces a bill, or potential law. Then the bill goes to a committee for study. After studying the bill, the committee recommends that the bill be changed or voted on. If a bill is introduced in the Senate, all senators discuss and vote on it. Next, the representatives do the same thing in the House. When both the Senate and the House approve it, the bill goes to the president. If the president signs the bill, it finally becomes a law. However, the president can veto the bill, but even with a veto, the bill can still become a law if two-thirds of the Senate and the House vote in favor of it. Because of this process, many bills get blocked, detoured, or totally changed along the way.

Respond to the reading. How are steps in making a law shown in the time line (or chart)? How are they given in the paragraph?

Use Order of Location

Often, you can organize descriptive details by order of location. For example, a description may move from left to right, from top to bottom, or from one direction (north) to another (south). Words or phrases like *next to, before, above, below, east, west, north,* and *south* may be used to show location. A drawing or map can help you organize your details.

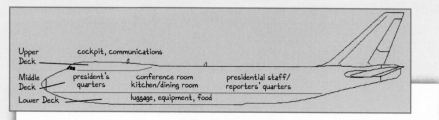

**Topic
sentence**

Body

**Closing
sentence**

The President's Plane

Air Force One, the president's plane, is a 747 jet with many special features. The lower level holds luggage, ultra-modern electronic equipment, and enough food for 100 people to eat 20 meals each. The 747's middle deck, which looks more like a hotel than an airplane, has the most sections. The president's quarters, at the front of the plane, include an office, an exercise room, and a bedroom. A large conference room and a kitchen make up the center section. The conference room doubles as a dining room. At the rear of the plane, the president's staff and the television and print reporters have work and rest areas. On the upper deck is the cockpit and a very sophisticated communications room. Air Force One has been modified in other ways, too, but that information is considered top secret.

BASIC ELEMENTS

Respond to the reading. With what part of *Air Force One* does the description begin? Where does it end?

Use Order of Importance

Persuasive and expository paragraphs are often organized by order of importance—from *most* to *least* important, or from *least* to *most* important.

> Most important
> 1. _____
> 2. _____   **or**
> 3. _____
> Least important
>
> Least important
> 3 _____
> 2. _____
> 1. _____
> Most important

Topic sentence

Body

Closing sentence

Presidential Powers

The president of the United States is the nation's most powerful leader. The president's most important duty is to "preserve, protect, and defend the Constitution of the United States." The Constitution serves as the blueprint for governing this country and for safeguarding the rights and freedoms of its citizens. Serving as commander in chief of the armed forces is probably the president's second-most important duty. In this role, the president can deploy troops to protect the country and its people. In times of national emergency, Congress can give the president even more control over the armed forces. The president can also appoint judges and make treaties, but he cannot make any laws. Only Congress has that power. Finally, as head of the executive branch, the president is in charge of 4 million employees. This might be the president's least-favorite job! All in all, the job of being president carries a lot of responsibility.

Respond to the reading. How are the details organized in this paragraph? On your own paper, list them in reverse order (most to least or least to most). Which order works better?

Use Comparison-Contrast Order

Expository paragraphs are often organized by comparison-contrast order, which shows how two subjects are both alike and different. A Venn diagram can be used to show differences (**A** and **B**) and similarities (**C**).

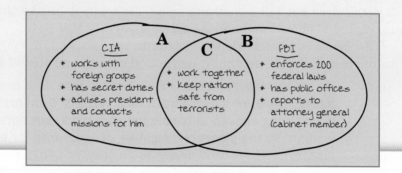

A **C** **B**

CIA
* works with foreign groups
* has secret duties
* advises president and conducts missions for him

* work together
* keep nation safe from terrorists

FBI
* enforces 200 federal laws
* has public offices
* reports to attorney general (cabinet member)

Topic sentence
· · · · · · · · · ·

Spy vs. Spy

     The Central Intelligence Agency (CIA) and the Federal Bureau of Investigation (FBI) help protect the United States. Although they share a goal and sometimes work together, the two groups are very different. The CIA's job is to collect information about foreign groups and people that may harm the United States. The CIA also works with the FBI to watch for spies or terrorists in the United States. Not only

Body

does the FBI hunt for spies, but it also enforces more than 200 federal laws in this country. CIA agents depend on secrecy to do their duties, while FBI agents work in offices across the country and do not hide their identities. The CIA advises the president and conducts special missions ordered by the president. The

Closing sentence
· · · · · · · · · ·

FBI reports to the attorney general, who is a member of the president's cabinet. Despite their differences, these two groups help keep the nation safe from terrorists and other threats.

BASIC ELEMENTS

Respond to the reading. Find two body sentences that include contrasting details. What words show the contrast?

Write

Write a paragraph. Choose two teams, groups, or organizations to compare. Use a Venn diagram to list the details. Then write your paragraph.

How can I be sure all my details work well?

Create Unity in Your Writing

In a well-written paragraph, each detail tells something about the topic. If a detail does not tell something about the topic, it breaks the *unity* of the paragraph and should probably be cut.

The detail (sentence) shown in blue in the following passage does not fit with the rest of the paragraph. It disrupts the unity and should be cut.

> In the 1800s, pioneers who headed west used oxen and mules instead of horses to pull their wagons. Oxen and mules were strong enough to handle the daily work, but horses weren't. So the pioneers bought six or eight oxen for each wagon. Cowboys used horses to drive cattle herds. The strength and endurance of oxen helped settlers cross the Rocky Mountains.

Try IT In the paragraph below, find three details (sentences) that do not support the topic sentence. Then read the paragraph aloud without those sentences. How does cutting those details affect the paragraph's unity?

1 A "prairie schooner" was a type of covered wagon used by
2 pioneers. It was about four feet wide and ten feet long. That's
3 much smaller than my bedroom at home. With the cover on, a
4 prairie schooner stood about ten feet tall. The wagon box was
5 made of hardwood and was about three feet deep. The pioneers
6 made the wagon box watertight by using tar. People also used
7 tar to patch a leaky roof. A watertight prairie schooner could
8 float across slow-moving rivers. The side boards were slanted
9 outward so that river water didn't come in under the edges of
10 the cover. River water has bacteria in it. The wagon box was
11 packed tight with everything the pioneers planned to take to
12 their new home.

Look at your paragraph. Study the comparison-contrast paragraph you wrote (page 537). Do all your details support your topic? Would the unity of your paragraph be improved if you cut a detail or two?

Develop Coherence from Start to Finish

An effective paragraph reads smoothly and clearly. When all the details in a paragraph are tied together well, the paragraph has *coherence* and is easy for the reader to follow. One way to make your writing smooth and coherent is to use transitions.

 Number your paper from 1 to 6. Use the transitions in black to help tie the paragraph below together. (Use each transition only once.) When you finish, read the paragraph. Does it read smoothly? If not, switch some transitions.

first	**in addition**	**besides**	**although**
then	**also**	**second**	**finally**

There are several simple ways in which kids can help the
environment. _____ , they can recycle things like plastic,
(1)
glass, cans, newspapers, and magazines. _____ , they can
(2)
pick up trash on school grounds and playgrounds. _____
(3)
they can clean up their own yards. _____ it takes some
(4)
work, kids can plant trees. _____ looking nice, trees help
(5)
the environment by producing oxygen, by removing pollution
from the air, and by providing food and shelter for birds.

_____ , kids can help even more by giving
(6)
Planet Earth a voice. They can speak up and
remind other people to take care of the
environment, too.

 Read your paragraph. Read your comparison-contrast paragraph from page 537. Underline any parts that don't flow smoothly. Then use transitions to make the writing smoother. (See pages 572–573.)

BASIC ELEMENTS

How can I turn my paragraphs into essays?

Use an Essay Plan

Turning a group of paragraphs into an essay is not simply a matter of placing one after another. To begin with, each paragraph needs to be well written and well organized. Here are some additional tips to follow.

1 Plan the organization.

Organize your essay in a way that fits your topic—chronological order, order of importance, logical order, order of location, and so on.

2 State the topic and focus in the first paragraph.

Begin with an interesting fact or example to catch the reader's attention. Then tell what your essay is about in a focus statement, which includes the topic and a main idea or feeling about it.

3 Develop your writing idea in the middle paragraphs.

Use each paragraph in the body of your essay to explain and support one part of your focus statement. Each paragraph must have a topic sentence, which deals with one part of the focus, followed with supporting details.

4 Finish with a strong ending.

The final paragraph is usually a review of the main points in the essay. Your ending may emphasize the importance of the topic or may leave the reader with something to think about.

5 Use transition words or phrases to connect paragraphs.

For a complete list of transitions, see pages 572–573.

A PARAGRAPH HAS . . .	AN ESSAY HAS . . .
a topic sentence.	a focus (thesis) statement.
sentences that develop the topic sentence.	body paragraphs that develop the focus.
a closing or transitional sentence.	a concluding paragraph.

How do I know if I have a strong paragraph?
Use a Paragraph Checklist

You'll know that you have a strong paragraph if it gives the reader complete information on a specific topic. One sentence should identify the topic, and the other sentences should support it. Use the checklist below to help you plan and write effective paragraphs.

Ideas

_____ **1.** Do I focus on an interesting idea?
_____ **2.** Do I use enough specific details?

Organization

_____ **3.** Is my topic sentence clear?
_____ **4.** Have I organized the details in the best order?

Voice

_____ **5.** Do I show interest in—and knowledge of—my topic?
_____ **6.** Does my voice fit my audience? My purpose? My topic?

Word Choice

_____ **7.** Do I use specific nouns and active verbs?
_____ **8.** Do I use specific adjectives and adverbs?

Sentence Fluency

_____ **9.** Have I written clear and complete sentences?
_____ **10.** Do I use a variety of sentence beginnings and lengths?

Conventions

_____ **11.** Do I use correct punctuation and capitalization?
_____ **12.** Do I use correct spelling and grammar?

improve

support

A Writer's Resource

organize

REFERENCE

select

A Writer's Resource

If you're like most students, you often have questions when you are in the middle of a writing assignment. If a question pops up when you're in class, you can ask your teacher or a classmate. If, however, a question pops up when you're not in class, you need to find another source to ask or check.

This "Writer's Resource" chapter can be a great source for answering many of your questions, like "How can I find the best topics to write about?" or "How can I make my voice more expressive?" or "What can I do to make my final copy look better?"

Mini Index

You will learn how to . . .

- find topics and get started.
- collect and organize details.
- write terrific topic sentences.
- use new forms.
- create a voice.
- improve your writing style.
- expand your vocabulary.
- write more effective sentences.
- connect sentences and paragraphs.
- improve your final copy.
- set up practical writing.

How can I find the best topics to write about?

Try a Topic-Selecting Strategy

A distinguished writer once said, "There are few experiences quite so satisfactory as getting a good writing idea." This may be overstating it a little, but getting a good writing idea is certainly an important step in the writing process. Let's say, for example, you are asked to write a report about a topic you have studied in a science unit. Your job would be to select a "good writing idea," a specific topic, to write about.

> **General Subject Area:** bacteria
> **Specific Writing Topic:** fighting harmful bacteria

The following strategies will help you select effective, specific topics that you can feel good about.

Journal Writing Write on a regular basis in a personal journal, recording your thoughts and experiences. Review your entries from time to time and underline ideas that you would like to write more about later. (See pages **431–434**.)

Clustering Begin a cluster (also called a web) with a key word. Select a general term or an idea that is related to your writing assignment. Then cluster related words around the key word, as in the model below.

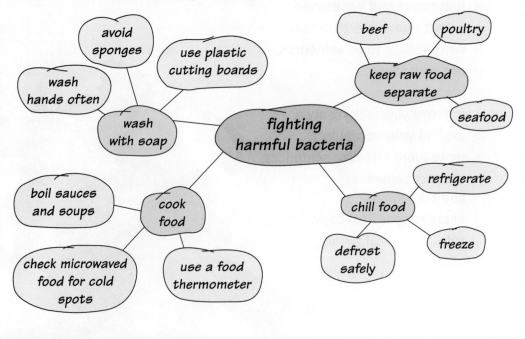

Listing List ideas as they come to mind when you think about your assignment. Keep your list going as long as you can. Then look for words in your list that you feel would make good writing topics.

Freewriting Write nonstop for 5 to 10 minutes to discover some possible writing ideas. Begin writing with a particular idea in mind (one related to the writing assignment). Underline the ideas that might work as topics for your assignment.

Sentence Completion Complete a sentence starter in as many ways as you can. Try to word your sentence so that it leads you to a topic you can use for a particular writing assignment.

Reading is . . .	I think it would be fun . . .	I like to share . . .
Journal entries help me . . .	I would not mind . . .	My favorite animal . . .
Painting can be . . .	My friend is . . .	My part-time job . . .
Last year my writing . . .	I wish my parents . . .	

Review the "Basics of Life" List

The words listed below name many of the categories or groups of things that most people need in order to live a full life. The list provides an endless variety of possibilities for topics. Consider the first category, *work/occupation.* You could write about . . .

- the occupation of a friend or a family member,
- what you think your all-time favorite occupation would be, or
- why your work is rewarding.

work/occupation	senses	rules/laws
clothing	machines	tools/utensils
housing	intelligence	heat/fuel
food	history/records	natural resources
communication	agriculture	personality/identity
exercise	land/property	recreation/hobby
education	community	trade/money
family	science	literature/books
friends	plants/vegetation	health/medicine
purpose/goals	freedom/rights	art/music
love	energy	faith/religion

What can I do to get started?

Use a List of Writing Topics

The writing prompts listed below and the sample topics listed on the next page provide plenty of starting points for writing assignments.

Writing Prompts

Every day is full of experiences that make you think. You do things that you feel good about. You hear things that make you angry. You wonder how different things work. You're reminded of a past experience. These common, everyday thoughts can make excellent prompts for writing.

Compare-Contrast

A shark and a manta ray
A llama and a camel
Soccer and football
Breakfast on Monday/breakfast on Sunday
Two seasons
Two months
Living in a city/small town
Yourself and a relative

Describe

The perfect bedroom
My favorite store
A parrot, a guinea pig, a ferret
Newborn lambs, calves, chickens
Stalking cats, galloping horses
Pioneer days, wagon-train life
Life in ancient Egypt, Greece, or Rome
Solar or lunar eclipses, rainbows
Meteor showers, hailstorms, sun dogs

Tell Your Story

My biggest surprise
Learning a lesson
Learning something amazing, surprising
Visiting a special place
Overcoming a challenge
A sudden or a big change

Problem-Solution

School rule about clothing
Being late to school
Keeping my cat off my bed
Keeping my brother out of my room
Getting to soccer practice
Convincing the city council we need
   a teen center
Getting my homework done on time

Editorial

Individual sports in school
More field trips for students
An environment-friendly idea
Ways to help your community
Supporting a worthwhile cause
Putting an end to something unfair

Respond to . . .

A book that changed your thinking
A character you identify with
A poem that expressed a feeling
The biography of someone you admire

Research

Aquifers, oil wells, salt mines
Hot springs, mud slides, droughts
Deserts, tide pools, glaciers

Sample Topics

You come across many people, places, experiences, and things every day that could be topics for writing. A number of possible topics are listed below for descriptive, narrative, expository, and persuasive writing.

Descriptive

People: teacher, relative, classmate, coach, neighbor, bus driver, hero, someone you spend time with, someone you admire, brothers and sisters, someone with a special talent, someone from history

Places: hangout, garage, room, rooftop, historical place, zoo, park, hallway, barn, bayou, lake, cupboard, yard, empty lot, alley, valley, campsite, river, city street

Things: billboard, poster, video game, cell phone, bus, boat, gift, drawing, rainbow, doll, junk drawer, flood, mascot, movie

Animals: dolphin, elephant, snake, armadillo, eagle, deer, toad, spoonbill, squirrel, pigeon, pet, coyote, catfish, octopus, beaver, turtle

Narrative

A time I . . . did something mean, embarrassed myself or someone else, acted without thinking

A time someone . . . said the wrong thing, discovered an unexpected friend, made the wrong decision

Expository

Comparison-Contrast . . . Two friends, two places, two jobs, two teachers, two pets, two types of transportation, a house cat and a lion, a lake and the ocean

The causes of . . . sunburn, acne, hiccups, tornadoes, rust, computer viruses, arguments, success, failure, frostbite

Kinds of . . . crowds, friends, commercials, dreams, neighbors, pain, clouds, joy, stereos, heroes, chores, homework, frustration

Definition of . . . a good time, a conservative, "soul," a grandmother, loyalty, one type of music, advice, courage, hope, strength, fun, freedom, pride

Persuasive

School: homework, school government, hot/cold classrooms, lunchroom vending machines, closed-campus lunches, crowded hallways, crowded library/computer lab

Environment: beautifying a neighborhood, cleaning up a local park, petitioning for cleaner air, volunteering at the library

Home: too many chores, pet troubles, changing a curfew, getting enough computer time, sharing a bathroom/bedroom

How can I collect details for my writing?

Try Graphic Organizers

Graphic organizers can help you gather and organize your details for writing. Clustering is one method. (See page **544**.) These two pages list other useful organizers.

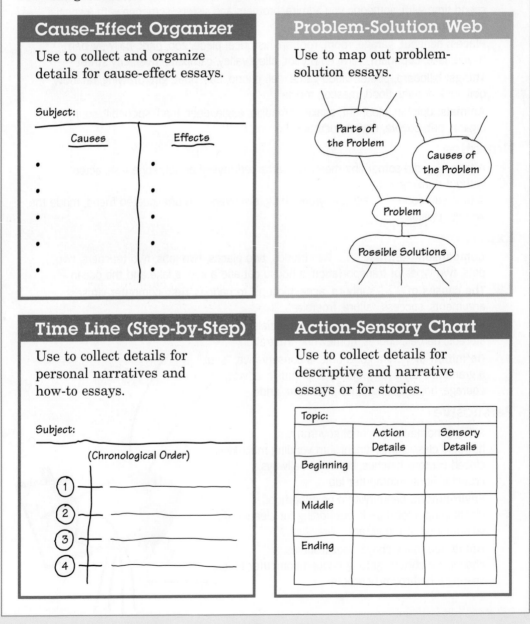

Cause-Effect Organizer

Use to collect and organize details for cause-effect essays.

Subject: _____

Causes	Effects
•	•
•	•
•	•
•	•
•	•

Problem-Solution Web

Use to map out problem-solution essays.

Parts of the Problem

Causes of the Problem

Problem

Possible Solutions

Time Line (Step-by-Step)

Use to collect details for personal narratives and how-to essays.

Subject: _____

(Chronological Order)

1 _____
2 _____
3 _____
4 _____

Action-Sensory Chart

Use to collect details for descriptive and narrative essays or for stories.

Topic:	Action Details	Sensory Details
Beginning		
Middle		
Ending		

organize
REFERENCE
select support
improve
549
A Writer's Resource

Venn Diagram

Use to collect details to compare and contrast two subjects.

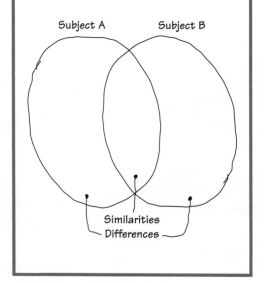

Subject A   Subject B

Similarities
Differences

5 W's Chart

Use to collect the *Who? What? When? Where?* and W*hy?* details for personal narratives and news stories.

Subject:

Who?	What?	When?	Where?	Why?

Sensory Chart

Use to collect details for descriptive essays and observation reports.

Subject:

Sights	Sounds	Smells	Tastes	Feelings

Process Chain (5 Step)

Use to collect details for science-related writing, such as how a process or cycle works.

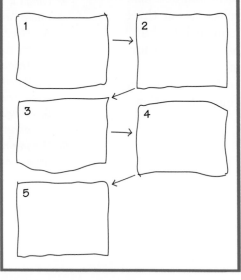

1
2
3
4
5

What can I do to organize my details better?

Make Lists and Outlines

List Your Details

You can use a variety of ways to organize details as you prepare to write an essay or a report. For most writing, you can make a simple list.

Ginga's background
— born in 1583, western coast of Africa
— father fought the Portuguese slave traders
— brother took throne when father died, but he was weak
— Ginga helped him and took over when he died
— she died in 1663

Good diplomat
— dealt with Portuguese effectively
— became allies of other African nations
— moved her people to avoid slavery

Good war ruler
— she and her two sisters led army regiments
— used jungle to hide armies

Outline Your Information

After gathering facts and details, select two or three main points that best support your focus. Write an outline to organize your information.

I. Ginga lived from about 1583 to 1663 in western Africa, where Angola is now located.
   A. Her father was the king of Ndongo.
   B. He fought three wars against the Portuguese slave traders, winning the first two but losing the third.
   C. When he died, Ginga's brother became king, and she carried out some of his responsibilities.
   D. Ginga used diplomacy, warfare, and alliances with other nations to protect her people.
II. Ginga showed her skill for diplomacy when her brother first became king.
   A. . . .
   B. . . .

Use Patterns of Organization

■ **Chronological (Time) Order** or **Step-by-Step** You can arrange your details in the order in which they happen (*first, then, next,* and so on). Use these patterns for narratives, history reports, directions, and explaining a process. (See page **534**.)

> With a groan, I pulled on my heavy backpack and headed off barefoot up the giant sand hills at Sleeping Bear Dunes. At first, I thought this hike would be easy. Then, about halfway up, I began huffing and puffing . . .

■ **Order of Location** You can arrange details in the order in which they are located (*above, below, beside,* and so on). Use order of location for descriptions, explanations, and directions. (See page **535**.)

> Some of my most important stuff is attached to the inside of my locker door. Near the top, I've taped two pictures of my favorite rock group. Around the edges, I've jammed in a bunch of notes from my friends. Below the notes, a collection of fridge magnets from my favorite pizza places hold up a . . .

■ **Order of Importance** You can arrange details from the most important to the least—or from the least important to the most. Persuasive and expository essays are often organized this way. (See page **536**.)

> The president of the United States is the nation's most powerful leader. The president's most important duty is to "preserve, protect, and defend the Constitution of the United States". . . . Serving as commander in chief of the armed forces is probably the president's second-most important duty. . . . Finally, as head of the executive branch, the president is in charge of . . .

■ **Comparison** You can write about two or more subjects by showing how they are alike and how they are different. Compare each subject separately or compare both, point by point, as in the example below. (See page **537**.)

> Tacos and pizza might seem totally different, but they actually have a lot in common. Even though tacos come from Mexico, and pizza comes from Italy, each food is an American favorite. . . . Tacos have a tortilla shell made from ground corn or flour. Pizzas are cooked on a crust that is basically a . . .

■ **Logical Order** You can organize information in a way that makes sense. Begin with a main idea followed by details, or start with details and lead up to the main point.

> As the chart below shows, you don't even have to be a smoker to die from cigarette smoke. Between 1995 and 2000, the number of Americans who died from secondhand smoke was more than a hundred thousand. Among smokers, there were nearly half a million deaths per year. The message is . . .

How can I write terrific topic sentences?

Try Eight Special Strategies

Writing a good topic sentence is a key to writing a great paragraph. A good topic sentence names the topic and states a specific feeling about it. Use the following strategies the next time you need to write a terrific topic sentence. (Also see page 525.)

Use a Number

Topic sentences can use number words to tell what the paragraph will be about.

Books come in a variety **of sizes.**

Mary Anne loves her job for a number **of reasons.**

NUMBER WORDS		
two	couple	a pair
few	three	a number
several	four	many
a variety	five	a list

Create a List

A topic sentence can list the things the paragraph will talk about.

Mars has a faint reddish hue **and** unusual brightness.

In the next chapter, more rockets blasted off, ripped through the clouds, **and** tried to reach new galaxies.

Start with *To* and a Verb

A topic sentence that starts with "to" and a verb helps the reader know why the information in the paragraph is important.

To analyze **a character in a novel, you need to look at how he or she changes.**

To understand **the rules of basketball, listen to your coach.**

Use Word Pairs

Conjunctions that come in pairs can help organize a topic sentence.

Our car needs not only **new tires** but also **new brakes.**

Your teacher can be both **your mentor** and **your instructor.**

WORD PAIRS
if . . . then
either . . . or
not only . . . but also
both . . . and
whether . . . or
as . . . so

Join Two Ideas

A topic sentence can combine two equal ideas by using a comma and a coordinating conjunction: *and, but, or, for, so, nor, yet.*

A kite is fun to fly, and a boomerang is fun to throw.

A lot of bacteria are useful, but some bacteria cause illness.

Use a "Why-What" Word

A "why-what" word is a subordinating conjunction that shows how ideas are connected.

Because all of the students love astronomy, the teacher scheduled a trip to a planetarium.

When you have a cold, be careful not to spread germs.

"WHY-WHAT" WORDS	
So that	Once
Before	Since
Until	Whenever
Because	While
If	As long as
As	After
In order that	When

Use a "Yes, But" Word

A "yes, but" word is a subordinating conjunction that tells how two ideas are different.

Even though our choir is small, we have gotten great reviews.

Friends help each other instead of turning away.

"YES, BUT" WORDS
However
Instead of
Although
Even though
Even if
Unless
Whether
Whereas

Quote an Expert

Sometimes the best way to start a paragraph is to quote someone who knows about your topic.

Michael Jordan once said, "You have to expect things of yourself before you can do them."

Amelia Earhart put it best: "It is far easier to start something than to finish it."

What other forms can I use for my writing?

Try These Forms of Writing

Finding the right *form* for your writing is just as important as finding the right topic. When you are selecting a form, be sure to ask yourself who you're writing for (your audience) and why you're writing (your purpose).

Anecdote	A brief story that makes a point
Autobiography	A writer's story of his or her own life
Biography	A writer's story of some other person's life
Book review	A brief essay giving a response or an opinion about a book (See pages **287–322**.)
Character sketch	Writing that describes a specific character in a story
Composition	A longer piece of writing, such as a story or an essay
Descriptive writing	Writing that uses details to help the reader clearly imagine a certain person, a place, a thing, or an idea (See pages **71–91**.)
Editorial	Newspaper letters or articles giving an opinion
Essay	A piece of writing in which ideas are presented, explained, argued, or described in an interesting way
Expository writing	Writing that explains by presenting the steps, the causes, or the kinds of something (See pages **157–217**.)
Fable	A short story that often uses talking animals as the main characters and teaches a lesson or moral
Fantasy	A story set in an imaginary world in which the characters usually have supernatural powers or abilities
Freewriting	Writing whatever comes to mind about any topic
Historical fiction	A made-up story based on something real in history in which fact is mixed with fiction
Myth	A traditional story intended to explain a mystery of nature, religion, or culture
Narrative	Writing that relates an event, an experience, or a story (See pages **93–155**.)

Novel	A book-length story with several characters and a well-developed plot
Personal narrative	Writing that shares an event or experience from the writer's personal life (See pages **97–134**.)
Persuasive writing	Writing that is meant to persuade the reader to agree with the writer about someone or something (See pages **219–281**.)
Play	A form that uses dialogue to tell a story and is meant to be performed in front of an audience
Poem	Writing that uses rhythm, rhyme, and imagery (See pages **353–361**.)
Proposal	Writing that includes specific information about an idea or a project that is being considered for approval
Research report	An essay that shares information on a topic that has been researched well and organized carefully (See pages **381–410**.)
Response to literature	Writing that is a summary or a reaction to something the writer has read (novel, short story, poem, article, and so on)
Science fiction	Writing based on real or imaginary science and often set in the future
Short story	A short piece of literature with only a few characters and one problem or conflict (See pages **343–349**.)
Summary	Writing that presents only the most important ideas from a longer piece of writing (See pages **377–380**.)
Tall tale	A humorous, exaggerated story (often based on the life of a real person) about a character who does impossible things
Tragedy	Literature in which the hero is destroyed because of some serious flaw or defect in his or her character

How can I create a voice in my writing?

You can create your writing voice by using dialogue and by *showing* instead of *telling*.

Use Dialogue

Each person you write about has a unique way of saying things, and well-written dialogue lets the reader *hear* the speaker's personality and thoughts. For example, notice how the message below can be spoken in several different ways.

> *Message:* **Your new car is impressive.**
>
> *Speaker 1:* **"Whoa, Dad! Cool new wheels!"**
>
> *Speaker 2:* **"Nice coupe, Bill. I've always been a sedan man myself."**
>
> *Speaker 3:* **"Such a fancy car, Son! Hope you didn't spend too much."**

Each of these speakers delivers the same message in a unique way. The dialogue tells as much about the speaker as it does about the topic.

One way to improve your dialogue is to think about the speaker and his or her personality. Look at the three personality webs below and try to decide which one is *Speaker 1, Speaker 2,* or *Speaker 3* from above. How does the dialogue show their personalities?

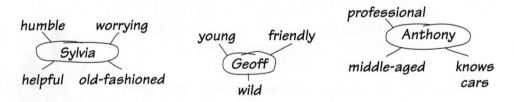

Tips for Punctuating Dialogue

- Indent every time a different person speaks.
- Put the exact words of a speaker in quotation marks.
- Set off the quoted words from the rest of the sentence by using a comma.
- At the end of quoted words, put a period or comma inside the quotation marks.

For more information and examples on how to punctuate dialogue, see **588.1, 598.1,** and **600.1** in the "Proofreader's Guide."

Show, Don't Tell

The old saying "Seeing is believing" is especially true in writing. Writing that *tells* the reader something is not as strong as writing that *shows* the reader something, allowing him or her to decide how to feel about it. Notice the difference between the two paragraphs below.

Telling: **I rode on the roller coaster. It was frightening but fun.**

Showing: **As the roller coaster topped the first big hill, I could see my mom down below. She looked so small. Then the coaster began to surge down the hill. My hands went up, my heart jumped into my throat, and I let out a sound that was half laugh and half scream.**

The first paragraph simply *tells* the reader that the roller coaster ride was "frightening but fun." The second paragraph *shows* just how "frightening but fun" it really was.

Key Strategies for Showing

Next time you realize your writing is telling rather than showing, try one of these strategies.

- **Add sensory details.** Include sights, sounds, smells, tastes, and touch sensations. That way, the reader can "experience" the event.

  Telling: **The sandwich was difficult to eat.**

  Showing: **The cucumbers slipped out first. I squeezed the Kaiser roll together more tightly. But a tomato was soon hanging out and dripping. Next came a slice of onion. I carefully rebuilt the sandwich. Again, the cucumber was the first to escape.**

- **Explain body language.** Write about facial expressions and the way people stand, gesture, and move.

  Telling: **Sharissa was upset with me.**

  Showing: **Sharissa glared at me, tapped her foot, pursed her lips, and snorted.**

- **Use dialogue.** Let the people in your writing speak for themselves.

  Telling: **Dr. Mike told me I had a broken bone.**

  Showing: **"You won't have to take the garbage out or do other chores until your broken bone heals," said Dr. Mike.**

What can I do to improve my writing style?

Learn Some Writing Techniques

Writers put special effects into their stories and essays in different ways. Look over the following writing techniques and then experiment with some of them in your own writing.

Analogy : A comparison of similar objects to help clarify one of the objects

Personal journals are like photograph albums. They both share personal details and tell a story.

Anecdote : A brief story used to illustrate or make a point

Abe Lincoln walked two miles to return several pennies he had overcharged a customer. (This anecdote shows Lincoln's honesty.)

Exaggeration : An overstatement or a stretching of the truth used to make a point or paint a clearer picture (See *overstatement*.)

After getting home from summer camp, I slept for a month.

Foreshadowing : Hints or clues that a writer uses to suggest what will happen next in a story

Halfway home, Sarah wondered whether she had locked her locker.

Irony : A technique that uses a word or phrase to mean the opposite of its normal meaning

Marshall just loves cleaning his room.

Local color : The use of details that are common in a certain place or local area (A story taking place on a seacoast would contain details about the water and the life and people near it.)

Everybody wore flannel shirts to the Friday fish fry.

Metaphor : A figure of speech that compares two things without using the word *like* or *as* (See page 360.)

In our community, high school football is king.

Overstatement : An exaggeration or a stretching of the truth (See *exaggeration*.)

When he saw my grades, my dad hit the roof.

Parallelism	Repeating similar words, phrases, or sentences to give writing rhythm (See page **522**.) **We will swim in the ocean, lie on the beach, and sleep under the stars.**
Personification	A figure of speech in which a nonhuman thing (an idea, object, or animal) is given human characteristics (See page **360**.) **Rosie's old car coughs and wheezes on cold days.**
Pun	A phrase that uses words in a way that gives them a humorous effect **The lumberjack logged on to the site to order new boots.**
Sarcasm	The use of praise to make fun of or "put down" someone or something (The expression is not sincere and is actually intended to mean the opposite thing.) **Micah's a real gourmet; he loves peanut butter and jelly sandwiches.** (A *gourmet* is a "lover of fine foods.")
Sensory details	Specific details that help the reader see, feel, smell, taste, and/or hear what is being described (See page **488**.) **As Lamont took his driver's test, his heart thumped, his hands went cold, and his face began to sweat.**
Simile	A figure of speech that compares two things using the word *like* or *as* (See page **360**.) **Faye's little brother darts around like a water bug.** **Yesterday the lake was as smooth as glass.**
Slang	Informal words or phrases used by particular groups of people when they talk to each other **chill out hang loose totally awesome**
Symbol	An object that is used to stand for an idea **The American flag is a symbol of the United States. The stars stand for the 50 states, and the stripes stand for the 13 original U.S. colonies.**
Understatement	Very calm language (the opposite of exaggeration) used to bring special attention to an object or an idea **These hot red peppers may make your mouth tingle a bit.**

RESOURCE

How can I expand my writing vocabulary?

Study Writing Terms

This glossary includes terms used to describe the parts of the writing process. It also includes terms that explain special ways of stating an idea.

Antonym	A word that means the opposite of another word: *happy* and *sad; large* and *small* (See page **563**.)
Audience	The people who read or hear what has been written
Body	The main or middle part in a piece of writing that comes between the *beginning* and the *ending* and includes the main points
Brainstorming	Collecting ideas by thinking freely about all the possibilities
Closing	The ending or final part in a piece of writing (In a paragraph, the closing is the last sentence. In an essay or a report, the closing is the final paragraph.)
Coherence	Tying ideas together in your writing (See page **539**.)
Connotation	The "feeling" a word suggests (See page **80**.)
Denotation	The dictionary meaning of a word
Dialogue	Written conversation between two or more people
Figurative language	Special comparisons, often called figures of speech, that make your writing more creative (See page **360**.)
Focus statement	The statement that tells what specific part of a topic is written about in an essay (See *thesis statement* and page **36**.)
Form	A type of writing or the way a piece of writing is put together (See pages **554–555**.)
Grammar	The structure of language; the rules and guidelines that you follow in order to speak and write acceptably
Jargon	The special language of a certain group, occupation, or field **Computer jargon: byte digital upload**
Journal	A notebook for writing down thoughts, experiences, ideas, and information (See pages **431–434**.)

Limiting the subject	Taking a general subject and narrowing it down to a specific topic

General subject   Specific topic
sports → **golf** → **golf skills** → **putting**

Modifiers	Words, phrases, or clauses that describe another word Our black **cat** slowly **stretched and** then **leaped** onto the wicker chair. (Without the blue modifiers, all we know is that a "cat stretched and leaped.")
Point of view	The angle from which a story is told (See page **352**.)
Purpose	The specific reason that a person has for writing **to describe** **to narrate** **to persuade** **to explain**
Style	How an author writes (choice of words and sentences)
Supporting details	Facts or ideas used to tell a story, explain a topic, describe something, or prove a point
Synonym	A word that means the same thing as another word (*dog* and *canine*) (See page **563**.)
Theme	The main point, message, or lesson in a piece of writing
Thesis statement	A statement that gives the main idea of an essay (See *focus statement*.)
Tone	A writer's attitude toward his or her subject **serious** **humorous** **sarcastic**
Topic	The specific subject of a piece of writing
Topic sentence	The sentence that contains the main idea of a paragraph (See page **525**.) **Blue jeans are a popular piece of American clothing.**
Transition	A word or phrase that connects or ties two ideas together smoothly (See pages **572–573**.) **also** **however** **lastly** **later** **next**
Usage	The way in which people use language (*Standard usage* generally follows the rules of good grammar. Most of the writing you do in school will require standard usage.)
Voice	A writer's unique, personal tone or feeling that comes across in a piece of writing (See page **40**.)

RESOURCE

What can I do to increase my vocabulary skills?

Try Vocabulary-Building Techniques

Technique	Description	Why It Works
Learn common roots, prefixes, and suffixes.	**If you know common word parts, you will be able to figure out many new words. (See pages 564–569.)**	Tens of thousands of English words come from Greek and Latin word parts.
Use context.	**Look at the passage surrounding a word you don't know. (See page 563.)**	Words and ideas around a word often give hints as to what the word means.
Look up words in the dictionary.	**Read the dictionary meaning. Also read the history of the word. (See pages 374–375.)**	Sometimes the word history helps you connect the new word with one you already know.
Keep a vocabulary notebook.	**Write down words you don't know. Find out their meaning and use each word in a sentence.**	Writing reinforces your learning. The notebook is also a handy study guide.
Say your new words out loud.	**Read your new words out loud and look for places in your writing where you can use them effectively.**	Saying new words out loud means you hear them. Using that extra sense helps you remember.
Use your new words often.	**Concentrate on using new words whenever possible in your writing.**	Research shows that you need to use a new word to make it your own.

Use Context

When you come across a word you don't know, you can often figure out its meaning from the other words in the sentence. The other words form a familiar context, or setting, for the unfamiliar word. Looking closely at the surrounding words will give you clues to the meaning of the new word.

When you come to a word you don't know . . .

- **Look for a synonym**—a word or words that have the same meaning as the unknown word.

  Sara had an ominous feeling when she woke up, but the feeling was less threatening when she saw she was in her own room. (An *ominous* feeling is a threatening one.)

- **Look for an antonym**—a word that has the opposite meaning as the unknown word.

  Boniface had always been quite heavy, but he looked gaunt when he returned from the hospital.
  (*Gaunt* is the opposite of *heavy*.)

- **Look for a comparison or contrast.**

  Riding a mountain bike in a remote area is my idea of a great day. I wonder why some people like to ride motorcycles on busy six-lane highways.
  (A *remote* area is out of the way, in contrast to a *busy* area.)

- **Look for a definition or description.**

  Manatees, large aquatic mammals (sometimes called sea cows), can be found in the warm coastal waters of Florida.
  (An *aquatic* mammal is one that lives in the water.)

- **Look for words that appear in a series.**

  The campers spotted blue jays, chickadees, and indigo buntings on Saturday morning.
  (An *indigo bunting*, like a *blue jay* or *chickadee*, is a bird.)

- **Look for a cause and effect relationship.**

  The amount of traffic at 6th and Main doubled last year, so crossing lights were placed at that corner to avert an accident.
  (*Avert* means "to prevent.")

RESOURCE

How can I build my vocabulary across the curriculum?

On the next several pages, you will find many of the most common prefixes, suffixes, and roots in the English language. Learning these word parts can help you increase your writing vocabulary.

Learn About Prefixes

A **prefix** is a word part that is added before a word to change the meaning of the word. For example, when the prefix *un* is added to the word *fair (unfair)*, it changes the word's meaning from "fair" to "not fair."

ambi *[both]*
ambidextrous (skilled with both hands)

anti *[against]*
antifreeze (a liquid that works against freezing)
antiwar (against wars and fighting)

astro *[star]*
astronaut (person who travels among the stars)
astronomy (study of the stars)

auto *[self]*
autobiography (writing that is about yourself)

bi *[two]*
bilingual (using or speaking two languages)
biped (having two feet)

circum *[in a circle, around]*
circumference (the line or distance around a circle)
circumnavigate (to sail around)

co *[together, with]*
cooperate (to work together)
coordinate (to put things together)

ex *[out]*
exhale (to breathe out)
exit (the act of going out)

fore *[before, in front of]*
foremost (in the first place, before everyone or everything else)
foretell (to tell or show beforehand)

hemi *[half]*
hemisphere (half of a sphere or globe)

hyper *[over]*
hyperactive (overactive)

im *[not, opposite of]*
impatient (not patient)
impossible (not possible)

in *[not, opposite of]*
inactive (not active)
incomplete (not complete)

inter *[between, among]*
international (between or among nations)
interplanetary (between the planets)

macro *[large]*
macrocosm (the entire universe)

mal *[bad, poor]*
malnutrition (poor nutrition)

micro *[small]*
microscope (an instrument used to see very small things)

organize
select **support**
REFERENCE
improve
565
A Writer's Resource

mono *[one]*
monolingual (using or speaking only one language)

non *[not, opposite of]*
nonfat (without the normal fat content)
nonfiction (based on facts; not made-up)

over *[too much, extra]*
overeat (to eat too much)
overtime (extra time; time beyond regular hours)

poly *[many]*
polygon (a figure or shape with three or more sides)
polysyllable (a word with more than three syllables)

post *[after]*
postscript (a note added at the end of a letter, after the signature)
postwar (after a war)

pre *[before]*
pregame (activities that occur before a game)
preheat (to heat before using)

re *[again, back]*
repay (to pay back)
rewrite (to write again or revise)

semi *[half, partly]*
semicircle (half a circle)
semiconscious (half conscious; not fully conscious)

sub *[under, below]*
submarine (a boat that can operate underwater)
submerge (to put underwater)

trans *[across, over; change]*
transcontinental (across a continent)
transform (to change from one form to another)

tri *[three]*
triangle (a figure that has three sides and three angles)
tricycle (a three-wheeled vehicle)

un *[not]*
uncomfortable (not comfortable)
unhappy (not happy; sad)

under *[below, beneath]*
underage (below or less than the usual or required age)
undersea (beneath the surface of the sea)

uni *[one]*
unicycle (a one-wheeled vehicle)
unisex (a single style that is worn by both males and females)

Numerical Prefixes

deci *[tenth of a part]*
decimal system (a number system based on units of 10)

centi *[hundredth of a part]*
centimeter (a unit of length equal to 1/100 meter)

milli *[thousandth of a part]*
millimeter (a unit of length equal to 1/1000 meter)

micro *[millionth of a part]*
micrometer (one-millionth of a meter)

deca, dec *[ten]*
decade (a period of 10 years)
decathlon (a contest with 10 events)

hecto, hect *[one hundred]*
hectare (a metric unit of land equal to 100 ares)

kilo *[one thousand]*
kilogram (a unit of mass equal to 1,000 grams)

mega *[one million]*
megabit (one million bits)

Study Suffixes

A **suffix** is a word part that is added after a word. Sometimes a suffix will tell you what part of speech a word is. For example, many adverbs end in the suffix *ly*.

able *[able, can do]*
agreeable (able or willing to agree)
doable (can be done)

al *[of, like]*
magical (like magic)
optical (of the eye)

ed *[past tense]*
called (past tense of *call*)
learned (past tense of *learn*)

ess *[female]*
lioness (a female lion)

ful *[full of]*
helpful (giving help; full of help)

ic *[like, having to do with]*
symbolic (having to do with symbols)

ily *[in some manner]*
happily (in a happy manner)

ish *[somewhat like or near]*
childish (somewhat like a child)

ism *[characteristic of]*
heroism (characteristic of a hero)

less *[without]*
careless (without care)

ly *[in some manner]*
calmly (in a calm manner)

ology *[study, science]*
biology (the study of living things)

s *[more than one]*
books (more than one book)

ward *[in the direction of]*
westward (in the direction of west)

y *[containing, full of]*
salty (containing salt)

Comparing Suffixes

er *[comparing two things]*
faster, later, neater, stronger

est *[comparing more than two]*
fastest, latest, neatest, strongest

Noun-Forming Suffixes

er *[one who]*
painter (one who paints)

ing *[the result of]*
painting (the result of a painter's work)

ion *[act of, state of]*
perfection (the state of being perfect)

ist *[one who]*
violinist (one who plays the violin)

ment *[act of, result of]*
amendment (the result of amending, or changing)
improvement (the result of improving)

ness *[state of]*
goodness (the state of being good)

or *[one who]*
actor (one who acts)

Understand Roots

A **root** is a word or word base from which other words are made by adding a prefix or a suffix. Knowing the common roots can help you figure out the meaning of difficult words.

aster *[star]*
asteroid (resembling a star)
asterisk (starlike symbol [*])

aud *[hear, listen]*
audible (can be heard)
auditorium (a place to listen to speeches and performances)

bibl *[book]*
Bible (sacred book of Christianity)
bibliography (list of books)

bio *[life]*
biography (book about a person's life)
biology (the study of life)

chrome *[color]*
monochrome (having one color)
polychrome (having many colors)

chron *[time]*
chronological (in time order)
synchronize (to make happen at the same time)

cide *[the killing of; killer]*
homicide (the killing of one person by another person)
pesticide (pest [bug] killer)

cise *[cut]*
incision (a thin, clean cut)
incisors (the teeth that cut or tear food)
precise (cut exactly right)

cord, cor *[heart]*
cordial (heartfelt)
coronary (relating to the heart)

corp *[body]*
corporation (a legal body; business)
corpse (a dead human body)

cycl, cyclo *[wheel, circular]*
bicycle (a vehicle with two wheels)
cyclone (a very strong circular wind)

dem *[people]*
democracy (ruled by the people)
epidemic (affecting many people at the same time)

dent, dont *[tooth]*
dentures (false teeth)
orthodontist (dentist who straightens teeth)

derm *[skin]*
dermatology (the study of skin)
epidermis (outer layer of skin)

fac, fact *[do, make]*
factory (a place where people make things)
manufacture (to make by hand or machine)

fin *[end]*
final (the last of something)
infinite (having no end)

flex *[bend]*
flexible (able to bend)
reflex (bending or springing back)

flu *[flowing]*
fluent (flowing smoothly or easily)
fluid (waterlike, flowing substance)

forc, fort *[strong]*
forceful (full of strength or power)
fortify (to make strong)

fract, frag *[break]*
fracture (to break)
fragment (a piece broken from the whole)

Learn More Roots

gen *[birth, produce]*
congenital (existing at birth)
genetics (the study of inborn traits)

geo *[of the earth]*
geography (the study of places on the earth)
geology (the study of the earth's physical features)

graph *[write]*
autograph (writing one's name)
graphology (the study of handwriting)

homo *[same]*
homogeneous (of the same birth or kind)
homogenize (to blend into a uniform mixture)

hydr *[water]*
dehydrate (to take the water out of)
hydrophobia (the fear of water)

ject *[throw]*
eject (to throw out)
project (to throw forward)

log, logo *[word, thought, speech]*
dialogue (speech between two people)
logic (thinking or reasoning)

luc, lum *[light]*
illuminate (to light up)
translucent (letting light come through)

magn *[great]*
magnificent (great)
magnify (to make bigger or greater)

man *[hand]*
manicure (to fix the hands)
manual (done by hand)

mania *[insanity]*
kleptomania (abnormal desire to steal)
maniac (an insane person)

mar *[sea, pool]*
marine (of or found in the sea)
mariner (sailor)

mega *[large]*
megalith (large stone)
megaphone (large horn used to make voices louder)

meter *[measure]*
kilometer (a thousand meters)
voltmeter (device to measure volts)

mit, miss *[send]*
emit (to send out; give off)
transmission (sending over)

multi *[many, much]*
multicultural (of or including many cultures)
multiped (an animal with many feet)

numer *[number]*
innumerable (too many to count)
numerous (large in number)

omni *[all, completely]*
omnipresent (present everywhere at the same time)
omnivorous (eating all kinds of food)

onym *[name]*
anonymous (without a name)
pseudonym (false name)

ped *[foot]*
pedal (lever worked by the foot)
pedestrian (one who travels by foot)

phil *[love]*
Philadelphia (city of brotherly love)
philosophy (the love of wisdom)

phobia *[fear]*
acrophobia (a fear of high places)
agoraphobia (a fear of public, open places)

phon *[sound]*
phonics (related to sounds)
symphony (sounds made together)

photo *[light]*
photo-essay (a story told mainly with photographs)
photograph (picture made using light rays)

pop *[people]*
population (number of people in an area)
populous (full of people)

port *[carry]*
export (to carry out)
portable (able to be carried)

psych *[mind, soul]*
psychiatry (the study of the mind)
psychology (science of mind and behavior)

sci *[know]*
conscious (being aware)
omniscient (knowing everything)

scope *[instrument for viewing]*
kaleidoscope (instrument for viewing patterns and shapes)
periscope (instrument used to see above the water)

scrib, script *[write]*
manuscript (something written by hand)
scribble (to write quickly)

spec *[look]*
inspect (to look at carefully)
specimen (an example to look at)

spir *[breath]*
expire (to breathe out; die)
inspire (to breathe into; give life to)

tele *[over a long distance; far]*
telephone (machine used to speak to people over a distance)
telescope (machine used to see things that are very far away)

tempo *[time]*
contemporary (from the current time period)
temporary (lasting for a short time)

tend, tens *[stretch, strain]*
extend (to stretch and make longer)
tension (stretching something tight)

terra *[earth]*
terrain (the earth or ground)
terrestrial (relating to the earth)

therm *[heat]*
thermal (related to heat)
thermostat (a device for controlling heat)

tom *[cut]*
anatomy (the science of cutting apart plants and animals for study)
atom (a particle that cannot be cut or divided)

tract *[draw, pull]*
traction (the act of pulling)
tractor (a machine for pulling)

typ *[print]*
prototype (the first printing or model)
typo (a printing error)

vac *[empty]*
vacant (empty)
vacuum (an empty space)

vid, vis *[see]*
supervise (to oversee or watch over)
videotape (record on tape for viewing)

vor *[eat]*
carnivorous (flesh-eating)
herbivorous (plant-eating)

zoo *[animal or animals]*
zoo (a place where animals are kept)
zoology (the study of animal life)

What can I do to write more effective sentences?

Study Sentence Patterns

Sentences in the English language follow the basic patterns below. Use a variety of patterns to add interest to your writing. (Also see page **571**.)

1 Subject + Action Verb

     S   AV
Wanda skateboards. (Some action verbs, like *skateboards,* are intransitive. This means that they *do not need* a direct object to express a complete thought. See **728.3**.)

2 Subject + Action Verb + Direct Object

     S   AV   DO
Jerome completed a wood carving at camp. (Some action verbs, like *completed,* are transitive. This means that they *need* a direct object to express a complete thought. See **728.2**.)

3 Subject + Action Verb + Indirect Object + Direct Object

        S   AV IO   DO
Nick's girlfriend gave him a watch.

4 Subject + Action Verb + Direct Object + Object Complement

       S   AV DO   OC
The committee voted Jayne the best actor.

5 Subject + Linking Verb + Predicate Noun

     S   LV   PN
Elephants are huge animals.

6 Subject + Linking Verb + Predicate Adjective

 S LV PA
He is funny.

> In the patterns above, the subject comes before the verb. In the patterns below, the subject (called a *delayed subject*) comes after the verb.

7   LV S   PN
Is Larisa a poet? (A question)

8   LV   S
There was a meeting. (A sentence beginning with *there* or *here*)

Practice Sentence Diagramming

Diagramming sentences can help you understand how the different parts of a sentence fit together. Here are the most common diagrams.

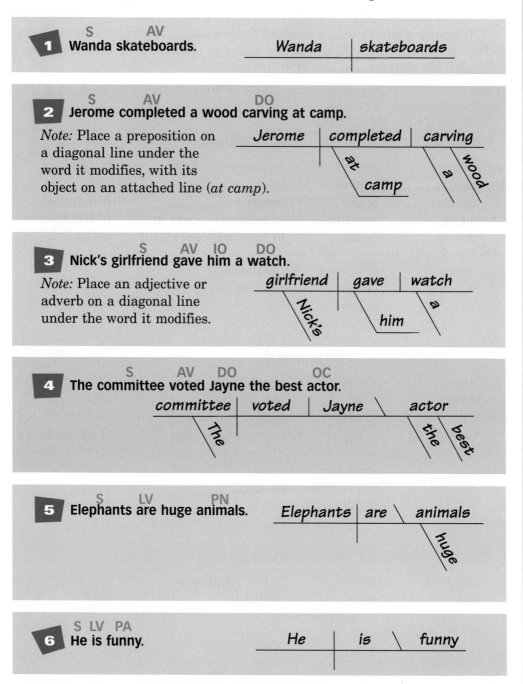

1   S   AV
Wanda skateboards.

Wanda | skateboards

2   S   AV   DO
Jerome completed a wood carving at camp.

Note: Place a preposition on a diagonal line under the word it modifies, with its object on an attached line (*at camp*).

Jerome | completed | carving
at camp   a   wood

3   S   AV   IO   DO
Nick's girlfriend gave him a watch.

Note: Place an adjective or adverb on a diagonal line under the word it modifies.

girlfriend | gave | watch
Nick's   him   a

4   S   AV   DO   OC
The committee voted Jayne the best actor.

committee | voted | Jayne \ actor
The   the   best

5   S   LV   PN
Elephants are huge animals.

Elephants | are \ animals
huge

6   S LV PA
He is funny.

He | is \ funny

RESOURCE

How can I connect my sentences and paragraphs?

Use Transitions

Transitions can be used to connect one sentence to another sentence or one paragraph to another within a longer essay or report. The lists below show a number of transitions and how they are used.

Note: Each colored list below is a group of transitions that could work well together in a piece of writing.

Words that can be used to show location

above	around	between	inside	outside
across	behind	by	into	over
against	below	down	near	throughout
along	beneath	in back of	next to	to the right
among	beside	in front of	on top of	under

Above	In front of	On top of
Below	Beside	Next to
To the left	In back of	Beneath
To the right		

Words that can be used to show time

about	during	yesterday	until	finally
after	first	meanwhile	next	then
at	second	today	soon	as soon as
before	to begin	tomorrow	later	in the end

First	To begin	Now	First	Before
Second	To continue	Soon	Then	During
Third	To conclude	Later	Next	After
Finally			In the end	

Words that can be used to compare two things

likewise	as	in the same way	one way
like	also	similarly	both

In the same way	One way
Also	Another way
Similarly	Both

Words that can be used to contrast things (show differences)

but	still	although	on the other hand
however	yet	otherwise	even though

On the other hand	Although
Even though	Yet
Still	Nevertheless

Words that can be used to emphasize a point

again	truly	especially	for this reason
to repeat	in fact	to emphasize	

For this reason	Truly	In fact
Especially	To emphasize	To repeat

Words that can be used to conclude or summarize

finally	as a result	to sum up	in conclusion
lastly	therefore	all in all	because

Because	As a result	To sum it up	Therefore
In conclusion	All in all	Because	Finally

Words that can be used to add information

again	another	for instance	for example
also	and	moreover	additionally
as well	besides	along with	other
next	finally	in addition	

For example	For instance	Next	Another
Additionally	Besides	Moreover	Along with
Finally	Next	Also	As well

Words that can be used to clarify

in other words	for instance	that is	for example

For instance	For example
In other words	Equally important

RESOURCE

What can I do to make my final copy look better?

Add Graphics to Your Writing

You can add information and interest to essays and reports by using diagrams, tables, and graphs.

Diagrams are drawings that show the parts of something.

Picture diagrams show how something is put together. A diagram may leave out some parts to show only the parts you need to learn.

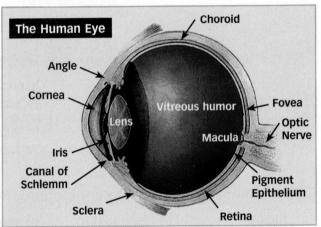

Line diagrams show something you can't really see. Instead of objects, line diagrams show ideas and relationships. This diagram shows how the Germanic languages are related to one another.

Tables are another form of diagram. Tables have two parts: rows and columns. Rows go across and show one kind of information or data. Columns go up and down and show a different kind of data.

To read a table, find where a row and a column meet. In the table below, to compare the size of Canada and the United States, find where the first row meets the first and third columns. Canada is slightly larger than the United States.

Comparing Countries			
	Canada	**Mexico**	**United States**
Size (Sq. Miles)	3.85 million	759,000	3.8 million
Type of Government	Parliamentary	Republic	Republic
Voting Age	18	18	18
Literacy	99%	87%	98%

organize
select support
REFERENCE
improve
575

A Writer's Resource

Graphs are pictures of information. **Bar graphs** show how things compare to one another. The bars on a bar graph may be vertical or horizontal. (*Vertical* means "up and down." *Horizontal* means "from side to side.") Sometimes the bars on graphs are called *columns*. The part that shows numbers is called the *scale*.

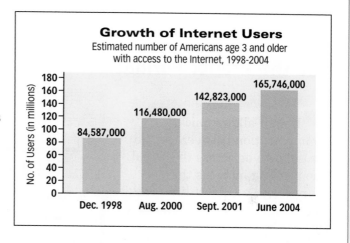

Growth of Internet Users
Estimated number of Americans age 3 and older with access to the Internet, 1998-2004

No. of Users (in millions)

84,587,000 — Dec. 1998
116,480,000 — Aug. 2000
142,823,000 — Sept. 2001
165,746,000 — June 2004

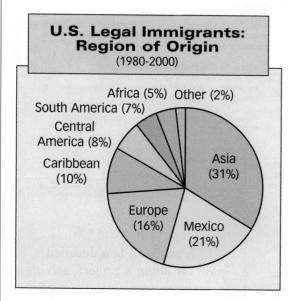

U.S. Legal Immigrants: Region of Origin
(1980-2000)

Africa (5%) Other (2%)
South America (7%)
Central America (8%)
Caribbean (10%)
Asia (31%)
Europe (16%)
Mexico (21%)

Pie graphs show how all the parts of something add up to make the whole. A pie graph often shows percentages. (A percentage is the part of a whole stated in hundredths: 35% = 35/100.) It's called a pie graph because it is usually in the shape of a pie or circle.

A pie graph begins with the largest segment at the top and moves clockwise around the circle by size. (Notice the example at the left.)

RESOURCE

Line graphs show how something changes as time goes by. A line graph always begins with an L-shaped grid. One axis of the grid shows passing time; the other axis shows numbers.

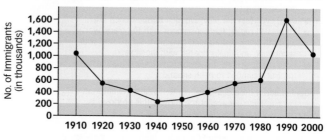

Legal Immigration to the United States

No. of Immigrants (in thousands)

1,600
1,400
1,200
1,000
800
600
400
200
0

1910 1920 1930 1940 1950 1960 1970 1980 1990 2000

How should I set up my practical writing?

Use the Proper Format

E-Mail Messages

E-mail allows quick communication between people across town or across the world. The heading includes the address and a subject line. The body should be set up in letter format.

Send Mail or Discussion Group Message

Send | Quote | Address | Attach | Spelling | Save | Security | Stop

To: wteja@inlandnet.com

Subject: Questions from Mr. Cooper's homeroom | Priority: Normal

Normal | 12 | A A A A | := := := := | F | ☞

Dear Ms. Teja:

My name is Susan Jackson, and I am in Mr. Cooper's homeroom class at Wilsburg Middle School. The class chose me to write to you to thank you for taking us on a tour of Inland Steel. The blast furnaces were huge, and the heat from the coke batteries was amazing!

In our class discussion, we came up with three more questions for you. We would really appreciate it if you could take a moment to answer them.

1. What is the difference between coal and coke?
2. How does annealing change steel?
3. You showed us how the slag is removed, but is there any use for slag?

...so much for taking us on the tour! We look forward to ...g from you.

...n Jackson
...son@wilsburgmiddleschool.edu

Traction and Four-Wheel Drive

Description: I'd like to test how well a motorized model truck climbs surfaces made of different materials and at different angles. I will create graphs to show how far and how fast the truck climbs in each situation.

Materials: I will use a radio-controlled four-wheel drive model truck, a plank, a protractor, a stopwatch, graph paper, and colored pencils. The different surface materials will include the following: water, aluminum foil, sandpaper, and loose sand.

Schedule: By March 7, I will have the materials collected and assembled. By March 14, I will have performed all my tests for different materials at different angles. By March 21, the total display will be ready for the science fair.

Procedure:
- For each surface, the plank will be pitched at 10°, 20°, 30°, 40°, and 50°.
- First, I will test the plain wooden ramp at each pitch.
- Then I will repeat the experiment with the plank wet, with the plank coated with aluminum foil, coated with sandpaper, and finally coated with loose sand.
- I will create graphs displaying how far and how fast the truck climbed in each situation.

Conclusion: I believe this experiment will show different levels of traction. Please let me know if this proposal is accepted. Any suggestions are welcome.

Proposals

A proposal is a detailed plan for doing a project, solving a problem, or meeting a need.

Follow Guidelines

Letters

A letter is a written message sent through the mail. Letters follow a set format, including important contact information, a salutation (greeting), a body, and a closing signature. (See pages **274–277** for more information.)

1212 Maple Park
Voree, IN 46300
March 24, 2004

Bruce Reynolds, Owner
Pet Project Pet Store
341 Jones Street
Voree, IN 46300

Dear Mr. Reynolds:

Last year I bought two long-haired guinea pigs from your store, and this year we have five guinea pigs. Are you interested in buying the three babies? They are all female and six weeks old, and I have included pictures of them. We would like to sell them back to you if you are interested.

Our veterinarian checked the three babies, and they are in fine health. We also had the veterinarian neuter the father so that we won't have more pigs to care for.

Please let me know if you are interested in buying our guinea pigs. You may call me at 555-9770 after 3:30 p.m. Otherwise, I will create fliers to sell them myself. Thanks for your time.

Sincerely,

Jessica Botticini

Jessica Botticini

Envelope Addresses

Place the return address in the upper left corner, the destination address in the center, and the correct postage in the upper right corner.

JESSICA BOTTICINI
1212 MAPLE PK
VOREE IN 46300

BRUCE REYNOLDS
PET PROJECT PET STORE
341 JONES ST
VOREE IN 46300

U.S. Postal Service Guidelines

1. Capitalize everything and leave out ALL punctuation.
2. Use the list of common address abbreviations at **634.1**. Use numerals rather than words for numbered streets and avenues (9TH AVE NE, 3RD ST SW).
3. If you know the ZIP + 4 code, use it.

capitalize
SPELL
punctuate

Proofreader's Guide

revise *edit*

Marking Punctuation

Periods

Use a **period** to end a sentence. Also use a period after initials, after abbreviations, and as a decimal point.

579.1
At the End of Sentences

Use a period to end a sentence that makes a statement or a request. Also use a period for a mild command, one that does not need an exclamation point. (See page 518.)

> **The Southern Ocean surrounds Antarctica.** (statement)
> **Please point out the world's largest ocean on a map.** (request)
> **Do not use a laser pointer.** (mild command)

NOTE It is not necessary to place a period after a statement that has parentheses around it if it is part of another sentence.

> **The Southern Ocean is the fourth-largest ocean (it is larger than the Atlantic).**

579.2
After Initials

Place a period after an initial.

> **J. K. Rowling** (author)
> **Colin L. Powell** (politician)

579.3
After Abbreviations

Place a period after each part of an abbreviation. Do not use periods with acronyms or initialisms. (See page 636.)

> Abbreviations: **Mr. Mrs. Ms. Dr. B.C.E. C.E.**
> Acronyms: **AIDS NASA**
> Initialisms: **NBC FBI**

NOTE When an abbreviation is the last word in a sentence, use only one period at the end of the sentence.

> **My grandfather's full name is William Ryan James Koenig, Jr.**

579.4
As Decimal Points

Use a period to separate dollars and cents and as a decimal point.

> **The price of a loaf of bread was $1.54 in 1992.**
> **That price was only 35 cents, or 77.3 percent less, in 1972.**

Question Marks

A **question mark** is used after an interrogative sentence and also to show doubt about the correctness of a fact or figure. (See page 518.)

580.1

At the End of Direct Questions

Use a question mark at the end of a direct question (an interrogative sentence).

Is a vegan a person who eats only vegetables?

580.2

At the End of Indirect Questions

No question mark is used after an indirect question. (An indirect question tells about a question you or someone else asked.)

Because I do not eat meat, I'm often asked if I am a vegetarian.

I asked the doctor if going meatless is harmful to my health.

580.3

To Show Doubt

Place a question mark within parentheses to show that you are unsure that a fact or figure is correct.

By the year 2020 (?) the number of vegetarians in the United States may approach 15 percent of the population.

Exclamation Points

An **exclamation point** may be placed after a word, a phrase, or a sentence to show emotion. (The exclamation point should not be overused.)

580.4

To Express Strong Feelings

Use an exclamation point to show excitement or strong feeling.

Yeah! Wow! Oh my!

Surprise! You've won the million-dollar sweepstakes!

Caution: Never use more than one exclamation point in writing assignments.

Incorrect: **Don't ever do that to me again!!!**

Correct: **Don't ever do that to me again!**

End Punctuation

For each numbered sentence below, write the last word in the sentence and the correct end punctuation after it.

Example: The blue whale is the largest animal that has ever lived

Answer: lived.

(1) Whales may look like fish and swim like fish, but did you know that whales are really mammals **(2)** Just like other mammals, they have a heart with four chambers, they are warm-blooded, and they give birth to live young **(3)** They even have some hair

(4) Whales travel in small groups called pods **(5)** They communicate with each other using a series of clicks and whistles **(6)** The sounds are just remarkable **(7)** People think of them as songs and have even recorded them **(8)** Have you heard any of these recordings

(9) Gentle and friendly, many whale species seem to trust people **(10)** Scientists say that whales are very intelligent and that their vision and hearing are excellent **(11)** Would you believe that whales can live for quite a long time **(12)** Just imagine: Some large whales have probably lived for more than 100 years

Next Step: Based on the reading above, write two sentences about whales: one should be a question you would like to ask, and one should be an emotional personal comment. Use the correct end punctuation for each.

Commas

Use a **comma** to indicate a pause or a change in thought. This helps to keep words and ideas from running together so that the writing is easier to read. For a writer, no other form of punctuation is more important to understand than the comma.

582.1
Between Items in a Series

Use commas between words, phrases, or clauses in a series. (A series contains at least three items.) (See page 513.)

Chinese, English, and Hindi are the three most widely used languages in the world. (words)

Being comfortable with technology, working well with others, and knowing another language are important skills for today's workers. (phrases)

My dad works in a factory, my mom works in an office, and I work in school. (clauses)

582.2
To Keep Numbers Clear

Use commas to separate the digits in a number in order to distinguish hundreds, thousands, millions, and so on.

More than 104,000 people live in Kingston, the capital of Jamaica.

The population of the entire country of Liechtenstein is only 29,000.

NOTE Commas are not used in years.

The world population was 6.1 billion by 2003.

582.3
In Dates and Addresses

Use commas to set off items in an address and items in a date.

On August 28, 1963, Martin Luther King, Jr., gave his famous "I Have a Dream" speech.

The address of the King Center is 449 Auburn Avenue NE, Atlanta, Georgia 30312.

NOTE No comma is placed between the state and ZIP code. Also, when only the month and year are given, no comma is needed.

In January 2029 we will celebrate the 100th anniversary of Reverend King's birth.

Commas 1

■ Between Items in a Series
■ To Keep Numbers Clear
■ In Dates and Addresses

 For each sentence below, write the series, date, address, or number that should include a comma. Add the commas.

1. The Civil War was caused by differences in opinion about slavery economics and politics.

   slavery, economics, and politics

2. The war officially began on April 12 1861 when Confederate troops fired upon Fort Sumter, South Carolina.

3. Today Fort Sumter is a national monument at 1214 Middle Street Sullivan's Island South Carolina 29482.

4. South Carolina left the Union, and Virginia Arkansas Tennessee and North Carolina soon followed.

5. More than 13000 Union soldiers and 10000 Confederates lost their lives during the Battle of Shiloh.

6. Three other major battles of the war were fought at Wilderness Spotsylvania and Cold Harbor.

7. After four years of fighting, the war officially ended with the Confederates' surrender on April 9 1865 in Appomattox Virginia.

8. The final death toll of the Civil War was more than 620000 soldiers from both the North and the South.

9. You can learn about the Civil War by reading government papers diaries and letters written during that time period.

10. You can read records of soldiers who fought in the Civil War at the National Archives 700 Pennsylvania Avenue Washington DC 20408.

Commas . . .

584.1
To Set Off Nonrestrictive Phrases and Clauses

Use commas to set off nonrestrictive phrases and clauses—those not necessary to the basic meaning of the sentence.

People get drinking water from surface water or groundwater, which makes up only 1 percent of the earth's water supply.
(The clause *which makes up only 1 percent of the earth's water supply* is additional information; it is nonrestrictive—not required. If the clause were left out, the meaning of the sentence would remain clear.)

Restrictive phrases or clauses—those that are needed in the sentence—restrict or limit the meaning of the sentence; they are not set off with commas.

Groundwater that is free from harmful pollutants is rare.
(The clause *that is free from harmful pollutants* is restrictive; it is needed to complete the meaning of the basic sentence and is not set off with commas.)

584.2
To Set Off Titles or Initials

Use commas to set off a title, a name, or initials that follow a person's last name. (Use only one period if an initial comes at the end of a sentence.)

Melanie Prokat, M.D., is our family's doctor. However, she is listed in the phone book only as Prokat, M.

NOTE Although commas are not necessary to set off "Jr." and "Sr." after a name, they may be used as long as a comma is used both before and after the abbreviation.

584.3
To Set Off Interruptions

Use commas to set off a word, phrase, or clause that interrupts the main thought of a sentence. These interruptions usually can be identified through the following tests:

1. You can leave them out of a sentence without changing its meaning.
2. You can place them other places in the sentence without changing its meaning.

Our school, as we all know, is becoming overcrowded again. (clause)

The gym, not the cafeteria, was expanded a while ago. (phrase)

My history class, for example, has 42 students in it. (phrase)

There are, indeed, about 1,000 people in my school. (word)

The building, however, has room for only 850 students. (word)

Commas 2

■ To Set Off Nonrestrictive Phrases and Clauses
■ To Set Off Titles or Initials
■ To Set Off Interruptions

 For each of the following sentences, write the information that should be set off with a comma. Include the word before the information and add the commas.

1. The ferret which is a cousin of the weasel can make a good pet.
   ferret, which is a cousin of the weasel,

2. Ferrets once only wild animals of the Great Plains are now a common tame breed.

3. Victoria Patterson D.V.M. claims they are as smart and loving as dogs and cats.

4. John Carpenter M.D. says he has never had to treat a ferret bite.

5. Ferrets need toys to keep them busy—old socks for instance.

6. Any pet as you know needs a lot of care.

7. Ferrets are known for their active and curious nature which sometimes gets them into trouble.

8. Ferrets on the loose will for example dig in your houseplant dirt.

9. They will "steal" small things and hide them in or under the furniture which could be annoying.

10. Ferrets which are like cats in some ways can be trained to use a litter box.

Next Step: Write two sentences about your favorite pet. Include a nonrestrictive phrase or clause in one and an interruption in the other. Use commas to correctly set off these items.

Commas . . .

Commas set off an appositive from the rest of the sentence. An appositive is a word or phrase that identifies or renames a noun or pronoun.

> **The capital of Cyprus, Nicosia, has a population of almost 643,000.** (*Nicosia* renames *capital of Cyprus*, so the word is set off with commas.)

> **Cyprus, an island in the Mediterranean Sea, is about half the size of Connecticut.** (*An island in the Mediterranean Sea* identifies *Cyprus,* so the phrase is set off with commas.)

Do not use commas with appositives that are necessary to the basic meaning of the sentence.

> **The Mediterranean island Cyprus is about half the size of Connecticut.** (*Cyprus* is not set off because it is needed to make the sentence clear.)

Use commas to separate two or more adjectives that equally modify the same noun.

> **Comfortable, efficient cars are becoming more important to drivers.** (*Comfortable* and *efficient* are separated by a comma because they modify *cars* equally.)

> **Some automobiles run on clean, renewable sources of energy.** (*Clean* and *renewable* are separated by a comma because they modify *sources* equally.)

> **Conventional gasoline engines emit a lot of pollution.** (*Conventional* and *gasoline* do not modify *engines* equally; therefore, no comma separates the two.)

Use these tests to help you decide if adjectives modify equally:

1. Switch the order of the adjectives; if the sentence is clear, the adjectives modify equally.

    Yes: Efficient, comfortable cars are becoming more important to drivers.

    No: Gasoline conventional engines emit a lot of pollution.

2. Put the word *and* between the adjectives; if the sentence is clear, use a comma when *and* is taken out.

    Yes: Comfortable and efficient cars are becoming more important to drivers.

    No: Conventional and gasoline engines emit a lot of pollution.

Commas 3

■ To Set Off Appositives

For each sentence below, write the appositive phrase as well as the noun it renames. Set off the appositive with commas.

1. Reginald Fessenden a Scotsman living in Canada made the first voice broadcast on radio in 1906.

   Reginald Fessenden, a Scotsman living in Canada,

2. Edwin Armstrong developed FM radio a signal offering clearer sound than AM radio.

3. Lee DeForest the "father of radio" used some of Armstrong's and some of Fessenden's ideas.

4. David Sarnoff another radio pioneer later moved into television, forming NBC.

5. Many other inventors people from all over the world added to the growth of radio.

■ To Separate Equal Adjectives

For each sentence below, write the adjectives that need commas between them. Add the commas.

6. Lee DeForest was a vain determined inventor.

   vain, determined

7. In the wild crazy years of the 1920s, radios become very popular.

8. During the Depression, even poor jobless people had radios to brighten their lives.

9. Soon, companies were designing radios with beautiful stylish cabinets.

10. A huge powerful radio was often the main piece of furniture in a living room.

11. Now the demand is for smaller lighter radios.

Commas . . .

588.1
**To Set Off
Dialogue**

Use commas to set off the exact words of a speaker from the rest of the sentence. (Also see page **556**.)

> The firefighter said, "When we cannot successfully put out a fire, we try to keep it from spreading."

> "When we cannot successfully put out a fire, we try to keep it from spreading," the firefighter said.

NOTE Do not use a comma or quotation marks for indirect quotations. The words *if* and *that* often signal dialogue that is being reported rather than quoted.

> The firefighter said that when they cannot successfully put out a fire, they try to keep it from spreading. (These are not the speaker's exact words.)

588.2
**In Direct
Address**

Use commas to separate a noun of direct address from the rest of the sentence. (A noun of direct address is a noun that names a person spoken to in the sentence.)

> Hanae, did you know that an interior decorator can change wallpaper and fabrics on a computer screen?

> Sure, Jack, and an architect can use a computer to see how light will fall in different parts of a building.

588.3
**To Set Off
Interjections**

Use commas to separate an interjection or a weak exclamation from the rest of the sentence.

> No kidding, you mean that one teacher has to manage a class of 42 pupils? (weak exclamation)

> Uh-huh, and that teacher has other classes that size. (interjection)

588.4
**To Set Off
Explanatory
Phrases**

Use commas to separate an explanatory phrase from the rest of the sentence.

> English, the language computers speak worldwide, is also the most widely used language in science and medicine.

> More than 750 million people, about an eighth of the world's population, speak English as a foreign language.

Commas 4

■ **To Set Off Dialogue**
■ **In Direct Address**
■ **To Set Off Interjections**
■ **To Set Off Explanatory Phrases**

 For each of the following sentences, write the word or words that should be set off with a comma. Add the commas.

1. Jenni let's go see a movie.
 Jenni,

2. Hey do you want to go see a movie with us?

3. I answered "It depends on what movie."

4. Today's movies especially the computer-animated films are pretty amazing.

5. The earliest films lasting no more than 10 minutes were just brief looks at sports or fashions of the early 1900s.

6. Wow it cost a whole nickel to see one of those movies!

7. Did you know Curtis that movies were silent until 1927?

8. Music usually played on a piano often accompanied films, but they were still called "silent" movies.

9. In the first movie with sound, Al Jolson said "Wait a minute. You ain't heard nothin' yet!"

10. A few silent-film stars including the famous Charlie Chaplin didn't think "talkies" would last.

11. Of course sound movies soon replaced the silent ones.

12. "I'm glad" Jennie said "that I can hear people talk in movies!"

Next Step: Write a brief conversation between yourself and a friend about a movie you've both seen. Include commas where needed in the dialogue and for nouns of direct address and interjections.

Commas . . .

590.1
To Separate Introductory Clauses and Phrases

Use a comma to separate an adverb clause or a long phrase from the independent clause that follows it.

If every automobile in the country were a light shade of red, we'd live in a pink-car nation. (adverb clause)

According to some experts, solar-powered cars will soon be common. (long modifying phrase)

590.2
In Compound Sentences

Use a comma between two independent clauses that are joined by a coordinating conjunction (such as *and, but, or, nor, for, so,* and *yet*), forming a compound sentence. An independent clause expresses a complete thought and can stand alone as a sentence. (Also see page **516**.)

Many students enjoy working on computers, so teachers are finding new ways to use them in the classroom.

Computers can be valuable in education, but many schools cannot afford enough of them.

Avoid Comma Splices: A comma splice results when two independent clauses are "spliced" together with only a comma—and no conjunction. (See page **506**.)

SCHOOL DAZE

Ann, we've completed two-thirds of the quarter, and you haven't turned in one assignment. What do you have to say for yourself?

Ah . . . is there anything I can do for extra credit?

Commas 5

■ To Separate Introductory Clauses and Phrases
■ In Compound Sentences

 For each sentence below, write the word that should be followed by a comma. Add the comma.

1. Often considered a Canadian sport hockey has also grown in popularity in the United States.

sport,

2. To be a good hockey player a person must be an excellent skater and a superb athlete.

3. Hockey players have a lot of gear but their most important pieces of equipment are their skates.

4. Since the skates must be kept clean and sharp every team has an equipment manager to sharpen the skates.

5. Although a skate appears to have one sharp blade each skate actually has two blades along a hollow center.

6. A deeper hollow means two sharp blades and that can mean faster skating.

7. Because they move from side to side a lot goalies prefer the control a flatter blade gives.

8. Regular skating dulls blades but they can be dulled even more quickly by crashing against another skater's blades.

9. The quality of the ice affects skating so stadiums take care to maintain their rinks.

10. While "fast ice" is hard and slick "slow ice" is soft and rough.

Next Step: Write four sentences about your favorite winter sport. Include two sentences with introductory clauses or phrases and two compound sentences. Place commas correctly.

Test Prep

Number your paper from 1 to 12. For each underlined part of the paragraphs below, write the letter (from the next page) of the best way to punctuate it.

Throughout parts of the United States caves have been carved out
1
of thick layers of limestone. Why does this happen Natural acids in
2
water dissolve limestone so the constant trickle of groundwater over
3
thousands of years forms a cave. Sometimes there is enough dripping
water and minerals to form a stalactite, a kind of stone icicle hanging
4
from the roof of the cave. A stalagmite is a column built up on the
floor of the cave and it is also formed from the dripping water. People
5
have found fantastic odd formations in caves.
6

Some places in caves are so small that spelunkers cave explorers
7
must stretch their arms out in front of them while squeezing through
the tight opening Other places open into huge dark rooms big enough
8   **9**
to offer shelter. In fact, birds, animals, and people actually use caves
10
for this reason.

When water stops dripping from the ceiling the cave stops
11
growing. Eventually, an earthquake the weight of the ground above the
12
cave or natural erosion can mean the end of a cave.

1. **A** United States caves,
   B United States' caves
   C United States, caves
   D correct as is

2. **A** happen? Natural acids
   B happen. Natural acids
   C happen; natural acids
   D correct as is

3. **A** limestone, so, the constant
   B limestone so, the constant
   C limestone, so the constant
   D correct as is

4. **A** a stalactite a kind,
   B a stalactite, a kind,
   C a stalactite a kind
   D correct as is

5. **A** the cave and, it
   B the cave, and, it
   C the cave, and it
   D correct as is

6. **A** fantastic, odd formations
   B fantastic, odd formations,
   C fantastic, odd, formations
   D correct as is

7. **A** spelunkers, cave explorers
   B spelunkers, cave explorers,
   C spelunkers cave explorers,
   D correct as is

8. **A** tight opening? Other places
   B tight opening. Other places
   C tight opening, other places
   D correct as is

9. **A** huge, dark, rooms
   B huge dark, rooms
   C huge, dark rooms
   D correct as is

10. **A** birds animals and people
    B birds, animals, and people,
    C birds, animals and people
    D correct as is

11. **A** the ceiling, the cave
    B the ceiling, the cave,
    C the ceiling the cave,
    D correct as is

12. **A** an earthquake, the weight of the ground above the cave, or natural erosion
    B an earthquake the weight of the ground above the cave, or natural erosion,
    C an earthquake, the weight of the ground above the cave or natural erosion
    D correct as is

Semicolons

Use a **semicolon** to suggest a stronger pause than a comma indicates. A semicolon may also serve in place of a period.

594.1

To Join Two Independent Clauses

In a compound sentence, use a semicolon to join two independent clauses that are not connected with a coordinating conjunction. (See **744.1**.)

> The United States has more computers than any other country; its residents own more than 164 million of them.

594.2

With Conjunctive Adverbs

A semicolon is also used to join two independent clauses when the clauses are connected by a conjunctive adverb (such as *as a result, for example, however, therefore,* and *instead*). (See **738.1**.)

> Japan is next on that list; however, the Japanese have only 50 million computers.

> You might think that the billion people of China own a lot of computers; instead, the smaller country of Germany has twice as many computers as China.

594.3

To Separate Groups That Contain Commas

Use a semicolon between groups of words in a series when one or more of the groups already contain commas.

> Many of our community's residents separate their garbage into bins for newspapers, cardboard, and junk mail; glass, metal, and plastic; and nonrecyclable trash.

SCHOOL DAZE

It's true that I have only a few minutes to finish this; **however,** I am not worried.

Well, that makes one of us.

Semicolons

For each of the following sentences, write the words on either side of the needed semicolons and insert the semicolons.

1. Animation has become very popular however, artists actually began animating cartoons in the early 1900s.

popular; however

2. The first cartoons were hand drawn frame by frame as a result, each cartoon took a long time to create.

3. Winsor McCay took his time making his cartoons his five-minute cartoon *Gertie the Dinosaur* took more than a year to make.

4. Early cartoons created by individual artists took a lot of time their quality was very high compared to some later cartoons.

5. Some of the most well-known names in animation include Walt Disney, who led the way Max Fleischer, who thought up Popeye and Walter Lantz, the creator of Woody Woodpecker.

6. Computer-generated animation is now fairly common it can make animation look very real.

7. Computer-animated movies include Disney's *Toy Story, A Bug's Life,* and *Finding Nemo* Dreamworks' *Shrek, Antz,* and *Spirit: Stallion of the Cimarron* and Columbia Tri-Star's *Final Fantasy: The Spirits Within.*

8. Lately, *anime* has caught on in this country it is a Japanese style of animation.

9. Animated movies used to be made for children today, they are just as likely to be aimed at the parents, too.

Next Step: Write two independent clauses (sentences) about a cartoon you like and join them with a semicolon.

Colons

A **colon** may be used to introduce a list or an important point. Colons are also used in business letters and between the numbers in time.

596.1
To Introduce Lists

Use a colon to introduce a list. The colon usually comes after words describing the subject of the list (as in the first example below) or after summary words, such as *the following* or *these things*. Do not use a colon after a verb or preposition.

> Certain items are still difficult to recycle: foam cups, car tires, and toxic chemicals.

> To conserve water, you should do the following three things: fix drippy faucets, install a low-flow showerhead, and turn the water off while brushing your teeth.

> Incorrect: To conserve water, you should: install a low-flow showerhead, turn the water off while brushing your teeth, and fix drippy faucets.

596.2
To Introduce Sentences

A colon may be used to introduce a sentence, a question, or a quotation.

> This is why air pollution is bad: We are sacrificing our health and the health of all other life on the planet.

> Answer this question for me: Why aren't more people concerned about global warming?

> Joaquin shared this with us: "Iceland is the world's leader in the use of renewable energy."

596.3
After Salutations

A colon may be used after the salutation of a business letter.

> Dear Ms. Manners: Dear Dr. Warmle: Dear Professor Potter:

> Dear Captain Elliot: Dear Senator:

596.4
For Emphasis

Use a colon to emphasize a word or phrase.

> The newest alternative energy is also the most common element on earth: hydrogen.

> Here's one thing that can help save energy: a programmable thermostat.

596.5
Between Numbers in Time

Use a colon between the parts of a number that indicates time.

> My thermostat automatically sets my heat to 60 degrees between 11:00 p.m. and 6:00 a.m.

Colons

The following letter needs colons placed correctly. Write the line number and the words or numbers that need colons. Then add the colons.

1 March 9, 2005

2 JoAnne White Cloud

3 1315 Wells Road

4 Colfax, WA 99201

5 Dear Ms. White Cloud

6   The Colfax Junior Heritage Club would like you to be the

7 guest speaker at our next meeting on April 6. During the last three

8 months, we have been studying the goals of the Spokane Tribe

9 independence, honesty, and tradition. These goals have inspired

10 many of us with Native American roots.

11   We meet in the large lecture hall at the community center.

12 The meeting will begin at 730 p.m. and end at about 900 p.m.

13 Here is our plan for the evening a short business meeting, your

14 presentation, time for questions, and refreshments.

15   Let me add one final thought Our club's goal is "peace through

16 understanding," and your visit could help us all to learn more about

17 our common history. I hope you will be able to join us in April.

18 Sincerely,

19 Carolyn Mose

Next Step: Write a note to a friend. Ask him or her to meet you at a certain time and place. Include colons after the salutation, between numbers in a time, and to introduce a list.

Quotation Marks

Quotation marks are used in a number of ways:
- to set off the exact words of a speaker,
- to punctuate material quoted from another source,
- to punctuate words used in a special way, and
- to punctuate certain titles.

598.1
To Set Off a Speaker's Exact Words

Place quotation marks before and after a speaker's words in dialogue. Only the exact words of the speaker are placed within quotation marks.

> Marla said, "I've decided to become a firefighter."
> "A firefighter," said Juan, "can help people in many ways."

598.2
For Quotations Within Quotations

Use single quotation marks to punctuate a quotation within a quotation.

> Sung Kim asked, "Did Marla just say, 'I've decided to become a firefighter'?"

When titles occur within a quotation, use single quotation marks to punctuate those that require quotation marks.

> Juan said, "Springsteen's song 'The Rising' really inspired her."

598.3
To Set Off Quoted Material

When quoting material from another source, place quotation marks before and after the source's exact words.

> In her book *Living the Life You Deserve,* Tess Spyeder explains, "Choose a job you'll enjoy doing day after day over one that will fatten your bank account."

598.4
To Set Off Long Quoted Material

If more than one paragraph is quoted from a single source, quotation marks are placed before each paragraph and at the end of the last paragraph.

Quotations that are more than four lines are usually set off from the rest of the paper by indenting each line 10 spaces from the left. Quotations that are set off in this way require no quotation marks either before or after the quoted material.

Quotation Marks 1

- ■ To Set Off a Speaker's Exact Words
- ■ For Quotations Within Quotations

 For each of the following sentences, write the first and last word of each quotation or title, adding the correct quotation marks. Use ellipses as shown.

1. Bettina said, My science project, which I will call Communicating with Your Pet, is a sure winner.
   "My . . . 'Communicating . . . Pet,' . . . winner."

2. I don't know, I said. Are you sure Ms. Lazarus knows about your plans?

3. Sure. She even said, That's a wonderful idea, Bettina stated.

4. I said, That's not what *I* would have said. I would have told you that it's a crazy idea.

5. Then I asked, What are you going to do for scientific research? We're supposed to show our research for this project, you know.

6. Bettina replied, I'm going to keep track of how my dog, Moose, communicates with me when he wants something. I will record all my information in a chart.

7. Do you think Moose will cooperate? I asked.

8. I already asked him, Bettina replied, and he said, Go for it!

9. Bettina, you are incredible, I said.

10. Woof! Moose joined in from his spot under the table.

Next Step: Write a short conversation you might have with your pet or the pet of a friend. Use quotation marks correctly.

Quotation Marks . . .

600.1
Placement of Punctuation

Always place periods and commas inside quotation marks.

"I don't know," said Lac.

Lac said, "I don't know."

Place an exclamation point or a question mark inside the quotation marks when it punctuates the quotation.

Ms. Wiley asked, "Can you actually tour the Smithsonian on the Internet?"

Place it outside when it punctuates the main sentence.

Did I hear you say, "Now we can tour the Smithsonian on the Internet"?

Place semicolons or colons outside quotation marks.

First, I will read the article "Sonny's Blues"; then I will read "The Star Café" in my favorite music magazine.

600.2
For Special Words

Quotation marks also may be used (1) to set apart a word that is being discussed, (2) to indicate that a word is slang, or (3) to point out that a word or phrase is being used in a special way.

1. Renny uses the word "like" entirely too much.
2. Man, your car is really "phat."
3. Aunt Lulu, an editor at a weekly magazine, says she has "issues."

600.3
To Punctuate Titles

Use quotation marks to punctuate titles of songs, poems, short stories, lectures, episodes of radio or television programs, chapters of books, and articles found in magazines, newspapers, or encyclopedias. (Also see 602.3.)

"21 Questions" (song)

"The Reed Flute's Song" (poem)

"Old Man at the Bridge" (short story)

"Birthday Boys" (a television episode)

"The Foolish and the Weak" (a chapter in a book)

"Science Careers Today" (lecture)

"Teen Rescues Stranded Dolphin" (newspaper article)

NOTE When you punctuate a title, capitalize the first word, last word, and every word in between—except for articles (*a, an, the*), short prepositions (*at, to, with,* and so on), and coordinating conjunctions (*and, but, or*). (See 624.2.)

Quotation Marks 2

■ Placement of Punctuation
■ To Punctuate Titles

Copy the following sentences and properly place quotation marks, commas, and end punctuation.

1. We're going on vacation next week Dan said to Chicago
   "We're going on vacation next week," Dan said, "to Chicago."

2. He began singing lines from the song My Kind of Town

3. What do you know about Chicago I asked

4. Dan said, I know that Carl Sandburg wrote poems, such as Clark Street Bridge and Skyscraper, about Chicago

5. I know they have an elevated train system he added and it can get you just about anywhere in the city

6. Oprah Winfrey's show is taped there, so Mom wants to get tickets She loved the episode Bargain Shopping with Oprah he said

7. You just said Mom wants to get tickets But what about you What do you want to see I asked

8. I want to see Buckingham Fountain, the Sears Tower, and Navy Pier Dan said

9. Are you going to go shopping for some souvenirs on Michigan Avenue I teased

10. Oh, yeah Dan winked

Next Step: What would be your dream vacation? Write a brief discussion you might have with a friend, explaining your dream vacation. Punctuate it correctly with quotation marks and properly placed commas and end punctuation.

Italics and Underlining

Italics is slightly slanted type. In this sentence, the word *happiness* is typed in italics. In handwritten material, each word or letter that should be in italics is **underlined**. (See an example on page **403**.)

602.1
In Printed Material

Print words in italics when you are using a computer.

In *Tuck Everlasting*, the author explores what it would be like to live forever.

602.2
In Handwritten Material

Underline words that should be italicized when you are writing by hand.

In <u>Tuck Everlasting</u>, the author explores what it would be like to live forever.

602.3
In Titles

Italicize (or underline) the titles of books, plays, book-length poems, magazines, newspapers, radio and television programs, movies, videos, cassettes, CD's, and the names of aircraft and ships.

Walk Two Moons (book)	*Teen People* (magazine)
Fairies and Dragons (movie)	*Everwood* (TV program)
The Young and the Hopeless (CD)	**U.S.S.** *Arizona* (ship)
Columbia (space shuttle)	*Daily Herald* (newspaper)

Exception: Do not italicize or put quotation marks around your own title at the top of your written work.

A Day Without Water (personal writing: do not italicize)

602.4
For Scientific and Foreign Words

Italicize (or underline) scientific and foreign words that are not commonly used in everyday English.

Spinacia oleracea is the scientific term for spinach.

Many store owners who can help Spanish-speaking customers display an *Hablamos Español* sign in their windows.

602.5
For Special Uses

Italicize (or underline) a number, letter, or word that is being discussed or used in a special way. (Sometimes quotation marks are used for this same reason.)

Matt's hat has a bright red *A* on it.

Italics and Underlining

For each of the following sentences, write the word or words that should be italicized and underline them.

1. Ancient Greek drama grew from dithyrambs, choral songs honoring the god Dionysus.

dithyrambs

2. One book about early drama in ancient Greece is I Came, I Saw, I Applauded.

3. Plays were acted out on a stage called a skene, the source of our modern words scene and scenery.

4. The book Ancient Greek Drama explains the interesting special effects used back then.

5. One of the most famous writers of Greek theater was Sophocles, who wrote the two plays Oedipus Rex and Antigone.

6. Another Greek writer, Homer, wrote a book-length poem called The Odyssey.

7. A recent article in the New York Times said that all modern drama stems from the early Greek tragedies.

8. Obviously confused, Ted thought the '60s movie Zorba the Greek was based on a 2,000-year-old play.

9. He had missed the day the class watched the video Ancient Greece: A Journey Back in Time.

10. Ted thinks he can prove his point if he brings in Imiskoubria 2030, a CD of Greek hip-hop he found at a resale shop.

Next Step: What special words are used in a hobby or an activity that you enjoy? Write a brief paragraph explaining the activity, correctly underlining the special words.

Apostrophes

Use **apostrophes** to form contractions, to form certain plurals, or to show possession.

604.1
In Contractions

Use an apostrophe to form a contraction, showing that one or more letters have been left out of a word.

Common Contractions

can't (cannot)	**couldn't** (could not)	**didn't** (did not)
doesn't (does not)	**don't** (do not)	**hasn't** (has not)
haven't (have not)	**isn't** (is not)	**I'll** (I will)
I'd (I would)	**I'm** (I am)	**I've** (I have)
they'll (they will)	**they'd** (they would)	**they've** (they have)
they're (they are)	**you're** (you are)	**wouldn't** (would not)
you'll (you will)	**you'd** (you would)	**you've** (you have)

604.2
In Place of Omitted Letters or Numbers

Use an apostrophe to show that one or more digits have been left out of a number, or that one or more letters have been left out of a word to show a special pronunciation.

> **class of '99** (*19* is left out)
>
> **g'bye** (the letters *ood* are left out of *good-bye*)

NOTE Letters and numbers should not be omitted in most writing assignments; however, they may be omitted in dialogue to make it sound like real people are talking.

604.3
To Form Some Plurals

Use an apostrophe and *s* to form the plural of a letter, a sign, a number, or a word being discussed as a word.

> **A's   +'s   8's   *to*'s**
>
> Don't use too many *and*'s in your writing.

604.4
To Form Singular Possessives

To form the possessive of a singular noun, add an apostrophe and *s*.

> **the game's directions   Dr. Mill's theory**
> **Ross's bike   Roz's hair**

NOTE When a singular noun with more than one syllable ends with an *s* or *z* sound, the possessive may be formed by adding just an apostrophe.

> **Texas' oil** (or) **Texas's oil   Carlos' mother** (or) **Carlos's mother**

Apostrophes 1

- In Contractions
- In Place of Omitted Letters or Numbers
- To Form Singular Possessives

 For each numbered sentence below, correctly write the words or numbers that need an apostrophe.

Example: Uncle Pauls farm isnt the kind you might imagine.

Answer: Paul's isn't

(1) Its a tree farm in Vermont, and Uncle Paul "grows" maple syrup! **(2)** A maple trees sap looks clear and is slightly sweet. **(3)** The common brown color and maple flavor happen when its boiled.

(4) "Sugarin season" lasts four to six weeks, from February to April. **(5)** It doesnt seem to me that hanging a bucket on a tree is hard work. **(6)** "But ysee," says Uncle Paul, "theres a lot more to it than that. **(7)** Horse-drawn sleds have to carry the syrup buckets because the maple forests arent open or level enough for tractors. **(8)** Also, a sleds runners dont damage the tree roots like a tractors wheels would. **(9)** Then we cook the collected sap until its a thick syrup."

(10) I couldnt believe that it takes 40 gallons of sap to make one gallon of syrup! **(11)** Each states maple tree sap has its own taste, so Massachusetts syrup doesnt taste the same as Vermonts. **(12)** Of course, you havent tasted the best until youve tried Uncle Pauls syrup.

Next Step: Explain the process for something you like to do. Include contractions and singular possessives. Properly place the apostrophes for each.

Apostrophes . . .

The possessive form of plural nouns ending in *s* is usually made by adding just an apostrophe.

> students' homework   teachers' lounge

For plural nouns not ending in *s*, an apostrophe and *s* must be added.

> children's book   people's opinions

Remember: The word immediately before the apostrophe is the owner.

> student's project (*student* is the owner)
>
> students' project (*students* are the owners)

When possession is shared by more than one noun, add an apostrophe and *s* to the last noun in the series.

> Uncle Reggie, Aunt Rosie, and my mom's garden
> (All three own the garden.)
>
> Uncle Reggie's, Aunt Rosie's, and my mom's gardens
> (Each person owns a garden.)

The possessive of a compound noun is formed by placing the possessive ending after the last word.

> her sister-in-law's hip-hop music (singular)
>
> her sisters-in-law's tastes in music (plural)
>
> the secretary of state's husband (singular)
>
> the secretaries of state's husbands (plural)

The possessive of an indefinite pronoun is formed by adding an apostrophe and *s*.

> no one's   anyone's   somebody's

NOTE In pronouns that use *else*, add an apostrophe and *s* to the second word.

> somebody else's   anyone else's

Use an apostrophe with an adjective that is part of an expression indicating time (month, day, hour) or amount.

> In today's Spanish class, we talked about going to Spain.
>
> My father lost more than an hour's work when that thunderstorm knocked out our power.
>
> I bought a couple dollars' worth of grapes at the roadside stand.

Apostrophes 2

■ **To Form Plural Possessives**
■ **To Show Shared Possession**
■ **To Form Possessives with Compound Nouns and Indefinite Pronouns**
■ **To Express Time or Amount**

For each of the following sentences, correctly write the word or words that need an apostrophe.

1. Everyones schedule is upset when a blackout occurs.
   everyone's

2. The eastern United States and Canadas worst blackout happened August 14, 2003.

3. Many people lost several hours work on their computers.

4. Annes, Jeremys, and Geoffs baseball games were canceled because of darkness.

5. My sister-in-laws candle store was very busy that night.

6. Nora, Kiki, and Sandys school had a generator, so people gathered there for the night.

7. It was anyones guess as to when the power would be restored.

8. Surprisingly, people didn't panic at the nights unusual darkness.

9. Peoples attention turned to skies unusually bright with stars.

10. Next door, the Wagners house was lit with some oil lamps.

11. Their childrens voices could be heard through the open windows.

12. Articles in the next days newspapers indicated how widespread the blackout was.

13. One editor in chiefs column asked why the blackout happened.

14. The electric companies reports blamed it on Ohio power lines that short-circuited.

Hyphens

Use a **hyphen** to divide words at the end of a line and to form compound words. Also use a hyphen between the numbers in a fraction and to join numbers that indicate the life span of an individual, the scores of a game, and so on.

608.1
To Divide Words

Use a hyphen to divide a word when you run out of room at the end of a line. A word may be divided only between syllables. Here are some additional guidelines:

- Never divide a one-syllable word: *raised, through.*
- Avoid dividing a word of five letters or fewer: *paper, study.*
- Never divide a one-letter syllable from the rest of the word: *omit-ted,* **not** *o-mitted.*
- Never divide abbreviations or contractions: *NASA, wouldn't.*
- Never divide the last word in more than two lines in a row or the last word in a paragraph.
- When a vowel is a syllable by itself, divide the word after the vowel: *epi-sode,* **not** *ep-isode.*

NOTE Refer to a dictionary if you're not sure how to divide a word.

608.2
In Compound Words

A hyphen is used in some compound words, including numbers from twenty-one to ninety-nine.

about-face	warm-up	time-out
down-to-earth	ice-skating	high-rise
thirty-three	seventy-five	

608.3
To Create New Words

A hyphen is often used to form new words beginning with the prefixes *self, ex, all,* and *great.* A hyphen is also used with suffixes such as *elect* and *free.*

self-cleaning	ex-friend	all-natural	mayor-elect
self-esteem	ex-president	great-aunt	germ-free

608.4
Between Numbers in a Fraction

Use a hyphen between the numbers in a fraction. Do not, however, use a hyphen between the numerator and denominator when one or both are already hyphenated.

four-tenths	five-sixteenths	seven thirty-seconds (7/32)

Hyphens 1

- ■ **To Divide Words**
- ■ **In Compound Words**
- ■ **To Create New Words**

 For each of the following sentences, correctly write the words that are incorrectly hyphenated or that should be hyphenated but are not.

1. My dad and his brother in law often go golfing together.

2. Thirty eight people bought lemonade from our stand.

3. Our troop's ex scoutmaster visited our last scout meeting.

4. Although Eileen is an excellent athlete, sometimes she does-n't have the right attitude.

5. Marta is taking a course in self defense at the community center.

6. Joan put a scoop of fat free ice cream on each brownie.

7. People could not believe that Arnold Schwarzenegger was the governor elect of California.

8. Rex's speed in the mile run was an all time high for any student at Greenville Junior High.

9. Luke couldn't believe what a low price he paid when he bought some kneepads for football.

10. Aaron's little sister begged him to take her on the merry go round.

11. Once we complete our essays, the teacher hands out some forms for self assessment.

12. Uncle Walter bought some souvenirs for us at the airport's duty free shop.

Next Step: Write two sentences in which you use some of the hyphenated words from the facing page.

Hyphens . . .

Use a hyphen to join two or more words that work together to form a single-thought adjective before a noun. Generally, hyphenate any compound adjective that might be misread if it is not hyphenated—use common sense. (See page **488**.)

smiley-face sticker   dress-up clothes   fresh-breeze scent

Use the tests below to determine if a hyphen is needed.

1. When a compound adjective is made of a noun plus an adjective, it should be hyphenated.

microwave-safe cookware   book-smart student

2. When a compound adjective is made of a noun plus a participle (*ing* or *ed* form of a verb), it should be hyphenated.

bone-chilling story   vitamin-enriched cereal

3. Hyphenate a compound adjective that is a phrase (includes conjunctions or prepositions).

heat-and-serve meals   refrigerator-to-oven dishes

Do *not* hyphenate compound adjectives in these instances:

1. When words forming the adjective come after the noun, do not hyphenate.

This cookware is microwave safe.
The cereal was vitamin enriched.

2. If the first of the two words ends in *ly,* do not hyphenate.

newly designed computer   rarely seen species

3. Do not use a hyphen when a number or letter is the final part of a one-thought adjective.

grade A milk   level 6 textbook

Use a hyphen to join a capital letter to a noun or participle.

U-turn   Y-axis   T-bar   A-frame
PG-rated movie   X-ray

Use a hyphen with prefixes or suffixes to avoid confusion or awkward spelling.

Re-collect (not recollect) **the reports we handed back last week.**
It has a shell-like (not shelllike) **texture.**

Hyphens 2

■ To Form Adjectives
■ To Join Letters to Words
■ To Avoid Confusion

For each of the following sentences, correctly write the words that should be hyphenated.

1. Cholesterol can be an artery clogging substance.
artery-clogging

2. Lyndeen pointed to some geese flying south in a V formation.

3. The chameleon had escaped from its cage, and the hard to spot creature was not found for days.

4. The patient complained of hearing belllike sounds all the time.

5. Dashiel used several C clamps to hold the pieces of wood together while the glue dried.

6. The souvenir that Alex showed the class was a miniature recreation of a famous sculpture in Paris.

7. Grandpa likes to have a soft boiled egg for breakfast.

8. I am going to use a stain covering paint in my bedroom.

9. Mary Anne grew up on a 2,000 acre farm in North Dakota.

10. As she took apart the kitchen faucet, Mom hoped that simply replacing the O ring would fix the leak.

11. The majority of shark species are not man eating fish.

Next Step: Write two sentences in which you use hyphenated adjectives. (Check the rules on the facing page to make sure your adjectives actually need hyphens.)

Dashes

The **dash** can be used to show a sudden break in a sentence, to emphasize a word or clause, and to show that someone's speech is being interrupted. There is no space before or after a dash.

612.1
To Indicate a Sudden Break

A dash can be used to show a sudden break in a sentence.

> The three of us came down with colds, lost our voices, and missed the football game—all because we had practiced in the rain.

612.2
For Emphasis

A dash may be used to emphasize or explain a word, a series of words, a phrase, or a clause.

> Vitamins and minerals—important dietary supplements—can improve your diet.

> The benefits of vitamin A—better vision and a stronger immune system—are well known.

612.3
To Indicate Interrupted Speech

Use a dash to show that someone's speech is being interrupted by another person.

> Well—yes, I understand—no, I remember—oh—okay, thank you.

Parentheses

Parentheses are used around words that are included in a sentence to add information or to help make an idea clearer.

612.4
To Add Information

Use parentheses when adding information or clarifying an idea.

> Cures for diseases (from arthritis to AIDS) may be found in plants in the rain forest.

> Only about 10 percent (27,000) of the plant species in the world have been studied.

Dashes

Rewrite the sentences below, adding dashes where appropriate.

1. Gingivitis that is, swollen gums is a common disease.
   Gingivitis—that is, swollen gums—is a common disease.

2. I was going to I mean I *am* going to take the subway.

3. Only one thing will get Winifred to leave that island a hurricane.

4. Excuse me yes, I know that have you but I okay.

5. People's donations will fund this research research that could save many lives.

6. Danielle, be sure to bundle up it's below zero out there.

Parentheses

Write the parts of the sentences below that should be enclosed in parentheses. Add the parentheses.

1. Randall got a majority 62% of the votes in the class election.
   (62%)

2. Derek acting totally unlike himself yelled at his friend.

3. Genny wore her new shirt the sparkly blue one to the dance.

4. Oliver's mom my aunt will drive us to the theater.

5. John's constant itching led him to make an appointment with a dermatologist a skin doctor.

6. Three northeastern states Maine, New Hampshire, and Vermont had ice storms yesterday.

Ellipses

Use an **ellipsis** (three periods) to show a pause in dialogue or to show that words or sentences have been left out. Leave one space before, after, and between each period.

614.1

To Show Pauses

Use an ellipsis to show a pause in dialogue.

> "My report," said Reggie, "is on . . . ah . . . cars of the future. One place that I . . . uh . . . checked on the Internet said that cars would someday run on sunshine."

614.2

To Show Omitted Words

Use an ellipsis to show that one or more words have been left out of a quotation. Read this statement about hibernation.

> Some animals, such as the chipmunk and the woodchuck, hibernate in winter. During this time, the animal's heart beats very slowly—only a few times per minute. Its body cools down so much that it nearly freezes, and this is called going into torpor.

Here's how you would type part of the above quotation, leaving out some of the words. If the words left out are at the end of a sentence, use a period followed by three dots.

> Some animals . . . hibernate in winter. During this time, the animal's heart beats very slowly . . . and this is called going into torpor.

SCHOOL DAZE

Max, where is your project? Today is the last day to turn it in!

Well . . . ah . . . can I e-mail it to you before midnight?

Ellipses

■ **To Show Omitted Words**

Read each of the following passages. Decide what the important parts are and rewrite each paragraph, leaving some of the words out. Use ellipses to show where you've left words out.

Passage A:

Spanish explorers of the late sixteenth century brought horses with them to North America. At first, the Native Americans thought the horses were big dogs. Then the Pueblo Indians learned to manage herds of horses. In a short time, horses became very important to other tribes, as well. Men riding horses were able to follow bison, which the people depended upon for food and shelter. Horses also became valuable for trading. As a result, tribes such as the Lakota and Crow grew and prospered.

Passage B:

Winter storms can be quite dangerous, and many people don't realize it. Icy roads lead to traffic accidents, or people become trapped in their cars during a blizzard. A storm may knock out power and leave homes without heat. People who remain outside risk injury due to exposure. Hypothermia, which results when body temperature falls below 90 degrees, and frostbite can result in permanent damage to a person's body. In addition, the heart is stressed by cold temperatures; add shoveling snow to that stress, and the heart can fail. The best way to avoid these dangers is to know the risks and be prepared with cold-weather supplies.

Next Step: Write a brief conversation between two friends discussing a recent storm. Use ellipses to show pauses in the dialogue.

Test Prep

For each sentence below, write the letter of the line that does NOT contain a mistake. If all lines contain a mistake, choose "D."

1. A Shari has a new book a-
    B bout cats; and its called
    C Cats of Ancient Egypt.
    D mistake in every line

2. A Franks' sister wears one
    B of his T-shirts, but it
    C does'nt really fit her.
    D mistake in every line

3. A I asked Bell, "May I
    B borrow a rarely-used
    C CD of yours"?
    D mistake in every line

4. A These are the be-
    B st songs; "White
    C Flag" and Stand Up.
    D mistake in every line

5. A A headline in todays
    B Daily Trumpet read
    C Man Bites (Hot)dog.
    D mistake in every line

6. A Did you just say, "We
    B ca'nt go to the movie
    C with you?"
    D mistake in every line

7. A Marc said, When I'm
    B done painting, my walls
    C will be clean and white.
    D mistake in every line

8. A My two best friend's
    B moms are doctors
    C theyr'e pediatricians.
    D mistake in every line

9. A Dana saw the G rated
    B movies Toy Story 2
    C and "Pokemon" on video.
    D mistake in every line

10. A Carl Sandburgs' poem
    B Chicago is about a
    C proud, fierce city.
    D mistake in every line

11. A Irene was a very bright
    B student, however, she
    C did'nt always get A's.
    D mistake in every line

12. A Did you see the art-
    B icle about mutts
    C in *Dog Fancy* magazine?
    D mistake in every line

PUNCTUATION

For each line, write the letter of the correct way (listed below) to write the underlined part .

13. The book "Cast About" should be on everyone's reading list

14. for <u>these reasons</u>: First, it is a creative story that keeps the

15. reader interested. Second, the characters are <u>well-developed</u>.

16. Last, the chapter "Home Again" is some of the most amazing

17. writing Kathryn Danielson has ever done. It is an <u>extremely e-</u>

18. motional <u>book, therefore,</u> be prepared to experience feelings

19. you <u>havent</u> had for a while.

13. A Cast About
   B *Cast About*
   C "Cast About
   D correct as is

14. A these reasons,
   B these reasons;
   C these reasons
   D correct as is

15. A well developed
   B well de-veloped
   C welldeveloped
   D correct as is

16. A Home Again"
   B Home Again
   C *Home Again*
   D correct as is

17. A extremely *(move letter "e" to next line)*
   B extremely emoti-
   C extreme-
   D correct as is

18. A book, therefore
   B book; therefore,
   C book therefore,
   D correct as is

19. A havent'
   B haven't
   C have'nt
   D correct as is

Editing for Mechanics

Capitalization

618.1
Proper Nouns and Adjectives

Capitalize all proper nouns and all proper adjectives. A proper noun is the name of a particular person, place, thing, or idea. A proper adjective is an adjective formed from a proper noun.

Common Noun: country, president, continent

Proper Noun: Canada, Andrew Jackson, Asia

Proper Adjective: Canadian, Jacksonian, Asian

618.2
Names of People

Capitalize the names of people and also the initials or abbreviations that stand for those names.

Samuel L. Jackson   Aung San Suu Kyi

Mary Sanchez-Gomez

618.3
Titles Used with Names

Capitalize titles used with names of persons; also capitalize abbreviations standing for those titles.

President Mohammed Hosni Mubarak   Dr. Linda Trout

Governor Michael Easley   Rev. Jim Zavaski

Senator John McCain

618.4
Words Used as Names

Capitalize words such as *mother, father, aunt,* and *uncle* when these words are used as names.

Uncle Marius **started to sit on the couch.** (*Uncle* is a name; the speaker calls this person "Uncle Marius.")

Then Uncle **stopped in midair.** (*Uncle* is used as a name.)

"So, Mom, **what are you doing here?"** I asked. (*Mom* is used as a name.)

Words such as *aunt, uncle, mom, dad, grandma,* and *grandpa* are usually not capitalized if they come after a possessive pronoun (my, his, our).

My aunt **had just called him.** (The word *aunt* describes this person but is not used as a name.)

Then my dad and mom **walked into the room.** (The words *dad* and *mom* are not used as names in this sentence.)

punctuate *edit* capitalize
SPELL
improve
Editing for Mechanics

619

MECHANICS

Capitalization 1

- Proper Nouns and Adjectives
- Names of People
- Titles Used with Names
- Words Used as Names

For each of the following sentences, correctly write the words that should be capitalized but are not.

1. Yesterday grandpa told me he'd never seen the american capital.

Grandpa, American

2. A nickname people often use when talking about the united states government is uncle sam.

3. A congressperson from new york, senator hillary clinton, is married to a former president.

4. From 1993 to 2005, the two men who held the highest office in the country were president william clinton and president george w. bush.

5. In england and canada, queen elizabeth II has reigned since the 1950s.

6. Canada's governor general adrienne clarkson represents the queen, who is the country's head of state.

7. After the 2003 election, prime minister paul martin became the head of the canadian government.

8. Uncle Richard, who is mom's brother, lives in montreal, quebec.

9. One summer, grandma and I visited him.

10. Uncle Rich introduced mom to a friend of his, dr. sylvia hill, and they keep in touch with e-mail.

Next Step: Write two or three sentences that include the name of a person, a title used with a name, and a word used as a person's name. Also include a proper adjective. Use correct capitalization.

Capitalization . . .

620.1
School Subjects

Capitalize the name of a specific educational course, but not the name of a general subject. (Exception—the names of all languages are proper nouns and are always capitalized: *French, English, Hindi, German, Latin*.)

Roberto is studying accounting **at the technical college.**
(Because *accounting* is a general subject, it is not capitalized.)

He likes the professor who teaches Accounting Principles.
(The specific course name is capitalized.)

620.2
Official Names

Capitalize the names of businesses and the official names of their products. (These are called trade names.) Do not, however, capitalize a general word like "toothpaste" when it follows the trade name.

Old Navy	**Best Buy**	**Microsoft**	**Kodak**
Sony Playstation	**Tombstone pizza**	**Mudd jeans**	

620.3
Races, Languages, Nationalities, Religions

Capitalize the names of languages, races, nationalities, and religions, as well as the proper adjectives formed from them.

Arab	**Spanish**	**Judaism**	**Catholicism**
African art	**Irish linen**	**Swedish meatballs**	

620.4
Days, Months, Holidays

Capitalize the names of days of the week, months of the year, and special holidays.

Thursday	**Friday**	**Saturday**
July	**August**	**September**
Arbor Day	**Independence Day**	

Do not capitalize the names of seasons.

winter, spring, summer, fall (autumn)

620.5
Historical Events

Capitalize the names of historical events, documents, and periods of time.

World War II	**the Bill of Rights**	**the Magna Carta**
the Middle Ages	**the Paleozoic Era**	

Capitalization 2

- ▪ School Subjects
- ▪ Official Names
- ▪ Races, Languages, Nationalities, Religions
- ▪ Days, Months, Holidays
- ▪ Historical Events

 For each of the following sentences, correctly write any word that is incorrectly capitalized.

1. Sue had lunch at Burger king last thursday.

   King, Thursday

2. At the catholic church that Ramón's family attends, the priests speak spanish.

3. More than a million soldiers fought the battle of the bulge in Europe during World war II.

4. Cassandra's first class of the day is fundamentals of music.

5. After that, she has Science, math, gym, and english.

6. The handlin Museum has a new exhibit of african art.

7. Independence day falls on the first sunday of july this year.

8. My favorite sandwich is made with Skippy Peanut Butter.

9. During the period of time called the renaissance, people made many advances in Art, Literature, and Science.

10. Shabbat, a day of rest and prayer in the jewish religion, begins on friday evening and ends saturday evening.

Next Step: Write a sentence that tells your favorite brand of soda. Write another sentence about a holiday you enjoy. Capitalize words correctly.

Capitalization . . .

622.1
Geographic Names

Capitalize the following geographic names.

Planets and heavenly bodies . . . . **Venus, Jupiter, Milky Way**

Lowercase the word "earth" except when used as the proper name of our planet, especially when mentioned with other planet names.

What on earth are you doing here?

Sam has traveled across the face of the earth several times.

Jupiter's diameter is 11 times larger than Earth's.

The four inner planets are Mercury, Venus, Earth, and Mars.

Continents . . . . **Europe, Asia, South America, Australia, Africa**

Countries . . . **Morocco, Haiti, Greece, Chile, United Arab Emirates**

States . . . . . **New Mexico, Alabama, West Virginia, Delaware, Iowa**

Provinces . . . . **Alberta, British Columbia, Quebec, Ontario**

Counties . . . . **Sioux County, Kandiyohi County, Wade County**

Cities . . . . **Montreal, Baton Rouge, Albuquerque, Portland**

Bodies of water . . . . **Delaware Bay, Chickamunga Lake, Indian Ocean, Gulf of Mexico, Skunk Creek**

Landforms. . . . . **Appalachian Mountains, Bitterroot Range**

Public areas . . . . **Tiananmen Square, Sequoia National Forest, Mount Rushmore, Open Space Park, Vietnam Memorial**

Roads and highways . . . . **New Jersey Turnpike, Interstate 80, Central Avenue, Chisholm Trail, Mutt's Road**

Buildings . . . **Pentagon, Paske High School, Empire State Building**

Monuments . . . . **Eiffel Tower, Statue of Liberty**

622.2
Particular Sections of the Country

Capitalize words that indicate particular sections of the country. Also capitalize proper adjectives formed from names of specific sections of a country.

Having grown up on the hectic East Coast, I find life in the South to be refreshing.

Here in Georgia, Southern hospitality is a way of life.

Words that simply indicate a direction are not capitalized; nor are adjectives that are formed from words that simply indicate direction.

The town where I live, located east of Memphis, is typical of others found in western Tennessee.

Capitalization 3

◼ **Geographic Names**
◼ **Particular Sections of the Country**

Write the answer to each of the following questions.

1. What is the name of the country located just south of the United States?

Mexico

2. What are the two continents not listed on the facing page?

3. Which four planets are closest to the sun?

4. What section of the country is famous for cowboys?

5. If you flew from New York to London, England, what body of water would you fly over?

6. What is the name of a mountain range in Colorado?

7. Which state is completely surrounded by an ocean, and what ocean is it?

8. What is the large, centrally located park in New York City?

9. What are two European countries?

10. What is the capital of Canada, and which province is it located in?

11. Which city is the second largest in the United States?

12. What is the name of the street where you live?

13. In what part of the country is Alabama located?

14. What is the name of the building in which the U.S. president lives?

15. What large canyon is located in Arizona?

Next Step: Write two sentences about your favorite place. Include geographic names in both sentences.

Capitalization . . .

624.1
First Words

Capitalize the first word of every sentence and the first word in a direct quotation.

> In many families, pets are treated like people, according to an article in the *Kansas City Star*. (sentence)

> Marty Becker, coauthor of *Chicken Soup for the Pet Lover's Soul*, reports, "Seven out of ten people let their pets sleep on the bed." (direct quotation)

> "I get my 15 minutes of fame," he says, "every time I come home." (Notice that *every* is not capitalized because it does not begin a new sentence.)

> "It's like being treated like a rock star," says Becker. "Now I have to tell you that feels pretty good."

Do not capitalize the first word in an indirect quotation.

> Becker says that in the last 10 years, pets have moved out of kennels and basements and into living rooms and bedrooms. (indirect quotation)

624.2
Titles

Capitalize the first word of a title, the last word, and every word in between except articles (*a, an, the*), short prepositions, and coordinating conjunctions. Follow this rule for titles of books, newspapers, magazines, poems, plays, songs, articles, movies, works of art, pictures, stories, and essays. (See **600.3**.)

> *Locked in Time* (book)

> *Boston Globe* (newspaper)

> *Dog Fancy* (magazine)

> "Roses Are Red" (poem)

> *The Phantom of the Opera* (play)

> *Daddy Day Care* (movie)

> "Intuition" (song)

> Mona Lisa (work of art)

Capitalization 4

- First Words
- Titles

For each of the following sentences, correctly write any word that is incorrectly capitalized.

1. Kai bought four tickets to the play *the Phantom Of the Opera*.
   The, of

2. He said, "as long as I can get the tickets I want, I really don't mind waiting in line."

3. The *New York times* had a fantastic review of the play in an article called "Phantom appears; Here to stay."

4. Shar read the poem "the Road not Taken" by Robert Frost.

5. "That poem," said Shar, "Really makes me think."

6. it is one of his best-known poems.

7. Danté enjoys the electronic magazine *EEK!: Environmental education for Kids*.

8. "I learned about the careers of park rangers," he said, "And wildlife biologists."

9. after we saw the movie *The Cat In The Hat*, Bruce got a hat just like the cat's.

10. He said that It made him look cool.

Next Step: Write a sentence for each of the following: a name of a book, a song, and a movie. Make sure you capitalize correctly.

Capitalization . . .

626.1
Abbreviations

Capitalize abbreviations of titles and organizations.

Dr. (Doctor)   **M.D.** (Doctor of Medicine)

Mr. (Mister)   **UPS** (United Parcel Service)

SADD (Students Against Destructive Decisions)

626.2
Organizations

Capitalize the name of an organization, an association, or a team.

New York State Historical Society	**the Red Cross**
General Motors Corporation	**the Miami Dolphins**
Republicans	**the Democratic Party**

626.3
Letters

Capitalize the letters used to indicate form or shape.

T-shirt   **U-turn**   **A-frame**

Capitalize	Do Not Capitalize
American	un-American
January, February	winter, spring
Missouri and Ohio Rivers	the rivers Missouri and Ohio
The South is humid in summer.	Turn south at the stop sign.
Duluth Middle School	a Duluth middle school
Governor Bob Taft	Bob Taft, our governor
President Luiz Lula Da Silva	Luiz Lula Da Silva, Brazil's president
Nissan Altima	a Nissan automobile
The planet Earth is egg shaped.	The earth on Grandpa's farm is rich.
I'm taking World Cultures.	I'm taking social studies.

Capitalization 5

■ Abbreviations
■ Organizations
■ Letters

Capitalize the words that need to be capitalized in the following sentences.

1. The construction crew carefully lowered the i-beam onto the foundation.

   I-beam

2. The green bay packers won the first two Super Bowls.

3. Our substitute teacher, ms. Lukas, will complete her m.a. degree this spring.

4. After I fell off the bleachers and broke my arm, mr. Stevenson took me to see dr. Bell at the clinic.

5. One of the largest ships in the United States Navy is the u.s.s. *Enterprise*.

6. Over the years, the smithsonian institution has become a world-famous museum.

7. The city council passed a new ordinance outlawing u-turns on Davis Avenue.

8. Most politicians seek public office as either a republican, a democrat, or an independent.

9. Did you see the new a-frame picnic shelter in Franklin Park?

10. The Northwest High School panthers' football games are broadcast on radio station kyxx.

11. Engineers at General motors corporation changed the angle of the b-pillar on their new sedan.

12. On the last day of school, the entire seventh-grade science class wore t-shirts with the words "mr. Kall is the coolest."

Test Prep

For each underlined part of the paragraphs below, choose the letter on the next page that shows the correct capitalization. If the underlined part is correct, choose "D."

<u>In Science Class</u>, we talked about the invention of the windchill
    1
chart. <u>Mr. Land said That</u> two scientists in <u>antarctica, Paul Sipel</u> and
     2   **3**
P. F. Passel, noticed how wind speed affected people and <u>animals. they</u>
                                                          4
<u>developed</u> a formula in the 1940s to measure the "windchill factor." Why

do low temperatures feel even colder in the wind—especially in <u>january</u>
                                                                 5
<u>and february</u>? It's because wind removes any heated air around your

body. It also evaporates moisture from your skin.

Every <u>Winter here in chicago</u>, we get a lot of windchill warnings.
          6
<u>Mom and dad</u> have a <u>membership with aaa</u> that helps them if their <u>ford</u>
    7   **8**   **9**
<u>Focus</u> sedan won't start in the bitter cold. And they're always telling me,

"<u>Don't forget chapstick</u> lip balm, and make sure you wear a hat!"
      10

Even in states like <u>Florida, Texas, and California</u>, the wind can
                              11
make temperatures seem colder than they actually are. A windy day in

<u>the gulf of Mexico</u> might trick people into thinking they won't get a
      12
sunburn. (When <u>Ms. Huang, our Principal</u>, returned from a vacation in
                      13
New Orleans, her fair skin was all pink.) Windchill factors, however,

are not usually printed in the <u>*Miami herald*</u> or the *Brownsville Sun.*
                                    14
Perhaps such cities should publish a "sun warmth factor" instead!

1. **A** In Science class
   B In science class
   C in science class
   D correct as is

2. **A** Mr. Land said that
   B Mr. land said That
   C mr. Land said that
   D correct as is

3. **A** antarctica, Paul sipel
   B Antarctica, paul sipel
   C Antarctica, Paul Sipel
   D correct as is

4. **A** Animals. they developed
   B animals. They developed
   C Animals. They developed
   D correct as is

5. **A** January and february
   B January and February
   C january and February
   D correct as is

6. **A** winter Here in Chicago
   B Winter here in Chicago
   C winter here in Chicago
   D correct as is

7. **A** mom and dad
   B Mom and Dad
   C mom and Dad
   D correct as is

8. **A** membership with Aaa
   B Membership with AAA
   C membership with AAA
   D correct as is

9. **A** Ford focus
   B Ford Focus
   C ford focus
   D correct as is

10. **A** Don't forget Chapstick
    B don't forget chapstick
    C don't forget Chapstick
    D correct as is

11. **A** florida, Texas, and california
    B Florida, Texas, and california
    C Florida, texas, and California
    D correct as is

12. **A** the Gulf of Mexico
    B The gulf of Mexico
    C The Gulf Of Mexico
    D correct as is

13. **A** Ms. Huang, Our Principal
    B Ms. huang, our Principal
    C Ms. Huang, our principal
    D correct as is

14. **A** *miami herald*
    B *Miami Herald*
    C *miami Herald*
    D correct as is

Plurals

630.1
Most Nouns

The **plurals** of most nouns are formed by adding *s* to the singular.

cheerleader — **cheerleaders**   wheel — **wheels**

bubble — **bubbles**

630.2
Nouns Ending in *ch, sh, s, x,* and *z*

The plural form of nouns ending in *ch, sh, s, x,* and *z* is made by adding *es* to the singular.

lunch — **lunches**   dish — **dishes**   mess — **messes**

buzz — **buzzes**   fox — **foxes**

630.3
Nouns Ending in *o*

The plurals of nouns ending in *o* with a vowel just before the *o* are formed by adding *s*.

radio — **radios**   studio — **studios**   rodeo — **rodeos**

The plurals of most nouns ending in *o* with a consonant just before the *o* are formed by adding *es*.

echo — **echoes**   hero — **heroes**   tomato — **tomatoes**

Exceptions: Musical terms and words of Spanish origin always form plurals by adding *s*.

alto — **altos**   banjo — **banjos**   taco — **tacos**

solo — **solos**   piano — **pianos**   burro — **burros**

630.4
Nouns Ending in *ful*

The plurals of nouns that end with *ful* are formed by adding an *s* at the end of the word.

three platefuls   six tankfuls   four cupfuls   five pailfuls

630.5
Nouns Ending in *f* or *fe*

The plurals of nouns that end in *f* or *fe* are formed in one of two ways: If the final *f* sound is still heard in the plural form of the word, simply add *s*; if the final sound is a *v* sound, change the *f* to *ve* and add *s*.

roof — roofs   chief — chiefs   belief — beliefs
(plural ends with *f* sound)

wife — wives   loaf — loaves   leaf — leaves
(plural ends with *v* sound)

Plurals 1

■ Nouns Ending in *ch, sh, s, x,* and *z*
■ Nouns Ending in *o, ful, f* or *fe*

For each of the following sentences, write the plural form of the underlined word or words.

1. The class collected five <u>box</u> of books for the book drive.
   boxes

2. Before the final bell rang, eight <u>bus</u> lined up in front of the school.

3. Several coral <u>reef</u> form a natural barrier for the chain of <u>island</u> off the South American coast.

4. <u>Farmer</u> in Idaho have a history of raising huge <u>potato</u>.

5. Jill likes two <u>spoonful</u> of sugar in her tea.

6. Clear the <u>ash</u> out of the fireplace before building a new fire.

7. Our school's music teacher wants 10 more <u>soprano</u> in the choir.

8. We saw 30 <u>calf</u> during our field trip to the Pell dairy farm.

9. Salid and Jerry decided to rent three <u>video</u> for the weekend.

10. After eating just one jalapeño pepper, Frank needed five <u>mouthful</u> of milk to cool his tongue.

11. Diego loves to play the <u>bongo</u>.

12. The drawing board in Mom's office faces a row of four <u>window</u>.

13. She enjoys watching the <u>leaf</u> change every fall.

14. Zack packed three <u>lunch</u> for the family's day of hiking.

Next Step: Write three sentences using the plurals of *radio, capful,* and *life.*

Plurals . . .

632.1
Nouns Ending in y

The plurals of common nouns that end in *y* with a consonant letter just before the *y* are formed by changing the *y* to *i* and adding *es*.

fly — **flies** baby — **babies** cavity — **cavities**

The plurals of common nouns that end in *y* with a vowel before the *y* are formed by adding only *s*.

key — **keys** holiday — **holidays** attorney — **attorneys**

The plurals of proper nouns ending in *y* are formed by adding *s*.

There are three Circuit Citys **in our metro area.**

632.2
Compound Nouns

The plurals of some compound nouns are formed by adding *s* or *es* to the main word in the compound.

brothers-in-law **maids of honor** **secretaries of state**

632.3
Plurals That Do Not Change

The plurals of some words are the same in singular and plural form.

deer **sheep** **trout** **aircraft**

632.4
Irregular Spelling

Some words (including many foreign words) form a plural by taking on an irregular spelling; others are now acceptable with the commonly used *s* or *es* ending.

child — **children** woman — **women** man — **men**

goose — **geese** mouse — **mice** ox — **oxen**

tooth — **teeth** octopus — **octopuses** or **octopi**

index — **indexes** or **indices**

632.5
Adding an 's

The plurals of letters, figures, symbols, and words discussed as words are formed by adding an apostrophe and an *s*.

Dr. Walters has two Ph.D.'s.

My dad's license plate has three 2's **between two** B's.

You've got too many but's **and** so's **in that sentence.**

For information on forming plural possessives, see 606.1.

Plurals 2

■ **Nouns Ending in** *y*
■ **Compound Nouns**
■ **Plurals That Do Not Change**
■ **Irregular Spelling**
■ **Adding an** *'s*

For each of the following sentences, write the correct form of any underlined plural that is not correct. If an underlined plural is correct, write "C."

1. Aaron's mother said one of her <u>sister-in-laws</u> worked in a circus for three years.
   sisters-in-law

2. The circus announcer shouted out, "<u>Ladys and gentlemans</u>, welcome to the finest show on earth!"

3. For the next five days, <u>people</u> entered the Fair Wing Circus Grounds through several <u>archwaies</u> set up near the roads.

4. Flags full of <u>Fs and Ws</u> flew above the tents.

5. Elaine expected to see elephants, but she did not expect to see <u>mooses!</u>

6. Faleena wondered if there were many <u>mouses</u> running around the circus grounds that might scare the elephants.

7. When a little girl saw the lion's sharp <u>tooths</u>, she started to cry.

8. The three clowns with <u>donkies</u> were so funny!

9. We could see the acrobats doing their <u>warm-ups</u> before climbing the ladder.

10. After the evening's performance, both Jane and Camille wrote in their <u>diarys</u>.

Abbreviations

An **abbreviation** is the shortened form of a word or phrase. The following abbreviations are always acceptable in any kind of writing:

Mr.	**Mrs.**	**Ms.**	**Dr.**	**a.m., p.m.** (A.M., P.M.)

B.C.E. (before the Common Era)   **C.E.** (Common Era)

B.A.   **M.A.**   **Ph.D.**   **M.D.**   **Sr.**   **Jr.**

Caution: Do not abbreviate the names of states, countries, months, days, or units of measure in formal writing. Also, do not use signs or symbols (%, &) in place of words.

Common Abbreviations

AC alternating current
a.m. ante meridiem
ASAP as soon as possible
COD cash on delivery
DA district attorney
DC direct current
etc. and so forth
F Fahrenheit
FM frequency modulation
GNP gross national product
i.e. that is (Latin *id est*)

kg kilogram
km kilometer
kW kilowatt
l liter
lb. pound
m meter
M.D. doctor of medicine
mfg. manufacturing
mpg miles per gallon
mph miles per hour
oz. ounce

pd. paid
pg. (or p.) page
p.m. post meridiem
ppd. postpaid, prepaid
qt. quart
R.S.V.P. please reply
tbs., tbsp. tablespoon
tsp. teaspoon
vol. volume
vs. versus
yd. yard

Address Abbreviations

	Standard	Postal		Standard	Postal		Standard	Postal
Avenue	Ave.	AVE	Lake	L.	LK	Rural	R.	R
Boulevard	Blvd.	BLVD	Lane	Ln.	LN	South	S.	S
Court	Ct.	CT	North	N.	N	Square	Sq.	SQ
Drive	Dr.	DR	Park	Pk.	PK	Station	Sta.	STA
East	E.	E	Parkway	Pky.	PKY	Street	St.	ST
Expressway	Expy.	EXPY	Place	Pl.	PL	Terrace	Ter.	TER
Heights	Hts.	HTS	Plaza	Plaza	PLZ	Turnpike	Tpke.	TPKE
Highway	Hwy.	HWY	Road	Rd.	RD	West	W.	W

Abbreviations 1

Write out the words that the abbreviations in the following sentences stand for.

1. The field is 50 m wide, not 50 yd. wide.
   meters, yards

2. There are 16 oz. in a lb.

3. The article is on pg. 345 of vol. 2.

4. This item is COD, so the bill must be pd. when you get it.

5. The DA needs an M.D. ASAP!

6. TicTec is a mfg. company located near the Virginia Tpke.

7. If this car gets 32 mpg, how far will it go on a qt. of gas?

Write the standard abbreviations of the following addresses.

8. 2103 East Fremont Court
   2103 E. Fremont Ct.

9. 7828 West Greentree Road

10. 697 Samson Highway

11. 992A Ryan Avenue

12. 5 South Elm Lane

13. 1218 North Adobe Terrace

14. 22223 Maple Parkway

15. 250 High Street

Next Step: Create an imaginary address for a place you would like to live some day.

MECHANICS

Abbreviations . . .

An **acronym** is an abbreviation that can be pronounced as a word. It does not require periods.

WHO — World Health Organization   **ROM** — read-only memory

FAQ — frequently asked question

An **initialism** is similar to an acronym except that it cannot be pronounced as a word; the initials are pronounced individually.

PBS — Public Broadcasting Service

BLM — Bureau of Land Management

WNBA — Women's National Basketball Association

Common Acronyms and Initialisms

AIDS	acquired immune deficiency syndrome	**ORV**	off-road vehicle
CETA	Comprehensive Employment and Training Act	**OSHA**	Occupational Safety and Health Administration
CIA	Central Intelligence Agency	**PAC**	political action committee
FAA	Federal Aviation Administration	**PIN**	personal identification number
FBI	Federal Bureau of Investigation	**PSA**	public service announcement
FCC	Federal Communications Commission	**ROTC**	Reserve Officers' Training Corps
FDA	Food and Drug Administration	**SADD**	Students Against Destructive Decisions
FDIC	Federal Deposit Insurance Corporation	**SSA**	Social Security Administration
FHA	Federal Housing Administration	**SUV**	sport-utility vehicle
FTC	Federal Trade Commission	**SWAT**	special weapons and tactics
HTML	Hypertext Markup Language	**TDD**	telecommunications device for the deaf
IRS	Internal Revenue Service	**TMJ**	temporomandibular joint
MADD	Mothers Against Drunk Driving	**TVA**	Tennessee Valley Authority
NAFTA	North American Free Trade Agreement	**VA**	Veterans Administration
NASA	National Aeronautics and Space Administration	**VISTA**	Volunteers in Service to America
NATO	North Atlantic Treaty Organization	**WAC**	Women's Army Corps
OEO	Office of Economic Opportunity	**WAVES**	Women Accepted for Volunteer Emergency Service
OEP	Office of Emergency Preparedness		

Abbreviations 2

- ■ Acronyms
- ■ Initialisms

 **In each sentence below, write what the abbreviation stands for. (Be careful; some abbreviations can stand for more than one thing!) Choose from the list at the bottom of the page.**

1. Rachel's family makes a yearly donation to CARE.
Cooperative for American Relief to Everywhere

2. The newest model of this car has an ABS.

3. Grandma always writes "P.S. I love you" at the end of the letters that she sends to me.

4. Is this toothpaste approved by the ADA?

5. Jake's car stereo has AFT.

6. The awards program begins at seven o'clock CST.

7. Mom said that she has to get some cash from the ATM.

8. The HVAC technician came to our house to fix the furnace.

9. I used to go to PS 106 in Far Rockaway, New York.

10. Each of the math instructors is a member of the AFT.

American Dental Association
American Federation of Teachers
antilock braking system
automatic fine tuning
automatic teller machine
Central Standard Time
Cooperative for American Relief to Everywhere
heating, ventilation, and air conditioning
postscript
public school

Next Step: Use your imagination to write what these acronyms might stand for: *COMB, SMED,* and *TRIK.*

Numbers

638.1
Numbers Under 10

Numbers from one to nine are usually written as words; all numbers 10 and over are usually written as numerals.

two   seven   nine   10   25   106

638.2
Numerals Only

Use numerals to express any of the following forms:

money **$2.39**

decimals **26.2**

percentages . . . . **8 percent**

chapters . . . . **chapter 7**

pages . . . . **pages 287–289**

time (with "a.m." or "p.m.") . . . . **4:30 p.m.**

telephone numbers **1-800-555-1212**

dates . . . . **44 B.C.E.; July 6, 1942**

identification numbers . . . . **Highway 36**

addresses . . . . **2125 Cairn Road**

ZIP codes **60004**

statistics . . . . **a vote of 23 to 4**

When abbreviations and symbols are used (for instance, in science or math), always use numerals with them.

12° C   7%   33 kg   9 cm   55 mph

638.3
Very Large Numbers

You may use a combination of numerals and words for very large numbers.

Of the 17 million residents of the three Midwestern states, only 1.3 million are blondes.

You may spell out a large number that can be written as two words. If more than two words are needed, use the numeral.

More than nine thousand people attended the concert.

About 3,500 people missed the opening act.

Numbers 1

■ **Numbers Under 10**
■ **Numerals Only**
■ **Very Large Numbers**

If a number in the sentences below is written incorrectly, write the correct form. Otherwise, write "correct."

1. Yesterday morning at five-fifteen, Mom's cell phone rang once and stopped.
5:15

2. My family has 2 phone numbers: one for the regular telephone and one for the cell phone.

3. The cell phone number, 555-989-9889, is easy to remember.

4. Since we got the cell phone, our other phone bill has gone down nine percent.

5. Some businesses have ten or more phone numbers.

6. Alpha International, a company at Ten-Twenty Visible Lane, has 66 phone numbers.

7. Area codes were introduced in the United States about fifty years ago, when there were 87 of them.

8. As of June First, 1999, there were 215 area codes in use.

9. Each area code has almost eight million phone numbers.

10. With one point three billion phone numbers currently available, when will the United States run out of phone numbers?

11. In the U.S., people make 30 million long distance calls a day.

12. They make 1.5 billion local calls, which is a twenty-five percent increase since 1990.

Next Step: Write a sentence about the number of times you talk on the phone in a week. Write another sentence that includes the page numbers of the pages you're looking at.

Numbers . . .

640.1
Comparing Numbers

If you are comparing two or more numbers in a sentence, write all of them the same way: as numerals or as words.

> Students from 9 to 14 years old are invited.

> Students from nine to fourteen years old are invited.

640.2
Numbers in Compound Modifiers

A compound modifier may include a numeral.

> The floorboards come in 10-foot lengths.

When a number comes before a compound modifier that includes a numeral, use words instead of numerals.

> We need eleven 10-foot lengths to finish the floor.

> Ms. Brown must grade twenty 12-page reports.

640.3
Sentence Beginnings

Use words, not numerals, to begin a sentence.

> Nine students had turned in their homework. Fourteen students said they were unable to finish the assignment.

640.4
Time and Money

When time or money is expressed with a symbol, use numerals. When either is expressed with words, spell out the number.

> 6:00 a.m. (or) six o'clock

> $25 (or) twenty-five dollars

SCHOOL DAZE

Jerry, haven't you finished your paper yet?

No, it's not due until **three o'clock**, and Mrs. Wright told me to add a few new twists and wrinkles.

Numbers 2

■ **Comparing Numbers**
■ **Numbers in Compound Modifiers**
■ **Sentence Beginnings**
■ **Time and Money**

 For each of the following sentences, write the correct form of the number, word, or phrase that is incorrect.

1. There were 18 15-pound babies at the audition for the diaper commercial.

   eighteen

2. 12 of the babies were less than a year old.

3. Those selected would be paid 500 dollars for their "work."

4. The director said, "Will the people sitting in rows eight through 15 please stand up?"

5. 25 people stood up.

6. "Go to soundstage B at 10 o'clock," she said.

7. "The audition should be over by two p.m.," she added.

8. After almost 20 10-minute auditions, the director had to make a decision.

9. She whispered, "I can't decide between Baby Six and Baby 11."

10. 16 of the babies were sent home, and the two remaining babies were in the commercial together.

Next Step: Write a sentence comparing your age and the age of a baby you know. In another sentence, tell how much money you might get to baby-sit that baby.

Improving Spelling

Write *i* before *e* except after *c*, or when sounded like *a* as in *neighbor* and *weigh*.

Some Exceptions to the Rule: *counterfeit, either, financier, foreign, height, heir, leisure, neither, science, seize, sheik, species, their, weird.*

If a word ends with a silent *e*, drop the *e* before adding a suffix that begins with a vowel. There are exceptions, for example, *knowledgeable* and *changeable*.

state—stating—statement	use—using—useful
like—liking—likeness	nine—ninety—nineteen

NOTE You do not drop the *e* when the suffix begins with a consonant. Exceptions include *truly, argument,* and *ninth*.

When *y* is the last letter in a word and the *y* comes just after a consonant, change the *y* to *i* before adding any suffix except those beginning with *i*.

fry—fries—frying	happy—happiness
hurry—hurried hurrying	beauty—beautiful
lady—ladies	

When forming the plural of a word that ends with a *y* that comes just after a vowel, add *s*.

toy—toys	play—plays	monkey—monkeys

When a one-syllable word ends in a consonant (*bat*) preceded by one vowel (*bat*), double the final consonant before adding a suffix that begins with a vowel (*batting*).

sum—summary	god—goddess

When a multisyllable word ends in a consonant preceded by one vowel (*control*), the accent is on the last syllable (*contról*), and the suffix begins with a vowel (*ing*)—the same rule holds true: double the final consonant (*controlling*).

prefer—preferred	begin—beginning

Spelling 1

■ *i* before *e*
■ Silent *e*

For each of the following sentences, write the correct choice from each set of words in parentheses.

1. Our (*nieghbor, neighbor*) Esteban bought his (*nineth, ninth*) wrench yesterday; soon he'll have a complete set.
neighbor, ninth

2. The (*cheif, chief*) reason he buys these tools is that he likes (*useing, using*) them for home-improvement projects.

3. Manuel, Esteban's seventh-grade son, is (*hopeful, hopful*) he will own his father's tools someday.

4. A tool (*reveiw, review*) in *Popular Mechanics* magazine rated his father's new scroll saw first out of 20 models.

5. Manuel and Esteban showed some of the tools to Mrs. Gomez, who shares (*thier, their*) enthusiasm for home improvement.

6. She likes to watch that (*fameous, famous*) TV show about fixing up old houses.

7. Mrs. Gomez was impressed with the (*variety, vareity*) of tools and asked Manuel to lend her a saw.

8. Using his best (*judgement, judgment*), Manuel said he would have to ask his father if she could borrow the scroll saw.

9. After practicing for a while, Mrs. Gomez successfully cut a difficult design out of a (*peice, piece*) of oak.

10. She could not (*believe, beleive*) how smoothly the saw worked.

11. With great (*excitment, excitement*), she ordered the same scroll saw for herself.

Next Step: Add a suffix to the words *arrive, care,* and *true*; then use each word in a sentence.

Spelling 2

■ Words Ending in *y*
■ Consonant Endings

 For each sentence below, write the correct spelling of any underlined word that is misspelled.

1. The <u>boys</u> bought three bags of <u>frys</u> for lunch.
   fries

2. Mrs. Bock <u>enjoys</u> going to each of the six <u>librarys</u> in our city.

3. When the hurricane <u>occured</u>, it seemed that people were <u>running</u> everywhere.

4. Relief workers knew the food <u>supplies</u> would be greeted with <u>happyness</u> by the storm victims.

5. Samuel's father keeps busy repairing antique <u>toies</u> at his shop and <u>shipping</u> them back to their owners.

6. Workers' <u>salaries</u> could be <u>droping</u> since business is slow.

7. February's blizzard <u>buryed</u> Springfield under two feet of snow—even more in the <u>valleys</u>.

8. Students must stay within the school's <u>boundaries</u> during school <u>dayes</u>.

9. Phil <u>trys</u> to walk two miles every evening, and last week, he saw several rabbits <u>hoping</u> all over the city park.

10. Ms. Stanton needs three students to help her buy <u>groceries</u> for the retreat that our class is <u>planing</u>.

11. We <u>beged</u> the teacher to give us more time to write our <u>essays</u>.

12. The <u>journies</u> of Lewis and Clark led them through beautiful and dangerous <u>territorys</u>.

13. All the <u>canaries</u> took off at once, <u>flaping</u> their yellow wings.

Next Step: Write sentences using the plurals of the following words: *memory, chimney,* and *city.*

Yellow Pages Guide to Improved Spelling

Be patient. Becoming a good speller takes time.

Check your spelling by using a dictionary or list of commonly misspelled words (like the list that follows). And, remember, don't rely too much on computer spell-checkers.

Learn the correct pronunciation of each word you are trying to spell. Knowing the correct pronunciation of a word will help you remember how it's spelled.

Look up the meaning of each word as you are checking the dictionary for pronunciation. (Knowing how to spell a word is of little use if you don't know what it means.)

Practice spelling the word before you close the dictionary. Look away from the page and try to see the word in your mind's eye. Write the word on a piece of paper. Check the spelling in the dictionary and repeat the process until you are able to spell the word correctly.

Keep a list of the words that you misspell.

Write often. As noted educator Frank Smith said, "There is little point in learning to spell if you have little intention of writing."

SPELLING

A

	account	after	almost
	accurate	afternoon	already
	accustom (ed)	afterward	although
abbreviate	ache	again	altogether
aboard	achieve (ment)	against	aluminum
about	acre	agreeable	always
above	across	agree (ment)	amateur
absence	actual	ah	ambulance
absent	adapt	aid	amendment
absolute (ly)	addition (al)	airy	among
abundance	address	aisle	amount
accelerate	adequate	alarm	analyze
accident	adjust (ment)	alcohol	ancient
accidental (ly)	admire	alike	angel
accompany	adventure	alive	anger
accomplice	advertise (ment)	alley	angle
accomplish	advertising	allowance	angry
according	afraid	all right	animal

anniversary
announce
annoyance
annual
anonymous
another
answer
Antarctic
anticipate
anxiety
anxious
anybody
anyhow
anyone
anything
anyway
anywhere
apartment
apiece
apologize
apparent (ly)
appeal
appearance
appetite
appliance
application
appointment
appreciate
approach
appropriate
approval
approximate
architect
Arctic
aren't
argument
arithmetic
around
arouse
arrange (ment)
arrival
article
artificial

asleep
assassin
assign (ment)
assistance
associate
association
assume
athlete
athletic
attach
attack (ed)
attempt
attendance
attention
attitude
attorney
attractive
audience
August
author
authority
automobile
autumn
available
avenue
average
awful (ly)
awkward

B

baggage
baking
balance
balloon
ballot
banana
bandage
bankrupt
barber
bargain
barrel

basement
basis
basket
battery
beautiful
beauty
because
become
becoming
before
began
beggar
beginning
behave
behavior
being
belief
believe
belong
beneath
benefit (ed)
between
bicycle
biscuit
blackboard
blanket
blizzard
bother
bottle
bottom
bough
bought
bounce
boundary
breakfast
breast
breath (n.)
breathe (v.)
breeze
bridge
brief
bright
brilliant

brother
brought
bruise
bubble
bucket
buckle
budget
building
bulletin
buoyant
bureau
burglar
bury
business
busy
button

C

cabbage
cafeteria
calendar
campaign
canal
cancel (ed)
candidate
candle
canister
cannon
cannot
canoe
can't
canyon
capacity
captain
carburetor
cardboard
career
careful
careless
carpenter
carriage

carrot
cashier
casserole
casualty
catalog
catastrophe
catcher
caterpillar
catsup
ceiling
celebration
cemetery
census
century
certain (ly)
certificate
challenge
champion
changeable
character (istic)
chief
children
chimney
chocolate
choice
chorus
circumstance
citizen
civilization
classmates
classroom
climate
climb
closet
clothing
coach
cocoa
cocoon
coffee
collar
college
colonel
color

colossal
column
comedy
coming
commercial
commission
commit
commitment
committed
committee
communicate
community
company
comparison
competition
competitive (ly)
complain
complete (ly)
complexion
compromise
conceive
concerning
concert
concession
concrete
condemn
condition
conductor
conference
confidence
congratulate
connect
conscience
conscious
conservative
constitution
continue
continuous
control
controversy
convenience
convince
coolly

cooperate
corporation
correspond
cough
couldn't
counter
counterfeit
country
county
courage
courageous
court
courteous
courtesy
cousin
coverage
cozy
cracker
cranky
crawl
creditor
cried
criticize
cruel
crumb
crumble
cupboard
curiosity
curious
current
custom
customer
cylinder

D

daily
dairy
damage
danger (ous)
daughter
dealt

deceive
decided
decision
declaration
decorate
defense
definite (ly)
definition
delicious
dependent
depot
describe
description
desert
deserve
design
desirable
despair
dessert
deteriorate
determine
develop (ment)
device (n.)
devise (v.)
diamond
diaphragm
diary
dictionary
difference
different
difficulty
dining
diploma
director
disagreeable
disappear
disappoint
disapprove
disastrous
discipline
discover
discuss
discussion

SPELLING

disease
dissatisfied
distinguish
distribute
divide
divine
divisible
division
doctor
doesn't
dollar
dormitory
doubt
dough
dual
duplicate

E

eager (ly)
economy
edge
edition
efficiency
eight
eighth
either
elaborate
electricity
elephant
eligible
ellipse
embarrass
emergency
emphasize
employee
employment
enclose
encourage
engineer
enormous
enough

entertain
enthusiastic
entirely
entrance
envelop (v.)
envelope (n.)
environment
equipment
equipped
equivalent
escape
especially
essential
establish
every
evidence
exaggerate
exceed
excellent
except
exceptional (ly)
excite
exercise
exhaust (ed)
exhibition
existence
expect
expensive
experience
explain
explanation
expression
extension
extinct
extraordinary
extreme (ly)

F

facilities
familiar
family

famous
fascinate
fashion
fatigue (d)
faucet
favorite
feature
February
federal
fertile
field
fierce
fiery
fifty
finally
financial (ly)
foliage
forcible
foreign
forfeit
formal (ly)
former (ly)
forth
fortunate
forty
forward
fountain
fourth
fragile
freight
friend (ly)
frighten
fulfill
fundamental
further
furthermore

G

gadget
gauge
generally

generous
genius
gentle
genuine
geography
ghetto
ghost
gnaw
government
governor
graduation
grammar
grateful
grease
grief
grocery
grudge
gruesome
guarantee
guard
guardian
guess
guidance
guide
guilty
gymnasium

H

hammer
handkerchief
handle (d)
handsome
haphazard
happen
happiness
harass
hastily
having
hazardous
headache
height

hemorrhage
hesitate
history
hoarse
holiday
honor
hoping
hopping
horrible
hospital
humorous
hurriedly
hydraulic
hygiene
hymn

icicle
identical
illegible
illiterate
illustrate
imaginary
imaginative
imagine
imitation
immediate (ly)
immense
immigrant
immortal
impatient
importance
impossible
improvement
inconvenience
incredible
indefinitely
independence
independent
individual
industrial

inferior
infinite
inflammable
influential
initial
initiation
innocence
innocent
installation
instance
instead
insurance
intelligence
intention
interested
interesting
interfere
interpret
interrupt
interview
investigate
invitation
irrigate
island
issue

J

jealous (y)
jewelry
journal
journey
judgment
juicy

K

kitchen
knew
knife
knives

knock
knowledge
knuckles

L

label
laboratory
ladies
language
laugh
laundry
lawyer
league
lecture
legal
legible
legislature
leisure
length
liable
library
license
lieutenant
lightning
likable
likely
liquid
listen
literature
living
loaves
loneliness
loose
lose
loser
losing
lovable
lovely

M

machinery
magazine
magnificent
maintain
majority
making
manual
manufacture
marriage
material
mathematics
maximum
mayor
meant
measure
medicine
medium
message
mileage
miniature
minimum
minute
mirror
miscellaneous
mischievous
miserable
missile
misspell
moisture
molecule
monotonous
monument
mortgage
mountain
muscle
musician
mysterious

SPELLING

N

naive
natural (ly)
necessary
negotiate
neighbor (hood)
neither
nickel
niece
nineteen
nineteenth
ninety
ninth
noisy
noticeable
nuclear
nuisance

O

obedience
obey
obstacle
occasion
occasional (ly)
occur
occurred
offense
official
often
omission
omitted
operate
opinion
opponent
opportunity
opposite
ordinarily
original
outrageous

P

package
paid
pamphlet
paradise
paragraph
parallel
paralyze
parentheses
partial
participant
participate
particular (ly)
pasture
patience
peculiar
people
perhaps
permanent
perpendicular
persistent
personal (ly)
personnel
perspiration
persuade
phase
physician
piece
pitcher
planned
plateau
playwright
pleasant
pleasure
pneumonia
politician
possess
possible
practical (ly)
prairie
precede
precious

precise (ly)
precision
preferable
preferred
prejudice
preparation
presence
previous
primitive
principal
principle
prisoner
privilege
probably
procedure
proceed
professor
prominent
pronounce
pronunciation
protein
psychology
pumpkin
pure

Q

quarter
questionnaire
quiet
quite
quotient

R

raise
realize
really
receipt
receive
received

recipe
recognize
recommend
reign
relieve
religious
remember
repetition
representative
reservoir
resistance
respectfully
responsibility
restaurant
review
rhyme
rhythm
ridiculous
route

S

safety
salad
salary
sandwich
satisfactory
Saturday
scene
scenery
schedule
science
scissors
scream
screen
season
secretary
seize
sensible
sentence
separate
several

sheriff
shining
similar
since
sincere (ly)
skiing
sleigh
soldier
souvenir
spaghetti
specific
sphere
sprinkle
squeeze
squirrel
statue
stature
statute
stomach
stopped
straight
strength
stretched
studying
subtle
succeed
success
sufficient
summarize
supplement
suppose
surely
surprise
syllable
sympathy
symptom

 T

tariff
technique
temperature
temporary
terrible
territory
thankful
theater
their
there
therefore
thief
thorough (ly)
though
throughout
tired
tobacco
together
tomorrow
tongue
touch
tournament
toward
tragedy
treasurer
tried
tries
trouble
truly
Tuesday
typical

 U

unconscious
unfortunate (ly)
unique
university
unnecessary
until
usable
useful
using
usual (ly)
utensil

 V

vacation
vacuum
valuable
variety
various
vegetable
vehicle
very
vicinity
view
villain
violence
visible
visitor
voice
volume
voluntary
volunteer

 W

wander
wasn't
weather
Wednesday
weigh
weird
welcome
welfare
whale
where
whether
which
whole
wholly
whose
width
women
worthwhile
wouldn't
wreckage
writing
written

Y

yellow
yesterday
yield

SPELLING

Using the Right Word

652.1
a, an

A is used before words that begin with a consonant sound; *an* is used before words that begin with any vowel sound except long "u."

> a **heap**, a **cat**, an **idol**, an **elephant**, an **honor**, a **historian**, an **umbrella**, a **unicorn**

652.2
accept, except

The verb *accept* means "to receive"; the preposition *except* means "other than."

> **Melissa graciously** accepted **defeat.** (verb)
> **All the boys** except **Zach were here.** (preposition)

652.3
affect, effect

Affect is almost always a verb; it means "to influence." *Effect* can be a verb, but it is most often used as a noun that means "the result."

> **How does population growth** affect **us?**
> **What are the** effects **of population growth?**

652.4
allowed, aloud

The verb *allowed* means "permitted" or "let happen"; *aloud* is an adverb that means "in a normal voice."

> **We aren't** allowed **to read** aloud **in the library.**

652.5
allusion, illusion

An *allusion* is a brief reference to or hint of something (person, place, thing, or idea). An *illusion* is a false impression or idea.

> **The Great Dontini, a magician, made an** allusion **to Houdini as he created the** illusion **of sawing his assistant in half.**

652.6
a lot

A lot is not one word, but two; it is a general descriptive phrase meaning "plenty." (It should be avoided in formal writing.)

652.7
all right

All right is not one word, but two; it is a phrase meaning "satisfactory" or "okay." (Please note, the following *are* spelled correctly: *always, altogether, already, almost.*)

Using the Right Word 1

■ accept, except; affect, effect; allowed, aloud; a lot

For each of the following sentences, write the correct choice from each set of words in parentheses.

1. When Josie reads her writing (*allowed, aloud*), she hears the mistakes she needs to fix.
   aloud

2. Sari's gentle touch and her soft voice had a calming (*affect, effect*) on the frightened collie.

3. Everyone at the school assembly stood and cheered when Franklin went forward to (*accept, except*) the community service award.

4. The use of pocket calculators is not (*allowed, aloud*) during the final exam.

5. That quiz won't (*affect, effect*) my grade (*a lot, alot*).

6. Marlyn put all the wood (*accept, except*) the heaviest piece in his pickup truck.

7. Oil spills around the world (*affect, effect*) future generations of wildlife.

8. Greta volunteers at a senior center, reading the residents' mail (*allowed, aloud*) for them.

9. "Please (*accept, except*) our late report," we begged Mr. Potter.

10. Matthew's little brother is not (*allowed, aloud*) to cross the street unless his mom or dad is there.

11. Troy was upset when everyone (*accept, except*) him was able to walk to the playground.

12. The rule can have a bad (*affect, effect*) on him, it seems.

Next Step: Read the text about "a lot" on the opposite page. Think of a type of writing where you might use this phrase, and write two sentences using it.

RIGHT WORD

654.1
**already,
all ready**

Already is an adverb that tells when. *All ready* is a phrase meaning "completely ready."

> We have already eaten breakfast; now we are all ready for school.

654.2
**altogether,
all together**

Altogether is always an adverb meaning "completely." *All together* is used to describe people or things that are gathered in one place at one time.

> Ms. Monces held her baton in the air and said, "Okay, class, all together now: sing!"

> Unfortunately, there was altogether too much street noise for us to hear her.

654.3
among, between

Among is used when speaking of more than two persons or things. *Between* is used when speaking of only two.

> The three friends talked among themselves as they tried to choose between trumpet or trombone lessons.

654.4
amount, number

Amount is used to describe things that you cannot count. *Number* is used when you can actually count the persons or things.

> The amount of interest in playing the tuba is shown by the number of kids learning to play the instrument.

654.5
**annual,
biannual,
semiannual,
biennial,
perennial**

An *annual* event happens once every year. A *biannual* (or *semiannual*) event happens twice a year. A *biennial* event happens once every two years. A *perennial* event happens year after year.

> The annual PTA rummage sale is so successful that it will now be a semiannual event.

> The neighbor has some wonderful perennial flowers.

654.6
ant, aunt

An *ant* is an insect. An *aunt* is a female relative (the sister of a person's mother or father).

> My aunt is an entomologist, a scientist who studies ants and other insects.

654.7
ascent, assent

Ascent is the act of rising or climbing; *assent* is agreement.

> After the group's ascent of five flights of stairs to the meeting room, plans for elevator repairs met with quick assent.

Using the Right Word 2

■ already, all ready; **altogether, all together;** among, between; **amount, number;** ascent, assent

For each of the following sentences, write the word "correct" if the underlined word is used correctly. If it is incorrect, write the right word.

1. The <u>amount</u> of professional football teams has grown over the last 30 years.
   number

2. In a "draft," the teams choose new players from <u>between</u> the hundreds who want to join the NFL.

3. A team might think it <u>already</u> has the best players possible.

4. In that case, it is <u>altogether</u> possible they will be the champions.

5. When the team is <u>altogether</u> in the locker room, the coach encourages the players to do their best.

6. A good running back can dash <u>between</u> two defenders and avoid being tackled.

7. A quarterback needs the <u>ascent</u> of all the players to make a successful play.

8. Some players are on the field for a greater <u>amount</u> of time than other players.

9. On the day of the game, professionals must be <u>already</u> to play.

10. If they play well, their team's <u>ascent</u> in the rankings may mean a trip to the Super Bowl.

Next Step: Show that you understand the words *between* and *assent* by using them in a sentence. Then write another sentence using the words *amount* and *already*.

RIGHT WORD

656.1
bare, bear

The adjective *bare* means "naked." A *bear* is a large, heavy animal with shaggy hair.

Despite his bare feet, the man chased the polar bear across the snow.

The verb *bear* means "to put up with" or "to carry."

Dwayne could not bear another of his older brother's lectures.

656.2
base, bass

Base is the foundation or the lower part of something. *Bass* (pronounced like "base") is a deep sound or tone.

The stereo speakers are on a base so solid that even the loudest bass tones don't rattle it.

Bass (rhymes with "mass") is a fish.

Jim hooked a record-setting bass, but it got away . . . so he says.

656.3
beat, beet

The verb *beat* means "to strike, to defeat," and the noun *beat* is a musical term for rhythm or tempo. A *beet* is a carrot-like vegetable (often red).

The beat of the drum in the marching band encouraged the fans to cheer on the team. After they beat West High's team four games to one, many team members were as red as a beet.

656.4
berth, birth

Berth is a space or compartment. *Birth* is the process of being born.

We pulled aside the curtain in our train berth to view the birth of a new day outside our window.

656.5
beside, besides

Beside means "by the side of." *Besides* means "in addition to."

Besides a flashlight, Kedar likes to keep his pet boa beside his bed at night.

656.6
billed, build

Billed means either "to be given a bill" or "to have a beak." The verb *build* means "to construct."

We asked the carpenter to build us a birdhouse. She billed us for time and materials.

656.7
blew, blue

Blew is the past tense of "blow." *Blue* is a color and is also used to mean "feeling low in spirits."

As the wind blew out the candles in the dark blue room, I felt more blue than ever.

Using the Right Word 3

■ bare, bear; base, bass; berth, birth; beside, besides; billed, build

For each of the following sentences, write the correct choice from each set of words in parentheses.

1. In rural areas, families (*billed, build*) small shelters so that students who have to wait for the bus can stay out of the cold wind.

   build

2. Julian claims that even on a cold, windy day, his (*bare, bear*) hands stay very warm.

3. (*Beside, Besides*) the strong north winds, last year's big storm brought a great deal of snow.

4. In only an hour, the snow completely covered the flagpole's stone (*base, bass*).

5. A small tree (*beside, besides*) the library was bent over by the weight of the snow.

6. During that storm, Jake wore a hat that looked like it was made out of (*bare, bear*) fur.

7. Rena knew that the rumbling (*base, bass*) sound she heard meant a snowplow was coming down the street.

8. An ambulance with a woman about to give (*berth, birth*) was able to get through to the hospital.

9. My dad, who has a plow on his truck, (*billed, build*) his customers for plowing their driveways.

10. A passenger traveling through the storm by train was very happy to be in a comfortable (*berth, birth*).

11. Incredibly, the storm didn't bother the people who were ice fishing for fresh (*base, bass*).

Next Step: Write two sentences that show your understanding of the two meanings of the word *bass*.

658.1
board, bored

A *board* is a piece of wood. *Board* also means "a group or council that helps run an organization."

The school board approved the purchase of 50 pine boards for the woodworking classes.

Bored means "to become weary or tired of something." It can also mean "made a hole by drilling."

Dulé bored a hole in the ice and dropped in a fishing line. Waiting and waiting for a bite bored him.

658.2
borrow, lend

Borrow means "to *receive* for temporary use." *Lend* means "to *give* for temporary use."

I asked Mom, "May I borrow $15 for a CD?"

She said, "I can lend you $15 until next Friday."

658.3
brake, break

A *brake* is a device used to stop a vehicle. The verb *break* means "to split, crack, or destroy"; as a noun, *break* means "gap or interruption."

After the brake on my bike failed, I took a break to fix it so I wouldn't break a bone.

658.4
bring, take

Use *bring* when the action is moving toward the speaker; use *take* when the action is moving away from the speaker.

Grandpa asked me to take the garbage out and bring him today's paper.

658.5
by, buy, bye

By is a preposition meaning "near" or "not later than." *Buy* is a verb meaning "to purchase."

By tomorrow I hope to buy tickets for the final match of the tournament.

Bye is the position of being automatically advanced to the next tournament round without playing.

Our soccer team received a bye because of our winning record.

658.6
can, may

Can means "able to," while *may* means "permitted to."

"Can I go to the library?"

(This actually means "Are my mind and body strong enough to get me there?")

"May I go?"

(This means "Do I have your permission to go?")

Using the Right Word 4

■ board, bored; **borrow, lend**; brake, break; bring, take;
by, buy, bye

For each of the following sentences, write a word from the list above to fill in the blank. Use each word once.

1. Students who enjoy working with tools almost never complain about being _____ in shop class.
   bored

2. Protective glasses are required for a student driving a nail into a _____ .

3. Lucinda said, "Mr. Johnson, I will need to _____ my uncle's band saw to cut this wood."

4. Brenda _____ five evenly spaced holes into the top of the trunk she is building.

5. The emergency _____ on the high-speed drill quickly stops its motor.

6. Mr. Johnson asked Lyle to _____ the extra plywood sheet back to the storage room.

7. Esai, the football team's quarterback, was able to finish his project because the team had a _____ last weekend.

8. Curtis said he could not afford to _____ the wood he wanted for his project.

9. As Lawrence walked _____ the pile of lumber, it fell over and hit his left leg.

10. Mr. Johnson asked the school nurse to _____ an ice bag to the classroom.

11. Lawrence was glad he didn't _____ his leg in the accident, but he did require crutches for a few days.

12. Angela said her family had some crutches that they could _____ to Lawrence.

660.1
canvas, canvass

Canvas is a heavy cloth; *canvass* means "ask people for votes or opinions."

Our old canvas tent leaks.

Someone with a clipboard is canvassing the neighborhood.

660.2
capital, capitol

Capital can be either a noun, referring to a city or to money, or an adjective, meaning "major or important." *Capitol* is used only when talking about a building.

The capitol building is in the capital city for a capital (major) reason: The city government contributed the capital (money) for the building project.

660.3
cell, sell

Cell means "a small room" or "a small unit of life basic to all plants and animals." *Sell* is a verb meaning "to give up for a price."

Today we looked at a human skin cell under a microscope.

Let's sell those old bicycles at the rummage sale.

660.4
cent, sent, scent

Cent (1/100 of a dollar) is a coin; *sent* is the past tense of the verb "send"; *scent* is an odor or a smell.

After our car hit a skunk, we sent our friends a postcard that said, "One cent doesn't go far, but skunk scent seems to last forever."

660.5
chord, cord

Chord may mean "an emotion or a feeling," but it is more often used to mean "the sound of three or more musical tones played at the same time." A *cord* is a string or rope.

The band struck a chord at the exact moment the mayor pulled the cord on the drape covering the new statue.

660.6
chose, choose

Chose (chōz) is the past tense of the verb *choose* (chōōz).

This afternoon Mom chose tacos and hot sauce; this evening she will choose an antacid.

660.7
coarse, course

Coarse means "rough or crude." *Course* means "a path" or "a class or series of studies."

In our cooking course, we learned to use coarse salt and freshly ground pepper in salads.

Using the Right Word 5

■ capital, capitol; cell, sell; cent, sent, scent; chose, choose;
coarse, course

**For each of the following sentences, write the correct choice from each
set of words in parentheses.**

1. Last month, the entire seventh-grade class went to our state's
(*capital, capitol*) city to watch a debate.
capital

2. Ben began sanding the (*coarse, course*) wood on the old desk.

3. Every student in science class gets a chance to look through a
microscope at a single skin (*cell, sell*).

4. After looking carefully at each toy, Darien (*chose, choose*) the
model car kit.

5. Will opened the door and immediately smelled the
(*cent, sent, scent*) of a burning candle.

6. Ms. Jur said that José, Cana, Fran, and Carmen could
(*chose, choose*) the next film for the class to watch.

7. Senators from every state meet regularly in the
(*Capital, Capitol*) building in Washington, D.C.

8. Julian will (*cell, sell*) candy for the school's fund-raiser.

9. The art class students picked the best drawings of the city and
(*cent, sent, scent*) them to the mayor's office.

10. Teachers of each (*coarse, course*) expect that students will
complete homework assignments on time.

11. Julio saw that the "sale" price of the CD was $9.99, which was
only one (*cent, sent, scent*) less than its regular price of $10.

Next Step: Using the pairs of words in this exercise, write two
sentences that offer a choice (as in the sentences above).
Exchange papers with a partner and pick the right words
for each other's sentences.

662.1
complement,
compliment

Complement means "to complete or go with." *Compliment* is an expression of admiration or praise.

> Aunt Athena said, "Your cheese sauce really complements this cauliflower!"

> "Thank you for the compliment," I replied.

662.2
continual,
continuous

Continual refers to something that happens again and again; *continuous* refers to something that doesn't stop happening.

> Sunlight hits Peoria, Iowa, on a continual basis; but sunlight hits the earth continuously.

662.3
counsel, council

When used as a noun, *counsel* means "advice"; when used as a verb, *counsel* means "to advise." *Council* refers to a group that advises.

> The student council asked for counsel from its trusted adviser.

662.4
creak, creek

A *creak* is a squeaking sound; a *creek* is a stream.

> I heard a creak from the old dock under my feet as I fished in the creek.

662.5
cymbal, symbol

A *cymbal* is a metal instrument shaped like a plate. A *symbol* is something (usually visible) that stands for or represents another thing or idea (usually invisible).

> The damaged cymbal lying on the stage was a symbol of the band's final concert.

662.6
dear, deer

Dear means "loved or valued"; *deer* are animals.

> My dear, old great-grandmother leaves corn and salt licks in her yard to attract deer.

662.7
desert, dessert

A *desert* is a barren wilderness. *Dessert* is a food served at the end of a meal.

> In the desert, cold water is more inviting than even the richest dessert.

The verb *desert* means "to abandon"; the noun *desert* (pronounced like the verb) means "deserving reward or punishment."

> A spy who deserts his country will receive his just deserts if he is caught.

Using the Right Word 6

■ complements, compliments; **counsel, council**; creak, creek;
cymbal, symbol; desert, dessert

For each sentence below, write a word from the list above to fill in the blank.

1. I would offer this _____ to any visitor to my city: Visit Becker Park.
counsel

2. Although my city is located in the _____, Becker Park is full of green trees and colorful flowers.

3. What I like most about the park is the little _____ that runs through it.

4. I like to hear the _____ of the boards when I walk on the bridge over the water.

5. Every six months, the city _____ organizes a day for volunteers to pick up trash and work in the gardens.

6. Last time, the cleanup day followed a parade, and someone found a _____ from the marching band!

7. The volunteer work _____ the work done by city employees.

8. On the day of the cleanup, each participant receives a T-shirt with a huge oak tree on the back, a _____ of Becker Park.

9. A local restaurant offers free coffee and _____ to the volunteers.

10. The city newspaper always _____ the volunteers' work in the next day's issue.

Next Step: Write two sentences that show your understanding of the words *complement* and *compliment*.

664.1
die, dye

Die (dying) means "to stop living." *Dye* (dyeing) is used to change the color of something.

The young girl hoped that her sick goldfish wouldn't die.
My sister dyes her hair with coloring that washes out.

664.2
faint, feign, feint

Faint means "feeble, without strength" or "to fall unconscious." *Feign* is a verb that means "to pretend or make up." *Feint* is a noun that means "a move or an activity that is pretended in order to divert attention."

The actors feigned a sword duel. One man staggered and fell in a feint. The audience gave faint applause.

664.3
farther, further

Farther is used when you are writing about a physical distance. *Further* means "additional."

Alaska reaches farther north than Iceland. For further information, check your local library.

664.4
fewer, less

Fewer refers to the number of separate units; *less* refers to bulk quantity.

I may have less money than you have, but I have fewer worries.

664.5
fir, fur

Fir refers to a type of evergreen tree; *fur* is animal hair.

The Douglas fir tree is named after a Scottish botanist.

An arctic fox has white fur in the winter.

664.6
flair, flare

Flair means "a natural talent" or "style"; *flare* means "to light up quickly" or "burst out" (or an object that does so).

Jenrette has a flair for remaining calm when other people's tempers flare.

664.7
for, four

The preposition *for* means "because of" or "directed to"; *four* is the number 4.

Mary had grilled steaks and chicken for the party, but the dog had stolen one of the four steaks.

Using the Right Word 7

■ farther, further; fewer, less; fir, fur; flair, flare; for, four

For each of the following sentences, write the correct choice from each set of words in parentheses.

1. Native Americans of the 1700s had a (*flair, flare*) for traveling through deep forests.

   flair

2. Today, experienced hikers take compass readings before hiking (*farther, further*) than they've ever been in an unknown forest.

3. They don't want to meet a bear, whose dark, thick (*fir, fur*) can camouflage it in a deep, shadowy forest.

4. Forests in northern Minnesota usually have (*fewer, less*) oak trees than forests in the southern part of the state.

5. Birch, elm, maple, and ash are (*for, four*) common types of trees in Minnesota.

6. In the fall, the brilliant colors of these trees really add (*flair, flare*) to the woods.

7. A (*fir, fur*) is a pine tree with soft, flat needles.

8. Studies show that young trees have (*fewer, less*) resistance to forest fires than old trees.

9. In a forest fire, a burning tree can look like a giant (*flair, flare*).

10. Scientists seek (*farther, further*) information about forests in order to preserve them.

11. College scholarships are available (*for, four*) those who wish to study forestry.

12. Unfortunately, there are (*fewer, less*) forests worldwide than ever before.

Next Step: Write two sentences about trees to show your understanding of the words *fewer* and *less*.

RIGHT WORD

666.1
good, well

Good is an adjective; *well* is nearly always an adverb.

The strange flying machines flew well. (The adverb *well* modifies *flew*.)

They looked good as they flew overhead. (The adjective *good* modifies *they*.)

When used in writing about health, *well* is an adjective.

The pilots did not feel well, however, after the long, hard race.

666.2
hare, hair

A *hare* is an animal similar to a rabbit; *hair* refers to the growth covering the head and body of mammals and human beings.

When a hare darted out in front of our car, the hair on my head stood up.

666.3
heal, heel

Heal means "to mend or restore to health." *Heel* is the back part of a human foot.

I got a blister on my heel from wearing my new shoes. It won't heal unless I wear my old ones.

666.4
hear, here

You *hear* sounds with your ears. *Here* is the opposite of *there* and means "nearby."

666.5
heard, herd

Heard is the past tense of the verb "to hear"; *herd* is a group of animals.

The herd of grazing sheep raised their heads when they heard the collie barking in the distance.

666.6
heir, air

An *heir* is a person who inherits something; *air* is what we breathe.

Will the next generation be heir to terminally polluted air?

666.7
hole, whole

A *hole* is a cavity or hollow place. *Whole* means "entire or complete."

The hole in the ozone layer is a serious problem requiring the attention of the whole world.

666.8
immigrate, emigrate

Immigrate means "to come into a new country or area." *Emigrate* means "to go out of one country to live in another."

Martin Ulferts immigrated to this country in 1882. He was only three years old when he emigrated from Germany.

Using the Right Word 8

■ good, well; **heal, heel**; heard, herd; **heir, air**; hole, whole

 For each of the following sentences, write a word from the list above to fill in the blank.

1. Exercise is _____ for a person's health.
good

2. It can help someone who's out of shape feel _____ again.

3. Some runners say they can get more _____ in their lungs if they run with their mouths open.

4. My _____ family exercises at least three times a week.

5. We warm up slowly because we know that a pulled muscle takes a long time to _____.

6. Since Lora injured her _____, she is not participating for a while.

7. Exercising when you feel severe pain is usually not a _____ idea.

8. Shea dropped the barbells and put a _____ in the floor.

9. While hiking near his cousin's farm, Denzel _____ some rustling noises.

10. Then he saw a _____ of deer.

11. The team played _____ and won the game.

12. They have a _____ chance of making the play-offs.

13. A person who inherits property is called an _____.

14. Raymond might inherit a _____ bunch of old baseball cards from his grandpa.

Next Step: Write two sentences—one using the word *well* as an adjective and another using the word as an adverb.

668.1 imply, infer

Imply means "to suggest indirectly"; *infer* means "to draw a conclusion from facts."

"Since you have to work, may I infer that you won't come to my party?" Guy asked.

"No, I only meant to imply that I would be late," Rochelle responded.

668.2 it's, its

It's is the contraction of "it is." *Its* is the possessive form of "it."

It's a fact that a minnow's teeth are in its throat.

668.3 knew, new

Knew is the past tense of the verb "know." *New* means "recent or modern."

If I knew how to fix it, I would not need a new one!

668.4 know, no

Know means "to recognize or understand." *No* means "the opposite of yes."

Phil, do you know Cheri?

No, I've never met her.

668.5 later, latter

Later means "after a period of time." *Latter* refers to the second of two things mentioned.

The band arrived later and set up the speakers and the lights.
The latter made the stage look like a carnival ride.

668.6 lay, lie

Lay means "to place." (*Lay* is a transitive verb; that means it needs a word to complete the meaning.) *Lie* means "to recline." (*Lie* is an intransitive verb.)

Lay your sleeping bag on the floor before you lie down on it.
(*Lay* needs the word *bag* to complete its meaning.)

668.7 lead, led

Lead (lēd) is a present tense verb meaning "to guide." The past tense of the verb is *led* (lĕd). The noun *lead* (lĕd) is the metal.

Guides planned to lead the settlers to safe quarters. Instead, they led them into a winter storm.

Peeling paint in old houses may contain lead.

668.8 learn, teach

Learn means "to get information"; *teach* means "to give information."

I want to learn how to sew. Will you teach me?

Using the Right Word 9

■ it's, its; lay, lie; lead, led; learn, teach

 For each sentence below, write the word "correct" if the underlined word is used correctly. If it is incorrect, write the right word.

1. Our science teacher said, "<u>Its</u> no secret that I love to challenge students to do their best."
It's

2. A good teacher will <u>learn</u> students more than just school subjects.

3. Classroom visitors usually just <u>lie</u> their coats over the back of a chair.

4. Hahn was selected to <u>lead</u> the students on the field trip through the state forest.

5. I will <u>teach</u> you how to make a sound with your thumbs, your mouth, and a piece of grass.

6. The winner of the race <u>lead</u> all the other runners from the beginning.

7. <u>It's</u> not a very exciting race when that happens.

8. Some paints made before 1978 contain <u>led</u>, which is dangerous if young children eat it.

9. After Shawn saw the museum exhibit, he decided to <u>learn</u> more about spiders.

10. The wolf spider has <u>it's</u> eyes arranged so it can see in all directions at once.

11. This spider will <u>lay</u> very still as it waits for its prey.

12. The female spider <u>lays</u> her eggs in a sac that she carries around with her.

Next Step: *Its* and *it's* can be challenging words to use correctly. Write two sentences that show you understand their meanings.

670.1 leave, let

Leave means "fail to take along." *Let* means "allow."

Rozi wanted to leave her boots at home, but Jorge wouldn't let her.

670.2 like, as

Like is a preposition meaning "similar to"; *as* is a conjunction meaning "to the same degree" or "while." *Like* usually introduces a phrase; *as* usually introduces a clause.

The glider floated like a bird. The glider floated as the pilot had hoped it would.

As we circled the airfield, we saw maintenance carts moving like ants below us.

670.3 loose, lose, loss

Loose (lüs) means "free or untied"; *lose* (lo͞oz) means "to misplace or fail to win"; *loss* (lôs) means "something lost."

These jeans are too loose in the waist since my recent weight loss. I still want to lose a few more pounds.

670.4 made, maid

Made is the past tense of "make," which means to "create," "prepare," or "put in order." A *maid* is a female servant; *maid* is also used to describe an unmarried girl or young woman.

The hotel maid asked if our beds needed to be made.

Grandma made a chocolate cake for dessert.

A maid strolled in the garden before the concert.

670.5 mail, male

Mail refers to letters or packages handled by the postal service. *Male* refers to the masculine sex.

My little brother likes getting junk mail.

The male sea horse, not the female, takes care of the fertilized eggs.

670.6 main, mane

Main refers to the most important part. *Mane* is the long hair growing from the top or sides of the neck of certain animals, such as the horse, lion, and so on.

The main thing we noticed about the magician's tamed lion was its luxurious mane.

670.7 meat, meet

Meat is food or flesh; *meet* means "to come upon or encounter."

I'd like you to meet the butcher who sells the leanest meat in town.

Using the Right Word 10

■ leave, let; like, as; made, maid; mail, male

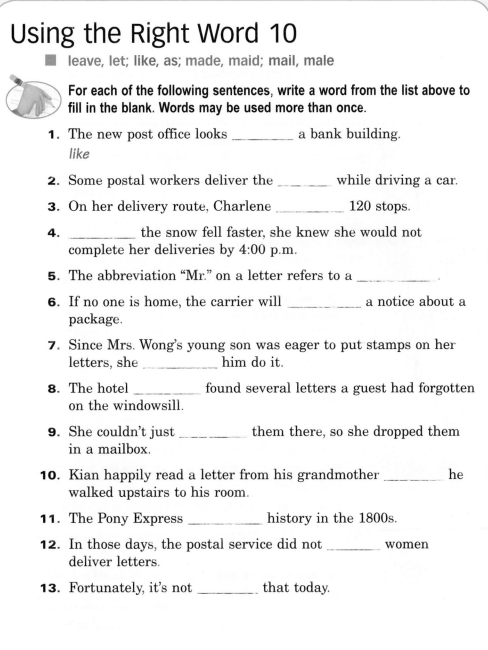

For each of the following sentences, write a word from the list above to fill in the blank. Words may be used more than once.

1. The new post office looks _____ a bank building.
like

2. Some postal workers deliver the _____ while driving a car.

3. On her delivery route, Charlene _____ 120 stops.

4. _____ the snow fell faster, she knew she would not complete her deliveries by 4:00 p.m.

5. The abbreviation "Mr." on a letter refers to a _____ .

6. If no one is home, the carrier will _____ a notice about a package.

7. Since Mrs. Wong's young son was eager to put stamps on her letters, she _____ him do it.

8. The hotel _____ found several letters a guest had forgotten on the windowsill.

9. She couldn't just _____ them there, so she dropped them in a mailbox.

10. Kian happily read a letter from his grandmother _____ he walked upstairs to his room.

11. The Pony Express _____ history in the 1800s.

12. In those days, the postal service did not _____ women deliver letters.

13. Fortunately, it's not _____ that today.

Next Step: Write two sentences about getting mail. Use the words *like* and *as.*

RIGHT WORD

672.1
medal, metal,
meddle, mettle

A *medal* is an award. *Metal* is an element like iron or gold. *Meddle* means "to interfere." *Mettle*, a noun, refers to quality of character.

Grandpa's friend received a medal for showing his mettle in battle. Grandma, who loves to meddle in others' business, asked if the award was a precious metal.

672.2
miner, minor

A *miner* digs in the ground for valuable ore. A *minor* is a person who is not legally an adult. *Minor* means "of no great importance" when used as an adjective.

The use of minors as miners is no minor problem.

672.3
moral, morale

Moral relates to what is right or wrong or to the lesson to be drawn from a story. *Morale* refers to a person's attitude or mental condition.

The moral of this story is "Everybody loves a winner."

After the unexpected win at football, morale was high throughout the town.

672.4
morning,
mourning

Morning refers to the first part of the day (before noon); *mourning* means "showing sorrow."

Abby was mourning her test grades all morning.

672.5
oar, or, ore

An *oar* is a paddle used in rowing or steering a boat. *Or* is a conjunction indicating choice. *Ore* refers to a mineral made up of several different kinds of material, as in iron ore.

Either use one oar to push us away from the dock, or start the boat's motor.

Silver-copper ore is smelted and refined to extract each metal.

672.6
pain, pane

Pain is the feeling of being hurt. A *pane* is a section or part of something.

Dad looked like he was in pain when he found out we broke a pane of glass in the neighbor's front door.

672.7
pair, pare, pear

A *pair* is a couple (two); *pare* is a verb meaning "to peel"; *pear* is the fruit.

A pair of doves nested in the pear tree.

Please pare the apples for the pie.

Using the Right Word 11

■ medal, metal, meddle, mettle; miner, minor; moral, morale; pair, pare, pear

 For each of the following sentences, write the correct choice from each set of words in parentheses.

1. Gold is used in electrical circuits because it is a (*metal, mettle*) that does not weaken with time.
   metal

2. A (*pair, pare, pear*) of contact points is needed to make a simple on/off electrical switch.

3. An electrician will (*pair, pare, pear*) two inches of insulation from a wire before working with it.

4. A line worker shows (*meddle, mettle*) when he or she climbs a tower and begins working on high-voltage power lines.

5. After installing a new outlet, the electrician turned to the (*miner, minor*) problem of replacing a burned-out lightbulb.

6. The employees of Western Hills Electric Power won a (*medal, meddle*) for resource conservation.

7. Many people consider conservation of natural resources to be a (*moral, morale*) issue.

8. A coal (*miner, minor*) rides in a special cage that drops deep into the earth.

9. These workers dig for (*metal, mettle*) ore.

10. As long as working conditions and income are good, the (*moral, morale*) in the mine is good.

11. Thomas decided that he would no longer (*medal, meddle*) in matters that were really his sister's concern.

12. Try an apple or a (*pair, pare, pear*) as an afternoon snack.

Next Step: Write a sentence for each of the following words: *medal, meddle, metal,* and *mettle.*

RIGHT WORD

674.1 past, passed

Passed is always a verb; it is the past tense of *pass*. *Past* can be used as a noun, as an adjective, or as a preposition.

A motorcycle passed my dad's 'Vette. (verb)

The old man won't forget the past. (noun)

I'm sorry, but I'd rather not talk about my past life. (adjective)

Old Blue walked right past the cat and never saw it. (preposition)

674.2 peace, piece

Peace means "harmony, or freedom from war." A *piece* is a part or fragment of something.

In order to keep peace among the triplets, each one had to have an identical piece of cake.

674.3 peak, peek, pique

A *peak* is a "high point" or a "pointed end." *Peek* means "brief look." *Pique*, as a verb, means "to excite by challenging"; as a noun, it means "a feeling of resentment."

Just a peek at Pike's Peak in the Rocky Mountains can pique a mountain climber's curiosity.

In a pique, she marched away from her giggling sisters.

674.4 personal, personnel

Personal means "private." *Personnel* are people working at a job.

Some thoughts are too personal to share.

The personnel manager will be hiring more workers.

674.5 plain, plane

A *plain* is an area of land that is flat or level; it also means "clearly seen or clearly understood" and "ordinary."

It's plain to see why the early settlers had trouble crossing the Great Plains.

Plane means "a flat, level surface" (as in geometry); it is also a tool used to smooth the surface of wood.

When I saw that the door wasn't a perfect plane, I used a plane to make it smooth.

674.6 pore, pour, poor

A *pore* is an opening in the skin. *Pour* means "to cause a flow or stream." *Poor* means "needy."

People perspire through the pores in their skin. Pour yourself a glass of water. Your poor body needs it!

Using the Right Word 12

■ past, passed; **peace, piece**; peak, peek, pique; plain, plane; pore, pour, poor

 For each numbered sentence below, write the word "correct" if the underlined word is used correctly. If it is incorrect, write the right word.

Example: Mr. Johnson decided his front walk was in <u>pore</u> condition.

Answer: *poor*

(1) During the <u>passed</u> week, Mr. Jackson replaced his front walk. **(2)** He smashed the old concrete with a sledgehammer until he could pick up each <u>peace</u> with one hand. **(3)** Some neighbors heard the noise and <u>peaked</u> out their windows to see what he was doing. **(4)** At last he was done hammering, and <u>peace</u> returned to the neighborhood.

(5) Mr. Jackson needed help to <u>poor</u> the new cement, so he asked his neighbor, Mr. Gupta. **(6)** <u>Poor</u> Mr. Gupta—he didn't know what he was getting into! **(7)** It was a very hot day, and sweat flowed from every <u>poor</u> of his body. **(8)** Mr. Jackson kindly <u>passed</u> Mr. Gupta a glass of cold lemonade.

(9) Finally, Mr. Jackson carefully smoothed the surface of the wet cement until it was a perfect <u>plain</u>. **(10)** Then he stamped a design that looked like <u>peaks</u> and valleys in the wet cement. **(11)** It was <u>plain</u> to see that the new walk would be quite different from the old one! **(12)** As people <u>past</u> his house, they admired his work. It made Mr. Jackson feel proud.

Next Step: Write two sentences about a difficult project you completed that made you feel proud. Use at least two of the following words: *past, piece, poor,* and *peak.*

676.1 principal, principle

As an adjective, *principal* means "primary." As a noun, it can mean "a school administrator" or "a sum of money." *Principle* means "idea or doctrine."

My mom's principal goal is to save money so she can pay off the principal balance on her loan from the bank.

Hey, Charlie, I hear the principal gave you a detention.

The principle of freedom is based on the principle of self-discipline.

676.2 quiet, quit, quite

Quiet is the opposite of "noisy." *Quit* means "to stop." *Quite* means "completely or entirely."

I quit mowing even though I wasn't quite finished.
The neighborhood was quiet again.

676.3 raise, rays, raze

Raise is a verb meaning "to lift or elevate." *Rays* are thin lines or beams. *Raze* is a verb that means "to tear down completely."

When I raise this shade, bright rays of sunlight stream into the room.

Construction workers will raze the old theater to make room for a parking lot.

676.4 real, very, really

Do not use the adjective *real* in place of the adverbs *very* or *really*.

The plants scattered throughout the restaurant are not real.

Hiccups are very embarrassing.

Her nose is really small.

676.5 red, read

Red is a color; *read*, pronounced the same way, is the past tense of the verb meaning "to understand the meaning of written words and symbols."

"I've read five books in two days," said the little boy.

The librarian gave him a red ribbon.

Using the Right Word 13

■ principal, principle; **quiet, quit, quite**; raise, rays, raze;
real, **very, really**

 For each of the following sentences, write the correct choice from each set of words in parentheses.

1. While Hugh Jackman is a (*real, really*) person, Wolverine is not.
real

2. Sal wanted to (*quit, quite*) the soccer team, but her mom insisted she play until the end of the season.

3. Tomas heard his parents talking about paying off the (*principal, principle*) on their loan.

4. The sun's (*raise, rays*) finally burst through the heavy cloud cover.

5. City crews will have to (*raise, raze*) the storm-damaged park shelter.

6. Ms. Show said that we must be (*quiet, quite*) during tests.

7. She said, "The (*principal, principle*) reason for my request is so that no one disturbs anyone else."

8. After playing in the snow for several hours, the boys admitted they were (*real, very*) cold.

9. Since there aren't (*quiet, quite*) enough books for everyone in the class, some kids must share.

10. I can better control my anger if I do not (*raise, raze*) my voice.

11. One (*principal, principle*) to live by is "honesty is the best policy."

12. Evan's shoes got (*real, really*) wet as he walked through the deep, dew-covered grass.

Next Step: Write two sentences that show your understanding of the words *real, really,* and *very.*

678.1
right, write, rite

Right means "correct or proper"; *right* is the opposite of "left"; it also refers to anything that a person has a legal claim to, as in "copyright." *Write* means "to record in print." *Rite* is a ritual or ceremonial act.

We have to write an essay about how our rights are protected by the Constitution.

Turn right at the next corner.

A rite of passage is a ceremony that celebrates becoming an adult.

678.2
scene, seen

Scene refers to the setting or location where something happens; it also means "sight or spectacle." *Seen* is a form of the verb "see."

The scene of the crime was roped off. We hadn't seen anyone go in or out of the building.

678.3
seam, seem

A *seam* is a line formed by connecting two pieces of material. *Seem* means "appear to exist."

Every Thanksgiving, it seems, I stuff myself so much that my shirt seams threaten to burst.

678.4
sew, so, sow

Sew is a verb meaning "to stitch"; *so* is a conjunction meaning "in order that." The verb *sow* means "to plant."

In Colonial times, the wife would sew the family clothes, and the husband would sow the family garden so the children could eat.

678.5
sight, cite, site

Sight means "the act of seeing" or "something that is seen." *Cite* means "to quote or refer to." A *site* is a location or position (including a Web site on the Internet).

The Alamo at night was a sight worth the trip. I was also able to cite my visit to this historical site in my history paper.

678.6
sit, set

Sit means "to put the body in a seated position." *Set* means "to place." (*Set* is a transitive verb; that means it needs a direct object to complete its meaning.)

How can you just sit there and watch as I set up all these chairs?

Using the Right Word 14

■ right, write, rite; seam, seem; sew, so, sow; sight, cite, site

For each sentence below, write the word "correct" if the underlined word is used correctly. If it is incorrect, write the right word.

1. All the computers in the lab <u>seam</u> slow today.
   seem

2. Whenever the lab gets a new computer, the computer club has a special <u>rite</u> of initiation.

3. Some computer screen savers are quite a <u>site</u>.

4. Jamal likes using a computer to <u>right</u> letters to his grandmother.

5. Can you find the Write Source Web <u>sight</u>?

6. My computer had crashed, <u>so</u> the teacher restarted it.

7. When you write research reports, make sure you correctly <u>site</u> information from the Internet.

8. Nathan didn't think the Web site's information was <u>rite</u>.

9. Being allowed to enter a chat room is a <u>right</u> of passage for some people.

10. A chat room makes it <u>seam</u> like you're right there talking to someone.

11. Our teacher showed us how to <u>sow</u> a simple case to hold CD's.

12. I stitched the <u>seam</u> twice to make it superstrong.

13. A computer can help a farmer determine the proper time to <u>sew</u> seeds.

14. It can also specify the best <u>site</u> for each crop.

Next Step: Write two sentences that show your understanding of the words *cite* and *site*.

RIGHT WORD

680.1 sole, soul

Sole means "single, only one"; *sole* also refers to the bottom surface of a foot or shoe. *Soul* refers to the spiritual part of a person.

Maggie got a job for the sole purpose of saving for a car.

The soles of these shoes are very thick.

"Who told you dogs don't have souls?" asked the kind veterinarian.

680.2 some, sum

Some means "an unknown number or part." *Sum* means "the whole amount."

The sum in the cash register was stolen by some thieves.

680.3 sore, soar

Sore means "painful"; to *soar* means "to rise or fly high into the air."

Craning to watch the eagle soar overhead, we soon had sore necks.

680.4 stationary, stationery

Stationary means "not movable"; *stationery* is the paper and envelopes used to write letters.

Grandpa designed and printed his own stationery.

All of the built-in furniture is stationary, of course.

680.5 steal, steel

Steal means "to take something without permission"; *steel* is a metal.

Early ironmakers had to steal recipes for producing steel.

680.6 than, then

Than is used in a comparison; *then* tells when.

Since tomorrow's weather is supposed to be nicer than today's, we'll go to the zoo then.

680.7 their, there, they're

Their is a possessive pronoun, one that shows ownership. (See **714.2**.) *There* is an adverb that tells where. *They're* is the contraction for "they are."

They're upset because their dog got into the garbage over there.

680.8 threw, through

Threw is the past tense of "throw." *Through* means "passing from one side to the other" or "by means of."

Through sheer talent and long practice, Nolan Ryan threw baseballs through the strike zone at more than 100 miles per hour.

Using the Right Word 15

■ **sole, soul; stationary, stationery; than, then;**
their, there, they're; threw, through

**For each of the following sentences, write the correct choice from each
set of words in parentheses.**

1. The (*sole, soul*) of the boot was completely worn out.
sole

2. With only one play left to win the game, the quarterback
(*threw, through*) the ball as far as he could.

3. The scouts set up (*their, they're*) tents in a clearing in the forest.

4. Rain began to fall, and (*than, then*) the temperature dropped
and turned the rain to snow.

5. Some superheroes can see (*threw, through*) walls.

6. Sanjay, please put that box of books over (*their, there*).

7. Hoping to strengthen his injured leg, Frank plans to pedal a
(*stationary, stationery*) bike for 30 minutes a day.

8. This year, students have to attend school later in June
(*than, then*) they did last year.

9. Many people feel that music is good for the (*sole, soul*).

10. Tonya writes letters on homemade (*stationary, stationery*).

11. When Mom and Dad get home from work, (*there, they're*) often
exhausted.

12. I would rather read a good book (*than, then*) watch daytime
television any day.

13. Am I the (*sole, soul*) book lover in this class?

Next Step: Write a sentence that shows your understanding of the
words *than* and *they're*. Exchange papers with a classmate
and check each other's sentences.

682.1

to, too, two

To is the preposition that can mean "in the direction of." (*To* also is used to form an infinitive. See **730.4**.) *Too* is an adverb meaning "very or excessive." *Too* is often used to mean "also." *Two* is the number 2.

Only two of Columbus's first three ships returned to Spain from the New World.

Columbus was too restless to stay in Spain for long.

682.2

vain, vane, vein

Vain means "worthless." It may also mean "thinking too highly of one's self; stuck-up." *Vane* is a flat piece of material set up to show which way the wind blows. *Vein* refers to a blood vessel or a mineral deposit.

The weather vane indicates the direction of wind.

A blood vein determines the direction of flowing blood.

The vain mind moves in no particular direction and thinks only about itself.

682.3

vary, very

Vary is a verb that means "to change." *Very* can be an adjective meaning "in the fullest sense" or "complete"; it can also be an adverb meaning "extremely."

Garon's version of the event would vary from day to day. His very interesting story was the very opposite of the truth.

682.4

waist, waste

Waist is the part of the body just above the hips. The verb *waste* means "to wear away" or "to use carelessly"; the noun *waste* refers to material that is unused or useless.

Don't waste your money on fast-food meals. What a waste to throw away all this food because you're concerned about the size of your waist!

682.5

wait, weight

Wait means "to stay somewhere expecting something." *Weight* is the measure of heaviness.

When I have to wait for the bus, the weight of my backpack seems to keep increasing.

682.6

ware, wear, where

Ware means "a product to be sold"; *wear* means "to have on or to carry on one's body"; *where* asks the question "in what place or in what situation?"

Where can you buy the best cookware to take on a campout—and the best rain gear to wear if it rains?

Using the Right Word 16

■ vain, vane, vein; **waist, waste; wait, weight; ware, wear, where**

For each of the following sentences, write the correct choice from each set of words in parentheses.

1. If people need blood in an emergency, they should not have to (*wait, weight*) for it.

   wait

2. People may boast about how much blood they give, yet it is not something to be (*vain, vane, vein*) about.

3. Sometimes a nurse who needs to draw some blood searches in (*vain, vane, vein*) for a usable blood vessel.

4. A (*vain, vane, vein*) carries blood from body cells back to the heart.

5. The lungs are the place (*ware, wear, where*) blood picks up oxygen.

6. The circulatory system carries some (*waist, waste*) products to the kidneys, which are located near the (*waist, waste*) toward the back of the body.

7. A person's (*wait, weight*) can affect his or her blood pressure.

8. Some medical equipment shows the direction of blood flow like a weather (*vain, vane, vein*) shows the direction of the wind.

9. The hard(*ware, wear, where*) used for blood transfusions can be costly.

10. Red blood cells eventually (*ware, wear, where*) out.

11. Fortunately, healthy people don't have to (*wait, weight*) long for their bones to replace worn-out blood cells.

12. Since the bones continually produce new blood cells, people do not (*waist, waste*) their own blood by donating it.

Next Step: Pick two or three of the words used above that sometimes confuse you. Write a sentence for each word.

684.1 way, weigh

Way means "path or route" or "a series of actions." *Weigh* means "to measure weight."

What is the correct way to weigh liquid medicines?

684.2 weather, whether

Weather refers to the condition of the atmosphere. *Whether* refers to a possibility.

The weather will determine whether I go fishing.

684.3 week, weak

A *week* is a period of seven days; *weak* means "not strong."

Last week when I had the flu, I felt light-headed and weak.

684.4 wet, whet

Wet means "soaked with liquid." *Whet* is a verb that means "to sharpen."

Of course, going swimming means I'll get wet, but all that exercise really whets my appetite.

684.5 which, witch

Which is a pronoun used to ask "what one or ones?" out of a group. A *witch* is a woman believed to have supernatural powers.

Which of the women in Salem in the 1600s were accused of being witches?

684.6 who, which, that

When introducing a clause, *who* is used to refer to people; *which* refers to animals and nonliving beings but never to people (it introduces a nonrestrictive, or unnecessary, clause); *that* usually refers to animals or things but can refer to people (it introduces a restrictive, or necessary, clause).

The idea that pizza is junk food is crazy.

Pizza, which is quite nutritious, can be included in a healthy diet.

My mom, who is a dietician, said so.

684.7 who, whom

Who is used as the subject in a sentence; *whom* is used as the object of a preposition or as a direct object.

Who asked you to play tennis?

You beat whom at tennis? You played tennis with whom?

NOTE To test for who/whom, arrange the parts of the clause in a subject–verb–direct-object order. *Who* works as the subject, *whom* as the object. (See page **570**.)

Using the Right Word 17

■ weather, whether; wet, whet; who, which, that; who, whom

For the following sentences, write a word from the list above to fill in each blank.

1. "Have you heard today's _____ forecast?" Jay asked.
   weather

2. Steve said, "I did, but I don't know _____ you should get out your skis or not."

3. Last night, Vince Stevens, the meteorologist _____ I usually trust, forecasted clouds but no snow.

4. The forecast _____ is in today's paper, however, predicts heavy, _____ snow.

5. Just thinking about the possibility of a snowstorm will _____ my desire to go skiing.

6. My new skis, _____ I received as a gift, are ready to go!

7. Aunt Winnie, _____ is as big a ski nut as I am, gave them to me for my birthday.

8. Unlike some other athletes, people _____ ski really have to rely on the right _____.

9. The idea _____ I might get to ski today sure is a nice one!

10. _____ or not it snows today, I guess I'll get my gear ready.

RIGHT WORD

Next Step: Write two sentences that show your understanding of the words *who* and *whom*.

686.1
who's, whose

Who's is the contraction for "who is." *Whose* is a possessive pronoun, one that shows ownership.

Who's the most popular writer today?

Whose bike is this?

686.2
wood, would

Wood is the material that comes from trees; *would* is a form of the verb "will."

Sequoia trees live practically forever, but would you believe that the wood from these giants is practically useless?

686.3
your, you're

Your is a possessive pronoun, one that shows ownership. *You're* is the contraction for "you are."

You're the most important person in your parents' lives.

SCHOOL DAZE

Using the Right Word 18

■ who's, whose; wood, would; your, you're

For each of the following sentences, write the correct choice from each set of words in parentheses.

1. (*Whose, Who's*) book is this?

2. The math teacher said that (*your, you're*) the only one who got an *A* on the test.

3. Danica has a pen that's made of (*wood, would*).

4. Dominic, (*whose, who's*) dad is from Italy, speaks Italian.

5. Excuse me, I think you dropped (*your, you're*) calculator.

6. (*Whose, Who's*) going to the basketball game Friday night?

7. I (*wood, would*) go, but I have to baby-sit for my neighbors.

Using the Right Word Review

For each of the following sentences, write the correct choice from each set of words in parentheses.

1. Sanford plays football (*real, very*) (*good, well*).

2. Shalonda (*heard, herd*) a blue jay this morning.

3. They are noisier (*than, then*) the other birds by her window.

4. I found the missing items (*altogether, all together*) in one place.

5. Donovan puts his homework (*besides, beside*) his shoes so he doesn't forget it.

6. My old dog loves to (*lay, lie*) right on top of a heat vent.

7. This large, empty lot is the (*sight, cite, site*) where the town will (*billed, build*) the new middle school.

8. A peregrine falcon flew (*among, between*) two trees.

9. After 20 minutes had (*past, passed*), Barry stopped counting the (*amount, number*) of concrete blocks he had to load on the truck.

Test Prep

For each sentence below, write the letter of the line in which the underlined word or words are used incorrectly. If there is no mistake, choose "D."

1. A Since her cut didn't <u>heal</u>
   B <u>good</u>, she will have
   C a <u>minor</u> scar there.
   D correct as is

2. A My dog, <u>that</u> loves
   B to <u>lie</u> on a big dog pillow,
   C has beautiful, soft <u>fur</u>.
   D correct as is

3. A The guide <u>led</u> us
   B <u>farther</u> into the ruins
   C of the archaeological <u>site</u>.
   D correct as is

4. A Would eating a <u>whole</u>
   B pizza have a bad <u>affect</u>
   C on Don's <u>weight</u>?
   D correct as is

5. A Mae used a <u>peace</u> of her
   B mom's <u>stationery</u> to
   C <u>write</u> a letter to Mr. Oh.
   D correct as is

6. A Josie and I <u>made</u>
   B a <u>real</u> big birthday cake
   C <u>for</u> our cousin.
   D correct as is

7. A Jamal's <u>ascent</u> to the top
   B of the rope was <u>like</u> a
   C climb up a mountain <u>peek</u>.
   D correct as is

8. A Will you <u>borrow</u> me
   B some money so I <u>can</u>
   C <u>buy</u> lunch today?
   D correct as is

9. A For some, the dry <u>air</u>
   B of the <u>desert</u> is its
   C <u>principle</u> appeal.
   D correct as is

10. A <u>Poor</u> Chantel must
    B <u>choose</u> the best ice cream
    C from <u>among</u> 20 flavors.
    D correct as is

11. A When Troy broke a <u>metal</u>
    B string on his <u>base</u> guitar,
    C he was <u>quite</u> angry.
    D correct as is

12. A The twins <u>take</u> the bus
    B to <u>they're</u> aunt's house,
    C <u>where</u> they stay for dinner.
    D correct as is

13. A It's hard for Angela
    B to except any kind
    C of compliment.
    D correct as is

14. A Besides learning some
    B history, we had alot of
    C fun in the state capital.
    D correct as is

15. A Deitrich, whom is very
    B smart, will teach us how to
    C build a model of an atom.
    D correct as is

16. A Albert eats less
    B then I do, but his
    C waist is as big as mine.
    D correct as is

17. A Time passed slowly as
    B Tina threw a tennis ball
    C against the wood door.
    D correct as is

18. A I asked Dad to leave me
    B go to your birthday party
    C at the mini-golf course.
    D correct as is

19. A Sandy, who's parents have
    B a pear tree in their yard,
    C cannot bear to eat them.
    D correct as is

20. A Martina turned a plain
    B object into a weather
    C vain in shop class.
    D correct as is

RIGHT WORD

Understanding Sentences

Sentences

A **sentence** is a group of words that expresses a complete thought. A sentence must have both a subject and a predicate. A sentence begins with a capital letter; it ends with a period, a question mark, or an exclamation point.

> I like my teacher this year.
>
> Will we go on a field trip?
>
> We get to go to the water park!

Parts of a Sentence

690.1
Subjects

A subject is the part of a sentence that does something or is talked about.

> The kids on my block play basketball at the local park.
>
> We meet after school almost every day.

690.2
Simple Subjects

The simple subject is the subject without the words that describe or modify it. (Also see page 502.)

> My friend Chester plays basketball on the school team.

690.3
Complete Subjects

The complete subject is the simple subject and all the words that modify it. (Also see page 501.)

> My friend Chester plays basketball on the school team.

690.4
Compound Subjects

A compound subject has two or more simple subjects. (See page 502.)

> Chester, Malik, and Meshelle play on our pickup team.
>
> Lou and I are the best shooters.

Parts of a Sentence 1

■ Simple, Complete, and Compound Subjects

For each numbered sentence in the paragraphs below, write the complete subject. Then circle the simple subject or the compound subject. (*Remember:* Compound sentences have two subjects.)

Example: Car problems made me late for school.
Answer: Car ⟨problems⟩

(1) I was on my way to school in my dad's car. **(2)** Suddenly, a light mist came from the vents, and an odd, sweet smell filled the car. **(3)** Dad pulled over and called a tow truck. **(4)** Thinking about yet another trip to the repair shop, he sighed deeply.

(5) A mechanic at the repair shop took a look at the engine. **(6)** Cars are so complex these days! **(7)** How does the mechanic know what to look for? **(8)** In most cases, training programs prepare mechanics for their work. **(9)** A two-year degree from a technical college is required for employment at many automobile dealerships. **(10)** Today's cars call for special training on computerized shop equipment. **(11)** Additionally, mechanics need some knowledge of electronics. **(12)** Of course, they must also work with traditional hand tools. **(13)** Besides a complete knowledge of automobiles, a good mechanic also needs the ability to solve problems.

(14) Dad's mechanic gave him the news. **(15)** "The problem is probably with the heater core." **(16)** Poor, stressed-out Dad had the repair shop fix his car . . . again.

Next Step: Write two sentences about a career that interests you. Exchange papers with a classmate. Underline your partner's complete subjects and circle the simple (or compound) subjects.

SENTENCES

Parts of a Sentence . . .

692.1
Predicates

The predicate, which contains the verb, is the part of the sentence that shows action or says something about the subject.

Hunting has reduced the tiger population in India.

692.2
Simple Predicates

The simple predicate is the predicate (verb) without the words that describe or modify it. (See page **502**.)

In the past, poachers **killed** too many African elephants.
Poaching **is** illegal.

692.3
Complete Predicates

The complete predicate is the simple predicate with all the words that modify or describe it. (See page **501**.)

In the past, **poachers** killed too many African elephants.
Poaching is illegal.

692.4
Direct Objects

The complete predicate often includes a direct object. The direct object is the noun or pronoun that receives the action of the simple predicate—directly. The direct object answers the question *what* or *whom*. (See page **570**.)

Many smaller animals need friends **who will speak up for them.**

The direct object may be compound.

We all need animals, plants, wetlands, deserts, **and** forests.

692.5
Indirect Objects

If a sentence has a direct object, it may also have an indirect object. An indirect object is the noun or pronoun that receives the action of the simple predicate—indirectly. An indirect object names the person *to whom* or *for whom* something is done. (See page **570**.)

I showed the class **my multimedia report on endangered species.** (*Class* is the indirect object because it says *to whom* the report was shown.)

Remember, in order for a sentence to have an indirect object, it must first have a direct object.

692.6
Compound Predicates

A compound predicate is composed of two or more simple predicates. (See page **502**.)

In 1990 the countries of the world **met** and **banned** the sale of ivory.

Parts of a Sentence 2

■ Simple, Compound, and Complete Predicates
■ Direct and Indirect Objects

For each numbered sentence below, write the complete predicate.
(*Remember:* Compound or complex sentences will have two.)
Underline any direct objects once and indirect objects twice.

Example: Some people innocently plant weeds.
Answer: *innocently plant <u>weeds</u>*

(1) Kudzu is a vine found in the southern states. **(2)** The climate there encourages the vine's rapid growth—as much as a foot per day! **(3)** The vine climbs trees, signposts, and barns. **(4)** It covers anything in its way. **(5)** Giant kudzu-covered trees that look like monsters are pretty scary!

(6) Although kudzu grows so well in the Southeast, it is not a native plant in the United States. **(7)** For Philadelphia's 1876 U.S. Centennial Exposition, the Japanese government created a delightful garden. **(8)** Plants from Japan, including kudzu, gave Americans ideas. **(9)** Japanese gardeners sold people the lush, sweet-smelling vine.

(10) Kudzu helped prevent soil erosion, so people planted the vine throughout the South. **(11)** Kudzu now covers seven million acres of land in the region. **(12)** Unfortunately, the thick vines prevent trees from getting sunlight, and valuable forests are dying as a result.

Next Step: Now go back and circle the simple or compound predicates within the complete predicates you wrote down.

SENTENCES

Parts of a Sentence . . .

694.1
Understood Subjects and Predicates

Either the subject or the predicate (or both) may not be stated in a sentence, but both must be clearly understood.

> [You] **Get involved!** (*You* is the understood subject.)
>
> **Who needs your help? Animals** [do]. (*Do* is the understood predicate.)
>
> **What do many animals face?** [They face] **Extinction.** (*They* is the understood subject, and *face* is the understood predicate.)

694.2
Delayed Subjects

In sentences that begin with *there* followed by a form of the "be" verb, the subject usually follows the verb. (See page **570**.)

> **There are** laws **that protect endangered species.** (The subject is *laws*; *are* is the verb.)

The subject is also delayed in questions.

> **How can** we **preserve the natural habitat?** (*We* is the subject.)

SCHOOL DAZE

John, I've got all the projects. Now which one is yours?

I'm not sure. See if there's one with a missing piece.

694.3
Modifiers

A modifier is a word (adjective, adverb) or a group of words (phrase, clause) that changes or adds to the meaning of another word. (See pages **486–493**.)

> **Many North American zoos and aquariums** voluntarily **participate** in breeding programs that help prevent extinction.

The modifiers in this sentence include the following: *many, North American* (adjectives), *voluntarily* (adverb), *in breeding programs* (phrase), *that help prevent extinction* (clause).

Parts of a Sentence 3

■ **Understood Subjects and Predicates**

For the answer to each question below, write the word or words that are not stated but are understood. Identify them as "subject," "predicate," or "both."

1. *How do we get to Turner Road?*
Turn right at the first stoplight.   *You (subject)*

2. *Who is the substitute teacher today?*
Mr. Ross.

3. *When is our next test?*
Friday.

4. *May I go outside after lunch?*
Yes.

5. *How do I cut this?*
Use a pair of scissors.

6. *What has been added to this popcorn?*
Oil, butter, and salt.

7. *What did Marva get from Johnny?*
A box of chocolates.

■ **Delayed Subjects**

Rewrite each of the following sentences so that the subject is not delayed.

8. Would you like to go for a walk?
You would like to go for a walk.

9. Is that a Siamese cat?

10. May I ride my bike to the arcade?

11. Are we having dinner with the Thorsens tonight?

12. After the movie, will Marcus need a ride home?

Test Prep

Number your paper from 1 to 15. For each underlined part in the following paragraphs, choose the letter or letters from the list below that best describe it. (Some answers will have two letters.)

A simple subject   **D** simple predicate

B complete subject   **E** complete predicate

C compound subject   **F** compound predicate

In 1883, <u>a volcano in eastern Indonesia</u> erupted. As a result,
<u>1</u>
100-foot ocean waves traveling at 400 miles per hour

<u>crashed</u> onto some nearby islands. <u>More than 36,000 people</u>
<u>2</u>   <u>3</u>
died. The disaster was a *tsunami*, a series of huge ocean

waves. Usually <u>an earthquake or a volcanic eruption</u> causes
<u>4</u>
a tsunami.

A tsunami's <u>waves</u> are vast amounts of water pushed by a
<u>5</u>
sudden movement of the earth. These incredible waves

<u>can travel great distances without losing power</u>. Near shore,
<u>6</u>
the shallow seafloor <u>makes</u> the first wave slow down.
<u>7</u>
Meanwhile, the waves behind it are still coming in fast. They

all <u>start to pile up and, therefore, become a high wall of water</u>.
<u>8</u>
The waves are so powerful that, when they finally do come

ashore, they can go inland for half a mile.

Although a <u>tsunami</u> can travel 450 miles per hour along the
<u>9</u>

ocean floor, it may not be noticed in the open ocean. Though these
gigantic waves extend thousands of feet deep, they <u>may be only</u>
10
<u>three feet higher than usual on the surface</u>. For this reason, it may
be impossible to see an approaching tsunami. However, <u>the</u>
11
<u>International Tsunami Warning System</u> was set up in 1965. This
organization <u>tries to predict tsunamis</u>. The workers <u>detect</u>
12   **13**
<u>earthquakes on the ocean floor and use wave gauges</u>. <u>They</u> also
14
look at satellite measurements of sudden sea-level changes.

There is no way to stop a tsunami, but areawide alerts allow
people to get away from the coast. <u>Loss of life and damage to</u>
15
<u>property</u> are greatly reduced thanks to the early warnings.

Parts of a Sentence . . .

698.1
Clauses

A clause is a group of related words that has both a subject and a verb. (Also see pages **513–515**.)

> **a whole chain of plants and animals is affected**
> (*Chain* is the subject, and *is affected* is the verb.)

> **when one species dies out completely**
> (*Species* is the subject; *dies out* is the verb.)

698.2
Independent Clauses

An independent clause presents a complete thought and can stand alone as a sentence.

> **This ancient oak tree may be cut down.**

> **This act could affect more than 200 different species of animals!**

> **Why would anyone want that to happen?**

698.3
Dependent Clauses

A dependent clause does not present a complete thought and cannot stand as a sentence. A dependent clause *depends* on being connected to an independent clause to make sense. Dependent clauses begin with either a subordinating conjunction (*after, although, because, before, if*) or a relative pronoun (*who, whose, which, that*). (See pages **710** and **744** for complete lists.)

> If this ancient oak tree is cut down, **it could affect more than 200 different species of animals!**

> **The tree**, which experts think could be 400 years old, **provides a home to many different kinds of birds and insects.**

SCHOOL DAZE

Boy, are you in for a real blockbuster next hour!

Yeah . . . Mr. Runge is showing a movie called *A Day in the Life of a Dependent Clause*.

Parts of a Sentence 4

■ Clauses

Some "sentences" in the following paragraphs are actually dependent clauses. Combine these clauses with a nearby independent clause to form a complex sentence.

Example: Before a bee is able to make a pound of beeswax. It must eat about 10 pounds of honey.

Answer: *Before a bee is able to make a pound of beeswax, it must eat about 10 pounds of honey.*

(1) There are three types of bees in a colony, including the queen. Who produces the eggs. **(2)** The male bees are called drones. **(3)** The thousands of female worker bees gather nectar, build the cells of a honeycomb, and make and store honey. **(4)** Worker bees also feed the larvae. **(5)** Until they reach mature size.

(6) Bees know where to find food. **(7)** Because they communicate with each other by "dancing" in a certain pattern. **(8)** Most bees get all of their food from flowers. **(9)** Which provide pollen and nectar. **(10)** The nectar is converted to honey. **(11)** When it reaches the bee's digestive tract.

(12) A beekeeper knows how to care for honeybees so that they produce and store more honey than they need. **(13)** The beekeeper collects the excess honey. **(14)** After the bees have been made sleepy with smoke. **(15)** The bees can then refill the honeycombs, or the beekeeper might melt the honeycomb. **(16)** If he or she wants to use the beeswax.

Next Step: In two columns labeled "relative pronouns" and "subordinating conjunctions," write all of the words that begin the dependent clauses in the paragraphs above.

SENTENCES

Parts of a Sentence . . .

700.1
Phrases

A phrase is a group of related words that lacks either a subject or a predicate (or both). (See pages **519–520**.)

guards the house (The predicate lacks a subject.)

the ancient oak tree (The subject lacks a predicate.)

with crooked old limbs (The phrase lacks both a subject and a predicate.)

The ancient oak tree with crooked old limbs guards the house. (Together, the three phrases form a complete thought.)

700.2
Types of Phrases

Phrases usually take their names from the main words that introduce them (prepositional phrase, verb phrase, and so on). They are also named for the function they serve in a sentence (adverb phrase, adjective phrase).

The ancient oak tree (noun phrase)

with crooked old limbs (prepositional phrase)

has stood its guard, (verb phrase)

very stubbornly, (adverb phrase)

protecting the little house. (verbal phrase)

For more information on verbal phrases, see page **730**.

SCHOOL DAZE

Give me an example of a **verbal phrase** used as a subject.

Hanging upside down refreshes my brain.

Parts of a Sentence 5

■ **Phrases**

Combine each of the following groups of phrases to write a sentence that forms a complete thought.

Example: of water and land   animals called amphibians
are creatures

Answer: *Animals called amphibians are creatures of water and land.*

1. belong in this classification
salamanders, toads, frogs, and newts

2. to the water   but their connection
on land   spend most of their lives
is clear   these animals

3. will slowly dry out   any amphibian
without a moist environment

4. in addition, they   to lay their eggs
need water

5. in body shape   most amphibians
go through a change

6. is probably   the best-known example
the everyday frog

7. a frog   as a tadpole
in the water   begins life

8. develops legs and lungs   during its growth period
and the tail   the tadpole
eventually disappears

9. onto land   will crawl
a fully developed frog   at last

Next Step: Label each of the phrases in numbers 5, 7, and 9 above as a "noun phrase," "verb phrase," or "prepositional phrase."

Using the Parts of Speech

Nouns

A **noun** is a word that names a person, a place, a thing, or an idea.

Person: **John Ulferts** (uncle)   Thing: **"Yankee Doodle"** (song)

Place: **Mississippi** (state)   Idea: **Labor Day** (holiday)

Kinds of Nouns

702.1
Common Nouns

A common noun is any noun that does not name a specific person, place, thing, or idea. These nouns are not capitalized.

woman   museum   book   weekend

702.2
Proper Nouns

A proper noun is the name of a specific person, place, thing, or idea. Proper nouns are capitalized.

Hillary Clinton   Central Park   *Maniac McGee*   Sunday

702.3
Concrete Nouns

A concrete noun names a thing that is physical (can be touched or seen). Concrete nouns can be either proper or common.

space station   pencil   Statue of Liberty

702.4
Abstract Nouns

An abstract noun names something you can think about but cannot see or touch. Abstract nouns can be either common or proper.

Judaism   poverty   satisfaction   illness

702.5
Collective Nouns

A collective noun names a group or collection of persons, animals, places, or things.

Persons: **tribe, congregation, family, class, team**

Animals: **flock, herd, gaggle, clutch, litter**

Things: **batch, cluster, bunch**

702.6
Compound Nouns

A compound noun is made up of two or more words.

football (written as one word)

high school (written as two words)

brother-in-law (written as a hyphenated word)

punctuate *edit* capitalize
improve SPELL
703
Using the Parts of Speech

Nouns 1

■ **Kinds of Nouns**

Write the answers to the questions following each paragraph.

After 300 years of Spanish rule, Mexico gained its <u>independence</u> in 1810. Like the <u>United States</u>, Mexico is a federal republic headed by a <u>president</u>. The country is divided into 31 states.

Which of the underlined nouns is . . .

1. a common, concrete noun?

2. a common, abstract noun?

3. a proper, concrete noun?

The <u>population</u> of the entire country is nearly 105 million. A full 89 percent of the people are <u>Roman Catholics</u>. The country's official language is <u>Spanish</u>.

Which of the underlined nouns is . . .

4. a collective noun?

5. a proper, abstract noun?

6. a proper, concrete noun?

Mexico's geography ranges from <u>mountains</u> to desert to low coastal plains. As a <u>result</u>, its climate also varies; there are hot, temperate, and cool regions. <u>Mexico</u> can be an enjoyable place for a <u>family</u> to vacation.

Which of the underlined nouns is . . .

7. a proper, concrete noun?

8. a collective noun?

9. a common, abstract noun?

10. a common, concrete noun?

Nouns . . .

Number of Nouns

The number of a noun is either singular or plural.

704.1
Singular Nouns

A singular noun names one person, place, thing, or idea.

boy   group   audience   stage   concert   hope

704.2
Plural Nouns

A plural noun names more than one person, place, thing, or idea.

boys   groups   audiences   stages   concerts   hopes

Gender of Nouns

704.3
Noun Gender

Nouns are grouped according to gender: *feminine, masculine, neuter,* and *indefinite*.

Feminine (female): **mother, sister, women, cow, hen**

Masculine (male): **father, brother, men, bull, rooster**

Neuter (neither male nor female): **tree, cobweb, closet**

Indefinite (male or female): **president, duckling, doctor**

Uses of Nouns

704.4
Subject Nouns

A noun that is the subject of a sentence does something or is talked about in the sentence.

The roots of rap can be traced back to West Africa and Jamaica.

704.5
Predicate Nouns

A predicate noun follows a form of the *be* verb (*am, is, are, was, were, being, been*) and renames the subject.

In the 1970s, rap was a street art.

704.6
Possessive Nouns

A possessive noun shows possession or ownership.

Early rap had a drummer's beat but no music.

The rapper's words are set to music.

704.7
Object Nouns

A noun is an object noun when it is used as the direct object, the indirect object, or the object of the preposition.

Some rappers tell people their story about life in the city.
(indirect object: *people*; direct object: *story*)

Rap is now a common music choice in this country. (object of the preposition: *country*)

punctuate *edit* capitalize
SPELL
improve
705
Using the Parts of Speech

Nouns 2

■ **Number and Gender of Nouns**

Draw a chart like the one below. Classify the underlined nouns in the
following paragraph by writing them in the correct box.

Gender	Singular	Plural
feminine		
masculine		*men*
neuter		
indefinite		

Antarctica was a
continent without <u>men</u> or
<u>women</u> until explorers
and <u>researchers</u> from
other parts of the world
arrived. Only penguins
and seals lived on the
land. In December 1911, <u>Roald Amundsen</u> and four other men made
their way across Antarctica using skis and dogsleds. They were the first
people to reach the South Pole, which is the point in the earth's southern
hemisphere where all the lines of longitude start. The <u>group</u> traveled
quickly across snow and <u>mountains</u>. When they reached the pole, they
set up the Norwegian <u>flag</u>. A month later, a team led by British explorer
Robert Scott arrived at the South Pole. It wasn't until 1969, however,
that the first <u>woman</u> reached the pole.

■ **Uses of Nouns**

Number your paper from 1 to 4. List each underlined noun from the
following paragraph and identify it as a "subject noun," a "predicate
noun," a "possessive noun," or an "object noun."

Example: Twelve <u>nations</u> signed the International Antarctic
Treaty in 1961.

Answer: *nations, subject noun*

The <u>treaty's</u> rules say that people can use Antarctica only for
peaceful purposes. The rules also promise <u>freedom</u> to do scientific study.
Today, many <u>countries</u> have permanent research stations in Antarctica,
and about 4,000 people are full-time <u>residents</u> during its summer months.

Pronouns

A **pronoun** is a word used in place of a noun. Some examples are *I, you, he, she, it, we, they, his, hers, her, its, me, myself, us, yours,* and so on.

Without pronouns: **Kevin said Kevin would be going to Kevin's grandmother's house this weekend.**

With pronouns: **Kevin said he would be going to his grandmother's house this weekend.**

706.1
Antecedents

An antecedent is the noun that the pronoun refers to or replaces. All pronouns (except interrogative and indefinite pronouns) have antecedents. (See page **474**.)

Jamal and Rick tried out for the team, and they both made it.
(*They* refers to *Jamal* and *Rick*; *it* refers to *team*.)

NOTE Pronouns must agree with their antecedents in number, person, and gender. (See pages **477–478**.)

Types of Pronouns

There are several types of pronouns. The most common type is the personal pronoun. (See the chart on page **710**.)

706.2
Personal Pronouns

A personal pronoun takes the place of a specific person (or thing) in a sentence. Some common personal pronouns are *I, you, he, she, it, we,* and *they.*

Suriana would not like to live in Buffalo, New York, because she does not like snow.

706.3
Relative Pronouns

A relative pronoun is both a pronoun and a connecting word. It connects a dependent clause to an independent clause in a complex sentence. Relative pronouns include *who, whose, which,* and *that.* (See page **514** and **684.6**.)

Buffalo, which often gets more than eight feet of snow in a year, is on the northeast shore of Lake Erie.

The United States city that gets the most snow is Valdez, Alaska.

706.4
Interrogative Pronouns

An interrogative pronoun helps ask a question.

Who wants to go to Alaska?

Which of the cities would you visit?

Whom would you like to travel with?

What did you say?

punctuate edit capitalize SPELL 707
improve
Using the Parts of Speech

Pronouns 1

■ Personal, Relative, and Interrogative Pronouns

 For each of the following sentences, identify the underlined pronouns as "personal," "relative," or "interrogative."

1. Great horned owls, <u>which</u> are the second-largest owls in North America, rely on their night vision to find prey in the dark.
   relative

2. An owl near Madison, Wisconsin, was starving in the wild because <u>it</u> had gone blind.

3. <u>Who</u> was brave enough to capture the creature?

4. Sue Theys, the woman <u>who</u> netted the owl, suspected that it had cataracts.

5. <u>She</u> and her husband took the owl to the veterinarian.

6. <u>What</u> does a vet do when an owl can't see?

7. Dr. Chris Murphy, a veterinary eye doctor, decided that <u>he</u> could perform surgery on the bird.

8. Dr. Murphy supervised two other doctors, and <u>they</u> implanted a pair of contact lenses into the bird's eyes.

9. <u>Whose</u> were they?

10. The lenses were originally made for another owl <u>that</u> ended up not having the surgery.

11. The Theyses gave the bird antibiotics and fed <u>it</u> mice during its recovery.

12. The great horned owl, <u>whose</u> wingspan can reach 55 inches, eats a variety of other animals.

Next Step: Go back to the previous sentences and write the antecedent for each of the personal and relative pronouns.

Pronouns . . .

Types of Pronouns

A demonstrative pronoun points out or identifies a noun without naming the noun. When used together in a sentence, *this* and *that* distinguish one item from another, and *these* and *those* distinguish one group from another. (See page **710**.)

> This **is a great idea;** that **was a nightmare.**

> These **are my favorite foods, and** those **are definitely not.**

NOTE When these words are used before a noun, they are *not* pronouns; rather, they are demonstrative adjectives.

> **Coming to** this **picnic was fun—and** those **ants think so, too.**

An intensive pronoun emphasizes, or *intensifies*, the noun or pronoun it refers to. Common intensive pronouns include *itself, myself, himself, herself,* and *yourself.*

> **Though the chameleon's quick-change act protects it from predators, the lizard** itself **can catch insects 10 inches away with its long, sticky tongue.**

> **When a chameleon changes its skin color—seemingly matching the background—the background colors** themselves **do not affect the chameleon's color changes.**

NOTE These sentences would be complete without the intensive pronoun. The pronoun simply emphasizes a particular noun.

A reflexive pronoun refers back to the subject of a sentence, and it is always an object (never a subject) in a sentence. Reflexive pronouns are the same as the intensive pronouns— *itself, myself, himself, herself, yourself,* and so on.

> **A chameleon protects** itself **from danger by changing colors.**
> (direct object)

> **A chameleon can give** itself **tasty meals of unsuspecting insects.**
> (indirect object)

> **I wish I could claim some of its amazing powers for** myself.
> (object of the preposition)

NOTE Unlike sentences with intensive pronouns, these sentences would *not* be complete without the reflexive pronouns.

Pronouns 2

■ **Demonstrative Pronouns**

Write whether the underlined word is a demonstrative adjective or a demonstrative pronoun. *Extra Challenge:* **Rewrite any sentence that contains a demonstrative adjective, changing the sentence so that the word is used as a pronoun instead.**

1. <u>This</u> cave is deep and dark.

demonstrative adjective   *This is a deep and dark cave.*

2. <u>That</u> concert was awful.

3. <u>This</u> is my absolute favorite meal!

4. <u>Those</u> are some of the birds I told you about.

5. <u>This</u> diagram is very confusing.

6. <u>That</u> was an unusual discovery.

■ **Intensive Pronouns**
■ **Reflexive Pronouns**

For each sentence below, write whether the underlined pronoun is "intensive" or "reflexive."

7. Have you <u>yourself</u> ever tried inventing something?

intensive

8. Many famous inventors have found <u>themselves</u> doing unusual things to prove their points.

9. Even Benjamin Franklin <u>himself</u>, a remarkable inventor, took risks.

10. I <u>myself</u> would be afraid to fly a kite during a lightning storm.

11. A metal wire on the kite drew the lightning's electricity to <u>itself</u>.

12. Mr. Franklin just wanted to prove something to <u>himself</u>.

Pronouns . . .

Types of Pronouns

An indefinite pronoun is a pronoun that does not have a specific antecedent (the noun or pronoun it replaces). (See page **475**.)

> Everything **about the chameleon is fascinating.**
>
> Someone **donated a chameleon to our class.**
>
> Anyone **who brings in a live insect can feed our chameleon.**

Types of Pronouns

Personal Pronouns

I, me, mine, my, we, us, our, ours, you, your, yours, they, them, their, theirs, he, him, his, she, her, hers, it, its

Relative Pronouns

who, whose, whom, which, what, that, whoever, whomever, whichever, whatever

Interrogative Pronouns

who, whose, whom, which, what

Demonstrative Pronouns

this, that, these, those

Intensive and Reflexive Pronouns

myself, himself, herself, itself, yourself, yourselves, themselves, ourselves

Indefinite Pronouns

all	both	everything	nobody	several
another	each	few	none	some
any	each one	many	no one	somebody
anybody	either	most	nothing	someone
anyone	everybody	much	one	something
anything	everyone	neither	other	such

Pronouns 3

■ Indefinite Pronouns

Number your paper from 1 to 3. Write the indefinite pronouns that appear in each of the three paragraphs below.

> *Example:* "Neither of my sisters will believe me," I thought.
>
> *Answer:* *neither*

"Marisol," I said, "you are someone who is trustworthy. I couldn't tell this to just anyone."

"You have nothing to worry about," Marisol said. "No one will hear a word from me."

I explained, "Something happened last night. I had one of those strange dreams again."

Pronoun Review

For each sentence below, identify the underlined pronoun as "relative," "demonstrative," or "indefinite."

1. The neighbors have a parrot <u>that</u> talks.

   relative

2. Anthony, <u>whose</u> family lives in the blue house, borrowed my bike.

3. <u>Everyone</u> was looking at a stereo in the cafeteria.

4. It was there for the dance, <u>which</u> would take place that evening.

5. Delia pointed and said, "I want to get <u>that</u> for my room."

6. If you asked <u>any</u> of the other kids, they'd say the same thing.

7. <u>This</u> is my favorite song of the CD!

Pronouns . . .

Number of a Pronoun

Pronouns can be either singular or plural in number.

    Singular: **I, you, he, she, it**   Plural: **we, you, they**

NOTE The pronouns *you, your,* and *yours* may be singular or plural.

Person of a Pronoun

The person of a pronoun tells whether the pronoun is speaking, being spoken to, or being spoken about. (See page **474**.)

A first-person pronoun is used in place of the name of the speaker or speakers.

    I am speaking.   **We are speaking.**

A second-person pronoun is used to name the person or thing spoken to.

    Eliza, will you please take out the garbage?

    You better stop grumbling!

A third-person pronoun is used to name the person or thing spoken about.

    Bill should listen if he wants to learn the words to this song.

    Charisse said that she already knows them.

    They will perform the song in the talent show.

Uses of Pronouns

A pronoun can be used as a subject, as an object, or to show possession. (See the chart on page **714**.)

A subject pronoun is used as the subject of a sentence (*I, you, he, she, it, we, they*).

    I like to surf the Net.

A subject pronoun is also used after a form of the *be* verb (*am, is, are, was, were, being, been*) if it repeats the subject. (See "Predicate Nouns," **704.5**.)

    "This is she," Mom replied into the telephone.

    "Yes, it was I," admitted the child who had eaten the cookies.

punctuate *edit* capitalize
SPELL
improve
713
Using the Parts of Speech

Pronouns 4

■ **Number of a Pronoun**
■ **Person of a Pronoun**

Write the antecedent for the missing pronoun in each sentence. Is it singular or plural? Is it first, second, or third person? Then, for each blank, write the correct pronoun.

1. The first time Maggie and I saw the movie *Bambi*, _____ cried.
   Maggie and I   *(plural, first person)*   *we*

2. Carlota bought a new leash for _____ dog.

3. Since the leash is leather, _____ will last a long time.

4. Franklin and John have soccer practice, so _____ will be late for dinner.

5. "Boys, you will have to make _____ own meal," Mom said.

6. I don't wake up in the morning until my cat licks _____ nose.

7. Theo isn't very tall, but _____ can really shoot hoops.

8. Grandpa gave this book to Kyle and me, and it is now _____ most prized possession.

9. Darcy, when you grab luggage off the carousel at the airport, make sure it's really _____.

10. Mr. and Mrs. Gunderson are trying to sell _____ house.

11. The towering maple tree has lost all of _____ leaves early this year.

12. I asked Jason to give _____ a ride to school.

13. Jessi and I don't like brussels sprouts, and _____ won't eat lima beans, either.

Next Step: Write a sentence in which you use a singular, second-person pronoun. Write a second sentence using a plural, first-person pronoun.

PARTS OF SPEECH

Pronouns . . .

Uses of Pronouns

An object pronoun (*me, you, him, her, it, us, them*) can be used as the object of a verb or preposition. (See **692.4**, **692.5**, and **742.1**.)

I'll call her as soon as I can. (direct object)

Hand me the phone book, please. (indirect object)

She thinks these flowers are from you. (object of the preposition)

A possessive pronoun shows possession or ownership. These possessive pronouns function as adjectives before nouns: *my, our, his, her, their, its,* and *your*.

School workers are painting our classroom this summer. Its walls will look much better.

These possessive pronouns can be used after verbs: *mine, ours, hers, his, theirs,* and *yours*.

I'm pretty sure this backpack is mine and that one is his.

NOTE An apostrophe is not needed with a possessive pronoun to show possession.

Uses of Personal Pronouns

	Singular Pronouns			Plural Pronouns		
	Subject Pronouns	Possessive Pronouns	Object Pronouns	Subject Pronouns	Possessive Pronouns	Object Pronouns
First Person	I	my, mine	me	we	our, ours	us
Second Person	you	your, yours	you	you	your, yours	you
Third Person	he	his	him	they	their, theirs	them
	she	her, hers	her			
	it	its	it			

punctuate *edit* capitalize SPELL 715
improve
Using the Parts of Speech

Pronouns 5

■ **Uses of Pronouns**

For each numbered sentence below, write the underlined pronoun or pronouns and identify each as a "subject pronoun," an "object pronoun," or a "possessive pronoun."

Example: Are <u>you</u> aware of the strange creatures of the sea?
Answer: *you (subject pronoun)*

(1) <u>It</u> is home to lobsters, octopuses, and jellyfish, but one of its most unusual inhabitants has to be the squid. Squid range in size from a few inches to more than 50 feet. **(2)** Ten arms help <u>them</u> swim. **(3)** <u>They</u> move—always backward—by forcing water through a special valve that acts like a jet engine. **(4)** This backward motion probably confuses any fish that might want to eat <u>them</u>. **(5)** A squid can also release an inky cloud that covers <u>its</u> escape.

(6) Even though giant squid live in deep, dark water, <u>their</u> eyes are the largest in the animal kingdom, and they have excellent eyesight. **(7)** <u>This</u> allows them to find food easily. Their one great natural enemy is the sperm whale; however, people also catch tons of squid. **(8)** <u>We</u> use them as bait for other fish and, of course, as food for <u>us</u>, too. **(9)** (<u>My</u> dad loves to eat squid at restaurants.)

Steve O'Shea is a New Zealand zoologist and an expert on squid. **(10)** <u>He</u> and <u>his</u> team of researchers recently caught what they call a "colossal" squid—even larger than the 50-foot giant squid. **(11)** He says, "<u>You</u> are not going to want to meet these in the water." **(12)** I have to believe <u>him</u>!

Next Step: Write two or three sentences about a sea creature. Use the pronoun *it* in its subject, object, and possessive forms.

Test Prep

Number your paper from 1 to 16. For each underlined word in the paragraphs below, choose the letter of the answer that best describes it from the following list.

A common subject noun   **E** proper object noun

B common object noun   **F** subject pronoun

C common predicate noun   **G** object pronoun

D proper subject noun   **H** possessive pronoun

The <u>man</u> whose face appears on the $100 bill was never a
<u>1</u>

<u>president</u>, but Benjamin Franklin was a very smart man. During
<u>2</u>

his 84 years, <u>Franklin</u> was an <u>inventor</u>, a writer, and a politician.
<u>3</u>　　　　　<u>4</u>

<u>Everyone</u> knows about Franklin's famous experiment with
<u>5</u>

lightning and a kite. But even before <u>that</u>, he discovered that
<u>6</u>

electricity has positive and negative charges. With this <u>knowledge</u>,
<u>7</u>

<u>he</u> created the first batteries.
<u>8</u>

As the owner of his own print <u>shop</u>, Franklin could publish <u>his</u>
<u>9</u>　　　　　　　　　<u>10</u>

essays. When he bought the *Pennsylvania Gazette*, he published
<u>11</u>

both his and others' opinions. A free <u>press</u> was important to him.
<u>12</u>

Franklin became a member of the <u>Pennsylvania Assembly</u> in
<u>13</u>

1751. The <u>Second Continental Congress</u> welcomed <u>him</u> 24 years
<u>14</u>　　　　　　　　　　　<u>15</u>

later. Franklin and the other members wanted independence from

Britain. <u>Their</u> creation of an army to defend the colonies was the
<u>16</u>

beginning of a new country.

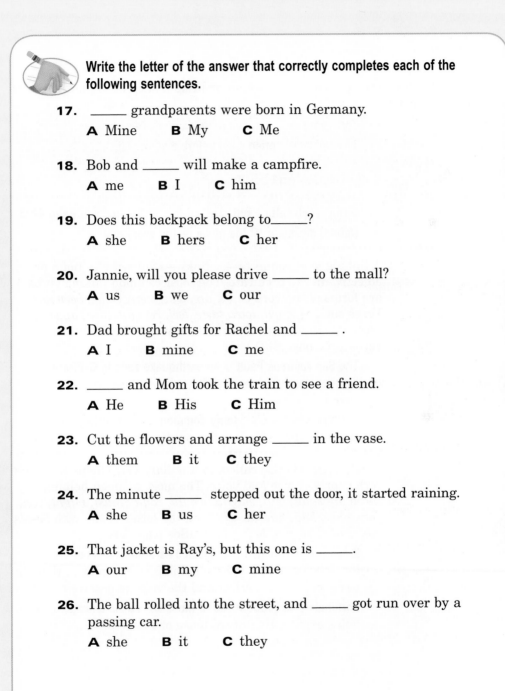

Write the letter of the answer that correctly completes each of the following sentences.

17. _____ grandparents were born in Germany.
    A Mine   **B** My   **C** Me

18. Bob and _____ will make a campfire.
    A me   **B** I   **C** him

19. Does this backpack belong to_____?
    A she   **B** hers   **C** her

20. Jannie, will you please drive _____ to the mall?
    A us   **B** we   **C** our

21. Dad brought gifts for Rachel and _____ .
    A I   **B** mine   **C** me

22. _____ and Mom took the train to see a friend.
    A He   **B** His   **C** Him

23. Cut the flowers and arrange _____ in the vase.
    A them   **B** it   **C** they

24. The minute _____ stepped out the door, it started raining.
    A she   **B** us   **C** her

25. That jacket is Ray's, but this one is _____.
    A our   **B** my   **C** mine

26. The ball rolled into the street, and _____ got run over by a passing car.
    A she   **B** it   **C** they

Verbs

A **verb** is a word that shows action or links a subject to another word in a sentence.

> Tornadoes cause tremendous damage. (action verb)
>
> The weather is often calm before a storm. (linking verb)

Types of Verbs

718.1
Action Verbs

An action verb tells what the subject is doing. (See page **480**.)

> Natural disasters hit the globe nearly every day.

718.2
Linking Verbs

A linking verb connects—or links—a subject to a noun or an adjective in the predicate. The most common linking verbs are forms of the verb *be* (*is, are, was, were, being, been, am*). Verbs such as *smell, look, taste, feel, remain, turn, appear, become, sound, seem, grow,* and *stay* can also be linking verbs. (See page **480**.)

> The San Andreas Fault is an earthquake zone in California. (The linking verb *is* connects the subject to the predicate noun *zone*.)
>
> Earthquakes there are fairly common. (The linking verb *are* connects the subject to the predicate adjective *common*.)

718.3
Helping Verbs

A helping verb (also called an auxiliary verb) helps the main verb express tense and voice. The most common helping verbs are *shall, will, should, would, could, must, might, can, may, have, had, has, do, did,* and the forms of the verb *be—is, are, was, were, am, being, been.* (See page **481**.)

> It has been estimated that 500,000 earthquakes occur around the world every year. (These helping verbs indicate that the tense is present perfect and the voice is passive.)
>
> Fortunately, only about 100 of those will cause damage. (*Will* helps express the future tense of the verb.)

punctuate edit capitalize
improve SPELL
719
Using the Parts of Speech

Verbs 1 ■ Action, Linking, and Helping Verbs

For the numbered sentences in the following paragraphs, write the underlined verb and identify each as an "action verb," a "linking verb," or a "helping verb."

Example: A boat <u>will</u> not float unless there is enough water.
Answer: will (helping verb)

(1) You know that boats <u>need</u> a certain depth of water in order to float. **(2)** What happens when people <u>must</u> take a boat where the water level is too low? **(3)** Engineers can build a dam, which <u>raises</u> the water level on one side of the dam. This enables boats to travel there. **(4)** But how <u>do</u> the boats get from one side of the dam to the other?

A "lock" in the dam allows boats through. **(5)** A lock <u>is</u> a huge container with massive gates on each end, built right into the wall of the dam. **(6)** When a boat <u>approaches</u> the dam, the gates on one end of the lock open so that the boat <u>can</u> enter. Once it's all the way in, the gates close. **(7)** The boat <u>remains</u> steady in the lock while the lock operators either add water (to raise the boat) or remove water (to lower the boat). **(8)** When the water level <u>reaches</u> the water level on the other side of the dam, the opposite gates open, and the boat continues on its way.

(9) Both small boats and large ships can <u>be</u> lifted or lowered in this way. **(10)** The process <u>seems</u> very slow, but boats and ships can go places that <u>would</u> have been impossible to reach without a system of locks.

Next Step: Write two or three sentences about being on a boat. Use all three types of verbs.

Verbs . . .

Tenses of Verbs

A verb has three principal parts: *present, past,* and *past participle*. (The part used with the helping verbs *has, have,* or *had* is called the past participle.)

All six of the tenses are formed from these principal parts. The past and past participle of regular verbs are formed by adding *ed* to the present tense. The past and past participle of irregular verbs are formed with different spellings. (See the chart on page **722**.)

720.1

Present Tense Verbs

The present tense of a verb expresses action (or a state of being) that is happening now or that happens continually or regularly. (See page **483**.)

> The universe **is** gigantic. It **takes** my breath away.

720.2

Past Tense Verbs

The past tense of a verb expresses action (or a state of being) that was completed in the past. (See page **483**.)

> To most people many years ago, the universe **was** the earth, the sun, and some stars. The universe **reached** only as far as the eye could see.

720.3

Future Tense Verbs

The future tense of a verb expresses action that *will* take place. (See page **483**.)

> Maybe I **will visit** another galaxy in my lifetime.
>
> Somebody **will find** a way to do it.

SCHOOL DAZE

I **know** the answer!

Okay, but I **said** you **will have** to sing the answer . . . go ahead!

punctuate *edit* capitalize
SPELL
improve
721
Using the Parts of Speech

Verbs 2

■ Present Tense, Past Tense, and Future Tense Verbs

**Make three columns with the headings "Present," "Past," and "Future."
Write each of the underlined verbs in the appropriate column.**

Imagine that you <u>are standing</u> near a friend and talking.
Suddenly, someone tickles you. First, you scream, and then you can't
stop laughing. What is going on? Why are people ticklish, anyway?

The answer goes back in time to the beginning of humanity.
Feeling a tickle was simply a natural defense. It <u>warned</u> a person
that something (say, a spider) <u>was touching</u> the skin.

When feeling a light tickle, hardly anyone <u>will laugh</u>. It's the
heavy tickle that causes uncontrollable laughter. The tickle really
<u>causes</u> a panic reaction, especially when it is a surprise. Although
heavy tickling <u>results</u> in laughter, it is not always a pleasant
experience. The sensation of a tickle actually <u>affects</u> the nerves the
same way pain does. In fact, tickling that went on and on <u>was</u> a
form of torture in the Middle Ages.

Scientists aren't sure why laughing automatically goes along
with tickling, but they <u>do know</u> that it has also been seen among
apes. Apes who <u>were tickled</u> in the armpits <u>made</u> an uncontrollable
sound much like human laughter.

So now you know how you <u>will react</u> the next time you're
tickled. First, you will have a brief point of panic (though you
probably <u>won't realize</u> it). Then you <u>will laugh</u>, even if you don't
think it's funny!

Next Step: Write a sentence in present tense about your thoughts on
tickling. Then write it in past and future tenses, too.

Common Irregular Verbs and Their Principal Parts

The principal parts of the common irregular verbs are listed below. The part used with the helping verbs *has, have,* or *had* is called the **past participle**. (Also see page 481.)

Present Tense: I write.   She hides.
Past Tense: Earlier I wrote.   Earlier she hid.
Past Participle: I have written. She has hidden.

Present Tense	Past Tense	Past Participle	Present Tense	Past Tense	Past Participle
am, is, are	was, were	been	lead	led	led
begin	began	begun	lie (recline)	lay	lain
bid (offer)	bid	bid	lie (deceive)	lied	lied
bid (order)	bade	bidden	make	made	made
bite	bit	bitten	ride	rode	ridden
blow	blew	blown	ring	rang	rung
break	broke	broken	rise	rose	risen
bring	brought	brought	run	ran	run
burst	burst	burst	see	saw	seen
buy	bought	bought	set	set	set
catch	caught	caught	shake	shook	shaken
come	came	come	shine (polish)	shined	shined
dive	dived, dove	dived	shine (light)	shone	shone
do	did	done	shrink	shrank	shrunk
draw	drew	drawn	sing	sang, sung	sung
drink	drank	drunk	sink	sank, sunk	sunk
drive	drove	driven	sit	sat	sat
eat	ate	eaten	sleep	slept	slept
fall	fell	fallen	speak	spoke	spoken
fight	fought	fought	spring	sprang, sprung	sprung
flee	fled	fled	steal	stole	stolen
fly	flew	flown	strive	strove	striven
forsake	forsook	forsaken	swear	swore	sworn
freeze	froze	frozen	swim	swam	swum
get	got	gotten, got	swing	swung	swung
give	gave	given	take	took	taken
go	went	gone	tear	tore	torn
grow	grew	grown	throw	threw	thrown
hang (execute)	hanged	hanged	wake	woke, waked	woken, waked
hang (dangle)	hung	hung	wear	wore	worn
hide	hid	hidden, hid	weave	wove	woven
know	knew	known	wring	wrung	wrung
lay (place)	laid	laid	write	wrote	written

punctuate *edit* capitalize
improve SPELL **723**
Using the Parts of Speech

Verbs 3

■ **Irregular Verbs**

For each blank, write the correct form of the irregular verb given in parentheses at the end of each sentence.

1. Last summer, we spent most of our time at the community pool, and we _____ for hours. (*swim*)

   swam

2. We _____ our swimsuits just about everywhere. (*wear*)

3. Always hungry after swimming, we _____ popcorn. (*make*)

4. I don't think I have ever _____ so much popcorn in one summer! (*eat*)

5. When we returned to school, the teachers remarked how we had _____. (*grow*)

6. Diego told us all how he _____ while rock climbing with his dad. (*fall*)

7. He had _____ his leg. (*break*)

8. Dan said, "Our family _____ to Brazil for a few weeks." (*fly*)

9. He _____ some of his souvenirs to show to the class. (*bring*)

10. Teresa reported that her grandmother had _____ her a surprise birthday party. (*throw*)

11. Jaimie explained that her family was bigger now—since her cousin had _____ to live with them. (*come*)

12. Lara stayed at a ranch and _____ a horse every day. (*ride*)

13. Steve said he just _____ as much as he could. (*sleep*)

14. Ms. Logan reminded us, "The school year has _____, so let's get to work." (*begin*)

Next Step: Write some sentences about your summer activities. Use the past tense and past participle of the verbs *see* and *take*.

Verbs . . .

Tenses of Verbs

724.1

Present Perfect Tense Verbs

The present perfect tense verb expresses action that began in the past but continues or is completed in the present. The present perfect tense is formed by adding *has* or *have* to the past participle. (Also see page **484**.)

> I have wondered **for some time how the stars got their names.**

> A visible star **has emitted light for thousands of years.**

724.2

Past Perfect Tense Verbs

The past perfect tense verb expresses action that began in the past and was completed in the past. This tense is formed by adding *had* to the past participle. (Also see page **484**.)

> I had hoped **to see a shooting star on our camping trip.**

724.3

Future Perfect Tense Verbs

A future perfect tense verb expresses action that will begin in the future and will be completed by a specific time in the future. The future perfect tense is formed by adding *will have* to the past participle. (Also see page **484**.)

> By the middle of this century, we probably will have discovered **many more stars, planets, and galaxies.**

724.4

Present Continuous Tense Verbs

A present continuous tense verb expresses action that is not completed at the time of stating it. The present continuous tense is formed by adding *am, is,* or *are* to the *ing* form of the main verb.

> Scientists are learning **a great deal from their study of the sky.**

724.5

Past Continuous Tense Verbs

A past continuous tense verb expresses action that was happening at a certain time in the past. This tense is formed by adding *was* or *were* to the *ing* form of the main verb.

> Astronomers were beginning **their quest for knowledge hundreds of years ago.**

724.6

Future Continuous Tense Verbs

A future continuous tense verb expresses action that will take place at a certain time in the future. This tense is formed by adding *will be* to the *ing* form of the main verb.

> Someday astronauts will be going **to Mars.**

This tense can also be formed by adding a phrase noting the future (*are going to*) plus *be* to the *ing* form of the main verb.

> They are going to be performing **many experiments.**

punctuate edit capitalize SPELL
improve
Using the Parts of Speech
725

Verbs 4

■ **Perfect Tense Verbs**

For each sentence below, choose the helping verb that best fits the sentence. Then write whether the entire verb tense is "present perfect," "past perfect," or "future perfect."

1. My family (*has, will have*) taken a driving vacation every year for the past eight years.
has (present perfect)

2. Last year, we (*had, will have*) decided to drive from our home in Ohio to New Mexico.

3. Taking two-lane highways instead of the interstates, we (*had, will have*) wanted to see the "real" America.

4. This year, we're going someplace we (*have, will have*) wanted to see for several years: Maine.

5. By the time we complete this year's vacation, we (*had, will have*) driven in every state except Hawaii.

■ **Continuous Tense Verbs**

For each sentence below, identify the underlined verb tense as "present continuous," "past continuous," or "future continuous."

6. I <u>am looking</u> forward to our time in Maine.
present continuous

7. Originally, we <u>were thinking</u> of going to Montana.

8. I <u>was trying</u> to persuade everyone that we should go someplace we haven't been before.

9. My suggestion worked; now we <u>are planning</u> the route we'll take to Maine.

10. In just a few weeks, we <u>will be loading</u> the car for our trip.

11. For the first time, my brother <u>is going to be driving</u> some of the way.

Verbs . . .
Forms of Verbs

The voice of a verb tells you whether the subject is doing the action or is receiving the action. A verb is in the active voice (in any tense) if the subject is doing the action in a sentence. (See page **482**.)

> I dream **of going to galaxies light-years from Earth.**

> I will travel **in an ultra-fast spaceship.**

A verb is in the passive voice if the subject is not doing the action. The action is done *by* someone or something else. The passive voice is always indicated with a helping verb plus a past participle or a past tense verb.

> **My daydreams often** are shattered **by reality.** (The subject *daydreams* is not doing the action.)

> **Of course, reality** can be seen **differently by different people.** (The subject *reality* is not doing the action.)

Tense	Active Voice		Passive Voice	
	Singular	**Plural**	**Singular**	**Plural**
Present Tense	I find	we find	I am found	we are found
	you find	you find	you are found	you are found
	he/she/it finds	they find	he/she/it is found	they are found
Past Tense	I found	we found	I was found	we were found
	you found	you found	you were found	you were found
	he found	they found	he/she/it was found	they were found
Future Tense	I will find	we will find	I will be found	we will be found
	you will find	you will find	you will be found	you will be found
	he will find	they will find	he/she/it will be found	they will be found
Present Perfect	I have found	we have found	I have been found	we have been found
	you have found	you have found	you have been found	you have been found
	he has found	they have found	he/she/it has been found	they have been found
Past Perfect	I had found	we had found	I had been found	we had been found
	you had found	you had found	you had been found	you had been found
	he had found	they had found	he/she/it had been found	they had been found
Future Perfect	I will have found	we will have found	I will have been found	we will have been found
	you will have found	you will have found	you will have been found	you will have been found
	he will have found	they will have found	he/she/it will have been found	they will have been found

punctuate *edit* capitalize SPELL 727
improve
Using the Parts of Speech

Verbs 5

■ Active or Passive Voice

Write whether each sentence below is in the active or passive voice.

1. Marta is going to run in a marathon.
   active

2. The distance of a marathon, 26.2 miles, can be driven in about half an hour by someone going 60 miles per hour.

3. Marta has already spent 15 weeks getting ready.

4. She will finish her training in the next six weeks.

5. Marta was told by her doctor that she is in great shape.

6. Stretches are done by all the runners before they compete.

7. First-time competitors are advised by experienced runners to go slow and save up their energy.

8. A runner's endurance is improved by this strategy.

9. During a race, many runners walk for a minute or two to get a little rest.

10. Some people are energized by running a long distance.

11. I would only feel exhausted!

12. Two benefits of running in marathons are increased energy and a sense of accomplishment.

Next Step: Choose two or three of the sentences above that you marked "passive" and rewrite them in the active voice.

Verbs . . .

Forms of Verbs

728.1
Singular and Plural Verbs

A singular subject needs a singular verb. A plural subject needs a plural verb. For action verbs, only the third-person singular verb form is different: *I wonder, we wonder, you wonder, she wonders, they wonder*. Some linking verbs, however, have several different forms.

| First Person | Singular: I am (or was) a good student. |
| | Plural: We are (or were) good students. |

| Second Person | Singular: You are (or were) a cheerleader. |
| | Plural: You are (or were) cheerleaders. |

| Third Person | Singular: He is (or was) on the wrestling team. |
| | Plural: They are (or were) also on the team. |

728.2
Transitive Verbs

A transitive verb is a verb that transfers its action to a direct object. The object makes the meaning of the verb complete. A transitive verb is always an action verb (never a linking verb). (See page **570**.)

An earthquake shook **San Francisco in 1906.** (*Shook* transfers its action to the direct object *San Francisco*. Without *San Francisco* the meaning of the verb *shook* is incomplete.)

The city's people spent **many years rebuilding.** (Without the direct object *years*, the verb's meaning is incomplete.)

A transitive verb transfers the action directly to a direct object and indirectly to an indirect object.

Fires destroyed **the city.** (direct object: *city*)

Our teacher gave **us the details.** (indirect object: *us*; direct object: *details*)

See **692.4** and **692.5** for more on direct and indirect objects.

728.3
Intransitive Verbs

An intransitive verb does not need an object to complete its meaning. (See page **570**.)

Abigail was shopping. (The verb's meaning is complete.)

Her stomach felt queasy. (*Queasy* is a predicate adjective describing *stomach*; there is no direct object.)

She lay **down on the bench.** (Again, there is no direct object. *Down* is an adverb modifying *lay*.)

punctuate edit capitalize
improve SPELL **729**
Using the Parts of Speech

Verbs 6

■ **Transitive Verbs**

The following sentences have transitive verbs. Write the direct object from each one.

1. Ruby keeps her jewelry in a tackle box.
   jewelry

2. She especially likes the ring that was her grandmother's.

3. She chose it from her grandma's velvet-lined jewelry box.

4. Ruby wants a real jewelry box, too.

5. Her mom will buy one at a rummage sale.

6. Ruby will put her best rings and bracelets in it.

■ **Intransitive Verbs**

For each of the following pairs of sentences, write the letter of the sentence that has an intransitive verb.

7. **A.** Luke sees well.
   B. Luke sees a red-tailed hawk.
   A

8. **A.** Ken tasted green peppers in the meat loaf.
   B. The meat loaf tasted funny.

9. **A.** Corinne walked the dog between 3:30 and 4:00 p.m.
   B. Corinne walked briskly along the path.

10. **A.** Mr. Moss speaks quite softly.
    B. Mr. Moss speaks three languages.

11. **A.** He is growing sunflowers in his backyard.
    B. They are growing so big!

12. **A.** Naomi sketches with charcoal and colored pencils.
    B. Naomi sketches pictures of wild animals.

PARTS OF SPEECH

Verbs . . .

Forms of Verbs

Some verbs can be either transitive or intransitive.

> Transitive: **She** reads **my note.**   **Albert** ate **an apple.**
>
> Intransitive: **She** reads **aloud.**   **Albert** ate **already.**

Verbals

A **verbal** is a word that is made from a verb but acts as
another part of speech. Gerunds, participles, and infinitives
are verbals. (Also see page **485**.)

A gerund is a verb form that ends in *ing* and is used as a
noun. A gerund often begins a gerund phrase.

> **Worrying is useless.** (The gerund is the subject noun.)
>
> **You should stop** worrying about so many things. (The gerund
> phrase is the direct object.)

A participle is a verb form ending in *ing* or *ed*. A participle is
used as an *adjective* and often begins a participial phrase.

> **The idea of the earth** shaking **and** splitting **both fascinates and
> frightens me.** (The participles modify *earth*.)
>
> Rattling in the cabinets, **the dishes were about to crash to the
> floor.** (The participial phrase modifies *dishes*.)
>
> **Why doesn't this** tired **earth just stand still?** (The participle
> modifies *earth*.)

An infinitive is a verb form introduced by *to*. It may be used
as a *noun*, an *adjective*, or an *adverb*. It often begins an
infinitive phrase.

> **My need** to whisper **is due to this secret.** (The infinitive is an
> adjective modifying *need*.)
>
> **I am afraid** to swim. (The infinitive is an adverb modifying
> the predicate adjective *afraid*.)
>
> To overcome this fear **is my goal.** (The infinitive phrase is
> used as a noun and is the subject of this sentence.)

punctuate *edit* capitalize
improve   SPELL   731
Using the Parts of Speech

Verbs 7 ■ Verbals

For the sentences below, write the word or words that function as a verbal. The number of each type of verbal is indicated in parentheses at the end of each sentence.

1. Every living thing needs water to survive. (*1 participle, 1 infinitive*)

   living, to survive

2. Living for several weeks without food is possible, but a person would last only a few days without water. (*1 gerund*)

3. Water allows the human body to work better by helping every system run more smoothly. (*1 infinitive, 1 gerund*)

4. Water is a required part of blood circulation and muscle movement.
   (*1 participle*)

5. To keep cool, the body releases water (sweat) through pores in the skin. (*1 infinitive*)

6. Cushioning joints and organs, water plays an important part in protecting the body from harm. (*1 participle, 1 gerund*)

7. Skin needs water to preserve its softness and flexibility.
   (*1 infinitive*)

8. Drinking enough water is a key to good health. (*1 gerund*)

9. Without enough water, the body can easily become dehydrated.
   (*1 participle*)

10. Feeling irritable and restless can be a sign of a lack of fluid.
    (*1 gerund*)

11. Increased thirst and decreased stretchiness of the skin are other symptoms. (*2 participles*)

12. It is vital to get water into a person with these symptoms.
    (*1 infinitive*)

Next Step: Write a sentence about being in water. Use one of the verbal forms.

Adjectives

An **adjective** is a word used to describe a noun or a pronoun. Adjectives tell *what kind, how many,* or *which one.* They usually come before the word they describe. (See pages **486–489.**)

ancient **dinosaurs**   800 **species**   that **triceratops**

Adjectives are the same whether the word they describe is singular or plural.

small **brain**—or—small **brains**   large **tooth**—or—large **teeth**

732.1
Articles

The articles *a, an,* and *the* are adjectives.

A brontosaurus was an animal about 70 feet long.

The huge dinosaur lived on land and ate plants.

732.2
Proper Adjectives

A proper adjective is formed from a proper noun, and it is always capitalized. (See **618.1.**)

A Chicago museum is home to the skeleton of one of these beasts. (*Chicago* functions as a proper adjective describing the noun *museum.*)

732.3
Common Adjectives

A common adjective is any adjective that is not proper. It is not capitalized (unless it is the first word in a sentence).

Ancient mammoths were huge, woolly creatures.

They lived in the ice fields of Siberia.

Special Kinds of Adjectives

732.4
Demonstrative Adjectives

A demonstrative adjective points out a particular noun. *This* and *these* point out something nearby; *that* and *those* point out something at a distance.

This mammoth is huge, but that mammoth is even bigger.

NOTE When a noun does not follow *this, these, that,* or *those,* these words are pronouns, not adjectives. (See **708.1.**)

732.5
Compound Adjectives

A compound adjective is made up of two or more words. (Sometimes it is hyphenated.)

Dinosaurs were egg-laying animals.

The North American Allosaurus had sharp teeth and powerful jaws.

punctuate *edit* capitalize
improve SPELL **733**
Using the Parts of Speech

Adjectives 1

■ **Proper and Common Adjectives**

Write one common adjective and one proper adjective from each sentence below. (Do not include the articles *a, an,* **or** *the.***)**

1. Guion Bluford, Jr., was the first African American astronaut to travel in space.

first, African American

2. On a hot August day in 1983, the space shuttle *Challenger* blasted off.

3. Bluford was the mission specialist on that *Challenger* expedition.

4. Bluford was a successful pilot in the air force after he graduated from an East Coast college.

5. Then he joined the NASA training program and went through four years of difficult training.

6. In 1991 and 1992, Bluford traveled with the *Discovery* crew on his last two trips into space.

■ **Demonstrative and Compound Adjectives**

Write one demonstrative adjective and one compound adjective from each sentence below.

7. "Alpacas are semi-tame mammals, and this one lives on my uncle's farm," said Abrita, showing a photograph to the class.

this, semi-tame

8. "What an awesome-looking animal! May I see that picture again?" asked Tommy.

9. "These animals live in South American grasslands," she said.

10. "Is this animal classified as a plant-eating mammal?" asked Anne.

11. "Yes," she said, "and notice those two-toed feet! Aren't they funny?"

Adjectives . . .

Special Kinds of Adjectives

734.1
Indefinite Adjectives

An indefinite adjective gives approximate, or indefinite, information (*any, few, many, most,* and so on). It does not tell exactly how many or how much.

Some **mammoths were heavier than today's elephants.**

734.2
Predicate Adjectives

A predicate adjective follows a linking verb and describes the subject.

Mammoths were once abundant, **but now they are** extinct.

Forms of Adjectives

734.3
Positive Adjectives

The positive form describes a noun or pronoun without comparing it to anyone or anything else.

The Eurostar is a fast **train that runs between London, Paris, and Brussels.**

It is an impressive **train.**

734.4
Comparative Adjectives

The comparative form of an adjective (*er*) compares two persons, places, things, or ideas. (See page **487**.)

The Eurostar is faster **than the Orient Express.**

Some adjectives that have more than one syllable show comparisons by their *er* suffix, but many of them use the modifiers *more* or *less*.

It is a speedier **commuter train than the Tobu Railway trains in Japan.**

This train is more impressive **than my commuter train.**

734.5
Superlative Adjectives

The superlative form (*est* or *most* or *least*) compares three or more persons, places, things, or ideas. (See page **487**.)

In fact, the Eurostar is the fastest **train in Europe.**

It is the most impressive **commuter train in the world.**

734.6
Irregular Forms

Some adjectives use completely different words to express comparison.

good, better, best   bad, worse, worst

many, more, most   little, less, least

punctuate *edit* capitalize SPELL
improve
735
Using the Parts of Speech

Adjectives 2

■ **Indefinite and Predicate Adjectives**

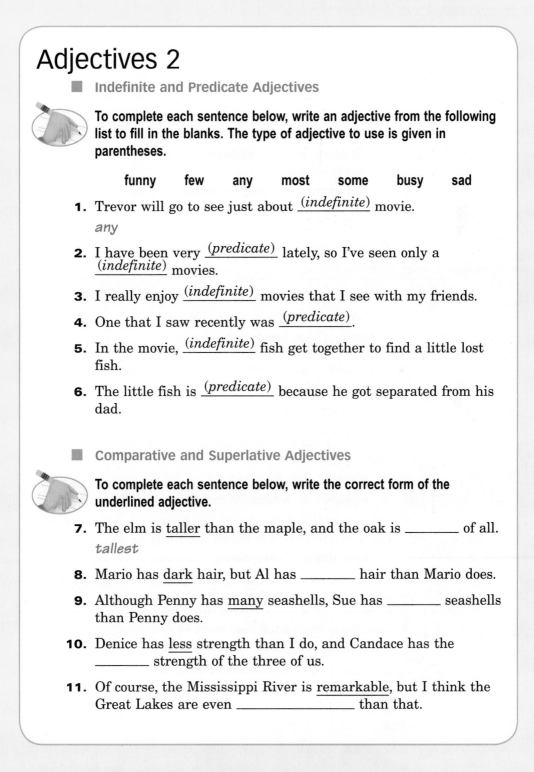

To complete each sentence below, write an adjective from the following list to fill in the blanks. The type of adjective to use is given in parentheses.

> funny   few   any   most   some   busy   sad

1. Trevor will go to see just about _(indefinite)_ movie.
any

2. I have been very _(predicate)_ lately, so I've seen only a _(indefinite)_ movies.

3. I really enjoy _(indefinite)_ movies that I see with my friends.

4. One that I saw recently was _(predicate)_.

5. In the movie, _(indefinite)_ fish get together to find a little lost fish.

6. The little fish is _(predicate)_ because he got separated from his dad.

■ **Comparative and Superlative Adjectives**

To complete each sentence below, write the correct form of the underlined adjective.

7. The elm is <u>taller</u> than the maple, and the oak is _____ of all.
tallest

8. Mario has <u>dark</u> hair, but Al has _____ hair than Mario does.

9. Although Penny has <u>many</u> seashells, Sue has _____ seashells than Penny does.

10. Denice has <u>less</u> strength than I do, and Candace has the _____ strength of the three of us.

11. Of course, the Mississippi River is <u>remarkable</u>, but I think the Great Lakes are even _____ than that.

Adverbs

An **adverb** is a word used to modify a verb, an adjective, or another adverb. It tells *how, when, where, how often,* or *how much.* Adverbs can come before or after the words they modify. (See pages **490–493**.)

Dad snores loudly. (*Loudly* modifies the verb *snores.*)

His snores are really **explosive.** (*Really* modifies the adjective *explosive.*)

Dad snores very **loudly.** (*Very* modifies the adverb *loudly.*)

Types of Adverbs

There are four basic types of adverbs: *time, place, manner,* and *degree.*

736.1
Adverbs of Time

Adverbs of time tell *when, how often,* and *how long.*

tomorrow   often   never   always

Jen rarely **has time to go swimming.**

736.2
Adverbs of Place

Adverbs of place tell *where, to where,* or *from where.*

there   backward   outside

We'll set up our tent here.

736.3
Adverbs of Manner

Adverbs of manner often end in *ly* and tell *how* something is done.

unkindly   gently   well

Ahmed boldly **entered the dark cave.**

Some words used as adverbs can be written with or without the *ly* ending. When in doubt, use the *ly* form.

slow, slowly   deep, deeply

NOTE Not all words ending in *ly* are adverbs. *Lovely,* for example, is an adjective.

736.4
Adverbs of Degree

Adverbs of degree tell *how much* or *how little.*

scarcely   entirely   generally   very   really

Jess is usually **the leader in these situations.**

Adverbs 1

■ **Types of Adverbs**

For each numbered, underlined adverb in the paragraph below, write whether it tells "how," "when," "where," "how often," or "how much." Then write whether it is an adverb of "time," "place," "manner," or "degree."

    Example: The human ear is <u>rather</u> amazing.
    Answer: *how much; degree*

People can hear <u>very</u> loud sounds and <u>extremely</u> soft sounds.
     1   **2**

How does an ear hear? The vibration of molecules <u>constantly</u>
                      3

produces sound waves. The waves enter the ear canal and strike the

eardrum, causing it to vibrate <u>rapidly</u>. These vibrations travel
                 4

<u>forward</u> through the rest of the middle ear, hitting the three tiny
  5

bones <u>there</u>. Their vibrations make waves in the fluid inside the
    6

cochlea, activating tiny, hair-like nerve cells that <u>immediately</u> turn
                      7

the vibrations into electrical signals. The auditory nerve <u>then</u>
                    8

transmits the information to the brain, and the brain interprets the

information as sound. When both ears work <u>together</u>, people can
                 9

<u>almost</u> always tell where a sound is coming from.
 10

Next Step: Use a thesaurus to look up synonyms for three of the underlined adverbs in the paragraph above. Write sentences using these synonyms.

Adverbs . . .
Special Kinds of Adverbs

738.1
Conjunctive Adverbs

A conjunctive adverb can be used as a conjunction and shows a connection or a transition between two independent clauses. Most often, a conjunctive adverb follows a semicolon in a compound sentence; however, it can also appear at the beginning or end of a sentence. (Note that the previous sentence has an example of a conjunctive adverb.)

| also | besides | however | instead |
| meanwhile | nevertheless | therefore | |

Forms of Adverbs

Many adverbs—especially adverbs of manner—have three forms: *positive, comparative,* and *superlative.*

738.2
Positive Adverbs

The positive form describes but does not make a comparison.

Juan woke up late.

He quickly **ate some breakfast.**

738.3
Comparative Adverbs

The comparative form of an adverb (*er*) compares two things.

Juan woke up later **than he usually did.** (See page **491**.)

Some adverbs that have more than one syllable show comparisons by their *er* suffix, but many of them use the modifiers *more* or *less*.

He ate his breakfast more quickly **than usual.**

738.4
Superlative Adverbs

The superlative form (*est* or *most* or *least*) compares three or more things. (See page **491**.)

Of the past three days, Juan woke up latest **on Saturday.**

Of the past three days, he ate his breakfast least quickly **on Saturday.**

738.5
Irregular Forms

Some adverbs use completely different words to express comparison.

Positive	Comparative	Superlative
well	better	best
badly	worse	worst

punctuate *edit* capitalize
SPELL
improve 739
Using the Parts of Speech

Adverbs 2

■ **Conjunctive Adverbs**

Number your paper from 1 to 3. In the following paragraph, find and write the three conjunctive adverbs.

> *Example:* Sojourner Truth did not dwell on her past; instead, she helped others pursue freedom.
>
> *Answer:* *instead*

We often think of the South when we think of slavery in the United States; however, one of the most famous slaves was a Northern-born woman named Sojourner Truth. She was first sold at the age of 11, going from owner to owner after that. Nevertheless, she remained proud and had a strong faith. She finally gained her freedom and went to New York City. There she took the name Sojourner Truth and preached her faith. Meanwhile, she met and joined others who spoke out for freedom and equality. Their strong voices made a difference for many people.

■ **Forms of Adverbs**

For each sentence below, write the correct form (comparative or superlative) of the underlined adverb.

4. Sojourner Truth worked <u>hard</u> than any of her owners.
   harder

5. As a slave, she was treated <u>badly</u> than the animals on a farm.

6. Her first language was Dutch, yet she spoke English <u>well</u> than many others.

7. Sojourner pushed <u>early</u> for equal rights than most other women.

8. Her voice boomed <u>deeply</u> than some men's voices.

9. Of all the speakers' messages, her call for justice was delivered <u>effectively</u>.

Test Prep

Number your paper from 1 to 12. For each underlined part of the paragraphs below, write the letter (from the next page) of the best choice.

The pancreas, an organ <u>finded</u> beneath and behind the
1
stomach, <u>produce</u> a hormone called insulin. Insulin is released into
2
the bloodstream when a person <u>ate</u>. It "unlocks" the cells in the
3
body so that they can use the glucose (a form of sugar) in the blood
for energy.

A person whose body doesn't make its own insulin (or doesn't
use it <u>well)</u> <u>have</u> diabetes. Since the cells <u>remains</u> "locked," they
4   **5**   **6**
<u>doesn't</u> use the glucose in the blood. A diabetic must use other
7
methods to control the level of sugar in the blood. Otherwise, he or
she could <u>became</u> very sick.
8

Diabetics have to be <u>carefuller</u> than others about their diets
9
and exercise habits. For some people with diabetes, taking insulin is
one of the <u>effectivest</u> ways for them to maintain a natural blood
10
sugar level. Since scientists <u>will have known</u> more about the disease
11
than they used to, a person with diabetes can live a <u>more normal</u>
12
life today than ever before.

punctuate *edit* capitalize **SPELL** 741
improve
Using the Parts of Speech

1. **A** find
   B found
   C founded
   D correct as is

2. **A** produces
   B produced
   C producing
   D correct as is

3. **A** eat
   B eaten
   C eats
   D correct as is

4. **A** good
   B wellest
   C goodly
   D correct as is

5. **A** has
   B had
   C haves
   D correct as is

6. **A** remaining
   B remain
   C remained
   D correct as is

7. **A** done
   B don't
   C didn't
   D correct as is

8. **A** becomed
   B becamed
   C become
   D correct as is

9. **A** carefullest
   B most careful
   C more careful
   D correct as is

10. **A** most effective
    B more effective
    C effectiver
    D correct as is

11. **A** know
    B knew
    C known
    D correct as is

12. **A** normaler
    B more normaler
    C normalest
    D correct as is

Prepositions

Prepositions are words that show position, direction, or how two words or ideas are related to each other. Specifically, a preposition shows the relationship between its object and some other word in the sentence.

> **Raul hid** under **the stairs.** (*Under* shows the relationship between *hid* and *stairs*.)

742.1

Prepositional Phrases

A preposition never appears alone; it is always part of a prepositional phrase. A prepositional phrase includes the preposition, the object of the preposition, and the modifiers of the object. (See pages **494–495**.)

> **Raul's friends looked** in the clothes hamper. (preposition: *in*; object: *hamper*; modifiers: *the, clothes*)

A prepositional phrase functions as an adjective or as an adverb.

> **They checked the closet** with all the winter coats. (*With all the winter coats* functions as an adjective modifying *closet*.)

> **They wandered** around the house **looking for him.** (*Around the house* functions as an adverb modifying *wandered*.)

NOTE If a word found in the list of prepositions has no object, it is not a preposition. It is probably an adverb.

> **Raul had never won at hide 'n' seek** before. (*Before* is an adverb that modifies *had won*.)

Prepositions

aboard	apart from	beyond	from	like	outside	under
about	around	but	from among	near	outside of	underneath
above	aside from	by	from between	near to	over	until
according to	at	by means of	from under	next to	over to	unto
across	away from	concerning	in	of	owing to	up
across from	back of	considering	in addition to	off	past	up to
after	because of	despite	in front of	on	prior to	upon
against	before	down	in place of	on account of	regarding	with
along	behind	down from	in regard to	on behalf of	since	within
along with	below	during	in spite of	on top of	through	without
alongside	beneath	except	inside	onto	throughout	
alongside of	beside	except for	inside of	opposite	to	
amid	besides	excepting	instead of	out	together with	
among	between	for	into	out of	toward	

punctuate edit capitalize SPELL 743
improve
Using the Parts of Speech

Prepositions

Write each prepositional phrase that appears in the following paragraphs. Underline the preposition and circle the object of the preposition.

Example: Spiders live everywhere, even in the finest houses.

Answer: in the finest (houses)

Although many people cringe at the sight of spiders, even dangerous spiders don't look for people as prey. Spiders prefer insects, and they eat billions of these pests.

Spiders capture different kinds of insects in the air and on the ground. Sticky spiderwebs trap insects. Some spiders jump out of special burrows to catch grasshoppers. Other spiders stand very still, just waiting for insects that run into their waiting jaws. All spiders have powerful venom that paralyzes their victims. Fortunately, spiders do not prey on humans. They simply go about their business looking for their next insect meal, and people can be glad about that.

For each of the following sentences, write whether the underlined word is a preposition or an adverb.

1. When I see a spider in my room, I scoop it up and throw it <u>outside</u>.

adverb

2. When my mom sees a spider, she runs <u>around</u> the house, yelling for someone to get rid of it.

3. In the garden, there are quite a few spiders walking <u>about</u>.

4. Yesterday I found a big yellow one <u>under</u> the watering can.

5. Another one was crawling <u>down</u> a sunflower stalk.

6. I wanted to look <u>around</u> for more.

7. However, I had to cut the grass, and I was running <u>behind</u>.

Conjunctions

A **conjunction** connects individual words or groups of words. There are three kinds of conjunctions: *coordinating, correlative*, and *subordinating*. (See pages 496–498.)

(See pages 496–498.)

744.1
Coordinating Conjunctions

A coordinating conjunction connects a word to a word, a phrase to a phrase, or a clause to a clause. The words, phrases, or clauses joined by a coordinating conjunction must be equal, or of the same type.

> **Polluted rivers** and **streams can be cleaned up.** (Two nouns are connected by *and*.)

> **Ride a bike** or **plant a tree to reduce pollution.** (Two verb phrases are connected by *or*.)

> **Maybe you can't invent a pollution-free engine,** but **you can cut down on the amount of energy you use.** (Two equal independent clauses are connected by *but*.)

NOTE When a coordinating conjunction is used to make a compound sentence, a comma always comes before it.

744.2
Correlative Conjunctions

Correlative conjunctions are conjunctions used in pairs.

> **We must reduce** not only **pollution** but also **excess energy use.**

> Either **you're part of the problem,** or **you're part of the solution.**

Conjunctions

Coordinating Conjunctions
and, but, or, nor, for, so, yet

Correlative Conjunctions

either, or   neither, nor   not only, but also   both, and   whether, or   as, so

Subordinating Conjunctions

after, although, as, as if, as long as, as though, because, before, if, in order that, provided that, since, so, so that, that, though, till, unless, until, when, where, whereas, while

punctuate *edit* capitalize **SPELL**   **745**
improve
Using the Parts of Speech

Conjunctions 1

■ **Coordinating Conjunctions**

Do this activity with a partner. Each of you must follow the directions in one of the two columns. Then put the columns together to make some funny sentences!

COLUMN A	COLUMN B
1. Write a compound subject connected with the conjunction *or*.	**1.** Write a compound predicate connected with the conjunction *and*.
2. Write one sentence followed by a comma and the conjunction *yet*.	**2.** Write one sentence.
3. Write a compound subject connected with the conjunction *and*.	**3.** Write a compound predicate connected with the conjunction *or*.
4. Write one sentence followed by a comma and the conjunction *but*.	**4.** Write one sentence.

■ **Correlative Conjunctions**

Write the correlative conjunctions that make the most sense in the following sentences.

5. We are going to the beach _____ it's sunny _____ cloudy.
   whether, or

6. _____ whales _____ dolphins are fish.

7. Dad put up a basketball hoop for _____ my brother _____ me.

8. Josh can _____ shoot three-pointers _____ get nothing but net!

9. Because of his busy schedule, he will join _____ the school team _____ a local league team.

Conjunctions . . .

746.1
Subordinating Conjunctions

A subordinating conjunction is a word or group of words that connects two clauses that are not equally important. A subordinating conjunction begins a dependent clause and connects it to an independent clause to make a complex sentence. (See page 517 and the chart on page 744.)

> Fuel-cell engines are unusual because they don't have moving parts.

> Since fuel-cell cars run on hydrogen, the only waste products are water and heat.

As you can see in the sentences above, a comma sets off the dependent clause only when it begins the sentence. A comma is usually not used when the dependent clause follows the independent clause.

NOTE Relative pronouns and conjunctive adverbs can also connect clauses. (See 706.3 and 738.1.)

Interjections

An **interjection** is a word or phrase used to express strong emotion or surprise. Punctuation (a comma or an exclamation point) is used to separate an interjection from the rest of the sentence.

> Wow, would you look at that!   Oh no! He's falling!

SCHOOL DAZE

> **Forget it!** We aren't using activity money for that.

> **Yikes,** I've told everyone that we could buy a plasma-screen TV for our classroom!

punctuate *edit* *capitalize*
SPELL
improve   **747**
Using the Parts of Speech

Conjunctions 2

■ Subordinating Conjunctions

Use a subordinating conjunction from the following list and write one complex sentence out of each pair of sentences below.

if   while   since   although   when

1. Ancient people looked at the sky. They saw shapes of animals, people, or objects in the stars.

When ancient people looked at the sky, they saw shapes of animals, people, or objects in the stars.

2. They mapped out the sky as early as 2000 B.C.E. The constellations in the zodiac were named only 2,000 years ago.

3. There are almost 90 known constellations. There are only 12 in the zodiac.

4. People can use the zodiac. They want to find a particular star in one of its constellations.

5. The zodiac is divided into 12 parts. It's easy to divide a 360-degree circle into 30-degree "slices."

Interjections

Use an appropriate interjection in each of the following sentences. Punctuate it with a comma or an exclamation point.

1. _____ That was some race!

Wow!

2. _____ I dropped the cake.

3. You passed the test? _____

4. _____ I need you here right now!

5. _____ I've discovered the cure for the common cold!

Quick Guide: Parts of Speech

In the English language, there are eight parts of speech. Understanding them will help you improve your writing skills. Every word you write is a part of speech—a noun, a verb, an adjective, and so on. The chart below lists the eight parts of speech.

Noun

A word that names a person, a place, a thing, or an idea

Alex Moya   Belize   ladder   courage

Pronoun

A word used in place of a noun

I   he   it   they   you   anybody   some

Verb

A word that shows action or links a subject to another word in the sentence

sing   shake   catch   is   are

Adjective

A word that describes a noun or a pronoun

stormy   red   rough   seven   grand

Adverb

A word that describes a verb, an adjective, or another adverb

quickly   today   now   bravely   softer

Preposition

A word that shows position or direction and introduces a prepositional phrase

around   up   under   over   between   to

Conjunction

A word that connects other words or groups of words

and   but   or   so   because   when

Interjection

A word (set off by commas or an exclamation point) that shows strong emotion

Stop! Hey, how are you?

punctuate *edit* capitalize
SPELL   749
improve
Using the Parts of Speech

Parts of Speech Review

For each numbered sentence below, write whether the underlined word is a "noun," a "pronoun," a "verb," an "adjective," an "adverb," a "preposition," a "conjunction," or an "interjection."

Example: <u>Wow</u>, an Eastern diamondback rattlesnake at Brookfield Zoo gave birth to nine babies last week!

Answer: *interjection*

(1) <u>Our</u> class went on a field trip to the Brookfield Zoo last week. **(2)** This zoo features <u>natural</u> settings for the animals. **(3)** The zoo's designers wanted people to be able to get close to the animals, but they didn't want to use <u>cages</u> or bars. **(4)** So the exhibits are separated <u>from</u> visitors with a high wall and a deep ditch or moat.

(5) We enjoyed looking at all the wonderful <u>animals</u> from around the world. **(6)** We <u>saw</u> Amur tigers, Indian rhinoceroses, Siberian ibexes, orangutans, blue poison frogs, Galapagos tortoises, and giant anteaters. **(7)** We stopped at the elephant house <u>and</u> talked about the amazing size of these animals.

(8) <u>Suddenly</u> Peter yelled, "Watch out! That elephant is going to spray us with water." **(9)** <u>Before</u> any of us could move, the elephant blasted us. **(10)** Those closest to the fence got hit the <u>worst</u>.

(11) "<u>Oh</u>, I'm so sorry," said the guide. **(12)** "<u>She</u> meant no harm."

(13) "Does she <u>always</u> do that?" Jill asked.

(14) The guide <u>answered</u>, "No. I guess she thought that the bunch of you needed to cool off!" **(15)** It *was* a <u>hot</u> day, so no one really complained. **(16)** Later, on the bus, we all laughed <u>about</u> our morning shower.

Next Step: Write a few sentences about a time you visited the zoo. Include all the parts of speech.

Credits

Photos:

comstock.com: pages vi, viii, 36, 63, 71, 93, 97, 101, 106, 107, 113, 125, 129, 157, 165, 171, 177, 189, 227, 233, 239, 251, 261, 291, 295, 301, 305, 313, 329, 387, 396, 405, 407, 419, 423, 430, 459, 474, 449, 501, 509, 521, 531, 533

Getty Images: pages v, 27, 65, 75, 77, 219, 229, 363, 376, 460, 524, 547, 555

Hemera: pages iii, ix, x, xi, xii, xviii, 1, 5, 9, 10, 11, 16, 29, 33, 45, 55, 57, 60, 65, 68, 83, 135, 161, 193, 199, 205, 223, 255, 261, 267, 287, 317, 323, 343, 353, 358, 377, 381, 409, 411, 417, 422, 431, 441, 445, 449, 461, 469, 523, 539

Ulead Systems: pages 143, 283, 441, 445

www.jupiterimages.com: pages 105, 173, 324, 354, 359, 360, 361, 471, 476, 492

Credits:

Page 375: Copyright © 2003 by Houghton Mifflin Company, Adapted by permission from *The American Heritage Student Dictionary.*

Acknowledgements

We're grateful to many people who helped bring *Write Source* to life. First, we must thank all the teachers and students from across the country who contributed writing models and ideas.

In addition, we want to thank our Write Source/Great Source team for all their help:

Steven J. Augustyn, Laura Bachman, Ron Bachman, William Baughn, Heather Bazata, Colleen Belmont, Lisa Bingen, Evelyn Curley, Sandra Easton, Chris Erickson, Jean Fischer, Sherry Gordon, Mariellen Hanrahan, Kathy Henning, Mary Anne Hoff, Kathy Kahnle, Rob King, Lois Krenzke, Joyce Becker Lee, Ellen Leitheusser, Douglas Niles, Sue Paro, Pat Reigel, Jason C. Reynolds, Susan Rogalski, Janae Sebranek, Lester Smith, Richard Spencer, Julie Spicuzza, Thomas Spicuzza, Jean Varley, Sandy Wagner, and Claire Ziffer.

Index

The **index** will help you find specific information in the handbook. Entries in italics are words from the "Using the Right Word" section. The colored boxes contain information you will use often.

G

H

process BASICS resource
forms proofreader's guide 763
Index

process BASICS resource
forms **proofreader's guide**
765

Index

Y